Ballparks of North America

Ballparks of North America

*A Comprehensive Historical Reference
to Baseball Grounds, Yards
and Stadiums, 1845 to Present*

by

Michael Benson

McFarland & Company, Inc., Publishers
Jefferson, North Carolina, and London

Frontispiece: Cover from sheet music for "Tally One for Me" by John T. Rutledge (Cincinnati: F.W. Helmick, 1877). From the Lester F. Levy Collection of Sheet Music, Special Collections, Milton S. Eisenhower Library, The Johns Hopkins University. Used by permission.

British Library Cataloguing-in-Publication data available

Library of Congress Cataloguing-in-Publication Data

Benson, Michael.
  Ballparks of North America.

  Bibliography: p. 423.
  Includes index.
  1. Baseball fields — America — History.   2. Baseball fields — North America — History.   3. Baseball fields — Central America — History.   4. Baseball fields — Caribbean Area — History.   I. Title.
  GV879.5.B46 1989   796.357′06′81812   89-45007

ISBN 0-89950-367-5 (lib. bdg. : 50# alk. paper) ∞

Printed in the United States of America

McFarland & Company, Inc., Publishers
  Box 611, Jefferson, North Carolina 28640

*This book is lovingly dedicated to my parents,
who, among other smart things,
took me to the ballpark at a very young age.*

Table of Contents

TABLE OF CONTENTS viii

Acknowledgments

The author would like to thank the following persons, institutions and organizations for their help in the preparation of this work:

Rick Erickson and David Pietrusza, research consultants

Aberdeen Parks, Recreation and Forestry Department
Akron/Summit Convention and Visitors Bureau
Alabama Bureau of Tourism and Travel
Alabama Mountain Lakes Tourist Association
Alabama Recreation and Parks Society, Inc.
Albuquerque Dukes
Alexander Mitchell Library (Aberdeen, S.D.)
Alexandria Town Talk (Jim Butler, Alexandria, La.)
Allen County-Fort Wayne Historical Society
Amarillo Chamber of Commerce
Amarillo, City of
American Association of Professional Baseball Clubs
Amsterdam Recreation Commission
Ann Arbor Convention and Visitors Bureau
Arizona Historical Society
Arizona State University
Arkansas Department of Parks and Tourism
Arkansas Industrial Development Commission
Asheville Tourists
Atlanta Braves
Atlanta Historical Society
Austin Convention and Visitors Bureau
Babe Ruth Birthplace/Baltimore Orioles Museum
Bakersfield Chamber of Commerce
Bakersfield Dodgers
Ball State University
Baltimore City Archives and Records Center
Baltimore Commission for Historical and Architectural Preservation
Baltimore Orioles
Baseball America

Baseball for Peace (Boaco, Nicaragua)
Baseball Opportunities (Santa Cruz, California)
Batavia Trojans
Beaumont Convention and Visitors Bureau
Jack H. Bell (Hopwood, Pennsylvania)
Bell & Stanton, Inc., Public Relations (Atlanta Braves)
Belleville Public Library
Bellingham, City of
Bellingham Visitors and Convention Bureau
Beloit Association of Commerce
Beloit Brewers
Bend Metro Park and Recreation District
Billings Chamber of Commerce
Birmingham Barons
Birmingham Convention & Visitors Bureau
Black Music Foundation (Nashville, Tenn.)
Bloomfield Chamber of Commerce
Bloomfield Public Library
Bloomington Chamber of Commerce
Bloomington Public Library
Robert F. Bluthardt
Boise Public Library
Boston Anthenaeum
Boston Red Sox
Wanda Boudreaux (New Orleans)
James H. Bready (Baltimore)
Keith Brenner (Shea Stadium)
Mitch and Marlene Brenner (Reading, Pa.)
Bristol (Tenn.-Va.) Visitors and Convention Council
Warren Broderick (Troy)
Brooklyn Historical Society (Claire Lamers, Librarian)
Brooklyn Public Library
Brownsville Chamber of Commerce
Buffalo and Erie County Historical Society
Buffalo Bisons
Bureau of Archives Division of Historical and Cultural Affairs (Wilmington, Del.)
Burlington Recreation and Parks Department
Busch Stadium (St. Louis)
Butler County (Pa.) Chamber of Commerce
Calgary Cannons
California Angels
California Historical Society (San Francisco)

California Office of Tourism
California State Library (Sacramento)
California State University at Fullerton
John T. Campbell (Missoula, Montana)
Carnegie Library of Pittsburgh (The Pennsylvania Room)
Carnegie-Stout Public Library (Dubuque, Iowa)
Cedar Rapids Reds
Central Berkshire Chamber of Commerce (Pittsfield, Massachusetts)
Chandler Public Library
Chapin Memorial Library (Myrtle Beach)
Chapman Historical Museum (Glens Falls, N.Y.)
Charleston (S.C.) Division of Archives and Records
Charleston (S.C.) *Post-Courier*
Chattanooga Area Convention and Visitors Bureau
Chemung County Historical Society (Elmira, N.Y.)
Chicago Cubs
Chicago Historical Society
Chicago White Sox
Jean Booth Chiemingo (Yeadon)
Clearwater Chamber of Commerce
Cleveland Indians
Cleveland Stadium Corp.
Clinton Baseball Club
Paul Cockerham
Cocoa Beach Area Chamber of Commerce
Cocoa Expo
Colorado Springs Chamber of Commerce
Columbia Mets
Columbus (Ga.) Astros
Columbus (Oh.) Clippers
Columbus (Oh.) Public Library
Connecticut Historical Society (Hartford)
Connecticut Trust for Historic Preservation (New Haven)
Consulado General de Mexico
Convention/Visitors Bureau of Greater Lansing
Cumberland County Public Library (Fayetteville, N.C.)
Dallas Convention and Visitors Bureau
Davenport Chamber of Commerce
Dayton and Montgomery County Public Library
Dayton Area Chamber of Commerce
Daytona Beach, City of
Decatur (Ill.) Public Library
Del Webb's Sun City West

Delaware Development Office
Denver Metro Convention & Visitors Bureau
Des Moines Convention and Visitors Bureau
Detroit Baseball Club (Tigers)
District of Columbia Armory Board
Dubuque Convention & Visitors Bureau
East Baton Rouge Parish Library (Ms. E.J. Carter)
East Orange Public Library
Edmonton Trappers
Elizabethton (Tenn.), City of
Erie County Library System
Eugene Public Library
Fenton Historical Society (Jamestown, N.Y.)
Filson Club (Louisville)
Finger Lakes Association, Inc.
Flagstaff, City of
Flatbush Historical Society
Florence Chamber of Commerce
Florence County Library
Florida State University
Ft. Lauderdale Stadium Complex
Fort Myers Historical Museum
Fort Myers/Lee County Public Library
Franklin County Historical Society (Columbus)
Bob Freitas, former president of the Northwest League
Fresno State University
Galveston County Beach Park Board of Trustees
Gaston County Public Library (Gastonia, N.C.)
Georgia Department of Industry and Trade
Georgia Tech Athletic Association
Grapevine Parks and Recreation Department
Anthony J. Grasso
Great Falls Dodgers
Greater Cincinnati Convention and Visitors Bureau
Greater Middletown Preservation Trust
Greater Syracuse Chamber of Commerce
Green Bay Area Visitors and Convention Bureau
Hagley Museum and Library (Wilmington, Del.)
Hurley and Roberta Hagood (Hannibal, Mo.)
Hannibal Chamber of Commerce
Hannibal Parks and Recreation
Harrisburg Senators
Crawford and Jean Harte

Hawaii Visitors Bureau
Mitch Highfill
Historic Richmond Foundation
Historical Society of Delaware
Historical Society of Pennsylvania (Philadelphia)
Historical Society of Western Pennsylvania (Pittsburgh)
Dr. Lawrence D. Hogan, Professor of History, Union County College
  (New Jersey)
Houston Sports Association, Inc. (Astros)
Huntsville Stars
The Idaho Falls Post-Register (John P. McDermott)
Idaho State Historical Society
Eric Illidge (Negro Leagues)
Illinois Department of Commerce and Community Affairs
Indiana State Library (especially Manuscripts Librarian Marybelle Burch,
  who hand-copied old newspaper articles when her Reader-Printer broke
  down.)
Indianapolis Indians
International League of Professional Baseball Clubs
Iowa Cubs
Jackson Hole Chamber of Commerce
Jackson Mets
Jacksonville Expos
Jacksonville University
Jamestown Chamber of Commerce
Jefferson County Office of Historic Preservation and Archives (Louisville)
Jervis Public Library (Rome, N.Y.)
Johnson City (Tenn.), City of
Kevin Johnston at The Clubhouse (for all your sports memorabilia needs,
  Rochester, N.Y.)
Gerwyn A. Jones (Walla Walla, Wash.)
Kanawha County Public Library (Charleston, W.Va.)
Kansas Department of Economic Development
Kenton County Public Library
Kentucky Department of Travel Development
Keokuk Chamber of Commerce
Kingsport Parks and Recreation
Kingston Parks and Recreation Commission
Kinston Indians
Kokomo/Howard County Chamber of Commerce
Kokomo Parks and Recreation Department
Kathy Krassner
Lafayette Chamber of Commerce

Lafayette Public Library
Lake Champlain Regional Chamber of Commerce
Lamar University (Beaumont, Tex.)
Lancaster County Library
Landmarks Center (St. Paul)
Rochelle Larkin
Las Vegas News Bureau
Lee County Historical Society (Keokuk, Ia.)
Lee County Parks and Recreation (Fort Myers, Florida)
Lehigh Valley (Pennsylvania) Convention and Visitors Bureau
Lenoir County (North Carolina) Chamber of Commerce
Lester S. Levy (author of *Picture the Song,* The Johns Hopkins University
    Press)
Lewiston Chamber of Commerce (Jennifer Babino)
Lincoln Library (Springfield, Illinois)
Little League Baseball
Lodi Public Library
Los Angeles Dodgers
Los Angeles Memorial Coliseum Commission
Los Angeles Public Library
Louisiana Office of Tourism
Louisiana State Library
Louisville Convention & Visitors Bureau
Barbara Lucas
Lycoming County (Pa.) Tourist Promotion Agency
Lynchburg Chamber of Commerce
Lynchburg Red Sox
McCord Museum (Montreal)
Mike McCormick (Terre Haute)
McLean County Historical Society (Bloomington, Illinois)
Macon Chamber of Commerce
Madison Convention & Visitors Bureau
Madison County (Ala.) Tourism Board
Madison Department of Public Works (Parks Division)
Al Maes (Rapid City and Green Bay)
Nick Mahoney, Esq.
Maine Guides (and Mick Mixon, their play-by-play announcer)
Major League Baseball, Office of the Commissioner
Marion County Historical Society (Indianapolis)
Melbourne (Fla.), City of
Memphis Chicks
Memphis State University
Metropolitan Detroit Convention and Visitors Bureau

Metropolitan Government of Nashville and Davidson County
Michigan State University (East Lansing, Michigan)
Michigan Travel Bureau
Middlesex County Historical Society (Middletown)
Middletown (Ohio) Public Library
Midland (Texas) Chamber of Commerce
Milwaukee Brewers
Milwaukee County Historical Society
Minnesota Historical Society
Minnesota Office of Tourism
Modesto Chamber of Commerce
Monessen Public Library and District Center
Monroe County May Hill Russell Library (Key West, Fla.)
Montana Department of Commerce
Montana Magazine
Montgomery County (Amsterdam, New York) Chamber of Commerce
Moorland-Springarn Research Center (and James P. Johnson, in Washington)
Museum of the City of New York
Nashua Public Library
Nashville Area Chamber of Commerce
National Baseball Library (especially Pat Kelly, in Cooperstown, N.Y.)
Nebraska Department of Economic Development
New Britain Public Library
New Hampshire Department of Resources and Economic Development
New Haven Chamber of Commerce
New Haven Colony Historical Society
New Haven Free Public Library
New Haven Preservation Trust
New Jersey Historical Society
New Orleans Public Library
New York Chamber of Commerce
New York Convention and Visitors Bureau, Inc.
New York Historical Society
New York Public Library (Albert G. Spalding Collection)
New York State Department of Commerce
New York State Museum in Albany
New York Yankees
Niagara Falls Public Library
Niagara Gazette
Norfolk Convention and Visitors Bureau
North Carolina Department of Commerce, Travel and Tourism Division, Hugh Morton, Jr., Director

Oakland Athletics Baseball Company
Office of the Japanese Baseball Commissioner
Ohio Department of Development
Ohio Historical Society (Columbus)
Oklahoma City 89ers
Old Dominion University
Oregon Economic Development Department
Oregon State University
Osceola County Stadium and Sports Complex (Kissimmee, Fla.)
Ouachita Parish (Monroe, La.) Public Library
Joseph Overfield (Buffalo)
Pacific Coast League
Palm Beach County Convention and Visitors Bureau
Peninsula (Hampton, Va.) White Sox
Pennsylvania Bureau of Travel Development
Peoria Chiefs
Philadelphia Convention and Visitors Bureau
Philadelphia Eagles
Philadelphia Phillies
Phoenix & Valley of the Sun Convention & Visitors Bureau
Pioneer Baseball League
Pittsburgh History and Landmarks Foundation
Portsmouth (Va.) Department of Parks and Recreation (Frankie Sperber)
James Prendergast Library Association (Jamestown, N.Y.)
Prince William (Va.) Library
Providence Preservation Society
Providence Public Library
Public Library of Charlotte (N.C.) and Mecklenberg County
Putnam County (Fla.) Chamber of Commerce
Quad City (Ia.) Angels
Rapides Parish Library (Alexandria, La.)
Reading Phillies
Redwood City Public Library
Reno-Sparks Chamber of Commerce
Rensselaer County Historical Society (Troy, N.Y.)
Rhode Island Department of Economic Development
Rhode Island Historical Society
Richmond Braves Baseball Club
Richmond Memorial Library (Batavia, N.Y.)
Richmond (Va.) Public Library
Riverhead (N.Y.) Chamber of Commerce
Roanoke Valley Convention and Visitors Bureau
Rochester (Minn.) Parks and Recreation Department

Rochester (N.Y.) Historical Society
Rochester (N.Y.) Museum and Science Center Library
Rockford Historical Society
Rockford Museum Association
Rockwood Museum (Wilmington, Del.)
Rocky Mount (N.C.) Area Chamber of Commerce
Rocky Mount City Schools
Rome Historical Society
Rosenberg Library (Galveston, Tex.)
Steve Rossi
St. Louis Convention and Visitors Commission
St. Petersburg Area Chamber of Commerce
St. Petersburg Historical Society
Salinas Area Chamber of Commerce
Salt Lake Trappers
San Antonio Convention and Visitors Bureau
San Diego Hall of Champions
San Diego Historical Society
San Diego Padres
San Francisco Giants
San Jose Convention and Visitors Bureau
San Jose Public Library
Sarasota, City of
Savannah Area Chamber of Commerce
Schenectady Chamber of Commerce
Schenectady County Historical Society
Scotia History Center (Michelle J. Norris, Scotia Village Historian)
Scottsdale Chamber of Commerce
Seattle Mariners
Sedona-Oak Creek Canyon Chamber of Commerce
Philip Semrau
Silas Bronson Library (Waterbury, Conn.)
Sioux Falls Parks and Recreation Department
Smithsonian Institution
Society of American Baseball Research
South Bend White Sox
South Brevard (Fla.) Chamber of Commerce
South Carolina Department of Parks, Recreation and Tourism
The Southern League
S.P.A.C.E.S. (Los Angeles)
Spartanburg County Public Library
Spartanburg Tourism and Convention Center
Spectacor Management, Inc. (Three Rivers Stadium, Pittsburgh)

Spokane Indians
Spokane Public Library
Springfield (Mass.) City Library (Margaret Humberston)
Springfield (Mass.) Convention & Visitors Bureau
Stanford University
Stockton Parks and Recreation
Stockton/San Joaquin Convention & Visitors Bureau
Marlys A. Svendsen (Davenport, Ia.)
Syracuse Chiefs Baseball Club
Tacoma/Pierce County Visitors and Convention Bureau
Tampa/Hillsborough Convention and Visitors Association, Inc.
Taos County (New Mexico) Chamber of Commerce
Tecolotes de los Laredos
Tempe Chamber of Commerce
Temple University Library
Texas A&M (College Station)
Texas Department of Commerce
Texas Gulf Coast Historical Society
Texas Rangers
Thibodaux Chamber of Commerce
Virginia Hege Tobiassen
Toledo Mud Hens
Toronto Blue Jays Baseball Club (Howard Starkman)
Kermit Torve (Rapid City, S.D.)
Mark Treu (Rochester Dead Head)
Tucson Public Library
Tulare County Free Library System (Annie Mitchell History Room,
    Visalia, California)
Tulsa Drillers (Brian Carroll)
University of Alabama
University of Florida (Gainesville)
University of Houston
University of Iowa
University of Louisville Eckstrom Library Photographic Archives
University of Maine
University of Miami
University of Minnesota
University of Nevada at Las Vegas
University of the Pacific
University of Portland
University of Richmond
University of South Alabama (Mobile)
University of South Florida

University of Southern California
University of Southern Mississippi
University of Tennessee (Knoxville)
Utah Travel Council
Vancouver Canadians
Vermont Agency of Development and Community Affairs
Vicksburg, City of
Vicksburg-Warren County Tourist Commission
Vigo County Historical Society
Vigo County Public Library (Terre Haute, Ind.)
Virginia Historical Society
Virginia State Library
Visalia Chamber of Commerce
Walla Walla (Wash.) Area Chamber of Commerce
Washington State University
Waterloo Indians
James Wells (Keokuk, Ia.)
West Virginia Department of Commerce
Western Reserve Historical Society (Cleveland)
Wichita State University
Earl Williams (East Orange, N.J.)
Wilson (N.C.) Chamber of Commerce
Wilson County (N.C.) Public Library
Winter Haven Red Sox
Wisconsin Department of Development
Miles Wolff (minor league ballparks)
Bob Wolfman (Hoboken, N.J.)
Marty Wolfson (Pittsburgh)
Worcester Historical Museum
Wythe County Public Library (Wytheville, Va.)
Yuma, City of
Yuma City-County Library
Yuma Department of Parks and Recreation

and special thanks to my wife, Lisa Maria Grasso, Esq.

Introduction:
Diamonds in the Dust

A ballpark is a ballpark, with or without a grandstand—or a scoreboard, or peanut vendors, or an usher wiping the seats with a furry mitten. It is a ballpark even if there are no spectators—although we'd rather believe otherwise, for spectator is the best role most of us can hope for.

A ballpark needs only baseball. That's where the magic is.

We know the ballpark. In the country it's the enclosure just off, but always within sight of, the main road. In the city it's an agrarian illusion, a splash of emerald in a chimney-stacked urbanscape. It's a place (in the Northeast anyway) where some men come in May to bare their winter-whitened beer bellies to the sun. Whether it be a seat of wooden bleachers beside a baseline or the wondrous beauty of Yankee Stadium, we know the ballpark by the feeling it gives us, that feeling of harmony with the music of the spheres—or at least that of the ballpark organ. The beer comes in plastic cups and the hot dogs, though indigestible, taste better there than anywhere else.

Many of us have early memories of the ballpark, the smell of rust and cigars, the first realization that peanut shells could be thrown on the "floor." You could yell as loud as you wanted. If far enough away, you saw the ball pop the catcher's glove a fraction of a second before hearing it. Like so many places discovered in childhood, the ballpark was magic—but it is one of the few places that remains magic after we grow up.

Yet it is the variety of ballparks from community to community that makes them so fascinating. The same game with the same rules was played in Baker Bowl and Braves Field, yet the Boston ballpark's outfield seemed twice as big as the one in Philadelphia. Look at photos of Fenway Park in Boston, Russwood Stadium in Memphis, Borchert Field in Milwaukee. Ballparks are shaped like the block upon which they sit. (Nowadays the larger of our ballparks usually sit in the center of their own parking lots.)

Baseball history has been exhaustively recorded. We know the exact number of games Will Foley played for the Chicago White Stockings in 1875: three. But where were those games played? What was it like there? How far out were the fences? How did the shape of the park affect the game? How much did it cost to get in? Questions like that led to this obsession of mine: to create a statistical and atmospheric setting for the history of baseball.

The Evolution of the Ballpark. After Alexander Cartwright first wrote down the rules to baseball in 1846 (see entry for Hoboken, New Jersey, *The Elysian Fields*) baseball stayed in the Northeast — with the exception of some high-society contests in New Orleans — until the Civil War, when intermingling armies in the camps and stockades whacked yarn-wrapped walnuts with trimmed hickory limbs and spread the game throughout the continent. By the time the war ended, baseball was the United States' national pastime.

In 1866, Charles A. Peverelly wrote in his *Book of American Pastimes,* "The game of Base Ball has now become beyond question the leading feature of the outdoor sports of the United States. . . . It is a game which is peculiarly suited to the American temperament and disposition."

Long before there were professional leagues, baseball's predominant attraction began to shift from the participatory to the vicarious. The best liked to play the best and the rest were willing to pay to watch, so increasingly impressive enclosures called "base-ball grounds" were constructed for the sole purpose of keeping freeloaders from viewing the game. The first superteam, the Cincinnati Red Stockings of the late 1860s, helped spread baseball fever by going on extensive barnstorming tours, taking on all comers, and winning just about every time.

In the nineteenth century, baseball was a shaky business proposition — similar in modern economic terms to a brand new traveling circus. The best way to make a buck in baseball was to lay a smart bet. Baseball grounds lasted no more than five or six years in the 1860s and 1870s. Wooden fences were raised on whatever land the club owner had bought or leased. Bench bleachers were erected. Maybe a dugout was built. There probably were no clubhouses. To save expenses the players often assisted in construction. Franchises in the first professional baseball league, the National Association (1871-75), bounced from place to place. Teams in what would be known as the big leagues changed home grounds routinely. Sometimes they just changed sides of town. Sometimes they changed states. Sometimes they moved abruptly right in the middle of the season. There was no reason to build ballparks to last. If a franchise did outlive its ballpark — which wasn't hard to do, as ballparks quickly grew decrepit and frequently burned — a new park was sometimes constructed in its place in a matter of days, maybe during a road trip.

Baseball's popularity grew slowly. Professional baseball attendance figures were aided in the 1890s by the introduction of electric trolley cars, which made it easier for people to travel to the games.

Through time, there were improvements and experiments in ballpark architecture (the cantilever construction of Philadelphia's Baker Bowl, for example), as well as in the scope of the ballpark's effect on its community (Ebbets Field in Brooklyn on the positive side and Shibe Park in Philadelphia on the negative). Lakefront Park in 1880s Chicago was the first to feature vanity in its design, a glib hint that maybe, just a little bit, the ballpark was the thing. It certainly gave the paying customers something to look at when bad baseball was being played.

After 30 years of trouble with burning ballparks, major league parks began the conversion to fireproof materials in 1909, and within a few years just about all of the big league arenas were constructed of concrete and steel. New materials, a new financial security, and a need for increased seating capacity resulted in the building of beauties like Shibe Park in Philadelphia and Forbes Field in Pittsburgh, again betraying the vanity of the club owners with their modern conveniences and grand sturdiness. For most of those people watching the birth of the new brand of stadium (Comiskey Park was next), these big league ballparks would be the only home their team would ever know.

The major league ballpark, like F.D.R. and Joe Louis and the Pope Piuses, just never changed during the long years of the Depression and World War II. Baseball might not have survived those years if it hadn't been for America's newfound ability to play ball at night.

When there were no jobs, Franklin Roosevelt put men to work building baseball parks in minor league towns. Some of those parks are still around. In the big leagues the classic parks lasted into the 1960s, when the big show moved to the suburbs and ballparks got round.

A quantum leap in baseball arena construction came in 1923 in the form of Yankee Stadium. This was the first to be called a *stadium* – the reason we still call ballparks stadiums. There had been many pretty churches, but this was a cathedral. Only Cleveland ever really tried to duplicate Yankee Stadium's magnitude and grandeur, and they created only a barren hulk.

The magic in the Bronx ballpark is only partially architectural. Yankee Stadium (even the new one) vibrates with an *urgency* for championship brand ball, rattles the girders every night with an arrogant demand for Ruthian superiority that would be comically out of place in any other setting.

In 1908, George A. Baird of Chicago started a trend toward high-tech ballparks when he invented the first electronic scoreboard. ("Electronic" meaning that balls, strikes, and outs were shown with electric lights; the line score still had to be changed manually.) The new scoreboard was attached by wire to a keyboard behind the umpire. Scoreboard operators no longer had to perch on top of the outfield fence with a pair of binoculars trying to figure out if the umpire called that last pitch a ball or a strike. (Instead, they sat inside the scoreboard, peeping out through the holes where no numbers were needed—leading generations of children to believe the operators lived there.)

The new scoreboard made its debut in the parks of the Boston clubs. A couple of years later, brand-new Shibe Park in Philadelphia installed one.

The scoreboard Baird manufactured was 50 by 24 feet. It could be purchased or leased. Rental was $2500 for the first year, and $750 a year after that. Baseball owners sold advertising space on their scoreboards at a dollar per square foot, and the new scoreboards paid for themselves after a time.

Once unleashed, the high-tech tide could not be turned back, and now we have computerized scoreboards (which *still* get the count wrong at least once a game)—along with computerized, plasticized ballparks, some of them indoors. Astroturf was invented when the grass in the Houston Astrodome died, and ballpark fashion took a big step in the wrong direction. Now there's DiamondVision. Even when you're at the ballpark, you have to watch commercials between innings.

Maybe we've lost sight of a crucial point: that there is something in the rhythms of baseball that will always go better with a handlebar mustache (and maybe a foamy mug of Pabst Blue Ribbon) than with the Jetsons.

How to Use This Book. The ballparks in this book are arranged chronologically under their cities, which are listed alphabetically (thus the history of ballparks in Albuquerque is near the front of the book; the essay for Griffith Stadium in Washington is near the back). To look up Wrigley Field, see the section on Chicago, under C. (Ballparks may also be found alphabetically by name in the Index.)

When determining chronology, the park first used for baseball is considered the older, even if the structure is younger. The listings are comprehensive for (white and integrated) major league play, and partial for the black leagues (major and minor), minor leagues and college play. The current ballparks used in the Mexican Leagues are all here.

Entries for ballparks contain two types of information: a "stat" section and an essay. The "stat" section shows as much as possible of the following information:

Name of ballpark (Alternative names of ballpark)
League of first team to play there, when they played (name of first team),
    League of second team to play there, when (name), etc.
Location
Dimensions of the field of play

Seating capacity
Attendance records.

Where available, other noteworthy tidbits are inserted into appropriate spots. The essays try to show what the numbers can't: that ballparks are like snowflakes, no two quite the same.

The listings tend to follow the history of the land on which the ballparks stood. Therefore (usually) if two ballparks stood on the same site, there is only one listing, but if the same ballpark is moved and existed in two locations, there are two listings.

For the purposes of this book, a twentieth-century ballpark is one you had to pay to get into. For the nineteenth century, almost any documented site of an 18-man ball game qualifies. There are exceptions.

In the nineteenth century, before ballparks became thought of as permanent structures, they weren't always given names. Some ballpark entries begin *Name of park unknown.* In some cases, this means the name of the park has been lost; in others it means the park never had a name.

There are no doubt mistakes in the entries on nineteenth century ballparks, as much of the information is based on the accounts of old men. We can't always distinguish tall tales from history. Luckily, this is only baseball. A tall tale every now and again won't hurt anyone.

During research, three different locations for Eastern Park in Brooklyn surfaced in written reports. Each writer knew exactly where the place was, having been there as a boy. Each knew the four streets that bordered the park. The three proposed sites, when plotted on a map, form three corners of a square. At the center of the square is the train station, equidistant from each proposed site. The men agreed on which train station you got off at and how far the ballpark was from the station, but disagreed on which direction they headed.

This book may be imagined as a brightly painted backdrop for the history of baseball. Some sections of the painting will always be missing, and others unclear. On the other hand, I am able to present here for the first time many ballparks recently rediscovered with the help of libraries and historical societies all over the nation.

This is a series of street corners, a set of outfield fences determining the boundaries of the sport with a variety unknown to any other competition. This is a nation's worth of neighborhoods, with one thing in common — they're within earshot of the crack of the bat. Here's the cast of characters that frequented those worlds: the all-powerful owners, the players and managers who provided most of the entertainment, the vendors who hawked the hot dogs, and the grounds crews who (except in Arizona in the 1890s, where there was dirt, just dirt) kept the grass greener than anything found outside their magical gardens.

Come with me now to other times and places, to a ballfield nestled in a small village. There are apple trees in the outfield. The sun is shining. Smell the rosin. Listen to the infield chatter, the rhythmic barking of the vendors, the cranky complaints of the rooters, and the popping of fists into leather. There's a foul ball into the stands and the scramble is on...

Ballparks of North America

Aberdeen, South Dakota

Johnson's Grove

Location: Near the town of Columbia.

The first baseball game reported in Brown County was played here on July 4, 1879 after a "public meeting."

Johnson Field

Home of weekday baseball before World War II, Dakota League circa 1920. *Location:* Present site of the Johnson Arts Center.

A Northern Normal and Industrial School football field with a wooden grandstand. A tiny press box sat atop the slanted pavilion roof.

Name of park unknown

Home of Sunday baseball before World War II, Dakota League circa 1920. *Location:* South of Wylie Park.

This park, which included a grandstand, sat on land owned by the Krueger brothers. Outfield fence was erected in 1910. Streetcar fare to the park was ten cents.

Municipal Ball Park

Northern League 1946–71 (Golden Pheasants, Pheasants). *Location:* Currently part of the Northern State College campus. *Built:* 1936. *Lights:* June, 1946. *Fire:* Friday, August 3, 1951.

A lighted field with grandstand and bleachers, built amid farm land plains divided by irregular fences. Here, the short porch was in left.

In 1951 the Municipal Ball Park was the site of a tremendous, all-consuming fire. The fire started hours after the ballpark had been jammed by one of the structure's largest crowds. Temporary bleachers were quickly built so that the Pheasants could complete the season and a $65,000 bond issue was passed so a new grandstand could be built for 1952.

The park was originally built for amateur local ball with WPA funds, but pro ball came to Aberdeen after World War II and stayed until 1971. Every day in the *Aberdeen American News* Philbert the Pheasant, a cartoon by Gordon Haug, would appear, the bird's mood telling the results of the previous day's game. Philbert carried a fishing pole for a bye and an umbrella when it rained.

In the 1940s a group of leather-lunged young men always sat together in the bleachers and referred to themselves as "The Fan Club."

In 1947 the ace of the Pheasant pitching staff was Ralph Schwamb, who later was convicted of murder and spent 15 undefeated years as the star hurler at San Quentin.

Earl Weaver managed the 1959 club. His star pitcher was Steve Dalkowski. That year Dalkowski pitched a no-hitter. He struck out 23 and walked 16. They tried to measure the speed of Dalkowski's fastball but, in order to make such measurements back in those days, one had to hit a set target, and this proved to be impossible for Dalkowski.

The Municipal Ball Park's grandstand was razed in the 1970s, but the diamond remains in use by Northern State College.

Fossum Field

Aberdeen's only present municipal ball field. *Location:* 8th Avenue Northeast and Highway 19. *Built:* 1974.

Aguascalientes, Mexico

Estadio Alberto Romo Chavez

Mexican League (Zona Norte), present (Rieleros). *Dimensions:* Left field, 330 feet; center field, 402 feet; right field, 330 feet. *Seating capacity:* 10,000.

Albany, New York

Washington Parade Grounds

Location: Washington Park.
On July 2, 1860, in what has been called the first road game, the Excelsiors of South Brooklyn made the trek to the Washington Parade Grounds in Albany to play the local champions.

Riverside Park (I)

National League 1880–82 (Troy Trojans, few games each season), home of Albany baseball 1880–1900. *Location:* Herkimer, Quay, and Westerlo streets; Broadway.

Riverside Park (II)

Home of Albany baseball circa 1901. *Location:* Bonaker's Island (privately owned island), across from State Street in Albany. *Seating capacity:* No grandstand.

Chadwick Park

New York State League, Eastern League, before 1928. *Location:* Menands.

Hawkins Stadium

Eastern League 1928–60. *Location:* Became the Mid-City Plaza. Now holds the offices of the State Workers Compensation Board. *Built:* 1928. *Construction cost:* $240,000. *Last game:* September 6, 1959. *Torn down:* 1960.
Named after team owner Michael J. Hawkins.

Bleecker Stadium

Eastern League 1982–83 (A's).
A concrete football stadium built in the 1930s. Along with one and a half seasons of baseball by the Albany-Colonie A's, who played here while Heritage Park was being built, the early 1980s saw a simultaneous appearance at Bleecker Stadium by the South African rugby team, the largest force of security ever seen in the city of Albany, and a communist splinter group. There were a few arrests.

Heritage Park

Eastern League 1983–present (Albany-Colonie Yankees). *Location:* Albany-Shaker Road (Route 155). *Construction cost:* $1.2 million. *Opened:* August 20, 1983. *Dimensions:* Left field, 325 feet; center field, 401 feet; right field, 335 feet. *Seating capacity:* 5000. *1987 season attendance:* 285,016.
Boring park. The aluminum bench seating is set too far from the playing field, and the food is overpriced. The first game here (in August, 1983) went 12 innings, and 66 kegs of beer were sold.

Albuquerque, New Mexico

Tingley Field (Apprentice Field)

Location: Tenth Street, Stover Avenue, Atlantic Street SW. *Built:* 1932. *Dimensions:* Left field, 348 feet; center field, 480 feet; right field, 348 feet.
There was as much dirt as grass on the field. Folding chairs were used for box seats. The dugouts were tiny. So was the grandstand, which was flanked by the high school–type bleachers.

Albuquerque Sports Stadium

Texas League 1961–71 (Dodgers); Pacific Coast League, 1972–present (Dukes). *Location:* Stadium Boulevard, east off Interstate 25. *Opened:* 1969. *Construction cost:* $1.5 million. *Dimensions:* Left field, 360 feet; center field, 410 feet; right field, 340 feet.

Heritage Park, Albany, N.Y. (Compliments of the New York State Dept. of Commerce.)

Seating capacity: 10,510 (6312 "theater-type" seats, 5560 bench seats). *Lights:* 85 footcandles per square foot for entire field. Also used for football and soccer—fields' layout parallel to left field bleachers.

Though each spectator in the Albuquerque Sports Stadium's grandstand gets an astonishing view of the Sandia Mountains, this park is best known for its "drive-in baseball." There is an elevated drive-in area beyond the outfield fence. The area is built upon 12,000 square feet of New Mexico lava rock, quarried from the volcanoes west of the city. Fans can park and watch.

The field is built in a bowl dug into the earth; 320,000 cubic yards of earth were moved in ten days. The pitcher's mound is 40 feet below the original ground level. Over 5000 cubic yards of concrete are in the project. The 20,000 square feet of factory-painted steel roof deck above the grandstand is secured with 15,000 waterproof bolts. The steel "bents" supporting the roof cantilever 50 feet to give an unobstructed view through 3000 square feet

of specially treated "nicot" (nylon and cotton) netting protecting grandstand spectators from foul balls.

The outfield grass was planted at the site while the stadium was under construction. The infield grass was planted on city-owned golf courses and sodded at site after the contractor was through using heavy machinery in the area during construction. All of the grass is planted over an eight-inch planting bed of locally produced fertilizer, Espanola pumice and selected native earth. The bed permits quick drainage of surface water and the deep root growth of the grass.

The base paths are composed of 60 percent red mountain clay from LaBajada Hill, 25 percent Diamond Grit (Calcined Clay) and 15 percent masonry sand, producing a fast, firm, moisture-absorbing playing surface. The watering hoses are on motorized reels located in a concealed space beside the dugouts.

The outfield fence advertisements are mounted upon a common background color, unifying the whole while

Albuquerque (N.M.) Sports Stadium. (Compliments of the Albuquerque Dukes.)

retaining the individuality of each advertiser. There is carpeting in the clubhouse areas, the press box, and a portion of the women's rest rooms.

In 1983, the new scoreboard and message center was added. Features of the Fairplay Integrated Systems computer include: 1) the capability to hold 100 animations and recall them instantly, 2) the ability to recall one- and two-line pictorials that are permanently stored on the computer tape, 3) the ability to store all animations and pictorials on a cassette tape for easy recall.

Lobo Field

Home of the University of New Mexico Lobos (Western Athletic Conference), present. *Location:* University of New Mexico campus. *Seating capacity:* 500.

Alexandria, Louisiana

On page two of the May 31, 1871 issue of the *Louisiana Democrat* there is an item that reads, "The Base Ball Clubs of Alexandria and Pineville, have decided to play for the Champion-

ship of Red River. They intend playing ... the best two out of three.... The first game came off on Saturday, in Pineville, which resulted in favor of the Rapides Base Ball Club, of Alexandria, beating the Lone Stars of Pineville, by a score of nine (sic). The next game comes off on Friday, on this side, weather permitting."

City Park Diamond

Home of Alexandria baseball before 1934.

Used as a practice field by the semi-pros and amateurs of Alexandria, after the Evangeline League began to play at Bringhurst Field.

Bringhurst Field

Evangeline League 1934–42, 1946–57, Texas League 1972–74. *Built:* 1934. *Dimensions:* (1934–87) Left field, 330 feet; center field, 410 feet; right field, 330 feet. (1988) Left field, 315 feet; left center, 360 feet; center field, 385 feet; right center, 360 feet; right field, 315 feet. *Fences:* (1934–87) 12 feet all the way around (metal). *Seating capacity:* (1934) 1500; (1938) 3200. *First night game:* May, 1938.

Cecil Coombs, business manager of the Alexandria entry in the Evangeline League, was in charge of building Bringhurst Park. Bringhurst, the commissioner of streets and parks, provided the land, so Coombs' biggest problem was acquiring supplies and labor for the building of the grandstand. The team was managed by former Shreveport skipper Art Phelan. The manicuring of the playing field was managed by Alex Thomas, a black groundskeeper and trainer from Fort Worth—who'd also been Phelan's right-hand man when the pair worked in Shreveport. The park Coombs built with the lumber and nails he eventually bought was described as "intimate."

Lights were installed at Bringhurst in 1938, but at first night games were restricted to Friday and Saturday nights, because of the drag on the municipal power supply. Also in 1938, Bringhurst Field had its first Ladies' Night. For Bringhurst's entire existence, there were no games Sundays or Wednesdays because of church services.

After the Evangeline League fell apart in 1957, the field was used by high school and local summer league teams. It deteriorated until 1972, when it was refurbished to serve as the home of the San Diego Padres' Texas League affiliate.

The city of Alexandria spent another $300,000 in 1987 for new lights, sod, and seats so that the facility could again be used for high school games, and as the summer league's 14-state World Series for players 15 to 18 years old.

According to Jim Butler at the *Alexandria Daily Town Talk,* "It is a grand old park, though old-timers miss the 12-foot metal outfield fence finally razed last year (1987)."

Alexandria, Virginia

Gentlemen's Driving Park
American Association 1891 (Wash-

ington, Sundays only), National League 1892–99 (Washington, Sundays only). *Location:* Four Mile Run.

A horsetrack used for baseball on Sundays to avoid blue laws. It was just outside the District of Columbia.

Municipal Stadium (Four Mile Run Park)
Carolina League 1976–82 (Independents). *Location:* Jefferson Davis Drive, Leslie Avenue, Duncan Avenue.

The franchise struggled for the entire seven years of its existence. The financial maladies were largely attributed to an Alexandria ordinance that prohibited beer sales at the park.

Allentown, Pennsylvania

Fairview Field
Interstate League 1947 (Cardinals). *Seating capacity:* 3500.

A bandbox ballpark. Built next to the Allentown trolley barn, Fairview had the short fence and high wall in left *à la* Fenway. The field was abandoned and facilities removed until 1976 when it was rebuilt as a bicentennial year community project.

Max Hess Stadium (Breadon Field)
Eastern League circa 1960–65. *Location:* Seventh Street in Whitehall. *Seating capacity:* 5500.

The stadium changed names when a local businessman bought it and named it for himself. The ball club disbanded after the 1965 season, and the land upon which Max Hess Stadium stood was sold for the building of Lehigh Valley Mall. There's been no pro ball in Allentown since.

Altoona, Pennsylvania

Columbia Park (Fourth Avenue Grounds)
Union Association 1884 (Pride). *Location:* Lower Sixth Street, 32nd

Street, Fourth Avenue, Mill Run Road. *First game:* April 30, 1884. *Last game:* May 31, 1884.

Altoona, a team rumored to be backed by Philadelphia bigwigs, withdrew from the Union Association after only six weeks of play. This was one of the two non-major league cities represented in the U.A., the other being Wilmington. Kansas City substituted for Altoona, and finished the rest of the season, at which time the whole league disbanded.

The site is currently used for gasoline storage tanks and railroad tracks.

Pennsylvania Railroad Park

Home of some Negro National League games by the Homestead Grays. The right field fence was only 150 feet from home. Balls driven over that fence counted as doubles.

Amarillo, Texas

Before 1926, ballgames in Amarillo were played in parks and fields just off of Fourth Street at Glenwood, and on a location where Ted Lokey's Service Station was located in the 1930s. The town team was known as the Greys and was composed of local talent. After games the men would get drunk and bury live chickens in the sand, so that just the heads were sticking out. Then the men would ride horses past the birds, lean down from the saddle and pull the chicken heads off. The rider who pulled off the most heads won. Some Greys games were not completed at all, especially those against nearby Tulia and Lubbock, because fist fights broke out.

The Greys played from the turn of the century until the mid-twenties, sometimes ad-libbing a schedule and sometimes participating in a loose union known as the Pecos Valley League.

Metro Park

Home of the Metros 1926–36. *Construction cost:* $80,000. *Burned:* 1936.

For part of this time, the Metros played in the Western League. This site later became Butler Field, the high school football stadium.

The Baseball Diamond Northwest of Town

Home of the Black Sandies circa 1938.

Negro minor league park. Games were reported in the *Amarillo News and Globe.* The Black Sandies played tough competition like the Sudan Black Cats.

Potter County Stadium (later Memorial Stadium)

Texas League 1959–63, 1965–70, 1972 (Gold Sox, Giants, franchise still operating as of 1980 in Texas League as Padres farm club. Franchise no longer exists.) Dixie Association 1971. *Seating capacity:* 4800.

A steel and concrete, roofed grandstand sits behind home plate. On the roof are two light towers with a press box in the middle.

Amsterdam, New York

Guy Park

Home of Amsterdam baseball in the 1900s. *Location:* Guy Park Avenue, western section of the city.

The New York Giants once played an exhibition game here.

Mohawk Mills Park (Crescent Park, Jollyland, Herbert L. Shuttleworth II Park)

Canadian American League 1938–42, 1946–51 (Rugmakers). *Location:* Crescent Street. *Dimensions:* Left field, 279 feet; center field, 406 feet; right field, 309 feet. *Seating capacity:* 3200. *Fences:* Left field, 26 feet; center field, 16 feet; right field, 16 feet (all wood). *Lights:* 1940. *Cost of lights:* $10,000.

Site was formerly an amusement

park called Crescent Park, and was first used for baseball Memorial Day 1914 for a game between the Amsterdam Empires and the Philadelphia Colored Giants. The Mohawk Colored Giants from Schenectady played many games here, along with traveling teams through the 1920s.

The amusement park was known as Jollyland for a time, and in the 1930s was sold to Mohawk Carpet Mills, the same company that had just bought the Gloversville franchise in the Canadian American League. The team, called the Rugmakers because of the rugmaking mills, was operated by Herb Shuttleworth, son of the mill proprietor. Much money was poured by the elder Shuttleworth into his son's ballpark. Lights were installed, a new fence was put in. (The old fence had been held up by supports that protruded into the outfield.) The infield remained all-dirt.

Head groundskeeper was Hall of Famer Chief Bender, who was known to get down on his hands and knees on the mound to make sure everything was just so.

The Magic Light Towers. Here's a story Herb Shuttleworth tells. Believe it or not... On July 20, 1942, the New York Yankees were booked to play at Mohawk Mills Park against the Rugmakers, a Yankee farm club. Eight days before the game (Sunday morning, July 12), an arsonist burned the park to the ground, causing a blaze so hot that the light towers softened and lowered, seemingly falling asleep above the outfield.

The Shuttleworths decided the show must go on, so everyone who worked in the mill was given the task of rebuilding the ballpark, with the exception of the grandstand roof. That didn't help the problem with the light towers. The Yankee exhibition was a day game, but those towers were going to make catching fly balls hazardous.

Then a miracle happened.

The light towers rose back to an erect position of their own volition as the

steel cooled, and were stiff and straight as ever—though maybe a little scorched—by the time the Yankees showed up. The exhibition was played on schedule before a packed house of 4032.

According to New York State ballpark aficionado David Pietrusza, "the park deteriorated after the league's demise, finally being deeded over to the City of Amsterdam in September 1964. The City had planned on buying it, but instead the Mills turned it over to the municipality for one dollar. From August 1, 1955, to June 12, 1980, there were no night games at the field. It was rebuilt with Federal Community Development Agency funds in the mid-1970s, but in the process ... much, if not all, of its charm was lost."

Anaheim, California

LaPalma Park
California League 1941, Sunset League 1947–48.

In 1950, used in the film *The Jackie Robinson Story*.

Anaheim Stadium
American League 1966–present (California Angels). *Location:* State College Boulevard (third base side), Katella Avenue (left field side), Orangewood Boulevard (first base), Orange Freeway and Santa Ana River (right field), Douglas Road (center field). Owned by the city of Anaheim. *Nickname:* The Big A. *Constructed by:* Del E. Webb Company. *Groundbreaking:* August 31, 1964 (soil turned by Gene Autry, Del Webb, and Anaheim Mayor Chuck Chandler). *Construction cost:* $24 million. *Dimensions:* Left field, 333 feet; left center, 375 feet; center field, 400 feet; right center, 375 feet; left field, 333 feet. 60 feet between home plate and the backstop. Big A scoreboard, 230 feet high. *Fences:* Ten feet, until 1966; lowered to eight feet 1966, padded in 1981, except in the

corners between the foul poles and the bullpens, where the fences are 4¾ feet. *Seating capacity:* (Until 1979) 43,250. Club boxes, 6900; field boxes, 11,076; terrace boxes, 8334; upper reserved, 9579; general admission, 7361. (After 1980) 65,158 for baseball, over 70,000 for football. *Size of entire site:* 140 acres. *Parking:* 15,000 cars. *First game:* April 19, 1966 (Chicago 3, California 1, night).

Before this site held a ballpark it was farm land. Camille Alec grew orange trees here. Roland Reynolds grew alfalfa, and John Knutgen, Bill Ross and George Lenney grew corn.

After a year in Los Angeles' Wrigley Field, and two years sharing Chavez Ravine with the Dodgers, the expansion Angels moved into Anaheim Stadium in 1966. It was announced by owner Gene Autry that the name of the club was being changed from the Los Angeles Angels to the California Angels.

When the ballpark was first built there were no stands in center field. The outfield was enclosed with two decks of seats in 1980. The park's nickname comes from the 230-foot A-frame scoreboard originally in left field. That scoreboard, the tallest ever, had a gold halo around its pointy tip, and bore the Chevron emblem of Standard Oil of California. During the 1980 enlargement the scoreboard was moved outside the right field stands and currently overlooks the parking lot and the Orange Freeway.

In 1980, a video scoreboard was installed by Stewart-Warner, the same company that made the old scoreboard. The new scoreboard is on the facade of the left center roof. The expansion was designed to provide additional seating for the Los Angeles Rams, who were moving here from the Coliseum.

This is one of the easiest ballparks to get into and out of by car. It is surrounded by three highways. The parking lots have 26 entrance lanes and 28 exit lanes.

Angels have signed a lease here through 2001, the Rams through 2015. There are 106 executive luxury boxes, ranging in yearly price from $16,000 to $50,000. There are several fancy dining areas throughout the stadium, including the Stadium Club.

This park was the site of the 1967 All-Star Game, the longest of all time, a 15-inning classic ending with Tony Perez's home run off Catfish Hunter.

Anderson, South Carolina

Memorial Stadium
Western Carolina League 1970–72, South Atlantic League circa 1985 (franchise no longer exists). *Seating capacity:* 4000.

Appleton, Wisconsin

Goodland Field
Three-I League 1958–61, Midwest League 1962–present (Foxes). *Location:* Spencer and South Outagamie streets. *Dimensions:* Left field, 330 feet; center field, 405 feet; right field, 330 feet. *Seating capacity:* 4300. *Season attendance:* (1985) 76,860; (1986) 60,001; (1987) 81,208. *Record season attendance:* 94,730 (1978).

Among the regulars up in the stands at Goodland Field is Patti McFarland, who can remember Earl Weaver playing second base for the Fox Cities. She recalls the night Dean Chance won all those stuffed animals throwing baseballs at the carnival. She held Cal Ripken, Jr., in her arms when he was just a baby. Back in those days (around 1960) Appleton, Wisconsin played in the Three-I (Indiana, Illinois, and Iowa) League, a bit of geographical oddity to be filed with the Atlanta Braves' placement in the National League West.

In 1986, team cut-up Tim Haller made such a fuss over his singing voice that his teammates challenged him to

Top: *Mohawk Mills Park, Amsterdam, N.Y., circa 1938. (From the personal collection of David Pietrusza.)* Bottom: *Anaheim Stadium, Anaheim, California—view from the upper deck. (Compliments of the California Angels.)*

sing the National Anthem before a game at Goodland. It took him two tries over three days, but he did it. His voice was fine, but the first time he forgot the words. He got as far as the bombs bursting in air, and then everything went blank.

The brick ballpark has a classic roofed grandstand built the old-fashioned way, with obstructing support beams. There are other obstructions as well. The wooden light poles stand in front of the bleachers and grandstand. There are advertisements on the wall, a Marlboro man in right center, and a small Miller High Life electric scoreboard on top of the fence in left center. Growing behind the fences are tall hedges which are neatly pruned flat. As of 1986, popcorn cost 50 cents, beer a dollar, and $1.25 got you a Cheese Brat.

Most nights you can get seats directly behind home—but on especially warm nights, open bleacher seats behind the third base dugout are recommended for the breeze.

Arlington, Texas see also Dallas, Texas, and Fort Worth, Texas

Arlington Stadium (Turnpike Stadium 1965–71)

Texas League 1965–71 (Dallas–Fort Worth Spurs), American League 1972–present (Texas Rangers). *Location:* On the Dallas–Fort Worth Turnpike (State Highway 157), north of the former Arlington Downs Race Track, not far from the Six Flags Over Texas Amusement Park. Collins Street (first base side), Copeland Road (third base),

Randol Mill Road (right field), Stadium Drive East (left field). *Built:* 1964 (by Tarrant County). *Construction cost:* (1964) $1.9 million. Owned by the City of Arlington 1971–present. *Total renovation cost:* (three renovations) $19 million. *Dimensions:* Left field, 330 feet; left center, 380 feet; center field, 400 feet; right center, 380 feet; right field, 330 feet. 60 feet between home plate and the backstop. *Seating capacity:* (1965) 10,000; (1970, all wooden bleachers) 20,000; (1971) 35,698; (1978–83) 41,284; (1984–present) 43,508. In 1971, seating broke down this way: field boxes, 6478; lower club boxes, 2666; lower reserved, 2042; upper loge boxes, 2758; upper plaza boxes, 2929; general admission (terrace), 18,825. Current (1988) seating breakdown: super boxes, 632; field boxes, 8851; mezzanine boxes, 6148; reserved, 2875; plaza, 5021; grandstand reserved, 3649; general admission, 16,332. *First Texas League game:* April 23, 1965 (Spurs defeat Albuquerque). *First American League game:* April 21, 1972 (Texas 7, California 6; attendance, 20,105).

When the site was first used as a ballpark, it was called Turnpike Stadium, held 10,000, and was used by the Dallas Spurs of the Texas League. The field was built at the bottom of a natural bowl in the earth. Except for behind the infield where there were wooden bench seats, fans sat on the grassy slopes of the bowl looking down at the action. The only excavation necessary for the construction of the park — or for its various enlargements — was the digging done to connect the dugouts to the clubhouses. In 1970, the seating capacity was doubled, and after 1971 it was nearly doubled again. A third enlargement in 1978 brought the seating capacity to over 41,000. The park remains single-decked, for the most part, with a small (by major league standards) upper deck directly behind home plate.

The name was changed to Arlington Stadium when the Rangers came to play here in 1972. The first major league home run in Arlington was hit by Frank Howard on April 21 in the first inning of the 1972 opener.

No fair ball has ever been hit out of Arlington Stadium. In 1981, this was the third worst hitter's park since 1900. Only 82 percent of the league-average number of runs were scored here.

The ballpark is close to other Arlington attractions like Wet'n Wild and Six Flags Over Texas, a proximity known to cause major traffic jams when there is more than one thing going on at once.

Concerts are never booked into Arlington Stadium — city policy. In 1983, director of stadium operations Stan McIlvaine said, "Whatever revenue a concert would generate, it would cost you more to re-sod the field."

The park derives little income outside of the Rangers. Major league baseball has a measurable effect on the Arlington economy. A 1980 study showed $6 million per year is spent outside the park by visiting fans — and 28 percent of all fans are visiting from outside the Arlington area.

The park employs 527 concession workers (concessions account for ⅔ of the park's income), 75 parking attendants and off-duty Arlington police officers for security.

Each rain-out costs the city $60,000. Texas rarely draws over 40,000 for a baseball game. The team has never won its division.

These days the Rangers have a little more to be excited about, like new stars Pete Incaviglia, Ruben Sierra, and Oddibe (18 Again) McDowell.

Asheville, North Carolina

Barn Field (Smith's 118-Acre Tract)
Location: Around Grove Street to the northeast corner of Aston Park.

In 1866, this was the site of the first recorded baseball game in Asheville. The area also served as a tournament

Arlington (Tex.) Stadium. (Compliments of the Texas Rangers.)

ground for Confederate veterans engaging in cavalry competitions, and as a public gathering place for political speeches or picnics.

Name of park unknown

Southeastern League 1897, home of Asheville baseball circa 1890–1904. *Location:* Hillside and Charlotte streets.

Kids watched the games from the branches of a big sycamore tree next to the field.

Riverside Park

Southeastern League 1910 (Skylanders), Appalachian League 1911 (Skylanders), also home of the Skylanders 1905–9. *Location:* In the flat plain across from Riverside Cemetery.

Riverside was Asheville's most celebrated park, with the most magnificent facilities in city history. Along with an "elaborate" ballpark there was a large exposition pavilion, a boathouse, daily canoe and sailboat excursions on the French Broad River, a penny arcade, a merry-go-round, and stables with weekly horse shows. The Skylanders were forced to move in the middle of

the 1911 season because of flooding. The ballpark was finally destroyed completely by the Great Flood of 1916.

The park was considered small even by dead-ball standards, the fences easily reachable to all fields. Fly balls to right field went into an artificial lake while drives to left went into the French Broad or sometimes bounced into the streetcar barn.

Oates Park

Appalachian League 1911–12 (Mountaineers), North Carolina State League 1913–17 (Mountaineers, Tourists). *Location:* Southside Avenue, McDowell and Choctaw streets. *Seating capacity:* 1200.

It was in this cramped park, squeezed into a triangle formed by its boundary streets, that Asheville resident Thomas Wolfe gained his appreciation of baseball. As was the case at Riverside, ground rule home runs were easy to hit here. Homers to center often shattered windows on Choctaw Street. One neighbor found a side business in selling the balls that landed on his roof to kids for 25 cents apiece.

According to Asheville historian

Milton Ready, "Oates was one of the finest baseball facilities in the South." Touring teams such as the Philadelphia A's and the Boston Red Sox arrived by streetcar for exhibition games from 1911 to 1922. In 1915, the Mountaineers won the championship of the North Carolina State League and afterward came in second three straight years.

On August 31, 1916, Oates Park was the site of the shortest game in organized baseball history. It was a meaningless last game of the season against Winston-Salem, with the visitors looking to catch an early train. The game started at 1:28 and was over at 1:59. Nobody took a pitch, nobody remembers who won, and spectators got their money back.

After the white players moved to new McCormick Field, Asheville's black professional ballplayers took up residence in Oates Park for many years.

McCormick Field

South Atlantic League 1924 (Skylanders), 1925-30, 1959-62, 1980-present (Tourists), Piedmont League 1931-42 (Tourists), Tri-State League 1946-55 (Tourists), Southern League 1963-66, 1968-70, 1972-75 (Tourists), Carolina League 1967 (Tourists), Dixie Association 1971, West Carolina League 1976-79 (Tourists). *Location:* Valley Street, McCormick Place. *Built:* 1924. *Dimensions:* Left field, 328 feet; center field, 397 feet; right center, 326 feet; right field, 301 feet. Deepest part of the field, just to the right of center, 404 feet. *Seating capacity:* (1960) 3200; (1975-85) 3500. *First game:* April 3, 1924 (Detroit Tigers 18, Asheville Skylanders 14, exhibition). *Lights installed:* 1940. *1987 season attendance:* 104,060.

The country's oldest wooden ballpark still in use. Like Wrigley Field in Chicago, McCormick Field is known for the thick vines covering the outfield wall. A colorful sign out front says, "Welcome to Historic McCormick Field."

The park was named after Dr. L.M. McCormick, the first and only Asheville bacteriologist. He started the germ-conscious "Swat That Fly" movement in Asheville, which spread throughout the United States, and even overseas. Flyswatter sales went way up.

At first, McCormick Field had no outfield fences. Outfielders had to chase fly balls up the side of the big hill out there. Since the 1950s the field has had a fence full of billboard signs, doubledecked in right next to the scoreboard. Sitting on top of the scoreboard is the clock from the Ebbets Field scoreboard, transplanted after the Dodgers went west. The park was a favorite of Dodger owner Branch Rickey, who used to love the smell of honeysuckle about the outfield.

Belly Ache Heard 'Round the World. Babe Ruth once called McCormick Park the prettiest park in America, and he might have meant it — despite his reputation as a man with a lot of charm. The field snuggles into the side of a mountain, the hill starting to rise just outside the outfield fences. A fan sees nothing but trees and sky above the home run barriers.

Not all of Ruth's experiences in Asheville were pleasant ones. It was here, in April of 1925, that the Babe collapsed at the train station and was carted off to the hospital, starting rumors flying that he had died. Many thought Babe was suffering the side-effects of carousing. Official word was that he'd, ahem, eaten too many hot dogs.

First Game. Baseball was first played at McCormick Field on April 3, 1924, an exhibition game between the home nine and the great Detroit Tigers. A crowd of 3199 watched — far from capacity. The grandstand from third to first was filled, but there was a second roofed grandstand out in left field. Those seats were "sparsely occupied." Tiger right-fielder Harry Heilmann, who had hit .403 the year before, abused the minor league pitching for three home runs that day, two of which bounced off the top of the left field grandstand. Ty Cobb added a homer of his own in the slugfest, as the Tigers won 18–14.

The park does not look very different today. The grandstand is still made of wood—but the left field stands have been gone since before World War II.

There was no baseball in McCormick Field between 1955 and 1957 after the collapse of the Tri-State League, and the site was used for car races for three years.

Folks still talk about the home runs Willie Stargell hit for Asheville in 1961. The Hall of Famer hit 22 that year, some of which looked to be heading for Wilmington, on the North Carolina coast.

In 1988 historic McCormick Field served as background in the film *Bull Durham*.

Atlanta, Georgia

Name of park unknown
Location: Hunter Street, west of Oakland Cemetery.

In 1866, this was the site of a 4½-hour marathon between the Atlantas and the Gate City Nine. Gate City emerged victorious 127–29, behind the home run hitting of third baseman Tom Johnson.

After the game the Atlantas disbanded, and the Gate Cities went 36–1 across the Southeast, their only loss to an Athens college team. The Gate Cities became popular and spread baseball fever through an area burned only two years before by Union soldiers.

Peters Park
Southern League 1885–86, 1888–89. *Location:* North Avenue and West Peachtree Street. *Built:* 1885.

A familiar face at Peters Park was Henry W. Grady, president of the Southern League and managing edi-

tor and sports writer for *The Atlanta Constitution.* Grady could be seen greeting the society figures whose attendance he had urged, and dictating game accounts for the paper to his personal secretary. Other notable fans of the time were Georgia political powerhouse Ben Hill, and Civil War general and ex-senator Bob Toombs.

The construction of Peters Park was subsidized by the Atlanta Street Railway. That company also oversaw the park's operation.

Named after baseball enthusiast Richard Peters, the park consisted of a small grandstand and bleachers. The grounds were enclosed by a tall wire fence.

Brisbane Park
Southern League 1892–93, 1896–98 (Crackers). *Location:* Cumley, Glenn, and Ira streets.

Baseball historian Steven A. Riess, in his book *Touching Base,* calls the location of short-lived Brisband Park "the fashionable southern part of town."

The Crackers moved to Athletic Grounds for two years, then came back to Brisbane for three years until the Southern League collapsed shortly into the 1898 season.

Athletic Grounds
Southern League 1894–95 (Crackers). *Location:* Jackson and Irwin streets.

Just as the construction of Brisbane Park was financed by the Atlanta Street Railway, one-upmanship led Consolidated Railway to build Athletic Grounds, called by Steven A. Riess "the second largest field in the south." Consolidated bragged that they could get a man from downtown to the ballpark in five minutes.

Show Grounds
Southern League 1896 (Crackers, some games). *Location:* Boulevard, Jackson, and Irvin streets.

Piedmont Park

Southern Association 1902–06 (Crackers). *Location:* 10th Street and Piedmont Avenue. *Built:* 1896. *Seating capacity:* (1902) 1000; (1904) 2000.

In 1902, after a three-year absence, minor league baseball returned to Atlanta in the form of the new Southern Association. Games were played at Piedmont Park in the old Exposition Grounds north of the city, a field built for college sports six years before.

In 1904, the city bought the park, rearranged the diamond, built a fence, and doubled the seating capacity to 2000. Smokers had a separate seating section. The park was easily accessible, as it was near both rail lines. The rent was cheap for the Crackers, $600 a year, and the field was kept in good shape—but it eventually proved unsatisfactory because of its lack of seating. Money was being lost turning away customers on weekends.

Ponce de Leon Park (Spiller Park 1924–32)

Southern Association 1907–59 (Crackers), Negro American League 1938 (Black Crackers), International League 1962–64 (Crackers). *Location:* 650 Ponce de Leon Boulevard (first base), North Boulevard (third base), Southern Railroad tracks (right field). *Construction cost:* (1906) $60,000, (1923) $250,000. *Dimensions:* (1923–50) Left field, 365 feet; center field, 462 feet; right field, 321 feet. (1951–64) Left field, 330 feet; center field, 410 feet; right field, 321 feet. *Fences:* Left field, four feet (once a two-foot hedge); left center, 25 feet (scoreboard); center field, six feet; right field, 15 feet. *Seating capacity:* (1907–23) 8000, (1923–64) 14,500. *Record attendance:* 21,812 (Opening Day, 1948, Crackers versus Birmingham). *Size of site:* 23 acres. *First game:* May 23, 1907 (attendance 8426). *Fire:* September 9, 1923 (rebuilt in concrete and steel for 1924 season). *Torn down:* 1967.

In 1906, the Crackers were purchased from Consolidated by the Georgia Railway and Electric Company and the ball club was moved to a new park—coincidence of all coincidences—right across the street from an amusement park (the original Ponce de Leon Park) owned by GR&E. The wooden grandstand had a separate section for black people.

The park burned in 1923, spectacularly, and with one injury—a club secretary who had fallen asleep in his office was burned before he was rescued. It was rebuilt in concrete and steel, and renamed Spiller Park after club president Tell J. Spiller. This was the structure that remained the home of Atlanta baseball for (almost) the remainder of the minor league days, Atlanta's last ballpark before the cookie-cutter. There was a slope deep in right field which eventually held as many as four rows of painted billboards, each row behind and above the one previous.

During the 1930s, Ponce de Leon Park hosted Georgia Tech baseball, and it remains the site of the longest game in Georgia Tech history. On May 1, 1933, Oglethorpe took 15 innings to beat Tech 5–3.

For a short time in 1949, a two-foot hedge was planted from the left field corner straight across to center field—to cut down the home run distance. But the hedge was too short and was dangerous. Ballplayers sometimes caught fly balls and then tumbled over the hedge to the other side—and this was a ground rule home run. A magnolia tree grew deep in right center.

This was the home of the Crackers until the end of the 1964 season. Atlanta-Fulton County Stadium was ready for use, so the minor league team played its last season (1965) in the big league park, waiting for the 1966 arrival of the Braves from Milwaukee.

Grant Field

Southern Association 1923 (Crackers), also home of the Georgia

Tech Yellow Jackets before 1931. *Location:* Georgia Tech campus.

The home of the Georgia Tech athletic teams was used by Crackers while Ponce de Leon Park was being rebuilt following its fire, September 9, 1923.

Chandler Stadium (Rose Bowl Field)

Home of the Georgia Tech University Yellow Jackets (Atlantic Coast Conference) 1931–present. *Location:* Fifth Avenue (first base side), Fowler Street (right field) on the edge of the Georgia Tech University campus. *Current grandstand built:* 1985. *Construction cost:* $650,000. *Dimensions:* Left field, 320 feet; left center, 375 feet; center field, 400 feet; right center, 385 feet; right field, 330 feet. *Seating capacity:* (1929–84) 6000; (1985–present) 2500 (reserved, 500). *Single game attendance record:* 4071 (May 1, 1983, versus the University of Georgia). *Lights:* 1983.

Chandler Stadium, part of the Rose Bowl Field athletic complex, is named after A. Russell Chandler III (Class of 1967), who donated the money for its construction in 1985, Georgia Tech's centennial year. In addition to the nine-row concrete grandstand which wraps around home plate, the stadium received new restroom and concessions facilities, a press level complete with radio and television booths, a V.I.P. box, and a working press area for 20 reporters. In 1986 a new clubhouse was constructed, which was connected to the Tech dugout by a tunnel.

The original stadium, whose stone walls are still there behind the new billboarded baseball fences, was constructed after the 1929 Rose Bowl, from funds received because of Tech's participation in the post-season college football classic.

The original configuration had home plate in the current right field corner, but it had to be changed to its current location in 1971, when Fifth Street was extended through the campus, forcing the demolition of the old grandstand.

The current outfield fence has been there since 1972. There have been advertisements (26 billboards) on the outfield fence since 1983, and the original revenue from these went to pay for the stadium's lights. The current scoreboard was installed in 1983 as well.

Atlanta-Fulton County Stadium

International League 1965 (Crackers), National League 1966–present (Braves). *Location:* Junction of interstate highways 20, 75, and 85 (one mile south of midtown Atlanta). Georgia Avenue (third base side), Capitol Avenue (first base side), Fulton Street (right field side), Pullman Street (left field side). *Nickname:* The Launching Pad. *Cost of construction:* $18 million. *Architects:* Heery & Heery, and Finch, Alexander, Barnes, Rothschild & Paschal, both of Atlanta. *General contractor:* Thompson & Street Co., of Charlotte, North Carolina, and Atlanta. *Construction begins:* April 15, 1964. *Dimensions:* Left field, 330 feet; left center, 385 feet; center field, 402 feet; right center, 385 feet; right field, 330 feet. 60 feet between home plate and backstop. *Fences:* Ten feet all the way around (six feet of wire topped by four feet of plexiglass). The wall behind fence is 22 feet high. *Seating capacity:* 53,043. Dugout level boxes, 173; field boxes, 2952; field reserved, 16,757; upper boxes, 2796; upper reserved, 19,869; general admission, 10,496. Holds 60,749 for football. *First game:* April 9, 1965 (Braves defeated Tigers 6–3 in exhibition). *First National League game:* April 12, 1966 (Pittsburgh 3, Atlanta 2, 13 innings, night). *Sports played at the stadium:* Braves baseball, Falcons football, annual Peach Bowl college football game, and Motocross Race in March.

The story of how Atlanta got their new stadium has been described as a "two-year municipal juggling act." Star performers were Atlanta Mayor Ivan Allen, Jr.; Mills Lane, chairman of the board of the Citizens and Southern Bank; Arthur Montgomery, Atlanta Coca-Cola bottler; Opie Shelton, executive director of the Atlanta Chamber of Commerce; Furman Bisher, sports editor of the *Atlanta Journal;* and Atlanta architects Bill Finch and George Heery.

In 1963, the city of Atlanta, desperately wanting major league baseball, had a predicament. It was described later by Mayor Allen: "We had to find a club which might want to move, then persuade them to move to Atlanta, where we offered them a stadium not yet designed, to be built with money we didn't yet have, on land we didn't yet own."

While Furman Bisher began looking for a team, influential citizen Mills Lane decided to build a stadium. Lane, with no more than a handshake, persuaded two separate architectural firms to work in conjunction on the ballpark project. They were Heery and Heery, and Finch, Alexander, Barnes, Rothschild and Paschal.

Next the land was bought, 62 ideal acres at the confluence of three interstate highways. Lane provided nearly three-quarters of a million dollars in unsecured loans to finance the initial steps toward building Atlanta a ballpark worthy of the Georgian capital. Arthur Montgomery of Coca-Cola took charge of the newly formed Atlanta and Fulton County Recreational Authority, a quasi-public organization which was to own the stadium and hold the revenue bonds with which it would be built.

Now for the juggling act: "Montgomery had to have absolute confidence that we would get a stadium built," said Mayor Allen, "yet to get a stadium agreement out of the Board of Aldermen, we had to have assurance that there was in fact a team ready to move in."

Chamber of Commerce head Opie Shelton worked out a deal. If Atlanta fans supported a bond issue for a new

auditorium and cultural center, then— Shelton promised—the Chamber of Commerce would support the drive for a stadium.

In the spring of 1964, the revenue bonds were authorized, the plans were approved, and the land under option was delivered to the Recreation Authority. One of the enhancements used to lure the Braves from Milwaukee was that the new Atlanta Stadium could be built in one year— this in spite of the fact that it had taken over two years to build the recently opened Shea Stadium in New York.

As it turned out, Atlanta-Fulton County Stadium was built in an amazing 50 weeks using a newly developed system of electronically computed scheduling. A rush job, and architecturally bland—just like the Braves of the late 1980s.

The longest home run hit here was by Cubs outfielder Willie Smith off Braves rightie Ron Reed, on June 10, 1969. The ball crashed into the upper deck in right, just to the left of the exit ramp in aisle 329. Other notable upper deck blasts have been hit by Willie McCovey, Earl Williams and, as one might suspect, Hank Aaron.

Among the memorable games that have been played here were the first two games of the 1969 National League Championship Series, the Braves losing both to the Mets.

In the 1972 All-Star Game, Aaron hit a sixth-inning home run here, off Gaylord Perry of the Indians. The National League won that game in 10 innings, 4-3.

But the most memorable game of all played in Atlanta-Fulton County Stadium was Opening Night, April 8, 1974, when Aaron became baseball's all-time home run champion by hitting number 715 off the Dodgers' Al Downing.

In 1966, a large figure named Big Victor, styled after a totem pole, stood behind the outfield fence. Victor tilted

Atlanta–Fulton County Stadium. A cookie-cutter! *(Compliments of the Atlanta Braves.)*

his head and rolled his eyes whenever the Braves hit a home run.

In 1967, Chief Noc-A-Homa's wigwam was put out there in place of Big Victor. Until 1971, the wigwam sat on top of a twenty-foot platform behind the left field fence. The wigwam (teepee) spent a few years out in right, and then found a new home up in the stands. On a couple of occasions management decided to take out the wigwam to fit in more paying customers, but each time the team began to tailspin, so the Chief's home was put back.

From 1972 to 1979, Atlanta-Fulton County Stadium was known for its last-place ball clubs and tacky promotions. Fans raced on ostriches. Camels threw cow chips at one another. Thirty-four couples were married at home plate followed by Championship Wrestling — "Headlock and Wedlock Night." A local deejay almost suffocated after diving head first into a huge ice cream sundae. Seriously, the man almost *died.* A wet tee-shirt contest kept 27,000 fans inside the ballpark until

1:30 in the morning, waiting out several rain delays and an 11–0 loss by the Braves. When the ballgame was finally over — thank God! — each of the 43 ladies in the feature event received standing ovations.

Atlantic City, New Jersey

Bacharach Park
Eastern Colored League 1923–28 (Bacharach Giants). *Location:* McKinley, North New York, and South Carolina avenues.

Mayor Henry Bacharach of Atlantic City went to see a black ball game in Jacksonville, and was so impressed by one team's skills that he hired them — actually, he put them on the city payroll — and built a ballpark for them to play in, naming everything he could after himself.

Ballpark was the site of Game Two of the 1926 Negro League World Series. The block currently holds the Carver Hall housing projects.

Atlantic Park Dog Track
Eastern Colored League 1923-28 (Bacharach Giants, some games). *Location:* Absecon Boulevard, at the Municipal Market, current site of the Shop'n Bag Supermarket.

Auburn, New York

Falcon Park
Canadian American League (Class C) 1938 (Boulies), 1940 (Falcons), Border League (Class C) 1946-50, New York-Pennsylvania League 1981-present (Astros). *Dimensions:* Left field, 326 feet; center field, 382 feet; right field, 325 feet. *Seating capacity:* 3500. *1987 season attendance:* 29,740. *Lights:* 1940.

Because of a dip in the outfield, outfielders have to be tall to play here, or they can't see the batter. The infield is noted for being hard as a rock, hell on pitchers who like to throw ground balls.

The ballpark was twice the home for a franchise in the Canadian American League, a disaster both times. It housed Border League baseball too, during the sole year of that league's existence. The Border League was founded by Father Martin (see Ogdensburg).

Augusta, Georgia

Heaton Park
South Atlantic League 1988 (Pirates). *Location:* Lake Olmstead, on Milledge Avenue, off Broad Street. *Dimensions:* Left field, 335 feet; center field, 400 feet; right field, 335 feet. *Seating capacity:* 4000.

Franchise moved here from Macon.

Austin, Texas

Clark Field
Texas League 1956-67, also home of the Texas Longhorns baseball team 1928-73. *Location:* University of Texas campus. *Dimensions:* Left field, 350 feet; left center, 375 feet; center field, 401 feet; right center, 363 feet; right field, 300 feet. *Seating capacity:* 5500. *First game:* March 24, 1928 (Detroit Tigers 12, Longhorns 8, exhibition). *Last game:* April 27, 1974 (Longhorns 4, Texas A&M 3).

A truly unique ballpark, one that added a whole new dimension to games played there—like 3D chess or something. The outfield was built on two tiers, with a 12-foot cliff separating them. Outfielders had to play in or out, out being on the upper tier. If they played out, infielders would be responsible for the lower tier. The cliff in straightaway center was very rocky, and became known as "Billy Goat Hill."

Those playing on the upper tier must have been reluctant on occasion to come in hard on a ball, and balls hit onto the upper tier when only one outfielder patroled it could easily roll free for inside-the-parkers. The upper tier was largest in center field, where the cliff was 53 feet from the fence. It also bulged in left, where there were 31 feet between the fence and the drop-off. Between the bulges, in left center, the cliff ran a slender 18 feet from the wall. There was no cliff in right.

The ballpark was torn down in 1974 when the main campus of the University of Texas needed the land for more academic reasons. Luckily, Disch-Falk Field, the park the university built to replace Clark, was a beauty.

Disch-Falk Field
Home of the Texas Longhorns baseball team 1975-present. *Location:* Martin Luther King Boulevard, between Comal Street and Interstate 25, just southeast of the main University of Texas campus. *Construction cost:* $2.5 million. *Dimensions:* Left field, 340 feet; left center, 375 feet; center field, 400 feet; right center, 375 feet; right

Zaragosa Amateur Baseball Field, Austin, Tex. (Compliments of the Austin Convention and Visitors Bureau.)

field, 325 feet. *Fences:* Left field, ten feet; center field, 20 feet; right field, ten feet. *Surface:* AstroTurf. Warning track is made of a rubberized Tartan material (last replaced 1985). *Seating capacity:* 7000 (5000 grandstand, 2000 bleachers). *Record single game attendance:* 10,000 (April 5, 1977, Texas Rangers versus Texas Longhorns, exhibition). *First game:* February 17, 1975 (Longhorns 4, St. Mary's 0, first game of doubleheader. Longhorns won second game, 11–0). *Dedication:* April 19, 1975 (Longhorns sweep two from TCU, 18–3, 14–0).

Named after two former Longhorn coaches, the late Billy Disch and Bibb Falk. William J. (Uncle Billy) Disch coached the Longhorns from 1911 to 1939, going 513–180 (.740) during that time, and earning 20 Southwest Conference Championships. He was called "the Connie Mack of collegiate baseball" because of his physical resemblance to Mr. McGillicuddy, and was inducted into the Texas Sports Hall of Fame.

Bibb Falk was the Longhorn skipper 1940–42, 1946–67. His record was 468–176. Like Disch before him, he

won 20 Southwest Conference pennants, as well as two NCAA championships in 1949 and 1950.

Money was first authorized for the ballpark by the university in 1973, when it was decided Clark Field was to be overrun by a growing campus. The field has been the site of NCAA post-season play from 1979 to the present. It is universally recognized as one of the best college baseball facilities in the nation.

The ballpark has eight light towers, plus banks of lights mounted on top of the grandstand roof, so the candlepower is comparable to major league levels. Bleachers run down the right field line.

Zaragosa Amateur Baseball Field

Home of the Zaragosa Amateur League, present. *Location:* 741 Pedernales.

Part of the City of Austin Parks and Recreation System. Also site of *Diez y Seis de Septiembre Celebration,* Soccer, Flag football, and Little League baseball.

Bakersfield, California

According to a story in *The Visalia Delta* in July 1879, the Visalia Empires amateur baseball team traveled to Bakersfield for a road game, which they won 44–21. The Visalia Silver Cornet Band and the Shooting Club went along for the ride. The paper reported, "During the game, an Irishman stole the umpire's coat and 50 men went after him. They stopped at the Willows with him and we thought we were going to see some 'Bakersfield justice.'"

Sam Lynn Park

California State League (Class C) 1941–42, 1946–56 (Badgers 1941–42, Indians 1946–55, Boosters, 1956), California League 1957–75, 1978–79, 1982–present (Bears 1957–67, Dodgers 1968–75, Outlaws 1978–79, Mariners 1982–83, Dodgers 1984–present). *Location:* Chester Street (California Avenue exit on Highway 99). *Opened:* 1941. *Dimensions:* Left field, 328 feet, center field, 354 feet, right field, 328 feet. *Seating capacity:* (1960) 3600, (1985) 3000. *Record season attendance:* 140,389 (1949). *Record low season attendance:* 23,234 (1965). *1987 season attendance:* 109,120.

People in Bakersfield are still trying to figure out who blundered. Some writers, like local baseball historian Bill Underwood, like to think that it was done on purpose—but there's a chance this was just a major snafu, a bit of vertigo that proved to be very expensive.

Like Vince Genna Stadium in Bend, Sam Lynn Park is out of whack, with straightaway center running slightly west of northwest, about a right angle off the direction stipulated in Rule 1.04 of the *Official Baseball Rules*, east-northeast. This means the sun sets behind left center, into batters' and catchers' eyes, turning pitchers into silhouettes, rendering hitting impossible—not to mention dangerous. Catchers have been known to wear sunglasses beneath their masks. Hitters

have been known to grow sick to their stomachs. Games in Bakersfield start at 8:00 instead of 7:00 so that fewer innings are played under these conditions. Over the years this has cost the team a lot of money in concession sales as more folks eat before coming to the ballpark. Fans have to stare out into the sun too.

So who blundered? Here are the suspects.

Sam Lynn was the local Coca-Cola distributor. He sponsored many local sports teams and donated the land for the ballpark. He also became personally involved with planning and promoting the project. When the time came he saw to it that Bakersfield had a spot in the newly formed California State League for the 1941 season. The ballpark, built with a combination of community and WPA funds, was ready just in time.

It was not Lynn's intention to name the park after himself. After seeing to it that every nail was pounded in correctly, Lynn dropped dead, days before the home opener, and the ballpark was named after him in memoriam.

Another possible suspect is R.H. Hubbard, a county official who advised Lynn. Hubbard toured Southern California ballparks seeking ideas for the Bakersfield construction. There's a chance Hubbard's idea was a doozy.

The ballpark was built out on the old fairgrounds, adjacent to a rodeo arena and a racetrack. Some locals think the grandstand was built on the wrong side just to make it accessible to the existing parking lot.

It has also been noted that the current grandstand placement faces fans into the prevailing wind, keeping the place a lot cooler on summer afternoons. It can get very hot in Bakersfield.

The center field fence is only 354 feet out. That's the softest straightaway home run touch in pro ball.

Bakersfield has had farm clubs in seven major league franchises since

Sam Lynn Park, Bakersfield, Calif. (Compliments of the Bakersfield Dodgers.)

1941. The Bakersfield teams that played at Sam Lynn Park have been known as the Badgers, Indians, Boosters, Bears, Outlaws, Dodgers, Mariners, and then Dodgers again.

Baltimore, Maryland

Newington Park
National Association 1872–74 (Lord Baltimores), American Association 1882 (for one week, Orioles). *Location:* Baker, Gold, and Calhoun streets, Pennsylvania Avenue. *First National Association game:* April 22, 1872. *Last National Association game:* October 14, 1874. *First American Association game:* May 9, 1882. *Last American Association game:* May 16, 1882.

Madison Avenue Grounds (Monumental Park, Pastime Base Ball Grounds)
National Association 1873 (Marylands), Union Association 1884 (Unions). *Location:* Bloom Street, later called Boundary Avenue, now called North Avenue (third base), Madison Avenue (home), old road between what is now Roberts Street and Laurens Street (first base), Linden Avenue (center field). *First National Association game:* April 14, 1873. *Last National Association game:* July 11, 1873. *First Union Association game:* August 25, 1884. *Last Union Association game:* September 23, 1884.

Oriole Park (I) (Huntingdon Avenue Park, American Association Park)
American Association 1882–89 (Orioles). *Location:* Huntingdon Avenue, later called Sixth Street, now called 25th Street (right field), York Road, later called Greenmount Avenue (first base), Fifth Street, now 24th Street (third base), Barclay Street (left field). Grandstand sat at what is now the southeast corner of Barclay and 25th streets. *Cost of construction:* $5000. *Seating capacity:* 5000 (grandstand 1200, bleacher 3800). *First game:* May 17, 1882 (Baltimore 8, St. Louis 5). *Last game:* October 10, 1889.

There were 1200 "elegant" chairs in the grandstand behind home. Bleachers sat on either side of the roofed section, down the baselines.

Every Thursday was Ladies Day, starting in 1883 — an idea that proved so popular that it soon caught on at other parks.

This was the neutral site of a World Series game October 21, 1887, between Detroit of the National League and St. Louis of the American Association. Detroit won 13–3. Attendance was 2707 for Game 11 of the 15-game series. The only home run of the game was hit by Detroit's Lawrence Twitchell, who played outfield that day and had gone 10–1 that year as a pitcher. Game 10 had been played that morning in Washington, St. Louis the victor. Detroit ended up winning ten of the 15 games while touring the country.

This park was eventually torn down and a new one (Union Park) was built directly across Barclay Avenue.

Union Association Park (Belair Lot)

Union Association 1884. *Location:* East Baltimore. Gay Street, Forrest Street, Low Street, and Chestnut Street (now Colvin Street), across Forrest from the Belair Market. Current site of the Old Town Mall parking lot. *First game:* April 17, 1884. *Last game:* September 24, 1884.

Only local ballpark to be located in East Baltimore.

Oriole Park (II)

American Association 1890–91 (Orioles). *Location:* York Road between Ninth and Tenth streets, bordered by Barclay to the east. (Now Greenmount Avenue between 28th and 29th streets. Grandstand located at what is now the southwest corner of Greenmount Avenue and 29th Street.) *First game:* August 27, 1890. *Last game:* May 10, 1891.

Union Park

American Association 1891 (Orioles), National League 1892–99 (Orioles). *Location:* Barclay Street (left field), Huntingdon Avenue, later called Sixth Street, now called 25th Street (third base), St. Paul Street, now

Guilford Avenue (first base), Sumwalt Street, now 24th Street and Brady's Run. Grandstand located on what is today the southwest corner of Barclay and 25th streets, across Barclay from site of Oriole Park (I). *Dimensions:* Left field, 300 feet; right field, 350 feet. *Fences:* 16 feet. *Seating capacity:* (1891) 6000, (1894) 6500. *Record single game attendance:* 30,000 (estimated), September 27, 1897. *Last American Association game:* October 3, 1891 (Philadelphia 8, Baltimore 2). *First National League game:* April 15, 1892 (Brooklyn 10, Baltimore 6). *Last National League game:* October 10, 1899 (Baltimore 5, Washington 5, five innings, darkness). *Fire:* 1894. *Major refurbishment:* 1895 (following '94 fire).

Across Barclay Street from the location of Oriole Park (I), beer wholesaler and Oriole owner Harry von der Horst leased a lot and built Union Park. He charged a nickel to get in and made $30,000 in 1893 alone. The park burned in 1894 and had to be rebuilt. Four National League parks burned that year, leading some to think an arsonist was at work. As was the case with many other parks, the stands were rebuilt larger than before. The ballpark was next to an amusement park where, after games, fans went for dining, dancing and concerts. The team wasn't doing well, so von der Horst gave fans reasons other than baseball to come out to the park. He set up picnic tables and a beer garden. There was plenty of stable space for those who brought horses. Dances immediately followed ball games, with the band starting to tune up as soon as the last out was made.

In 1892 the Orioles became members of the National League. Gradually they got better, then much better. Still, the carnival atmosphere at the park remained.

It turned out that ballplayers liked the beer garden picnic area just as much as the fans — so much that in 1899 a rule was made saying players "must

come in from the field and seat themselves on the players bench at the con-
clusion of their half in the field."

The park was in a residential area,
and the wooden stands sported a small
roofed upper deck behind home plate.
When 30,000 showed up to watch the
Orioles try (unsuccessfully) to win a
fourth consecutive National League
pennant on September 27, 1897, a large
number of fans sat in the open bleachers, along the foul lines from third and
first to the outfield corners. Many fans
stood in front of the high board
wooden outfield fence, while the remainder sat downstairs or upstairs in
the comparatively small grandstand.
Eight hundred of those grandstand
seats had come from Forepaugh's
Theater.

There were "bike barns" along Barclay Street outside the park, and these
were always filled by game time, with
both men's and women's bicycles.
Society women who came to be seen
rather than to watch the game sat all
together behind first base. Frequent
among spectators were Jim Corbett,
the heavyweight champion whose kid
brother was an Oriole, and Jake Kil-
rain, a pugilist from the bareknuckle
days who owned a saloon on West
Pratt Street.

It was here that John McGraw,
Willie Keeler and others invented "inside baseball," which forever removed
the word gentleman from the sport.
The new rules were: winning's the thing
and cheating's okay, as long as you
don't get caught.

McGraw's philosophy necessitated
larger umpiring crews as he liked to
trip, grab or get in the way of base runners at third whenever the ump wasn't
looking.

Even the grounds crew got into the
act—and it was here that the chalk foul
lines were first built up to keep bunted
balls fair.

The head groundskeeper was Thomas
J. Murphy, a man with an incredibly
long mustache. When an opposing

pitcher was awesome (such as Amos
"The Hoosier Thunderbolt" Rusie,
who won 230 games in eight years with
the New York Giants), Murphy would
mix soap shavings with the dirt on the
pitcher's mound. Every time the pitcher
would wipe his hands in the dirt his
fingers would get slipperier and slipperier, until he could no longer find the
strike zone. Naturally, the Oriole
pitcher (maybe Sadie McMahon) was
savvy to the scam and carried fresh dirt
for his own hands in his hip pocket.

The grass in the outfield was kept
high so the grounds crew could hide
baseballs out there. When an opponent
hit a ball into the grass, Baltimore
outfielders didn't have to waste time
looking for it; they could grab the
nearest hidden ball and fire it back in.
Visiting hitters found doubles hard to
come by. (It's hard to figure out how
the Orioles kept visiting outfielders
from discovering the hidden baseballs.
Some system must have been worked
out.)

The Baltimore crowds knew what
was going on and decided to join in the
unscrupulous fun. Fans in the stands
with small mirrors sometimes reflected
sunlight directly into the eyes of visiting
fielders or hitters. Sometimes there
were over a dozen mirrors working at
once.

You can argue about the morality of
the Orioles' play, but not about their
success. Between 1893 and 1898, Baltimore won four out of five National
League pennants.

A stream called Brady's Run ran
behind the right field fence. The outfield sloped downhill toward the fence
and waters oozed under the fence to
turn the outfield into marshland. Even
when the rest of the field was dry, out
in right it was visibly muddy at the bottom of the slope.

Baseball and the Orioles flourished
in Baltimore until the Spanish-American War (1898) strained America's
sports economy. Von der Horst
deserted to Brooklyn and took the

nucleus of his team with him. Left behind were McGraw and Wilbert Robinson, who refused to switch.

American League Park

American League 1901–02, International League 1903–15 (Orioles). *Location:* Same as Oriole Park (II). *First American League game:* April 26, 1901 (Baltimore 10, Boston 6). *Last American League game:* September 29, 1902 (Boston 9, Baltimore 5).

The outfield fence met the outfield at an obtuse angle, like the right field barrier in Ebbets Field. Only the top third of the American League Park fence was plumb.

This is where the International League Orioles were playing when the Federal League Terrapins began play on the other side of 29th Street. There was a big to-do about the Federal League at first, so everyone forgot about the Orioles. That's why fewer than 200 persons showed up at the old American League Park to see the professional debut of a 19-year-old hometown boy named George Herman Ruth, who pitched a six-hit shut-out. By the end of that season Ruth was pitching in Boston. By the following year, the International League team had moved to Richmond.

Back River, Glen Burnie, Driving Park

Sites of Sunday International League Oriole games before repeal of the blue laws.

Terrapin Park [Oriole Park (III) 1916–44]

Federal League 1914–15 (Terrapins), International League 1916–44 (Orioles). *Location:* Eleventh Street (left field), Tenth Street (first base), Vineyard Street (third base), and York Road (right field), across Tenth Street from American League Park. (Now known as 30th Street, 29th Street, Greenmount Avenue, and Vineyard Street.) *Construction cost:* $82,000+.

Dimensions: Left field, 305 feet; center field, 412 feet; right field, 310 feet. *Seating capacity:* 15,000. *Single game attendance record:* 28,000 (April 13, 1914, Opening Day). *Burned:* July 4, 1944.

Fire had become such a renowned hazard in ballparks by 1914 that all the new parks built to house the Federal League teams were concrete and fireproof — except Terrapin Park, which was built of wood. It wasn't the only wooden park in the league, however, as some franchises moved into already existing wooden parks. The stands lasted for over 30 years before they finally burned as a result of a Fourth of July fireworks accident.

The park was built between February 1, 1914, and the start of the 1914 season. Stands were constructed. Seats and turnstiles were installed. The field was drained, graded and sodded. For Opening Day, over 28,000 showed up. Folks were paying up to $10 to scalpers for tickets. The Governor of Maryland was there. The Mayor of Baltimore threw out the first ball.

The wood-above-concrete construction was cooler than the all-concrete parks being built elsewhere. When the park finally did burn, in 1944, it had long been home of the Baltimore International League franchise.

At 4 a.m. people all over Baltimore were awakened by the sound of the fire bell, or maybe the glow from the burning structure. Once the tarred roof of the stadium caught fire, there was no hope of saving anything. The loss was estimated at $150,000, and firemen failed even to save the Orioles' trophies and photographs.

The Orioles had to move to Municipal Stadium, a converted football stadium, where they drew huge crowds and promptly won the International League pennant, the post-season playoffs and the Junior World Series.

Bugle Field (Moore's Field)

Eastern Colored League 1923–28

(Black Sox), Negro American League 1929 (Black Sox), Negro East-West League 1932 (Black Sox), Negro National League 1933-34 (Black Sox), Negro American League 1938-49 (Elite Giants). *Location:* Biddle Street, Edison Highway.

It was here, in 1938, that a teenaged Roy Campanella played weekends for the Black Elites while he was still in school. He was a teammate of Biz Mackey—a great defensive catcher who taught Campy the ropes. Campanella earned $35 a week, and the check went straight to his Italian dad, who sat behind home plate at Bugle Field, shouting encouragement to his kid.

The ballpark was named after the Bugle Coat and Apron Supply Company, a large laundry owned by the Washington Senators' top scout, Joe Cambria—who also owned the ballpark and the Black Sox during the 1930s.

Druid Hill

Eastern Colored League circa 1925 (Black Sox, some games). *Location:* Druid Hill Park, Madison Avenue.

Municipal Stadium (Venable Stadium, Baltimore Stadium, Metropolitan Stadium, Babe Ruth Stadium, 1949-50)

International League 1944-49 (Orioles). *Location:* Same as Memorial Stadium, see below. *Dimensions:* Configured for football with the short fence in left. Left field, 290 feet. *Seating capacity:* Once held as many as 55,000 for baseball. *Single game attendance record:* 52,833 (October 9, 1944, Game 4, Junior World Series, Louisville 5, Baltimore 4). *Season attendance record:* 620,726 (1946).

This football bowl became the emergency home of baseball in Baltimore after Oriole Park burned down on the Fourth of July, 1944. The diamond was set up within the oval much like the diamond at the Los Angeles Coliseum, with the short porch in left.

In 1946, taking advantage of Municipal Stadium's ample seating capacity, the AAA Orioles set an International League attendance record that still stands. The structure was torn down in 1950 to make way for the new ballpark, Memorial Stadium.

Maryland Baseball Park (Westport Park)

Negro American League 1950 (Elite Giants). *Location:* In nearby Westport, Maryland. Westport Boulevard, between Russell and Bush streets.

Memorial Stadium

International League 1950-53 (Orioles), American League 1954-present (Orioles). Also former home of the Colts (National Football League). Owned by the City of Baltimore. *Location:* East 33rd Street [Babe Ruth Plaza] (home plate side), Ellerslie Avenue (third base), 36th Street (center field), Ednor Road (first base). Same as Municipal Stadium. *Designer:* L.P. Kooken Company. *Builder:* DeLuca-Davis and Joseph F. Hughes companies. *Dimensions:* (Original) left field, 309 feet; center field, 445 feet; right field, 309 feet. (Current) left field, 309 feet; left center, 390 feet; center field, 410 feet; right center, 390 feet; right field, 309 feet. 78 feet between home plate and the backstop until 1961. After that, 58 feet. *Seating capacity:* (1950-53) 31,000; (1954-60) 46,000; (1961-present) gradual rise from 49,000 to 54,076. When the capacity was 52,137, seating broke down this way: lower boxes, 7488; lower reserved, 8617; mezzanine boxes, 2117; upper reserved, 12,424; general admission, 18,087; bleacher, 3404. *First American League game:* April 15, 1954 (Baltimore 3, Chicago 1).

Here is where Brooks Robinson and Mark Belanger worked their glove wizardry; where Boog Powell hit awesome towering shots; where Earl Weaver turned his cap backwards so

Top: *Memorial Stadium, Baltimore, Md. (Photo by Morton Tadder. Compliments of the Baltimore Orioles.)* Bottom: *interior view.*

he could get his face that much closer to the umpire's face; where Palmer and McNally and Dobson and Cuellar all won 20 the same year (1971); where Frank Robinson won the American League Triple Crown in 1966; where the Orioles have won five pennants and one World Championship.

Where Memorial Stadium opened for major league baseball in 1954, the city hadn't quite completed the $6.5 million project. The bowl of Municipal Stadium had been torn down and replaced by Memorial Stadium, a double-decked horseshoe designed to accommodate both baseball and football.

It was a good thing that Opening Day didn't go into extra innings, because the lights in the outfield still hadn't been installed. The first pitch that day was thrown out by Vice-President Richard Nixon. Hours earlier there had been a grand welcoming parade for the new team and the new park.

For years the big advertisement on top of the Memorial Stadium scoreboard read, "Happiest Hit in Beer! Gunther!"

One of the major complaints about Memorial Stadium has always been that there is too little parking. Fans are forced to use the nearby parking lots belonging to Morgan State University and the Poly-Western Complex.

Sadly, Memorial Stadium was, in 1964, the site of a tragic accident as one child was killed and 46 others injured in an escalator mishap.

Now there is talk of scrapping old Memorial Stadium and building a new ballpark in Camden Yards. Ballpark historian David Pietrusza likes Memorial Stadium just fine.

"Sure, sight lines are obstructed by columns with some regularity in the lower deck, but the management is very careful not to sell any seats so obstructed. Crab cakes at Memorial Stadium are quite tasty. So are 'Half Smokeds,' a kielbasa-like sausage that is very spicy. Ushers are quite distinguished in their orange jackets."

Baseball City, Florida see Orlando, Florida

Batavia, New York

Dwyer Stadium

New York-Pennsylvania League (Formerly known as the P-O-N-Y League) 1939–present (Trojans). *Location:* Denio Street. *Built:* 1939 (WPA). *Dimensions:* Left field, 326 feet; center field, 382 feet; right field, 325 feet. *Seating capacity:* 3000. *1987 season attendance:* 25,339.

In 1939 Batavia's Mayor Mahaney personally called President Roosevelt in Washington to request WPA funds for a ballpark. His request was answered.

The park is named after Ed Dwyer, one of the original directors of Batavia

baseball, and the current president of the club.

Though the place has been fixed up here and there since it was built, it remains structurally the same — and is likely to for some time to come, despite recent discussion of tearing it down and starting from scratch.

Baton Rouge, Louisiana

City Park

Evangeline League (Class C) 1946–55 (Rebels)

Not centrally located. Lacked parking facilities.

Pete Goldsby Park

Evangeline League (Class C) 1956–57 (Rebels). *Location:* Off Scenic Highway. *Construction cost:* $140,421.16.

Goldsby Park was dedicated on August 30, 1956 at 7:30 in the evening, with the game between the Rebels and the Monroe Sports starting fifteen minutes later. The park had been built by the Recreation and Parks Commission on a 9.45 acre plot of land obtained from the state between the '55 and '56 baseball seasons. It had been in use since the beginning of the '56 season. The first game at Goldsby Park was between the Rebels and Thibodaux. Much of the work on the new park remained to be done for the opener, including the building of the overhead canopy. Rev. James L. Stovall, pastor of the North Baton Rouge Methodist Church, gave the invocation at the dedication ceremonies before officials from the city and the ball club — as well as Pete Goldsby's widow.

For years Goldsby, an advertising man, had been active sponsoring playground activities around Baton Rouge. He was in charge of youth baseball in Baton Rouge before the formation of the Recreation and Parks Commission. He had died in 1955.

Only a week before the dedication the director of parks, A.E. Champion, gave Goldsby Park's architect a list of items needing correction in the grandstand. The walls in the Negro restrooms needed to be shifted and sunk. A glass shield needed to be placed in front of the fluorescent light fixtures in the press box.

"No Negroes Can Play Evangeline League Here." That was the headline on April 5, 1956, in the Baton Rouge newspapers. For three years, blacks had been playing in Baton Rouge, but the whites in this community were strict segregationists and battled against this mixing of the races. Vice Chairman of the East Baton Rouge Parish Recreation and Parks Commission Norman David said a new ruling by his committee "will mean no Negroes will be permitted to play in the Baton Rouge park." Baton Rouge didn't have blacks on their team, but other teams in the league did. So, by the time Pete Goldsby Park was dedicated, it was already the beginning of the end for organized baseball in Baton Rouge. The segregation issue tore up the Evangeline League. By the middle of the 1957 season, Baton Rouge and Lafayette were out of the league—which was trying to make it as a four-team circuit.

Alex Box Stadium

Home of Louisiana State University Tigers (Southeastern Conference), present. *Dimensions:* Left field, 330 feet; left center, 370 feet; center field, 400 feet; right center, 370 feet; right field, 330 feet. *Seating capacity:* 6000.

Beaumont, Texas

Magnolia Ballpark

Texas League 1912-17, 1919-22 (Exporters), home of the Sluggers 1912-14 (semi-pro). *Location:* Magnolia Avenue, between Hazel and Long streets.

Stuart Stadium

Texas League 1923-54 (Exporters, 1923-45, Roughnecks 1946-54). *Location:* Avenue A (at the present site of the Stadium Shopping Center). *Dimensions:* Right field, 260 feet. *Lights:* 1942.

Starting pitcher for the Beaumont Exporters the day Stuart Stadium was dedicated (Opening Day, 1923) was Jerry Mallett, a rookie from Arkansas. Mallett stayed in Beaumont to marry and raise a family. Mrs. Mallett earned her master's degree while bringing up four children. One of the Malletts' daughters was crowned Miss Texas and went on to be a finalist in the Miss America pageant. Another daughter led a Crusade for Christ before graduating from Baylor. One son (Jerry, Jr.) played briefly for the Boston Red Sox in 1959, and another played in the Houston Astros organization. In 1973, the Beaumont Chamber of Commerce gave the Malletts a citation for their contribution to the culture of their hometown.

Stuart Stadium had a right field fence that was only 260 feet from home, so a vertical line was painted on it toward right center. Anything hit over the fence to the right of the line counted a double.

The ballpark was considered out in the country when it was built—but not for long. The community was already four times larger than at the turn of the century, with a 1920 population of 40,000. Beaumont soon engulfed the park.

The early 1920s were an exciting time in Beaumont, brought on by Frank Yount's second Spindletop oil strike. The city was busy paving the streets—which had become a necessity for the first time after a 1923 flood floated away the wooden blocks that had previously served as a road surface.

The Hotel Beaumont was built downtown in 1922. New churches, schools, and public buildings had to be built to accommodate the exploding population. Stuart Stadium was surrounded by fields on three sides and a farm on the fourth only when it was new.

As was the case everywhere, Beaumont's prosperity ended in 1929, and by the early 1930s Beaumont's refineries were laying off hundreds of men, putting others on a short work week. Still, those were the ball club's glory years. As a farm club of the Tigers, the Exporters had talent like Schoolboy Rowe, Hank Greenberg, Dizzy Trout and Rip Sewell passing through.

Sitting up in the Stuart Stadium press box during those years was William Thomas "Tiny" Scurlock, sports editor for the Beaumont *Journal*. Sitting beside him doing his rewrites was his wife, Ruth Garrison Scurlock. During the Depression years, the Scurlock household became a home away from home for homesick ballplayers and out-of-work newspaper people.

The ballpark's boomerang-shaped grandstand went past the bases down either line. There were bleachers between the grandstand and the left field fence. Between the grandstand and the right field fence was a pavilion, or a smaller jury box–type grandstand.

R.L. Stuart built the stadium and gave it his name. He got into baseball in 1923 as a stockbroker in a company formed by the Young Men's Business League to buy the franchise from B.A. Steinhagen. Rogers Hornsby ended his baseball career in 1950 as manager of the Beaumont Roughnecks. The team's name had changed in 1946 when purchased by Guy Airey. The Beaumont franchise was sold to Allen Russell and moved to Austin in 1955. Stuart Stadium was torn down.

According to John Walker, in his book *Beaumont: A Pictorial History,* "all that remains of (Stuart Stadium) are baseball fans' memories and a plaque set in concrete marking the location of home plate."

Vincent-Beck Stadium (Cardinal Field, before 1981)

Texas League 1983–present (Golden Gators), home of the Lamar University Cardinals (American South Conference), present. *Location:* Lamar University campus. *Dimensions:* Left field, 325 feet; left center, 370 feet; center field, 380 feet; right center, 370 feet; right field, 325 feet. *Fences:* 20 feet all the way around. *Scoreboard:* 9 feet by 54 feet (14-foot message board). *Seating capacity:* (originally) 1200; (1983) 4500 (910 chairback seats for season ticket holders). *Parking lot:* 1200 automobiles.

Since $1 million was funneled into Lamar University's Vincent-Beck Stadium in 1983 to make it suitable for the Texas League, it has been one of the elite college baseball facilities in the Southwest. The park was expanded from a 1200 seating capacity to hold 4500 for the Golden Gators. The press box is air conditioned and there are two broadcast booths.

The park is named after Al Vincent and Bryan Beck. Vincent was a former professional baseball player who for years helped head coach Jim Gilligan with the Lamar Cardinals on a volunteer basis. Beck is a former member of Lamar's Board of Regents who personally financed many of Lamar's athletic facilities.

A tropical storm badly damaged the fence and the clubhouse in 1986.

Belleville, Illinois

Name of park unknown

Home of Belleville baseball before 1900. *Location:* Northwest corner of 20th and West Main streets.

Roofed, wooden grandstand. No screen. No seats behind home either, just an open press box.

Belleville Athletic Field

Negro American League, August 7, 1950 (Monarchs). *Location:* 901 South Illinois Street.

The Monarchs made a tour appearance in Belleville, and played at a

Vincent-Beck Stadium, Beaumont, Texas, as it appeared before the 1983 enlargement. (Compliments of Lamar University.)

high school field in what turned out to be one of the last barnstorming Negro League games. Belleville is about 15 miles from St. Louis.

Bellingham, Washington

Joe Martin Field (Civic Field)
Northwest League 1973–present (Mariners), also home of Western Washington University baseball, present. *Location:* Two blocks from the Lakeway Drive exit on Interstate 5; Moore Street (right field), Potter Street (left field), adjacent to Civic Stadium (Bellingham's football facility, seating capacity 5000) and Downer Field (Bellingham's youth baseball facility). *Dimensions:* Left field, 325 feet; center field, 381 feet; right field, 320 feet. *Seating capacity:* 1450. *1987 season attendance:* 22,183.

The Civic Field Complex is 65 acres and contains picnicking and multi-sport facilities. The ballpark was renamed in 1981 after a longtime Bellingham baseball supporter.

This is also the home baseball field for Bellingham and Sehome high schools, American Legion and Babe Ruth teams, and a semi-pro club.

Beloit, Wisconsin

Harry C. Pohlman Field (in Telfer Park)
Midwest League, 1983–present (Brewers). *Location:* Off Cranston Road. Also accessible from Prairie Avenue. *Dimensions:* Left field, 325 feet; center field, 380 feet; right field, 325 feet. *Seating capacity:* 3100. *1987 season attendance:* 87,208. *Record season attendance:* 101,127 (1986).

On December 19, 1986, at the Annual Beloit Brewers Hot Stove League Banquet, it was announced that the ballpark in Telfer Park would be officially named Harry C. Pohlman Field. Ceremonies were to be held Opening Day, April 10, 1987. In attendance for the announcement was Pohlman himself. He didn't make it to Opening Day, dying of a heart attack at age 82 on Valentine's Day.

Pohlman first came to Beloit in 1941. The school system had hired him as a baseball coach and a junior high school teacher. He took over the town Legion team and organized Cub Baseball—a forerunner of today's Little League programs. Pohlman was involved in Legion ball for 20 years, taking his team to the state tournament eleven times, winning it three times. He served as high school coach from 1953 to 1961 and compiled a 247-58-5 record. The Beloit Brewers' general manager chose Pohlman first for his board of directors because Pohlman's "impact on baseball in the city was tremendous," and it was Pohlman who was elected to throw out the first ball at the Beloit Brewers' first Opening Day in 1983.

Along with the ballpark, Telfer Park has five lighted tennis courts, an open air pavilion, a hockey box, and a lighted softball field. Park is on the northeast side of town.

Bend, Oregon

O'Donnell Field and Rodeo Grounds

Location: "The city center." Home of semi-pro baseball before World War II.

Replaced in 1946 by Vince Genna Stadium as the site became more valuable for commercial development.

Vince Genna Stadium (Municipal Ball Park)

Northwest League 1970–present (Rainbows 1970–77, Timberhawks 1978, Hawks 1979–86, Bucks 1987–present). *Location:* 4th Street (left field), Roosevelt and Wilson streets, 3rd Avenue. *Constructed:* 1946. *Seating capacity:* 1000. *Dimensions:* (1946) Left field, 299 feet; right field, 299 feet. (1962) Left field, 330 feet; left center, 385 feet; center field, 390 feet; right center, 385 feet; right field, 330 feet. *Fences:* (1946) Wood. (1962) 10-foot, 6-inch steel sign panels. *1987 season attendance:* 36,131. *Lights installed:* 1950, 1973, 1985.

After World War II, baseball players,

softball players, sponsors, and the city of Bend joined forces to build the Municipal Ball Park on the south fringe of the city, where there was little or no development. The ballpark was built on 6.19 acres of land surrounded by pine trees and trailer homes, deeded to the city of Bend by Deschutes County on April 20, 1946.

Donated materials from the lumber mills were used to build the grandstand, bleachers and fence. Crews from the city leveled and seeded the field. This was no simple task because of the tremendous amount of lava rock so close to the surface. Hundreds of yards of topsoil were hauled by excavation contractors. Skilled volunteers — carpenters, plumbers, laborers and electricians — pooled their efforts to build the facility.

Too bad the ballfield was laid out 90 degrees out of alignment, so that the sun sets over left center. The error was blamed on the city manager at the time of construction, with an assist to his engineers. The construction crew thought all games would be played at night — this was before Daylight Savings Time — and were more concerned about cut and fill conditions when they laid out the diamond.

The original lights at the ballpark were financed by the Bend Elks. The city paid the lodge back at the rate of $2000 down, $1000 per year, for six years. The final payment was made in 1956.

The infield needed more intense grooming because it frequently switched from a baseball field to a softball field and back again. The field was used both for the semi-pro Oregon League Baseball Championships and the Oregon Softball Championships. In the '50s and '60s the Bend American Legion team won the town's affection. The Legion team won the state championship in 1958. Because of that success, the ballpark was the site of several National American Legion tournaments.

Vince Genna Stadium, Bend, Ore. (Compliments of the Bend Metro Park and Recreation Department.)

By 1962, the Municipal Ball Park was in bad shape. The bleachers had been condemned and the outfield fences were ridiculously short. The Park and Recreation Department was instrumental in getting one-half of Fourth Street, which ran behind the left field wall, closed off so that the fence could be moved back. The old wooden outfield fence was replaced by steel advertisement panels. New bleachers were built on the third base side, parking was improved, the restrooms were enlarged, and a concession stand was built. The lights were pushed back in the outfield.

In 1970, Bend (elevation 4000 feet) got its first professional franchise, in the Northwest League. The team was known as the Rainbows, and was managed by Charlie Silvera.

The Oakland Athletics had a farm team known as the Timberhawks playing in Vince Genna Stadium in 1978. Bend was a Philadelphia Phillies farm club from 1979 through 1986, and were known as the Hawks. The city operated an independent team called the Bucks in 1987, before joining the Angels organization.

On June 21, 1972, the City Commission changed the name of the ballpark to Vince Genna Stadium, in honor of the perennial Park and Recreation director. Genna did a large portion of the stadium remodeling, and went to Portland to haul special materials back to Bend. For years he'd been the coach of Bend American Legion baseball teams, and instrumental in creating many successful baseball and softball programs within Bend.

Also in 1972, the city applied for a federal grant to update the field lighting. The old incandescent lights were inadequate, and they were replaced in 1973 with mercury vapor lights. By 1985, the lights again needed upgrading. The mercury vapor lights were replaced with metal halide fixtures for energy savings and a greater number of lumens.

In 1979, the first year the Bend team played as a farm club of the Philadelphia Phillies, that major league organization built a clubhouse to their own specifications.

By autumn 1987 the wooden bleachers on the first base side had been replaced by aluminum benches, with plans for all of the seating to be aluminum before long. There are also plans to build a sunshade in left center, and to pave the parking lot. Inside the park, in the left field foul territory, there is an 18- by 150-foot structure that houses a hitting and pitching tunnel for practice. Spring comes late in Oregon. This handicaps school and recreation programs. The hitting tunnel can be used all year. It must work, since the Bend high school baseball team won the state championship in 1987 for the first time since 1958. The tunnel project was paid for by the Greater Bend Rotary Club.

Billings, Montana

Cobb Field
Pioneer League 1969-present (Mustangs). *Location:* Ninth Avenue. *Dimensions:* Left field, 335 feet; center field, 405 feet; right field, 335 feet. *Seating capacity:* 4500 (578 box seats). *1987 season attendance:* 104,732.

This amphitheatric ballpark under the Big Sky sits at the foot of Yellowstone Rim. According to Montana baseball expert Bob Decker, those cliffs form a "stunning concentric backdrop to the outfield wall." It is named after Bob Cobb—not Ty as is often assumed—who founded the Mustangs in 1948. Cobb was a Los Angeles restaurateur and part-owner of the Pacific Coast League's Hollywood Stars. To raise the $100,000 start-up money needed for the team, Cobb used his Hollywood connections, who included Barbara Stanwyck, Cecil B. DeMille and Bing Crosby. A contest was held to name the team. Among the losing suggestions were Rimrockers, Sugar Beeters, Yellowstone Chiefs and Crosby's Colts.

Current Mustang General Manager Bob Wilson says he has no problem selling out his 578 box seats. The fran-

chise sells 1200 to 1400 season tickets a year and averages 2800 fans per game. Baseball is Billings' favorite sport. The Mustangs' 14-year affiliation with the Cincinnati Reds is the longest stint of farm monogamy in the Pioneer League.

Binghamton, New York

Johnson Field
Eastern League 1967-68, circa 1985 (franchise no longer exists). *Seating capacity:* 5200.

Birmingham, Alabama

The Slag Pile
Home of Birmingham baseball circa 1887. *Location:* Sixth Street, between First Avenue North and the Great Southern Railroad tracks. *Seating capacity:* 600.

Adults who didn't fit in the tiny grandstand sat on the slag pile above and beyond the outfield fence, while the kids of Birmingham saved a climb and bored holes in the wooden fence to get a view.

Rickwood Field
Southern Association 1910-61, 1964-65 (Barons), Negro National League 1924-25, 1927-30 (Black Barons), Negro American League 1937-38, 1940-50, Southern League 1967-75, 1980-87 (Barons). *Location:* 1137 West Second Avenue (first base), East 18th Street (third base). *Built:* 1910 (first concrete and steel minor league park). *Dimensions:* (Original) left field, 405 feet; center field, 470 feet; right field, 334 feet. (Later) left field, 325 feet; center field, 393 feet; right field, 335 feet. *Fences:* Left field, five feet; center field to right field, 15 feet. In the 1940s the scoreboard in left center was 35 feet high. *Seating capacity:* (1960) 14,500; (1975) 9312; (1985) 10,400. *Record Barons season attendance:* 445,926 (1948). *Record Barons low season*

attendance: 21,016 (1973). *1987 season attendance:* 139,808. *Record Barons Opening Day attendance:* 14,237 (1928). *Record low Barons Opening Day attendance:* 830 (1974). *First game:* August 18, 1910 (45 days after the first game at Comiskey; Birmingham 3, Montgomery 2, attendance: 10,000). *First night game:* May 19, 1938 (Nashville 3, Barons 0). *Site of Game 6 of the 1943 Negro World Series, site of Game 1 and Game 3 of the 1944 Negro World Series.*

Until Rickwood Field was retired following the 1987 Southern League season, it was the second oldest ballpark in use, second only to Comiskey in Chicago. Both Comiskey and Rickwood were first used for the 1911 baseball season, but the American League opened its season first.

The park was named after Rick Woodward, owner of the Barons from the time the park was built until the Depression. It was built, with Forbes Field in mind, in an older residential neighborhood not far from the State Fairgrounds. Railroad tracks ran past the right field fence.

In 1921, the outfield fence and bleachers were dismantled by a cyclone. Reparations cost $30,000.

In 1927, the Birmingham Black Barons acquired Satchel Paige, already on his third Negro League team. Paige spent a couple of years here before moving up north, where he could pitch against white guys every now and then and make more money. It was in Rickwood Field that Paige first started bragging about his control by putting a gum wrapper on home plate. "That's my base," he'd say.

By the 1930s, the single-decked grandstand was roofed from third base to the right field foul pole. Bleachers extended from third to the left field corner, and in right, pushing only slightly into home run territory.

On Sunday, August 11, 1935, a New Orleans Pelican named Eddie Ross pulled a fastball in his kitchen off

Baron pitcher Legrant Scott, Sr., and was scored an infield single after breaking the neck of a low-flying pigeon with his line drive. Both ball and bird came down between third and short. Ross had the carcass stuffed and mounted.

Rickwood's fences were pulled in, as became the common practice, after the Babe started America's home run fetish, and the original walls were left standing.

The original wall went around the outside of the grandstand and defined the boundaries of the property. In the outfield the light towers were built between the old and new fences.

The scoreboard was in straightaway left back in the days when it was hand-operated. It was black with white numbers, and stood twice as high as the rest of the fence.

A railroad track passed close to the outer fence in right. The only immediate neighbors lived across the street on the first base side.

The Barons were a farm club of the Chicago White Sox, when the team last used Rickwood in 1987. Then the wooden walls were painted green. The original ticket windows were in use. The infield was red clay. The computerized scoreboard had been around since 1981. The old wooden fences so close that line drives off them were frequently held to singles. In right center, there was a "Mello Yello" sign with a basketball backboard and hoop on it — a hundred bucks for a homer over the sign, five hundred if the ball went through the hoop.

Samford Field

Home of the Samford University Bulldogs (Trans-America Conference), present. *Location:* Samford University. *Dimensions:* Left field, 300 feet; center field, 390 feet; right field, 330 feet. *Seating capacity:* 300.

Youns Memorial Field

Home of the University of Alabama at Birmingham Blazers (Sunbelt Con-

Interior view from the grandstand of Rickwood Field, Birmingham, Ala. (Photo by Don Newton, Jr. Compliments of the Birmingham Area Chamber of Commerce.)

ference), present. *Dimensions:* Left field, 330 feet; left center, 370 feet; center field, 390 feet; right center, 370 feet; right field, 330 feet. *Seating capacity:* 500.

Hoover Stadium
Southern League. 1988–present (Barons). *Location:* Hoover, Alabama. Junction of Highways 150 and 459. *Dimensions:* Left field, 340 feet; center field, 405 feet; right field, 340 feet. *Seating capacity:* 10,000.

A suburban ballpark.

The Hoover Park and Recreation Board began leasing the stadium to the Barons for 10 years beginning March 15, 1988, with an option to renew for five more years.

The stadium is planned in three stages. The initial facility cost $10 million and seated 10,000. The second phase will add 5500 seats, and the third will boost seating to 23,000.

An artist's depiction of the proposed stadium shows a single-decked and roofed grandstand whose tiering is graded into the land, so that all seats are at ground level. The playing field is well below the level of the parking

lot — and there seems to be plenty of land out beyond the outfield fences, where the game could be watched from a parked car.

Blackstone, Virginia

High School Stadium
Virginia League. *Seating capacity:* 2000.

Bloomfield, New Jersey

Bloomfield Green
Site of early baseball games, 1860–79. *Location:* Park Place and Beach Street, north of Monroe Place.

On July 4, 1860, two eight-man teams (no shortstops) played a post-picnic game on the Bloomfield Green. The Passaic Club beat the Excelsior Club 20–19.

In 1879, in a game at the Green between the Oneida nine and the Actives of Irvington, one of the longest home runs in Bloomfield history was struck by Big Ben Baldwin of Frankling Street.

The Oneidas were down by two and had two men on in the ninth when Baldwin stepped to the plate. According to a March 12, 1948, *Bloomfield Independent Press* recollection, "He swung. The ball soared into the clouds, landed at Park Place and Beach Street, rolled down Beach Street toward Beach mansion (now the Colonial Village). Rooters rooted so loudly that local shopkeepers rushed from their stores to see 'what's going on at the Green?'"

Williamson Oval

Atlantic League 1914, site of Bloomfield baseball 1880–1914. *Location:* Williamson Avenue and Liberty Street, running through Berkeley Avenue.

Back in the 1880s, when baseball was first played in the Williamson Oval, there were plenty of other sporting events in town to compete with—and not all of them are legal today. According to the *Bloomfield Independent Press,* March 12, 1948, "It was not infrequent to see a greyhound covered with a blanket taking his workout along Bloomfield streets or a bulldog with gashed head following its trainer, or a rooster nursing the wounds of war. Dog racing, bulldog fighting and cock fighting were popular among Bloomfielders in early days."

There were no clubhouses at the Williamson Oval, so teams dressed at the nearby Fairview School.

From 1909 to 1914, the local baseball team was owned by Orrin Dodd, who also bought the Williamson Oval to protect his investment. His team was the best in the state for a while, and frequently filled the house. Then the quality diminished. Crowds shrunk. Dodd tried to sell the Oval to the Board of Education at cost, but the board was not interested. He ended up selling the land to a speculator, who turned the property into the Bloomfield Tennis Club and other various building lots.

The Williamson Oval was the site of many community activities, including Fourth of July celebrations.

Glen Ridge Outing Grounds

Home of Bloomfield baseball circa 1895. *Location:* between Douglas Road and Lincoln Street.

Name of park unknown

Home of the Watsessing (section of Bloomfield) team circa 1903. *Location:* Off MacArthur Avenue, near the current site of Westinghouse.

Sprague Field (General Electric Field)

Negro East-West League 1932 (Browns). *Location:* Bloomfield, Arlington, Floyd, and LaFrance avenues. *Dimensions:* Left field, 330 feet; center field, 385 feet; right field, 325 feet.

New Jersey has an East Orange, a West Orange, and a South Orange, but there's no North Orange. That's because they put Bloomfield in that spot.

Bloomington, Illinois

Wilder Field

Home of the Bloomington Pastimes circa 1888. *Location:* Later the site of Illinois Wesleyan's concrete stadium.

In the late 1880s, the Chicago National League team managed by Cap Anson came to Wilder Field, and beat the Pastimes 10–0 before an overflow crowd. Clark Griffith earned the shutout victory.

East Side Fairgrounds

Home of the Pastimes circa 1890.

It was here that, in 1890, the Pastimes' Frank Will won an 11-inning 6–5 victory over Kenney's Mutes. The Mutes were managed by Pacer Smith, who later murdered his wife and was publicly hanged in Decatur.

Other parks used for baseball before 1900 were the *Brewery Ball Park,* where Highland Park now stands, *West Side Park, Forty Acres Grounds, Water Works Grounds, Market Street Park, Lannigan's Pasture,* and *East Side Park.*

Fans Field (Three-I Park)
Three-I League (Class B) 1901–43
(Bloomers). *Built:* 1902. *Rebuilt:* 1919,
1935. *Location:* Lafayette and Main
streets, at Berenz Place near the Armory. *Dimensions:* Left field, 327 feet;
center field, 410 feet. *First night game:*
June 14, 1930 (attendance, 3500).

Fans Field in the 1930s was a modern
baseball plant, built on 15 acres of land
on Bloomington's south side, owned by
a nonprofit community group. At that
time the word Bloomfield was written
in grass along the dirt foul territory between the first base line and the grandstand.

Dame Fashion, covering the female
beat, attended the first night game at
Fans Field in June 1930, and filed this
report: "Far in the distance the big
lights shone out like a series of lighthouses along a rocky seacoast.... Just
as at any party, there were refreshments for those who wished, but most
women seemed to be following the
game too closely to be much interested
in food or drink. To be in the midst of
the 4000 people, all interested, and all
taking deep breaths of good fresh air,
is an experience that renews.... Dame
Fashion declares she never saw so many
prosperous looking young men of
Bloomington together in one place
before in her life—and nine-tenths of
them had a pretty date with them."

The star of the Bloomers that year
was Carl Dorley, who hit 31 home runs.

By 1944, the diamond had been
removed from the Fans Field, and had
been replaced by a 260-by-155-foot dirt
oval for the Society Horse Show, which
was to become an annual event at the
site. Bleachers crossed the area that had
once been the outfield, and the original
stands, though aging, still stood.

O'Neil Park
Location: Route 150, Hinshaw Avenue, Chestnut Street, Graham Street.
Currently the site of the only lighted
baseball diamond in Bloomington.

Bluefield, West Virginia

Bowen Field
Appalachian League 1957–present
(Orioles). *Location:* Route 460 at
Westgate. *Dimensions:* Left field, 335
feet; center field, 365 feet; right field,
335 feet. *Seating capacity:* 3000. *1987
season attendance:* 35,862.

Boaco, Nicaragua

Geronimo Robles Stadium
According to *The Sporting News* in
1987: "The unchecked civil war and
rampant inflation in Nicaragua notwithstanding, northern California
sportswriter Jay Feldman is going
ahead with plans for his third annual
goodwill baseball tour of the Central
American hotspot.

"'We're an American institution
now,' Feldman said of his Baseball for
Peace organization, which has distributed thousands of dollars' worth of
baseball equipment in the barnstorming tours of the Nicaraguan countryside."

Along with playing Nicaraguan
teams, the group planned to rebuild the
ballpark in the mountain town of
Boaco. In 1986, local officials announced plans for a new stadium. (A
section of the old stadium had collapsed, injuring a spectator.)

The people thought the money had
already been allocated and dismantled
the old one for firewood. (The same
thing happened in Oswego, New York,
in the 1940s, when poverty caused the
residents to steal the ballpark piece by
piece for firewood.) By the time the
town officials figured out what was happening, the old ballpark was already
missing its bleachers, dugouts and the
outfield fence.

Money for the new park has been
donated by Bill Edison of Elk, California.

In the spring of 1988, Baseball for
Peace said through its newsletter, "Last

December a delegation of fifteen ball-players and construction workers spent a week in Boaco, playing ball and helping with the beginning of the construction of Geronimo Robles Stadium. A week was barely enough time to begin the work, but when we left, the foundation for the outer wall had been completed and a good portion of the outfield fence was built." (Geronimo Robles was a promising young ballplayer from Boaco who was killed by Somoza's National Guard in 1978.)

By press time, the newsletter stated, the outer wall along the right field line had been completed, funds had run out, and work had stalled. Another $6000 was needed.

Boise, Idaho

The Public Square
Home of Boise baseball 1869.

Games played on an area reserved for the future construction of a territorial capitol building. Before the first game could be played here (between the Boise Pioneer Baseball Club and all comers), brush and rubbish had to be cleared from the site.

Joe Devine Stadium (Airway Park)
Pioneer League 1939–63 (Pilots 1939–52, Yankees 1953–54, Braves 1955–63). *Location:* Maple Avenue, Park Boulevard, near the Municipal Tourist Park. *Built:* 1939. *Enlarged:* 1948. *Seating capacity:* 4500. *Record season attendance:* approximately 110,000 (1947). *First game:* May 2, 1939.

The park was finally abandoned in 1963 when structural problems were discovered in its light poles. The poles needed replacing, which would have cost $35,000 the club didn't have.

On April 30, 1939, *The Idaho States-man* described a ballpark in much better condition:

"The planners have had foresight. They have constructed a grandstand that is airtight enough to prevent westerly breezes from whistling around women's silk clad ankles or up men's trouser legs. They have built seats that, although as hard as any wooden seats, have back rests low enough to permit comfortable lounging while watching the game and provide rests for both elbows or outstretched arms. And if you are a baseball fan, you know what those comforts mean.

"There's no roof to the stand and there may never be. Games are to be played at night in the summer time, when weather is warm and it is a pleasure to have a star-studded sky above. And no roof means no posts or pillars behind which ushers can hide the fans. Every seat offers a perfect, unobstructed view of the field....

"The lights, say officials, are equal to those lighting any major league park.... For the first time in history, Boise is getting a baseball park that is modern and will eventually equal any park in a city of comparable size in the nation."

The outfield was enclosed by a double deck of billboards. There was no roof on the grandstand. The hand-operated scoreboard was atop the hitters' background and beneath an advertisement for the local CBS affiliate, radio station KGSH.

Wigle Field
Northwest League 1975–76 (A's), 1987–present (Hawks). *Location:* Borah High School. *Dimensions:* Left field, 330 feet; center field, 405 feet; right field, 330 feet. *Seating capacity:* 3000. *1987 season attendance:* 71,344.

Wigle Field is a high school baseball field. Among the players who started their professional baseball careers here is Rickey Henderson.

Boston, Massachusetts

South End Grounds (Grand Pavilion, Walpole Street Grounds, Boston Base-

ball Grounds)
National Association 1872–75 (Red Stockings), National League 1876–1915 (Beaneaters, Doves, Red Caps, Braves). *Location:* Boston and Providence Railroad tracks; New York, New Haven and Hartford Railroad tracks (left field), Walpole Street (home plate), Columbus Avenue and Berlin Street (right field), Tremont and Gainsborough streets (center field). *Dimensions:* Left field, 250 feet; left center, 445 feet; center field, 440 feet; right center, 440 feet; right field, 255 feet. *1875 club expenses:* $617.50 rent of grounds; $888.82 care of grounds and wages; $689.27 repair of grounds. *First National Association game:* May 16, 1871. *Last National Association game:* October 30, 1875. *First National League game:* April 29, 1876 (Hartford 3, Boston 2, 10 innings). *Last National League game:* June 3, 1915 (New York 10, Boston 3). *Fire:* 1894.

Theories on the relationship between groundskeeping at the South End Grounds and the weather were discussed in the March 29, 1874, edition of the *Boston Herald:*

"With the exception of some unevenness caused by the frost, the ground on Thursday and Friday was in better condition than it had been at this season of the year for a long time. The snow of Saturday morning will, if anything, have the effect of improving the surface, as it will soften it and prepare for the roller and two or three sunny days will bring it into order."

Photos at the Boston Public Library of this playing field don't show much grass. Just patches here and there, and a lot of dirt. Like the ballfields on many of today's playgrounds, it is a diamond created by wear. No grass can survive the natural footpaths of baseball's pattern. There was no schematic sodding.

Signs on the grandstand advertised the sale of "SODA" and "REFRESHMENTS." The pavilion looked like a big volunteer fireman's carnival booth. There were spaces between the horizontal planks of the rear wall wide enough to let the sunlight through. Four rows of primitive box seats and a smaller wooden bleacher section sat in front of the grandstand behind a three-foot wooden fence. Bleachers ran down the first base line.

Lack of parity helped kill the National Association. In 1875, the Boston Red Stockings were undefeated at home. Al Spalding had a win-loss record of 57–5. The team finished 71–8.

The Grand Pavilion 1883–94. The original grandstand was torn down. The replacement was a classic.

South End Grounds had the most distinctive grandstand of its time, a steep, majestic beauty, though certainly not the most comfortable for spectators. Mr. Soden, the owner of Boston's National League franchise, believed wholeheartedly in making money and crammed as many people as possible into his park.

Soden really was tight. He once ripped out the press box to make room for more paying customers. Players' wives had to buy tickets to get in.

The Grand Pavilion was a double-decked grandstand, highest of its day, rivaled only by the bunting-covered structure on the Old Polo Grounds. The Boston Pavilion had six spires on top of its roof. It was built after Boston's 1883 pennant-winning season, and lasted until it burned in 1894, the year so many ballparks burned that there were rumors of conspiracy.

Rectangular Grounds. The playing field was a lot longer than it was wide – like a bowling alley. It only had one field: center. Exploiting the low fence in left, Boston led the league in home runs in 1883. They hit 34.

Cigar manufacturer F. Norton offered a box of "Sleeper's Perfectos" to any Red Cap player who hit a homer. Also known for his generosity with boxes of cigars was Boston's number one baseball fan, the dubiously titled General Hi Hi Dixwell, who sometimes traveled on the road with the club.

The bleachers extended from the sides of the Grand Pavilion to the corners—which was not a great distance—at the same height as the pavilion's lower deck. The South End Grounds and the Huntington Avenue Grounds (built in 1901) were almost adjacent, with nothing but railroad tracks separating their locations.

In the late 1880s and early 1890s the Boston team was one of the greatest ever—Dan Brouthers, John Clarkson, Ol' Hoss Radbourne, King Kelly. The inspiration for *Casey at the Bat* probably came from here. Suspicion is the poem is about the K of Kelly.

Boston dominated all league ball during that time. Counting the National League, the American Association, and the Players League, there were seven big league seasons played. Boston teams won five pennants.

The big pavilion caught fire during a Boston-Baltimore game (in the bottom of the third), May 15, 1894. The fire, caused by a tossed cigarette, burned $70,000 worth of equipment as well as the park. Gone was the only truly double-decked grandstand Boston would ever have.

The team moved to the Congress Street ballpark, former home of the Players League and American Association teams, and returned after a couple of months to a rebuilt but smaller Walpole Street Grounds.

The original park had been underinsured for fire so there wasn't enough money to rebuild the park to its previous size. This time there were only two spires on the roof. These have been saved and still sit on top of a building on Columbus Avenue.

By 1908 the *Boston Globe* referred to the South End Grounds as the "oldest baseball park in the country." It had been home to eleven pennant-winning teams.

The park was next refurbished in 1912 by Braves owner James Gaffney so it would last until Braves Field on Commonwealth Avenue was completed.

Union Park (Dartmouth Street Park)
Union Association 1884 (Unions). *Location:* Huntington Avenue, Dartmouth Street (Back Bay section). *First game:* April 30, 1884. *Last game:* September 24, 1884.

Congress Street Park

Players League 1890 (Reds), American Association 1891 (Reds), National League 1894. *First Players League game:* April 19, 1890. *Last Players League game:* September 10, 1890. *First American Association game:* April 18, 1891. *Last American Association game:* October 3, 1891. *First National League game:* May 16, 1894. *Last National League game:* July 19, 1894.

The Players League Reds featured outfielder Hardy Richardson's 143 runs batted in, Big Dan Brouthers, the playing/managing of King Kelly, and the 27-12 pitching of Ol' Hoss Radbourne—all from the National League Boston team.

The 1891 American Association Reds also had Brouthers and Richardson. Both teams won their pennant.

Huntington Avenue Grounds

American League 1901-11 (Pilgrims). *Location:* Huntington Avenue (left field), Rogers Avenue, later Forsyth Street (third base), New York, New Haven and Hartford Railroad tracks (first base), New Gravelly Point Road and Gainsborough Street (right field), just north of the site of South End Grounds. *Dimensions:* Left field, 440 feet; center field, approx. 635 feet; right field, 280 feet. Distance from home to backstop, 60 feet. *Seating capacity:* 9,000. *First game:* May 8, 1901 (Boston 12, Philadelphia 4). *Last game:* October 7, 1911 (Boston 8, Washington 1).

On October 1, 1903, the first World Series game between the American and National League pennant winners was played at Huntington Avenue Grounds, Pittsburgh beating the Pilgrims 7-3.

Boston won the series in eight games, however, finishing the Bucs off on October 13, 3–0, also at home. Bill Dineen pitched his second shutout and third victory of the series before 7400.

Cy Young pitched the first perfect game of the twentieth century here, May 5, 1904, shutting out the Athletics 3–0.

In 1911, Ban Johnson tried to speed up American League games by outlawing warm-up pitches between innings. Ballgames were running as long as two and a half hours. Things were getting out of hand.

The rule caused a freak home run in the Huntington Avenue Grounds on June 27. Boston pitcher Ed Karger, seeing that his outfielders were slow to take their positions, lobbed a few home to keep from stiffening up. The Athletics' Stuffy McInnis ran up to the plate and lined one of Karger's warm-ups into the right center gap and quickly circled the bases. Boston outfielders failed to take any of this seriously and didn't even chase the ball. The ump said it had to be a homer. League president Ban Johnson backed him up after the Pilgrims protested the ball had been struck before all of the Athletics had left the field.

Advertisements painted on the walls sold "C.M.C. Garters for Men" and "Emerson Shoes." The outfield was huge. Plenty of standing room when the grandstand was full. The scoreboard was a small hand-operated model that sat on top of the outfield fence near the right field foul pole.

Before the ballpark was built, the site had been used for circuses and carnivals. Northeastern University's Godfrey Lowell Cabot Physical Education Center, featuring a World Series Exhibit Room, is there now. A metal plaque commemorating the ballpark at the former location of the left field foul line was unveiled May 16, 1956.

Fenway Park

American League 1912–present (Red Sox), National League 1914–15, 1946 (Braves, some games). Owned by the Boston Red Sox. *Location:* Lansdowne Street (left field), Yawkey Way (third base), Ipswich Street (right field), Van Ness Street (first base). *Seating capacity:* (Originally) 27,000; (eventually) 33,583. Roof, 1,568; boxes, 13,250; reserved grandstand, 12,202; bleachers, 6,563. *Dimensions:* (Original) Left field, 321 feet; center field, 488 feet; right field, 313½ feet. (Current) Left field, 315 feet; left center, 379 feet; center field, 390 feet; deep center, 420 feet; deep right, 380 feet; right field, 302 feet. Originally 68 feet from home plate to the backstop; after 1934, 60 feet. *Height of fences:* (Original) Left field, 10 feet (wood). (Current) Left field, 37 feet (screen extends another 23 feet); center field, 17 feet; bullpens, five feet; right field, three to five feet. *Record attendance:* 47,627 (September 22, 1935, doubleheader versus the New York Yankees). *Post-war and single game attendance record:* 36,388 (August 22, 1978, versus the Cleveland Indians). *Night game attendance record:* 36,228 (June 28, 1949, versus the New York Yankees). *Opening Day attendance record:* 35,343 (April 14, 1969, versus the Baltimore Orioles). *First game:* April 20, 1912 (Boston 7, New York 6, attendance: 27,000, estimated). *Major refurbishing:* 1934. *Lights installed:* 1947.

Baseball appeals because of its close analogy to life, and Boston's pea-green bandbox captures the bizarre tragicomedy of the summer game better than any current setting. According to John Updike, Fenway "seems in curiously sharp focus, like the inside of an old-fashioned peeping-type Easter egg ... a compromise between Man's Euclidean determinations and Nature's beguiling irregularities."

Overview. Construction on the ballpark started in 1911, and it was called Fenway Park because it was located in a marshy area of the city known as the Fens. The first game was scheduled for

Fenway Park, Boston, Mass.

April 18, 1912, but was rained out. The park did not get to open until April 20, for a doubleheader.

A single-deck grandstand stood behind home, and there were large wooden bleachers between the grandstand and the left field corner, wooden bleachers out in center and a wooden pavilion in the far right field corner.

The formal dedication of the park was delayed until May 17 so the finishing touches could be put on the park. At the dedication ceremony, the first pitch was thrown out by Mayor John F. Fitzgerald, "Honey Fitz," grandfather of President John F. Kennedy. Tris Speaker became the first and best centerfielder to roam Fenway's strange center field.

During the first year of the park's existence, Speaker not only showed an aptitude for his home park's eccentricities, but hit .383 to boot. Smokey Joe Wood was the star Red Sox pitcher that year, going 34–5.

On October 16, 1912, Fenway Park was the site of Game 7 of the World Series, between the Red Sox and John McGraw's New York Giants. It was to be one of the most famous ballgames in history. In the top of the tenth inning, the Giants took a 2–1 lead, then quickly

brought in Christy Mathewson to save the lead. The Giants then self-destructed. A lazy fly ball by pinch hitter Clyde Engle was muffed by Giant centerfielder Fred Snodgrass. Having blown the easy one, Snodgrass made a three-exclamation-point catch of Harry Hooper's diving liner for the first out. Steve Yerkes walked. Speaker was up. Speaker popped up the first pitch to the foul side of the first base line. Catcher Chief Meyers and first baseman Fred Merkle stared at each other while the ball dropped between them. With new life, Speaker took advantage, and drove in the tying run with a scorching double to right. McGraw ordered Matty to walk the next batter intentionally, but this didn't work, as Larry Gardner promptly knocked in the championship-winning run with a fly ball to right field.

In 1914, when the "miracle" Braves won the National League pennant, they played their World Series games at Fenway because it had a greater seating capacity than South End Grounds. The next two years the Braves repaid the favor, allowing the Bosox to use brand new Braves Field, which held more than Fenway.

The Red Sox fell upon hard times in

It's a great day for a game, and crowds gather outside Fenway Park in Boston. (Photo by Steve Rossi.)

the 1920s, which is why theater producer and Red Sox owner Harry Frazee sold Babe Ruth to the Yankees for $125,000. In July, 1923, the club itself was sold to Bob Quinn, who was also the vice president and business manager of the St. Louis Browns.

Nothing improved until 1933, when Quinn sold both club and park to lumberman and sportsman Austin Yawkey, who immediately began to put money into improvements. The place burned, so he rebuilt it bigger and better than ever.

There've been changes in the ballpark's look over the years. The 23-foot screen on top of the Green Monster was erected in 1936, thus ending the frequent broken windows among the storefronts of Lansdowne Street. The bullpens were not constructed until 1940, and then primarily to offer Ted Williams a softer home run touch. The lights were not put in until 1947, the same year the Green Monster was first painted green. Until then, the big wall had served as an advertisement billboard. Runways between clubhouses and dugouts were installed in 1952, which ended the fights that sometimes broke out when all of the ballplayers had to leave the field via the same exit. Between 1975 and 1976, the press boxes were finally air conditioned and enclosed in glass, and the park was given its electronic scoreboard atop the bleachers.

The Cliff. Before the era of warning tracks, it was not uncommon for inclines to be built into the landscape in front of fences to keep outfielders from killing themselves. Fenway Park had one of the largest, and most famous inclines, in front of its still-famous left field wall.

The incline was ten feet high, and became known as Duffy's Cliff because of Hugh Duffy's uncanny ability to climb the mountain and catch fly balls at the same time. The slope lasted until 1934, when the warning track was put in. At the same time the original wooden fence was replaced by a metal one. (Roger Angell says in *Five Seasons* that the *Boston Globe* remeasured the distance from home to the left field foul pole and came up with 304 feet, eleven feet less than advertised.)

Out in the Bleachers. Bleacherite George Kimball described the land out in center and right in the 1950s when the Red Sox were not at peak popularity:

"There were the beaten old men who looked like they'd just panhandled the 50 cent admission price, the retired gentlemen with their transistor radios and the truckdrivers who took their shirts off on summer days. There were two old ladies from Dorchester, both named Mary, who attended the afternoon games as faithfully as they attended Mass. They left home early in the morning, bringing their Official Big League Scorebook along to Church, and after lunch in Kenmore Square, showed up at the park before batting practice started.... And there was Fat Howie. Fat Howie was on speaking terms with every centerfielder in the league.... Howie would lean over the wall between innings and yell out to Bob Allison: 'Hey, Bob, what's happening in Cleveland?' (The scoreboard on the left field wall can't be seen from the bleachers in center.) And Allison would check the score and holler back: '4 to 2 Indians, Howie.' Howie was always there day or night."

Fires. There have been two major fires at Fenway. The first came in the middle of the 1926 season. The left field bleachers burned down and there was no time to rebuild them, so play continued with left-fielders being allowed to run through the opened space and behind the grandstand to catch a fly ball. Until 1934, when the park was rebuilt to look as it does today, there were two sets of wooden bleachers—in center field and right field—with a space between them.

The second fire, in January of 1934, was the four-alarmer necessitating the total reconstruction of the park in concrete, including the bleachers.

On June 22, 1927, on his way to a 60-home-run season, Babe Ruth smacked two at Fenway. The first cleared the wall in left center, and the second went between the center and right field bleachers. According to the *New York Times* the following day, the homer "rolled across a vacant lot, and brought up smartly against the wall of a garage where six men and two boys fell on it and engaged in a battle royale."

Fenway has always been known as a hitters' park, and not just because of the wall. Everyone seems to hit better here. That sharp focus Updike so perceptively noticed works for batters as well. They see better here, just like the spectators. So it is strange that in 1918, with baseball turned inside out by World War I, Fenway Park was the fourth worst hitters' park of the century. This according to John Thorn and Pete Palmer in *The Hidden Game of Baseball,* who also note that, statistically speaking, Fenway was the best hitters' park of all time in 1955. It is cruelest to left-handed pitchers.

Like Wrigley Field, this is a place where a ballgame can get out of hand. Mercurial earned run averages explode out the top of the thermometer. Some examples: The Red Sox scored 17 runs in one inning against Detroit in 1953, winning the game 23–3. In 1950, they defeated lowly St. Louis 20–4 and 29–4, back to back. Washington came in and got trounced 24–4 in 1940. The 1923 Red Sox lost to the Yankees 24–4. And so on, and so on.

Yet it was here that Walter Johnson pitched his only no-hitter.

Five hitters have hit homers to the right of the flagpole, at the park's deepest point. Hank Greenberg did it in 1937, Jimmie Foxx in 1937, Moose Skowron in 1957, Carl Yastrzemski in 1970, Bobby Mitchell in 1973, and Jim Rice in 1975.

"Beguiling Irregularities." The outfield's configuration is determined by seventeen different facets and barriers—hellish on visiting outfielders, but learnable if you call it home.

Dom DiMaggio, the Red Sox centerfielder for many years, was asked by sportswriter Ned Martin if he liked playing amid the meandering contours of Fenway's mean pasture. DiMaggio said, "I liked it. It wasn't an easy place to play, what with the caroms off the left-center field wall. And it is improved now that they filled in the little triangle at the base of the flagpole. I played fairly shallow ... the fences were my friends ... I felt like I had control of all corners."

Sure, Fenway is a great place to hit but, as has been said before, "The wall giveth and the wall taketh away." (It gaveth to Bucky Dent. It gaveth to Carlton Fisk with the help of some body English.) Line drives off the wall, however, if played properly can be returned to the infield very quickly, so slow runners are held to singles, and mediocre runners get tossed out at second.

A runner has to be careful of any ball hit down the left field line, even those on the ground. Since there is no foul territory, ground balls past the third baseman sometimes strike the stands and bounce straight back to the shortstop. Runners trying for two or rounding first too far can get nailed.

The Wall Today. It's covered with dents.

A vertical home run line is painted in yellow on the big green wall where the bleachers begin. A ball striking the wall to the right of the line is a home run. The wall is made of concrete everywhere except for where it is in play. In between the yellow home run line and the flagpole is netting to protect television equipment.

There is a ladder on the wall at the foul pole side of the old scoreboard, so field attendants can get the balls out of the screen. The concrete wall must have been there before the ballpark. Certainly before the bleachers existed in

Fenway Park, Boston, Mass. Top: *Balls stuck in the screen atop the Green Monster.*
Bottom: *Jim Rice and the wall. (Photos by Steve Rossi.)*

Fenway Park as seen from the worst seat in the house. (Photo by Steve Rossi.)

their current configuration. There are slatted windows in that wall that serve no purpose and are cut off diagonally by the seats.

Pigeons. Fenway Park was then, as it is now, known for its pigeon population. Of course, during DiMaggio's day, pigeons didn't relax around the ballfield, as Ted Williams brought his rifle to the park and loved to take target practice before games. There's no telling how many dirty birds he plugged before the Humane Society put a halt to it.

Though foul balls and balls hit in batting practice have struck pigeons, the birds came into play in a game only once, when Philadelphia outfielder Hal Peck brained a squab with a throw from the outfield. The ball deflected to the second baseman, who tagged out Skeeter Newsome trying to stretch his single.

A Great Day for a Game. It's a great day for a game during the summer of 1985. Outside the park along Yawkey Way, the air is filled with the vendors' roasting peanuts. Twenty cents a bag.

On Lansdowne Street, the wall looks shorter, the field being ten feet below street level. "BLEACHERS CREA-

TURES" tee-shirts are for sale. A representative of this organization barks, "It's more than a tee-shirt, it's a way of life."

Inside, the sunshine enhances the green of the Monster. The warning tracks are gray, the color of crushed stone rather than the color of the infield.

The foul pole in right is even closer than the one in left. But only ten feet from the foul pole, the right field wall bellies out to 370.

The bullpens are cute cubbyholes in front of the bleachers and behind the short right field fence. They have miniature dugouts in them. The only place the stands meet the home run fence is where the grandstand wraps around the right field foul pole.

The two decks of roof seats are tiny, with only four rows in each. In the lower deck, the old wooden slat seats are painted red at the bottom, blue on top.

The only bad seats in the house are deep up in the left field corner, under the roof behind one of the obstructing poles, where there's a lot of crowd between a fan and the game. The grandstand doesn't rise steeply, so when

Fenway Park, Boston, Mass. A slice of bleacherites, and the knuckleheads who climbed the Gilbey's Gin sign. (Photo by Steve Rossi.)

people stand up, its tough to see—and people stand up for all sorts of things. If there's a fight, you miss an inning.

The light towers are of the old erector set variety, two above the wall, five on the roof of the grandstand. The tree out front pokes into the skyline above the press boxes behind home. Just before the game begins, a man disappears behind a door in the scoreboard at the base of the left field wall and is never seen again. There is no foul territory, providing lots of souvenirs and lots of second chances.

Against the Blue Jays, Wade Boggs lines one off the wall, so what's new? You get the impression he can do that any time he wants to. Baserunning foolishness by Boggs and Jim Rice wipes out the inning.

The electronic scoreboard, mounted on the corner of the green concrete wall at the peak of the bleachers in straightaway center, looks out of place. Out of time. Too technological for this setting. It casts a shadow on some seats, and looks ready to fall like the Phantom of the Opera's chandelier. If you sit at the very top of the bleachers you are sitting behind the scoreboard.

There's no beer sold in the stands, and even if you wait in line you are limited to two eight-ounce cups.

Vending in Fenway is difficult because there are so few aisles. One ice cream vendor uses the toss method. Every ice cream sandwich lands on target, and money is passed to him in an orderly manner.

The Fenway Park men's rooms still don't have urinals. They have trenches. Lines move along efficiently.

Falling behind 6-3, the Red Sox rally for four in the eighth, to take the lead. Above the concrete wall in left center towers the GILBEY'S DOUBLE PLAY sign. There are twelve men standing on that sign, perched on wooden planks eighty feet above the sidewalk. The Red Sox hold the Blue Jays in the ninth for the win, and now those guys have to climb all the way back down without

breaking their necks and they're in no hurry...

Braves Field (National League Field, 1936-40)

National League 1912-52 (Braves, Bees), American League 1915-16 (World Series only), 1929-32 (Sundays only). Owned by the Boston Braves. *Location:* Commonwealth Avenue (first base side), Babcock Street (third base), Gaffney Street (right field), Boston and Albany Railroad tracks (left field). *Dimensions:* (1915-28) Right field, 402 feet; center field, 550 feet; left field, 402 feet. (1928-52) Right field, 320 feet; deepest part of right center, 390 feet; center field, 370 feet; left field, 340 feet. From 1915-36, 75 feet from home plate to the backstop. After that, 60 feet. *Fences:* Left field to right center, (1915) 10 feet, (1928) 8 feet, (1946) 19 feet; (1946) left field scoreboard, 68 feet at its highest point; right center exit gate, 8 feet; right field, 10 feet. *Seating capacity:* 40,000. Grandstand, 18,000; two pavilions, 10,000 apiece; small bleacher (jury box), 2000. *Day game attendance record:* 41,527 (versus Chicago, August 8, 1948). *Doubleheader attendance record:* 47,123 (versus Philadelphia, May 22, 1932). *Night game attendance record:* 39,549 (Brooklyn, August 5, 1946). *Opening game attendance record:* 25,000 (New York, April 16, 1935). *Season high attendance record:* 1,455,439 (1948). *Season low attendance record:* 84,938 (1918). *First game:* August 18, 1915 (Boston 3, St. Louis 1). *Lights installed:* 1946. *Refurbished:* 1946 (cost: $500,000). *Last game:* September 21, 1952 (Brooklyn 8, Boston 2, attendance 8822).

It was here that Babe Ruth had his career as a pitcher, here that Warren Spahn began his.

According to some, there was a cave-in during construction. Twelve horses and mules were buried alive underneath third base—and were there the whole time ball was played on the site!

On May 1, 1920, Braves Field was the site of the longest game in major league history, a 1–1 tie, Boston against Brooklyn. Leon Cadore of the Dodgers and Joe Oeschger pitched complete games. This was the start of a long three-day stretch for the Dodgers. They returned home the following day to lose to the Phillies 4–3 in 13 innings, then went back to Boston on May 3, where they lost 2–1 in 19 innings. That's 58 innings and two train rides in three days.

In 1915 and 1916, the Red Sox won the American League pennant and played their World Series games here, because, at that time, Braves Field held 4300 more fans than Fenway Park.

Because of its huge original dimensions, it was ten years before a ball was hit over one of the outfield fences. The first ground rule home run in Braves Field was struck May 28, 1925, by Pancho Snyder off Larry Benton. In the dozen years between the opening of the park and the construction of the inner fence to aid the Braves' frustrated power hitters, this was by far the largest outfield in the major leagues. Using the original configuration, only seven balls *total* were hit over the fence on the fly. Seven other blows bounced over the wall into the stands or rolled under a gate so the outfielder couldn't get to them.

In the meantime 209 inside-the-park home runs were hit. Braves Field during the 1920s was the inside-the-park homer's last great stand. In fact, on April 29, 1922, during a game played in the sort of wind that makes outfielders look bad, the visiting New York Giants hit four inside-the-park home runs in Braves Field in a single game, two of them by George Kelly. The dimensions were originally shortened in 1928 by placing bleacher seats in the outfield, but the seats weren't used much and were taken down. From then on the home run distances were determined by a double deck of advertisement signs, except in left, where there was a short screen in front of the jury box, gently curving at the corners, well inside the original wall. The whole jury box was inside the original wall, for that matter.

Originally the Braves Field scoreboard was on the ground level in left field, so that balls could occasionally go into the open holes and disappear. By 1949, Braves Field had one of the tallest scoreboards in baseball. The middle arch above the Waltham clock was 68 feet above the ground out in left field. On either side of the clock were advertisements reading, "The Six Little Tailors," and "It's Okay to Owe Kay Jewelry."

Fans stopped coming to see the Braves play before the team moved to Milwaukee in 1953, only seven years after lights were installed here and a half million dollars was spent on refurbishing Braves Field. The season attendance for the 1952 Boston Braves was 281,000.

Much of Braves Field still stands. It has been turned into Nickerson Field, home of Boston University football. The open first base side stands, original outfield fence, and office building are still there. Field is astroturfed. The university owns the stadium, and the place is still looking sharp. Nickerson was also the home of the United States Football League's Boston Breakers.

Before Braves Field was built the site was the Allston Golf Club.

Bradenton, Florida

McKechnie Field

Spring home of the St. Louis Cardinals 1930s (Gas House Gang), also former spring home of the Boston and Milwaukee Braves. Current spring home of the Pittsburgh Pirates; Gulf Coast League (Rookie), present (Blue Jays). *Location:* Route 19, 26th Avenue East, Ninth Street West. *Dimensions:* Left field, 342 feet; center field, 433 feet; right field, 385 feet.

According to Red Sox announcer Ken Coleman, "Rickety McKechnie Field has a charm that evokes baseball in its simpler, more pastoral time. Attendants park cars in nearby grassy fields, and the feeling is not so much that of major league baseball but more like a country fair."

When Dizzy Dean had spring training here as a Cardinal, he liked it so much that he bought a Bradenton gas station.

Pirate City

Gulf Coast League (Rookie), present (Braves, Dodgers, Pirates, three franchises). *Dimensions:* Left field, 340 feet; center field, 410 feet; right field, 340 feet. *Size of site:* 49 acres.

This is also the spring training facility for the Pittsburgh Pirates' farm system. Facility includes dorms for 200 ballplayers. Four fields are arranged like slices of a pie. Visitors are allowed to watch four games at once from a tower in the center.

Sprinkler system is computer controlled.

Brenham, Texas

Fireman's Park

Used for Brenham high school ball, present. *Fences:* Twelve feet, painted wood.

According to *Sports Illustrated,* this park, with its smell of honeysuckle, "has to be one of the nicest high school ballparks in America. The covered wooden grandstands form a horseshoe behind home plate. . . . Behind the left-field wall, oh, 360 feet from home plate, is an electric scoreboard, donated by Blue Bell ice cream. . . . The park is hard by the Santa Fe train tracks, which are set on an earthen embankment, so that the trains go by at about the level of the grandstand roof. Three times a game, at 7:05, 7:30, and 8:30, a train rumbles past, loaded with coal. It takes two minutes for the train

to pass, and since there is a crossing just beyond the park, the engineer, leaning out of his cab, blows the whistle long and loud."

Bristol, Virginia

Devault Memorial Stadium

Appalachian League 1969–present (Tigers). *Location:* Euclid Avenue exit on Interstate 381. *Dimensions:* Left field, 365 feet; center field, 410 feet; right field, 310 feet. *Seating capacity:* 2000. *1987 season attendance:* 15,337.

Brockville, Ontario

Fulford Field

Canadian American League 1936–37 (Pirates). *Location:* First Avenue (left field). *Dimensions:* Left field, 275 feet; left center, 300 feet. *Seating capacity:* 2000.

Land for Fulford Field was donated to the city of Brockville by George Taylor Brockville in 1908. At that time the infield was all dirt and the next-door neighbors were the baseball-rabid residents of the Fulford Home for Retired Ladies. The outfield fence and clubhouse were constructed in the 1920s.

There was still no grass on the infield when the park was used for organized baseball by the Pirates of the Canadian American League in 1936–37.

The dimensions were a little ridiculous. Because of the proximity of First Avenue, the left field fence was on top of the infield. This is one of the few parks where a ball struck over the outfield barrier on the fly counted as a ground rule double.

Park still exists and is used today by the Brockville Bunnies of the Ontario Baseball Association.

Brooklyn, New York

York Street Park

Home of the Brooklyn Atlantics 1855–65. *Location:* York Street (near the current site of the Brooklyn Bridge).

Union Grounds

National Association 1871-75 (New York Mutuals), 1871-72 (Eckfords), 1873-75 (Atlantics), 1877 (Hartfords of Brooklyn). *Location:* Lee Avenue and Rutledge Street. *Built:* 1862. *Seating capacity:* 1500. *First National Association game (Eckfords):* May 9, 1871. *First National Association game (Mutuals):* May 25, 1871. *Last National Association game (Eckfords):* October 22, 1872. *Last National Association game (Mutuals):* October 29, 1875. *First National Association game (Atlantics):* May 7, 1873. *Last National Association game (Atlantics):* October 9, 1875. *First National League game:* April 30, 1877. *Last National League game:* September 21, 1877.

The first enclosure constructed just for baseball was the Union Grounds, built in 1862 by William Cammeyer in the Williamsburg section of Brooklyn. The park was located at the corner of Lee Avenue and Rutledge Street, just across the East River from Lower Manhattan. It opened May 15, 1862.

A drawing of Brooklyn's Union Grounds appears on the sports page of the Saturday, September 12, 1868, *New York Clipper.* The illustration, in questionable proportion, depicts a game in progress, played five days before between the Brooklyn Atlantics and the Philadelphia Athletics. The grass diamond has only the basepaths worn to dirt. A horeshoe-shaped, single-decked grandstand, roofed behind the plate, surrounds the action on three sides. Those stands seated 1500 on long benches. Initially, the men preferred the old-fashioned way of viewing the game, standing along the edge of the field, and the bleachers were thought of as a place for the ladies to sit. But those feelings were gone by the start of organized play in the early 1870s. Grandstand seats became thought of as choice.

Home run distances appear quite reachable down the lines and unthinkable everywhere else. Most of the infrequent homers struck here got past the outfielders and rolled forever.

That winter Cammeyer put more money into the facility. Here is what *The Standard,* Saturday, April 19, 1869, had to say about that off-season's ongoing refurbishment:

"The lots situated on the corner of Lee ave. and Rutledge street, occupied last winter by the Union Skating Association, have been enlarged, levelled and laid out into ball grounds, with room enough to accommodate three clubs. Houses and benches, &c, will be erected, and everything to make the grounds complete will be done by the enterprizing President, Mr. Cammeyer.

"Which three clubs will occupy these grounds has not yet been settled, and none, we believe, have made application except the Rutledge Club. An admission fee of 10 cents will be charged on *match* days. These grounds, if managed properly — and there is little doubt but that they will be — could be made not only to prove very profitable, but a credit to the section in which they are located. They are conveniently situated, and accessible to both districts — the Flushing, Division avenue and Greenpoint cars running within a few blocks of the grounds."

At first Cammeyer, owner of the grounds but not the ball club, pocketed all of those dimes for admission. In return, he didn't charge the ball club any rent. That lasted only until the Union club refused to play unless Cammeyer shared profits. When the president caved in, the Union Nine of Brooklyn became a money-making proposition.

The notion of gate-sharing spread as more fields became enclosed, allowing ball clubs to avoid the red, and occasionally get into the black.

The Union Grounds were the home field for the New York Mutuals, a team made up of some firemen and some (pro) ringers, all with heavy-duty political connections.

In 1871, the Mutuals were New York's sole entry in the National Association because that was the way Boss Tweed wanted it. Tweed gave some of the ringer Mutuals, who were really professional ballplayers, no-show jobs—usually in the coroner's office where no one wanted to investigate.

In 1866, prices went from 10 cents to 25 cents for important games. In 1867, all games cost a quarter. By 1870, there was experimentation with a 50 cent price tag for big games.

The Original Big Red Machine. The Union Grounds were baseball's focal point on Tuesday, June 15, 1869. That was the day the Cincinnati Red Stockings, the world's first completely professional baseball team, came to Brooklyn to play the Mutuals, the City of Churches' finest "amateurs." Both teams considered themselves the best in the nation. The Mutuals were the undisputed "best team in the East," and the Red Stockings were in the middle of an undefeated transcontinental barnstorming tour. Traveling from city to city, the original Big Red Machine had won 14 games in a row.

Brooklyn was already known for its baseball fanatics. Even in 1869, many of Brooklyn's 300,000 citizens lived and died for the Mutuals, as their descendants would for the Dodgers. When the Red Stockings set foot into town they got the rude raspberry wherever they roamed. Cincinnati manager Harry Wright ran a tight ship, and wouldn't allow his players to lose their dignity under the onslaught of unspeakably vulgar Brooklynese.

It was threatening to rain on the day of the game, yet an undaunted crowd commenced gathering at the Union Grounds early in the morning. Game time was 2 o'clock. By noon, folks were coming from all over town, and even by ferry across the river from New

York. Brooklyn did something it had always been good at. It picked a special summer day, and it played hooky.

A traffic jam crippled Williamsburg's thoroughfares. Rutledge Avenue, outside the grounds, was a horse-rearing mess. Fights broke out, providing the entertainment. Management stopped selling tickets early, as the crowd spilled out of the stands and onto the field. The game started late, as Brooklyn police were forced to clear room for the game.

Folks who couldn't get into the ballpark jockeyed for position to see from nearby rooftops or through knotholes in the wooden fence. The crowd was rife with evidence of alcohol and chance, vices not unknown even to the players.

The only umpire for the "match" was Charles Walker, whose job was made more difficult by fans publicly discussing his olfactory effect.

Official scorer for the contest was Henry Chadwick, the journalist who invented the box score. He viewed the game, scoring with pen and ink, from beneath both his topper and an awning, along the first base line.

Chadwick spent much of his life trying to remove baseball's gambling element, which threatened to liquidate the embryonic professional sport. He didn't do much good. On that day, gambling was conducted openly in the stands and in the outfield where the overflow stood.

Also in attendance was ex-boxer and later to be U.S. Congressman John Morrissey. His money was on the Red Stockings.

Brooklynites chancing wages on the Mutuals staggered home—or into the comforting din of their neighborhood saloon—disappointed that day, as the Cincinnatis kept their winning streak alive, defeating the Mutuals 4-2 behind the crafty control pitching of Asa Brainard.

The Red Stockings' winning streak eventually reached 92 games. It was still alive the following year when Cincinnati again won their confrontation at the Union Grounds. This time the score was a crushing 16–3. Cincinnati was the most profitable baseball business ever. They proved just how financially successful baseball could be.

In 1871, the Union Grounds were the neutral site of the National Association Championship Game, between the Philadelphia Athletics and the Chicago White Stockings. The White Stockings' home grounds had been destroyed by the Great Chicago Fire, forcing the team to play all of the remaining games on the road. They were a ragtag bunch. Their uniforms had been burned, forcing them to bum extras from the other clubs in the National Association.

It was the first year of organized professional baseball. Chicago was the home team in a game won by the Athletics before a small crowd.

The winning pitcher was ex-cricketeer Dick McBride. McBride was one of the few ballplayers who didn't have a mustache—but he made up for it with outrageous sideburns that went all the way down to his chin. Hitting star was N.A. batting champ Long Levi Meyerle (.403).

The White Stockings looked so motley they made reporters sad. They looked even dingier on the field with the A's, who wore the league's sharpest blazers.

The Union Grounds' home team was still the "New York" Mutuals, who finished 1871 below .500 and in sixth place. At an early season game that year against Chicago a crowd of 6000 attended, returning $3000 in receipts. More than 3000 men seeking to hop the fence caused security problems. All over Brooklyn telegraph offices were crowded as play-by-play came over the wire.

In 1872, when the Mutuals finished fourth, their infielder/outfielder John Van Buren (Jack) Hatfield set the world long-distance baseball throwing record in the Union Grounds. Four hundred feet, 7½ inches on the fly. That year he led off and hit .303, appearing in 56 games, all at second base.

The grounds were the neutral site of two games by the Elizabeth Resolutes in 1873.

"A Disgraceful Scene on the Union Grounds." Gambling at the Union Grounds was a problem that got worse instead of better. All too frequently corruption spilled onto the lawns of play.

On September 21, 1876, the *New York Times* reported as follows: "Early in the afternoon the betting in the pool room was 25 to 10 in favor of the New-York team, but just before the game these odds turned in favor of the Brooklyn men. At this time it was openly asserted that at least two of the New-York players had arranged to lose the game, and the subsequent exhibition of fielding on the part of the two mentioned certainly gave color to the charge.... While the players were changing their uniforms in the clubhouse, some one accused Hovey of selling the game. A disgraceful fight ensued, to suppress which the Police had to be called in, a fitting finale to the most disreputable proceeding that has been witnessed on a ball field in this vicinity for years."

This wasn't a league game. Whoever Hovey was, he didn't last long, and never got into a real National Association or National League game.

After the collapse of the National Association in 1875, Brooklyn did not have another big league entry until 1884 in the American Association, where they first became the Trolley Dodgers.

On May 24, 1889, the Union Grounds were used for major league baseball for the last time, by Brooklyn of the American Association.

Capitoline Grounds

Home of the Atlantics 1865–71, and Excelsiors 1866–71, National Association 1872 (Atlantics), National League 1876 (New York Mutuals). Also the home of the Stars, and Enterprise. First used for baseball 1865. *Location:* Halsey Street and Marcy, Putnam and Nostrand avenues (in 1949 reported to be the site of the 13th Regiment Armory; current site of Boys' High School). *First National Association game:* May 6, 1872. *First National League game:* April 25, 1876. *Last National League game:* October 17, 1876.

An old-timer named Hamilton A. Gill recalls the Capitoline Grounds of the 1860s and 1870s in a 1934 article for the Brooklyn *Eagle:*

"Opposite the roadhouse south of Gates Avenue were open fields where the old Atlantic Baseball Club used to play ball until enclosed grounds were laid out. The field was laid out just opposite the school on the east side of Bedford Avenue, covering a plot about 600 or 700 feet, extending through to Nostrand Avenue's west side. That was the Decker Farm, owned by Reuben S. Decker. He and Hamilton A. Weed built the Old Capitoline Ground, which was situated on the east side of Nostrand Avenue and extending from Putnam Avenue, at the edge of Putnam Pond, to Halsey Street, and then to Marcy Avenue. It was here that the old Atlantic baseball team played their first game on enclosed ground, built in about 1868. The players at that time familiarly known by me were Dicky Pierce, Bob Ferguson, and Joe Stuart."

Ferguson was known as "Death to Flying Things."

The Excelsiors, one of the teams that made their home here, had their clubhouse in Brooklyn Heights, at 133 Clinton Street, in a house that still exists, with a plaque commemorating its historical status.

The Little House. There was a small round brick house, the use of which is never clearly specified, deep in center field. Its roof was cone-shaped, and there was a big flag sticking out of the roof. Perhaps it was divided into ladies and gentlemen sections.

Anyone clearing the roof of the "little house" with a drive received a bottle of champagne. This honor was earned most often by Lip Pike.

The house is shown in a drawing of the Capitoline Grounds that appeared in *Leslie's Illustrated Newspaper* on November 4, 1865. There don't appear to be seats, but men in tall top hats line the foul lines watching the action. There is a wooden fence in right field with carriages parked in front of it.

In 1865 the stolen base was invented at the Capitoline Grounds, by a visiting player named Eddie Cuthbert. Everyone laughed at him until it was discovered that there was no rule forbidding his thievery. Eddie was allowed to stay at second, and baseball was changed.

Chiming the News to Bedford Village. The grounds were 15 acres in area, and it was not an uncommon thing to see an improvised bar set up on one side of the field, at which beer and sandwiches were dispensed without hindrance from the authorities.

Crowds as large as 10,000 showed up for big games. Boys were allowed in free at the start of the eighth inning. If the Excelsiors or the Atlantics won, the bell atop the grounds' main building chimed out the news to Bedford Village.

In those days, there was a little ceremony after the game. A representative of the defeated nine formally, in a brief speech, presented the game ball as a trophy to the winners, who had it painted, and the score written between the stitches.

It was at the Capitoline Grounds, on July 2, 1870, that the Cincinnati Red Stockings' record 92-game winning streak came to an end. The Atlantics beat them that day 3–2, in 11 innings.

Here is what *Harper's Weekly* had to say at the time about the game and the locals who came out to watch:

"From 12,000 to 15,200 people passed into the inclosure to witness the sport and we are sorry to say that the crowd was boisterous and noisy, and greatly marred the pleasure of the game for those who wanted to look on quietly.

"The Red Stockings were not treated with the courtesy they had hitherto received, and, for the first time, and we trust the last, partisan feeling was allowed to display itself."

The crowd would have been even larger if the price of admission had not been jacked up to 50 cents a head.

That summer there was a great deal of controversy over the scientific possibility of the curveball, the old underhanded "inshoot" that was boggling batters even before league ball. In August, a demonstration was given to prove that the curve ball was all too real, a piece of physical possibility made to shatter a boy's dreams of turning pro.

Here is how the event was reported by Henry Chadwick in *The Brooklyn Eagle:*

"Yesterday (August 16, 1870), a large crowd assembled and cheered lustily as a youth from New Haven, Connecticut, Fred Goldsmith, demonstrated to the satisfaction of all that a baseball could be so manipulated and controlled by throwing it from one given point to another, as to make a pronounced arc in space."

Goldsmith, who went on to be a four-time 20-game winner in the National League for the Chicago White Stockings, proved his point by driving two eight-foot poles into the ground, one midway between the pitcher's box and the plate and the other just to the right of the plate. Using his 6'1", 195-lb. frame, he threw the ball outside the first pole and inside the second from the box. Goldsmith proved the inshoot was no optical illusion.

The Atlantics did not enter the National Association until their second year, in 1872, because William Marcy "Boss" Tweed had favored the firemen on the Mutuals. But Tweed had left power in handcuffs in 1871, leaving the Atlantics free to do as they wished, and the entrance fee to the National Asso-

tion was only ten dollars.

A studio-posed photograph of the Brooklyn Atlantics taken in 1871 and currently housed in the National Baseball Library in Cooperstown is labeled, "Champions of America 1864, 1865, 1866, 1868, 1870." (The claim to the 1866 championship is questionable, since 30,000 Philadelphians claimed to have seen their Athletics beat the Atlantics in that year's October 1 championship game.) Atlantics manager Peter O'Brien had a full beard, while his players were split evenly between clean-shaven and mustached.

After 1872, the Atlantics abandoned Capitoline for the Union Grounds, sharing that site with the Mutuals. The Mutuals plotted to make life difficult for the Atlantics. Cammeyer got Bob "Death to Flying Things" Ferguson, the Atlantics' star player, elected president of the National Association. Overworked to say the least, Ferguson's team deteriorated, eventually finishing last in a 13-team league by 1875, their last season.

On November 15 of every year the Capitoline Grounds were flooded with four feet of water and turned into a skating rink.

The Capitoline Grounds' last appearance on the Long Island Historical Society's maps is in 1880.

Satellite Grounds
Location: Unknown.

According to the *Brooklyn Daily Union,* October 4, 1867, two black teams played at the Satellite Grounds, the Philadelphia Excelsiors defeating the Brooklyn Uniques 37–24 in a game called after seven innings for darkness. The *Daily Union* reporter called the match the "championship of colored clubs."

In pre-game ceremonies the teams paraded around the field behind a fife and drum. The reporter complained, however, of the roughness of the black teams' play and the rowdiness of the racially mixed crowd.

Washington Park (I)

Interstate League 1883, American Association 1884–89 (Trolley Dodgers), National League 1890–91. *Location:* Between Third and Fifth streets and Fourth and Fifth avenues. *Seating capacity:* 2500. *First Interstate League game:* May 12, 1883 (Brooklyn 13, Trenton 6). *First American Association game:* May 5, 1884 (Brooklyn 11, Washington 3). *Last American Association game:* October 5, 1899 (Philadelphia 10, Brooklyn 2, 8 innings, darkness). *First National League game:* April 28, 1890 (Brooklyn 10, Philadelphia 0). *Last National League game:* April 16, 1891. *Fire:* 1886; May 23, 1889.

In 1883, New York businessmen Charles H. Byrne, R.I. Byrne, and Joseph J. Doyle, along with gambling house proprietor Ferdinand A. Abell, purchased the Camden, New Jersey, Merritts of the Interstate League, who moved across the Hudson to become Brooklyn's first professional baseball franchise in seven years.

The Brooklyn team played one year in the minor league, then moved to the American Association, a major circuit started in 1883 to compete with the National League.

R.I. Byrne, whose business was real estate, picked the site for the Brooklyn ballpark between the Park Slope and Red Hook sections. Land was leased from the Litchfield property and $30,000 was spent fixing up the grounds. There was wooden grandstand and bleacher seating for 2500, but on May 12, 1883, 6000 showed up for the Interstate League opener. Most sat on stools and camp chairs they had brought with them. After the famous 23rd Regiment Band played a few popular tunes, Brooklyn beat Trenton 13–6.

As this was the approximate site of the Continental Army of George Washington's Battle of Long Island, the ballpark was called Washington Park. It was here that Washington made his last stand prior to his retreat to Fort Lee, then to Trenton, New Jersey.

The old stone house, used in 1890 as the club room for the Brooklyn team, was used by Washington and his staff for several hours as headquarters before and during the battle. The most severe fighting of the battle took place here, General Stirling's troops performing a deadly delaying action upon Cornwallis' superior number of Redcoats, permitting Washington's successful retreat. The house was built in 1699. By the beginning of the twentieth century the "Old Stone House at Gowanus" had fallen into complete ruin and was recreated by the city's Parks Department, using at least some of the same stones from the original. The replica still stands (see photo) and is known as the Vechte-Cortelyou House.

Byrne named Doyle his team manager and assembled a staff to operate the new baseball business. One young ticket-seller and general handyman for the club went on to bigger and better things. His name was Charles H. Ebbets. At that time Ebbets lived near the ballpark, on 6th Street.

When the park opened, horse cars came from Fulton, Wall, and South ferries, via Fifth Avenue, to the main entrance. A few years later, the newfangled trolleys ran outside the ballpark along Fourth Avenue, and folks had to concentrate to avoid vehicles that didn't clomp.

The American Association team soon became known as the Trolley Dodgers, then, simply the Dodgers.

In 1889, Brooklyn fans were still the nastiest. Two St. Louis players particularly felt the heat. St. Louis outfielder Charles "Home Run" Duffee said he'd rather hoe cotton back home in Mobile for ten bucks a month than play a boy's game before the brutes of Brooklyn. Right-hander Elton "Icebox" Chamberlain, 32–15 that year, feared for his life in the Washington Park box.

In 1891, the American Association

Seen today, covered with graffiti and in need of a new roof, this is a precise replica of the stone house on the site of the original Washington Park (Brooklyn, N.Y.) that served as clubhouse for baseball and as headquarters for General George Washington during the Revoutionary War's Battle of Long Island. (Photo by MacIntyre Symms.)

Brooklyn team was forced to leave the original Washington Park due to inroads created by the Brotherhood War.

The lot is currently the Byrne Park playground, so there is still ball being played here — even if it is on blacktop.

Parade Grounds

Home of semi-pro ball around 1890. *Location:* Park Circle, Park Slope.

A happy crowd turned out for the 1883 championship game between the Peerless and Nameless at the Parade Grounds on the number two diamond.

Behind home, along the fence, and out on Caton Avenue, men and boys had climbed the trees for a view of the game, and the outfield had been roped off. Some folks weren't sure where the Nameless team came from, and some recognized the Peerless as the men who worked at the Miles Brush Factory at Hinsdale and Pitkin avenues in East New York.

The crowd was happy because it had money. Signs of cash were everywhere. The cake and candy vendor with the gray hair and whiskers was sold out by the third inning. He and his son then sat down and watched the rest of the game.

Also doing excellent business was a young man selling lemon drops and tutti-frutti chewing gum from a square wooden box, and others selling lemonade, two cents a glass.

Over 2000 Peerless fans came from East New York and Greenpoint. The favorites lost, making the considerably smaller Nameless contingent happy. Things would have been different, grumbled the Peerless many, if Jack Connelly, the Peerless catcher, hadn't gone down with an injury. Stuck, the team had to replace Connelly with Father Carr, known for his goodness but not for his fielding, and, well, that was that.

According to Joseph S. Halstead in a 1943 Brooklyn *Eagle* column, the best thing about the Parade Grounds, back in the late 1880s, was nearby Thomas Coyne's saloon on Coney Island Avenue behind which the cricket club had built and maintained a forty-feet-square clubhouse:

"The grounds were kept in tip-top shape, rolled daily by a horse-drawn roller. Teams that played there were the Resolutes, Peerless, Stars, Nameless, Bedford, Commercial, Dauntless, and the Cuban Stars, a colored team. On the weekends games were played between the drivers and conductors of the old horsecars. A keg was kept on the field, but a batter had to get on base to get a drink. One drink for a single, two for a double, three for a triple, and the limit for a home run. The good players had plenty of beer while others practically died of thirst."

By 1939, the Parade Grounds had become undoubtedly the most extensive free field in a large city for the exclusive use of ballplayers. Both baseball and cricket flourished from April to October, when the football players were allowed to take over. The grounds consisted of 40 acres, rectangular in shape, parallel with the southeastern extremity of Prospect Park. Most of it was level, well-kept turf. There was sufficient space for 26 diamonds.

The Parade Grounds and their diamonds are still there.

Eastern Park

Used as early as the 1870s on Sundays. Players League 1890 (Wonders), National League 1891–97 (Bridegrooms). *Location:* Eastern Parkway (now Pitkin Avenue), Belmont Avenue, Sackman Street, and Van Sinderen Avenue. (Another source says Van Sinderen, Glenmore, Williams and Liberty. Still another says Eastern Parkway to Blake Avenue. Everyone agrees it was near the junction between the Canarsie Line and the City Line el. *Dimensions:* 460 feet by 860 feet. *First Players League game:* April 28, 1890 (Brooklyn 3, Philadelphia 1). *Last Players League game:* September 12, 1890 (Brooklyn 8, Boston 7). *First National League game:* April 27, 1891 (New York 6, Brooklyn 5). *Last Na-*

tional League game: October 2, 1897 (Brooklyn 15, Boston 6).

As early as the 1870s, before there were stands to sit in, illegal games were played on this site on Sundays. Fans were alert; escape routes were planned. A collar by the constable cost ten dollars or ten days.

These were beer-in-the-bucket games. A contest could last four hours or more with all the fighting and jawing and clowning. A popular topic of zesty debate concerned whether the pitcher was throwing (raising his arm above his hip) instead of pitching.

McDevitts Hotel was opposite the grounds. On one side of the diamond was a row of houses. When the big leagues came, kids paid ten cents to watch from the roofs, or the Howard House stoop. Of course a kid could get in the ballpark for free if he knew enough to help the groundskeeper with some of the heavy work.

According to Albert Osterland in a 1943 Brooklyn *Eagle* column, East New York (a section of Brooklyn) contributed greatly in the nineteenth century toward making Brooklyn a major baseball city. When in use by the National League (because new ball club stockholder Chauncey owned East New York real estate) Eastern was one of the most popular professional ballparks, both with the players and the fans, swept as it was by the ocean breezes off Manhattan Beach. It was a double-decked grandstand with cone-shaped spires on its roof and bleachers running down its baselines.

Still, when the ballpark was used by the Bridegrooms, it was considered a hardship for the majority of fans to reach, and attendance slacked off. William Breen, writing in the Brooklyn *Eagle,* recalled going to Eastern Park as a child in the 1890s:

"I often scraped up 40 cents — 25 cents for a seat in the bleachers, ten cents carfare on the 'El' to Manhattan Junction and five cents for a hot dog or a bag of peanuts. Tommy Tucker was the first first baseman to wear a finger glove."

Mr. Breen had an excellent memory. Tucker played only 73 games for Brooklyn (all at first base) and was out of baseball after 1899. The rent at Eastern Park was $7500 for the National League team, which proved far too much. When Charles Ebbets assumed presidency of the team, they returned to South Brooklyn, as close as possible to the original Washington Park site (the old land wasn't available), to a lot catty-corner from the old park.

Ridgewood Park (also known as Wallace's Ridgewood Grounds, The Horse Market, Meyerrose's Union League Park) American Association 1889, 1890 Trolley Dodgers, Sundays only). *Location:* Onderdonk and Elm avenues (currently considered in the Borough of Queens). *Last American Association game:* August 3, 1890 (Toledo 9, Brooklyn 2).

Back in 1883, when Ridgewood Park was still just a vacant lot used for amateur ball, where the horse auctions had once been held, next to the Ridgewood Pumping Station, balls that rolled under the station's big iron gate were home runs.

In 1943, an old-timer named George Forbell recalled in the Brooklyn *Eagle* his most memorable moment as an amateur ballplayer in Ridgewood Park:

"While batting against Red Hughes and his Jersey City team one day, I misjudged one of his inshoots and it struck me squarely in the pit of the stomach. I contracted my diaphragm instantly, and the ball fell dead at my feet. I picked up the ball, threw it back to the pitcher, and took my base. Many times I have worried about that, for fear of cancer."

The only known picture of this park is in *Illustrated History of Greater Ridgewood,* a 1913 volume by George

Schubel. Onderdonk Avenue is a dirt road, cutting through an unkempt field of grass next to the baseball grounds. Ridgewood Park looks dilapidated. The wooden bleachers never reach as high as the second floor of the house nearby. "Meyerrose's Union League Park" is painted in white on the outside of the rickety wooden outfield fence. We don't know which Union League the sign refers to, as the photo is undated, captioned simply, "Ridgewood Park." Barely visible in the photo is a small roofed grandstand.

The park was 20 minutes by el from the Brooklyn Bridge.

Baseball Pioneer Henry Chadwick was almost 80 when he became official scorekeeper at the technically illegal Sunday games played out in Ridgewood, where Queens and Brooklyn came together. The American Association played 13 Sunday games there in 1889. Chadwick had always found Sunday baseball blasphemous, but mellowed when baseball-oriented work became harder to come by. He even accepted a small sum for his Sabbath scoring.

Ambrose Park
Home of the Bay Ridge Athletic Club 1896–97. *Location:* South Brooklyn.

A huge enclosure where once Buffalo Bill and his Congress of Rough Riders had been the main attraction.

Washington Park (II)
National League 1898–1912 (Superbas, Dodgers), Federal League 1914–15 (Tip Tops). *Location:* First Street (right field), Third Street (third base), Third Avenue (left field), Fourth Avenue (first base). *Construction cost:* $60,000. *Dimensions:* Left field, 335 feet; center field, 500 feet; right field, 295 feet. 90 feet from home plate to the backstop. *First National League game:* April 30, 1898 (Philadelphia 6, Brooklyn 4). *Last National League game:* October 5, 1912 (New York 1, Brooklyn 0).

First Federal League game: May 11, 1914 (Pittsburgh 2, Brooklyn 0). *Last Federal League game:* September 30, 1915 (Buffalo 3, Brooklyn 2).

Charles Ebbets became president of Brooklyn's National League ball club, moved the team out of Eastern Park, saving $7500 a year in rent for a lousy location, and instead bought land in South Brooklyn, catty-corner from the old Washington Park. He then built a $60,000 ballpark, the cost shared by the two nearby streetcar lines.

The uncovered seats out past the grandstand were called the "bleacheries." There was a small and tasteful front entrance, which was always done up with bunting for opening day. The largest sign, at the top of the entrance, read, "THE BROOKLYN BALL CLUB." A smaller sign below read, "WASHINGTON PARK," and then a smaller sign yet said, "Pavilion Entrance. 50 cents."

Watching baseball from the Ginney Flats (the rooftops across First Street) was free, but a fellow was expected to "rush the growler" every now and again—that is, hike over to Fourth Avenue and load up with dime-apiece buckets of beer. The pub keepers even furnished the rope, so the buckets could be hauled up to the fire-escape sitters. According to Frank Graham, "The Giant outfielders told of Brooklyn rooters on the rooftops or fire escape of the Ginney Flats fashioning spears out of umbrella ribs and hurling them at them; plus there were many brawls in the stands."

Brooklyn's dark ages came from 1902 to 1915. During those years the Dodgers never finished in the first division. The team was bad—decimated by deserters to the newfangled Junior Circuit. More people watched from the Flats than from the stands.

Part of baseball's circus atmosphere came to an end in 1906, when Ebbets got the National League to require all parks to install hot water locker rooms for visiting teams. This killed the custom of parading ballplayers from the hotel to the park, subjecting them to the wrath of opposing fans. Some, after all, saw these parades as target practice.

Most of the time Washington Park was big enough to handle Dodger crowds—but not so when the Giants crossed the river. The turnaround crowds that showed up for games against Brooklyn's arch-rivals gave Ebbets a practical excuse to expand the club's quarters. Ebbets was also sick and tired of looking out over the right field fence and seeing flocks of freeloaders on the Flats.

There was a major enlargement ($22,000 worth) before the 1908 season. The April 11 edition of the *Brooklyn Eagle* said:

"When fans reach the new Washington Park tomorrow they will realize what the improvements on the grounds mean.... The new twenty-five-cent seats in centerfield are substantially built and will afford an excellent view of the game. They are far and away ahead of any similar seats on the circuit. With the additional seats, and with the arrangements made to handle an overflow on big days, 20,000 people can be comfortably accommodated. The boxes, of which there are 42, will provide for 252. There are over 5200 seventy-five-cent seats and 600 more can be placed around on the inside of the field in three raised rows. There are 8500 fifty-cent seats and over 1500 twenty-five-cent seats. With benches in the outfield and standing room, almost 4000 more spectators can get into the grounds.

"The 'dugouts' of the new-fangled players' benches have been put into good shape. They are in their old positions but are made of cement foundations sunk into the ground about ten inches. They will not interfere in any way with the spectators view. The roof is covered with tar paper, and a comfortable bench has been placed in each."

Ebbets had squeezed so many additional seats into Washington Park that there were box seats 15 feet from home plate. It was almost impossible for a player to catch a foul ball. There were two sets of bleachers, side by side, along the right field line, one along left.

According to some reports, Washington Park II was not always the greatest place to watch a ball game because of its proximity to the aromatic Gowanus Canal and nearby factories. Foul, dark smoke often lingered in the ballpark during the dog days of August, without a wisp of wind to move it along.

The team moved out at the end of the 1912 season, for their new home on the other side of Prospect Park. Ebbets' first thought had been to fix Washington Park up and make it seat more people, maybe move the grandstand over from the Fourth to the Third Avenue side and enlarge the bleacher section. Fortunately for all concerned, he decided to build elsewhere.

The park remained idle for only one year. In 1914, it was used because of major league baseball's diluting expansion. Renovation for Federal League usage was delayed because the Ward brothers — the bakery owners who owned the club — used non-union help in their bakeries. Union men wouldn't fix up the ballpark and urged a league-wide boycott of the Brooklyn Tip Tops' games. The Tip Tops were named after the bakers' best-selling loaf. The name was considered silly for a baseball team, and people generally called them the BrookFeds. The team managed to siphon some gate receipts from the Dodgers, especially in 1915.

The BrookFeds were not a good team, but had a star in outfielder Benny Kauff, who won the Federal League batting crown by hitting .342. He also knocked in 83 runs, and led the league with 55 stolen bases.

Photographs of the ballpark during the 1914 season show hieroglyphics (human and animal figures, perhaps American Indian symbols) on the scoreboard, which was mounted in straightaway center, in front of the junction between the right and left field walls.

The lot is the current site of the Con Edison parking lot and garages.

Ryan's Oval

Atlantic League 1907 (Edisons), semi-pro Pioneers 1910–20. *Location:* Columbia and Pioneer streets in Red Hook.

The Pioneers were, at that time, Brooklyn's premiere semi-pro ballclub.

Ebbets Field

National League 1913–57 (Dodgers), Negro National League 1935 (Eagles), United States League 1945 (Brown Dodgers, partial season). Owned by the Ebbets-McKeever Exhibition Company. *Location:* Bedford Avenue (right field side), Montgomery Street (left field), McKeever Place (third base), Sullivan Place (first base). Current site of the Jackie Robinson Apartments. *Architect:* C.A. Van Buskirk. *Contractors:* Golliek & Smith. *Ground broken:* March 4, 1912. *Grandstand cornerstone laid:* July 6, 1912. *Construction material:* 230,000 feet of Clinton Electrically Welded wire. *Construction cost:* $750,000. *Dimensions:* (1913) Left field, 419 feet; center field, 477 feet; right field, 301 feet. (Later) left field, 315 feet; deepest left center, 395 feet; center field, 389 feet; deepest right center, 403 feet; right field, 297 feet. 71 feet between home plate and the backstop. *Seating capacity:* (1913–16) 18,000. (1917) 22,000. (Later) 31,497. (Lower boxes, 6803; lower reserved, 11,613; upper boxes, 1550; upper reserved, 10,053; general admission, 1478). *Single game attendance record:* 37,512 (versus New York, August 30, 1947). *Doubleheader attendance record:* 41,209 (versus New York, May 30, 1934). *Night game attendance record:* 35,583 (versus Philadelphia, September 24, 1949). *Opening game attendance record:* 34,530 (versus

New York, April 18, 1949). *Season high attendance record:* 1,807,526 (1947). *Season low attendance record:* 83,831 (1918). *Size of site:* Four and a half acres. *First exhibition game:* April 5, 1913 (Brooklyn 3, New York Highlanders 2, home run Stengel). *First National League game:* April 9, 1913 (Philadelphia 1, Brooklyn 0, attendance, 12,000, winning pitcher: Tom Seaton). *Lights installed:* 1938. *Last game:* September 24, 1957 (Brooklyn 3, Pittsburgh 0, attendance: 6702). *Torn down:* February 23, 1960.

Charles Ebbets found the site for his new ballpark in 1908: four and a half acres of land-filled marsh in Pigtown, on Crown Heights' lower slope, only a couple of blocks from what was then Flatbush Avenue's northernmost point — an Italian ghetto, made up of shanties, goats and dandelions.

Here's how Peter Golenbock described that land in his book *Bums:* "(In 1907) it was a wild, craggy piece of land with shanties scattered over it, and in the middle of this nest of poverty was a large, gaping pit into which the shantie dwellers threw their fetid, steaming garbage. Farmers from the area brought their pigs there to feed."

In order to obtain the entire block, which was only just big enough for a ballpark, Ebbets had to purchase 1200 individual parcels of land. Over four years, the parcels were bought from 15 different owners at a total cost of $200,000. To accomplish it he needed secrecy, so he formed a dummy company to make the purchases for him.

By the time Ebbets finally owned the complete site, he was practically broke. He tried to secure loans from other baseball owners but was unanimously refused. To pay for his new park, Ebbets sold half the club's stock to a pair of local contractors with political power. They were Edward J. and Stephen W. McKeever, sons of Irish immigrants. Two corporations were formed. The team was owned by the Brooklyn Baseball Club, Inc. (Ebbets,

president, Ed McKeever, vice president), while the park was owned by the Ebbets-McKeever Exhibition Company (Ed McKeever, president, Ebbets, vice president). Steve McKeever functioned as the treasurer for both corporations.

Ebbets had hoped to build his new park for under a half million dollars but found this impossible. There were delays. One parcel of land could not be purchased as the owner couldn't be found. Ebbets' people chased the landowner all over the world, and finally back to New Jersey. When they caught up with this traveling gentleman he proclaimed he'd all but forgotten his little piece of Brooklyn. Having no notion of the importance of the plot the man asked (and promptly received) a measly $500 for the land. Construction costs for Ebbets Field reached three-quarters of a million dollars.

By the groundbreaking (March 4, 1912) the shanties had all been torn down and the garbage hole filled in.

In the "it pays to have friends in high places" category, buildings superintendent John Thatcher helped in designing Ebbets Field's sewer system, and park commissioner M.J. Kennedy assisted in landscaping.

Built Despite Mrs. Boole's Warnings. On January 2, 1913, Mrs. Ella A. Boole made a speech at the Central Presbyterian Church in Brooklyn, in which she said that in order to attend the fine new baseball grounds on the East of Flatbush near Malbone, young people would have to arrive via an elevated railroad platform serving a brewery. She concluded that "many a fine boy is going to be ruined through the perfectly healthy sport of baseball." Since she never made it clear if she wanted the ballpark, the platform, or the brewery abolished, folks merely became perplexed, and nothing ever came of Mrs. Boole's comments.

Opening Day. To Ebbets' embarrassment, his construction plans had not included a press box, and the park opened without one. He roped off two rows of seats behind home in the front of the upper deck for the press. A real press box was not put in until 1929.

In his informal history of the Dodgers, Frank Graham described the first (exhibition) game at Ebbets Field on April 5, 1913:

"The stands were gaily draped; all the borough dignitaries were there; the Twenty-third Regiment band played bravely, and Ebbets and the two McKeevers marched, hay-foot, straw-foot, with the athletes to the flagstaff, where the colors and a bright, new Brooklyn Baseball Club flag were raised. The seating capacity of the stands, announced at 25,000, was taxed, and to make it a perfect day, Nap Rucker beat the Giants 3–2." (This was an exhibition game, and it was actually the Highlanders that Rucker beat.)

Four days later, it was a different story in the new park for the real opener. The Dodgers lost to the Phillies on a wind-chilled day, weather holding the crowd to 12,000. Still, things looked busy before the game in front of the fancy main entrance. Inside, in the marble rotunda (too nice to be called a lobby) under the stucco ceiling, folks milled about excitedly.

In the game, it was so cold hornets stung the hands of jammed batters. The Phillies' Tom Seaton (who later returned to Brooklyn as a Tip Top) outdueled lefty Nap Rucker, 1–0. The lone run scored on a muffed fly ball by Benny "Earache" Meyer—a Canadian whose scouting report had said he was all stick and no glove. "Earache" proved to be no stick either, hitting .195 for Brooklyn that year.

That opening game also featured an outstanding catch of a long fly by Casey Stengel. Tex Rickart gave the lineups. According to Golenbock, "The ticket sellers stood behind gilded cages like circus boxes."

When it was new, Ebbets Field was not in the "heart" of Brooklyn. Brooklyn grew up around the ballpark, which was between upper-class Bedford and suburban Flatbush. It wasn't as far into the outskirts as Eastern Park or Ridgewood Park, certainly, but it was not nearly as close to Downtown Brooklyn as Washington Park.

Still, the new park was accessible to 90 percent of Brooklyn's population via mass transportation. Four million people were within 45 minutes of the park's turnstiles by el, trolley, or subway. Nine trolley lines served Ebbets Field for the locals, while the subway and the el gave easy access to the park for those who worked in Manhattan's Wall Street and City Hall areas. For those who drove, a lot across the street was used for parking.

In its original configuration the park had 18,000 seats, with standing room for three thousand more. The double-decked grandstand extended down the right field foul line past the foul pole, and just past third base in left. Between the grandstand and the left field fence was a set of open wooden bleachers.

The ushers were known as thugs, once brutally beating a man for stealing a foul ball. The man protested that he only wanted to take the ball home as a souvenir for his boy, so they beat him some more.

Ebbets painted the brick wall around the field a dark olive green. Vines had been planted to cover the walls, an idea better manifested in Chicago's Wrigley Field.

The curved-back opera seats in Ebbets Field's grandstand were two inches roomier than chairs in other parks because they had an arm rest on only one side.

Before the stands were built out in left field, the distance to the fence down the left field line was 419 feet. It was a roomy 477 feet to center. The fence in right was originally nine feet high.

Washington Park had been known for its lack of foul territory, and Ebbets Field was not a lot better. The stands hugged the field. Fans could see the players' facial expressions. When it was quiet, you could hear the infield chatter.

Because the stands were so close to the field, the bullpens were squeezed between the foul lines and the stands. The visitors' bullpen was a hazardous place, easily within throwing distance of the Brooklynite partisans. When a righty and a lefty warmed up out there at the same time, the righty was on the inside, closest to the stands, and tended to get hit by the most garbage.

Both bullpens were subject to vicious line drives. Extra players always stood behind the bullpen catchers—who had their backs to home—to field balls hit in that direction.

Atop the grandstand the flags for the eight National League teams flew. They were arranged from left to right according to the league standings.

Quickly Obsolete. Ebbets had hoped his new ballpark would offer all the room he would ever need—but this did not turn out to be the case. By today's standards, the plot upon which the ballpark sat was minuscule. Today a four-and-a-half-acre plot wouldn't make a decent major league parking lot.

When the 1916 World Series was played here, only 21,000 were able to get in for the Dodgers' home games. Just as had been the case in Washington Park, fans were turned away. More seats were needed.

No expansion was possible out in right. Bedford Avenue was only 310 feet from home, and it wasn't moving. But there was room in left, so Ebbets had more open wooden stands built out there, in front of the original fence. A low wooden fence separated the new stands from the playing field. The new stands, used only for big crowds, went from the left field corner to almost straightaway center. They were actually bleachers but were called "the emergency grandstand section." Ebbets charged full grandstand prices to sit out there, resulting in some mild Brooklynese grumbling from fans.

The emergency grandstand increased the seating capacity to about 22,000, with room for 2000 more standees behind ropes in front of the new seats. Reacting to the million-plus fans who'd come to Ebbets Field in 1930, Ebbets decided to rip down the old wooden bleachers and build concrete bleachers that would seat more. The new steel and concrete bleachers opened in 1931, but weren't completely usable until 1932—when Ebbets was horrified to learn that they held the same number of people as the old wooden ones.

There were more refurbishments between 1938 and 1943 by Larry Mac-Phail. The seats were old, many broken, and the dugouts and clubhouses needed to be refurbished. During the pre-war years, MacPhail put over a quarter of a million dollars into fixing up Ebbets Field. The Dodgers continued to try to cram more seats into Ebbets Field as late as 1948.

With the coming of the rabbit ball, and the expansion of the double-decked grandstand all the way around the left field to straightaway center, Ebbets Field became a power hitter's delight. The left field foul line remained a hefty 347 feet, but the alleys weren't much deeper. The distance to the stands in the left field power alley was under 370 feet, and even in the deepest part of the park the home run distance did not reach 400 feet. It had once been quite a pasture, but seats cut the distance in center to 397.

Out in right field was the fence that kept line drives from going into Bedford Avenue. The fence sloped back away from the playing field for its first 15 feet and then straightened out to a total height of 30 feet.

On top of the fence was the screen. Unlike Fenway's screen, which functions as a net to catch home runs, balls bounced off Ebbets Field's screen back into play. Playing the screen was an acquired skill, acquired most admirably by Carl Furillo and Dixie Walker. Playing the screen well was a matter of luck

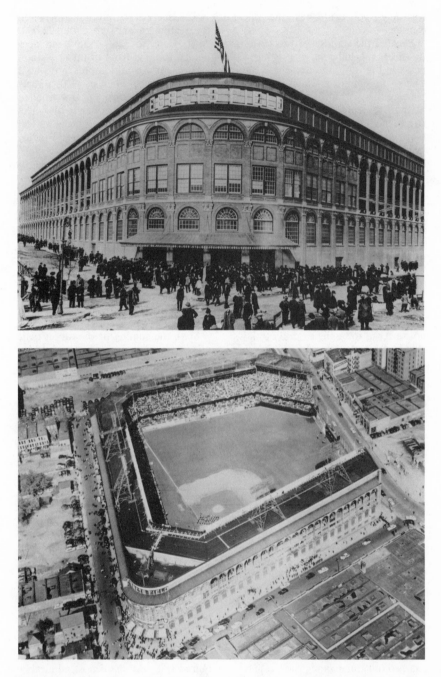

Ebbets Field, Brooklyn, N.Y. Top: *The main entrance. (Photo used with permission from the Brooklyn Historical Society.)* Bottom: *Aerial view.*

for visiting outfielders, who found the caroms unpredictable — sometimes ridiculous. Balls had been known to hit the screen and stick. That was a ground rule double.

For the first 13 years of Ebbets Field's existence, the outfield was roamed by one Zack Wheat. During much of that time an ad painted on the outfield fence cleverly read, "Zack Wheat caught 400 flies last season; Tanglefoot fly paper caught 10 million." This was false advertising. Wheat never hauled in more than 338 in a season.

Ebbets was slow to install a scoreboard that electronically gave the number of balls, strikes, and outs. Baseball historian Harold Seymour, who operated the scoreboard as a boy, says that until the 1920s operators used "a crude contraption of ropes weighted with bricks for adjusting the ball and strike signs."

Maybe the Lights Could Have Been Better, Maybe Nobody Was Going to Hit Vander Meer That Night Anyway. Larry MacPhail was the first general manager to install lights in his ballpark when he was in Cincinnati in 1935. After arriving in Brooklyn, putting lights in Ebbets Field was high on his priority list.

The first night game in Ebbets Field took place on June 15, 1938. A crowd of 38,748 saw the Reds' Johnny Vander Meer pitch his second consecutive no-hitter, winning 6–0.

Not all of the fans saw the whole game. There was a mix-up with the tickets, and brawls broke out all over the place as people assigned the same seats confronted one another. Later everyone claimed to have seen each and every one of Vandy's pitches.

The Incongruous General. Roger Kahn, author of the world's greatest baseball book, *The Boys of Summer,* wrote recently in *The Sporting News:* "The first celebrity who became addicted to Ebbets Field was General Douglas MacArthur. His wars were done — this was after Truman fired

him — and MacArthur would travel by limo from his home in the Waldorf Towers on Park Avenue. When he arrived, he rode the press elevator to Walter O'Malley's private box. With MacArthur aboard, the press elevator was closed to other V.I.P.'s, and indeed, even to the press. No one ever accused Doug MacArthur of being the people's general. He seemed as incongruous in Ebbets Field as a millionaire on The Bowery."

After World War II the Schaefer beer sign on top of the scoreboard gave the crowd scorers' decisions. The "H" and the "E" lit up. In those days the Dodgers took the field at the start of each game to the organ strains of Gladys Gooding.

It bothered Branch Rickey that he wasn't gaining the income from Negro League baseball the way Stoneham or Ruppert had at the Polo Grounds and Yankee Stadium. He decided, in 1945, to start his own Negro League, the United States League, in hopes that when integration came he would monopolize the contracts of the best black ballplayers.

The project failed for lack of interest after a couple of months, but one of the short-lived Brown Dodgers was Jackie Robinson, and Robinson reminded Rickey of himself.

America's Most Sincere Love Affair. Brooklyn loved its bums and dem bums loved Brooklyn — and everyone loved Ebbets Field. Among the Dodgers who wept when the team went west was Clem Labine, who came to the Dodgers as a 17-year-old in 1944 (though he didn't actually appear in a game), missed the next two seasons touring Europe the hard way and didn't make it back to the majors until 1950 — this time to stay. According to Maury Allen in the *New York Post,* Labine said, "I lived near the Dyker Beach Golf Course in Brooklyn and I would carpool to Ebbets Field with Pee Wee Reese, Russ Meyer, Preacher Roe, and Don Newcombe. I enjoyed Ebbets Field. Large parks made a pitcher careless. I really worked on my sinker in Ebbets Field. Those fans were down to earth. They knew the game. When we went west I knew it was a different game when I couldn't throw the ball in the stands because I couldn't reach it. We lost the closeness. The LA fans weren't as adept at telling you what you should do."

Dick Young's Tribute. On the one hundredth birthday of the Brooklyn Bridge, the late Dick Young wrote instead about another Brooklyn landmark. Here's a segment from his column in the *New York Post,* May 24, 1983:

"Ebbets Field was as famous as the Brooklyn Bridge, and perhaps the most famous part of the park was the Abe Stark sign. It invited the ballplayers to "Hit the sign and get a free suit" from Stark, the philanthropist who ran a men's clothing store on Pitkin Avenue.

"Trouble was, in order to hit the narrow painted sign painted along the base of the scoreboard in right-center, the batter had to bang a line drive past some of the best outfielders known to baseball, including Duke Snider and Carl Furillo, especially Furillo.

"One day it occurred to me that perhaps Abe Stark of Pitkin Avenue owed Furillo a suit of clothes for all of the merchandise Carl had saved him through the years with those great backhand catches of low line drives. At least a sports jacket. I mentioned it in the newspaper.

"Sure enough, Abe Stark invited Carl Furillo to pick out a new suit— and would Furillo be good enough to bring along a few autographed balls...."

Ebbets Field had personality coming out of its ears. In the upper deck of the center field bleachers rang the cowbell of the Dodgers' number one fan, Hilda Chester. When she screamed at Snider, she wanted the Duke to *respond!* Yes, ma'am.

Eddie Batan sat behind third in a white pith helmet. Lavagetto was his

favorite, so between innings he blew up balloons that read "COOOOKEEEEE." Shorty Laurice and his brass section/ drinking buddies (a.k.a. the Dodger Symphony) roamed the stands making a merry racket. Red Barber was in the press box.

One time management offered Hilda Chester permanent seats in the grandstand right behind the dugout, but she refused indignantly, preferring her regular seat in the bleachers. Hilda became irritated at the la-di-da offer. She is reported to have said, "Did any of those plush seat bums come near me when I was in the hospital? Not one! But the ballplayers did, and they sent me cards and letters and flowers, and the boys and girls out here were dropping in all the time. No, sir. I'll stay right here, thank you."

For a while Old Gold was a sponsor for the team. When a Dodger hit a home run, a carton of Old Golds slid from the press box down the screen to the playing field behind home.

There was always a bar under the stands where reporters, who were supposed to be watching the game, sipped suds and listened to Red Barber (or Sid Soberfeld, or Vin Scully, or Connie Desmond) on the radio. After World War II, the bartender, Bill Boylan, also pitched batting practice.

Cohesion for the Polyglot. Ebbets Field was maybe the best ballpark ever, home of the greatest pain and greatest joy, home of the biggest family. On Opening Day 1947, Ebbets Field provided the laboratory for Mr. Robinson and Mr. Rickey's noble experiment. It was here that Jackie Robinson began his courageous battle against an embarrassing American injustice.

When the Dodgers moved west, it was the end of baseball's most sincere love affair—the death of which was slower than perhaps we are led to believe—and a large part of Brooklyn died. After the last game at Ebbets Field, Roy Campanella eased the pain by kicking in for beer and crab fingers for the players and press.

Baseball was beloved by everyone in Brooklyn, and thus provided a great social function. The Dodgers were glue for an otherwise fragmented community. The Polish and Irish and Italians wouldn't have mixed in that melting pot if it weren't for baseball. They would have stuck to their own kind like their parents and grandparents.

The Dodgers gave the Brooklyn community a sense of just that, community — different and separate and maybe sometimes better than the New York City that had officially amalgamated Brooklyn into a borough in 1898, an uppity New York City that was always trying to show up Brooklyn in one way or another. The Dodgers gave everyone in Brooklyn something in common — a good, healthy hatred of the Giants.

Let's take solace from the fact that when Ebbets Field finally died and the wrecker's ball came crashing, the park proved to be an organ donor. Its light towers were moved to Downing Stadium on Randall's Island. The clock atop the scoreboard found a new home in McCormick Field in Asheville, North Carolina.

Dexter Park (Bushwick Park, Sterling Oval)

Western Colored League 1923–27 (Royal Giants), also home of the semipro Bushwicks 1930s and 1940s. *Location:* Bushwick Avenue in Woodhaven, Queens section, just on the Queens side of the Brooklyn-Queens border.

The most famous semi-pro ballpark of them all, home of the Bushwicks, who employed future- and ex-major leaguers and had success playing pro teams. During the 1930s and 1940s the biggest crowds showed up at Dexter Park for games against the Negro League teams (the Bushwicks were a white club) like the Pittsburgh Crawfords.

Once, when the Bushwicks were

playing the Crawfords at Dexter Park, Josh Gibson, never known for his glove, dropped a fly ball in the ninth, allowing the winning run to score. Those in the crowd with money on the Crawfords threw a fit, thinking Josh had thrown the game.

Someone told the black team there was a bomb on their bus. It took three squad cars to get the Crawfords and their bombless bus back to Harlem.

Because of the incident the Crawfords were called in before Judge Landis. The Commissioner of Baseball was convinced that everything was on the up and up. The Crawfords, it was clear, didn't have enough money to be on the take.

On the outfield wall, an advertisement for an optician read, "Don't kill the umpire — Maybe it's your eyes."

Buffalo, New York

Riverside Park

National League 1879–83 (Bisons). *Location:* Fargo and West avenues, Rhode Island and Vermont streets. *First game:* May 1, 1879. *Last game:* September 8, 1883.

Olympic Park (I)

National League 1884–85 (Bisons). *Location:* Richmond and Summer streets, Howard and Norwood avenues. *Cost of construction:* $6000. *Seating capacity:* 5000 (standing room 1000 more). *Size of grounds:* (length and width) 350 feet by 608 feet. *First game:* May 21, 1884. *Last game:* October 7, 1885.

After making a $5000 profit in 1883, Buffalo built a new park, with a new kind of grandstand. This stand was closed off at its back, ventilated only with louvers, to keep the wind off spectators.

In 1884, the "parking lot" consisted of a covered shed where carriage trade parked. Cost: 15 cents a game or $5 for the season.

It was about this time that John B. Sage, a Buffalo printer, began to sell posters, window hangers, and colored scorecards in 24 designs for 25 cents a set. In the meantime, at the ballpark, on special occasions, Poppenburg's band played.

On October 7, 1885, a paying audience of twelve saw the Bisons lose a doubleheader to the Providence Grays.

Olympic Park (II)

Players League 1890 (Bisons). *Location:* Michigan Avenue (first base), East Ferry Street (third base), Masten Street (left field), Woodlawn Avenue (right field). *Average attendance per game:* 942. *First game:* April 19, 1890. *Last game:* October 4, 1890.

Federal League Park (International Fair Association Grounds)

Federal League 1914–15 (Blues, Buf-Feds). *Location:* Northdale and Lonsdale avenues at Boston (now Hamlin) Road. *Dimensions:* reportedly "tiny." *First game:* May 11, 1914. *Last game:* September 29, 1915.

This is where Prince Hal Chase (boo, hiss) played, in 1915, when he led the Federal League in home runs with 17. The corrupt villain also led the league's first basemen in errors with 26.

Offermann Stadium (Robertson Park 1924, Bison Stadium 1925–34)

Location: Same as Olympic Park (II). *Built:* 1924. *Dimensions:* Left field, 321 feet; left center, 346 feet; center field, 400 feet; right center, 366 feet; right field, 297 feet. 21 feet from home plate to the backstop. *Fences:* (1924) left field, 12 feet; center field (scoreboard), 40 feet; right field, 12 feet. (1934) left field, 32 feet; center field (scoreboard), 60 feet; right field, 12 feet. *Record season attendance:* 413,263 (1959). *Last regular season game:* September 11, 1960 (Toronto 7, Buffalo 5, attendance 4285). *Last game (playoffs):* September 18, 1960 (Toronto 5, Buffalo 3, attendance 2020, Toronto wins best-of-seven series, 4–0). *Torn down:* 1960.

This park had a 60-foot scoreboard in center after 1934, one of the biggest. It featured almost all grandstand seating, with the only bleachers being a small set between the grandstand and the left field corner. The roofed grandstand went all the way down the right field line into the corner.

During the early years of Offermann Stadium, a neighbor across Master Street assembled bleachers atop his garage and charged admission. Bison management put an end to this by building a 32-foot concrete and wood fence in left field to block the view.

Despite the fact that Offermann had served Buffalo so well and for so long, the Buffalo papers made almost no mention of its passing in 1960. The team was battling for a spot in the playoffs and the papers focused on that.

Before the final regular season game at Offermann, there was a wheelbarrow race held between the opposing managers, Kirby Farrell of the Bisons and the Maple Leafs' Mel McGaha. McGaha won going away.

The team made the playoffs and played the actual last game at Offermann a week later. Losing pitcher in the final game was Bison Babe Birrer, who relieved the starting pitcher, right-hander Clarence Podbelian, in the second inning. Both pitchers were ex-Dodgers. The last home run hit in Offermann was struck by Billy Moran of Toronto. The Maple Leafs had Sparky Anderson playing second that day, Chuck Tanner in left, and Steve Demeter at third.

The site is now a junior high school.

War Memorial Stadium (Roesch Stadium, Grover Cleveland Stadium, Civic Stadium)

International League 1961–70 (Bisons), Eastern League 1979–82 (Bisons), American Association

1983–87 (Bisons). Also former home of the Buffalo Bills (All-America Conference Bills 1946–49, American Football League 1960–72). *Location:* Dodge Street, Best Street (right field), between Main and Jefferson streets. *Nickname:* The Rockpile. *Built:* 1937. *Construction cost:* $3 million. *Dimensions:* Left field, 350 feet; center field, 410 feet; right field, 310 feet [my foot—au.]. *Seating capacity:* 48,000 (originally 38,000). *1987 Bison season attendance:* 497,760. *High school football attendance record:* 50,988 (October 21, 1948, Kensington versus Bennett). *First event:* October 16, 1937, college football, Tulane 7, Colgate 6, attendance: 32,524. *First baseball game:* May 3, 1961 (Buffalo 4, Puerto Rico 3, attendance: 20,619). *Last International League game:* May 27, 1970 (Buffalo 6, Rochester 3, attendance: 150). *First Eastern League game:* April 17, 1979 (doubleheader; Buffalo 3, Reading 0; Reading 11, Buffalo 6). *Single (baseball) game attendance record:* 38,211 (July 26, 1987, versus Denver). *First American Football League game:* September 18, 1960, Denver 27, Buffalo 21).

Used as background in the film *The Natural.* A gray, lenticular football stadium built 1935–37 with WPA funds. It was named for a time Charles E. Roesch Stadium in memory of the late Buffalo mayor, and also Grover Cleveland Stadium, after the late United States president. It was rededicated War Memorial Stadium on August 24, 1960, by Buffalo Mayor Frank A. Sedita. The following spring it was used for baseball for the first time, with the big part of the grandstand — the part with the all-time highest obstructing roof supports—on the first base side and the necessary short screen in right. An inner fence kept the home run distance in left accessible. The seats beyond the far end zone were remote, dark, and seldom used. The location of the diamond on the football field was determined by Vince McNamara, who later went on to become chairman of the Buffalo Baseball Hall of Fame Committee. Once the diamond was laid out, tucked into its corner, it stayed put for the entire time War Memorial Stadium was used for baseball.

Firsts. The first home run hit here was by Rogers Robinson of the Puerto Rico Marlins, in the first inning of the first game played. The first Bison home run came two days later, on May 5, 1961, by Wally Shannon. The first shot onto the stadium roof in right was hit by Jersey City's Harry Anderson on August 4, 1961. Don Mincher became the first Buffalo player to do it. His home run on August 24, off of Toronto's Carl Mathias, is still discussed in Buffalo. The ball struck the top of the football press box and bounced over the roof onto Best Street, over 500 feet.

That International League franchise had trouble mustering a winner in the '60s. Seldom did more than a thousand people show up. War Memorial Stadium was in a deteriorating neighborhood.

Buffalo lost AAA in 1970, and didn't get it back until 1983. Summer riots erupted June 27, 1967, and forced a curfew in Buffalo, so the Bisons played only day games at the Rockpile, moving their night games to Niagara Falls. On July 19, 1969, a gang of knife-bearing youths invaded the home clubhouse during batting practice. The game was postponed due to "threatening weather."

Baseball returned in 1979, but struggled until Bob Rich, Jr., of Rich Products bought the club and revived community interest through interesting gimmicks and promotions.

The batboy weighed over 300 pounds. The beer vendor danced. Nights had ethnic themes. The new franchise in the American Association thrived here until 1987, when War Memorial Stadium was abandoned in favor of a new park (Pilot Field) that could be adapted for major league expansion.

In its final year of use, 497,760 came to the Rockpile, second best to Louisville that year in the minors. For the final game, 25,412 came to say goodbye. Near the end the ballpark stopped being the Rockpile and started being the Grand Old Dame. Some bad ballparks are like hookers—they gain respect with age.

War Memorial Stadium still stands, and is the home of Canisius College football.

Site of the 1938 National AAU Track and Field Championships, stock car racing in the 1950s, and professional soccer (the Blazers) in the 1960s.

Pilot Field

American Association 1988–present (Bisons). *Location:* Washington and Swan streets (in the heart of downtown Buffalo). *Architects:* Hellmuth, Obata and Kassabaum (HOK) of Kansas City. *Cost of construction:* $56.4 million (includes two parking garages; stadium alone, $42 million). *Dimensions:* Left field, 325 feet; left center, 384 feet; center field, 410 feet; right center, 384 feet; right field, 325 feet. *Scoreboard:* 79 feet high, 49 feet wide. *Seating capacity:* 19,500 (expandable during an off season to 40,000). *First game:* April 14, 1988 (Bisons 1, Denver Zephyrs 0), attendance 19,500.

In 1988, more people watched the Buffalo Bisons of the American Association play at Pilot Field than any other minor league club in history. With only a few days left in the season, the team was averaging 16,209 fans per game, had already passed the all-time season attendance record (1,052,438), previously held by the 1983 Louisville Colonels.

A gorgeous new ballpark has been built, and now they're packing the place. Best new ballpark in a long time. Built, unlike other new stadiums, in the center of the city, surrounded on all sides by real streets just like the good old days. The refreshingly fancy grandstand has an ornate roof, arched windows and pennant-topped cupolas reminiscent of Ebbets Field.

The location and some of the design might be old-fashioned, but nothing else is. There are 38 luxury suites at the club level of the stadium which include television, furniture, wet bar, and sliding glass doors leading to two rows of seats just outside each suite.

The green metal roof will have to come off if there's ever expansion.

Pettibone's Grille is a full-service restaurant on the main level of the stadium. It has a seating capacity of 350 and is open for breakfast, lunch, and dinner. This is downtown, remember. The restaurant has 250 feet of windows and a two-tiered patio to provide a panoramic view of the ballpark. It's become *the* place for singles to go after work.

The "Food Court" concession stands on the main level sell barbecued beef, Italian and Polish sausage, and Mexican food.

A 50-foot-high, 80-foot-wide scoreboard designed by the Daktronics Corporation is in center, with large advertisements on either side of it. The board has four-color animation capability.

Two "trivision" advertising signs are located above the left field fence. They are back-lit and rotate at set intervals during a game to reveal different ads.

Opening Day was cold and windy. Festivities started with a parade of antique cars and politicians from Niagara Falls to the ballpark in downtown Buffalo. The Oak Ridge Boys handled the National Anthem chores *a cappella* with a Royal Canadian Mounted Police color guard. Pigeons were released. Everybody was cold. Time of game: 2:02.

After years in War Memorial Stadium, one could have laid big bucks that the next home of the Bisons would have a symmetrical playing field. Baseball fever is burning hot in Buffalo, the only city proposed for big league expansion to have a crazed look in its eyes.

Burlington, North Carolina

Fairchild Park
Carolina League 1958-72. *Seating capacity:* 2500.

Burlington Athletic Field
Appalachian League 1986-present (Indians). *Location:* Beaumont Street. *Dimensions:* Left field, 335 feet; center field, 405 feet; right field, 335 feet. *Seating capacity:* 3500. *1987 season attendance:* 76,653.

Burlington, Iowa

Community Field
Midwest League 1962-present (Rangers, Expos, Braves). *Location:* East of Highway 61. *Dimensions:* Left field, 330 feet; center field, 372 feet; right field, 320 feet. *Seating capacity:* 3500. *Season attendance record:* 71,098 (1987).

Burlington, Vermont

Centennial Field
Eastern League 1984-present (Vermont Reds, Vermont Mariners). *Location:* On the campus of the University of Vermont. *Built:* 1922. *Dimensions:* Left field, 335 feet; center field, 405 feet; right field, 335 feet. (Deep power alleys.) *Seating capacity:* 5500. *1987 season attendance:* 85,261.

One of the oldest ballparks still in use. A concrete arena with a covered grandstand and slab seats. Painted on the seats are University of Vermont symbols inside baseballs.

Park had a hand-operated scoreboard until 1984. Still has no plumbing. Rest rooms are Port-o-Sans. As of the summer of 1988 there was a hornets' nest in the men's room.

Butler, Pennsylvania

Pullman Park
Middle American League (Class C) 1946-circa 1955 (Indians, Yankees, Tigers). *Location:* Pillow and Plum streets, Sullivan Run Creek. *Dedicated:* 1934.

Built on the site of the Pullman Railcar Manufacturing Plant, Pullman Park was used for professional baseball steadily from 1935 to the mid-1950s.

In 1946, Whitey Ford pitched here for the Butler Yankees. From the looks of pictures, he pitched in Butler before he shaved.

The franchise failed in the mid-1950s as Butlerites stayed home to watch their new television sets.

Butte, Montana

Alumni Coliseum
Pioneer League 1978-85, 1987-present (Copper Kings). *Location:* Park Street, on the Montana Tech campus. *Dimensions:* Left field, 350 feet; center field, 410 feet; right field, 355 feet. *Seating capacity:* 1900. *1987 season attendance:* 19,669.

The Copper Kings began in 1978 without a major league affiliation. It was a "co-op" team filled with castaways and nondraftees — one of whom was a 16-year-old Dominican named Julio Franco. That team set a modern-day Pioneer League record for most runs allowed in a season: 591. They won only 19 games. There were nine rain-outs, and the franchise lost $30,000.

The general manager of the Copper Kings that year, Bruce Manno, recalled in a recent *Montana Magazine* interview that the weather always seemed to be cold (it hailed in August), his coaches quit, his trainer quit, most of his ballplayers threatened to quit. Nonetheless more than 700 fans showed up per game, giving Manno the courage to continue.

Since then the Copper Kings in the Alumni Coliseum have functioned under working agreements with the Brewers, Royals and Mariners.

Caldwell, Idaho

Simplot Stadium (Canyon Multi-Purpose Stadium)
Rookie League 1964–71 (Treasure Valley/Caldwell Cubs). *Location:* Highway 30, across from the College of Idaho.
Cadlwell is a town on the Boise River in Canyon County.

Calgary, Alberta

Buffalo Stadium
Home of amateur baseball in Calgary before 1968. *Location:* Downtown, now a parking lot. *Torn down:* Late 1960s.

Foothills Baseball Stadium
Home of amateur baseball 1968–76, Pioneer League (Rookie) 1977–84, Pacific Coast League (AAA) 1985–present (Cannons). Owned by the city of Calgary. *Opened:* 1968. *Location:* 24th Avenue, Crowchild Trail. *Dimensions:* Left field, 345 feet; left center, 370 feet; center field, 400 feet; right center, 370 feet; right field, 345 feet. *Fences:* Left field foul pole to the right center scoreboard, 20 feet; right field, 10 feet. *Seating capacity:* (1977–87) 6000; (1988) 7500. *Single game attendance record:* 8426 (June 30, 1985, night, versus Hawaii, Canada Day/ Fireworks). *Day game attendance record:* 7432 (August 31, 1986, versus Edmonton, Fan Appreciation Day). *Doubleheader attendance record:* 5829 (August 22, 1985, versus Tacoma). *Opening Day attendance record:* 5395 (April 19, 1986, versus Albuquerque). *Low single game attendance record:* 1806 (April 23, 1985, night, versus Phoenix). *Low day single game atten-*

dance record: 2270 (May 10, 1985, versus Albuquerque). *Low doubleheader attendance record:* 2632 (May 7, 1985, versus Edmonton). *Low Opening Day attendance record:* 4313 (April 22, 1985, versus Tucson). *1987 season attendance:* 304,897. *First Pacific Coast League game:* April 22, 1985 (Calgary 7, Tucson 6, attendance: 4314). *First night game:* April 23, 1985.
During the winter of 1984–85, the stadium underwent extensive upgrading to bring it from Rookie League to AAA standards. As of 1987, a seat anywhere in the ballpark cost about $5.00, Canadian. Cannons crowds average 4000+ fans per game. They draw best against Edmonton, worst against Las Vegas.

Campeche, Mexico

Venustiano Carranza
Mexican League, Zona Sur, present (Piratas). *Dimensions:* Left field, 320 feet; center field, 400 feet; right field, 320 feet. *Seating capacity:* 12,500.

Cedar Rapids, Iowa

Name of park unknown
Two-I League 1891 (Canaries). *Location:* Second Avenue and Fourteenth Street S.E.
Here's how the *Cedar Rapids Gazette* described the scene at the ballpark for a Canaries Opening Day victory in the spring of 1891: "Every seat in the stands was filled and a large number of carriages were lined up along the left field fence. It was a splendid crowd made up of the best citizenship of Cedar Rapids and hundreds of people from neighboring villages. Our boys certainly did themselves proud."

Athletic Park
Western Association 1896–99 (Rabbits), Three-I League 1901–09 (Rabbits, Bunnies). *Location:* Ninth Street and

Foothills Baseball Stadium, Calgary, Alberta, Canada. (Compliments of the Calgary Cannons.)

F Avenue N.W. *Opened:* April 21, 1896.

Games were played in the middle of a ⅓ mile bicycle track.

Hill Park

Central Association 1913–17 (Bunnies), Three-I League 1920–21 (Bunnies), Mississippi Valley League 1922–32 (Bunnies), Western League 1934–37 (Raiders), Three-I League 1938–42 (Raiders). *Location:* E Avenue and 13th Street N.W. *Land purchased and ballpark dedicated:* 1913. *Torn down:* 1942.

The popular Chicago Cubs broadcaster Bert Wilson got his start in Cedar Rapids.

The Bunnies wouldn't let Wilson (who was known as Burt Puckett in his Cedar Rapids days) into Hill Park, fearing radio play-by-play would hurt attendance. Wilson outsmarted them and broadcast game descriptions from a porch roof overlooking the right field fence on E Avenue N.W.

Wilson went on to become the voice of the Cubs over a large radio network originating from WIND in Chicago, and it was there that he originated the saying, "I don't care who wins as long as it's the Cubs."

Veterans Memorial Park

Central Association 1949 (Rockets), Three-I League 1950–61 (Indians 1950–54, Raiders 1955–57, Braves 1958–61), Midwest League 1962–present (Braves 1962, Red Raiders 1963–64, Cardinals 1965–72, Astros 1973–74, Giants, Reds). *Location:* Rockford Road SW, Center Drive. *Dimensions:* Left field, 325 feet; left center, 350 feet; center field, 385 feet; right center, 350 feet; right field, 325 feet. *Seating capacity:* 6000. *Record season attendance:* 155,034 (1985). *1987 season attendance:* 144,279. *First game:* May 2, 1949 (Keokuk 9, Cedar Rapids 6, attendance: 4000 +). *First night game:* June 9, 1931 (Cedar Rapids 4, Moline 3, attendance: 3000).

From the stands fans see the Cedar Rapids skyline above the outfield fence. The old hand-operated scoreboard remains on top of the fence in left, while the larger electronic scoreboard is in right wearing a "Lite" advertisement. The outfield fence is covered with ads. There is even an ad painted on the hitters' background, painted in dark green on dark blue, for "Hames Mobile Homes, The Homes People."

The concrete grandstand has been voted the best in the Midwest League.

Chandler, Arizona

Compadre Stadium

Spring home of the Milwaukee Brewers 1986–present. *Location:* 1425 W. Ocotillo Road, 793 North Alma School Road, Chandler Heights Road. *Seating capacity:* 5000 (not counting lawn spectator area, with its estimated capacity 10,000, where it's sprawling room only). *First game:* Friday, March 7, 1986 (Milwaukee Brewers versus Chicago Cubs, attendance 8000, 6075 paid).

On Thursday morning, February 27, 1986, a gas explosion in the Brewers' clubhouse injured nine people, several seriously. According to the *Chandler Arizonian,* the explosion hurled coaches and players through the air, while "washing a wave of flame through halls and doorways."

The explosion was caused by a pilot light going on while a plumber drained air from a gas line. The hero of the day was Brewer manager George Bamberger, then 60 years old, who leaped upon the burning plumber (22-year-old Jeff Sutton) following the explosion and smothered his flames. Sutton suffered second- and third-degree burns in the incident. Bamberger no doubt saved his life. It was later learned that Sutton followed unsafe procedures before the explosion. Damage came to $50,000.

Also injured seriously was coach Tony Muser. Among the less seriously injured were bullpen coach Larry Haney, general manager Harry Dalton, first base coach Andy Etchebarren, pitching coach Herm Starrette, pitcher Bill Wegman, and catcher Bill Schroeder.

So, by the time the first Cactus League game was played in Compadre Stadium, the park was already notorious.

On Opening Day, ceremonies for the media started at 11 a.m. with a press luncheon. The Grand Opening for the fans and players started at 12:30 p.m.

The ballpark was packed. Traffic had run smoothly. The sun was shining. The first ball was thrown out by Jim Patterson, a partner in the developing firm (Ocotillo West) involved in the Compadre Stadium project. Over the left field fence of the stadium pitchers got some running in on the two other spring training practice fields. The National Anthem was played by bands from Chandler Senior and Junior High School, and Willis Junior High. Fans were in shorts, the men shirtless. Some were sprawled with coolers and blankets on the lawn spectator area in the outfield.

Thousands of blue and gold balloons were released, and everyone cheered, and for a second it felt like more than just a spring training game. It was a picture postcard, a deliverance from the pain of eight days previous.

Charleston, South Carolina

College Park

South Atlantic League 1940s, 1959–61 (White Sox), 1980–present (Royals, Rainbows), also home of the Citadel since at least the 1920s (collegiate). *Location:* Rutledge Avenue, between Grove and Cleveland streets. *Dimensions:* Left field, 310 feet; center field, 402 feet; right field, 298 feet. *Seating capacity:* (1960) 6000, (1985) 4500. *1987 season attendance:* 87,185. *Refurbishments:* 1980 ($50,000), 1984 ($94,000).

The land at Grove and Rutledge was leased by the city of Charleston in August 1907 to the College of Charleston for use as an athletic field. The original wooden ballpark was built on a portion of present-day Hampton Park. It served as the home of high school sports, and as home for the Citadel's athletic teams. The Citadel has been playing its college baseball games on the same site for over 60 years.

College Park was first used for professional baseball in the 1940s, beginning an off-again-on-again relationship with the Sally League that continues (on again) today.

The College Park of the 1940s consisted of steel bleachers and a grandstand, both 14 rows high. The roof was slanted to reflect sunshine off the stands below, so the ballpark looked like it kept the brim of its cap up.

On the first base side there was an eight-foot gap between the bleachers and the grandstand. Precariously perched between the roofed and unroofed sections of the stands, bridging the gap at the very top, supported by not a heck of a lot on either side, was the wooden press box where two men sat with their ties loose, occasionally pretending they were in a hot air balloon.

Elvis Presley performed here in 1956.

A tornado struck in 1966.

On July 11, 1965, the *Post-Courier* ran this headline: "College Park: An Eyesore With No Plans For Future." And this was fifteen years before the city got around to fixing the place up so it could again be a minor league park.

Between 1980 and 1984, the Kansas City Royals' farm system paid for a new infield, a new sprinkler system, and a new press box. New lights were installed. Actually the lights were used, transplanted to College Park from Johnson Hagood Stadium.

But there were still problems. The stands were dangerous. Most of the seats were still wooden bench bleachers (about 5 to 10 percent of which were replaced yearly), built with open spaces between the rows, so belongings and small children could fall right through. In the 1980s a girl did fall through, and filed a lawsuit. Earlier a man had stepped on a rotted plank, fallen through, and had also sued. During a three-year span in the '80s, College Park's liability insurance premium rose from $1200 to over $8000 a year.

Parking was always a problem when the crowds were large or if there was rain. The parking lot was dirt, and had a penchant for potholes.

In 1984, Charleston Rainbows co-owner Ray Passailaigue said to the *Post-Courier,* "I keep telling (the city) about the problems that we have, but they would like to keep College Park the way it is because it has a lot of charisma. And they are right. From an age standpoint, College Park is a nice old stadium. But from a fan's point of view, it's not such a good stadium."

According to Ernestine C. Fellers, the city of Charleston archivist, today's College Park looks different from the simple country bleachers of the 1940s and 1950s. Since 1984, the stands have been rebuilt so kids can't fall through.

Charleston, West Virginia

Organized baseball dates back to the nineteenth century in Charleston. According to *Kanawha County Images,* baseball was played at three sites before 1908. There were (1) just above Bradford Street on part of the old Comstock race track, (2) close to Florida Street, between Central Avenue and Kanawha Street on the city's West Side, and (3) on Elizabeth Street at the current site of the Board of Education Building.

Werhle Park

Virginia Valley League 1910 (Statesmen), Mountain States League 1911–12, Ohio State League 1913–16. *Location:* Virginia, Ruffner and Quarrier streets. *Constructed:* 1908. *First game:* May 5, 1910 (Statesmen defeat the Montgomery Mountebacks, attendance 1200).

In 1910, the automobile was still a bit of a novelty in the city of Charleston, so that was what management used to promote the new ball club, the Statesmen.

On Opening Day, a fleet of autos convoyed from the Capitol Building at Lee and Capitol streets to the ballpark, attracting more and more attention by the block. The park, located on land formerly used by Charleston High

School for its football games and its track meets, was named after the owner of the Statesmen.

The crowd of 1200, most of whom had arrived by trolley, watched West Virginia Governor William Ellsworth Glasscock throw the first ceremonial pitch, a toss that went two feet wide of the catcher. Glasscock's lack of control was famous, especially when it came to conflicts between coal miners and mine owners.

Watt Powell Park (Exhibition Park 1916-30, Kanawha Park 1931-42)
Middle Atlantic League 1931-42 (Senators), Central League 1949-51, American Association 1952-59 (Senators), International League 1961-62, 1971-78 (Charlies), Eastern League 1963-65 (Indians), South Atlantic League 1987-present (Wheelers). *Location:* Kanawha Park, Kanawha City, across the 35th Street Bridge from Interstate 77. *Constructed:* 1916, 1948. *Construction cost:* (1948) $350,000. *Dimensions:* (Original) left field, 360 feet; left center, 466 feet; center field, 527 feet; right center, 528 feet; right field, 330 feet. (Later) left field, 330 feet; center field, 400 feet; right field, 330 feet. *Seating capacity:* (1916) 3500; (1960) 5300; (1975) 8000. *1987 season attendance:* 97,563. *Fire:* 1939 (rebuilt without interruption in schedule). *Refurbished:* 1987.

Watt Powell was a native of Bath County, Virginia, and had played some minor league baseball (in Wheeling, Danville and Roanoke) before coming to Charleston to stay in 1915. The following year baseball was first played in Exhibition (later Kanawha) Park, on a field now named for Powell, who went on to become Charleston's best known baseball promoter.

When new, the field had only wooden bleachers. Fans were allowed to park their cars inside the outfield fence and watch from there. The streetcar line crossed Kanawha City Bridge and came close to the park. In the time that the

Class C Middle Atlantic League played here, the dimensions were so deep that only seven home runs were hit over the fence.

Behind the right field fence were railroad tracks, and many a power hitter wanted to hit one so far that it would land in one of the coal cars parked out there—but no one ever did (though it is said Rudy York and Luke Easter came closest).

Despite the dimensions, the park remained a good hitters' park. Hitters liked seeing the pitch come out of the dark green background of the hills behind the outfield.

For years, Powell managed the Kanawha Hotel pool hall. In 1931 he brought pro baseball back to Charleston in the form of the Senators of the Middle Atlantic League, and remained involved until 1942 when the league folded due to World War II.

In 1948, the ballfield in Kanawha Park was completely rebuilt with a $350,000 bond issue and renamed Watt Powell Park. Powell died that same year. It reopened on April 28, 1949, as over 8000—including marching bands from Charleston and Stonewall Jackson high schools—watched the Charleston Senators of the Class A Central League defeat the Saginaw Bears 11-5.

Charlotte, North Carolina

Clark Griffith Park (Crockett Park, Knights Park)
South Atlantic League 1954-1963, Southern League 1976-present (Orioles, Knights). *Location:* 400 Magnolia Avenue. *Dimensions:* Left field, 320 feet; center field, 390 feet; right field, 320 feet. *Seating capacity:* (1960) 6500, (1985) 5500, (1988) 3000. *Fire:* March 1987 (rebuilt immediately).

Knights are a farm club of the Baltimore Orioles.

Chattanooga, Tennessee

Joe Engel Stadium
Home of Chattanooga baseball since
1930, Southern League 1961, 1964–
present (Lookouts, Indians, circa 1980,
Lookouts), South Atlantic League
1963. *Location:* Fifth and O'Neal streets
(Fourth Street Exit on Interstate 124).
Constructed: 1930. *Dimensions:* (1930–
86) Left field, 368 feet; left center, 383
feet; center field, 471 feet; right field,
318 feet. (1987–present) Left field, 355
feet; center field, 413 feet; right field,
324 feet. *Fences:* (1930–86) 22 feet all
the way around. Scoreboard in left, 42
feet. *Seating capacity:* (1960) 10,000;
(1985) 7000. *1987 season attendance:*
110,893.

Built in 1930, this is now one of the
oldest ballparks in use. Ballpark used
in the making of the film *The Pete Gray
Story* (1958). It is currently the home of
a Seattle Mariners farm club.

In the '30s, for big games, temporary
bleachers were sometimes set up in
front of the right field fence. As late as
the '60s the large hand-operated scoreboard in left field gave the inning-by-
inning line scores for all American, National and Southern league games.

In left center the land inclines sharply
up five feet in straightaway center to
the Coca-Cola sign. That incline has
the word LOOKOUTS painted on it.
The incline also has steep shoulders.
Until 1986, the "terrace" was in play.
Any outfielder navigating it would have
to worry about falling off the sides. In
1987, an inner fence of chain link was
built to cut the home run distances.

In the 1930s, when the park was new,
and Joe Engel was still the owner of the
Lookouts, there was once a standing-
room-only crowd for House Day.
Engel raffled off a house.

Today, Engel Stadium has grown old
in a neighborhood that has grown old.
It is surrounded by rusty bridges across
the Tennessee River and warehouses.
Sitting in the stands, looking out over
the right field wall, you see what seems
like a thousand parked Southern Railway freight cars.

The park still uses the original high-
backed seats, now painted yellow and
blue to match the uniforms of the
Lookouts. The old outfield wall is
made of cinderblock, painted blue. It is
currently covered with a double deck of
advertising signs. Home runs fall in
front of it.

Cheney, Washington

Chissus Field
Home of the Eastern Washington
University Eagles (Pac-10 Conference,
Northern Division). *Seating capacity:*
2500.

Chicago, Illinois

Dexter Park
Home of the Chicago Atlantics.

In 1870, the Chicagos played in Dexter Park, in the infield of the racetrack
there. Baseball had been played at that
site since at least 1867.

On the day of games two or three extra trains were run by each of the two
railroads leading from the city to the
park. Trains were packed, and streets
were jammed with buggies and barouches. *The Western Monthly* at the
time called the streets around the
ballpark before a game "a continuous
caravan of vehicles and dust."

Business was great. A total of five
thousand dollars was made on one ball
game between the Chicagos and the
Forest Cities of Fort Wayne in June of
1870. *The Western Monthly* described
Dexter Park on a day like that this way:
"The immense audience disposed,
for the most part, on seats of the 'grand
stand,' a favored hundred or two in the
cool piazzas and balconies of the Club
House; an adventurous Gideon's band,
mostly made up of sports, amateur and
professional, congregating in front of
the Club House, a score of reporters

Sheet music cover from "Home Run Galop" shows the Chicago Atlantics playing in 1867. (From the Lester S. Levy Collection of Sheet Music, Special Collections, Milton S. Eisenhower Library, The Johns Hopkins University. Used by permission.)

thrown out, like a company of skirmishers, well onto the field, and the remainder of the throng scattered promiscuously about the skirts of the field, in carriages or otherwise, — the game commences. If it happens to run pretty evenly, or even if the score is kept down to a low figure, the interest of the crowd is intense. Every good play of any member on either side is hailed with huzzas, partly from amateurs who admire the feat, but chiefly from bettors who have put money on the player's side."

Lake Park

National Association 1871 (White Stockings). *Location:* Randolph, Michigan and Madison streets. *Seating capacity:* 7000. *First game:* May 8, 1871. *Last game:* September 29, 1871. *Fire:* Destroyed by Great Chicago Fire, October 8–11, 1871.

In 1871, Chicago's organized baseball history got off to a crispy start, and it was a crying shame because folks had been so optimistic at the beginning of the year. Business was booming. Chicago's population had grown almost a third of a million in the previous thirty years.

A dump beside Lake Michigan had been converted for National Association play. The rickety six-foot wooden fence that enclosed Lake Park read, "Post No Bills." The site was closer to the lake than it is now, as the shoreline has been pushed eastward over the years by lake-fill.

In the municipally owned ballpark, within walking distance of the business district, over 7000 could sit in the shade and watch from the splintery grandstand. Ladies and gentlemen were seated separately, men in the preferential seating, and there were private sections where only city officials could sit. A $15 season ticket, priced to keep the section elite, allowed one the same seat for every home game. The ball club promised not to sell the seat in the owner's absence.

The fences were an average of 375 feet from home. The *Tribune* called Lake Park as big as any field in the National Association.

On October 9, the Windy City became a canto of *The Divine Comedy*. The Great Fire consumed 2600 acres of Chicago, a few of which constituted Lake Park.

Along with their home the White Stockings lost their money and possessions. Only charity from the railroads and from other teams allowed the White Stockings to finish the season — and still they came close to winning the championship.

Chicago concentrated on more important matters than baseball for a few years. Folks rebuilt their homes. The city didn't have organized baseball again until 1874, the last time Chicago did not have at least one team in the big leagues.

Twenty-third Street Grounds

National Association 1874–75 (White Stockings), National League 1876–77 (White Stockings). *Location:* 22nd, 23rd, State and Clark streets. *First National Association game:* May 13, 1874. *Last National Association game:* Octo-

ber 2, 1875. *First National League game:* May 10, 1876 (Chicago 6, Cincinnati 0). *Last National League game:* October 5, 1877 (Louisville 4, Chicago 0).

In 1874, with a new National Association franchise, Chicago played in the Twenty-third Street Grounds on the South Side. During the few years this park was in operation, traveling time to and from was cut in half, as slow horsecars were replaced by steam-powered trains.

In 1876, the team acquired a clubhouse that was only a block away from the park. Before that the White Stockings suited up at home. There was only one clubhouse, for the home team, and it was reported to be the finest in the country. A reporter for the *Tribune* said Chicago's new locker room was "furnished in the most gorgeous style of the furniture dealer's art."

Four times this ballpark was used as a neutral site for a National Association game, twice for Cleveland versus the Lord Baltimores, once for the Philadelphia Athletics versus Troy in 1872, and once in 1873 for Boston versus the Philadelphia Pearls.

Lakefront Park

National League 1878–84 (White Stockings), Union Association 1884 (Unions, some games). *Location:* Same as Lake Park. *Dimensions:* Left field, 180 feet; left center, 300 feet; right center, 252 feet; right field, 196 feet. *First game:* May 14, 1878 (Indianapolis 5, Chicago 3). *Refurbished:* 1883. *Last game:* October 11, 1884.

Baseball's popularity still grew in the 1880s, offering owners the stability to put more money into the construction of their enclosures. Owners of franchises in the larger cities — New York, Chicago, Philadelphia — saw a need for larger seating capacity. By the 1880s, ballparks were getting bigger, as well as more familiar to the modern eye. Indeed, ballparks were starting to look like ballparks, not unlike modern minor league stadiums, though still made exclusively of wood.

The finest park of the era was Lakefront Park in Chicago, the house of Al Spalding's White Stockings. That's the same Al Spalding who was a pitching star in the National Association (207–56 in five years), the same Al Spalding who went on to be a sporting goods tycoon. According to Peter Levine in his book *A.G. Spalding and the Rise of Baseball,* "(P.T.) Barnum and Spalding were essential figures in satisfying the entertainment and leisure-time needs of late-nineteenth-century America." Spalding's grounds were indisputably the finest in the world "in respect of seating accommodations and conveniences."

An article in *Harper's Weekly* said the grounds were located on what was known as the Lake Front property, the title to which was in the name of the city of Chicago. The enclosure began at Randolph Street on the north, and extended along the east line of Michigan Avenue southward to a point about midway between Washington and Madison streets.

Toward the east were the switchyards and tracks of the Illinois Central Railroad Company, an unfriendly neighbor who repeatedly offered $800,000 to buy the land from Spalding, a figure representing less than half the property's worth. Because the city was not permitted to sell the land or build permanent buildings upon it, the White Stockings were allowed to play there within a two-minute walk of State Street, the city's chief retail drag.

Because the park was so close to downtown, and because the White Stockings had won three consecutive National League pennants, beginning with 1881, baseball was getting big in Chicago. Attendance there was the best in the nation. In 1882, the White Stockings drew 130,000 during 45 home games, an average of almost 3000 per game. The White Stockings appealed to a la-di-da Chicago crowd who paid big bucks for choice seats. Spalding could afford the best in players and accommodations.

By comparison with the usual style of 1880s ballpark accommodations, Lakefront Park was positively palatial. The ballpark had been completely refurbished following the 1882 season. The seating arrangements had been remodeled. Over $1800 was spent on paint alone. Each exposed surface was shiny and new. Spalding had seen to it personally.

The grandstand area behind home was enlarged to seat 2000, and there was room for 6000 more in the uncovered bleachers along the foul lines, arranged so that they cut the field off sharply on the right side. With standing room, Lakefront Park held 10,000 without hindering play. A six-foot wooden fence surrounded the playing field in front of the seats. The stands were raised to command the best view.

A handsomely ornamented pagoda watched over Lakefront Park's main entrance. Built for a bandstand, it was home for the First Cavalry Band throughout the 1883 season.

On the roof of the grandstand, on the third base side of home, was a row of 18 private luxury boxes — where Spalding made the real money. Society watched from armchairs, in boxes that were cozily draped with curtains to keep out sun and wind. One of the boxes, of course, belonged to Spalding. His was equipped with a telephone and a gong so he could conduct business, baseball and otherwise, without missing a pitch.

In addition to club officers and players, a 41-person crew was necessary to operate the stadium on game day: seven ushers, six policemen, four ticket-sellers, four gatekeepers, three groundskeepers, three "cushion-renters," six "refreshment boys," and eight musicians.

The most interesting thing about Lakefront Park's playing field was its diminutive size, especially in its right-field foul line, which measured only 196 feet to the wooden fence in front of the stands. In 1884, this became a distance the White Stockings learned to exploit—so successfully that they forgot to do everything else.

That year the most homers hit by a non-White Stocking was 14, yet Chicago boasted four players over 20. Third baseman Ned Williamson led the National League with an all-time record 27. Second baseman Fred Pfeffer had 25, left-fielder Abner Dalrymple had 22, and manager and first baseman Cap Anson had 21. (This was the same year that Providence pitching ace Hoss Radbourne won 60 games.)

The White Stockings barely managed to finish in the first division, but they poked so many homers over that short fence that their record became the mark to match through the remainder of the dead ball era. Too bad that fence was close for the opposition as well. The cheap homers became an embarrassment to the league.

After the end of the 1884 season, the National League passed a rule mandating a minimum distance for outfield fences at 210 feet. Balls hit over the already existing fence in Lakefront Park became ground rule doubles. The stats would lead us to believe that such blows were ground rule doubles before the 1884 season as well. The White Stockings hit 13 homers in 1883. They hit 142 the following year. If the fences stayed in place, the rules must have changed.

Spalding liked to handle all of the day-to-day business operations of the White Stockings himself. He scheduled non-league contests, hired mascots, made arrangements for umpires, got tickets printed, and advertised the games. Later, as his sporting goods business took up more of his time, he delegated these duties to his assistant, Jonathan Brown. But as long as the White Stockings were in Lakefront, Spalding was running the show. He personally contacted groups such as the

Calumet Lacrosse Club and Barnum and Bailey's Circus—two diverse groups who rented Lakefront Park for performances. Barnum and Bailey paid Spalding $2500 for the use of his ballpark.

Spalding maintained a temperance campaign throughout his years as a baseball mogul. No alcoholic beverages were sold at White Stockings games. Spalding went as far as to try to keep other ball club owners from selling beer and liquor in their parks. He tried particularly hard, and to no avail, to shut down the notoriously rowdy liquor bar in the Polo Grounds.

Spalding went out of his way to see to it that fans attending his ball games were comfortable. In September of 1884, Spalding wrote to the superintendent of the West Division Rail Company, John Lake, and told him that it would be in their mutual interest to improve service on the Van Buren Street and State Street lines. Spalding sold Lake on the idea, and in 1885 extra and larger trains ran before home games, so that it was more tempting than ever for Chicago businessmen to leave the office to go to the ballpark.

The dream was ephemeral. Lakefront Park's reign as America's pastime's best house lasted three years, when the White Stockings were forced off the land by legal restrictions.

To Spalding's horror, it was discovered why the city was unable to sell the land or build a permanent building on it. Turned out the land had been given to the city originally by the Federal Government, with the stipulation that it not be used for commercial venture.

South Side Park (Chicago Cricket Club Grounds 1884, White Sox Park 1900–10, Schorling Park)

Union Association 1884 (Unions, some games), American League 1900–10 (White Sox), Negro National League 1920–31, 1933–35 (American Giants), Negro Southern League 1932 (American Giants), Negro American League

1937–40 (American Giants). *Location:* Wabash, Wentworth (right field), and Michigan avenues at 39th Street (first base, now known as Pershing Road), four blocks from the eventual site of Comiskey Park. *Seating capacity:* (1900–09) 15,000. *First Union Association game:* May 2, 1884. *Last Union Association game:* August 1, 1884. *First American League game:* April 21, 1900 (Milwaukee 5, Chicago 4, 10 innings). *First (major league) American League game:* April 24, 1901 (Chicago 8, Cleveland 2, attendance: 14,000, time: 1:30). *Last American League game:* June 26, 1910 (Cleveland 5, Chicago 4). *Fire:* 1909; December 25, 1940.

For years the site of the Chicago Cricket Club, these grounds were first used for baseball by the Chicago franchise of the Union Association, a mediocre ball club that found no fan support here and wound up finishing out the season in Pittsburgh. Sixteen years passed before baseball returned to these grounds, but when it did it stayed for 40 years.

Last Wooden Ballpark in Chicago. A new grandstand holding approximately 15,000 was built for the White Sox of the brand new American League in 1900, and rebuilt in 1910 following a 1909 fire. That grandstand (actually a set of three small grandstands and no bleachers) survived 31 years, an amazing length of time for a wooden ballpark. It finally burned on Christmas Day, 1940.

From the beginning, the American League White Sox were owned by Charles Comiskey, the former St. Louis (American Association) pitcher and manager. The field was located in the Armour Square section, a working-class white ethnic neighborhood. South Siders loved the location of the new park, but those from the North and West found it difficult to get to. In spite of this, the White Sox quickly became the biggest draw in the newborn American League. The team was so popular the White Sox quickly outgrew their home and Comiskey Park had to be built.

All-Time Pitchers' Park. South Side Park was the all-time number-one pitchers' park. The outfield fences were irregularly shaped, dipping in toward the plate in straightaway center. The home run distance was shorter to center than to right or left, but practically unreachable in all directions. According to John Thorn and Pete Palmer in *The Hidden Game of Baseball,* "this cavernous stadium produced home run totals like the two in 1904, three in 1906, and four in 1909; in two years the Sox failed to hit *any* homers at home, thus earning the nickname 'hitless wonder.' In 1906, Chicago pitchers held opponents to 180 runs at South Side Park, an average of 2.28 runs per game, earned *and* unearned, in a decade when four out of every ten runs was unearned."

The record held until 1981, when Houston Astro pitchers held opponents to 2.08 during the 51 home games of the strike-shortened season.

The American Giants. After the White Sox were gone, the ballpark officially became known as South Side Park—which was what everyone had always called it anyway—and sometimes as Schorling Park, after John M. Schorling, the white promoter of South Side Park's black ball games.

The Chicago American Giants, the black team, played here as early as 1911, long before they were in an official league. They were the best black team of the teens.

When Jack Johnson (Heavyweight Champion of the World 1909–15) jumped bail after his arrest on morals charges in Canada—he'd crossed the border with a white woman—he snuck back into the country dressed as an American Giant, carrying baseball equipment.

The team was managed by the former pitching ace Rube Foster, who managed from a box seat rather than from a bench. According to Donn Rogosin in *Invisible Men,* Foster "puffed away on his meerschaum pipe or chomped his favorite Havana cigar." He went on to found the Negro National League, and it was for his entrepreneurial skills that he was elected to the Hall of Fame. Still, he was the most effective black pitcher of the 1900s, a submarine screwball pitcher. In 1907, while still a player, Foster gave a harbinger of his future when he convinced the owner of his Chicago Leland Giants, Frank Leland, to accept no less than half the take even when playing white semi-pro teams.

Congress Street Park (West Side Park)

National League 1885–91, Players League 1890 (Pirates, some games). *Location:* Congress, Loomis, Harrison and Throop streets. *Seating capacity:* 6000 (2500 numbered grandstand seats, 3500 open bleachers). *Construction cost:* $30,000. *First game:* June 6, 1885 (Chicago 9, St. Louis 2). *Last game:* October 6, 1892 (Chicago 5, Louisville 3, 7 innings, darkness). Also neutral site of Game 14 of the 1887 World Series, October 25, 1887 (Detroit NL 4, St. Louis AA 3, attendance: 378).

After getting the boot from his lakeside baseball palace (Lakefront Park), Al Spalding persuaded his fellow directors to invest $30,000 in a new ballpark at the corner of Congress and Loomis streets. Not as convenient as Lakefront Park—nothing could be—the new Congress Street Park was still only a 15-minute horsecar ride from the center of Chicago. This ballpark featured private boxes on the roof, a carriage entrance to the grounds on Congress Street, and a neatly furnished toilet with a private entrance for ladies.

The Congress Street Park was no larger in capacity than Lakefront, but presented a feeling of permanence. It was surrounded by a twelve-foot brick wall rather than the traditional wooden fence.

The visiting clubhouse was at the northeast corner (Throop and Congress) of the grandstand with a private gate leading to it. The home clubhouse was at the opposite end of the grounds and consisted of a one-story brick structure. Inside were a large dressing room and showers.

A two-story brick building at the corner of Loomis and Congress housed the ticket stands and the team offices. The woodwork was painted a terra-cotta color.

Eclectic Entertainments. Just in case the new ballpark couldn't recoup the directors' investment through baseball attendance alone, Spalding readied the facilities for other attractions, such as cycling, lacrosse, lawn tennis, and track.

In 1886, after Spalding's plans to play a baseball game at night fell through, he used the lights system he'd had built for an amusement park-skating rink combination right inside the ballpark. A 65-foot toboggan slide was rigged. Under Cap Anson's supervision, patrons could slide over 700 feet, arriving at ground level somewhere in short-center field. For non-daredevils there was a skating rink next to the slide.

The playing field was shaped like a modern home plate. The foul lines were not that much longer than they had been in Lakefront Park, at 216 feet, but center was deeper. Of the extra-curricular activities here, the cycling affected baseball play most, as the banked track encircled the field.

In 1891, on "Base Ball Day," 400 local amateur teams were let into the park free for a game because they'd come in uniform. The event was declared the largest gathering of ballplayers in history.

The park was located in a middle-class neighborhood that strongly objected to it, thinking it a threat to stability and safety. It probably didn't hurt the community, but it brought no good luck either. The neighborhood degenerated, becoming dominated by poor new European immigrants. To some degree, however, the ballpark's presence caused local property values to rise. Some new hopes were built. The sense of permanence in the brick was an illusion. This park lasted only five years before high rent again forced Spalding to move the White Stockings.

Brotherhood Park

Players League 1890 (Pirates, some games), National League 1891–93, 1894 (some games). *Location:* West 35th Street, Wentworth Avenue, and West 34th Place—across the street from the eventual site of Comiskey Park. *First Players League game:* May 5, 1890. *Last Players League game:* October 4, 1890.

In 1891, Al Spalding scheduled half of his National League team's home games at the former South Side site of the Brotherhood team. All White Stockings games were played in Brotherhood Park in 1892. The Players League park was newer and more modern than the facility on Congress Street, and the rent was $1500 a year, one-fifth the previous rent.

The lease on this park ran till 1897, so—after the ball club moved to West Side Grounds—the Chicago National League Baseball club rented out these grounds to other entertainments, such as bicycle races, college football games, and "Bedouin Wild East Shows."

Spalding moved his ball club again after only three years in Brotherhood Park, to quickly take advantage of land he owned in proximity to the Chicago Columbian Exposition of 1893.

West Side Grounds

Western Association 1888, National League 1893 (White Stockings, Sundays only), 1894–1915 (Colts, Cubs). *Location:* Polk Street (third base), South Lincoln Street (first base), South Wood Street (left field), and Taylor (now Wolcott) Street (right field). *Construction cost:* $30,000. *Dimensions:* Left field, 340 feet, center field, 560 feet, right field, 340 feet. *First game:* May 14, 1893 (Cincinnati 13, Chicago 12). *Last game:* October 3, 1915 (Chicago 7, St. Louis 2). *Fire:* August 5, 1894 (during game, which was suspended in seventh inning).

The Phillies' Big Ed Delahanty, a notorious bad ball hitter, went 5-for-5 at West Side Grounds in 1896, including four home runs. This was only the second time a player had hit four home runs in a game.

Delahanty hit only 13 roundtrippers that year, but was being super-productive nonetheless, driving in 126 runs in 123 games. On this day, against Colts pitcher Bill Terry, he couldn't lose. The 190-pound, six-foot slugger hit each home run farther than the one before it.

The first homer went into the left field bleachers, the second deep into the right field grass, and the third deep into center where few fielders ever trod. Delahanty also lined an infield single.

For Delahanty's fifth at-bat, Chicago center-fielder Bill Lange made the crowd laugh by playing in the uncut grass far out in center, in front of the clubhouses. He had to wave his arms to let the pitcher know he was ready.

Grinning, Big Ed smacked home run number four off the roof of one side of the clubhouse (out in deepest center field, just to the left field side of straightaway) to the other side, then back onto the playing field out of Lange's reach.

Lange did not even bother to throw the ball back in. He hid it under the home team clubhouse floor so he'd have it later for a souvenir.

One can tell from the story that there was quite a large outfield at this park. The field of play was *much* larger than that of any of Chicago's previous ballparks. In 1890, the Brotherhood team had considered and rejected this site before building its own park.

Al Spalding moved the White Stockings' Sunday games in 1893 from Brotherhood Park to this location, to take advantage of the draw of the nearby 1893 Chicago Columbian Exposition. The park was located in a native-born white area of the city, across the street from the Cook County Hospital. There was an elevated line under construction that would cut the travel time from downtown to seven minutes.

Spalding enjoyed the great success from those 1893 Sunday games, so the following year he moved all of his team's home games here. This was the same field where, in 1888, the Chicago Western Association franchise had played. In 1898, Cleveland of the National League played part of their home schedule here. This is the field where the Tinkers to Evers to Chance dynasty (1906–08) would play.

On August 6, 1894, the grandstand at West Side Park caught fire during the seventh inning of a game attended by 6000 fans. A human stampede toward safety slammed staight into a barbed wire fence in front of the grandstand, injuring hundreds. That year, there was a fire at one-third of all major league ballparks.

By 1906, when the Cubs won the first of three consecutive NL pennants, there were stands set up in the outfield. There were two long bleachers: one from the left field corner to left center, the other running all the way from left center, at the left corner of the clubhouse, to the right field corner. Above the right field bleachers, from straightaway center to the right field corner, was a large billboard sign that read, "The *Tribune* always makes a hit with its sporting news." The small hand-operated scoreboard, which displayed only the line score of the game in progress, sat on the clubhouse roof, while the four operators, only one of whom was really needed, sprawled on the clubhouse roof so as not to interfere with anyone's view of the score.

For the World Series, the outfield stands were filled. An especially large Stars and Stripes had been raised in center on a flagpole (with a platform

for a sitter) protruding from the clubhouse roof behind the scoreboard. There were many men packed upon the roofs of the houses across the street in all directions. That year the Cubs had won the pennant by a whopping 20 games, but ended up losing to their crosstown rivals, the White Sox, in six games. The Cubs lost all of the games at West Side Park.

In later years there was a small set of bleachers in straightaway center in front of the clubhouse. There was a high screen with billboards on it in right field, and a scoreboard in the right field corner. After 1908 there was an irregular U-shaped grandstand from corner to corner. Before that there were bleachers down the lines with a grandstand surrounding the infield only.

Following a fire at White Sox Park in 1910, after which the White Sox moved out, Chicago amended its building code. Ballparks could no longer be built of combustible materials unless seating capacity was below 5000. The wooden parts of all ballparks had to be treated annually with a fire retardant. A maximum number of seats between aisles was established. Roofstands, such as those atop the West Side Grounds, were permitted only in fireproof ballparks, and only after adequate means of escape had been allowed. The Cubs' home had two sets of roofstands sitting 125 persons apiece that had to be removed.

Every year the city would send fire marshals out to the ballpark to make sure the aisles were being kept clear in case there was a need for evacuation. Sometimes more seats were sold than existed and a fire hazard was created, but punishment was infrequent. Everyone could be bribed. Since the city had the authority to close down a ballpark, teams were vulnerable to political pressure.

In 1909, for example, the owner of the Cubs, Charles W. Murphy, incurred the wrath of county treasurer John R. Thompson by doubling the rent on Thompson's downtown restaurant. Thompson retaliated by sending the building commissioner out to the West Side Grounds where, naturally, many violations of the building code were discovered, resulting in a heavy fine for Murphy.

Generally, though, Chicago government and Chicago baseball tried to get along. Parks were lent for political functions, and free passes to games were liberally distributed to city officials.

When the Federal League folded, the Cubs moved out of the West Side Grounds, and moved into the park that was to become Wrigley Field.

The site currently holds the Illinois State Hospital and Medical School.

Comiskey Park (White Sox Park II)

American League 1910-present (White Sox), Negro American League 1941-50 (American Giants), National League 1918 (Cubs, World Series only). *Location:* 34th Place (left field side), 35th Street (first base), South Shields Avenue (third base), Wentworth Avenue (right field). One block west of Brotherhood Park. *Architect:* Zachary Taylor Davis. *Contractor:* George W. Jackson. *Groundbreaking:* February 15, 1910. *Cost of construction:* $750,000. *Dimensions:* (1910) Left field, 352 feet; center field, 440 feet; right field, 352 feet. (1949) Left field, 341 feet; left center, 374 feet; center field, 401 feet; right center, 374 feet; right field, 341 feet. (1977) Center field, 440 feet; other dimensions the same. (1982) Same as 1949. 86 feet from home plate to the backstop. *Outfield wall heights:* Left field, 9 feet, 10 inches; center field, 11 feet; right field, 9 feet, 10 inches. *Turf:* Natural grass (artificial turf on infield only 1968-75). *Seating capacity:* (1910) 32,000 (7000 of which were bleachers); (1927) 46,552; (Current) 44,492, broken down as follows: lower boxes, 7578; lower reserved, 7669; upper boxes, 5526; upper re-

served, 2895; general admission, 20,824. *Single game attendance record:* 54,215 (June 19, 1953, versus New York). *Season attendance record:* 2,136,988 (1984, also a city of Chicago season attendance record). *Doubleheader attendance record:* 55,555 (May 20, 1973, versus Minnesota). *Opening Day attendance record:* 51,560 (April 14, 1981, versus Milwaukee). *Night attendance record:* 53,940 (June 8, 1951, versus New York). *Twi-night doubleheader attendance record:* 52,592 (July 12, 1951, versus Boston). *Four-game series attendance record:* 172,264 (July 29- August 1, 1983, versus New York). *Three-game series attendance record:* 144,840 (August 8-10, 1960, versus New York). *Two-game series attendance record:* 84,783 (August 22- 3, 1977, versus New York. *Season low attendance record:* 195,081 (1918). *First game:* July 1, 1910 (St. Louis 2, Chicago 0, attendance: 24,900 paid, 28,000 total). *First night game:* August 14, 1939, White Sox beat Browns 5- 2.

Opening Day, July 1, 1910. Comiskey had the stands decorated with thousands of yards of colorful bunting. Five bands played. Comiskey's personal box was filled with flowers. Troops from the U.S. War Department conducted a flag raising ceremony. "Hail to the Chief" was played. The mayor presented a banner to Comiskey. The owner was aware of his working-class following and had put plenty of 25 cent seats in his stands. When the park was new those stands held 32,000.

The White Sox lost their home opener in their new park 2-0 to the St. Louis Browns. The losing pitcher was White Sox ace Ed Walsh, who had been on the committee to design "White Sox Park." That's why the new park almost made it through its first month without a home run being hit. The first was by the Sox's Lee Tannehill, on July 31, 1910, a grand slam against Detroit. The first Comiskey Park home run by an opponent was struck the same day by

Ty Cobb to give the Tigers a 6–5 victory. The fences were 362-420-362. Pitchers' paradise.

Planning a Pitchers' Park. On February 1, 1909, Comiskey announced he'd purchased from the estate of Chicago's first mayor, John Wentworth, for $100,000, the lot upon which Comiskey Park would be built. Comiskey assigned the task of designing his new concrete and steel park to Zachary Taylor Davis, a graduate of nearby Armour Institute (now known as the Illinois Institute of Technology).

In addition to Comiskey Park, Taylor's other architectural achievements included St. Ambrose Church at 47th Street and Ellis Avenue, the Kankakee Courthouse, the educational buildings of the downtown Loyola University campus, Wrigley Field (all in Chicago), and Wrigley Field in Los Angeles.

Comiskey Park was Davis's first ballpark, so he sent his assistant, Karl Vitzthum (along with Ed Walsh), on a research trip to visit brand new Forbes Field and Shibe Park. Vitzthum returned with stolen innovations such as ramps, allowing the crowd a safer and quicker exit from the upper levels, and a new drainage system of tile drains and gravel subsoil.

Though it was supposedly Walsh's idea to make the outfield large, thus creating a pitchers' park, Comiskey too was known to prefer large ballparks, with room to challenge outfielders' skills, creating the excitement of frequent extra base hits.

Walsh made his sole journey into ballpark design work for him. He won 26 games in 1911, followed that up with 27 in 1912, and ended up in the Hall of Fame.

Like Forbes Field, Comiskey Park had a double-decked grandstand between first and third, with unattached single-deck pavilions beyond. Original plans were to give Comiskey Park a Roman facade much like the one on Shibe Park. For reasons of budget, the fancy outer shell was never put on. Instead, a simple brick wall covered the stadium's steel skeleton, with the letter C repeatedly designed into the brick patterns.

Similarly, there was a time when cantilevered construction was considered, but it would have added $350,000 to the construction costs, so the notion was scrapped—and fans to this day have to deal with the resulting support beam obstructions.

Comiskey managed to hold the total cost of the project to $700,000, which included $550,000 for construction and $150,000 for the property.

Unlike other owners, whose financial interests were largely elsewhere, Comiskey made his living owning White Sox. Because of this he was willing to fight harder than the next guy to put a team of pennant-winning capabilities on the playing field.

He also went out of his way to make the fans happy. In the rain, those in the bleachers were allowed to move into the grandstand under the roof.

He was despised by his players, who found him maddeningly stingy, but loved by the people of Chicago. Any worthy Chicago organization that wanted to use his park for an event had it for free—assuming they were White Sox fans of course, and they always were. According to baseball historian David Voight, Comiskey said, "The fans built the park, didn't they?"

Comiskey was late to realize the economic dangers of building a ballpark in a changing neighborhood. According to Steven A. Riess in *Touching Base*, "important changes were taking place in the nearby Douglas community west of Wentworth Avenue. That area was an integral part of the growing blackbelt developing east of State Street between 12th and 39th Streets.... The proximity of a black neighborhood undoubtedly frightened away a number of white fans, especially after the 1919 race riots."

Several businesses (several bars and a

Comiskey Park, July 10, 1910 - Opening Day

Comiskey Park, July 6, 1933 - First All-Star Game

Comiskey Park, Early 1970's - Known as "White Sox Park"

Shots of Comiskey Park, Chicago, Ill., show its progress, 1910-1970. (Compliments of the Chicago White Sox.)

Greek ice cream parlor) moved into the immediate ballpark vicinity to take advantage of the crowds. One bar, called McCuddy's, had the prime location directly across the street from the park's main entrance. McCuddy opened up before the park was built, and word was an inside tip had led to the real estate coup. The value of the property tripled in the first five years his bar was open.

In 1913 there was a sign across the front entrance reading, "Auto Polo... America's Newest Craze...At This Park...June 5th, 6th, 7th, and 8th."

Experimental Night Game Played. On August 27, 1910, inventor George F. Cahill brought his new patented light-

ing system to White Sox Park and convinced Comiskey to let him stage a night baseball game here. Twenty 137,000-candlepower arc lights were used to illuminate the field of play for the game between the Logan Square and Rogers Park teams. Over 20,000 came to watch, and the experiment was deemed a success.

But Cahill was a man ahead of his time. He would be dead by the time the first major league night game was played on May 25, 1935, in Cincinnati. The first night game was not played at Comiskey Park until August 14, 1939, with the White Sox defeating the St. Louis Browns behind the pitching of John Duncan Rigney.

During its first decade, Comiskey Park (which became its name around 1913) was host to three consecutive World Series. In 1917 and 1918, the Sox played, and in 1918 it was the Cubs, who borrowed Comiskey for its larger seating capacity.

Of course, Comiskey Park was the site of the infamous Black Sox scandal of 1919, in which several White Sox players received money from gamblers in return for dumping World Series games. The scandal almost killed baseball, but the national pastime was saved by Judge Landis—the first commissioner of baseball, who forever removed the gambling element—and revived by Babe Ruth, who became the most popular man in America the instant he found his home run swing.

Enlargements. Comiskey Park was big enough for most games, but not nearly big enough to hold the crowds that showed up when the Yankees and the Babe came to play. To make room, Comiskey expanded his stadium.

Between the 1926 and 1927 seasons the wooden bleachers in the outfield were torn down and replaced by concrete stands. The outfield pavilions were double-decked. The original plans called for a 55,000 seating capacity, but fire codes held it to 52,000.

Zachary Davis, Comiskey Park's architect, also designed the enlargements. The park could expand eastward, because Comiskey had bought an additional parcel of land on that side, but was confined by city streets in all other directions. This may be the reason that the upper decks in left and right field vary in the steepness of their incline. The lower deck in right field has 31 rows, while out in left the lower deck only has 19 rows of seats. The upper deck has 20 rows of seats in both right and left field.

Until 1950 the bullpens were in foul territory, but it proved better for relief pitchers' peace of mind when they were moved behind the center field fence.

When the 1927 enlargements had been completed, Comiskey is said to have exclaimed, "Well, nobody is going to hit the ball over those stands." Wrong.

The home run virginity of the new Comiskey Park roof lasted until August 18, 1927, when a Babe Ruth blast off Tommy Thomas cleared the right field stands. The ball came down in the middle of the parking lot outside the ballpark, clearing at a point where the roof was 75 feet high, 360 feet from home. The second player to clear the roof with a homer was Lou Gehrig, off Red Faber, May 4, 1929. It's happened over 30 times since.

For the shirtless and thirsty and rowdy there are showers in the bleachers—a blessing during day games in August in the sun. There's not much of a chance of catching a home run out there, though. The center field bleachers, as they currently stand, have been reached only six times by a batted ball: Jimmie Foxx (1934), Hank Greenberg (1938), Alex Johnson (1970), Dick Allen (1972), Richie Zisk (1977), and Tony Armas (1984).

In 1940, Bob Feller and his Cleveland Indians were in town for the start of the season, and Feller pitched the only Opening Day no-hitter in baseball history, winning 1–0. It was the first no-hitter pitched at Comiskey Park by an opponent.

For one year (1934) home plate was moved 14 feet closer to the outfield fences to help Al Simmons hit more home runs. The next year Simmons was gone and the plate was put back in its original position. In 1949 and 1969–70, there were experiments with inner fences to cut down on the home run distances—and every year since 1949 there has been some sort of fence reducing the home run distance to straightaway center.

In 1941 and 1947, the narrow straight-backed seats were replaced with wider curved-back seats, and there was a corresponding drop in seating capacity.

Comiskey Park reached low points

in attendance in 1918 because of the war and in 1932 because of the Depression. It wasn't until after World War II, and the breaking of baseball's color line, that Comiskey's 1927 ballpark expansion became necessary. Between 1951 and 1965, annual attendance for the White Sox rose by about a million fans.

Veeck. The late Bill Veeck took over the club in 1959 and painted the park white. He knocked the bricks out of the left field wall, put in screens and built a picnic area behind the wall with a view of the game.

In 1960, in his most memorable move, he enabled the electronic scoreboard (which had been there since 1951) to make exploding noises each time a White Sox player hit a home run. It was the first exploding scoreboard in the big leagues. (The original scoreboard was replaced in 1982 by a computerized DiamondVision variety—but the new one explodes and has pinwheels that go around just like the old one.)

Veeck's effects can still be seen all over the park. The picnic area is still there. In left anyone can sit out there— so hoodlums usually do, the types that liked to get right up against Kirk Gibson's ear when Gibson still played for the Tigers. Now they like to plague visiting Rickey Henderson. In center and right, the seats behind the wall are reserved for private parties.

On July 12, 1979, Bill Veeck executed his (without a doubt) worst promotion idea: Disco Demolition Night. (Almost as stupid as "Ten Cent Beer Night" in Cleveland.) Admission was 98 cents, for a twin bill. Bring your disco records for the bonfire between games. Some hated disco so much that they brought cherry bombs. One fan brought the golf ball that almost beaned Ron LeFlore.

Between games of the doubleheader, the disco records were piled and set afire by a blonde bombshell using the professional name Lorelei. Seven thousand fire worshippers charged onto the field. Veeck and Harry Caray called for

order over the P.A. Police were called in. Fifty were arrested. Six suffered minor injuries. The second game of the doubleheader was forfeited by the home team.

All-Star Games. Three times, Comiskey Park has hosted the major league All-Star Game. The very first All-Star Game in 1933 was staged as part of the Century of Progress Exhibition occurring that summer on Chicago's Lake Front. The game drew 47,595, who saw the American League go home victorious after a two-run homer by Babe Ruth.

Fifty years later, on July 6, 1983, Fred Lynn hit the All-Star Game's first grand slam home run to lead the American League to a 13–3 victory.

In between, on July 11, 1950, Chicago fans saw the National League win a 4–3 victory in 14 innings.

Aged Yet Proud. In *Five Seasons*, Roger Angell says Comiskey Park looks like "a docked paddle-wheel steamer."

During its day, Comiskey Park was the site of the Negro League East-West All Star Game from 1933 to 1950. The ballpark also housed three Negro World Series games in 1924, five in 1926, and single Negro World Series games in 1943, 1946, and 1947.

The park has been the home of four white or integrated World Series as well: 1917 (White Sox defeated New York Giants four games to two), 1918 (Boston Red Sox defeated Chicago Cubs four games to two, with Babe Ruth pitching a 1–0 shutout in Game 1), 1919 (Black Sox allowed Redlegs to win five games to three), and 1959 (Los Angeles beat the Chisox four games to two).

Jerry Reinsdorf and Eddie Einhorn bought the White Sox in 1981, and soon thereafter spent $14 million on park improvements. DiamondVision was installed, everything got painted, and 27 luxury boxes were built.

Nonetheless, since Comiskey is the oldest ballpark still in use, it would be asking too much for it to be the most comfortable. State of the art, it ain't. Chip Atkison, who wrote a book about his pilgrimage to all 26 major league ballparks during the 1986 season, says of Comiskey, "The seats were too close together, the rows too narrow, the 24-inch roof supports made the number of good viewing seats rare, and the public address system sounded like a weekend electrician had wired a diaphragm inside a 55 gallon drum."

In 1974, everybody got a scare when a popcorn machine in the right field stands caught fire. Four thousand fans rushed onto the field, and it took over an hour before they could get the ball game started again.

These days, the underside of the roof above the upper deck is painted a flat black. The seats are green. Concession stands serve Mexican cuisine in addition to the regular baseball fare.

In 1984, Comiskey Park was the site of the longest by-the-clock game in American League history. The game (May 8–9) took 8:06 and 753 pitches to complete. Carlton Fisk, whose dawdling would explain about three hours of that record time, was probably catching.

In addition to baseball, Comiskey Park was, for many years, the home of the Chicago Cardinals of the National Football League—before the franchise moved to St. Louis. It was here that, on Thanksgiving Day, 1929, Ernie Nevers (who was also a major league pitcher) scored a record 40 points as the Cards beat the crosstown Bears (with George Halas and Red Grange) 40–6.

Leland Giants Field

Home of the Leland Giants circa 1910, Negro National League 1920s (American Giants, some games). *Location:* 6221 South Halsted Street, at 69th Street.

DePaul University Field

Federal League (minor league) 1913 (Whales). *Location:* Fullerton Campus,

a mile and a half from the Loop.

Wrigley Field (Weeghman Park, 1914–15, Cubs Park, 1916–26)

Federal League 1914–15 (Whales), National League 1916–present (Cubs). Owned by the Chicago Cubs. *Location:* North Clark Street (home plate side), Waveland Avenue (left field), Sheffield Avenue (right field), West Addison Street (first base). *Architect:* Zachary Taylor Davis. *Construction cost:* (1914) $250,000. *Dimensions:* (1920) Left field, 348 feet; center field, 447 feet; right field, 318 feet. (Present) Left field, 355 feet; left center, 357 feet; center field, 400 feet; right center, 363 feet; right field, 353 feet. 62 feet from home plate to the backstop. *Seating capacity:* (1914–21) 16,000. (1922–26) 20,000. (1927–present) 37,741. Field boxes, 3254; lower boxes, 6254; lower reserved, 2150; mezzanine boxes, 150; upper boxes, 4616; general admission, 18,017; bleacher, 3300. *Season low attendance record:* 337,256 (1918). *First Federal League game:* April 23, 1914 (Chicago 9, Kansas City 1). *Last Federal League game:* October 3, 1915 (Doubleheader, Pittsburgh 5, Chicago 4; Chicago 3, Pittsburgh 0). *First National League game:* April 20, 1916 (Chicago 7, St. Louis 6, 11 innings). *Cost of lights:* $5 million. *First night game:* August 9, 1988 (Cubs 6, Mets 4, winning pitcher: Frank DiPino, attendance: 36,399, time: 3:03).

As this is written, no one has seen the inside of Wrigley Field at night—and there's something about that exclusivity to the daylight that's reminiscent of childhood and grammar school. We rarely saw the inside of our school at night, and if we did, the experience was always dreamlike and bizarre, a world taken too far out of context to be real, certainly not the same place where we attended class during the day. The nighttime is an adult world. Wrigley Field is growing up now. So must we. The bleacher bums are going to feel silly pouring beer on their bare chests to enhance the moontan process. The first time you see Wrigley at night, it's going to feel like you just saw your second grade teacher in the supermarket. When ball games end at midnight, will they still raise the blue L flag and the white W flag to let those passing the ballpark know if the Cubbies won or lost?

"While it would be an exaggeration to suggest that time stops at Wrigley, evidence indicates it moves slowly there."—Skip Rozin in (of all places) *Audubon*.

The Federal League. In 1909, the De Cantillon brothers, realizing there was no baseball on the North Side of Chicago, bought a plot on Addison Street in a residential area, with the original intention of using it as home for an American Association franchise. This didn't pan out, so the brothers leased the property in 1914 to the Chicago Whales of the Federal League. The Whales belonged to Chicago lunchroom owner Charles Weeghman. The Federal League was an association that had operated as a minor league in 1913, and was in 1914 attempting to make a go of it as a major league for the first time. When news got out that there was to be a ballpark built on the North Side, in the Sheridan Park area, the area businessmen were pleased. Over 700 businessmen signed a resolution to that effect. On the other hand, many neighborhood property owners were displeased, and presented a petition of protest to Mayor Carter Harrison II. As had been the case at Comiskey Park a couple of years before, landlords on the blocks facing the park already had their new taverns operating before the park was built.

Weeghman Park was single-decked and—in accordance with the 1909 Chicago law following the fire at White Sox Park—100 percent fireproof.

While it was still a Federal League park, fans expressed annoyance at vendors who wandered the ballpark. The vendors, folks said, were noisy and tended to block people's view. In response, Weeghman set up vending stalls in the back of the stands manned with trained people.

When the Federal League disbanded after two years, Weeghman and others got together and bought the Cubs from Charles Taft. The National League club was moved from their home in the West Side Grounds to Weeghman Park, which was renamed Cubs Park.

In 1916, Joa, a real cub bear, lived on Addison Street in a cage outside the ballpark. That same year, Weeghman first allowed fans to keep batted balls that went into the stands. This was thought of as quite a generous policy on his part. It would still be years before this would become a standard practice, after a judge in 1923 in Philadelphia ruled keeping the baseball wasn't stealing.

In 1918, Weeghman's interest in the club was bought out by chewing gum magnate William Wrigley. Nine years later, the upper deck was built, and the park took on the new owner's name.

Ruth Calls His Shot. It was in the 1932 World Series, October 1, in Wrigley Field, that Babe Ruth hit one of the most famous home runs of all time. Ruth had already hit one three-run homer that day, and had botched a play badly out in right. On both occasions he played the crowd, tipping his cap to the jeers. By the time he came to the plate in the fifth, Ruth and the overflow Chicago crowd of 49,986 had what you might call a kind of rapport going on, a kind of hate-hate relationship.

Here's how John Drebinger told the rest of the story in *The New York Times:*

"...(It) seems decidedly unhealthy for anyone to taunt the great man Ruth too much and very soon the crowd was to learn its lesson. A single lemon rolled out to the plate ... and in no mistaken motions Babe notified the crowd that the nature of his retaliation would be a wallop right out of the confines of the park. (Charlie) Root pitched two balls and two strikes, while Ruth signaled with his fingers after each pitch to let the spectators know exactly how the situation stood. Then the mightiest blow of all fell. It was a tremendous smash that bore straight down the center of the field in an enormous arc, came down alongside the flagpole and disappeared behind the corner formed by the scoreboard and the end of the right-field bleachers."

The Bleachers. In the outfield are the bleachers, maybe the most famous bleachers in the world, built where there used to be outfield (and some smaller wooden bleachers that were there the day Ruth hit his homer), making the outfield dimensions a paradise—ask Andre Dawson—for anyone with power to the alleys. The bleachers start out narrow and then rise to a peak in center field, making them look like a steeply angled boomerang perched atop the outfield fence.

Construction of the bleachers as they look today began in the middle of the 1937 season. A pasteboard fence was thrown up to separate the playing field from the construction site, and there were immediately grumbles from fans about "the elimination of the outfield."

By September, however, when the new stands were finished, fans applauded the grace of their design, and expressed amazement that so many new seats could be put in while taking such a tiny chunk out of the former playing field.

In right field, the removal of the old bleachers (those put there in 1923) in right field had left the distance to the fence down the right field line 34 feet longer than it used to be. Only a few feet were cut off the left field foul line, with the center field dimension shrunken about 40 feet.

According to the enthusiastic and daydreamy voice of the *Chicago Tribune,* on September 12, 1937, the financial advantages of extra seats were secondary to Mr. Wrigley: "The desire for scenic distinction probably was more of an incentive than the desire to spring the capacity of the field."

The bleachers had also been constructed so that the houses on Waveland Avenue past the left field fence, and those on Sheffield Avenue in right field, could still use their roofs to watch games for free. The architects for the 1937 refurbishment were the firm of Holabird & Root.

The bleachers were originally solid seating. Only after frequent and bitter complaints from hitters about the white shirts in the outfield was one section of the bleachers, just to the left field side of the peak, blocked off to spectators to form a hitters' background.

Also in 1937, Bill Veeck had the scoreboard built atop the new center field bleachers, and the famous ivy planted along the base of the bricked outfield walls. The scoreboard was 27 feet high and 75 feet wide. Construction, which cost $200,000, was allowed to continue on game days until 2:30, with the first pitch scheduled for a half hour later. The walls were then, and always have been, kept free of advertising—with the exception of two small Wrigley Chewing Gum elves.

Originally, Chinese Elms were planted on the big steps that lead up the edges of the bleachers to the scoreboard. Ten times the trees were blown off the steps by winds off Lake Michigan, and management finally abandoned the idea. The steps are still there and are used for sunbathing and picnicking during ballgames.

Ah, the Friendly Confines. In the old days fans and ballplayers (hitters in anticipation, pitchers in dread) sniffed the air on game day for a whiff of the stockyards. That smell, not a pleasant one (particularly unpleasant to pregnant women), meant the wind was blowing out.

Hear Pat Peiper on the P.A.: "Ladies and gentlemen, boys and girls, have your pencil and scorecard ready, for the correct lineups, for today's game."

Wrigley's well-maintained, double-decked grandstand is tucked up close to the foul lines. As in Fenway and Ebbets Field, fans sit where foul territory would be in a modern park. It seems the whole Wrigley Field grandstand would fit inside that of the Oakland Coliseum (where the foul territory goes on and on before the seats begin), without a need to move the playing field.

The entire playing field is still surrounded by a brick wall, and the ivy Veeck planted in the late '30s is thicker than ever in the outfield, though it does tend to brown and thin out by the end of each playing season. Then again, so do the Cubs.

For years there was a large BABY RUTH sign on the roof of a building beyond the right-field fence. It came down during the Durocher years, but till then was rumored by fans under nine to be a marker commemorating the landing spot of the most mytho-logical of Ruthian homers.

In 1942, Wrigley Field came very close to having lights. But World War II was raging—and Philip K. Wrigley donated the lights to a shipyard, where the Pearl Harbor–decimated Pacific fleet was being rebuilt 24 hours a day. After the war, Wrigley found he had the only big league ballpark without lights, so he decided to keep it that way, to stick to a brand of ball most easily enjoyed by the whole family. And the ballpark remained forever—well, at least another 40 years—a place beautiful enough to make us all (and not just Ernie Banks) say, "Let's play three!"

The Lights Go On at Wrigley. Called it. The lights went on 8-8-88 and the animals in the bleachers took their shirts off. The switch was pressed by 91-year-old Cubs fan Harry Grossman at 6:06 p.m. central time. That morning Bryant Gumbel of the NBC "To-day" show had broadcast from Wrigley

Field, doing part of the broadcast from the bleachers, part from home plate, part from the first base grandstand, etc. The first balls for the game were thrown out by Ernie Banks, whose number 14 flies on a flag over the left field fence, and Billy Williams, whose number 24 is on a flag in right. Two weeks before, 3000 paying customers had come to see the testing of the lights and a home run hitting contest (won by Andre Dawson). The first organ song played was "You Light Up My Life." The first batter, Phil Bradley of the Phillies, hit a home run into the bleachers off Rick Sutcliffe. In the bot-tom of the first the megabuxom Mor-gana ran onto the field to kiss batter Ryne Sandberg, but was collared by security and tugged off the playing field before the second baseman got smooched. Sandberg then homered to tie the game. On TV the ballpark looked very different, smaller, almost minor league, like maybe we'd tuned in a nifty park in Japan or something. (Not to say that Japanese ballparks are nifty. Hardly. They seem to imitate the worst of America's ballparks rather than the best.) The Cubs led 3–1 in the fourth inning when the rains came. The game was stopped at 8:15, then post-poned at 10:15, so the first official night game at Wrigley was not played until the following night, when the Cubs beat the Mets. The first official night game home run was struck by Met centerfielder Lenny Dykstra, a two-run shot off Mike Bielecki in the top of the fifth inning. (The shirtless bums threw it back. So what if the ball might have been worth some money? Who wants Dykstra's stinkin' home run?) For the first night game, there was no big pro-test outside. There had been some minor squawking from neighbors who likened the density of their community to Tokyo, and feared the effect night baseball would have on their ability to sleep and feel secure. The Cubs prom-ised no beer sales after 9:20, no organ music after 9:50, which meant that

Two aerial views of Wrigley Field, Chicago, Ill., as it looked in the 1980s before lights. (Compliments of the Chicago Cubs.)

Harry Caray might on occasion have to sing "Take Me Out to the Ballgame" *a cappella*—but the lights would get to stay on for as long as they were needed. Chicago went gentle into that good night. Folks in the stands still wore goofy hats, and everyone stood and bowed when Andre Dawson came up to the plate. The scoreboard was still manually operated and for the first time could report the inning-by-inning results of the other night games. A streak of 6852 straight day games had been broken with kind of a collective so what. Eighteen night games a year are planned for the immediate future. Then, one day, there'll be a generation that doesn't remember all day baseball at Wrigley.

Asbury Ball Park
Negro National League 1920s (American Giants, some games). *Location:* 79th Street and Wentworth Avenue.

Name of park unknown
Negro National League 1920s (American Giants, some games). *Location:* 67th and Langley streets.

Name of park unknown
Negro National League 1920s (American Giants, some games). *Location:* 37th and Butler streets.

Pyott's Park
Negro National League 1920s (American Giants, some games). *Loca-*

tion: West Lake Street and 48th Avenue (later Kilpatrick Avenue). *Dimensions:* short porch in left.

Normal Park
Negro National League 1920s (American Giants, some games). *Location:* Normal, 61st, Racine, and 63rd streets. *Dimensions:* configured for football.

Soldier Field (Grant Park Municipal Stadium)
Negro National League 1920s (American Giants, some games). *Location:* 425 East McFetridge Place, 14th Street, Waldron Drive.
Still the home of the Chicago Bears of the National Football League.

Cincinnati, Ohio

Union Cricket Club Grounds
Home of the Red Stockings circa 1869, National Association 1871, 1875 (on five occasions used as a neutral site), National League 1876 (Buckeyes). *Location:* Lincoln Park, beside the Union Terminal.
Home of the first dynasty. The team, famous for its successful road trips and 92-game winning streak, proved there was money to be made in baseball with such pioneer professional players as captain and center-fielder Harry Wright ($1200 per annum), his shortstop brother George ($1400), Asa Brainard ($1100) and third baseman Fred Waterman ($1000). Everybody else got $800.

Avenue Grounds
National League 1876-77 (Buckeyes). *Location:* Monmouth Street, Alabama Avenue, at the Baltimore and Ohio railroad tracks; also reported as Spring Grove Avenue, currently Chester Park. *First game:* April 25, 1876 (Cincinnati 2, St. Louis 1). *Last game:* September 29, 1877 (Cincinnati 11, Chicago 10).

Bank Street Grounds
National League 1880 (Buckeyes), American Association 1882-83 (Red Stockings), Union Association 1884 (Outlaw Reds). *Location:* Bank, Duck and Cross streets, and Western Avenue. *First National League game:* May 1, 1880 (Chicago 4, Cincinnati 3). *Last National League game:* September 30, 1880. *First American Association game:* May 21, 1882 (Pittsburgh 10, Cincinnati 9). *Last American Association game:* September 29, 1883 (New York 4, Cincinnati 1). *First Union Association game:* May 1, 1884. *Last Union Association game:* October 12, 1884 (Cincinnati 11, Boston 5).
In 1880, when the Grounds were home of the National League's Buckeyes, a three-piece regimental ensemble was hired for five dollars a day to play before and during ball games. Every once in a while, the Cincinnati Grand Orchestra played. This franchise was given the boot for defying league rules and selling beer in the ballpark.
In 1883, when the Red Stockings of the American Association were playing here, there was a set of steps on the Bank Street Grounds, leading from the field to the stands, so ladies arriving by carriage could reach the special ladies' section without having to walk through the men's sections.
The ballpark was only three blocks north of the eventual site of Crosley Field along Western Avenue, and was known for being ravaged each spring with the flood from the Ohio River.
In 1884, the Red Stockings of the American Association left to play in their deadly abandoned brickyard, and this field was used by the Outlaw Reds of the Union Association. Word is, the two teams hated each other, and each hired thugs to menace the other nine.

Crosley Field (Cincinnati Base Ball Grounds 1884-89, Western Avenue Grounds 1891, League Park 1892-1901, Palace of the Fans 1902-11, Redland Field 1912-33)

Top: *Soldier Field, Chicago, Ill., best used by the Bears.* Bottom: *The Union Cricket Club Grounds in Lincoln Park, Cincinnati, Ohio. Opening Day, May 4, 1869, perhaps the earliest baseball action photo. Where's the catcher? The Red Stockings beat the Great Westerns that day 45-9. (Photo used with the permission of the National Baseball Library in Cooperstown, N.Y.)*

American Association 1884-89 (Reds), National League 1890-1970 (Reds), Negro National League 1921-30 (Cuban Stars West), Negro American League 1937, 1942-45 (Tigers, Clowns). Owned by the Cincinnati Reds. *Location:* Findlay Street (first base side), Western Avenue (center field), York Street (left field). From 1884 to 1894, home plate was located in what later would be the right field corner, at the corner of Findlay and Western. *Dimensions:* (Before 1925) left field, 360 feet; center field, 420 feet; right field, 360 feet. (After 1925) left field, 328 feet; left center, 382 feet; center field, 387 feet; right center, 387 feet; right field, 342 feet. 78 feet from home plate to the backstop. *Fences:* 14 feet from the top of the terrace to the top of the wall. Home plate six feet lower, making height of the wall from home plate level 20 feet. The left field scoreboard measured 50 feet, 2 inches, from ground level to the top of the signs. The clock was another 7 feet, 10 inches in height, making a total height of 58 feet. Scoreboard was 65 feet wide. *Seating capacity:* 29,488. Boxes, 11,449; reserved, 10,106; sundeck reserved, 4009; general admission, 3924. *Day game attendance record:* 35,747 (April 15, 1924, versus Pittsburgh). *Doubleheader attendance record:* 36,691 (April 27, 1947, versus Pittsburgh). *Night game attendance record:* 32,916 (June 29, 1936, versus Chicago). *Twi-night doubleheader attendance record:* 32,552 (August 8, 1966, versus San Francisco). *Opening game attendance record:* 35,747 (April 15, 1924, versus Pittsburgh). *Season high attendance record:* 1,125,928 (1956). *Season low attendance record:* 100,791 (1914). *First American Association game:* May 1, 1884 (Columbus 10, Cincinnati 9). *Last American Association game:* October 15, 1889 (doubleheader, Cincinnati 8, St. Louis 3; St. Louis 2, Cincinnati 1). *First National League game:* April 19, 1890 (Chicago 5, Cincinnati 4). *Last National League game:* June 24, 1970 (night, Cincinnati 5, San Francisco 4).

This ballpark, as it originally existed in 1884, and Baker Bowl have the notoriety of being the only two baseball arenas ever to fall down and kill people. (Baker Bowl did it twice — but only because it was given ample opportunity.) The lot for this quickly assembled wooden grandstand on the corner of Findlay and Western, at the site of an abandoned brickyard, was chosen by team owner Aaron S. Stern. The stands collapsed the very first time they held people, Opening Day, 1884. One person died and many others were hurt.

The park was rebuilt and would serve as the site of Cincinnati baseball for the next 86 years. But a lot of changes took place during that time. In 1885, for example, management painted the center field wall black, thus inventing the hitters' background.

When first built, the park sat among vacant lots. The neighborhood became increasingly industrial over the years until the Reds played in a park surrounded by factories.

It was here that the Reds, after 27 years, finally won a World Championship in 1919, only to have it tainted by the Black Sox scandal.

Stern's Tax Return. Here, according to baseball historian Harold Seymour, are the expenses incurred by the American Association franchise during an average year in the 1880s: sprinkling Western Avenue during the season, $52.50; repairing two lawn mowers, $2.50; fire insurance premium ($1000 policy), $12.50; building a 78' 8" fence 16 feet high, $64.00; water bill for the season, $25.00; one keg of nails, $2.60; attorney's retainer, $250.00; one gong bell, $10.00; plumbing, $55.27; carpenter work, $22.00; lumber for partitions, $24.34; sewer pipes, $2.76; rubber hose, $19.90; one neighbor's broken window, $2.50.

Stern had a reputation as a tightwad. He did not give away free passes. He paid his security personnel $1.75 per game, but at one point was "forced" to cut everybody's hours in half.

Stern was doing okay. In those days there were many breweries in Cincinnati, and the Red Stockings made $3000 a year from beer sales alone.

The park was rebuilt partially in concrete and steel, the first such ballpark — meeting new building codes passed to stem a rash of ballpark fires. Home plate was moved with this refurbishment to the spot where it was to stay for 76 years.

Palace of the Fans. Despite the new construction materials, the park burned in 1900 and 1901. When it was rebuilt for the 1902 season it was known as the Palace of the Fans and was designed to look like a palace, with pillars that made the joint look like a Greek ruin. The pillars could not be seen through.

In 1901, a record 50 inside-the-park home runs were hit here. Sam Crawford, later known for his triples, hit 12 of them. The park stayed conducive to inside-the-parkers. According to L. Robert Davids in his book *Insider's Baseball,* 360 inside-the-park home runs were hit here between 1900 and 1955.

The Palace's grandeur soon faded. By 1907 and 1908, the Cincinnati building inspector was starting to complain about it. Girders were cracked. Supports were decayed. Floors were unsafe. Fences needed rebuilding. A whole bleacher platform was defective. A signboard on the roof blew off onto the street. This park burned again after the 1911 season. When it reopened the place had lost its pillars and looked a lot more like the Crosley Field it was to become.

Experimental Night Game. The inventor of the pitching machine, George F. Cahill, from Holyoke, Massachusetts, devised a portable yet powerful lighting system. In 1909 he set out cross-country to persuade baseball teams to use his new invention for night baseball.

As the first to envision baseball's nocturnal future, Cahill certainly would have deserved the title "Father of Night Baseball," except for one thing: Nobody took him very seriously.

For Cahill, business was slow. His first chance to properly exhibit his wares came in Cincinnati on June 19, 1909. Reds president Garry Herrmann okayed a night game in the Palace of the Fans between the Elk lodges of Cincinnati and Newport, Kentucky. Around 3000 showed up to watch the novelty. Present were the Cincinnati and Philadelphia teams, who remained after their afternoon game to watch.

The players reported little trouble following the ball. Herrmann appeared impressed. But nothing came of it.

In less than a month, Cahill would once again get an opportunity to show off his wares, this time in Grand Rapids, Michigan—but night baseball was not about to catch on. Baseball's permanent move to prime time was still decades away.

Rooters' Row. Around the same time, the P.O.T.F. had a "spectators' paradise" beneath the grandstand directly behind home. It was a bar, actually, called Rooters' Row. Fans there drank lots, sat on a hard wood bench, and were so close to the action that they could participate in on-field conversations.

LeJeune's Toss. On October 10, 1910, Field Day at the Palace of the Fans, there was an organized competition between Sheldon LeJeune of the Evansville (Central League) Club and Eslar Foudrea of Springfield, Illinois. That day LeJeune threw a ball under standard (no supporting wind) conditions, 426 feet, 6¼ inches—breaking the previous record held by Jack Hatfield. (See Brooklyn, Union Grounds.) In his career, LeJeune only played 24 big league games in 1911 and 1915.

Crosley. When Garry Herrmann and other Cincinnatians took over the Reds in 1911, the ballpark underwent another metamorphosis. Harry Hake designed the new structure, Redland Field, which was formally dedicated May 18, 1912. The new facility on the same old site cost an estimated $225,000.

The top of the Redland Field flagpole stood 82 feet above the playing surface, yet balls striking it, even at the top, remained in play—making it one of the tallest structures "in play" in baseball history, surpassed only by the flagpole in Detroit's Tiger Stadium and the left field light tower in Savannah's Grayson Stadium. (The flagpole in Tiger Stadium is still there, but no longer in play above a certain point.)

During the 1920s, the park was rented for movies and dancing. These events caused the Cincinnati Juvenile Protective Association to repeatedly complain about "immoral dancing" and "vulgar conduct between boys and girls in unlighted portions of the grandstand." The complaints became so frequent that the Reds had to stop renting the park for these activities.

That same decade, the Cuban Stars of the Negro National League played at Redland Field, thus becoming the first black team to become a tenant of a big league team. The black team paid the Reds $4000 a year in rent. In return, the Reds provided four police officers for weekday games (ten on Sunday), tickets, ticket-takers, and a grounds crew.

About 5000 seats were added in 1925, mostly in field boxes. To make room home plate was moved twenty feet closer to the fences, reducing distances from 360-420-360 to 328-387-366.

In 1935, new concrete stands were built from foul pole to foul pole. The year before the ballpark had been rechristened after Reds owner, automobile designer and radio magnate Powell Crosley. The upper deck was extended down the baselines in 1939, adding 3000 more seats. Several times between 1946 and 1960, the Reds experimented with a screen in right field in front of the existing fence to shorten the home run distance.

First Big League Night Game. The major leagues were slow to accept night baseball, finding it repugnant to the nature of the sport. Like George F. Cahill in 1909, salesmen were trying to sell lights to baseball owners in the 1930s—and the magnates still weren't buying.

By 1935, night baseball was played in most minor leagues, and had been for several years. The Depression had struck baseball's smaller businesses first and hardest, so it was there that night baseball's financial necessity was first realized.

In December 1934, Larry MacPhail, general manager of the Reds, requested permission to light up Crosley. The National League agreed only because of the Reds' perilous financial difficulties.

The first big league night game was played May 24, 1935, before 20,422. President Franklin Roosevelt pushed a button in the White House—and in Cincinnati 1,090,000 watts of electric power lit up the ballpark. National League president Ford Frick threw out the first ball. The Reds beat the Phillies 2-1 that night, behind the six-hit pitch-ing of Paul Derringer.

One newspaper account didn't care for the artificially lit version of the game: "Birds roosting under the roof of cavernous Crosley Field flew over the field, singing as if it were daybreak. The game became a strangely colorless, synthetic affair. Like the lights, it was artificial, mechanical. Personal characteristics and facial expressions of the players became vague in the haze that hung over the field."

Here's the account of Douglas Wallop in his book, *Baseball—An Informal History:* "That night in Cincinnati the players were bitter. They were afraid to dig in at the plate, leery of taking toeholds, fearful of being beaned. One said that baseball was being turned into a 'five-and-ten-cent racket.'

"The fans didn't like it either. They were cold and they couldn't see the players very well. The consensus was clear: night baseball would never last."

In 1937, the Ohio River floods came to Cincinnati, covering Crosley Field as no other stadium of this size has ever been covered. Reds pitchers Lee Grissom and Gene Schott rowed a boat into the ballpark over the outfield wall.

In 1957, a new scoreboard was installed, a monster. It was 58 feet high and 65 feet wide. It stood at the top of the incline, dominating left field.

Beyond the left field wall was the Superior Towel and Linen Service Building. Every once in a while a home run would bounce off their wall. The Spiedler Suit Company bought billboard space on Superior's wall and put up a "Hit This, Win a Suit" sign.

Many pieces of Crosley Field, including the scoreboard, currently reside in the Cincinnati suburb of Blue Ash, Ohio. In July 1988, the ballfield was the site of an all-star game commemorating Cincinnati's bicentennial.

Pendleton Grounds

American Association 1891 (Kelly's Killers). *Location:* In the suburb of Pendleton; Ridgely and Watson streets.

First American Association game: April 25, 1891. Last American Association game: August 13, 1891.

Ballpark was built along the bank of the Ohio River, northeast of Tacoma Park.

Northside Park

Negro National League 1921 (Cuban Stars). Location unknown.

Riverfront Stadium

National League 1970–present (Reds). City-county owned. Location: Mehring Way (first base side), Second Street (third base), Suspension Bridge Approach (home plate). Dimensions: Left field, 330 feet; left center, 375 feet; center field, 404 feet; right center, 375 feet; right field, 330 feet. 51 feet from home plate to the backstop. Fences: Twelve feet from 1970 to 1983; eight feet from 1984 to the present. Seating capacity: 51,786. Club boxes, 2040; boxes, 17,987; reserved, 21,967; general admission, 9792. First game: June 30, 1970 (night, Atlanta 8, Cincinnati 2).

Built on top of its own parking garage. One of those round stadiums with artificial surface and symmetrical dimensions. This was the home of the Big Red Machine of the 1970s, with Johnny Bench, Pete Rose, George Foster, Tony Perez, and Joe Morgan. Wow.

Site of the annual Ohio Valley Kool Jazz Festival.

Clearwater, Florida

Jack Russell Field

Florida State League 1985–present (Phillies), spring home of the Philadelphia Phillies 1955–present. Location: 800 Phillies Drive, Palmetto Street. Dimensions: Left field, 340 feet; center field, 400 feet; right field, 340 feet. Seating capacity: 5347 (box seats, 1912; grandstand, 2435; bleachers, 1000). First Philadelphia Phillies game: March 10, 1955 (also dedication day).

1987 Florida State League season attendance: 55,370.

The Phillies have trained in Clearwater since 1947, and in this ballpark since 1955. On the day this stadium was dedicated, Philadelphia beat Detroit in a spring game 4–2. Before the game, the ballpark was named for Jack Russell, a former major league pitcher (85–141 lifetime with the Red Sox, Indians, Senators, Tigers, Cubs, and Cards) who'd become Clearwater City Commissioner. This dedication was a surprise to Russell, who was instrumental in the building of the ballpark. He'd thought the ballpark was going to be called something completely different.

In 1987, the city of Clearwater spent almost $750,000 refurbishing Jack Russell Stadium and the entire Carpenter Complex (spring training facility). New lockers and a new rubber floor were put in the clubhouses. All four practice fields received new fences and hitters' backdrops. To give youngsters experience they might need later on, the field out beyond Jack Russell Stadium's right field fence was Astroturfed.

Cleveland, Ohio

Case Commons

Home of the Forest Citys 1865–70. Location: East 38th Street, between Central (formerly Garden Street) and Community College avenues. Seating capacity: O. Fans stood behind ropes.

The Cleveland Forest Citys played their first game on October 21, 1865, against the Penfield Club of Oberlin, at the Case Commons. The Forest Citys went down to defeat miserably, 67–28. To add insult to injury, an outfielder named Leffingwell hurt his arm, and Mr. Smith lost two teeth in a collision. The Oberlin team did not come away unscathed either, as a ballplayer named Ryder had his day ended early by a line drive to the face.

Jack Russell Stadium, Clearwater, Florida, as it looked in the spring of 1988. (Photos by David Pietrusza.)

According to William Ganson Rose, in his book *Cleveland, the Making of a City,* "Woodland Avenue cars operated on a half-hour schedule carrying fans to Case Avenue, where they boarded a dinky horsecar that took them to the ball ground."

In 1869, 2000 fans watched the visiting Cincinnati Red Stockings, masters of all baseball, defeat the Forest Citys 25-6.

In 1870, for the first time, a 25-cent admission charge was initiated for Forest Citys games. The lowlight of that season, their last before the formation of the National Association and their last at the Case Commons, was an 85-11 defeat by the Philadelphia Athletics.

National Association Grounds

National Association 1871-72 (Forest Citys). *Location:* Willson Avenue (now East 55th Street) and Garden Street (now Central Avenue). *First game:* May 11, 1871. *Last game:* August 19, 1872.

National League Park

National League 1879-84 (Spiders). *Location:* Kennard Street (now East 46th Street), Silby Street (now Carnegie Street) and Cedar Avenue. *First game:* May 1, 1879. *Last game:* October 11, 1884.

As in Lakefront Park in Chicago, balls hit over the fence down the line (in this case left) were a ground rule double in 1880 and 1881. Tough to figure out why. Fifty-eight home runs were hit in the whole National League in 1879, when National League Park had regular ground rules, and the Spiders only hit eight of them both home and away. Boston hit 20. If anyone was exploiting the short fence it must have been visitors.

Out in center, where hitting a ball over the fence was out of the question, there were trees growing in play—but these were removed by the 1880 season.

Spider Park (Brookside Park)
American Association 1887–88 (Spiders), National League 1889–90 (Spiders). *Location:* East 39th and East 35th streets, Payne and Euclid avenues. *First American Association game:* May 4, 1887. *Last American Association game:* September 15, 1888. *First National League game:* May 3, 1889 (Chicago 4, Cleveland 0). *Fire:* June 1890 (grandstand splintered by lightning).

To get to the ballpark fans took the Robinson trolley line. That's because the Spiders were owned by Frank DeHaas Robinson, who also owned the Payne and Superior streetcar lines. When lightning blew his park apart, he built a new one, League Park, equally close to his streetcar lines.

Team featured James Toy, the first American Indian to play major league ball.

After professional baseball moved to the new League Park, this field was used by the Cleveland Athletic Club, the city's finest amateur baseball team.

Beyerle's Park
American Association 1888 (Spiders, Sundays only). *Location:* Cleveland and Canton Road.

To get around municipal blue laws, the Spiders played their Sunday games on the Cleveland and Canton Road, just beyond the city line.

Brotherhood Park
Players League 1890 (Infants). *Loca-* *tion:* Willson Avenue (now East 55th Street) at the Nickel Plate Railroad tracks. *Average attendance per game:* 927.

League Park (Dunn Field 1916–27)
National League 1891–99 (Spiders), American League 1900–47 (Broncos 1901, Blues 1902–04, Naps 1905–11, Molly McGuires 1912–14, Indians 1915–47), Negro American League 1939–40, 1943–48, 1950 (Bears, Buckeyes). Also home of the National Football League's Cleveland Browns. Owned by the Cleveland Indians. *Location:* East 66th Street [formerly Dunham Street] (first base), Lexington Avenue (right field), East 70th Street (left field), Linwood Avenue (third base). *Dimensions:* Left field, 375 feet; left center, 415 feet; center field, 420 feet (460 feet before 1920); right center, 340 feet; right field, 290 feet. *Fences:* Right field, 40 feet. *Seating capacity:* (1910) 18,000; (1947) 21,414 (field boxes, 2206; grandstand, 9535; pavilion, 8673; bleacher, 1000). *Fire:* 1894 (struck by lightning during game against Chicago, game postponed). *Major refurbishment:* 1910. *First National League game:* May 1, 1891. *Last National League game:* August 30, 1899 (Boston 8, Cleveland 5). *First American League (minor league) game:* April 26, 1900. *First American League (major league) game:* April 29, 1901. *Last American League game:* September 21, 1946 (Detroit 5, Cleveland 3).

Payne Avenue and Wade Park streetcars passed the main entrance to League Park, located at the corner of East 66th Street and Lexington Avenue. The site had been chosen by Spiders owner F.D. Robinson, who owned the streetcar company and saw to it that his public transportation system dropped patrons off no more than 20 feet from League Park's main entrance.

When the brick structure opened in 1891, with flags on top and adorned arches in the brickwork below, the Spiders arrived on the scene at the tail end of a parade (accompanied by balloons, circus animals and a 16-piece band) riding a decorated streetcar. It was May 1, and the Spiders' pitcher that day was Denton "Cyclone" Young, later just Cy, who stood only 55 feet from the plate as he threw to League Park's first batter, the Cincinnati Redlegs' Biddy McPhee. The first pitch was a called strike fastball, popping the glove of catcher Chief Zimmer.

There was very little foul territory. According to Cleveland baseball historian Peter Jedick, "The fans sat on wooden benches so close to the field they could watch the players sweat and hear them cuss."

In 1890, the average attendance per game at League Park was 668 fans, yet this was one of the few parks in baseball maintained all year round by a groundskeeper. The playing field here during those days has been described as "a millionaire's lawn."

On April 24, 1898, the Spanish-American War began. People stopped going to ball games. Seventy-five fans showed up for one game in Cleveland against the Orioles. The next year, Spiders owners sold the club, bought the St. Louis franchise, and took all of Cleveland's best players with them (including Cy Young and Jess Burkett), leaving the Spiders with the dregs of the league. Easily the worst team in major league history, the Spiders went 20-134. Only once during the entire season did the Spiders win two games in a row. The Opening Day twin bill in 1899 drew only 500 fans. By June the total attendance for the year was 3179. It was Cleveland's last season in the National League.

In 1900 Jack Kilfoyl, owner of a men's furnishing store on public square, and Charley Somers, who'd inherited his father's coal mine riches, bought the Grand Rapids franchise in Ban Johnson's Western (soon to be American) League — fully savvy to the fact that the league would be "major" within a year or so. The team called itself the Blues

because they wore the Spiders' blue uniforms.

Here's a story that sounds straight out of a Hollywood movie — *Damn Yankees* or *The Natural*. In 1902, the Cleveland club (who were known as the Broncos by this time) was managed by Bill Armour. The club wan't far into its season when Armour realized he lacked a player who could pitch, so he held an open tryout at League Park, and the young men of Cleveland showed up, seeking instant fame. All in one day, Armour discovered Otto Hess and started him against the Washington Senators. Hess won the game 7-6 in extra innings, and went on to win twenty that year.

Armour was a man of many ideas. That same year he decided he and some of his players could make some off-season scratch by turning the playing field into a skating rink. Dirt embankments were built all around the field and water was pumped in. The dirt embankments didn't come close to holding the water, and Armour managed to flood much of the neighborhood.

Between the 1909 and 1910 seasons, when Charles Somers was owner of both the ball club and the field, League Park was enlarged and rebuilt in steel. It held 18,000 for Opening Day.

Let's Play "Wall." Center field was originally quite deep, 460 feet, but was cut down to 420 in 1920 by the addition of seats out there. The right field wall hung very closely to the plate — like Fenway in reverse — and that fence was made particularly difficult for outfielders to play by the steel beams which protruded from its surface.

Balls came off the wall in bizarre ways. When it was clear a fly ball was going off the wall, outfielders converged, ready for anything. The wall in right was an easy mark for the Ruths and Gehrigs, who liked to pick up two or three home runs every time they came to town. Even right-handed batters punched the ball to right — as was the case in Philadelphia's lopsided Baker Bowl over in the National League.

The original wall out in right was made out of wood, with eye-level knotholes that magically reopened every time management filled them in. That wall tended to take some of the steam out of line drives that struck it. The new wall was 20 feet of concrete with 20 feet of screen on top of that. (In spite of its height, the Indians still had to pay for twenty or thirty broken windows per year.)

Balls hitting the concrete bounced back toward the infield—so outfielders had a crucial decision to make with each ball hit over their head. Go back and try to catch it, or *run forward* and play the carom? Balls striking the screen did one of three things: bounced off true, dropped dead to the base of the wall, or stuck in the wire for a ground rule double.

Kids in Cleveland, as in no other city, played "Wall," fielding carom after carom off garages or brick edifices overlooking vacant lots, in imitation of the right-fielder (Joe Jackson, maybe, or Homer Summa) they'd seen at the ballpark.

Kids on the Outside. Many kids went to the ballpark every day and never paid to get in. They'd hang out in groups on Lexington Avenue with one eye always on that right field screen. If they caught a home run and turned it in, they'd get in free.

Sometimes, during batting practice, an outfielder would lob a ball over that fence and smile, imagining the scramble going on only a few feet away.

One home run, chased down on August 11, 1929, turned out to be Babe Ruth's 500th career homer. The kid who turned the ball in, Jack Geiser, got a $20 bill from the Babe, an autographed ball, and a chance to sit next to the Babe in the Yankee dugout.

Some kids sought out alternative ways to watch the game for free, which always involved some climbing. The most popular perch for diminutive deadbeats was the Dunham School fire escape, but the view from here was poor. Only a slice of the field could be seen. A better view came from the top of the Andrews Storage building, but getting up there involved a scary climb that only the heartiest attempted.

Grownups on the Inside. In 1914, box seats cost $1.25, reserved seats were $1.00, $.75 for general admission, and $.50 for "pavilion admission," seats in the double-decked grandstand extensions that had been built between the original grandstand the the foul poles. Tickets were color coded.

For weekdays, just the main gate at East 66th Street and Lexington Avenue was open, but for special games, a second ticket booth and entrance opened up at East 66th Street and Linwood Avenue. Season tickets were $100.00 for a box of eight seats. There were Ladies Days, during which the purchaser of a grandstand ticket got to take a lady in free.

The double-decked grandstand went from foul pole to foul pole. The grandstand was in two pieces, with a break just behind third base where the grandstand ended and the roofed pavilion began. There was a single deck of stands from ten feet outside the left field pole to left center. The scoreboard was in dead center, just a little bit shorter than the right field screen.

It appeared in later years that the architect had not considered the necessity of bullpens, and sometime after the park was built, home plate was moved up, moving the foul poles in, creating room for bullpens between the foul lines and the stands. The bullpens were crammed into the corners. Between them and their respective dugouts, which were three-quarters of the way down the baselines toward the fences, seats had been added level with the playing field to compensate for the extra foul territory. But these extra seats were not built the same on either side of the field.

On the first base side, where the Indians had their dugout, the seats were back far enough so that only a few spectators could actually see into the dugout. The entire playing field could be seen from the Indian dugout, including the entire length of the right field foul line.

On the third base side, where the visitors had their dugout, the seats were between the dugout and the foul pole, all the way to the bullpen. If the bullpen was in play, an outfielder might field a ball and throw the ball over the box seats on its way back toward the infield.

As was the case in Griffith Stadium in Washington, seats on the visitors' side were arranged so fans could see the visitors' bench — and the visitors' bench could see them. The visiting bench couldn't see the left field corner. Whenever a bench-warming visitor tried to see the left field corner he found himself face to face with Indians fans just a few feet away. Imagine the sort of fans who chose those seats.

There were two identically tall flag poles in the outfield, one sticking up directly out of the top of the scoreboard and another from the top of the wall behind the left center bleachers.

Straightaway center was southeast from the plate. Home runs over the tall fence were struck due south. A setting sun must have been hell for the left-fielder. With a 375-foot foul line in left, that outfielder could have serious problems with any ball that got by him — and into the previously mentioned visitors' bullpen.

As more and more fans began to come to the ball games by automobile, neighbors allowed three or four cars to park on their lawns. Cost: 25 cents.

The press box in League Park was one of the most dangerous in baseball, open in front and very close to home plate. Reporters and announcers stayed alert up there — and always had the white flag ready when a savage foul tip sent them scattering.

Many say the hardest hit ball in League Park history wasn't even a home run, but a double blasted by Babe Ruth off the top of the screen in center field near the scoreboard, 460 feet from the plate, still going up when it hit.

Speaker. In 1916, Tris Speaker joined the Cleveland club. The superstar Boston center-fielder had been purchased for $55,000 and two players — the biggest deal in baseball history up to that time. He and teammates would impress League Park crowds before games, with sophisticated games of pepper. Too bad there wasn't anyone around to play "Sweet Georgia Brown."

Speaker led the Indians to their first World Series in 1920 — a series unjustly marred by the recent exposure of the Black Sox Scandal. That was the series that produced Bill Wambsganss' unassisted triple play. A crowd of 26,684 saw that game, Game 4, the same game that featured Elmer Smith's grand slam, the first salami in World Series history. Cleveland went on to win the World Championship — winning all four of their home games.

Scorecards. In 1922, under orders from management, the men who operated the scoreboard stopped putting the names of the starting lineups on the board, but rather just the number of each starter. They correctly assumed this would increase their scorecard sales. ("You can't tell the players without a scorecard.") The move also made fans grumble. Scorecards were a nickel.

In each scorecard there was a lucky number — lucky, that is, if they announced your number during the between-innings drawing. Winners received two free tickets. According to Cleveland baseball historian Peter Jedick, there was one occasion when the printer made a mistake and everyone who bought a scorecard that day had the lucky number.

The League Park scoreboard gave an inning-by-inning line score of each game in the American League and didn't know the National League existed.

Lindbergh's Landing. According to the *New York Herald-Tribune,* May 21, 1927, in an account of the game the previous day between the Yankees and the Indians, "Charles Lindbergh landing outside the gates of Paris at the completion of his trans–Atlantic flight stopped the ball game ... at Dunn Field this warm, sunny afternoon." (The ballpark was named after owner James Dunn from 1916 to 1927.) The *Herald-Tribune* continued:

"Word of his arrival came over the wires in the last half of the seventh inning and spread like a breeze through the stands. The national pastime came to a pause. Fifteen thousand persons bared their heads and stood silent, but proud, while the band played 'The Star-Spangled Banner.' It was a simple tribute to a great deed.

"The game went on."

In 1945, League Park hosted the first game of the Negro League World Series, played before a crowd of over 10,000. In 1947, games 2 and 5 were played here.

Between 1933 and 1947, the Cleveland Indians were the only major league team with two home fields, playing their Sunday and holiday games at larger Municipal Stadium.

During those years the Indians preferred to play their weekday games at League Park because it was cozier. In 1936, Bob Feller arrived, a teenager with a fastball that packed the ballpark. On September 13, 1936, Feller used the smoke to strike out 17 at League Park.

In the end it was old age that killed League Park. Near the end a strong windstorm hit Cleveland and part of the right field wall collapsed. The superstructure had deteriorated. It was no longer a safe facility.

In 1945, the Cleveland Rams played their games at League Park. On November 11 of that year, during the

National Football League's Western Division Championship game, temporary bleachers collapsed, sending 700 people hurtling to the ground. The police arrived and called for the ballpark to be evacuated. Ambulances screamed to the scene. But the football game went on, and everyone refused to leave — except for those that were carried away. The Rams won the game, and the division title. The next year the Rams were playing in Los Angeles.

In 1947, Bill Veeck, Jr., in his second year as owner of the ball club, signed Larry Doby, the first black player in the American League, and moved the Indians into Municipal Stadium for good.

In 1987, baseball historian (and pilgrim) David Pietrusza visited the site of League Park. Here's his report:

"I had correctly heard that it was in a rundown neighborhood, so I walked there at nine o'clock on a Saturday morning from downtown Cleveland. It's a playground now. The old League Park office building is still standing, along with a wall and a tunnel which once led from a dugout under the stands."

The site has been a playground since 1951, when the city of Cleveland demolished most of the park.

Western League Park
National League 1890s (Spiders, Sundays only). *Location:* Clarke Avenue and Kennard Street (now called East 46th Street).

Tate Park
Negro National League 1922, 1924, 1926 (Tate Stars, Browns, Elites). Location unknown.

Hooper Field
Negro National League 1927 (Hornets). Location unknown.

Cubs Stadium
Negro National League 1931 (Cubs). A very small park directly across the street from League Park.

Hardware Field
Negro East-West League 1932 (Stars). *Location:* Kinsman Road, East 79th Street.

Municipal Stadium (also known as Lakefront Stadium, Cleveland Stadium)
American League 1932-present (Indians). Also home of the National Football League and All-America Football Conference 1931-present (Indians, Browns 1946-present). Owned by the city of Cleveland 1931-74, by the Cleveland Stadium Corporation 1974-present. *Location:* 1085 West 3rd Street (first base), Boudreau Boulevard (left field), Lake Erie (third base). *Nickname:* The Mistake by the Lake. *Architect:* F.R. Walker of Walker & Weeks. *Engineers:* Osborn Engineering Co. *Groundbreaking:* June 28, 1930. *Construction completed:* July 2, 1931. *Construction cost:* $2,986,685. *Refurbished:* 1967, 1974. *Refurbishment cost:* (1967) $5,000,000 (escalators, stadium restaurant, office additions, field level seats, new dugouts). (1974) $3,600,000 (Installation of private loge boxes, plumbing and sewer repair, new parking lot lights, new seating and concession stands). *Dimensions:* (Before 1947) left field, 322 feet; center field, 470 feet; right field, 322 feet. (After 1947) left field, 320 feet; left center, 365-385 feet; center field, 400 feet; right center, 365-385 feet; right field, 320 feet. *Fences:* Eight feet all the way around. *Foul poles:* 32 feet, 8 inches high. *Current scoreboard:* 137 feet wide, 54 feet high. Total of 20,160 light bulbs. Computerized matrix is 86 feet by 29 feet. *Seating capacity:* 77,797. Loge boxes, 800; field boxes, 1880; lower boxes, 5448; lower reserved, 29,000; upper boxes, 7400; upper reserved, 22,051; general admission, 8218; bleacher, 3000. For football, 80,322. *Regular season attendance record:* 84,587 (September 12, 1954, doubleheader versus New York Yankees, largest crowd in American League

history). *World Series attendance record:* 86,288 (October 10, 1948, Game 5, Boston Braves 11, Cleveland 5, winning pitcher: Warren Spahn). *Night game attendance record:* 76,382 (August 20, 1948, versus Chicago, major league record). *Opening Day attendance record:* 74,420 (April 7, 1973, versus Detroit, American League record). *First game:* July 31, 1932 (Philadelphia 1, Cleveland 0, attendance 80,184, winning pitcher: Robert "Lefty" Grove). *First night game:* June 27, 1939 (Cleveland 5, Detroit 0). *Current lights:* 1310 halide lamps of 1500 watts each, producing 130,000 footcandles on the playing field.

The stadium building boom of 1910 to 1920 was long over when the city of Cleveland built Municipal Stadium, the largest baseball stadium in the world, on the shore of Lake Michigan. It was the first municipally owned major league baseball stadium—and it set quite a precedent. After this, no big league baseball owner would build a ballpark with his own money again.

Ground was broken June 28, 1930, five days after the grading contract was authorized by the city. The area on the lakefront was manmade, that is, mostly consisting of crushed automobiles and car tires. Years after its completion, the stadium suffered sagging in right field due to landfill settling. There have been other problems. Baseball fans have come close to freezing to death during night games in April due to the icy winds off of the lake. There are also stories that when the sewers back up, the dugouts fill up.

The original cost of the stadium's construction was just under $3 million. The largest initial expenses were for the construction contract, the engineering and design contract, the pile foundation, the grandstand seats, and the acquisition and erection of the structural steel. Municipal Stadium's first scoreboard cost $9700.

The first step in the construction of the stadium was the building of a strong foundation. For the structure, 2521 piles were sunk 65 feet into the ground. Of that 65 feet, 24 feet were concrete and the other 41 feet were wood. On top of these piles were put 4600 tons of structural steel, 500 tons of reinforced steel, 15,000 yards of concrete, 3,300,000 bricks, and 130,000 pounds of aluminum.

Why So Big? The city of Cleveland wanted to host the 1932 Olympics, and lost out to Los Angeles. As a consolation, the stadium housed an event on August 31, 1932, where the Olympians who participated in the L.A. games were invited to appear. Fifty-five thousand showed up to watch the games. One of the competitors was Jesse Owens, then a track and field star at East Tech High School, who would become world-famous four years later in the Berlin Olympics.

The original plan, in the works since as far back as 1917, called for a major urban renewal project along the waterfront—a combination stadium and mall shopping area, with the mall built on a pier in the lake. The ballpark was the only part of the plan actually undertaken. With the Olympics in mind, funds for the ballpark were first approved on November 6, 1928, when the people voted $2.5 million in stadium bonds.

The first event held at Municipal Stadium was the Civic Opening on July 2, 1931. Just over 8000 people paid 25 cents apiece to see several musical ensembles and a 2500-member chorus. The next evening the first sporting event was held there. Max Schmeling KO'd Young Stribling in the fifteenth round of their heavyweight bout in front of 38,000 fans.

The Indians played 77 games in Municipal Stadium in 1933, but weekday crowds seemed lonesome in its massiveness. The following year the Indians were back in League Park except for Sunday and holiday games.

Only when League Park deteriorated to the point of being unusable did the Indians once again begin to play all of their games in the Mistake by the Lake.

The first home run hit in Municipal Stadium was by infielder Johnny Burnett of the Indians in the sixth inning of the first game of a doubleheader against Washington on August 7, 1932. Cleveland won the game 7-4.

There was not a no-hitter here until July 10, 1947, when the Indians' Don Black authored a masterpiece at the A's expense. Final score: Cleveland 3, Philadelphia 0.

Those fans sitting at the top of the bleachers in center field at Municipal Stadium are paying money to sit farther from home plate than any other baseball fans in the world, including the unfortunate few who—a few games each season, when right field is full—have to sit in the left field bleachers at Yankee Stadium.

The longest home run ever struck at Municipal Stadium was hit by Luke Easter on June 23, 1950. The blast landed near the top of the grandstand's upper deck, section four, 477 feet from home. Mickey Mantle, Frank Howard and Rocky Colavito have hit home runs that came close to entering the bleachers in center, bouncing in front of the bleacher wall, 465 feet from home. No one has ever hit a home run into the bleachers.

Before the inner fence was built Babe Ruth said, "You'd have to have a horse to play outfield there."

The inner fence, built to drastically reduce the home run distance to center field (from 470 to 410 feet), was installed in April 1947. The move helped to improve the ballclub greatly. Indian homers climbed from 79 in 1946 to 112 in 1947, to 155 in 1948. In that same time period, the team's finishes rose from sixth to fourth to first.

A Headbanger's Dream Come True. On June 4, 1974, this ballpark was the scene of the dumbest promotion in the history of baseball: Ten Cent Beer Night. To a beer drinker that reads: Free Beer Night. It was a horrible

Top: *Municipal Stadium, Cleveland, Ohio, seen from the air in 1948, the first year the inner fence was used. (Compliments of the Cleveland Indians.)* Bottom: *Municipal Stadium as it appears today. (Compliments of the Cleveland Stadium Corporation.)*

dream come true for Cleveland's row-
diest of the rowdy. Many showed up
early.

"Gimme ten," they said in turn,
offering a crisp single.

The only amazing thing is that things
stayed reasonably under control for
most of the evening. Oh sure, the
visiting Texas Rangers' bullpen got
pelted with cherry bombs and lager —
but nothing serious. Things didn't get
out of hand until the bottom of the
ninth. With the score tied 5–5, fans
rushed the field. A menacing group surrounded Ranger right-fielder Jeff Burroughs. Burroughs and fans got into a
shoving match. Some punches were
thrown. Texas manager Billy Martin
sent his team onto the field to defend
the player, and the melee was on. The
players were seriously outnumbered
and in deep trouble.

Nestor Chylak, the veteran umpire,
forfeited the game to the Rangers, later
saying, "They were uncontrollable
beasts out there." Chylak received a cut
hand by a flying chair in the riot. Nine
were arrested. Seven went to the hospital with minor injuries. Later the Indians, who had reason to downplay the
event, said 60,000 cups of beer were
sold that night.

According to a 1987 issue of the
Cleveland Plain Dealer, Cleveland
Stadium has been placed on the National Register of Historic Places, a
move that would impede any planned
demolition of the stadium. The listing
on the register came because of hard
work by David Bush, director of the
Archaeology Laboratory at Case Western Reserve University, who had to
combat resistance to the listing from
city officials and members of the Cleveland Landmarks Commission.

The newest scoreboard, which began
operation April 7, 1978, has complete
message and animation capabilities.

Since 1931, the National Football
League has played games in Municipal
Stadium. The first NFL pro football
game here took place Saturday, De-

cember 26, 1931. The Cleveland Football Indians defeated the Brooklyn
Football Dodgers, 6–0. The Cleveland
Browns, then a member of the All-
America Football Conference, played
their first game here on Friday, September 6, 1946, the Browns defeating
Miami Seahawks 44–9, before a crowd
of 60,135. In 1945, the Cleveland Rams
of the NFL played their first season
here — and it was the second year that
Municipal Stadium ever made money.

Other events of note to take place at
Municipal Stadium are donkey baseball, midget auto racing, a Beatles concert, a National Drum & Bugle Corps
Convention, pro wrestling, chariot
races, dog races, the rodeo, high school
football championships, boxing, concerts, Navy–Notre Dame football, college baseball, and professional soccer.

Luna Bowl

Negro National League 1933–34
(Giants, Red Sox). *Location:* Woodland Avenue, Woodhill Road, Ingersoll Road, East 110th Street, currently
part of an amusement park. *Dimensions:* Configured for football.

Clinton, Iowa

Ringwood Park

Three-I League 1907–09 (Infants),
Northern Association 1910 (Teddies,
Tigers, partial season). *Location:* Cur-
rently known as Fourth Street and
Tenth Avenue North, now the site of
single homes. *Seating capacity:* 1500.

Baseball in Clinton did not fare well
in its first few attempts. The Infants,
owned by Clinton businessmen C.L.
Root and P.P. Crafts, played poorly
and struggled to draw 30,000 for a
season. In 1909 the team played a split
season. Playing half their games in
Clinton, half in Sterling, they were
known as the Clin-Ster Infants.

In 1910, Clinton salvaged a spot in
minor league baseball only by urging
the formation of a new league. By July,

it was all deemed a big mistake and abandoned. Pro baseball did not return to Clinton until the construction of Riverview Stadium.

Riverview Stadium

Three-I League 1937–41 (Owls), an industrial league 1942–45, Central Association 1947–49 (Cubs, Steers), Mississippi and Ohio Valley League 1954–58, Midwest League 1959–present (Giants). *Location:* Sixth Avenue North, Second Street. *Architect:* A.H. Morrell. *Cost of construction:* $125,000. *Dimensions:* Left field, 335 feet; center field, 390 feet; right field, 325 feet. *Fences:* (1937) Nine feet all the way around (sheet steel). *Seating capacity:* (1937) 4000; (1985) 3500; (present) 3600, broken down as follows: box seats 450, general admission 3150). *Record season attendance:* 112,826 (1987). *First game:* May 9, 1937 (Clinton 3, Bloomington 2, game protested by Bloomington because of supposed catcher's interference, protest denied). *First night game:* May 10, 1937 (versus Bloomington).

Otherwise known as "Project No. 500, Iowa Central Division, WPA." On May 1, 1937, the *Clinton Herald* called it "the most beautiful baseball park in America." Built upon a brackish bottomland that once housed the city dump, this ballpark is still standing due to its superior construction.

The father of the project was Peter Matzen, Clinton's WPA advisor. He saw to it that the city of Clinton and the WPA got together to cough up the funds for the park. Plans for the stadium were drawn by A.H. Morrell, a local architect. Construction foreman was Fred Grumstrup, electrical supervisor was Edward C. Doyne, and the supervisor of masonry and cement work was Lyle Hubbart. Herman Woehrle was in charge of sodding the land beside the mighty Mississippi. Fans would be able to watch the barges over the left field fence.

The Works Progress Administration

did all right by Clinton in 1937, turning over to the Clinton Board of Park Commissioners in its completed state a big, modern sports facility.

As the '37 season approached, only minor tasks needed to be completed. Spring rains had delayed some of the sodding—which had to be done at the last minute. Sod for the field was taken from Root Memorial Park. The desodded sections of Root were turned into parking lots and tennis courts.

When the park opened the capacity was 4000. Beneath the ballpark's tiered ramparts were the offices of the Clinton Board of Commissioners, headquarters for the board's maintenance department, and big modern clubhouses connected to the dugouts by tunnel. A private clubhouse for umpires was equipped the same as those for players. There was also a service room under the grandstand which housed the heating equipment. All of the facilities beneath the grandstand were steam-heated.

The project had been begun on November 29, 1935. Sixteen months later, it was ready for baseball. The project was designed to alleviate the local unemployment problem. During the construction of the ballpark, the WPA pumped $59,380.08 into the local economy in the form of labor payroll. That amounted to 107,680 man-hours of skilled, semi-skilled and common labor. The WPA spent $24,729.03 on building materials—and about half of that was purchased from local firms. The Clinton Board of Park Commissioners spent $32,000 on construction materials, all of which was purchased locally. The materials broke down as follows: cement, 5900 sacks (seven railroad carloads); sand and gravel, 2000 tons (36 carloads); reinforcing steel, 41 tons (one carload); lumber, 104,500 square feet (four carloads); structural steel, 68 tons (two carloads); cinder blocks and bricks (nine carloads); white crushed rock for parking lot surface (five carloads); paint, four

*Riverview Park, Clinton, Iowa, as seen from the clocktower in the old Clinton
courthouse. (Compliments of the Clinton Giants.)*

tons; sewer pipe, 1385 feet; conduit
pipe, 2500 feet; water pipe, 2000 feet;
armored underground cable, 260 feet;
electric wire, 9150 feet; seat supports,
1415 units; roofing, 190 squares; brick-
layer's cement, 7000 sacks; nails, 51
kegs.

The ballpark was built to be 99 9/10
percent fireproof. Six ramps allowed
entrance and egress to the concrete
apron around the stadium's outer rim.
The outer concrete walkway was 25 feet
wide and bounded by metal fencing.
For night games it was lit by small
floodlights mounted on the roof. The
restrooms were built adjacent to the
two center ramps.

When the park first opened, the seats
were made of redwood in all areas except the three rows at the head of the
ramps, where individual steel opera
chairs were divided into boxes.

The screen behind home was made of
heavy mesh wire mounted on steel
cables. It extended upward to the
grandstand roof, 60 feet to either side
of home. Under the roof, at the rear
and top of the center section of the
grandstand, was the screened-in press
box with telegraph and telephone
facilities. From the press box was
operated the public address system,
which consisted of two large speakers

mounted under the roof at either end of
the grandstand. The system could be
hooked up with microphones on the
field as well, for pre-game ceremonies.

The ballpark had lights for night ball
right from day one. In the beginning
there were forty reflectors, each with
three 1500-watt globes arranged in
varying numbers atop eight light
towers. The towers around the infield
were mounted on the stadium roof—
something that couldn't be done when
adding light towers to old ballparks
because the roofs couldn't take the
weight—so they weren't blocking the
spectators' view.

The ticket office and front gate were
facing Sixth Avenue North. In case of
overflow crowds, the original ballpark
had the capability of quickly installing
auxiliary bleachers down the left and
right field foul lines.

That first year there was a contest to
name the team. Because night baseball
was still such a novelty, the team was
called the Owls.

Across the street from the ballpark
back then was an A&W Root Beer
stand. It was a popular place for the
players, and therefore for the fans too.

On August 17, 1938, a pre-game exhibition was held in Riverview by 1936
Olympic Star Jesse Owens. He ran a

60-yard dash against local speedster Carl Nelson. Owens won going away with a time of :06.2. He beat two ballplayers in a 100-yard dash after giving them an eight-yard headstart, finishing in :09.6 — and then further proved his track and field superiority in the hurdles and jumping events.

Wartime. During World War II minor league baseball came to a halt. Only the wartime industrial league used Riverview Stadium. To qualify for the league, a player had to be employed in vital war-related occupations in the various essential industries. Each team played a 14-game schedule spread out over a three-month period. Managers battled to keep teams together, as players changed work shifts frequently and couldn't always be there at game time. War factories worked in three eight-hour shifts, so it was hard to find nine guys who all got up at the same time.

Among the touring teams to come to Riverview during this time period for exhibitions against semi-pro competition were the Tama Indians, the Indianapolis Clowns, the Arkansas Hillbillies, and the Chicago Black Barons.

Flooding was a problem during the war years. In June 1944, Riverview was completely flooded, with a measured highwater mark of 18.5 feet, breaking the record set in June 1943.

Professional baseball returned to Clinton in 1947 as a farm club for the Cubs. For one year the Clinton Cubs and the local industrial league teams shared Riverview. The industrial players used the park on weekdays and Sundays during their last year of play, while the Cubs played mostly at night. That same year the ballpark needed box seats. Wrigley Field in Chicago was having its replaced that year, so the Cubs' farm director appropriated the removed seats, picked out the best, and installed them in Riverview.

Baseball in Clinton slumped in the '60s, as it did almost everywhere. In 1965, professional baseball almost went belly up, but survived by the skin of its teeth after the season's first month was wiped out by floods. While Riverview dried out, games were played at Rock Island and Lowden. A dike system has since been set up to protect the lowland from these yearly ravages. In 1986, the Giants drew a near record 100,326. Among the major league stars to have played in Clinton are Denny McLain, Steve Sax, Darrell Porter, Ron LeFlore, Candy Maldonado, Ron Kittle, and Orel Hershiser.

Cocoa Beach, Florida

Cocoa Expo Stadium
Part of Cocoa Expo Spring Training Facilities (Size: 50 acres). Also the home of the Joe Brinkman Umpire School. *Location:* 500 Friday Road, at State Route 520. *Seating capacity:* 5000.

The Cocoa Expo Spring Training Facility includes bullpens, lighted batting cages, locker rooms, dormitory living quarters, five playing fields, the Ueberroth Hall Classroom, a lighted soccer field, basketball courts, hot tub, pool and a spa.

The stadium's field is set off by itself, while the other four identical playing fields extend outward from a single point, a pie sliced four ways. At the center of the four practice fields is a coaches' observation deck. Out past the left field fence of one of the practice fields is Expo Lake.

College Station, Texas

Name of park unknown
Home of the Texas A&M Aggies mid-1930s to 1977. *Location:* Land adjacent to current site of Kyle Field, and eventual site of Olsen Field, on the campus of Texas A&M.

C.E. "Pat" Olsen Field
Home of the Texas A&M Aggies

Top: *College Station, Texas: Texas A&M's Olsen Field is in the background; an older park, name unknown, is in the front.* Bottom: *Olsen Field. (Both photos compliments of Texas A&M.)*

1978–present. *Location:* Campus of Texas A&M, across road from site of old park. *Dedicated:* March 21, 1978. *Dimensions:* Left field, 330 feet; left center, 375 feet; center field, 400 feet; right center, 375 feet; right field, 330 feet. *Seating capacity:* 5053. *Lights:* (infield) 100 candlepower, (outfield) 80 candlepower. *Turf:* Tifway Bermuda grass.

An architecturally attractive grandstand, with a small lower deck, and larger roofed upper deck, named after Pat Olsen (Class of 1923).

In 1985, the Olsen Field groundskeeper, Leo Goertz, received the NCAA Division I Groundskeeper of the Year award, an honor sponsored by

Collegiate Baseball and Diamond Dry. In 1987, Goertz was presented the Sports Turf Managers/Beam Clay Baseball Diamond of the Year award for excellence and professionalism in maintaining a baseball facility.

The small electronic scoreboard is in left field. The outfield fence is painted dark green. Painted in big white numbers are the distances, maybe the biggest distance markers anywhere.

Colorado Springs, Colorado

Sky Sox Stadium
Pacific Coast League 1988 (Sky Sox).
Location: Powers Boulevard, Barnes

Road. *Dimensions:* Left field, 335 feet; center field, 410 feet; right field, 335 feet. *Seating capacity:* 6000.
The Sky Sox had to play their first 20 games on the road while the stadium was completed. The team is the former Hawaii Islanders, transplanted by minor league entrepreneur Dave Elmore, who has pumped $1.5 million into the new park.

Columbia, South Carolina

Capital City Park

South Atlantic League 1946–57, 1960–61 (Reds), 1983–present (Mets). *Location:* 300 South Assembly Street, Dreyfus Road. *Dimensions:* Left field, 330 feet; center field, 395 feet; right field, 320 feet. *Seating capacity:* (1960) 3500; (1985) 2500. *1987 season attendance:* 92,855.
It can get very hot in Columbia. On Sunday, August 21, 1983, it was 107 degrees on the playing field in Capital City Park at game time.
No professional baseball was played in the ballpark from August 30, 1961, when the final Columbia Reds home game was rained out, until April 15, 1983, when—again under wet conditions—the new Columbia Mets bowed to the Greenwood Pirates on a Friday night. A crowd of 2217 showed up, with umbrellas, despite heavy competition from the South Carolina Gamecocks two blocks away.
The ballpark has been regularly upgraded since 1982. New seats, a new scoreboard, and a new outfield fence have been installed. Until 1960, there was a screen outfield fence. There are now advertisements painted on wooden boards out there.
During the years of no pro baseball in Columbia, the ballpark was home of American Legion and Little League ball—which it continues to be when the Mets are on the road. Grandstand and bleachers are very tiny.

Columbus, Georgia

Golden Park

Southern League 1972–present (Astros). *Location:* 100 4th Street. *Constructed:* 1951. *Dimensions:* Left field, 315 feet; center field, 415 feet; right field, 315 feet. *Seating capacity:* (1975) 6000; (1985) 5700. *1987 attendance:* 128,845.
In the 1940s Golden Park was home of a minor league club called the Cardinals. In the 1960s, it housed a farm club of the Yankees. During that time the outside of the Golden Park grandstand had the New York Yankees' emblem and the Confederate flag painted side by side.

Columbus, Ohio

A very poor field in the suburbs was the site of an 1867 game between the professional Washington Nationals, accompanied by famed baseball writer Henry Chadwick, and Columbus's best nine. Columbus started James Williams in the box, a man who later became secretary of the American Association. Williams lost 90–10 to the barnstormers. Ruined his earned run average for the whole year.
Williams was better suited for management. He formed the first professional baseball team in Columbus, the Buckeyes, in 1876, and organized the International Association the following year. He became known in Columbus as "Father of Minor League Baseball" and died a few days before the end of World War I.

Recreation Park

American Association 1883–84, 1889–91 (Discoverers), Ohio State League 1887, Tri-State League 1888 (Senators), Western League 1892, Inter-State League 1895 (Statesmen). *Location:* Parsons Avenue, Meadow Lane (now Monroe Street), 17th Street and Mound Street. *Seating capacity:* 6500

Top: *Right field fence of Capital City Park, Columbia, S.C. Note the obligatory Marlboro man above the double deck of signs toward center. (Compliments of the Columbia Mets.)* Bottom: *Golden Park, Columbus, Ga., in 1965 — home of the Yankees. (Compliments of the Columbus Astros.)*

(grandstand 5000, bleachers 1500). *First American Association game:* May 1, 1883 (Columbus Discoverers 6, Louisville Eclipse 5). *Torn down:* April 1900.

It was a beautiful summer afternoon in 1887, and Harry M. Stevens was going door to door along 17th Street in Columbus selling copies of *The Life of General Logan,* the biography of the popular Civil War general and Ohio politician, John A. Logan. Stevens' feet were telling him it was time to call it a day when he happened upon Recreation Park at game time.

Stevens, only five years before, had been a native resident of Derby, England. Now, along with his English wife and three children, Stevens had settled in Niles, Ohio, in the Mahoning Valley Steel district near Youngstown. He worked in a steel mill until it was closed by labor strikes, forcing him to hit the road. Now he sat and watched his first baseball game. Before long, he noticed something missing — the visiting ballplayers' faces were unfamiliar, and the faces of the Columbus Discoverers were often far away. It was difficult to tell who was playing where and who was batting when.

He conceived the scorecard.

In those parts, listings of the rosters

had been distributed at ballparks before, but never on a card with a grid so the game could be scored. (Stevens didn't technically invent the scorecard as, unbeknownst to him, scorecards had been printed and used in Philadelphia as early as 1866.)

Stevens went to work right away on his new idea. He sold advertising space on the card to pay for the printing—which was arranged through the ball club—and went on a one-man campaign to convince the baseball fans of Columbus that a game could not be enjoyed unless it was scored.

Wearing a red coat and a straw hat, Stevens barked his way through the grandstands—sometimes quoting Byron or Shakespeare, sometimes sticking to the basics. They all look the same without a scorecard. You can't know the players without a scorecard. Five cents.

The idea caught on beyond Stevens' wildest dreams. Soon he was selling scorecards in Wheeling, Pittsburgh, Toledo, and Milwaukee. A generation later, his son was selling soft drinks and peanuts to a widening circuit of concessionaire franchises.

Today, Harry M. Stevens, Inc., remains one of the largest ballpark concessionaire services in America. "Score-Card Harry" still has his name on many of the things sold in ballparks. In the 1986 New York Mets scorebook, Harry M. Stevens, Inc., is listed as the National Advertising Consultant.

In 1884, Columbus finished second in the American Association (behind the New York Metropolitans). Ace twirler was Ed Morris (34–13).

In 1890, Henry Gastright went 30–14 for Columbus, with an E.R.A. under 3.00, by far his best year in baseball.

Columbus Central Athletic Park

Western League 1896–99. Location: Parsons Avenue, Jenkins and Moler streets. First game: April 22, 1896 (Columbus 14, Grand Rapids 4, attendance 3000). Torn down: April 5,

1900.

Columbus fans abandoned this whole enterprise and with good reason. In mid-July, 1899, very quietly, as though hoping no one would notice, the Western League switched the Columbus franchise to Grand Rapids and the Grand Rapids team to Columbus, the idea being to get the better team into the better drawing market. Gone was local favorite Rube Waddell, who was on his way to winning 26 games that year, including seven in the big leagues for Louisville. Ten days and maybe four customers later Columbus lost their new team too, to Springfield, Ohio.

John Riley purchased a club in the Inter-State League for the following year and immediately started looking for a place for a new ballpark, determining Athletic Park to be too far away to draw well on weekdays. Riley worked out a lease with Robert Neil on land across from the Columbus Barracks (now Ft. Hayes) on Cleveland Avenue, signing it March 14, 1900. Then the Athletic Park stands were moved to the new site.

Neil Park

Inter-State League 1900 (Senators), Western Association 1901 (Senators), American Association 1902–32 (Senators). Location: Cleveland Avenue, Buckingham Street. Built: April 1900; 1905. Construction cost: (1905) $64,000. Record single day attendance: 20,531 (Columbus versus Toledo, 9/1/07 doubleheader). Record season attendance: 316,980 (1907). First game: April 15, 1900 (Columbus versus Connie Mack's Milwaukee American League team, exhibition, game played before stands completed). First Inter-State League game: Sunday, April 28, 1900 (Wheeling 14, Columbus 10).

On April 5, 1900, contractor John D. Evans tore down Athletic Park very carefully, in large sections which were left unharmed. These sections were loaded onto flatcars and hauled via the

Columbus Street Railway System to Cleveland Avenue and the site of the new ballpark. Columbus did not take to the Senators right away. Only the year before their experience in the Western League had left a bitter taste. Out of financial necessity, owner John Riley played all home games after August 22 in Anderson, Indiana. Columbus was back in 1901, in the same league with a new name, now called the Western Association. After the 1901 season, Columbus withdrew from the Western Association and joined the new American Association, where they stayed, here in Neil Park, another 30 years.

As was the case in the Polo Grounds and Baker Bowl and other stadiums, the clubhouse at Neil Park was in straightaway center field. The star of the 1902 team, Terry (Cotton Top) Turner, the best third baseman in the league, once hit two home runs in one game at Neil Park. Both went through the clubhouse door.

Originally, the playing field at Neil Park was laid out with home plate in the southeast corner. From the beginning of the 1905 season, and the debut of the new grandstand, home plate was moved to the southwest corner. The new grandstand, affordable after early success in the American Association, cost $64,000.

Until recent successes in the International League, Columbus had always considered as their greatest team the Senators of 1905, 1906, and 1907. They won the American Association pennant all three of those years. On September 1, 1907, 20,531 crammed into Neil Park to see the Senators sweep a doubleheader from Toledo. The 1907 season attendance was 316,980, a local record until 1977. Hitting star was outfielder Doc Gessler, who went on to be a real dentist and a football star for the Ohio Medical College Medics. Star pitcher was Heine Berger. Both Gessler and Berger went on to play major league ball.

Neil Park was used between 1902 and 1905 for four American League games, "home" field for Cleveland twice and Detroit twice. Current site of the Ross Laboratories, the house that Similac built.

Cooper Stadium (Redbird Stadium 1931-54, Jets Stadium 1955-71, Franklin County Stadium 1977-84) Negro National League 1931, 1933, 1935 (Buckeyes, Bluebirds, Elite Giants), Negro Southern League 1932 (Turfs), American Association 1932-54 (Redbirds), International League 1955-71 (Jets), 1977-present (Clippers). Site of Game 4 of the 1943 Negro League World Series. *Location:* 1155 West Mound Street, Glenwood Avenue. *Dimensions:* (Original) left field, 415 feet; center field, 450 feet; right center, 337 feet; right field, 315 feet. (Current) left field, 355 feet; center field, 400 feet; right field, 330 feet. *Fences:* Left field, 6 feet; center field, 8 feet; right field, 8 feet. *Turf:* (1931-83) grass, (1984-present) artificial. *Seating capacity:* (1960) 12,000, (1985) 15,000. *Single game attendance record:* 20,131 (July 17, 1980, versus the Rochester Red Wings). *Season attendance record:* 599,544 (1979). *1987 season attendance:* 570,599. *First game:* June 3, 1932 (Columbus 11, Louisville 2). *First night game:* June 17, 1932 (Columbus 5, St. Paul 4, 11 innings).

The St. Louis Cardinals gained controlling interest of the Columbus team February 12, 1931. New president Larry MacPhail recognized a need for new grounds and chose Sunshine Park as his site. The new stadium on West Mound was considered one of the best in the minor leagues. In left field, there was a big hand-operated scoreboard that gave American Association scores. This was flanked by advertisement billboards and two auxiliary scoreboards that gave American and National League line scores.

Opening Day. On Friday, June 3, 1932, the Columbus Redbirds beat

Louisville 11–2 in the first game at Red-bird Stadium. In attendance were commissioner of baseball Judge Kenesaw Mountain Landis, Thomas J. Hickey, president of the American Association, and Branch Rickey, general manager of the Cardinals. Kenny Ash was the winning pitcher.

The first night game at Redbird Stadium was played two weeks later, Friday, June 17, 1932. Over 20,000 fans packed the park. Paul Dean, Pete Fowler and Ash shared the pitching duties. With the game tied 4–4 in the bottom of the eleventh inning, Ash won his own ball game by lining a single off the glove of St. Paul second baseman Irv Jeffries.

Currently, Columbus has led the International League in attendance for many years in a row, regularly drawing between 500,000 and 600,000 per season.

In 1981, the Clippers won their third consecutive International League pennant and Governor's Cup (the league's post-season playoff).

In 1984 the park was renamed after former Franklin County commissioner and current president and commissioner of the alliance (the International League and the American Association put together.) The park now has artificial turf — and that automatically means it's not as nice there as it used to be.

Behind the right field fence is the George P. Dysart Memorial Park, presented to the club as a gift from Mrs. Hester Dysart in 1978. Dysart was the former chairman of the Board of Directors for the Columbus Jets. The park's walkways form a small, stylized baseball diamond.

Cooperstown, New York

Abner Doubleday Field

Site of Hall of Fame games 1940–present. *Location:* Susquehanna Street (right field), Main Street (first

base), Pioneer Street (third base), Elm Street (left field). *Dimensions:* Left field, 296 feet; left center, 390 feet; center field, 385 feet; right center, 350 feet; right field, 312 feet. 30 feet from home plate to the backstop. *Fences:* Left field, 17 feet; right field, 10 feet.

Elihu Phinney's cow pasture has a concrete wall in right, a wood and wire screen fence in left. The field is built on the site of the Doubleday myth, partially using money donated by Tom Yawkey. The grandstand is brick. Used very seldom: for the Hall of Fame game of course, and sometimes for semi-pro ball. In 1942, the war forced the Quebec Athletics of the Canadian-American League to use Doubleday Field for spring training.

Coral Gables, Florida

Mark Light Stadium (The Light)

Home of the University of Miami Hurricanes (Independent Division I) 1973–present. *Location:* University of Miami campus. *Dimensions:* Left field, 330 feet; left center, 365 feet; center field, 400 feet; right center, 365 feet; right field, 330 feet. *Seating capacity:* 5000. *Record season attendance:* 163,261 (1981, NCAA record). *First game:* February 16, 1973 (University of Miami 5, Florida State University 1, attendance: 4235).

In 1971, local businessman George Light donated $100,000 to the University of Miami to build a baseball park. The park was dedicated in February 1973, to Light's son Mark, who was a victim of muscular dystrophy. During the first game ever played at Mark Light Field the Hurricanes executed a triple play.

Since then there has been a constant upgrading of the park, with the help of further donations by Light and others. An electronic scoreboard was installed late in the 1973 season. In 1976, a grandstand was built and the name of the park was changed to Mark Light Stadium.

Top: *Doubleday Field, Cooperstown, N.Y., in the snow, January 1988. (Photo by David Pietrusza.)* Bottom: *Doubleday in the bright sunshine of June 1988. (Photo by MacIntyre Symms.)*

As late as 1985, new improvements were being added. New locker rooms and offices were built, VIP seating was installed along the first base side, and additional radio and TV booth space was added.

In 1981, the former San Diego Chicken made his first appearance at an amateur event in Mark Light Stadium. The Hurricanes drew 163,261 to Mark Light Stadium in 1981, an NCAA record and a figure most minor league ballclubs would be more than satisfied with.

Cornwall, Ontario

Cornwall Athletic Grounds

Canadian-American League 1937– early 1940s (Royals, Bisons). *Built:* 1908. *Dimensions:* Left field, 360 feet; center field, 407 feet; right field, 400 feet. *Seating capacity:* 3000. *First night game:* July 6, 1937 (attendance: 1600).

A farm team of the Buffalo Bisons moved into the Athletic Grounds in the paper mill town of Cornwall after leaving Perth.

A traveling secretary for the Amsterdam Rugmakers remembered coming to the Athletic Grounds for games against Cornwall this way: "I don't know if the paper mills let out the sludge at night or what—but the ballpark stunk to high heaven. It was horrible."

Corvallis, Oregon

Coleman Field

Home of the Oregon State University Beavers (Pac-10 Conference, Northern Division) 1973–present. *Location:* Oregon State University campus. *Dimensions:* Left field, 355 feet; left center, 385 feet; center field, 400 feet; right center, 365 feet; right field, 330 feet. *Fences:* Left field, 20 feet; center field, 6 feet; right field, 6 feet. *Turf:* grass. *Seating capacity:* 2000. *Renovated:* 1983.

In 1981, this ballpark's name was changed to honor Ralph Coleman, coach of the OSU Beavers 1923–31 and 1938–66. Coleman compiled a 560–317 record (.639) during those years. During the 1983 renovation, funded by alumni donations, seats were covered with orange plastic and the entire seating area was paved. The Beavers play well at home. They were 183–59 (.756) here between 1973 and 1987.

Covington, Kentucky

Federal League Baseball Park
(Riverbreeze Park)

Federal League 1913 (Blue Sox). *Location:* Second and Scott streets. *Seating capacity:* 6000. *Groundbreaking:* April 16, 1913. *First game:* May 8, 1913.

In January, 1913, baseball fans with money from Covington and Newport applied for a Blue Grass League franchise—a request vetoed by the Cincinnati Reds. Covington and Newport were what would today be called suburbs of Cincinnati, just across the Ohio River, and the Reds invoked a clause in the organized baseball agreement giving an existing team veto rights over

any team attempting to operate within a five-mile radius. Six miles out, it was okay. The Covington businessmen did not give up. In March, they gave their pitch to the outlaw Federal League, an organization that did not abide by the baseball establishment's territorial restrictions. At first, Covington's chances seemed remote, even though the Federal League was still a year away from considering itself "major."

The city did not have a suitable ballpark. Proposed owner William Weierich said he would operate the franchise out of Cincinnati, at the Hippodrome Park there. That plan fell through—and the team switched back to Covington, where businessmen William Reidlin, president of Bavarian Brewery, and R.C. Stewart, president of Stewart Iron Works, raised $12,500 in capital stock for a park. Covington was officially granted a Federal League franchise.

The new Covington team incorporated under the name Covington Amusement Company. Sam Long was named business manager. Charles Eugene Clark, vice president of People's Savings Bank and Trust Company; Polk Lafoon, secretary of the C.N. and C. Street Railway Company; and architect Bernard Wisenall were selected to find a nice place for the new ballpark. With the start of the Federal League's 120-game schedule less than a month away, they picked part of Riverbreeze Park.

On April 14, Long was replaced as business manager by John A. Spinney. Two days later ground was broken at Second and Scott streets, and bleachers were built to hold 4200 at the southwest corner of that block. On April 17, Spinney named as the Covington manager "former twirler of the Pittsburgh Nationals" Sam Leever. Ball club stockholders commissioned P.J. Carroll and R.J. Dibowski to travel from town to town searching for players to sign. Tryouts were held at Crowe's ballpark, last stop on the Elberton car line in Price Hill.

By April 18, you could see the way the diamond was going to lie upon the land, and the grandstand was rising on the northwest corner of the site, with an entrance off Second Street. Real estate offices were closed Opening Day. Ticket prices ranged from a quarter to a dollar. The Blue Sox started the season on the road, and returned for the home opener with a winning record.

The grandstand was finished just in time. Seating capacity had been enlarged from the original plan of 4200 to 6000. Stories in the papers predicted the Blue Sox hitters would be "hammering the ball to the far corners of the lot," while on the mound there would be "twirling . . . replete with benders of every description."

Opening Day. The streets of Covington were lined with thousands of people. The parade commenced at Scott and 12th streets, and made its way to the ballpark via Madison and Fifth. In the ballpark bands were playing. Bombs containing tiny American flags were burst overhead. A young girl stood on the pitcher's mound beneath a canopy of American shields. She held a bouquet of roses in one hand, a gold ball in the other. Twelve carrier pigeons were released to wing news of Covington's ballpark splendor to the state capitals of the Midwest. The day's newspaper headline read "Covington Goes Baseball Crazy." The crowd at the ballpark was too big for the stands. Fans lined the edge of the playing field all the way around. Balls hit into the spectators were ground rule singles. Everyone went home happy, too. Blue Sox twirler Walter Justus shut out St. Louis 4-0.

The initial fanaticism didn't last. In fact, Covington lost interest and stopped going to the ballpark almost immediately. It had been a fad.

On June 19, 1913, a letter appeared in the *Kentucky Post* begging fans to come out and watch the Blue Sox play, saying Covington could still replace Cincinnati on the baseball map despite the inadequate ballpark.

On June 25, the Covington Amusement Company announced the team would leave town because of low attendance. The Blue Sox record was 21–31, fourth place in a six-team league, when the franchise shifted to Kansas City mid-season.

The old ballpark was used for many years by area youngsters as a playground, and is currently the site of the Gateway Motel.

Covington Ball Park

Home of Knothole baseball, plus touring attractions, until 1959. *Location:* Pike Street and Willow Run (current site of Interstate 75). *Dimensions:* Left field, 310 feet; left center, 335 feet; center field, 368 feet; right center, 372 feet; right field, 330 feet. Measurements reflect distances to fences, not to the base of sharp inclines. *Seating capacity:* 2500.

Built cozily at the base of a hill, the Covington Ball Park during the fifties was an all-purpose facility for community activities. It had three grandstands, two long ones the length of the baseline on either side, and a small one behind home. All three were roofed. Looking heavy atop the tiny grandstand behind home was the press box, which was slightly longer than the grandstand upon which it sat.

Perhaps the most interesting thing about the ballpark was its outfield terrain. The original green monster was in left, a steep cliff of grass-covered earth with a fence on top. This cliff tapered down to a rolling hill in straightaway center, atop of which sat the scoreboard, donated to the park by the Bavarian Brewing Company, maker of Bavarian Old Style, "A Man's Beer." In the fence behind that scoreboard was a hole large enough for a kid to crawl through. The field had lights and had once hosted a game by the Indianapolis Clowns, a touring baseball team patterned after the Harlem Globetrotters,

with young Henry Aaron in the outfield. (Another such touring black team
to play here was the Twenty Counts.)
Restrooms were under the grandstand
on the first base side.

It was not a pretentious place. The
groundskeeper and the concessions
man were the same guy. Pop Mulberry
would stop drawing in the batter's
boxes, come over to fix someone a hot
dog, then go back to linemaking.

In 1953, the Covington Ball Park was
looking pretty run down, so Mayor
John J. Moloney asked local flam-
boyant bachelor and entrepreneur Colonel Jake Wolking to take over operation of the ballpark. Wolking saw that
the park got a fresh coat of paint. His
workmen put in a new sod, new fences,
a refreshment stand, electric iceboxes
and showers in the locker room.

Wolking, as was his style, began to
use the ballpark imaginatively. The
King Brothers Circus performed there.
There were boxing matches. There was
even female mud wrestling, a concept
ahead of its time. And the charge to get
in was always the same. It was a buck
a head, 50 cents for a kid.

Covington Ball Park thrived until
1959, when highway engineers turned it
into I-75.

Dallas, Texas

Gaston Park
Texas League 1886-1918 (off and on).
Location: Second and Parry streets,
current location of the Texas State
Fairgrounds' Music Hall.

Gardner Park (I)
Texas League 1919-24 (Giants,
Steers). *Location:* Oak Cliff section,
Jefferson Boulevard and Comal Street,
down the street from the Texas The-
ater. Burned July 19, 1924 (after a
Steers game).

Gardner Park (II) (also known as
Steers Park, Rebels Park 1939-47,
Burnett Field 1948, Eagles Stadium
1949-50)
Texas League 1924-65 (Giants,
Steers, Rebels, Eagles). *Location:*
Across the street from Gardner Park
(I). 1500 E. Jefferson Boulevard (first
base), Brazos Street (third base), Col-
orado Boulevard (right field). *Seating
capacity:* (1924) 7000; (1965) 10,571.
Dimensions: Left field, 325 feet; center
field, 382 feet; right field, 335 feet.
Burned: September 10, 1940. *Reopened
and dedicated:* July 29, 1941.

Sitting in the stands at this house of
many names, fans saw the Trinity River
flowing by, just beyond the left field
fence.

The Cotton Bowl
Texas League 1950 (Eagles). Site of
home opener April 11, 1950 (attendance
53,578, then a minor league record).
Location: Second Avenue, in the Texas
State Fairgrounds.

Most of the record crowd was there
to see Ty Cobb, who made a rare playing appearance in an old-timers' game
before the Texas League contest.

Danville, Virginia

League Park
Virginia League circa 1900 (Tobac-
coists). *Seating capacity:* 3500.

Stonewall Jackson Park
Virginia League circa 1910 (Leafs).
Seating capacity: 2000.

Darby, Pennsylvania *see* Yeadon,
Pennsylvania

---

*The Covington (Ky.) Federal League Baseball Park as it appeared in the teens.
(Photo supplied by the Kenyon County Public Library.)*

Davenport, Iowa

John O'Donnell Stadium (Municipal Stadium)
Home of professional baseball in Davenport since 1931. Midwest League 1960-present (Quad-City Angels). *Location:* At the foot of Gaines Street off U.S. Route 61, along the waterfront of the Mississippi River. *Dimensions:* Left field, 350 feet; center field, 380 feet; right field, 350 feet. *Seating capacity:* (1960) 6200; (1985) 8500. *1987 season attendance:* 60,999. *First night game:* June 4, 1931.

For almost 60 years it's been so nice, so nice in the summer . . . sitting on the third base side, looking toward first, the Mississippi rolling by, spanned by a seemingly endless bridge. The city of Davenport is built on low, rolling hills in extreme Eastern Iowa, at the junction between the Mississippi and Rock rivers.

On January 21, 1930, the Levee Improvement Commission, an organization determined to turn the riverside dump into a landmark the city of Davenport could be proud of, and the American Legion, represented by a group headed by George Decker French, met to discuss the building of a Municipal Auditorium on the levee "in the nature of a memorial to all service men."

By September 8 of that year, $60,000 in bonds were allocated. Before they were through, over $150,000 would be spent on the project.

They had no way of knowing, of course, that, if they had been able to go without a ballpark for another five years, Roosevelt's WPA probably would have built one for them.

Plans originally called for a grandstand seating 3000, plus three movable stands, but soon escalated. The more planning that was done the bigger the plans got. Mr. Blandings builds his dream stadium.

On November 4, architectural services were contracted. By December 5, low bidders had been determined for construction. They were Tunnicliff Construction Company, $96,360; Ryan Plumbing and Heating, $9195; Raymond Concrete Pile Company (concrete), $10,500; and R.D. Speers Company (electrical work), $4062.

There were several changes over the next few months in the number of bleacher seats and the number of seats with backs. Plans were to open the park in the spring. After some debate, lights were included and built by Tri-City Electric for $17,829.44. The dedication of the park was held on May 26, 1931. A 25-piece band played. A cinder walk linked the new athletic field with LeClair Park. The stands overlooked the river. The curve of the outfield fence was in contour with the river bank. Though there was some parking between the river and the outfield fence, the stone levee made it look as if the river had been carved to fit the ballpark, as if the power of baseballs driven toward the fences had forced the river to bend outward.

In the next few years the stadium would be used for the National Junior Olympics, boxing, St. Ambrose College football games, and the Centennial Pageant.

The Levee Improvement Commission operated Municipal Stadium until 1953, when the Davenport Park Board took over. In 1960, the park was leased to the Quad-City Baseball Fan Association who instituted Class A baseball, circuses, high school football, and music concerts. In 1970, the name of the park was changed to John O'Donnell Stadium in tribute to the sports editor of the *Davenport Times-Democrat*.

In 1986, Quad-City drew 116,062 fans. Following the 1987 season, the ballpark began a $2.3 million renovation project. Until then, it was the same as in 1931.

The brick grandstand—single-decked with obstructing poles—does not make it as far as first and third, and there

John O'Donnell Stadium, Davenport, Ia. (Compliments of the Quad-City Angels.)

are bleachers, equally high, attached to the third base side. On the first base side, there are few seats past the dugout. The sign, carved into rock across the entrance to the park, still reads Municipal Stadium.

The park has two rows of box seats. So nice in the summer...

Dayton, Ohio

Fairview Park

Location: North Main and Fairview streets.

Used in June 1902 as the neutral site for an American League game between Cleveland and Baltimore. The North Main streetcar crossed the north end of the park.

Westwood Field

Negro National League 1920, 1926 (Marcos). Location unknown.

Right field was enclosed by a high brick wall.

North Side Park

Central League, Mid-Atlantic League 1933-34. *Seating capacity:* 3500.

Hudson Field (Young's Field 1931-33, West Side Park 1934, Ducks Park 1935-45)

Mid-Atlantic League 1934-42 (Ducks). *Location:* West of Roosevelt High School, West Third Street, between Kilmore and Ardmore streets. *First used for baseball:* 1931. *Grandstand constructed:* 1934. *Seating capacity:* 3500.

Since it has been a part of the William H. Young Estate, this was called Young's Field during the early years of the Depression. The field was part of an undeveloped tract of land when the Kessler Athletic Club first improved it for baseball in the spring of 1931. The manager of the Kessler team owned the field and sold the land to the new Mid-Atlantic League franchise, the Ducks, in 1933 so they could build Dayton's new ballpark. Fans would arrive via the Third Street cars. The grandstand was constructed under the supervision of Ducks owner Howard "Ducky" Holmes in 1934.

The Brooklyn Dodgers took over operation of the park in 1939, and ran things until 1942 when World War II all but ended minor league baseball.

After that, local sports promoter

Elwood Parsons ran the park for a while, and finally, the city of Dayton bought it and used it for local amateur ball.

In 1945, the park was rededicated Hudson Field, in honor of Sergeant Ben Hudson, killed in action near the end of the war.

Daytona Beach, Florida

City Island Park
Florida State League 1936-41, 1946-66, 1968-present (Islanders). *Dimensions:* Left field, 315 feet; center field, 400 feet; right field, 325 feet. *Seating capacity:* (1960) 3000; (1985) 4500.

In 1947, Islanders' General Manager Grover Hartley bought pitcher Elwin "Stubby" Stablefeld for $25. The pitcher lost 21 games that year, but won 28 in 1948. Both figures represent Florida State League records. Not waiting for the tide to turn again, Hartley was sold for $5000, and the money went toward the building of much-needed third base seats. The new seats were called "Stablefeld Bleachers" and stood until the 1970s, when they were replaced by the current stands. Shade seats are on the first base side, bleachers along third base. Ballpark is really on an island.

Decatur, Illinois

In 1866, Judge William C. Johns, just back from the Civil War, started a team called the McPhersons (named after Union officer General James Birdseye McPherson) who played their games on a diamond at the future site of the Wabash freight house.

According to county historian O.T. Banton, "Other early diamonds were developed east of the Illinois Central railroad tracks between East William and North streets; in the general area of Milliken Place just west of Pine Street, and one just west of Oakland Avenue approximately where Eisner's supermarket is located."

Downing Racetrack
Three-I League circa 1901 (Commodores). *Seating capacity:* 4500. Served both baseball and harness racing.

Name of park unknown
Three-I League circa 1909 (Commodores). *Location:* North Broadway, Garfield Avenue.

Staley Field
Three-I League circa 1915 (Commodores). *Location:* Eldorado and 22nd streets.

Fan's Field
Three-I League 1924-50 (Commodores), Midwest League 1956-72. *Location:* East Garfield and North Woodford streets. *Built:* 1924. *Construction cost:* $50,000+. *Dimensions:* Left field, 340 feet; center field, 370 feet; right field, 340 feet. *Seating capacity:* 4500. *Torn down:* 1975.

The grandstand is gone but the field is still used for softball.

Denver, Colorado

Merchants Park
Western League, before 1948. *Location:* Virginia Avenue, Bannock Street, Broadway.

Mile High Stadium (Bears Stadium 1948-68)
American Association 1948-present (Bears, Zephyrs). Former home of the United States Football League's Denver Gold. Current home to the National Football League's Broncos. *Location:* Interstate 25, Routes 88 and 287, and Routes 40, 287, and 70. Clay Street (left field), West 20th Street (third base), Elliot Street (first base), West 17th Street (right field). Built adjacent to the McNichols Sports Arena, home of the National Basketball Association's Nuggets. *Constructed:* 1948. *Dimensions:* Left field, 348 feet; left center, 395 feet; center field, 420 feet;

Top: *City Island Park, Daytona Beach, Fla. (Compliments of the city of Daytona Beach.)* Bottom: *Mile High Stadium, Denver, Colo.*

right center, 400 feet; right field, 366 feet. *Surface:* grass. *Seating capacity:* (1960) 19,000, (1975) 43,103, (1985) 75,123. (66,000 concert seating, 23,000 moveable seats can be arranged in football, soccer or baseball configurations). *1987 American Association season attendance:* 314,549. *Press box capacity:* 50–300. *Parking:* 5500 spaces.

When the park was first built it was single-decked, with seats to the corners, with a rounded outfield fence of uniform height. A second and third deck were added on the right side in

1968, on the left in 1976, and across the outfield in 1977, all to accommodate pro football crowds.

The ballpark is easily accessible from downtown Denver via the new Colfax Viaduct finished in 1986. Some seats offer a view of the Denver skyline.

Des Moines, Iowa

Name of park unknown
Western League (Class A) 1900–37.
First night game: May 2, 1930.

Sec Taylor Stadium, Des Moines, Ia. (Compliments of the Iowa Cubs.)

In late 1929, team president E. Lee Keyser announced, during a speech at the annual National Association convention, that he intended to host the first regular season official league night game. He came in second, beaten to the punch by Independence, Kansas, of the Western Association. Independence played their first night game on April 28, 1930. Des Moines opened the season on the road and didn't get to play theirs until May 2.

Sec Taylor Stadium (Pioneer Memorial Stadium, 1947–59)
American Association, midseason 1969–present (Cubs). *Constructed:* 1947 by the Chamber of Des Moines. *Location:* Junction of the Raccoon and Des Moines rivers. Elm Street (left field), SW Second Street (third base), Riverside Park (first base), SW First Street (right field). *Dimensions:* Left field, 330 feet; center field, 400 feet; right field, 330 feet. *Seating capacity:* (1975) 5000; (1985) 7500. *1987 season attendance:* 257,857.

The ballpark is near downtown at the junction of the Raccoon and Des Moines rivers. The Raccoon flows behind the first base stands, while the Des Moines crosses the entire outfield,

flowing from left to right.

Park was built by the Chamber of Des Moines, then turned over to the city. Since September 1, 1959, Pioneer Stadium has been known as Sec Taylor Stadium in honor of Garner W. (Sec) Taylor, a longtime sports editor for the *Des Moines Register and Tribune.* Taylor died February 26, 1965, at 78. He served as sports editor for 50 years.

The ballpark has changed since 1959. In 1982, new owners reshaped the outfield fence and added new locker rooms. The previous locker rooms had been under the grandstand. New bleachers were added.

High school, college and even Japanese Olympic baseball have been played here. Exhibition games between major and minor league clubs have also taken place. In 1986 and 1987, Sec Taylor Stadium was used for summer concerts.

Detroit, Michigan

Recreation Park
National League 1881–88 (Wolverines). *Location:* Willis, John R, Beaubien and Brady streets (Brady no longer there) and Alexanderine Avenue East,

where Brush Street is now. *First game:* May 2, 1881. *Last game:* September 22, 1888.

Recreation Park had a small roofed wooden grandstand behind home, extending past third base and into left field, but only halfway up the first base line. Along the remainder of the right field foul line were simple wooden bleachers. Neither the grandstand nor the bleachers went more than thirteen rows high at any point. On crowded days fans encircled the outfield, with the carriages and horses kept in deep right. There were no outfield fences, and fans stood as close to the outfielders' backs as authorities would allow. The field was so big that a cricket game could be played at the north end while a baseball game was played in the south. The press box was on the roof of the grandstand, twenty feet off the ground, on the third base side. Fans sometimes climbed atop buildings and scaffolding behind the right field bleachers for a view of the proceedings below. Light-colored and dark-banded boaters could be seen in the crowd. The number of broad-brimmed boaters (among the more staid derbys of a nearly past era) was ever increasing during the 1880s.

The Wolverines were operated out of the mayor's office. Hizzoner W.G. Thompson was president of the team. Although the team never finished higher than fourth during its first five seasons in the National League, it did feature some of the major stars of its day — outfielder Ned Hanlon and ill-fated catcher Charley Bennett. Next to Buck Ewing, Bennett was the era's best catcher, and is credited with being the first to wear a chest protector outside his uniform.

Following the 1884 season, Thompson became tired of his club's mediocre finishes, and decided to spend big bucks to shore up the troops. He shelled out $8000 to Buffalo in exchange for their "Big Four" infield of Dan Brouthers, Hardy Richardson, Jack Rowe, and Deacon White. The new players helped the Wolverines rise to a second place finish in 1886 — and then to the National League pennant in 1887.

That year Detroit played a 15-game "World Series" against St. Louis, winners of the American Association championship. Detroit won the series ten games to five. Played in barnstorm style, the series covered ten cities before the final game (October 26, in Chicago, attendance 659) was called in the sixth inning because of the cold.

The Wolverines never managed to make much money, and Detroit withdrew from the National League following a fifth place finish in 1888. The franchise moved to Cleveland. That was the end of play at Recreation Park, and the end of major league baseball for Detroit until 1901.

Name of park unknown

Western League 1894–99 (Tigers). *Location:* Helen Avenue and Champlain Street (now Lafayette Boulevard), near Detroit's eastern boundary.

Although Detroit never finished higher than third during their stint in the Western League — Ban Johnson's league, soon to be the American League — this was a time of great historical interest to Detroit. It was in 1895, with the team playing out on the eastern city limits, that the headline writers of the *Detroit Free Press* began calling the team "Tigers" because of their brown and black striped socks.

Burns Park

American League 1900–09 (Tigers, Sundays only). *Location:* Dix, Vernon and Waterman streets at Livernois Avenue, near the stockyards in Springwells Township just past the Detroit city line. *First American League (major league) game:* April 28, 1901.

There were no Sunday baseball games played at Bennett Park until 1910 because of Detroit's strict blue laws, so the Tigers crossed the western city limits to play. Named after Tigers president George D. Burns.

BASE BALL GAME
PLAYED AT
RECREATION PARK DETROIT, MICH.
ON
JUNE 19, 1886
BETWEEN DETROIT & CHICAGO

13 INNINGS WERE PLAYED ENDING IN A SCORE OF 1 TO 0
IN FAVOR OF THE HOME TEAM. RECREATION PARK
WAS LOCATED WHERE BRUSH ST. IS NOW BETWEEN
BRADY ST. AND ALEXANDERINE AVE. EAST.

Recreation Park, Detroit, Mich., 1886. (Used with permission from the Detroit Public Library.)

Tiger Stadium (Bennett Park 1900–1911, Navin Field 1912–37, Briggs Stadium 1938–60) American League 1900–present (Tigers). Owned by the Detroit Tigers. *Location:* Michigan Avenue (first base), National Avenue (third base), Kaline Drive [formerly Cherry Street] (left field), Trumbull Avenue (right field). Before 1911, home plate was in what is currently the right field corner. Previous site of the Haymarket and then Woodbridge Grove. *Refurbished, renovated or enlarged:* 1908, 1910, 1911–12, 1923, 1938. *Dimensions:* Left field, 340 feet; left center, 365 feet; center field, 440 feet; right center, 370 feet; right field, 325 feet. 66 feet from home plate to the backstop. *Seating capacity:* (1900–07) 8500; (1908–09) 10,500; (1910) 13,500; (1911–22) 23,000; (1923–37) 29,000; (1938–present) 54,220, broken down as follows: boxes, 10,335; reserved, 21,172; general admission, 11,502; bleacher, 11,211. *Season low attendance record:* 203,719 (1918). *Season high attendance:* 2,704,794 (1984). *First game:* April 19, 1900 (Buffalo 8,

Detroit 0). *First American League game:* April 25, 1901. *First night game:* 1948. *Designated a state historical site:* 1976.

Home of Charley Gehringer, Hal Newhouser, Al Kaline, Mark "The Bird" Fidrych ... and, of course, the orneriest of critters, Ty Cobb!

Bennett Park. Bennett Park was located in the Eighth Ward of Detroit in an Irish neighborhood called Corktown. The park was named after Charley Bennett, the catcher for the Detroit Wolverines 1881–88, who'd lost his legs in a train accident. The accident occurred in Wellsville, Kansas, just a few miles from Lawrence, when Bennett got off the train to speak to a friend. Within weeks of the accident he wrote a letter to *The Sporting Life* that said he was looking "forward to the time when I can stumble around with artificial limbs."

When Bennett Park opened, there was a planing mill between the right field wall and Cherry Street. The park was considered a rickety little place, even by the era's comparatively shabby

Tiger Stadium, Detroit, Mich. (Compliments of the Detroit Tigers.)

standards. It had the smallest seating capacity in the major leagues — only about 8500, not including the wildcat bleachers jerry-built on the other side of the outfield fence on land owned by the mill, where folks sat for anywhere from a nickel to 15 cents depending on the importance of the game.

Fans sat in a long grandstand along third, and a shorter pavilion on the first base side that went three-quarters of the way into the right field corner. There were long and shallow bleachers in both right and left fields. (It was from these bleachers that Walter O. Briggs, born February 27, 1877, learned baseball. In 1927, he became half-owner of the Tigers.)

The playing field itself was a mess. Not enough fill had been put on top of the cobblestone haymarket that used to be there. After being the haymarket, the land was the Woodbridge Grove. Cobblestones from the haymarket still poked up here and there through the dirt and grass, even in the infield, making grounders an adventure. The clubhouse was in the far corner of center field. It was for the Tigers, of course.

As per the custom of the day, no facilities were provided for visitors.

On Opening Day, 1903, the players and 500 Elks marched across the field, and the first ball was thrown out by the city's mayor.

Until 1910, Bennett Park was used on weekdays only, because of blue laws. (*See* Burns Park.)

Ty Cobb played his first game for Detroit on August 30, 1905. All in all, he played 3033 games as a Tiger. He once broke up a no-hitter with a bunt. That's just plain mean.

In 1907 the Tigers bought the mill property behind center and moved the fences back. The move didn't have anything to do with home run distances. They wanted to make room for more spectators to stand. That year, on August 12, 11,500 crammed into Bennett Park to see Rube Waddell and the A's beat the Tigers 7-3.

For the start of the 1908 season the ballpark was refurbished and enlarged, work supervised by part-owner Frank J. Navin over the winter. The park now seated over 10,000. Including the standees, 14,051 showed up for Opening

Day. Cobb went 3-for-6 and drove in two runs, but the Tigers lost to Cleveland 9–3, in 12 innings.

An area in front of the plate—soaked by the grounds crew to snuff out that part of Cobb's bunts that the backspin hadn't already killed—became known as Cobb's Lake.

Before the 1910 season, Navin again enlarged Bennett Park, this time adding 3000 more seats. All of the grandstand seats were still in foul territory.

There were three grandstands, one behind the infield, and two small ones in the corners. The only uncovered seats were a small set of bleachers in right center, nestled into the corner of Cherry and Trumbull.

Navin Field. Then Navin got tired of adding onto deteriorating Bennett Park. He decided to tear the whole thing down and start over. During construction, between the 1911 and 1912 seasons, the field was reoriented so that home plate was where left field had been.

By March of 1912, almost all of the new steel and concrete stands were finished. The construction of the new park cost $500,000. The new seating capacity was 23,000.

Now the Tigers had a ballpark they could be proud of. The stands behind the infield were roofed and single-decked. Between the grandstand and the outfield fences were covered pavilions. The bleachers were out in right field. The outfield wall in left was made of concrete, painted green and kept free of advertisements. There were now dressing rooms for both the home and visiting teams, because of Ban Johnson's rule. As of 1912, visiting teams had to dress on the baseball grounds. No more circus parades.

The new park was named Navin Field. Frank J. Navin had been with the team since 1902, the year Burns sold the Tigers to insurance man Samuel F. Angus. Angus brought along his bookkeeper named Navin, a student of law and business. Navin began to invest his

money in Tiger stock. When he owned half the club he became president.

The next enlargement came before the 1923 season when a second deck stretching from first to third gave Navin Field a seating capacity of 30,000. The Opening Day crowd was 36,000. On Sunday, May 13, 40,884 crammed in there to see George "Hooks" Dauss whip the Yanks for his sixth straight win.

Navin got to see the Tigers become the 1935 World Champions, then promptly died that fall at 64 of a heart attack while horseback riding.

Walter Briggs first invested into the team to help sign Mickey Cochrane as catcher-manager in 1934. Cochrane's career was eventually ended by a near-fatal beaning. Briggs soon ran the show.

Briggs Stadium. After the 1937 season, Navin Field was completely rebuilt, and at last it looked as it does today. To honor the man who had succeeded Frank Navin as president of the Tigers, Walter Briggs, the ballpark was named Briggs Stadium.

During the 1937–38 reconstruction, the distance from home to right was considerably shortened. Until '37, it was 370 feet to the fence down the right field line. Dead center had been 467 feet, shorter when the crowd was big, as that was where auxiliary bleachers were constructed. By 1938, the stadium had a seating capacity of 53,000.

Tiger Stadium did not have lights installed until 1948, the last in the American League.

The highest structure "in play" in baseball at one time was the flagpole at Tiger Stadium, whose top is 125 feet above the playing surface. Hypothetically, balls hitting the top of that pole and bouncing back onto the lawn below had to be fielded. Now balls hitting the flagpole above a certain point are ground rule homers.

The overhang of the upper deck, and the inviting power alleys, make Tiger Stadium more of a hitters' park than

Tiger Stadium, Detroit, Mich. (Compliments of the Michigan Travel Commission.)

ever in these days of the rabbit ball and corked bats. Next to the 1961 Yankees, the 1987 Tigers hit more home runs than any team in major league history.

On February 1, 1977, a fire destroyed the press box, which took $600,000 to replace. Later that year, the team invested another half million dollars into a "multi-vapor lighting system," and the stadium was sold by owner John E. Fetzer to the city of Detroit for one dollar, then leased back to the Tigers for 30 years with a 30-year renewal option.

By 1980 the seats had been replaced with new blue and orange plastic seats, there were structural improvements on the stadium itself, and a new $2 million scoreboard had been installed. Over the next few years the outside of the stadium was covered with an off-white and blue metal siding, with a band of blue spectra glaze block to highlight the street level. The renovation was completed in 1983.

In 1986 Detroit mayor Coleman A. Young called for the replacement of Tiger Stadium with a dome. He repeated his suggestion the following year, adding that the dome should be built near the present site of Tiger

Stadium. He estimated the cost at $150 million.

By 1987, Tiger Stadium was again in need of renovation. The *Detroit Free Press* took a poll of readers and found that two-thirds of their sample wanted the Tigers to remain at Tiger Stadium, rather than move to a new facility.

Mack Park

Negro National League 1920–31 (Stars). *Location:* Mack Avenue and Fairview Street, currently the site of the Fairview Greens Apartments.

Hamtramck Stadium (Keyworth Stadium)

Negro East-West League 1932 (Wolves), Negro National League 1933 (Stars). *Location:* Hamtramck, Michigan (suburban Detroit). Joseph Campau, Berris, Dan, Gallagher, and Roosevelt streets. *Dimensions:* Configured for football.

DeQuindre Park (Cubs Park, Linton Field)

Negro American League 1937 (Stars). *Location:* DeQuindre Avenue, Modern, Orleans and Riopelle streets — near Six Mile Road.

Sportsman's Park

Negro American League 1937 (Stars, one game). *Location:* Livernois Avenue, Burkhouse Street.

Dubuque, Iowa

26th Street Field (later Olinger Park, Comiskey Field)

Northwestern League 1879–81. *Location:* 24th, 26th and Jackson streets. *Seating capacity:* 2000.

According to a *Dubuque Herald-Tribune* photo caption on July 11, 1958, in a comment most likely based on hearsay, the park "had no equal anywhere in the country—Chicago parks included. The grounds were filled with a layer of sand which was covered with about six inches of black loam and was then seeded with a high grade seed. Two thousand persons could be accommodated in the park's two bleachers, one of which was covered, and the field was surrounded by a high board fence." The photo shows a diminutive but homey park surrounded by two-storied single-resident homes painted almost exclusively white.

The site became a ballpark again (actually a playground and recreation center) in 1929. Then it was named Comiskey Field, after Charles A., who played for Dubuque's 1879 Northwestern League pennant-winners.

The same nine won a 1–0 victory in an exhibition game over Cap Anson's Chicago White Stockings. The winning pitcher in that famous game was Ol' Hoss Radbourne.

Municipal Park (I)

Three-I League 1914–15, Central Association 1917, Mississippi Valley League 1922–32, Midwest League 1956–70. *Location:* Fourth Street extension. *Construction cost:* $30,000. *Seating capacity:* 5300. *First game:* April 30, 1914 (Decatur 9, Dubuque 5, attendance 5888 in the frigid cold).

This is the first municipally owned ballpark in the United States. Before its opening, Dubuque held its biggest parade ever. Too bad it was football weather. Everyone turned up their collar, shivered, and went on with the show.

At 1:30, Opening Day, 1914, the parade formed at Nineteenth Street and Couler Avenue—then marched to the new park. Once there, the overflow crowd shivered through more speeches, a ceremonial raising of the Stars and Stripes, and the address of dedication by A.F. Frudden, president of the Dubuque Industrial Corporation. A crowd favorite was the vested choir from St. Joseph's College. The Dubuque *Saengerbund* sang "Under the Double Eagle," accompanied by the Dubuque German College Band. Then the crowd sang "America," accompanied by every band there—a rendition lacking musical, if not spiritual, cohesiveness.

Eugene Adams, a prominent member of the Municipal Athletic Field Committee, climbed the mound to deliver the first pitch of the day to Mayor James Saul. The hurl was wide, and Hizzoner had to make a kick-save to keep the damned thing from going all the way to the backstop.

Municipal Park, with completely roofed-in stands, sat on the Fourth Street extension, between the city and the high bridge leading to East Dubuque.

According to the *Dubuque Telegraph-Herald* on April 30, 1914, "It is located on ground formerly occupied by millions of feet of lumber owned by the Standard Lumber Company, lumber which was destroyed in a monster conflagration about three years ago, a conflagration that cost the company nearly a million dollars."

Perhaps Standard Lumber had conflagration insurance.

The report goes on: "The field is located on what half a century ago was a network of sloughs and islands.... It was seen from the start that it would be a huge undertaking to convert this tract of ground into a modern athletic field. The refuse from the Standard Lumber Company had filled the sloughs but the greater part of the filling was sawdust and refuse comprising small pieces of lumber."

Construction began in 1913. It was ordered that all street cleanings and other garbage be sent immediately to the site. Businesses routinely sent their garbage there. It was the community thing to do. Naturally, all dirt from city excavations was hauled over. It is estimated that 20,000 loads of fill were hauled to the site, 10,000 paid for by the promoters, 5000 donated and 5000 hauled in "by individuals of whom no note has been taken."

By the winter of 1913 the land was filled. All that remained was the construction of the grandstand and the outfield fence. That job started as soon as weather permitted, only a few weeks before the beginning of the Three-I League season.

Cement piers were constructed, and on these the grandstand was built. The stands were made of wood on steel supports, with rows far enough apart for everyone to be comfortable even when there was a capacity crowd.

In front of the raised grandstand were 1000 "opera chairs," the park's equivalent of box seats. The bleachers were on the north side of the grandstand (the third base side) and were constructed as solidly as those under the roof.

According to the *Herald-Tribune,* "One of the pleasing features of the field as it will appear to persons seeing it for the first time will be the fine fences with their well lettered and beautifully colored advertisements. These advertisements are to be seen both inside and outside the park and are not all from Dubuque merchants, a number of manufacturers of national repute have taken space."

Dunedin, Florida

Grant Field

Spring home of the Toronto Blue Jays 1976–present, Florida State League 1987–present (Blue Jays). *Location:* 311 Douglas Avenue. *Dimensions:* (Before 1984) left field, 345 feet; left center, 365 feet; center field, 400 feet; right center, 380 feet; right field, 301 feet. (After 1984, when left field foul line moved closer to the stands) left field, 335 feet; left center, 365 feet; center field, 400 feet; right center, 380 feet; right field, 315 feet. *Fences:* Twelve feet all the way around, with net on top to catch home runs. *Seating capacity:* 3500. *1987 Florida State League season attendance:* 20,905.

Since taking over the field, the Blue Jays have put $2.5 million into it, including money for grading and resodding.

Durham, North Carolina

Durham Athletic Park

Carolina League 1945–71, 1980–present (Bulls). *Location:* West Geer Street (left field), Washington Street (third base), West Corporation Street (first base), Foster Street (right field). *Opened:* 1938. *Dimensions:* (1939) Left field, 360 feet; center field, 460 feet; right field, 290 feet. (1965) Left field, 330 feet; center field, 410 feet; right field, 307 feet. *Fences:* (1939) Left field, 24 feet; center field, 27 feet; right center, 20 feet; right field, 50 feet. (1965) Left field, 8 feet; center field, 8 feet; right center, 8 feet; right field, 16 feet. *Seating capacity:* 5000. *1987 season attendance:* 217,012.

When the park was first used, the outfield fences sat atop embankments, keeping as many balls as possible on the premises. In 1965, an inner fence was built all the way around. Before then, there was a flagpole, twelve bushes, a tree and eight telephone poles in play in center field. The telephone

The scoreboard at Grant Field, Dunedin, Fla., with a few lights out, April 1988. (Photo by David Pietrusza.)

poles were used to buttress the fence.

My editor for this book, who used to live near Durham, says that even though she never went to a game, the goings-on at this park were so legendary in their goofiness that they reached even into her non-athletic world. "My friend Bert had a pet chicken named Grant," she said, "and he swore that he took Grant to all the Durham Bulls' games. I only half-believed him until some mutual friends said they saw him at the ballpark with a chicken in his backpack."

Extensively used in the 1988 film *Bull Durham*.

East Lansing, Michigan

Kobs Field (Old College Field, before 1969)

Home of the Michigan State University Spartans, Big Ten Conference, 1902–present. *Location:* On the banks of the Red Cedar River. *Dimensions:* Left field, 340 feet; left center, 377 feet; center field, 400 feet; right center, 355

feet; right field, 301 feet. *Fire:* 1926.

Trees grow behind the outfield fence from left center, behind the hand-operated scoreboard in straightaway center, to the right field foul pole, so close to the fence in right that the branches overhang. Behind those trees is the Red Cedar River.

From the plate, the right field fence looks close, and the trees make it look closer. Still, ballplayers say it isn't the easy poke it should be to knock one over that wall. There are a couple of explanations for this. Psychologists say ballplayers may have their eye on the wall instead of the ball. Scientists say the heavy foliage out there holds moisture in the air, and the heavy air prevents fly balls from carrying.

Rob Ellis, a former Michigan State outfielder (class of '71), who's a philosopher and a poet more than a psychologist or scientist, was quoted by the *Lansing State Journal* as saying, "There's nothing prettier in baseball than when the trees (at Kobs Field) are in full bloom in mid-May. It's a beautiful sight to see the white ball just disappear

Kobs Field, East Lansing, Mich. (Compliments of the Michigan State University Sports Information Department.)

up there in all that green and rattle around the trees.... You're out there enjoying college life. There are people going by, there's the running water behind you, the trees are in bloom and you have kids yelling. Except you're in right field watching baseball and they're going to hit it to you."

This plot of land has been the home of Spartan baseball since 1902, and during that time has been the home of stars like Robin Roberts, Steve Garvey, and Kirk Gibson.

The trees' overhang is not the only eccentricity Kobs Field forces upon right-fielders. From the right field foul pole to center field there's a thirty-five-degree upward bank to the fence, an incline that's been likened to the one in left at Crosley. The hill's there to help prevent flooding. The Red Cedar's overflowing has washed out many ball games.

Even the outfield incline can't stop the waters if they rise high enough. In 1949, two feet of water stood in the outfield for the home opener. The ballplayers attempted to play a game with players and bases floating in canoes—but the first inning was never completed as the competition deteriorated into a demonstration of rowdy dunking techniques.

The likelihood of future flood is so great that no permanent seating has ever been built at Kobs Field. Fans still sit on open bleachers along either foul line. Crowds have been known to be as big as 10,000 (in 1979, for the game deciding the Big Ten title), with most of those fans standing between the sets of bleachers or in the outfield.

In 1902, thirteen acres beside the river were purchased by the State Board of Agriculture for $250. The school bought the land twenty years later. The baseball diamond has been at its current location in the Old College Field since 1923, when baseball stopped sharing the Michigan State football stadium.

The old baseball grandstand burned in 1926 following an 8–5 Michigan State victory over arch-rival Michigan. The fire was started by rambunctious students headed by cheerleader Skinny Skellinger.

During the 1950s, when a new budget took the golf team's nine-hole course away (the space was needed for the Jenison Field House and Demonstration Hall), they practiced for matches on a putting green on the far west side of the baseball field. This continued until 1957, when the Forest Akers Golf Course on Harrison Road became the permanent home of the Spartan Linksters.

By far the longest home run in Kobs Field history was struck by Kirk Gibson, a member of the 1979 Big Ten Championship team. The blast cleared the trees in right center and landed 550 feet from home on Landon Field, the nearby practice field for the marching band.

The field is named after the late John Kobs, who coached (that is, managed) the Spartans from 1925 to 1963.

East Orange, New Jersey

Grove Street Oval (East Orange Oval, Oval Playground, Monte Irvin Field)
Negro National League 1940–48 (Cubans), Negro American League 1949–50 (Cubans). *Location:* Greenwood Avenue (left field), Grove Place (third base), Grove Street North (first base), Eaton Place (right field).

Originally part of the Aaron Beck Estate, this land — beside the Erie Lackawanna Railroad in a residential neighborhood — was bought by the city for $45,000 and commissioned by the Board of Recreation Commissioners in July 1907 as a playground.

On Labor Day, 1908, the field was officially dedicated as the East Orange Oval. A month later additional property was purchased (the Grove Place entrance) for $7000, making the entire site 6½ acres large. About $70,000 was spent altogether. The original wooden grandstand seated 1800. There were also seven tennis courts, a shelter house, and a running track.

According to a 1932 edition of the *East Orange Record,* the crowd for the Labor Day dedication was 8000. The *Record* goes on:

"A feature of the dedication was a baseball game between the State Senate and General Assembly. . . . William H. Phillips became caretaker of the field when it first opened and served until he was made superintendent of grounds and buildings in 1911, a position he has held ever since. Antonio Renna has been a caretaker at the Oval Playground ever since it opened."

In 1923, the existing shelter house was torn down and replaced by a $12,750 tile and stucco model with a Spanish tile roof. It contained a large playroom, a fireplace and lockers. The fieldhouse was built out past center field. The concrete stands, often covered with the same flags used to decorate the entrance, were built in 1925. A seven-foot fence enclosed the entire field.

East Orange city clerk Earl Williams, who was 61 years old in 1988, visited the Grove Street Oval many times as a youth, both as a spectator and a player. Williams says, "My greatest personal moment at the Oval was seeing all the black teams and all those great players, Josh Gibson, Satchel Paige, Monte Irvin, Larry Doby, Mule Suttles. I saw Mule hit a ball that cleared the outfield fence and went all the way up onto the railroad tracks, far enough to be out of *any* major league park. For big games the stands were filled and men lined up along the railroad, sitting up on the wall."

There was a softball field and a playground out past left field. The oval held track meets.

The park is still there but the stands are gone. The ballfield in 1986 was rededicated Monte Irvin Field, who lived for many years in East Orange. The field is still used for community baseball.

Edenton, North Carolina

Hicks Field
Virginia League circa 1950 (Colonials). *Seating capacity:* 2500.

Edmonton, Alberta

John Ducey Park (Renfrew Park, before 1984)
Pacific Coast League 1981–present (Trappers). *Location:* 10233 96th Avenue. *Refurbished:* 1984. *Dimensions:* Left field, 335 feet; center field, 405 feet; right field, 320 feet. *Seating capacity:* 6200. *First Pacific Coast League game:* April 22, 1981. *Season attendance record:* 233,044 (1982). *1987 season attendance:* 229,381.

This was already an old park when it was first used by the Pacific Coast League.

The Trappers started the season on the road, and after three grueling hours getting through customs, they arrived at Renfrew Park for practice the day before the home opener, only to find a huge pile of dirt on their infield. *Edmonton Sun* reporter Scott Haskins noted at the time, "It's very doubtful that the dirt can be leveled, rolled, and prepared for Triple-A baseball overnight. (If they try to play, the) club will open its home stand in a gravel pit." But the grounds crew worked all night. By the day of the opener, the infield was smooth and ready.

Here's how Trappers' p.r. recalls that day, April 22, 1981:

"Just a few hundred feet from the edge of the North Saskatchewan River sits a rickety old ballpark. It's painted a dull, brownish red.... It's Renfrew Park, according to some dirty yellow letters over the main door....

"If the ballpark is not quite up to Yankee Stadium standards, that's okay to the fans. Maybe the ballpark staff is somewhat confused in its new jobs, but the fans don't care. So what if the Edmonton Oilers game is on the air from New York, most of these fans are packing radios, and some have even lugged in television sets....

"Right now, Edmonton's Mr. Baseball, John Ducey, is preparing to toss the ceremonial first pitch for the new team...."

On May 21, 1981, over 4000 fans turned out at Renfrew for a Trappers exhibition game against the Chicago White Sox. Tickets were $10.00 apiece. For the first time that night, fans could buy beer at an athletic event in Alberta. Attendance that year was 187,501. Because the old bleachers were being replaced section by section as the season went along, there was always construction, so the park usually never seated more than 3000.

In 1982 the Trappers drew well over 200,000, most of whom came to see Ron Kittle, who was having a great year (50 homers, 144 R.B.I.). The year started with some last minute resodding to get rid of the ledge at the outer lip of the infield, where the grass of the outfield started, then a 22–12 blow-out of Albuquerque. A dixieland band was hired to play between innings.

Also in '82, team owner Peter Pocklington was held hostage at gunpoint in his home and was wounded during his rescue. Two days out of the hospital, Pocklington went to the ballpark, showed off his scars, and signed autographs.

For the 1984 season, the park was completely refurbished and named John Ducey Park in honor of Edmonton's Mr. Baseball, who kept baseball alive in Edmonton when the going was tough. He was a member of the Alberta Sports Hall of Fame and the Canadian Baseball Hall of Fame.

Today, a double deck of advertisements covers the (maybe 16-foot) fence from the left field foul pole to right center. A dark green hitters' background, and a slightly shorter fence, also covered with ads, are in right field. There is a small grandstand with a press box on top and steep bleacher

John Ducey Park, Edmonton, Alberta, Canada, 1988. (Compliments of the Edmonton Trappers.)

sections along the baselines. The bleachers are larger along first base.

Commonwealth Stadium

Usually the home of Edmonton's Canadian Football League team, this was reconfigured for baseball for a 1983 exhibition game between the Edmonton Trappers and the California Angels. Twenty-five thousand fans showed up, only a portion of whom could have seen the game if it had been played at the baseball park. Reggie Jackson hit a double, then spent most of the game signing autographs in the end zone.

El Paso, Texas

Dudley Field

Texas League 1962–70, 1972–present (Diablos). *Location:* 3933 Findley Street, Boone Street. *Nickname:* The Dudley Dome. *Constructed:* 1945. *Dimensions:* Left field, 300 feet; center field, 400 feet; right field, 305 feet. *Fences:* Left field, 16 feet; left center, 24 feet. *Seating capacity:* (1975) 7500, (1985) 7000. *1987 season attendance:* 180,633.

The only baseball grandstand constructed of adobe bricks, this is the ballpark in the Miller beer commercial. A gorgeous little park, painted yellow and orange. The only shade seats are directly behind home. Roofless stands (general admission) run up either line, and there are bleachers in the right field corner.

Out in right there are double decked advertisement signs. In the center of this high fence, which goes all the way from the right field foul pole to the hitters' background, is the Texaco electric scoreboard. To the center field side of the scoreboard a Marlboro man sticks up above the fence.

The grandstand once had a huge venetian blind to protect fans from the sun, and there was a rise out in center field that served as a levee against a canal.

In 1985, a $6 million bond issue passed for the construction of a new ballpark. By 1988, El Paso had a site picked, but no design for the new park had been drawn. The proposed seating capacity is 11,000, and hopes are to have the new park open by the spring of 1989.

Two views of Dudley Field, El Paso, Tex. (Compliments of the El Paso Diablos.)

Elizabeth, New Jersey

Waverly Park (Weequahic Park)
National Association 1873 (Resolutes). *Location:* Lower Road, Haynes Avenue, and Frelinghuysen Street in the currently nonexistent town of Waverly. This is the current site of Weequahic City Park and the B'Nai Jeshuron Cemetery on the current Elizabeth/Newark border. *First game:* April 28, 1873. *Last game:* July 23, 1873.

Weequahic Park is currently oper-ated by the city of Newark and contains that city's only public golf course.

Elizabeth City, North Carolina

Memorial Park
Virginia League circa 1950 (Albemarles). *Seating capacity:* 2500.

Elizabethton, Tennessee

Joe O'Brien Field (Riverside Park)
Appalachian League 1974–present

(Twins). *Location:* Holly Lane, one block from Highway 321. *Dimensions:* Left field, 335 feet; center field, 414 feet; right field, 326 feet. *Seating capacity:* 1500. *1987 season attendance:* 13,101.

Joe O'Brien fell in love with Elizabethton upon his arrival in 1923. He organized the Cherokee Athletic Association in 1931 and served as its director from 1931 to 1959. For 15 consecutive years (1944–59) he was president of that association.

O'Brien made arrangements for the Minnesota Twins to place a rookie league team in Elizabethton in December of 1973. He served as chairman of the Elizabethton Twins Baseball Committee from 1974 until May 1981. In 1974, he was "Executive of the Year" in the Appalachian League.

In 1980 the Elizabethton City Council named the ball field at Riverside Park "Joe O'Brien Field" in honor of his contributions to professional baseball. O'Brien died November 16, 1981.

Elmira, New York

Luce St. Dunn Field

New York–Pennsylvania League 1973–present (Pioneers). *Location:* Church Street exit off Route 17, Luce Street. *Dimensions:* Left field, 325 feet; center field, 384 feet; right field, 325 feet. *Seating capacity:* 5100. *1987 season attendance:* 49,848.

Has a roofed grandstand with a press box on top, bleachers on the first base side.

Emmett, Idaho

This town, not far from Boise, had organized baseball as far back as 1889, when the town's ball field was located in an area currently bounded by Fourth Street and Boise Avenue. In later years, Emmett would field a professional team in the Idaho State League known as the Prune Pickers.

Emporia, Virginia

Slagle Stadium

Virginia League circa 1950 (Rebels, Nats). *Seating capacity:* 2000.

Erie, Pennsylvania

Ainsworth Field (Athletic Field, before 1947)

Negro American League 1940s (Kansas City Monarchs, some games), Middle Atlantic League 1938–41, 1946–51 (Sailors), New York–Pennsylvania League 1954–63, 1967 (Tigers), 1981–present (Cardinals 1981–87, Orioles). Owned by the Erie School District. *Location:* 22nd and Cranberry streets. *Built:* Fall, 1938. *Dimensions:* (Original) left field, 390 feet; center field, 500 feet; right field, 356 feet. (Current) left field, 320 feet; left center, 350 feet; center field, 385 feet; right center, 325 feet; right field, 300 feet. *Fence:* 16 feet all the way around (particle board). *Seating capacity:* 3500. *Lights:* 1939.

The current dimensions listed above represent the figures painted on the outfield fence. In 1981, the *Erie Daily Times* sent a surveyor to the ballpark to measure. The surveyor discovered that the distance to the fence down the left field line was 318.4 feet (rather than 320), in left center the marker was correct, in center the distance was 382.4 (not 385), right center was a measly 319.25 (not 325), and the right field foul line was 286.5 feet (not 300). The right field dimension represents the distance to an inner fence. Years ago, the right field barrier was the back of the Roosevelt School, which stands behind the current fence.

The inflated dimensions were painted on the walls in 1981 by Dave Masi, owner of the Erie Cardinals of the New York–Pennsylvania League, who thought a white lie might prevent scouts from diminishing the importance of his team's power stats, thus inhibiting careers.

Ainsworth Field was built in 1939 by the Erie School District, who still owns the facility. Since that time the field has been used by a variety of minor league franchises ranging from C- to A-level ball. Between 1967 and 1981, there was no professional baseball played at Ainsworth Field, and the field operated without lights for high school and American Legion ball only. During that time, the stands — a grandstand from first to third with a wooden press box on top — were allowed to deteriorate badly. Only the playing field itself was kept in decent shape.

The other lapse in professional play at Ainsworth came during World War II. During that stretch the field was used only for special attractions — such as the time Dizzy Dean and Honus Wagner brought their all-star pick-up teams to town for an exhibition.

Named after J.C. "Doc" Ainsworth. As of 1988, the Erie club was in the farm system of the Baltimore Orioles.

Eugene, Oregon

Bethel Park

Far West League (Class D) 1946–51 (Larks), Northwest League 1955–68 (Emeralds). *Location:* Seneca and Roosevelt roads in West Eugene. *Seating capacity:* 4000.

Park was privately owned, and was eventually torn down to make way for an expressway that was never constructed. This was one of the last wooden ballparks used for minor league ball.

As of 1983, the concrete foundation of the Bethel Park ballfield could still be seen in the vacant field near Seneca and Roosevelt roads.

Civic Stadium

Pacific Coast League 1969–73 (Emeralds), Northwest League 1974–present (Emeralds). *Location:* 20th and Willamette streets. *Built:* 1938. *Dimensions:* Left field, 335 feet; center

field, 402 feet; right field, 335 feet. *Seating capacity:* (1975) 5500; (1985) 6410. *First Pacific Coast League game:* April 26, 1969 (Eugene 6, Tacoma 3, attendance: 5217). *1987 season attendance:* 132,819.

Park was originally owned by the Eugene School District. It was constructed with WPA funds and money from the city, the school district, and a civic campaign. It was first used October 28, 1938, for a football game between Eugene and Corvallis high schools. The roof was yet to be completed and there was no grass on the field.

The park served as home of Eugene's semi-pro baseball until the late 1940s. When professional baseball came to Eugene for the first time in 1950, the school district forbade the use of its field, forcing the construction of Bethel Park.

By 1969, when Eugene acquired a franchise in the Pacific Coast League, the city proclaimed Bethel Park unfit for use, even if refurbished, and baseball returned to Civic Stadium. To make the park suitable for baseball again, the entire field had to be resodded, and a major excavation project made the right field corner, for the first time, on a level with the rest of the field. The lights' intensity was more than doubled. The light towers were moved from football to baseball configuration. Over 700 box seats were installed. Total cost: $250,000. About 60 percent of the total cost went toward the lights. Eugene, at that time, was the smallest city in the nation with a triple-A franchise.

Before the refurbishment, Civic Stadium had sadly deteriorated. It was no more than a cyclone fence surrounding a chewed-up football field and dilapidated bleachers, home of the South Eugene High School football team. The renovation began in January of 1969 and was completed in time for Opening Day.

At the Opening Day ceremonies,

Two views of Civic Stadium, Eugene, Ore. (Photos by Eileen Beban, used compliments of the Eugene Public Library and the Eugene Emeralds.)

1200 green gas-filled balloons were released in hopes of adding a carnival atmosphere to the proceedings. Unfortunately, in the still air, most of the balloons failed to rise, and the crowd laughed and laughed as the grounds crew ran around trying to pop them all so the game could begin. The first ball was thrown out by Pacific Coast League President William McKechnie of Phoenix.

Refurbishments were not quite done by game time. All of the box seats weren't in, so some had to sit on folding chairs. The right field fence was not completed, allowing a group of youngsters to watch for free. Other freeloaders watched from nearby roofs and from the Amazon Parkway overpass.

Swede Johnson Stadium

Home of high school, American Legion and semi-pro baseball 1988–present. *Construction cost:* $1 million. *Seating capacity:* 3000. *Dimensions:* Left field, 320 feet; center field, 390 feet; right field, 330 feet. *Fence:* 12 feet high. Plywood, bearing 42 advertisements.

Built upon land owned by the school district. Has a $40,000 scoreboard, and 95-foot light towers of AAA quality.

Evansville, Indiana

Bosse Field

American Association from 1970 at least to 1980 (Triplets, franchise no longer exists). *Location:* Maxwell, Morgan and Heidelbach avenues, at Main Street. *Constructed:* 1935. *Dimensions:* (Original) left field, 334 feet; center field, 447 feet; right field, 334 feet. (Current) left field, 315 feet; center field, 410 feet; right field, 315 feet. *Seating capacity:* 5000.

Everett, Washington

Everett Sports Complex
Northwest League 1984–present (Giants). *Location:* 38th Street (left field, north), Broadway (right field), Wetmore Street (first base). *Dimensions:* Left field, 330 feet; center field, 395 feet; right field, 335 feet. *Seating capacity:* 2350. *1987 season attendance:* 58,823.

Fayetteville, North Carolina

Cape Fear Fairgrounds Park
Site of Baltimore Orioles 1914 spring training. *Location:* Gillespie Street, current site of North Carolina Highway Commission District Office.

Near the site of this park on Route 301 stands a historical marker. It reads:

BABE RUTH

Hit his first home run
in professional baseball,
March, 1914, 135 yds. N.W.
In this town George
Herman Ruth acquired
the nickname "Babe."

Maurice Fleishman, a local clothier, was a 70-year-old man in 1973 when he was interviewed by the *Fayetteville News and Observer* about the historic blast. Fleishman had been a batboy for the intrasquad game that contained Ruth's first roundtripper as a pro.

"He was just a kid," Fleishman recalled. Ruth was 19, straight from St. Mary's Industrial School. "He had a real baby face. That's why they started calling him the Babe – and it happened right here."

Ballplayers walked a mile to the ballpark from the hotel. Fleishman remembered Babe would play catch with any kids who were tagging along for the walk.

"He also liked to have his fun in the hotel, spending the night running the elevator up and down," Fleishman said.

The historical marker was dedicated April 5, 1952. Present for the ceremony were Mrs. Clara Ruth and Connie Mack.

Highland Park
Location: Grove Street, current site of Cross Creek Court. *Seating capacity:* 300.

On April 5, 1935, Babe came back to Fayetteville to play in an exhibition game with his new ball club, the Boston Braves. The crowd, estimated at 15,000 in a park that sat 300, lined the foul lines, standing within a few feet of the first and third basemen. After drizzle all morning the sun broke through just in time for the start of the game, and that brought a roar. Babe grounded out twice and whiffed. When Ruth was taken out of the game in the sixth inning the crowd lost interest in the contest and lined up for autographs. The game was stopped when all 200 baseballs had been hit into the crowd and kept.

J.P. Riddle Park
South Atlantic League 1987–present (Generals). *Location:* Legion Road. *Dimensions:* Left field, 330 feet; center field, 400 feet; right field, 330 feet. *Seating capacity:* 3000. *1987 season attendance:* 95,008.

Farm club of the Tigers.

Flagstaff, Arizona

Mount Eden Park
Flagstaff's premiere diamond for

youth baseball. *Location:* Spruce and First streets, at First Avenue. *Dedicated:* 1925. *Size of site:* 2.12 acres.

Florence, South Carolina

American Legion Field
South Atlantic League circa 1985 (Blue Jays, franchise no longer exists). *Dimensions:* Left field, 315 feet; center field, 400 feet; right field, 315 feet. *Seating capacity:* 3500.

Ft. Lauderdale, Florida

Ft. Lauderdale Stadium Complex
Florida State League 1962–present (Yankees), spring home of the New York Yankees 1962–present. Owned by the city of Ft. Lauderdale. *Location:* 5300 NW 12th Avenue, three blocks west of I-95, just north of Commercial Boulevard. *Constructed:* 1962. *Dimensions:* Left field, 335 feet; center field, 401 feet; right field, 332 feet. *Turf:* grass. *Seating capacity:* (1975) 7500; (1985) 7061. *1987 Florida State League season attendance:* 50,074. *Parking lot:* 3500 cars.

Park has three concession stands, and night lighting sufficient for network television broadcasts. The big league Yanks draw over 100,000 each year to see their home spring training schedule. The restrooms and seating facilities are accessible to the handicapped.

The stadium also serves as the site for Mickey Mantle–Whitey Ford Dream Camps, high school baseball, professional wrestling, concerts — and something called Campus Life Scream in the Dark.

The ballpark is part of the Ft. Lauderdale Stadium Complex, which includes Lockhart Stadium, a football-soccer arena that holds 26,000. Lockhart has also been used for truck pulls, pro wrestling, polo matches, and dog shows.

Ft. Myers, Florida

Name of park unknown
Used for baseball 1896. *Location:* east of Hendry Street, just behind the present location of the Edison Theatre.

Park T. Pigott Memorial Stadium
(Terry Park, Fairgrounds)
Spring home of Philadelphia A's 1925–36, Cleveland Indians, Pittsburgh Pirates 1955–68, and Kansas City Royals 1969–87, Florida State League (Class A) 1978–87 (Royals). *Grandstand constructed:* 1954. *Location:* Terry Park, Palm Beach Boulevard in East Fort Myers. *Dimensions:* Left field, 360 feet; center field, 410 feet; right field, 360 feet. *Turf:* Artificial infield, grass outfield. *Seating capacity:* 6200 (all theater-type seats). *First major league exhibition game:* March 16, 1925 (Phillies 6, Athletics 3). *Last major league exhibition game:* April 4, 1987 (Kansas City 4, Texas 2, attendance 3781).

Through the efforts of R.Q. Richards, then president of the Kiwanis Club, the Philadelphia Athletics came to train in Terry Park in 1925 and stayed for twelve seasons. Then known as the Fort Myers Fairgrounds, the park would later be named after Mrs. Tootie McGregor Terry, who donated the land to the county in 1906.

The present stadium, built in 1955 for the Pittsburgh Pirates' spring games, sits in Terry Park beside Palm Beach Boulevard, a thoroughfare lined with royal palm trees. The roof is so big no one gets wet when it rains, except the players and the umpires.

The first game played in Terry Park by the Pirates at the new ballpark took place on March 12, 1955, as the Pirates beat the Kansas City Athletics 9–8 in 10 innings. The first home run was struck by Ben Wilson of the A's. The first ball was thrown out by 92-year-old Connie Mack.

The Pirates practiced in Fort Myers until 1968, when they moved their

Fort Lauderdale (Fla.) Stadium Complex. (Compliments of the Fort Lauderdale Stadium Complex.)

spring camp to Bradenton.

Between 1978 and 1987, the facility was the spring training home of the Kansas City Royals, who — along with Lee County — put money into improvements and expansion.

Abandonment. In 1988 the Royals moved to their new concept, Baseball City's Boardwalk and Baseball, taking their Florida State League team with them. The abandonment cost Lee County millions of dollars in yearly revenue. One hotel alone lost $400,000 in spring training business.

A lot of folks were out of a job. Folks like Albert Sprankle, who worked in the parking lot, collecting a buck and pointing to the proper parking spot; Jim Moore, who sold souvenirs for years; Ken Kern, who kept trespassers and beer moochers out of the press box during ball games; and Chris Barnes, who read the starting lineups for 10 years, then did the games on TV and radio. Also unemployed were Big Jim Maruca, who operated the scoreboard, and Hank Swanson, who collected tickets.

The oldest structure in Terry Park was the clubhouse, built in 1916. The clubhouse originally was the home of the Fort Myers Yacht and Country Club, then later served as offices for the Lee County Parks and Recreation Department and the Veterans Service Office before becoming the clubhouse for the Pirates and the Royals. It was torn down again in 1988 to make way for a playground and parking.

The last home run in Pigott Stadium was hit by Tom Paciorek of the Texas Rangers.

Fort Wayne, Indiana

The Grand Duchess (Hamilton Field 1862-70, Calhoun Street League Park)

Home of the Summit Citys 1862, 1866-70 and Kekiongas 1866-70 (independent schedules), National Association 1871 (Kekiongas), Northwestern League 1883-87, Western Association 1888-91, Western League 1892-97, Northwestern League, Tri-State League, Central League 1903-04, 1908-15, 1917, 1928-34 (Chiefs), Three-I League 1935 (Chiefs). *Location:* Lewis, Calhoun, and Clinton streets; Douglas Avenue. *First National Association game:* May 4, 1871. *Last National Association game:* August 29, 1871. Site of first National Association game. *Torn down:* circa 1940.

On May 4, 1871, the first major league baseball game — that is, the first game in the newly formed National Association — was played in a ballpark called the Grand Duchess.

Where the Record Books Begin. In Fort Wayne, in the spring of 1871, news of formalized competition for the Kekiongas spawned a zealous response in the community. A new ballpark was quickly approved and constructed at the site of Hamilton Field, which, without the stands, had been in use for baseball since 1862. The land, at the southwest corner of Lewis and Calhoun streets had been donated for Fort Wayne baseball by pioneer banker Allen Hamilton.

According to the *Old Fort News,* "The local citizenry, visualizing a possible championship for their fine team, jumped into the project with a vengeance and raised funds to erect a beautiful ornamented grandstand on the site of the (old) ballpark. The grandstand was finished and christened 'The Grand Duchess,' so lavish was its construction. The old ball grounds was located just west of the Main Street bridge on land to the north of Main Street running to the canal (presently the tracks of the Nickel Plate Railroad)."

The Fort Wayne Kekiongas won a pitcher's duel over the Cleveland nine 2-0. Kekionga ace Bobby Mathews notched the big league's first shutout. Spectators marveled at Fort Wayne's barehanded and error-free fielding, and the cunning of both underhanded pitchers.

Indeed, the game was something special. It would be four years before organized baseball would again see a score this low. The National Association consisted of nine teams who'd agreed to play each other six times apiece over the course of the summer. Some of the rules were different. Foul balls caught on one bounce were out. Pitchers delivered the ball from only 45 feet away, but had their effectiveness regulated by restrictions on their pitching motion. Balls had to be thrown from below the waist — so it was a hitters' game. Scores were also inflated by the lack of fielding gloves. Fewer line drives were stabbed, since a broken hand could result. Pitchers did not have to deliver the ball with their toe on a pitcher's rubber, but rather could get a running start, as in cricket, as long as they stayed within a six-foot-square pitcher's box. There was no mound. It took nine balls to walk a batter. Batters could choose from two strike zones, from waist to eyes or waist to knees. The chosen strike zone had to be crossed for a called strike. A ball striking the ground fair and then rolling foul was considered a fair ball — thus greatly increasing the effectiveness of bunting.

Teams wore baggy knickers, with long stockings, lace-up high-top leather shoes, long sleeves with cuffs, stiff-collared shirts (sometimes with the collars turned up), and ties. The team's city was usually spelled across the front, as today. Wide, dark belts held up the trousers.

The players, mostly tough Irish men, wore thick mustaches that sometimes covered the whole mouth, and short-brimmed caps more reminiscent of those in the military than today's baseball hats.

Since before the Civil War, Fort Wayne had been the site of spirited youth baseball. The Kekiongas formed the year after the war ended. In 1869, when the great Cincinnati Red Stockings came to town, the comparatively weak Kekiongas succumbed whole-heartedly, 86–0.

By the following year the Kekiongas were recognized as one of the best nines in baseball. That was the year a group from a disbanded Baltimore team came to town and infiltrated the Kekiongas' ranks — to the benefit of all except those cut.

Among the newcomers was Bobby Mathews, a right-handed pitcher. Though he stood only five feet five inches and weighed a mere 145 pounds, he possessed an uncanny curve. Pitching underhanded not only restricted the speed pitchers could get on the ball, but also their ability to make the ball break. Despite this, Mathews had learned to whip his elbow and snap his wrist just right, creating a pitch that broke severely down and away from a right-handed hitter. One moment the pitch would appear to be heading straight for the batter's head, and the next it would slash at the knees across the outside corner of the then-square home base. That pitch not only greatly improved the quality of the Kekiongas, but led Mathews to a 17-year career and 298 major league victories. If the 300-game victory mark had been the accepted milestone for immortality that it is today, it is doubtful that Mathews would have stopped pitching just when he did. Mathews won 30 games in a year three times in his career, and three times notched over 200 strikeouts in a season. The strike-out figures are especially high for the time, since common thinking had it that a pitcher did not even try for a strikeout until he was in a jam. Mathews

was already a feared man that after-noon when he blanked Cleveland in the 1871 opener.

The first major league pitch was a ball. Cleveland's Deacon White then doubled off Mathews to lead off the in-ning. White failed to score, however, when, after a pop-up out, shortstop Tom Carey caught a line drive and beat White back to second for the first unassisted double play.

Fort Wayne's catcher, Bill Lennon, scored the winning run when, after doubling, he came around on Joe McDermott's single. With the Keki-ongas batting in the bottom of the ninth — despite their being ahead, as per the day's custom — rain halted play. Mathews struck out six and walked one. The game took two hours to play.

Corruption Cracks the Kekiongas. That glorious Opening Day victory was no harbinger. Ugly rumors started almost immediately. Games were being dumped. Gamblers determined out-comes. After the Kekiongas were mobbed by angry spectators following a close victory over the Troy Hay-makers at the Bulls Head Tavern Grounds in Batestown, New York, the Kekiongas became incapable of win-ning on the road.

Back in Indiana, discouraged fans stopped visiting the Grand Duchess, whose empty seats signaled financial ruin for the franchise. After several weeks of losing, manager Henry C. Deane was replaced by Bill Lennon, the catcher. Things only got worse. Their record was 7–21 in July when they withdrew from the National Associa-tion. Big league baseball never came to Fort Wayne again. It would be 12 years before organized baseball of any kind would come to town. When it did, it came in the form of a franchise in the Northwestern League, where the town fielded a remarkable young shortstop named John W. "Pebbly Jack" Glass-cock, a former-day Ozzie Smith.

On June 2, 1883, the second game at night under lights was played on this site. (For the first, see **Hull, Massachusetts.**) The game was played between the Methodist College nine and the Quincy, Illinois, professional team. The lights (17 arc lamps) were provided, purely as a promotional stunt, by the Jenney Electric Light Company. Quincy won 19–11 in seven innings before 2000 spectators. Local consensus was that a lot more than 17 lamps were needed to simulate the sun. There would be more novelty night games such as this in the nineteenth century, but night baseball was not really considered until 1909—and even then it was hardly considered *seriously.*

In 1896, Fort Wayne, playing in the Western League—an association that would become the American League—had a 21-year-old first baseman who hit .374 and was known for his speed. His name was Zane Grey, and he later went on to write a western or two.

In 1913, a huge spring flood inundated the ballpark. The clubhouse and bleachers were demolished, and the receding waters left the site a mudhole. The team had to start the season on the road while their home grounds were repaired.

Swinney Park

Site of 1883 post-season play between the Chicago White Stockings and Providence Grays.

Lakeside Base Ball Grounds

Northwest League 1898. *Location:* Lakeside section. Anthony Boulevard, Delta Lake, Tilden Avenue, Columbia Street.

Baseball was played here for only one year, as the site was far from the beaten path and attendance was low. Team was managed by Jack Glasscock.

Jailhouse Flats

Location: Calhoun, North Clinton, and St. Clair streets.

On several occasions in 1902, park was used by the Cleveland Indians for American League games.

Dwenger Park

Central League 1948 (Generals)

Used for Fort Wayne baseball after the demolition of the Calhoun Street Park before World War II. Used predominantly by the semi-pro ball club, the General Electric Voltmen.

Fort Worth, Texas

Hayne's Park

Circa 1880–1900. *Location:* In the "Prairie" area near downtown.

Panther Park

Texas League 1900–25 (Panthers, Cats). *Location:* West side of North Main Street. *Built:* 1900. *Seating capacity:* 4600.

This was the first steel and concrete ballpark in the Texas League, also the first park with turnstiles and reserved seating. Panther Park didn't follow trends, it started them.

In June 1915, the ballpark was considerably damaged when the Trinity River overflowed its banks.

LaGrave Field

Texas League 1926–64 (Cats). *Location:* North Main, Calhoun, Sixth and Pecan streets, a few blocks from Panther Park. *Dimensions:* Left field, 335 feet; center field, 400 feet; right field, 300 feet. *Burned:* May 15, 1949. *Rebuilt and dedicated:* July 5, 1950.

Named after the owner of the Fort Worth Cats, Paul LaGrave. On May 15, 1949, LaGrave Field burned. The very next day came the rains and floods, which caused even more damage. By the start of the 1950 season, LaGrave had been rebuilt bigger and better than ever.

The site is now a grassy lot.

TCU Baseball Diamond

Home of the Texas Christian University Horned Frogs (Southwest Conference), present. *Location:* TCU campus. *Seating capacity:* 1500.

Franklin, Virginia

Franklin Field
Virginia League circa 1950. *Seating capacity:* 1500.

Fresno, California

John Euless Park
California State League 1941–42, California League 1946–present (Padres, Suns). *Location:* McKinley Street. *Dimensions:* Left field, 330 feet; center field, 400 feet; right field, 330 feet. *Seating capacity:* (1960) 3500, (1985) 2600. *1987 season attendance:* 107,908. Used for baseball as early as 1941.

Beiden Field (Varsity Park 1966–72)
Home of the Fresno State Bulldogs (Pacific Coast Athletic Association) 1966–present. *Location:* Fresno State University. *Dimensions:* Left field, 330 feet; left center, 366 feet; center field, 400 feet; right center, 366 feet; right field, 330 feet. *Playing surface:* grass, crushed dirt infield, rock dirt warning track. *Seating capacity:* (1984–present) 3575, all theater-type seating. *Lights installed:* 1969 (98 fixtures on eight towers, generating 70–100 foot candles of light in the infield, 32 foot candles in the outfield). *Stadium rebuilt:* 1984. *Cost of rebuilding:* $2.2 million.

The first game in the new superstructure, cast-in-place and pre-cast concrete Beiden Field was played March 16, 1984, Fresno State hosting Long Beach State. The stadium, one of the finest amateur ballparks in the nation, had cost over $2 million, money raised through a community-wide fund drive.

The horseshoe-shaped grandstand has four rows of box seats, a cross aisle, and then 16 rows of standard seating behind that. The restrooms, press box, and concession stands are all new. The FSU baseball coaching staff offices are located in the stadium concourse.

The scoreboard alone at the new park cost $140,000, and was made possible through donations by American National Bank, Pepsi-Cola, and Me-N-Ed's Pizza. It was designed and built by the American Sign and Indicator Company.

This park was originally known as Varsity Park. Since 1972, it has been named after former Fresno State baseball coach Pete Beiden, who coached the Bulldogs to 600 wins in 21 seasons (1948–69) and was later inducted into the College Baseball Coaches Association Hall of Fame.

Fullerton, California

Titan Field
Home of the California State University at Fullerton Titans (Pacific Coast Athletic Conference), present. *Location:* Cal State at Fullerton campus. *Seating capacity:* 1000.

A joint venture among the city of Fullerton, the Marriot Hotel chain and the state university system will soon produce a $6.7 million sports complex next to a new Marriot Hotel. The complex will include a soccer-football stadium, and a new grandstand and fan facilities around Titan Field. Plans are to have the new complex open by 1990.

The biggest name to thus far come out of the Cal State Fullerton baseball program is the Montreal Expos' Tim Wallach.

Gainesville, Florida

Perry Field
Home of the University of Florida Gators (Southeastern Conference) 1988–present. *Location:* University of Florida campus, just west of the O'Connell Center where the old park sat. *Designer:* Hansen Lind Meyer, Inc. *Constructor:* C.R. Perry Construction. *Construction cost:* $2.4 million. *Dimensions:* Left field, 330 feet; left center, 375 feet; center field, 400 feet;

right center, 365 feet; left field, 325 feet. *Seating capacity:* 4000. *Lights:* 1977 (donated by George Steinbrenner, since upgraded).

Galveston, Texas

Beach Park
Texas League 1888–90 (Giants). *Location:* Tremont Street, near the beach. A board fence surrounded the field. There were two grandstands, one 80 feet and one 50 feet long. Starting April 11, 1888, ladies were admitted free on Wednesdays. Out on the right field fence was "Houlihan's tally board," where Texas League scores off the wire were posted.

Gulfview Park
Texas League 1907–17 (Sandcrabs). *Location:* 2802 Avenue R. *Dimensions:* Right field, 260 feet.

The number one hero was pitcher and lush Eugene Moore, Sr., who, during batting practice, hit balls purposefully over the 260-foot right field fence. The rule was "he who hits it, gets it," and the Blue Goose Saloon was on the other side of that fence.

On August 15, 1915, Gulfview was rendered unusable for the rest of the season by a tropical storm.

Moody Stadium
Texas League 1931–37 (Buccaneers). *Location:* 5108 Avenue G.

Named for team owner Shearn Moody, who bought the Waco franchise and brought it to Galveston.

Gastonia, North Carolina

Sims Legion Park
South Atlantic League 1977–present (Jets). *Location:* North Marietta Street. *Dimensions:* Left field, 360 feet; center field, 400 feet; right field, 360 feet. *Seating capacity:* 4500. *1987 season attendance:* 71,110.

One of the few ballparks in the United States that does not serve beer.

Park looks like it was constructed during the Depression, atop a concrete foundation. Grandstand has an ornate facade. Steel beams hold up the heavy, all-covering roof.

Geneva, New York

McDonough Park
New York–Pennsylvania League 1958–present (Cubs). *Location:* Lyceum Street. *Dimensions:* Left field, 315 feet; center field, 370 feet; right field, 305 feet. *Seating capacity:* 1200. *1987 season attendance:* 19,918.

In 1988, when the Cubs started the season 1–10, 23-year-old general manager Ken Shephard vowed to sleep on a cot in the McDonough Park press box until the Cubs won again. Already on a six-game losing streak, the Cubs lost 12 more before allowing their general manager to sleep at home. The 18-game losing streak tied a New York–Pennsylvania League record set by Watertown in 1985. Because of Shephard's stunt, Geneva was the most highly publicized minor league team in the nation for a time.

One of the few parks with video games behind the stands. Concessions sell salt potatoes. Starting lineups are written just inside the entrance gate on a beat-up blackboard. The whole place could use a paint job.

This is where Pete Rose played minor league ball.

According to Karl Zimmermann in *Upstate* magazine, "McDonough's roofed, screened grandstand is a structure that speaks eloquently of an earlier, more leisurely time. . . . (It is) most quintessentially, beautifully bush-league."

Glens Falls, New York

East Field
Eastern League 1980–present (White

Top: *A drawing of Perry Field, Gainesville, Fla. (Compliments of the University of Florida.)* Bottom: *McDonough Park, Geneva, N.Y. (Photo by David Pietrusza.)*

Sox 1980–85, Tigers 1986–present). *Location:* Dix Avenue, Haskell Street. *Dimensions:* Left field, 315 feet; center field, 380 feet; right field, 330 feet. *Fences:* Eight feet all the way around. *Seating capacity:* 8000. *1987 season attendance:* 79,303.

When this site was first used for professional baseball, there was nothing but a field, bleachers, and a couple of Johnny-on-the-Spots for restrooms. Glens Falls had a good reason to be unprepared for minor league baseball, as the idea was sprung upon them just before the beginning of the 1980 season. Originally, the team was to play in Schenectady, but neighbors of Central Park there balked, so plans were changed.

Since then, East Field has developed into a beautiful little ballpark, with one luxury box up on the roof called the "Tiger's Den." Sound is piped in. The price of the box includes a keg of beer. Night games can get cold in Glens Falls, and those indoor seats are popular. Also, the luxury booth contains the only spectator seats in the park with a roof.

Glens Falls' answer to the San Diego Chicken is Sawhorse Sam. "He (or she) doesn't do much," says visitor David Pietrusza, "but seems popular with the smaller fry."

East Field, Glens Falls, N.Y. (Photo by David Pietrusza.)

Gloucester Point, New Jersey

Gloucester Point Grounds

American Association 1888–90 (Philadelphia Athletics, Sundays only).

Directly across the Delaware River from Philadelphia, and used to get around blue laws.

Gloversville, New York

JAG Park (Parkhurst Field)

New York State League 1904–07. *Location:* Off Route 30.

Johnstown, Amsterdam, and Gloversville shared a franchise — hence JAG. The Pittsburgh Pirates and Boston Red Sox came here for exhibitions before World War I. In 1922, the Cincinnati Reds visited.

Site is currently used for Little League baseball.

Glovers Park (The Fairgrounds, Berkshire Park)

Canadian-American League 1937, 1939–51 (Glovers). *Location:* Current site of Nichols Department Store. *Dimensions:* Left field, 330 feet; center field, 405 feet; right field, 333 feet. *Seating capacity:* 3000. *Lights:* 1940. *Refurbished:* 1948. *Torn down:* 1960.

First used for baseball on Decoration Day, 1898, for a game between two local teams (the McKeevers and the Adelphis), which ended in a tie when the only ball was lost. Used for horse racing during the first part of the century. By the time it was used exclusively for baseball, in the 1930s, it was a rundown wooden park. The racetrack and performing stage were removed. The Glovers were a St. Louis Browns farm team and turned out very good players. The outfield was described as a "hayfield" and home run distances were determined by snow fences. Lights were installed in 1940, financed by the selling of stock. The park was refurbished in 1948, and in 1950 received a new scoreboard. By 1960, when the place was torn down, it was known as Lovers Park because someone had painted out the G on the sign. The site became a shopping center. The light towers were all that remained of the old park until they too were removed in the mid-'70s.

Top: *Parkhurst Field, Gloversville, N.Y., in the snow, January 1988. (Photo by David Pietrusza.)* Bottom: *Glovers Park, Gloversville, N.Y., before the "G" on the sign was obliterated. (Photo from the personal collection of David Pietrusza.)*

Grambling, Louisiana

Haggard Diamond

Home of the Grambling State University Tigers (Southwestern Conference), present. *Seating capacity:* 1000.

Grand Rapids, Michigan

Ramona Athletic Park

Central League (Class B) 1903–17.

In the summer of 1909, inventor George F. Cahill (*see* Cincinnati) came to Grand Rapids with his latest invention: portable lights for night baseball. He was allowed to set up at the Ramona Athletic Park for a nocturnal contest July 7 between Grand Rapids and Zanesville. Grand Rapids Mayor George Ellis was the umpire. The ball game drew 4500 people, who saw Grand Rapids win 11–10 in seven innings. Hitters had no complaints, but outfielders had fits with fly balls above the lights. It was later decided the game shouldn't count in the Central League standings because of a league rule prohibiting games started later than two hours before sunset.

The next night baseball game was not played until the following year, when Cahill carted his equipment to Chicago and showed it to Mr. Comiskey.

Here's a switch: A 1908 photo of Ramona in the National Baseball Library photo archives in Cooperstown shows a field with a grass infield and a dirt outfield.

Grapevine, Texas

Oak Grove Park

A four-field complex built in 1975 as a cooperative project between the city and the Army Corps of Engineers. The fields are lighted and used predominantly for youth baseball.

Great Falls, Montana

Legion Park

Pioneer League 1948–1963, 1969–present (Selectrics, Dodgers, Giants 1969–83, Dodgers, again 1984–present). *Location:* 26th Street and River Road. *Dimensions:* Left field, 340 feet; center field, 410 feet; right field, 340 feet. *Seating capacity:* 3536. *1987 season attendance:* 64,226.

According to Montana baseball expert Bob Decker, "Legion Park rests atop the south flank of the Great Falls of the Missouri and opens to the abandoned Anaconda smelting complex sprawling on the broad hillside across the river. Although baseball lost an old friend with the 1982 demolition of the 500-foot Anaconda stack that commanded the horizon beyond left field, blazing Charlie Russell sunsets frequently glorify the sky above Legion Park." It's enough to make you overlook the little flaws—like the fact that the first base light tower sticks right up out of the seats, creating quite an obstruction.

The original park was built in 1940, using WPA funds and donated materials and labor. The facility was improved in 1948 by Great Falls brewer Emil Sick, who brought the Pioneer League into town for the first time. The league disbanded after the 1963 season. For five years Legion Park was used only as the home of the local American Legion team. Legion ball didn't generate funds for maintenance, and the park was allowed to deteriorate badly. Rain had washed away much of the dirt part of the infield. At one point there was a foot-deep drop-off from the grass of the infield to the skin. Forget about bad hops—you could break an ankle.

Great Falls began in the Pioneer League in 1948. They were then known as the Selectrics, a combination of the "Select" brand of beer sold by the brewery that owned the club and "Electric" after Great Falls' nickname, the Electric City. When the brewery sold

Top: *The bleachers and backstop at Field 2, Oak Grove Park, Grapevine, Tex. (Compliments of the Grapevine Parks & Recreation Department.)* Bottom: *Legion Park, Great Falls, Mont. (Compliments of the Great Falls Dodgers.)*

the ball club to the Great Falls Baseball Club in the late '50s, they became the Electrics. The city lost baseball for awhile, but it returned in 1969.

For the '69 season, a team was purchased in the new Pioneer League by Logan W. Hurlbert who, with the help of his wife Marie, built a well-respected minor league franchise. It wasn't easy. The ballpark he leased was, euphemistically put, a fixer-upper — more ready for demolition than for pro ball.

Here's an excerpt from the first lease Hurlbert signed with the city for Legion Park:

"Lessee agrees that the following will be completed by June 25, 1969: Repair and paint where needed of office area, visitor and home dressing rooms; repair plumbing (showers, toilets, drinking fountains) and replace hot water storage tank; replace dugout steps and fence screen along baselines; repair and paint scoreboard; repair infield and replace pitcher's mound to comply with new standards . . . replace broken windows . . . and conduct general cleanup of all areas. In addition to the above, Lessee agrees to repair the loose cement above the grandstand walking area."

Hurlbert watered the Legion Park infield himself during the franchise's first year in 1969, while Marie laundered uniforms. The team drew just 350 customers per game that first year. Successful promotion, however, made the franchise grow. They now average something like 2400 per game, and a three-piece band entertains crowds between innings.

Hurlbert's job was made easier by the work of the Great Falls Booster Club. New ballplayers are always given a welcome dinner. The club underwrites the team mascot, "Scruffy the Squirrel," pays ten-dollar incentives for shutout pitching and home run hitting, puts together a picnic for players and fans on the day of the major league All-Star Game, pays one-third of the cost for fan buses to away games, and pays the organist.

Legion Park sure isn't the shambles it used to be. Since the team has been in town, thousands of dollars have been spent on improvements on Legion Park. New lights have been installed, as have new seats, an underground watering system, new offices, more restrooms, and a handicap ramp. And of course, it has the advantage of being built beneath the Big Sky.

Hurlbert recently retired from day-to-day operation of the club, but remains with the ball club in an advisory capacity.

Green Bay, Wisconsin

Bluejay Field
Wisconsin State League 1946–53, Three-I League 1958–60 (Bluejays). *Location:* Joannes Park. *Torn down:* 1987.

According to former Bluejays business manager Al Maes, "the city of Green Bay tore down the old ball park [in 1987] and erected a bleacher park that is a disgrace to the city."

Bluejay Field had a roofed grandstand, and it came very close to losing it in 1959. While the Bluejays were on the road a tornado crossed the outfield. A light tower was knocked over, and

the wooden fence in the left field corner was destroyed.

Greensboro, North Carolina

War Memorial Stadium
Carolina League 1945–68, South Atlantic League 1979–present (Hornets). *Location:* Lindsay Street. *Dimensions:* Left field, 327 feet; center field, 401 feet; right field, 327 feet. *Seating capacity:* 10,000. *1987 season capacity:* 166,208.

Formerly doubled as a half-mile dirt track. The single-decked grandstand is shaped like a long-stemmed J, with the stem going down the left field line, past the fence and into the distance, to the other end of the track. Only the seats between home and first have a roof. Used briefly in the 1988 film *Bull Durham*.

In terms of attendance, Greensboro is the strongest franchise in the Sally League these days.

Greenville, South Carolina

Greenville Municipal Stadium
Carolina League 1984–present (Braves). *Location:* One Braves Avenue, Mauldin Road. *Dimensions:* Left field, 335 feet; center field, 405 feet; right field, 335 feet. *Seating capacity:* 7023. *1987 season attendance:* 203,549.

Concrete grandstand has 22 rows of bench seating and no roof. Reserved seats behind home are painted red and blue. Surrounded by rolling woody land.

Guadalajara, Mexico

Parque de Beisbol de la Universidad de Guadalajara
Mexican League, Zona Sur (Charros de Jalisco), present. *Dimensions:* Left field, 330 feet; center field, 400 feet; right field, 330 feet. *Seating capacity:* 18,000.

Bernie Arbour Stadium, Hamilton, Ontario, Canada. (Photo by David Pietrusza.)

Hagerstown, Maryland

Municipal Stadium
Interstate League 1947 (Owls), Carolina League 1981–present (Suns). *Location:* ½ mile off Highway 11 and Route 70. *Dimensions:* Left field, 335 feet; center field, 400 feet; right field, 335 feet. *Seating capacity:* 6000. *1987 season attendance:* 135,059.

The 1947 Interstate League franchise was a Detroit Tigers farm club. Park was described then, almost forty years before it was used by the Carolina League, as "old and beat up."

Hamilton, Ontario

Scott Park
Home of Hamilton baseball before 1972. *Location:* Downtown.

Bernie Arbour Park
Inter-County Major Baseball League circa 1972 (Cardinals), New York–Pennsylvania League 1988–present

(Redbirds). *Location:* Mohawk Road, Upper Kenilworth Avenue, "on the mountain." *Constructed:* 1972. *Dimensions:* Left field, 303 feet; left center, 375 feet; center field, 400 feet; right center, 375 feet; right field, 325 feet. *Fences:* Eight feet all the way around (chain link). *Seating capacity:* (1972) 600, (1988) 3200. *First game:* June 16, 1988.

Named after a late local police sergeant. On Opening Day 1988 the Hamilton-Wadsworth Regional Police Pipe Band wore their kilts and played their bagpipes. Skydivers parachuted onto the infield. Later the Sultans Six Jazz Band played between innings and Hamilton mascot Bud E. Bird cavorted in a feathery costume. Seats consist of metal bleachers.

Hampton, Virginia

Hampton Institute Field
Negro National League (Chicago American Giants 1920s, annual barnstorming games).

Hannibal, Missouri

League Park (League Field, Clayton's Showground)
Hannibal baseball's primary home 1871–1900. Home of the Nationals 1871, the Blues 1886–89, and the Eagles in the early 1900s. Central Association 1909 (Cannibals). *Location:* Lyon and Glascock streets.

According to Roberta and J. Hurley Hagood in their book *Hannibal, Too,* the infield at League Park often had huge clumps of grass in it, and the grass in the outfield was allowed to grow so high that baseballs kept getting lost in it. That conjures a familiar picture for any country boy: fellows toeing the weeds for horsehide, looking glum.

At the turn of the century, the streetcar company laid special tracks to the ballpark. Jake Beckley, now a Hall of Famer, was a local who arranged exhibition games between the Hannibal Eagles and major league competition, the Reds in 1902 and the Cardinals in 1904.

Judge Eby Leaves the Bench. By Opening Day, 1909, the last year League Park was used, this field had been the home of baseball for as long as just about anybody could remember. This was where the Nationals had played all the way back in 1871, and where the Blues had played in the 1880s, and now where the Cannibals of the Central Association made their home playing teams from Keokuk, Kewanee, and Ottumwa. Attendance Opening Day was 3327.

It was a day bright with warm golden sunshine—not a day to be cooped up inside. According to the Hagoods, "The enthusiasm for baseball was contagious. It even permeated the legal court system.... Judge David H. Eby, after listening to cases all morning, and with a proposed full docket for the afternoon, succumbed when the First Regiment Band marched by on its way to League Park. The balmy weather of a spring day also contributed to his

decision."

According to the May 4, 1909, *Hannibal Courier-Post,* Judge Eby said to his court stenographer, and we quote, "I think I will go to the ballgame." The man quickly grabbed his hat and exited, leaving a stunned courtroom to file out into the fresh air on their own volition.

By 1910, baseball moved to Mainland's Park at Oakwood, and the franchise moved to the Three-I League.

On September 12, 1914, this was the site of a performance by the Buffalo Bill Show. The park by this time was known as Clayton's Showground. As they had been since 1870, the grounds were used for circuses, carnivals, and medicine shows. The park was convenient for shows that traveled by train because of its proximity to a railroad spur. The circuses that most frequently came to town in those days were Lemon Brothers, Sells-Floto, Sells-Downs, John Robinson, Barnum and Bailey, and Wallace and Hagenbeck.

Mark Twain Cave Park
Used for baseball, 1890s.

Park, originally known as Cave Hollow, was renamed to exploit its appearance in *The Adventures of Tom Sawyer.* During the 1890s the baseball field outside the cave became popular because it was kept in excellent condition.

Mainland's Park (Robal Park)
Central Association 1910–15 (Cannibals), Three-I League 1916–18 (Mules), Illinois-Missouri League, early 1920s–1924. *Location:* Market Street in Oakwood, two and a half miles from downtown Hannibal.

When owner John Mainland, owner of the Hannibal Electric Company (the firm who furnished Hannibal's streetcar service), purchased Link-McMahon Park, renamed it Mainland's Park and fixed it up, all of the teams that had been playing in League Park moved to Mainland's for the the 1910 season.

Then Mainland built a home on the red sand bluffs behind the streetcar barns, up on the top level of the bluffs overlooking his ballpark.

After the end of World War I, Hannibal became a union town, and the name of Mainland's Park was changed to Robal Park—labor spelled backwards. Mainland continued to put improvements into the park. The playing field was finely groomed—an improvement over League Park, which had an infield of great relief. Here, the outfield grass was always kept cut short. A grandstand was built. Picnic benches were placed beneath neighboring sycamore trees. Picturesque bridges were repeatedly built across nearby Bear Creek, only to be washed away again and again by flooding. Fourth of July fireworks displays were held. Only when people sneaking into the ballpark without paying became a problem did Mainland build an eight-foot board fence all the way around the ballpark. A policeman walked the perimeter of the park continuously in search of those trying to climb over—but usually he was an understanding bloke who allowed boys to watch through the knotholes.

Hometown boy and future Hall of Famer (elected 1971) Jake Beckley, returned to Hannibal in 1911 after a glorious major league career and played 98 games for the team as a player-coach. Mainland's Park was used in 1915 as an outdoor movie theater, with the silent films projected on something Mainland called a "Sky Dome."

In 1916, Hannibal's first year in the Three-I League, the team drew 89,000 fans to Robal Park. Then the war took away Hannibal's interest in recreation, and the league disbanded in 1918. Baseball did not return to Hannibal and to Robal Park until the early 1920s, this time as a representative of the Illinois-Missouri League. The star player for that team was Perry Palmer, an osteopathy student with a moving fastball.

Robal Park was the site of various odd entertainments that passed through town. In 1920, for example, Red Liberty (probably not his real name) came to Robal Park and jumped a gap between two ramps in a four-cylinder Baby Overland. One of Hannibal's favorite entertainers who appeared yearly at Robal Park was Toby, a singer, guitar player, magician, and salesman of "Toby's Elixir."

Next to the ballpark Mainland built a dance pavilion, which was open-ended so night breezes could keep dancers cool in the days before air conditioning. The pavilion was used for dance marathons—a fad that was short-lived as it proved dangerous to the health of the competitors.

The Flood. Throughout its history, Robal Park was plagued by Bear Creek, which tended to overflow its banks. The creek ran right past the ballpark, between the park and Market Street. The problem was usually annoying, and one night it was disastrous.

On August 15, 1916, 3.82 inches of rain fell on Hannibal. At 1:30 a.m. on the 16th, Bear Creek was a mile wide in some places and ten feet deep in places where it wasn't supposed to be at all. At the ballpark, night watchman Thomas Rouse had to climb higher and higher up the grandstand to avoid the rising waters and was forced to spend the night on the very top row of seats. With lightning offering the only visibility, Rouse could see the boards of the outfield fence floating off. The little bridge was again washed away.

The ballpark was restored following the flood and was used for eight more years before it was replaced by Clemens Field. Into the 1930s Robal Park was considered a popular picnic area, but it gradually fell into disuse.

Clemens Field

Illinois-Missouri League 1925 (Travelers), Corn Belt League 1946, Central Association 1947 (Pilots). Also the site of Hannibal High School football games and track meets 1910–25. *Location:* Third and Collier streets. *Seating capacity:* (1925) 2000, wood. (1938) 2000, concrete. *Fire:* 1936. *Rebuilt:* 1937–38. *Lights:* 1947.

Named after Samuel, of course.

In 1924, a group of Hannibal businessmen decided it would be a sound financial move to build a facility to replace Robal Park for the town's existing Illinois-Missouri League franchise. L.H. Quirk was chairman of a campaign to raise funds to build the structure. The businessmen guaranteed the money in advance so construction could start before the money was raised. This was done out of necessity so the ballpark would be ready for the beginning of the 1925 season.

Land was purchased for the park at Third and Collier, which till then had been the site of the Cruikshank Lumber Mill. Beside the diamond was built a wooden grandstand holding 2000.

The first game in Clemens Field featured the Hannibal Travelers versus the Quincy Eagles. Perry Palmer was the pitcher for the Travelers. The Travelers lasted only one year. After 1925, Hannibal had a ballpark but no team.

In the spring of 1929, the Mississippi overflowed its banks severely. A photo of Clemens Field taken April 29 shows only the top of the wooden outfield fence and the top few rows of stands above water.

From 1925 on, Clemens Field was the home of Hannibal High School football. In 1929, Clemens Field was first used for Hannibal-LaGrange College's major games.

There were attempts to turn Clemens Field into a money-making proposition during the Depression years by booking events like carnivals into the grounds, but the original agreement stated that the facility could only be used as an athletic grounds, so these attempts were stifled.

The first night baseball game in Hannibal was played at Clemens Field on August 15, 1930, when the Kansas City Monarchs, a black team with their own portable lighting system, played a local nine in an exhibition. The Monarchs won the game 16–1—and did a lot of clowning around near the end.

Out with the Old and in with the New. In 1936, the wooden grandstand at Clemens Field burned down. The Works Progress Administration gave $40,000 and the city another $10,000 toward rebuilding the park in concrete and steel, with a large stone wall encircling the grounds to replace the rickety wooden one that had been there. Because of this stone wall, Clemens Field was literally used as a fortress on a couple of occasions, once to keep prisoners in and once to keep protesters out.

The rock for the wall was quarried by WPA workers from the top of Riverside Street. This had to be done by hand, a very slow process, so actual construction on the new park did not start until 1937. The concrete grandstand was built on the opposite end of the field from the old one. At the site of the wooden grandstand was built, also by the WPA, the Admiral Robert E. Coontz Armory, which was made of the same stone used to build the athletic grounds' wall.

In October 1939, the National Youth Administration sodded the field and painted the grandstand. The new park was used for baseball for the first time for a visit by the bearded baseball magicians of the House of David, who came from Benton Harbor, Michigan, to make a local nine look silly.

The playing field was so huge that a wooden fence was constructed inside the stone wall, with the additional space being used for softball diamonds.

The War. In the autumn of 1944, 200 German prisoners were detained in tents behind barbed wire and the stone walls of Clemens Field. The prisoners sorted military shoes that had been collected by the army to be sent to European refugees. Captain Elgin Fuller was in charge of bringing prisoners to Hannibal and seeing after their housing, feeding and security.

The war, in its way, helped the playing field. Preoccupation with matters overseas had caused the waterfront to be neglected, and four hundred truckloads of silt had gathered by 1945 in the cobblestone wharf between Broadway and Center streets. This silt was taken to Clemens Field, where it served to level and elevate the playing field, which was the worse for wear after its stint as a prisoner-of-war camp.

In 1946, the City Council appropriated $15,000 toward improving Clemens Field as pro ball came to town for the first time in over 20 years. The franchise in the Corn Belt League lasted only one year, as did the team in the Central Association the following year, for which $7500 worth of lights were installed. There has not been professional baseball in Hannibal since.

Since then the park has been used for carnivals (complete with amusement park rides), the rodeo (a practice eventually stopped because horseshoes tear up the playing field), and intramural softball and baseball.

The most controversial event at Clemens Field in the recent past took place on April 24, 1982, when the Ku Klux Klan were told they could have a rally in Hannibal, as long as they had it in Clemens Field. The city's thinking was that the stone wall would keep the Klan in and protesters out. It worked, and there was no trouble.

Clemens Field is still standing and is still used for local sports.

Harlingen, Texas

Giants Field
Texas League 1960–61. *Seating capacity:* 4000.

Harrisburg, Pennsylvania

Island Park
Tri-State League 1904–14, International League 1915, New York State League 1916–17, Eastern Colored League 1924–27 (Giants), Negro National League 1943 (Stars), Interstate League 1947 (Senators). *Seating capacity:* 3700.

There was minor league baseball in Harrisburg from 1900 to 1952, and then none for 35 years. Island Park was on an island in the middle of the Susquehanna River, and often flooded after a heavy rain.

RiverSide Stadium
Eastern League 1987–present (Senators). *Location:* On City Island, same as early minor league ballpark. *Construction cost:* $1.9 million. *Seating capacity:* 5200. *1987 season attendance:* 212,141.

The original grandstand was designed to last only two years. A small grandstand sits behind home, and open bleachers oversee the third base side. On the first base side are the trailers that serve as the clubhouses, offices and ticket stands. Plans are to enlarge the seating capacity for 1989, and to build permanent structures to replace the trailers.

The 62-acre park that surrounds this stadium also has softball fields, basketball and tennis courts, and a specialty foods area known as RiverSide Village.

Harrisonburg, Virginia

Municipal Field
Virginia League circa 1950 (Turks). *Seating capacity:* 2000.

Hartford, Connecticut

Hartford Baseball Grounds
National Association 1874–75, National League 1876–77 (Dark Blues). *Location:* Wyllys and Hendrixon.

Obstacles in the outfield no longer exist. The old Yankee Stadium had monuments in deep center field, and before fences were drawn in many flagpoles came right up out of the field. But these hazards were nothing compared to those found on the grounds Hartford used in the 1870s.

There were three trees (they appear to be apple trees from a bird's-eye drawing of the park done in 1877 by Oakley H. Bailey) in that outfield — one in left, one in center and one in right, all inside the outfield fence. One wonders how often and in what bizarre ways those trees came into play.

The tree in straightaway center was the most crucial. The centerfielder practically had to play in the shade of that tree when one of the big boys came up.

The fences themselves could not be reached with the batted ball. The Hartford Blues, as a team, hit four home runs in all of 1876 (58 games), and the odds are that none of them left the premises.

In the Shadow of the Steeple. During both of Hartford's big league stints teams played at the Hartford Baseball Grounds, located at the corner of Wyllys Avenue and Hendrixon Avenue, in the Fourth Ward, exactly one mile as the crow flies from the Union Railroad Depot. The street address was listed variously by the *Geer's Hartford City Directory* as 230 and 258 Wyllys Street.

The roofed wooden grandstand with a capacity of several thousand sat along Wyllys. The diamond was set up facing south so that the sun was in batters' eyes as days grew long. A small press box with a domed roof sat on top of the grandstand directly behind home. Hendrixon Avenue ran past third base.

A wooden fence surrounded the grounds, which were only four blocks from the Connecticut River and directly across Hendrixon Avenue from the Church of Good Shepherd. In modern ballparks the shadows of the grand-stand cross the infield heading toward second base. In Hartford, late in the season, the shadow of the church steeple crossed the infield toward home plate during the early innings. There were stables beyond the outfield fence.

The Hartford Baseball Club, the Dark Blues, had a man named Morgan Gardner Bulkeley as their president in 1874 and 1875. When the National League formed in 1876, Bulkeley was unanimously elected as its first president and agreed to serve one year. During that time he enhanced the image of the game by reducing drinking and gambling on games — but the season ended badly for the new league. The Chicago franchise won the pennant easily, while the Athletics of Philadelphia and the Mutuals of New York (Brooklyn) refused to make their last western trip and were tossed from the league. Bulkeley was replaced as league president in December of 1876 by William Hulbert.

The Hartford Baseball Club was organized on February 24, 1874, and maintained offices at 258 Main Street.

Pitcher for the 1876 Dark Blues was Candy Cummings, the man most often credited with the invention of the curveball. It was his pitch that caused the uproar among scientists. Curveballs were impossible, they said. It was an optical illusion. Cummings was 16–8 in 1876 with a 2.14 earned run average. He didn't care whether or not his pitch curved — just as long as they couldn't hit it.

Hitting star for that year's Dark Blues was John Cassidy, who hit .378, second in the league. Then something must have happened to him because he never hit as high as .270 again.

Bob "Death to Flying Things" Ferguson managed the ball club in 1876 to a 47–21 record, good for a third place finish behind Spalding's White Stockings and St. Louis. Ferguson hit one home run in 2306 major league at-bats.

Hattiesburg, Mississippi

C.J. "Pete" Taylor Park

Home of the University of Southern Mississippi Golden Eagles (Metro Conference), present. *Dimensions:* Left field, 340 feet; left center, 365 feet; center field, 400 feet; right center, 365 feet; right field, 340 feet. *Seating capacity:* 2000 (bleacher seating).

Dressing rooms are in the adjacent Green Coliseum, but the park has a new sprinkler system and new lights. The press facilities are lacking, but there are plans to change that in the near future. One of the more popular aspects of Taylor Park is the lounge area with picnic tables on the other side of the right field fence.

C.J. "Pete" Taylor was coach of the University of Southern Mississippi Golden Eagles from 1959 to 1983.

Havana, Cuba

Estadio Latino Americano (Gran Stadium)

International League 1954–60 (Cubans), site of the 1987 Inter-Continental Cup (amateur). *Built:* 1940s. *Dimensions:* Left field, 325 feet; left center, 380 feet; center field, 400 feet; right center, 380 feet; right field, 325 feet. *Fences:* Eight feet—four feet of plexiglass on top of four feet of wood. Plexiglass added to keep outfielders out of the stands. Ten feet in straightaway center (hitters' background). *Seating capacity:* (1960) 28,000; (1987) 55,000.

The light towers in center field come right up out of the seats, so it's easy to tell that the bleachers were there first. An electric scoreboard perches atop the bleachers in right center. The grandstand is an extremely high and roofed single deck with obstructing roof supports. The stadium is totally enclosed by seats, with bleachers all the way across the outfield.

The whole stadium is painted army-fatigue green. The foul poles are short,

but painted a shiny color to make them easily visible. The bullpens are in left and right between the stands and the foul lines.

For television broadcasts mini-cams are allowed on the playing field. It's strange to see a camera operator and a cable puller scurrying around behind home plate in between pitches.

Cubans don't boo, they whistle.

Helena, Montana

Kindrick Legion Field

Pioneer League 1978–present (Gold Sox). *Location:* Warren and Memorial streets. *Dimensions:* Left field, 324 feet; center field, 410 feet; right field, 340 feet. *Seating capacity:* 2500. *1987 season attendance:* 27,020.

According to Bob Decker, the best seat in the Pioneer League is in the upper corner of the right field bleachers in Kindrick Legion Field. In an article for *Montana Magazine* called "Baseball Under the Big Sky," Decker wrote:

"The visible urban landmarks, including the spires of St. Helena Cathedral and the dome of the Capitol, are charming, and I can ponder the surrounding landforms for innings on end—the Scratchgravel Hills ... the Big Belt and Elkhorn ranges ... the sprawling Helena Valley...

"Sometimes, when Old Glory rolls in a gentle evening breeze, when the setting sun dapples the hills under pastel skies, and when the crowd murmurs in summer complacency, my attention wanders from the playing of the game. But that's a common occurrence in the Pioneer League, and baseball forgives the indiscretion."

"The mountains and the streams are our competition," says Ward Goodrich, general manager of the Helena Gold Sox, a team that survives by drawing 750 per game from the Pioneer League's smallest city. The team started in the league as an affiliate of the Phillies in 1978. They were an independent team for a year in 1984, and have been a farm club of the Milwaukee Brewers since.

Hoboken, New Jersey

Elysian Fields
Location: Tenth, Eleventh, Hudson and Washington streets.

A bearded surveyor named Alexander Cartwright wrote down the rules to baseball for the first time in 1845, standardizing the game and allowing it to be played between towns. The rules made baseball a fast pitch game, too difficult to be played well by an average man—and it was to get significantly more difficult to play with later changes in the rules—yet splendid when played by exceptional athletes, such as a town's best nine. The first organized game under the new rules was played at the Elysian Fields in Hoboken, New Jersey, on June 19, 1846. The New York Nine defeated the Knickerbockers 23-1. Cartwright himself umped. During the game, decency forced him to fine a New York player named Davis six cents for using a cuss word.

The Elysian Fields was a large lawn with no fences—a real park. There were many mature shade trees growing deep in the outfield. History has chosen this game as the sport's official premiere, yet an illustration of the game drawn at the time shows a diamond with basepaths already worn bare. There were no seats, but interested spectators stood two or three deep all around the proceedings. Many stood behind the outfielders, perhaps for the shade. As far as we know, no women attended. Fielders played barehanded, and pitchers delivered the ball underhand. It was a slower, smaller game than today—but you'd recognize it right away if you saw it.

The Knickerbockers, under Alexander Cartwright's leadership, drew up a club constitution. For $75, the team rented both the Elysian Fields and its dressing room for a year.

Used for baseball as late as 1873, when the New York Mutuals of the National Association played the Brooklyn Atlantics here for a Fourth of July game.

The site is currently residential, consisting of both houses and apartment buildings. On the grassy median in the middle of Eleventh Street is a plaque commemorating the site.

Sergeant William Feskin Memorial Field
Present home of Hoboken Little League. Location: Hudson, Fourth, and Fifth streets; the Hudson River.

Named after Hoboken man killed in Vietnam.

Hollywood, California

Gilmore Field
Pacific Coast League 1939–57 (Stars). Opened: 1939. Location: 7700 Beverly Boulevard, Fairfax and Third streets, next to Gilmore Stadium. Current site of Farmers' Market and CBS's Television City. Dimensions: Left field, 335 feet; left center, 383 feet; center field, 400 feet; right center, 383 feet; right field, 335 feet. 34 feet from home plate to the backstop. Final Pacific Coast League game: September 5, 1957 (attendance 6354).

In the 1890s, Arthur Gilmore bought a small parcel of land within the Rancho La Brea, and there he ran a dairy farm. In 1903, Gilmore struck oil while drilling for water. Gilmore's son, Earl, developed the A.F. Gilmore Oil Company into the largest independent oil business in California. Gilmore Field and Gilmore Stadium were built to mark the spot of the discovery.

The park was solid-looking, much like Wrigley Field in Los Angeles. There was a sign on the outfield fence advertising the Brown Derby.

The Hollywood Stars moved here after playing for a time in Wrigley Field

Top: *Hoboken, N.J.: Plaque commemorates the first intertown game ever. (Photo by Katherine Krassner.)* Bottom: *Feskin Field, Hoboken, N.J., with the Hudson River and the Manhattan skyline in the background. (Photo by Bob Wolfman.)*

(Los Angeles), and then next door in Gilmore Stadium while the finishing touches were put on their new home. The Pacific Coast League franchise was owned by George Burns, Gracie Allen, Gary Cooper, Cecil B. DeMille, Walt Disney, William Frawley, George Stevens, and Bing Crosby. For them, Earl Gilmore would build a baseball park next to his football stadium.

Major league expansion destroyed the Stars, of course.

Gilmore Stadium
Pacific Coast League 1939 (Stars, some games). *Location:* Next to Gilmore Field. *Seating capacity:* 18,000.

A football stadium used for baseball briefly in 1939, while the finishing touches were put on Gilmore Field next door. Built by oil tycoon Earl Gilmore.

It was known as the working man's stadium because it offered popular Depression prices. It was here that Los Angeles got its first taste of pro football.

There was midget car racing. According to Bruce T. Torrence in *Hollywood: The First 100 Years,* "Every conceivable form of outdoor entertainment was promoted successfully at Gilmore Stadium."

Honolulu, Hawaii

Honolulu Stadium (The Old Lady)
Pacific Coast League 1961–75 (Hawaii Islanders). Also former home of the University of Hawaii Fighting Deans football team and former site of the annual Hula Bowl. *Location:* King Street. *Opened:* November 11, 1926. *Seating capacity:* about 25,000. *Last game:* September 8, 1975.

Honolulu Stadium was the brain-child of J. Ashman Beaven, a lawyer and sports promoter, who saw his dream come true when local sportsmen and business firms backed him to the tune of $100,000. Beaven purchased 14 acres of land, and it was upon this that Honolulu Stadium was built. It was designed to tide over baseball and football for 15 years. It lasted 49.

By the time the "Old Lady" was abandoned, she was termite-eaten and tottering on her steel frames. The ballpark bowed out in glory as the Islanders picked 1975 to win their first Pacific Coast League pennant since 1960. Organist Rollie Wray played "Aloha Oe" for the final Islander game.

Johnny Kerr, who also functioned as a pass receiver for Kamehameha Alumni, was the first person ever to hit a ball completely out of Honolulu Stadium. His home run on May 20, 1934, landed in the St. Louis Alumni Association Clubhouse grounds. Joe Di-Maggio duplicated the feat on June 4, 1944, before 26,000 fans as his 7th Air Force club lost to Navy, 6–2.

On October 25, 1935, Connie Mack's Major League All-Stars came to town for a game against a picked Hawaii baseball team. The Islanders were out-matched. Lou Gehrig slammed a home run, and Babe Ruth added a pair of doubles.

During its long life, Honolulu Stadium housed religious crusades, fairs, Boy Scout makahikis, stock car racing, polo, track, professional boxing, and lots of football.

Aloha Stadium
Pacific Coast League 1975–87 (Hawaii Islanders). Also home of the University of Hawaii Rainbow Warriors football team. Site of the annual Hula Bowl. *Location:* Halawa Valley, not far from Pearl Harbor. *Architect:* Charles Luckman. *Cost of construction:* $27 million. *Dimensions:* Left field, 325 feet; center field, 420 feet; right field, 325 feet. *Turf:* Artificial. *Seating capacity:* 50,063.

A truly different kind of ballpark. Whole sections of the huge grandstand are on sophisticated "wheels," so the configuration can be changed from baseball to football and back again. The sides of the stadium are parallel when football is being played. For baseball they swing out to form a right angle.

There are no wasted seats at Aloha Stadium. The four separate grandstand sections are movable into the best positions for viewing through the "air film" principle. Each moveable grandstand weighs 3.5 million pounds and rotates 200 feet through a 40-degree arc. Twenty-eight thousand seats are moved when the configuration is changed. According to the *Honolulu Star Bulletin,* the "air film" principle is applied by use of transporters manufactured by Rolair Systems of Santa Barbara, California. The transporters, located under the stands, travel on concrete runways. They are supplied with compressed air, and they lift the grandstand off the concrete runway. With friction minimized, the section of grandstand can be moved by a simple hydraulic system guided by a fixed rail. It's been said the stadium does the mechanical hula. Actually, the opening grandstand resembles an opening blossom.

The stands that do most of the moving are the makai (west) stands and the mauka (east) stands.

When architect Charles Luckman first came up with the idea to build a ballpark that changes itself back and forth from a football stadium to a

baseball stadium, he couldn't get anyone to believe that his system would
work. He finally had to demonstrate his
own confidence in the project by post-
ing a $1 million performance bond,
something he had never heard of an architect doing before. Among Luckman's other architectural achievements
are the Manned Spacecraft Center in
Houston, the 300-acre lineal acceler-
ator at Stanford University, the U.S.
Pavilion at the New York World's Fair,
and the Prudential Center in Boston.

When the stadium opened in September 1975, the Stadium Authority
threw an open house. There was a
parade with 10 bands, 14 high school
football teams and Governor George
Ariyoshi, who made the only speech of
the free event. Those attending the
event got the first look at the moving
grandstand, the fine lighting and sound
system, and the million-dollar scoreboard. That scoreboard became an instant favorite of the fans, as it provided
an entertaining side show with its
animated action of players and spectators, as well as slogans in local
jargon.

Stadium snack concessions offer the
usual ballpark fare, as well as some
uniquely Hawaiian taste treats. Also
served are boiled peanuts, Chinese
preserved seeds, and a steaming noodle
soup called saimin.

After all that work to build an adapt-
able stadium, one would have thought
pro baseball would have stayed in
Hawaii forever and ever. Not so. To
cut down on Pacific Coast League
travel expenses after the 1987 season,
the Islanders moved to Colorado
Springs, Colorado, and became the
Sky Sox. This was bad news to the players of the PCL, who had come to cherish
their periodic trips to paradise.

Houston, Texas

West End Park
Texas League 1907–27.

On August 15, 1915, West End Park
was rendered unusable for the rest of
the season by a tropical storm – the
same storm that wiped out the park in
Galveston.

Buffalo Stadium (Busch Stadium)
Texas League 1928–42, 1946–58 (Buffaloes), Negro American League 1949–
50 (Eagles), American Association
1959–61. *Location:* 4000 Harby Street
(third base), 4001 Gulf Freeway (first
base), Cullen Boulevard (right field).
Seating capacity: 11,500. *Dimensions:*
Left field, 345 feet; center field, 440
feet; right field, 325 feet.

Park opened in April 1928 as home
of the minor league Houston Buffaloes,
who were named after the Buffalo
Bayou, which cuts Houston in half.
Fans entered the park through a Span-
ish-style gate.

The park was renamed Busch Stadium for a time when the Buffaloes
became part of the St. Louis Cardinal
farm system.

When Houston received their major
league expansion franchise, it was
decided that Buffalo Stadium – or just
Buff Stadium as it tended to be called in
the newspapers – did not have the
seating capacity or the parking for a
major league facility.

The site currently holds Fingers Furniture Store, and the Houston Sports
Hall of Fame, where there is a plaque
commemorating the park.

Colt Stadium
National League 1962–64 (Colt .45s).
Owned by the Houston Colt .45s.
Location: Kirby Street (home plate
side), Route 610 (third base), currently
the Astrodome parking lot. *Construction cost:* $2,000,000. *Dimensions:*
Left field, 360 feet; left center, 395 feet;
center field, 420 feet; right center, 395
feet; right field, 360 feet. 60 feet from
home plate to the backstop. *Fences:*
Left field, 8 feet; center field, 30 feet
(hitters' background); right field, 8
feet. *Seating capacity:* 32,000. Lower

Colt Stadium, Houston, Tex., with the Astrodome under construction next door. (Photo courtesy of the Houston Astros.)

boxes, 8448; promenade boxes, 5541; reserved, 6348; general admission, 11,663. *Day game attendance record:* 26,697 (April 16, 1964, versus Milwaukee). *Doubleheader attendance record:* 30,027 (June 10, 1962, versus Los Angeles). *Night game attendance record:* 28,669 (September 12, 1962, versus Los Angeles). *Opening game attendance record:* 26,697 (April 16, 1964, versus Milwaukee). *Season high attendance record:* 924,456 (1962). *Season low attendance record:* 719,502 (1963). *First game:* April 10, 1962 (Houston 11, Chicago 2). *Last game:* September 27, 1964 (night, Houston 1, Los Angeles 0, 12 innings).

Colt Stadium was never known as a great place to play ball. The concrete was still wet when it opened in 1962. It was meant to be temporary, with a designed lifespan of three years. It ended up torturous. The park was in a swamp.

On a muggy August evening the heat and humidity and humongous Texas-sized mosquitoes made the Colt .45s home a lot like playing ball in Vietnam.

Once, during a Sunday twin bill, 100 fans needed first aid for the heat. The place was bad enough to warrant a mention in Bruce Nash and Allan Zullo's first volume of *The Baseball Hall of Shame.* Allan and Zullo wrote, "Colt Stadium's singular claim to fame is that it was the only park in history where the concession stands sold more mosquito repellent than beer."

Poor lights provided anemic hitting and a gloomy ambiance during night games.

Considering the hardship, there wasn't a lot of despair. All fans had to do was look to the other side of the parking lot, to where they were building the Eighth Wonder of the World (the Astrodome), and it was easier to ignore the grounds crew spraying insecticide on the field between innings. The highlight of the park was the Fast Draw Club under the stands, with an Old West–type bar. There, fans drank beer and ate big bowls of Hell Fire Stew.

Houston's major league baseball history got off to a fabulous start. After Opening Day ceremonies that involved a marching band, the team won their first three games at home, sweeping a series against the Cubs. The boys in the press box began to chant, "Break up the Colts!" Rumors of a dynasty were premature.

The ballpark had a single unroofed grandstand going from foul pole to foul pole. There were bleachers in both left and right field and no seats in straightaway center. Signs on the outfield fence advertised local banks and florists.

When the park first opened the public address announcer earned $10 a game. His name was Dan Rather.

The Astrodome (Harris County Domed Stadium)

National League 1965–present (Astros). Owned by Harris County. *Location:* Route 610 (first base side), Kirby Street (home plate). Adjacent to the site of Colt Stadium. *Dimensions:* (1965) Left field, 340 feet; left center, 378 feet; center field, 400 feet; right center, 378 feet; right field, 340 feet. (1988, blue inner fence) Left field, 330 feet; left center, 370 feet; center field, 400 feet; right center, 370 feet; right field, 330 feet. 61 feet from home plate to the backstop. *Turf:* (1965) grass; (1966–present) astroturf. *Seating capacity:* 45,011. Lower boxes, 10,532; mezzanine boxes, 3880; mezzanine reserved, 6712; loge, 4912; club boxes, 1266; upper level, 11,741; sky boxes, 2058; pavilion, 3910. *First game:* April 9, 1965 (Astros 2, New York Yankees 1, 12 innings, exhibition, attendance 47,876). *First National League game:* April 12, 1965 (Philadelphia 2, Houston 0, attendance 42,652).

The first indoor baseball game featuring major league caliber competition was played April 9, 1965. The first indoor home run was hit by Mickey Mantle. Governor John Connally threw out the first indoor ball.

The original intention was to play in the Astrodome on grass. The ballpark, known as the Harris County Domed Stadium when it opened in 1965, had real grass on the field (special Tifway 419 for indoor use), and clear glass panes in the roof for photosynthesis. But the sunlight through the glass made playing the outfield dangerous. So the glass was painted, and the Tifway 419 bit the dust. Then they had to invent the carpet — and now we have to watch baseball played on plastic. Artificial turf has injured baseball far closer to its heart than the designated hitter rule. If there isn't any grass, then it isn't a park.

To mark the sad occasion, the day the music died, the first game on artificial turf was April 8, 1966, the Astros versus the Dodgers.

In 1981, Astros pitchers held opponents to 2.08 runs per game at home, earned and unearned — beating the old record set by Chicago White Sox pitchers in South Side Park in 1906 of 2.28 runs per game.

In the summer of 1987, the Harris County Commissioners Court moved toward issuing $60 million in bonds for renovation of the Astrodome. The money is to go toward the installation of two new playing surfaces (baseball and football), a concrete subfloor, and the expansion of the seating by 10,000, so the Astrodome will hold 60,000 for baseball and 61,500 for football. Under the new planned system, the conversion from the baseball to football playing surfaces will be done in an hour with a crew as small as four men. Air jets will float the one-piece surface over the field with a minimum of friction, so that it can be installed or removed. When the surfaces are not being used, they will be rolled into a steel core and stored in compartments below the floor.

The Astrodome's $2 million, 300-ton, 474-foot message board is the longest scoreboard in the world. Lindsay Nelson once broadcast a game (April 28, 1965) from the roof's gondola over second base. It was here that Willie Mays struck his 500th home run. On June 15, 1976, a game was postponed

The Astrodome, Houston, Tex. (Photo courtesy of the Houston Astros.)

here because of rain—the storm was so bad that no one could get to the ballpark. It was on the mound here that J.R. Richard's brilliance burned brightly yet briefly, and here where his career was ended by a stroke in 1980.

Cameron Field

Home of the Rice University Owls (Southwest Conference), present. *Seating capacity:* 1200.

Cougar Field

Home of the University of Houston Cougars (Southwest Conference), present. *Seating capacity:* 1500.

The outfield fence is a ten-foot-high screen with canvas draped over it in center to provide the hitter with a background. Even if the canvas were not there, hitters would be looking into the dark foliage of the thick trees growing on the other side of the outfield fence.

The most famous players to come out of the University of Houston baseball program are Tom Paciorek and Doug Drabek.

Hull, Massachusetts

Nantasket Bay

Location: On the lawn behind Nantasket's Sea Foam House.

On Thursday, September 2, 1880, this was the site of the very first game ever played at night under the lights. The game was staged by Boston's Northern Electric Light Company.

Edison invented the incandescent lightbulb in 1879, and the electric company wanted to show just what their products could do. A demonstration like night baseball might speed the installation of electric streetlights.

The game was played between two of Boston's prominent department stores, Jordan Marsh and R.H. White. Nobody came to see the ball game. Everyone came to see the lights.

For the game three wooden towers were erected. Each held 12 lamps for a total strength of 30,000 candlepower. The towers were 100 feet apart. Each was operated by its own generator. The three generators, and the two small engines that ran them, were housed in a nearby shed.

According to the *Boston Post,* "A clear, pure, bright light was produced, very strong and yet very pleasant to the sight," but the game was played with "scarcely the precision as by daylight." The game ended in a 16–16 tie as the players and 300 spectators had to catch the last boat back to Boston. It would be three years before lights would again find their way around a baseball field. (*See* Fort Wayne, Indiana.)

Huntsville, Alabama

Joe W. Davis Stadium
Southern League 1985–present (Stars). *Location:* South Memorial Parkway (Highway 231), between Drake Avenue and Airport Road. *Dimensions:* Left field, 345 feet; center field, 405 feet; right field, 330 feet. *Seating capacity:* 10,250. *Single game attendance record:* 11,653 (August 2, 1985. An appearance was made at this game by the San Diego Chicken, a man dressed in a chicken costume.) *1987 season attendance: 254,417. First game:* April 19, 1985. *Construction costs:* $7.6 million.

The ballpark is named after a five-term mayor of Huntsville. It features aluminum bench seating, with an ample press box (built for both baseball and football) and VIP boxes up top. The single deck of seats goes all the way down the left field foul line and wraps slightly around the pole into fair territory. In right field the grandstand goes only as far as first base. Between first and the right field fence is a small set of bleachers.

Built in the middle of a flat plain, parking lots on two sides, the ballpark sits near a major thoroughfare, Highway 231. When sitting in the stands one can see tree-covered hills above the double deck of ads on the high right field wall. Also visible above that wall is the Governor's House Motel. The first base end of the grandstand contains the "no alcoholic beverages" section. Perhaps it is no coincidence that this section is behind the visitor's dugout.

The scoreboard is in left center field, rising above the fence. In straightaway center, mounted to the top of the fence, is a small electronic message board.

Because there is no roof, fans tend to stay away when the weather is threatening.

In 1985 the Huntsville Stars — freshly transplanted from Nashville — won the Southern League pennant. That year the Southern League MVP was Stars outfielder José Canseco. The franchise has been very successful in its new home, drawing nearly 600,000 total during the '85 and '86 seasons.

The father of the Stars, and their first general manager, is local boy and former major leaguer Don Mincher. When health reasons forced him to step down from that post he continued on with the club as the director of public and community relations.

Idaho Falls, Idaho

McDermott Field (Highland Park 1930s–1976)
Pioneer League 1942–present (Nuggets, Braves 1986–present). *Location:* 500 West Elva, near the Latter Day Saints Temple. *Dimensions:* Left field, 350 feet; center field, 408 feet; right field, 350 feet. *Seating capacity:* (1940) 5000, (present) 2200. *1987 season attendance:* 52,164. *Fire:* 1976.

Idaho Falls has the longest continuous franchise in the Pioneer League, and they have played all of their home games on the same site. The original wooden grandstand was built sometime in the 1930s. Described as "delightfully comfortable," it had a roof that kept everyone dry except those that remained in their box seats.

In the autumn of 1976 young arsonists — who were later caught and punished — burned Highland Park down.

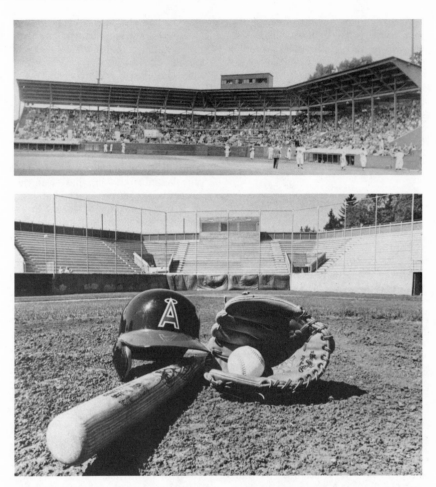

Top: *Highland Park, Idaho Falls, Ida. (Compliments of the* Post-Register.*)* Bottom: *McDermott Field, Idaho Falls, Ida. (Compliments of the* Post-Register.*)*

Forty years of paint went up very fast, so firemen could only concentrate on saving the outfield fences, the light towers, and one small section of bleachers.

The city immediately set about the task of rebuilding. The new concrete grandstand was built from the old park's insurance money. Out of financial necessity it was smaller and had no roof. The concession areas, locker rooms and offices were all improved over their predecessors, but fans

grumbled sometimes, wanting the old Highland back.

The new park—named McDermott Field in honor of E.F. McDermott, the local newspaper publisher and "Mr. Baseball of the Pioneer League"—was ready for the June start of the 1978 season. Rookie leagues start after school lets out.

McDermott served as president of the Idaho Falls Nuggets for over 20 years. He was 80 years old for the pre-game dedication ceremony, and died soon thereafter of cancer.

In the '80s, the Nuggets had financial difficulties, changing ownership and major league affiliation repeatedly. But, in 1987, in their second year in the Atlanta farm system, the Idaho Falls Braves drew 53,000 for the year, breaking the previous attendance record by 13,000.

Independence, Kansas

Riverside Park

Western Association (Class C) 1928–32 (Producers). *First night game:* April 28, 1930 (first minor league night game).

The first regular season night game was originally scheduled for Saturday, April 26, 1930, but was rained out. A Sunday afternoon game followed, so the lights weren't turned on till Monday night. More than a few breathed a sigh of relief. The honor of hosting the first official league night game could easily have slipped away if the weather had not been on Independence's side. The ballpark in Des Moines, Iowa, was equipped for night ball, but their home opener in the Western League was not scheduled until May 2.

It was a soggy Monday night and only 1000 people saw that first night game. Afterward, Producers catcher Sherman Walker said he thought the lights were pretty good, but he kept getting the impression there was only half a ball.

Indianapolis, Indiana

Camp Morton Field

There was a 25-cent admission charge to Camp Morton Field in 1870, to see the Indianapolis nine play teams like the Gad Flies, Shoo Flies, and Raging Tads. The Indianapolis team played the Cincinnati Red Stockings here on August 5, 1870, and the biggest crowd to see a game in Indiana up till

that time showed up. Final score: Cincinnati 61, Indianapolis 8. The team did have its major victories too. They beat Evansville 47–17 on August 22, but they did it on the road.

South Street Park

International Association 1876–77 (Capital Citys), National League 1878 (Blues). *Located:* Northeast corner of South and Delaware streets, between Delaware and Alabama streets, later the site of the "Big Four" freight houses. *First National League game:* May 1, 1878 (Chicago 5, Indianapolis 4, time: 2:30). *Last National League game:* September 14, 1878. Existed about three years.

Indianapolis got its first taste of major league baseball in 1876 when the city fielded the minor league Capital Citys. The team won the International Association championship and drew big crowds to the South Street Park whenever they played exhibition games against National League competition. At the end of the '76 season, National League officials announced that the team winning the most exhibition games against National League teams would be admitted to the league for the 1878 season. Nobody could hit Indianapolis's Edward "the Only" Nolan's inshoot—which he claimed to have invented—and it took a skilled batterymate like Frank "the Only" Flint to catch it. (Flint caught them with bare hands and would have laughed at the suggestion of shin guards or a mask.) "The Only" Blues defeated big league competition 14 times and were given a berth.

The biggest player on the team was Ned Williamson, later of the White Stockings, at 5' 11", 170 lbs. Even with the Only Nolan and the Only Flint as their battery, the team went 24–36 in 1878, and finished next to last.

On Opening Day at the South Street Park on May 1, 1878, Nolan struck out seven but lost to Chicago 5–4.

In those days there was a viaduct

over Delaware Street—not the old Virginia Avenue viaduct, but another. Fans approached along Washington Street (now U.S. Route 40), then crossed the viaduct to the ballpark, where all too few paid to get in.

When the club directors counted up the till at the end of the season they realized they were $2500 in debt and unable to make good on salary still due the players. A few of the players hired lawyers, but none of them ever got paid in full. The money just wasn't there.

Bruce Park

American Association 1884 (Hoosiers), National League 1887 (Hoosiers, Sundays only). *Location:* Bruce Street (now 23rd Street), College Avenue—in Broad Ripple, then outside the Indianapolis city limits. *First American Association game:* May 14, 1884. *Last American Association game:* September 21, 1884.

In 1884, the American Association was known as the "Beer and Whiskey League" because so many of its owners operated breweries and distilleries.

The members of the '84 Hoosiers tried to give the league's monicker a second application. More than once Indianapolis players had to be jailed for public drunkenness. In their daily reports the *Indianapolis Journal* complained ballplayers were showing up for games intoxicated.

The team left a bad taste in Indianapolis' mouth. Three years later, when the city was granted a franchise in the National League, citizens were worried that there would be a repeat of the rowdyism.

Because the park was in Broad Ripple, then outside the city limits, it was used by the National League Hoosiers in 1887 on Sundays to circumvent blue laws. Fans found the park inaccessible, and attendance here was never good.

Tinker Park (Seventh Street Field, Athletic Park)

National League 1887–89 (Hoosiers).

Location: Tinker Street (later known as Seventh Street, and today as 16th Street), Mississippi Street (now Senate Avenue), and Capitol Street. Current site of Methodist Hospital. *Dimensions:* Left field, 286 feet; right field, 261 feet. *Fences:* Tall screen in right.

Opening Day 1887 was a windy April afternoon, which kept the 100 or so ladies in attendance holding their hats on and keeping their bangs in order.

To get to the game people had to take the Illinois mule-car line to the turntable at Tinker Street (now Sixteenth Street)—and then walk the rest of the way. (By 1889, the mule-car line ran down Tinker all the way to the ballpark's entrance, and the jangle of the mule bells mingled with the yells of the fans.) The wind nearly blew pencils from the hands of reporters. The new Hoosier shortstop, Pebbly Jack Glasscock, was pulled aside by a fan and told that the new team would win public support only if they behaved themselves. Pebbly Jack assured the fan that the team was resolved to keep the good will of the citizens.

Some men read the newspaper as they waited for the game to start, and the stories were of actor Edwin Booth's performance at English's Theatre, John L. Sullivan's performance at the Grand Opera House, the construction of the Soldier's Monument, and an upcoming visit to Indianapolis by the Boston Symphony Orchestra.

The Hoosiers were owned by John T. Brush, owner of the When Store and organizer of the When Band. Brush went on to own the New York Giants.

Stores were closed Opening Day from three to six so employees could see the game. The When Band led a parade of dignitaries and players through the streets to the park. Crowds along the way cheered lustily, and already the wind was blowing a gale. Sadly, the game was won by visiting Detroit 4–3. Attendance was 3000.

The new Hoosiers, 75 percent of whom had handlebars across the upper lip, started off with a last place finish in 1887, and finished only a notch higher the next two seasons. Six managers saw duty in three years. Still the Indianapolis people loved them. The public was forced to release its embrace when National League owners got together before the 1890 season and gave the boot to the franchises in Indianapolis and Washington.

Indianapolis Park

National League 1888–89 (Hoosiers, Sundays only). *Location:* Hanna Street (now Oriental Street), New York and East Ohio streets, Arsenal Avenue.

This is where the National League Hoosiers played their Sunday games after they tired of the inaccessibility of Bruce Park. Also served as the home field for three Cleveland Spiders games in 1890.

Market-Oriental Park

Western Inter-State League 1890, Western League 1892, 1894–99. *Location:* Market and Oriental streets (formerly Noble's Pasture).

In Noble's Pasture, the founders of Indianapolis had held Fourth of July celebrations and Sunday School picnics. According to a 1932 retrospective in the *Indianapolis News,* the ballpark built there wasn't popular.

East Washington Street Park

American League 1900, American Association 1902–04. *Location:* East Washington (now U.S. Route 40) and Gray streets, later the site of Wonderland Amusement Park.

Indianapolis finished third in the American League's only year as a minor league. They were fifth in the eight-team league in attendance, drawing 76,000.

In November 1900, it was announced that for the following year, the first year of major league play, the Indianapolis franchise would be shifted eastward to Philadelphia.

The city's biggest sin in this case, it seems, was that it was too far away from the rest of the league.

The East Washington Street Park was then used to house a minor league team for three teams—and fans got to see the winning of the very first (new) American Association pennant.

It was during these years that the first Washington Park was home of popular George "Hoggy" Hogriever. The first thing Hoggy did when he put on a clean uniform was plug his cheek with a fresh chaw, then roll around on the ground until he was "looking like a hut on the Mud River." Folks just loved to call out, "Hit it, Hoggy!" because he usually did. He was known for hitting them to right and for telling the umpire what he was.

Hoggy died in 1961 a month and a half before his ninety-second birthday, no doubt in a very clean hospital bed.

When they stopped using this site for baseball, it became Wonderland, with shoot-the-chutes and other rides. The amusement park's biggest attraction was its replica of the Johnstown flood spectacle. When the water began to pour over the crevasse of the broken dam, the barker would shout, "My God! The dam has broke! Flee for your lives!"

West Washington Street Park

American Association 1905–12, 1915–31 (Indians), Federal League 1913–14 (Federal Hoosiers), Negro National League 1920s (ABCs). *Location:* West Washington Street (opposite the "car barns"). Current site of International Harvester, across the street from the Indianapolis Transit System property. *First Federal League (major league) game:* April 24, 1914. *Last Federal League game:* October 8, 1914. *First Negro National League game:* May 2, 1920 (ABCs 4, Chicago Giants 2).

Previous failures had not stifled Indianapolis' thirst for big league ball. In 1913, local investors raised $75,000 to join the upstart Federal League, founded by smooth-talking coal millionaire James Gilmore, who assured them the league would be operating at big league level by its second year. Technically, it did—but the talent made its major league status marginal.

The Federal Hoosiers had to play at the same time as the minor league franchise Indians, and a fierce competition went on for fans during these years.

The team clinched the 1914 Federal League pennant on October 3, and before the game the next day, there was a parade for the Hoosiers to the ballpark opposite the car barns.

According to the *Indianapolis Star,* "The Hoosiers were hauled around the city in benzine buggies, headed by Beiser's brass-bugle-blowing outfit. The parade was arranged by Prexy J. Ed Krause for copping the calico."

Boys found that the Big Four switchmen were a good-natured lot and always managed to slip a line of freight cars behind the right field fence, forming some do-it-yourself bleachers. The second the cars came to a halt the scramble was on for a viewing spot on their roofs.

Boys that didn't make it raced over to left field, where climbable power poles offered convenient perching. It wasn't as comfortable as a seat atop a freight car, but you could see the game.

In 1914, the Indy Feds fielded the best team Indianapolis would ever see. The team was managed by Bill Philips, and finished 88–65 behind the 25–18 pitching of Cy Falkenberg. The hitting star was right-fielder Benny Kauff, who hit a league-leading .370 while knocking in 95 runs, and second baseman Frank LaPorte, with a .311 average and 107 R.B.I.

Indianapolis won the Federal League pennant both years it was in the league, but attendance was lousy. The franchise was moved to Newark before the start of the 1915 season. Stockholders accepted a league offer of $76,000 for the club—and Indianapolis had seen its last big league baseball. This ballpark

remained in use by the American Association franchise until 1931. During the 1920s, Washington Park was the home (along with other fields) of the Indianapolis ABCs of the Negro National League.

The first Negro National League game—that is, the first game in league history—was played here May 2, 1920. The ABCs defeated Joe Green's Chicago Giants 4–2. Crowds of 8–10,000 came out to see the black team play on Sundays.

Brighton Beach Park
Circa 1905.

Located along the Broad Ripple canal, used for local play. Possibly used to house the American Association Indians while West Washington Street Park was being used by the Federal Hoosiers.

It was here that Owen "Donie" Bush learned how to play shortstop. Bush went on to be a star shortstop for the Detroit Tigers, and then returned to Indianapolis to become the mayor of the east end.

The splintery grandstand behind home was seven rows deep and held no more than 500 people. There were private boxes elevated to a second deck—maybe eight feet off the ground—attached to the third base side of the grandstand. Extending out toward third base were open bleachers. The players' bench was so close to the seats that only one person at a time could walk between them.

Northwestern Avenue Ballpark
Negro National League 1920s (ABCs, some games). *Location:* Northwestern Avenue, Holton Place, 17th and 18th streets.

Speedway Park
Negro National League 1920s (ABCs, some games). *Location:* Near the Indianapolis Motor Speedway.

After the 1924 season, the Negro

National League and the newfangled Eastern Colored League got into a player war, and the ABCs were all but wiped out, as ten of their ballplayers jumped. In 1925, there were a lot of new faces. Park appears in the film *The Big Wheel* (1949).

Bush Stadium (Perry Stadium 1931–42, Victory Field 1942–67) American Association 1931–1962 (Indians), Negro National League 1930s (ABCs), Negro American League 1944, 1946–50 (Clowns), International League 1963 (Indians), Pacific Coast League 1964–68 (Indians), American Association 1969–present (Indians). Site of Game 5 of the 1943 Negro League World Series. Site of the 1987 Pan-American Games baseball competition. *Location:* 1501 West 16th Street, 38th Street, White River. *Constructed:* 1931. *Cost of construction:* $500,000. *Dimensions:* (1931) Left field, 350 feet; center field, 500 feet; right field, 350 feet. (Present) Left field, 335 feet; center field, 395 feet; right field, 335 feet. *Seating capacity:* (1931) 13,000 + ; (1960) 12,934; (present) 12,500. *1987 season attendance:* 250,250.

In 1823 Fielding Geeter bought a large chunk of land along Fall Creek for growing corn, paying the federal government $309. Between Geeter's purchase and the present, that land has changed hands only four times. During the first third of the twentieth century, the 15½ acres of land that include the ballpark site belonged to Charles Rauh. When the land was purchased in 1931 by Norman A. Perry, owner of the American Association's Indianapolis Indians, an old house was standing where the ballpark was to be built. Adjoining the house was a popular well. The house had to be torn down, but the well, enclosed within the baseball grounds, continued to be used.

When the park was built, it seated over 13,000 with room for 2000 more standing in the outfield. At the time,

local sports writer William Herschell wrote, "The plant, although not the largest in the country, is called the most perfect in equipment, and has a playing field surpasssed in area by only a few. The new Perry Stadium joins the Indianapolis Motor Speedway in giving Indianapolis two sporting institutions of national note."

The new park removed Indianapolis from the list of cities with wooden ballparks. Perry Stadium was constructed entirely of steel and concrete, and the whole grounds were enclosed by a brick wall sixteen feet high. Stairways, such as those found in the old Washington Park, were replaced by wide ramps.

Business manager for the Indians, Jack Hendricks, bragged of the new ballpark's comfort and safety. Restrooms were modern for both men and women. Women patrons, he assured, did not have to worry about taking any seat in the house. Box seats, he said, had orange and green covers so that ladies could use them "even if wearing the daintiest raiment." Ushers and concessionaires wore uniforms. When lights were installed management rented the park out to the Indianapolis ABCs to help pay for the improvement.

Club offices were spacious and adjoined by a dining room and kitchen — the thought being that visiting officials might enjoy having dinner at the park before night games.

The players' clubhouses were equipped with "the newest of club devices" and were innovatively placed. The Indians no longer had to march from the dugout across the field to get to the clubhouse — a hike that subjected players to the wrath of the fans after losses. The new clubhouses were connected by tunnel to the dugouts, a feature now common in ballparks.

Even the umpires had been thought of kindly, and had been given quarters separate from those of the players. Showering after a game could be rough on an ump if he had to do it next to that guy he called out in the ninth.

The new stadium was surrounded by a large area for parking purposes, making it possible to approach the park from both 16th Street and Fall Creek Drive.

It was determined that there would be no advertising signs inside the park, and that trolley buses would be used to transport fans without automobiles to the park.

When it opened, the foul lines of Perry Stadium ran 350 feet to the wall, and the flagpole in deep straightaway center was 500 feet from home. As the *Indianapolis News* put it, "It is a far cry from the old parks to this present home of the great national game. Some of (Indianapolis') former parks could be laid down inside the new playing field and scarcely be observed."

The playing field is no longer quite as big, as it has been cut down by an inner home run wall. Other than this, the park has remained very much the same as when it was built.

During the Second World War, the name was changed to Victory Field. It held this name until August 30, 1967, when it was formally dedicated Owen J. Bush Stadium, in honor of the native son and shortstop who went on to fame with the Detroit Tigers and returned home.

Parking accommodations can now be made for 3000 cars in lots adjacent to the stadium, and across 16th Street where the Indians lease the CYO Field parking facilities.

A fan gets a good view from any seat, and the red brick wall covered with ivy provides a beautiful background for the action. All box and grandstand seats have backs and arm rests. The lighting in the parking lot, lobby and on the playing field has been excellent since new lighting units were installed in the 1970s. There are very few games called on account of wet grounds because there is drainage tile beneath the playing surface.

The stadium has been owned since June 1, 1967, by the City of Indianapolis, who bought it from the estate of Norman A. Perry. The city leases the park to the Metropolitan Park Board, who then subleases it to the Indianapolis Indians, Inc., annually for the period April 1 through September 15.

In 1987, phony billboards for early twentieth century products were thrown up against the real walls for the filming of "Eight Men Out," a film directed by John Sayles about the Black Sox scandal.

Bush Stadium is still considered one of the finest minor league stadiums in the country.

Iowa City, Iowa

Iowa Field

Home of the University of Iowa Hawkeyes (Big Ten Conference), present. *Seating capacity:* 3000.

The Iowa Hawkeye baseball program produced Mike Boddicker and Jim Sundberg.

Irvine, California

Crawford Field

Home of the University of California at Irvine Anteaters (Pacific Coast Athletic Conference), present. *Seating capacity:* 1500.

Jackson, Mississippi

Smith-Wills Stadium (Municipal Stadium)

Texas League 1975–present (Mets). *Location:* ¼ mile from the Lakeland Drive exit of Interstate 55. *Constructed:* 1974–75. *Dimensions:* Left field, 330 feet; center field, 405 feet; right field, 320 feet. *Seating capacity:* 5000. *1987 season attendance:* 131,248.

The most memorable wedding in recent Jackson history took place June 22, 1978, when South Carolina's Rosa

Top: *Bush Stadium, Indianapolis, Ind. (Compliments of the Indianapolis Indians.)*
Bottom: *Iowa Field, Iowa City, Ia. (Compliments of the University of Iowa.)*

Gilbert took as her groom one Mookie Wilson, center-fielder. The ceremony took place on home plate in Smith-Wills Stadium. Mets infielder Paco Perez was best man. The ceremony ended with the happy couple walking beneath an archway of Louisville Sluggers, held aloft by teammates. The honeymoon was a short one. The Mookster was back in the starting lineup the following night.

Jackson women and ballplayers have a thing going. If you're signed by the Mets and sent to Jackson, finding a wife seems to be the thing to do. Eleven Mets have married local beauties.

Soggy Start at Smith-Wills. In 1975, the Mets moved their AA club to Jackson, the capital of Mississippi, from Victoria, Texas. The move followed a campaign of civic leaders in Jackson to build a 5000-seat ballpark.

The ballpark was home of the 1981, 1984, and 1985 Texas League pennant winners. But the franchise got off to more humble beginnings, some caused by acts of God.

When Jackson entered the Texas

Foliage forms the backdrop at Smith-Wills Stadium, Jackson, Miss. (Compliments of the Jackson Mets.)

League, the city had been without organized baseball for 22 years, last participating in the Class C Cotton States League in 1953. "Smith-Wills" was selected as the stadium name, in honor of two teenaged Jacksonian amateur baseball players who'd been killed in separate car accidents.

During the ballpark's first season, 1975, the parking lot was unpaved, the front office was in a trailer, and there was no roof over the press box—the only place where it's really necessary to keep your scorecard dry. Somebody must have been assigned to keep an umbrella over the official scorer's book at all times, or maybe he just used the "hold it underneath your coat and try not to drip on it" method. It can rain in Jackson.

Johnny Antonelli managed the Mets to a 65–65 record in 1975. The team drew 77,046 for the year. That's 1572 per home date.

In 1979, there was much enthusiasm in the Jackson Mets organization. The season looked good for the players and the fans. The new general manager, Mike Feder, was promotion-minded and determined. Then the rains came.

The 1979 Easter Flood washed out the first home stand. Before the season was through, 20 home dates would be rained out. Nothing ever dried out, and the Mets failed to finish in the first division.

Considerably drier since that opening year, Smith-Wills Stadium has been the site of two exhibition games with the New York Mets, the 1984 Texas League All-Star Game, and an exhibition game against the 1984 U.S. Olympic Team. The Olympic team made a lengthy tour of the United States that year, but played only two games against professional competition.

In 1979 the season attendance was 68,340. It jumped to 98,833 in 1980, a drier year. By 1984, the attendance was up to 119,007. In 1985, 132,021.

In the "It Only Goes to Show" department, put the fact that in 1985, Darryl Strawberry's team record for Runs Batted In was broken by Barry Lyons, who knocked in 108. Wonder who walked the most.

Jackson Hole, Wyoming

Mateosky Ball Park
The current home of baseball in
Jackson Hole. Located next to the
rodeo grounds, the park is used for
Farm League and Little League baseball. There are restroom facilities, a
drinking fountain, and a concession
stand.

The park is named after native son
Ben Mateosky, a volunteer fireman and
owner of the Mateosky Construction
Company. Ben played twelve years of
minor league ball. For ten of them he
batted over .280, hit more than 27
home runs, and knocked in over 100
runs. He made ten all-star teams and
was MVP in four different leagues, yet
never made it to the majors. Ben and
Lila, his wife of over 30 years, have
three children.

Jacksonville, Florida

Red Cap Stadium (Barr's Field,
Douglas Field, Durkee Field)
Negro American League 1938, 1941–
42 (Red Caps), South Atlantic League
1936–42, 1946–54 (Tars, 1953, Braves).
Location: 1701 Myrtle Avenue, Durkee
and Moncrief avenues, Davis Street
and C Street, later Hopkins Street, now
West 7th Street.

Back in the late 1930s and early
1940s, the Red Caps officially played in
the Negro American League. Unoffi-
cially they played year round, and in
the winters beefed up their roster with
black stars from the north, offering the
northerners no-show jobs redcapping
at the Jacksonville Train Station.

Jacksonville writer Rex Edmondson
notes that the ballpark, with its rickety
propped up wooden stands and kid-
dotted fences, simply "*looked* like a
ballpark." He reports that the Tars,
Jacksonville's white team who used the
ballpark later, "played in the old South
Atlantic League with such hated, but
respected rivals as the Macon Peaches,

the Savannah Indians, the Augusta
Tigers, the Greenville Spinners, Columbus Cardinals, and a host of other
cities who almost annually swapped
franchises."

Sam W. Wolfson Baseball Park
(Jacksonville Baseball Park)
South Atlantic League 1955–61, In-
ternational League 1962–68 (Suns),
Southern League 1970–present (Royals,
Expos). *Location:* 1201 East Duval
Street. *Constructed:* 1955. *Dimensions:*
Left field, 325 feet; center field, 400
feet; right field, 325 feet. *Seating
capacity:* (1975) 10,264; (1985) 6312.
1986 season attendance: 164,772. *1987
season attendance:* 186,379.

The ballpark is named after a man
who helped bring AAA ball to Jacksonville in the early sixties. Jacksonville's acquisition of an International
League franchise actually required the
combined efforts of the city's civic and
government leaders and a revolution in
Cuba.

Robert Maduro, owner of the Havana Sugar Kings team, fled from
Castro and tried to make his franchise
go in Jersey City, but it didn't work
because of the proximity to New York.

Then Sam Wolfson, sportsman and
civic leader, convinced Maduro that
Jacksonville was the logical place to
move his team. The move was further
facilitated by Atlanta's inclusion in the
International League at the same time,
providing the schedule makers with a
southern trip for the northern teams.
Wolfson died during the Suns' second
season in AAA. The Suns were successful, affiliated with the Mets in the
International League, until Atlanta got
the Braves, leaving Jacksonville iso-
lated in a northern league. Since then
Jacksonville has returned to the lower
minor leagues and plays teams closer to
home. They are currently a farm club
of the Expos.

Wolfson's grandstand goes from first
to third, built with support beams supporting the roof. On the first base side

The back of the press box and the underside of the grandstand at Sam W. Wolfson Baseball Park, Jacksonville, Fla. (Compliments of the Jacksonville Expos.)

the end of the grandstand is flush with the end of the dugout. Since the bullpens are behind a fence beside the grandstand, adjacent to the dugouts, no phone communication is necessary. Flags stick up over the brick outfield wall, the flags of the other teams in the Southern League, as well as the Stars and Stripes.

The current advertising rates for 50-word-or-less messages on the park's electronic message board are $550.00 for a full season, $375.00 for a half-season. Companies can also lease the ballpark's concourse as a mini-showroom for display purposes. Rental for four consecutive nights costs $500.

To rent one of the 20-seat skyboxes, the best seats in the house, costs $300.00. That fee includes 30 hot dogs, eight nacho trays, two cases of beer and all the popcorn and soft drinks requested. The park also has a picnic area and restaurant for pre-game parties or dining.

Brest Field

Home of the Jacksonville University Dolphins (Sun Belt Conference), present. *Seating capacity:* 1000.

Field has no outfield fences in spots. Balls struck to left center, for example, roll up a tree-covered and grassy hill. According to Jacksonville University assistant athletic director Gary F. Izzo, the ballpark has been named since 1965 after Alexander Brest, "an elderly gentleman who resides in Jacksonville and who has donated a great deal of money and time to the university over the years."

Jamestown, New York

College Stadium

New York–Pennsylvania League 1961–present (Expos 1977–present). *Location:* Just off Route 17. *Dimensions:* Left field, 356 feet; center field, 404 feet; right field, 346 feet. *Seating capacity:* 5077. *1987 season attendance:* 46,324.

Jersey City, New Jersey

Oakland Park

National League 1889 (New York Giants, two games). *Location:* Oakland

and Hoboken avenues, Concord and Fleet streets.

Skeeters Park (West Side Park)
Home of minor league baseball in Jersey City before Roosevelt Stadium. *Location:* Not far from the Jersey Central Railroad Station.

Roosevelt Stadium
International League 1950s, National League 1956–57 (Brooklyn Dodgers, 15 games). Owned by Jersey City. *Location:* Danforth Avenue (first base side), Route 440 (right field), Hackensack River (third base). *Dimensions:* Left field, 330 feet; left center, 377 feet; center field, 411 feet; right center, 377 feet; right field, 330 feet. 60 feet from home plate to the backstop. *Fences:* Left field, four feet; right field, seven feet. *Seating capacity:* 24,167. Field boxes, 1230; loges, 4817; grandstand reserved, 6284; pavilion, 11,836. *Dodgers day game attendance record:* 12,214 (April 19, 1956, versus Philadelphia). *Dodgers night game attendance record:* 26,385 (August 15, 1956, versus New York). *Dodgers opening game attendance record:* 12,214 (April 19, 1956, versus Philadelphia). *First National League game:* April 19, 1956 (Brooklyn 5, Philadelphia 4). *Last National League game:* September 3, 1957 (night, Philadelphia 3, Brooklyn 2). *Torn down:* 1984.

Grounds were defined by a tall stone wall — with a gate in straightaway center — and a large single deck grandstand. All three outfield light towers stood well inside the wall, and eventually so did the inner fence determining the home run distances. The hand-operated scoreboard, with a clock on top, sat in the left field power alley, 40 feet high. Site of a famous Grateful Dead concert in the mid-'70s.

Johnson City, Tennessee

Howard Johnson Field
Appalachian League 1964–present

(Cardinals). *Location:* Off Interstate 81. *Dimensions:* Left field, 310 feet; center field, 410 feet; right field, 310 feet. *Seating capacity:* 2735. *1987 season attendance:* 22,271.

Johnstown, Pennsylvania

Point Stadium
Negro National League 1930s (Pittsburgh Crawfords, Homestead Grays, some games). *Location:* John Street (left field), Washington Street (third base), Route 56 Bypass (first base). *Dimensions:* Left field, 270 feet; center field, 475 feet; right field, 250 feet.

This park had a 70-foot left field screen, all of which was in play if struck by the ball. There was a ticket booth out beyond the center field fence.

The ballpark was built on the Point, where the Little Conemaugh joined Stoney Creek to form the Conemaugh River. The ballpark still stands, and is used for community baseball and football.

The park is now single-decked, but was formerly a double-decked structure.

Kansas City, Missouri

Riverview Park
Home of Kansas City baseball in the 1870s.

Athletic Park
Union Association 1884. *Location:* Southwest Boulevard, Summit Street. *First game:* June 7, 1884 (Chicago 6, Kansas City 5, 12 innings, attendance 1500). *Last game:* October 19, 1884.

The Union Association franchise from Altoona, Pennsylvania, moved to Kansas City mid-season.

Association Park (I)
National League 1886 (Cowboys), Western League 1887, American Association 1888 (Blues). *Location:* Lydia,

Tracy, Independence and Highland avenues. *Nickname:* The Hole. *First National League game:* April 30, 1886. *Last National League (Cowboys) game:* September 18, 1886. *Last National League game:* October 15, 1892 (St. Louis versus Chicago). *First American Association game:* April 18, 1888.

When Kansas City acquired the dirt for a new thoroughfare's road bed, they used the resulting hole for their ballpark, playing at the bottom, putting seats along the sides. On July 21, 1886, the Cowboys beat Detroit 12–2 in 11 innings here, a score only possible in an era when the home team could bat first.

Exposition Park

American Association 1889, 1902–19 (Blues). *Location:* 15th Street (now Truman Avenue), 20th Street, Prospect Avenue.

Used for baseball until 1920 and the building of Association Park II not far away. Burned down at least once.

Federal League Park (Gordon and Koppel Field)

Federal League 1914–15 (Packers). *Location:* 49th and Tracy streets, Brush Creek Boulevard, the Paseo. *First game:* April 16, 1914. *Last game:* September 28, 1915.

City had a Federal League franchise from July 1913 — when the league was still "minor" — until the end of the 1915 season, when the league went out of business.

The Federal League was the brainchild of James A. Gilmore, a coal and paper executive. Kansas City joined in mid-season, replacing the Covington, Kentucky, franchise, which had been representing an unresponsive Cincinnati area.

When the league practically went belly-up in its initial campaign, Gilmore actively recruited major league talent with his own bankroll, and stirred up enough interest to keep the thing going for two more years. Eighty-

one major leaguers jumped to the Federal League.

Association Park (II)

American Association 1920–23 (Blues), Negro National League 1920–22 (Monarchs). *Location:* 21st Street (center field), 19th Street (home), Olive Street (first base).

When the Monarchs organized and began to use Association Park in 1920, the lad who pulled the tarp over the field was Newt Allen. In return for his labor, the team gave Newt a few baseballs. The investment paid off, as Newt went on to play second base and shortstop — then later left field and first base — for the Monarchs from 1922 to 1944.

American Association Park was owned by George Tebeau, who restricted blacks in attendance to the top 14 rows of seats, even when black teams were using the field. There was a 30-foot screen out in right. The park was a single-decked wooden structure. Tebeau and George Muehlebach, a brewer who owned Kansas City's white team, the Blues, had a disagreement in 1922. Local sports writers hoped that if a fight between the two were to force Muehlebach to build a new stadium, the Monarchs could continue their lease with Tebeau for the park at 19th and Olive and thus have a park of their own. Muehlebach did build his own stadium in 1923 (see Municipal Stadium below), but J. Leslie Wilkinson (owner of the Monarchs) alone could not afford to pay Tebeau's operating expenses, so Wilkinson made an agreement with Muehlebach for use of the new field — so the Blues and the Monarchs continued to share.

The park is now a playground.

Paradeway Park

Negro National League 1920s (Monarchs, some games). *Location:* 17th Street at the Paseo.

Municipal Stadium (Muehlebach Field 1923-37, Ruppert Stadium 1938-42, Blues Stadium 1943-54) American Association 1923-54, Negro National League 1923-30 (Monarchs), home of Monarchs 1931-37 (independent), Negro American League 1938-50 (Monarchs), American League 1955-67 (Athletics), 1969-72 (Royals). Site of Games 5, 6, and 7 of First "Colored World Series," 1924, Monarchs versus Hilldale (Yeadon), attendance for each 15,000. Owned by Kansas City, Missouri. *Location:* 22nd Street (first base side), Brooklyn Avenue (right field), 21st Street (left field), Euclid Avenue (third base). *Constructed:* 1922. *Construction cost:* $400,000. *Rebuilt and enlarged:* 1954-55. *Cost of rebuilding:* $2.5 million. *Dimensions:* (1962) Left field, 369 feet; left center, 408 feet; center field, 421 feet; right center, 382 feet; right field, 353 feet. 60 feet from home plate to the backstop. *Seating capacity:* (1922) 16,000 (not counting bleachers which were seldom used); (1955-72) 35,020. Boxes, 10,534; reserved, 19,881; general admission, 4605. *Athletics day game attendance record:* 34,065 (August 27, 1961, versus New York). *Athletics doubleheader attendance record:* 34,865 (July 15, 1962, versus New York). *Athletics night game attendance record:* 33,471 (April 29, 1955, versus New York). *Athletics twi-night doubleheader attendance record:* 35,147 (August 8, 1955, versus New York). *Athletics opening game attendance record:* 31,895 (April 12, 1955, versus Detroit). *Athletics season high attendance record:* 1,393,054 (1955). *Athletics season low attendance record:* 528,344 (1965). *Royals day game attendance record:* 30,035 (May 24, 1970, versus Milwaukee). *Royals doubleheader attendance record:* 31,872 (April 20, 1969, versus Oakland). *Royals night game attendance record:* 16,406 (June 13, 1970, versus New York). *Royals twi-night doubleheader attendance record:* 18,248 (June 18, 1969,

versus Oakland). *Royals opening game attendance record:* 32,728 (April 12, 1971, night, versus Minnesota). *Royals season high attendance record:* 910,784 (1971). *Royals season low attendance record:* 693,647 (1970). *First Blues game:* July 3, 1923 (Blues 10, Milwaukee 7, attendance, 14,000, winning pitcher, Ferdie Schupp). *First Athletics game:* April 12, 1955 (Kansas City 6, Detroit 2). *Last Athletics game:* September 27, 1967 (doubleheader, Kansas City 5, Chicago 2; Kansas City 4, Chicago 0). *First Royals game:* April 8, 1969 (Kansas City 4, Minnesota 3, 12 innings).

The former frog pond, swimming hole and ash heap was first used as a ballpark on July 23, 1923. Between then and its last use in 1972, the dimensions of the playing field and the height of the fences changed more frequently than in any other ballpark.

For many years, this was the home of both the Blues and the Monarchs, Kansas City's white and black teams. Of the two, the Monarchs were the more interesting. They were the champions of the Negro Leagues many times, while the Blues functioned as an oft-abused farm of the New York Yankees. Seating was segregated for Blues games, but the lines of division were removed when the Monarchs played. In the mid-1930s, the Blues were bought by former Cubs catcher Johnny Kling, who refused to segregate seating. Segregation was again instituted in 1938 when the park was bought by Jacob Ruppert, owner of the Yankees, causing a furor in Kansas City's black newspaper, the *Kansas City Call*.

In the early days there was a large hill out in right field and there were two levels of signs, one running along the base of the hill defining the home run distance, the other running along the top of the hill, above and behind the first set. Even when it was single-decked this was a big ballpark with a tall and deep grandstand, roofed with obstructions, and bleachers in the outfield.

Monarchs games were events in the black section of Kansas City, where Muehlebach Stadium was built. People wore their finery to the ballpark. Mornings before Sunday games the streets of Kansas City's black neighborhood smelled of women frying their hair. The women wore furs and hats to church, and went straight from the church to the ballpark. Men wore suits, patent leather shoes and straw hats.

Merchants exploited the fashion scene at Monarchs games. According to Janet Bruce in her book *The Kansas City Monarchs,* one store's advertisement read, "The Monarchs Are Here! The opening game of the Monarchs is always a Fashion Parade and of course you will want to look your best."

During the 1920s, crowds for Monarchs games were 90 percent black. As long as white people didn't come, crowds could never get too big. There were only about 30,000 black people in Kansas City, a minority of whom had the discretionary income for something like attending baseball games. The same 5000 attended Sunday games, and the same 400 came on weekdays. The black community's economic woes started to mount almost a full decade before the Depression.

The owner of the Monarchs was J. Leslie Wilkinson, a former professional pitcher and owner of the traveling and integrated All Nations team who brought their own canvas fence and bleachers with them to a town, much like a circus pitched its own tent. Wilkinson was the only white owner in the Negro American League.

By 1926, Wilkinson was running promotions such as Ladies Day (ladies get in free), and Knothole Day (kids 15 and under get in free), and lowering box seat prices from $1.10 to 75 cents.

The franchise might have gone under if it hadn't been for the popularity of the Booster Club. It was, according to Janet Bruce, "a loose amalgam of neighborhood fans." When the Booster Club formed, its sole duty was to organize the Opening Day parade, which functioned like the Pied Piper to draw folks with it to the ballpark. Later the club became a popular civic organization including anybody who was anybody.

The Boosters did so much to put butts in the seats that Wilkinson played a number of benefit games in return for the Salvation Army, the NAACP, the Red Cross, and other organizations. The Opening Day parade, by the end of the decade, had become quite a to-do. It included Western University's band, the Second Regiment band, the Elks band, decorated cars for ballplayers, managers, and reporters—all led by a police escort, heading for Muehlebach Field along a criss-crossing route designed to get within earshot of every black person in the city.

Fans who had cars found a spot at the end of the parade and became part of the parade, and they brought along their musical instruments if they had them so that they could blow jazz at the roadside spectators, something sweet for a spring day. In 1923 one car in the Opening Day Parade bore a tooter who only knew one song—and was within earshot of a reporter, who later wrote that he never wanted to hear "Good Bye Tootsie" again.

Opening Day was almost always the largest crowd of the year. The league's seasons were so disorganized—teams never played the same number of league games—that there was seldom a tight finish or a "pennant race" or anything like that (when the Monarchs won they usually won by a mile), so Opening Day was the biggest event of the baseball year in black Kansas City.

According to Janet Bruce, "People came from all over the state, and the mayor traditionally gave city employees a half-day holiday so that they could greet the team. Three times in the 1920s the *Kansas City Call* alerted readers that 'moving pictures' would be taken of the parade, the opening ceremonies, and the game. These films were shown the following week at the Lincoln Theatre in the black neighborhood."

Though women continued to make up a substantial portion of the crowd at Monarchs games, they failed to diminish crowd rowdyism. Some thought that behavior at Muehlebach Field by some fans was an embarrassment to black people. These were prohibition days, but liquor was sold under the stands, only somewhat discreetly, and many brought their own booze in with them in hip flasks.

In 1929, Wilkinson paid the Giant Manufacturing Company between $50,000 and $100,000 to build a portable light system for night ball. Remember, this is a man who once brought his own bleachers with him when he was forced to hit the road. Now the Depression was on and he determined that night baseball was the salvation of the Monarchs. During much of the '30s the Monarchs stopped being a league team and started being an independent barnstorming team, traveling with their own light system for night games.

According to Janet Bruce, "Wilkinson's lighting system consisted of telescoping poles, which elevated lights forty-five to fifty feet above the playing field. Each pole supported six floodlights measuring four feet across. The poles were fastened on a pivot to truck beds and were raised by means of a derrick. Wilkinson positioned the trucks along the foul lines, behind a six-foot canvas fence that stretched around the outfield. If playing in a stadium, he placed a 'battery of light' on the roof of the grandstand; otherwise another truck was parked behind home plate. The whole system took about two hours to assemble."

The new system subjected players to horrible conditions. Hitters couldn't see pitches, and outfielders couldn't see fly balls. Ground rules were set up to account for the many fly balls that were lost in the night sky—anything landing

in front of an outfielder shielding his head counted a single or something like that. The electric generator to operate the lights was usually put out in center field and made so much noise that centerfielders couldn't hear what infielders were yelling out.

But the lighting system, as Wilkinson predicted, turned out to be the financial savior of the Monarchs during the Depression era. From 1941 to 1943, Satchel Paige pitched for the Monarchs, which, of course, added more financial support—he was the biggest drawing card in the Negro Leagues. Satchel's arm had died in the late '30s, but had been magically rejuvenated after Wilkinson acquired him (he was acquired as a novelty act to travel with Satchel Paige's All-Stars). The long wing of Satch was restored thanks to Frank "Jewbaby" Floyd, the Monarchs' trainer for thirty years, who rubbed Paige's shoulder daily with "deer oil."

Jackie Robinson played here briefly in 1945. His ingratiating manner made him unpopular with his teammates, so they were not upset when Mr. Rickey bought Robinson's contract for his new United States League.

Charley O. In 1955, a new scoreboard was put in right center—the same board that had, until the previous fall, stood in Braves Field in Boston.

In the "Obstacles in Play" category put the base of the left center light tower, which was in front of the fence, causing a drunken swerve in the warning tracks.

During the years when the ballpark was run by Charley O. Finley, there was a zoo out beyond the right field fence where a mule (named Charley O.), sheep, pheasants, monkeys, rabbits, and a dog lived. To add to the menagerie, a mechanical rabbit named Harvey popped up out of the ground and fed the home plate umpire fresh baseballs.

In 1963 Finley got it into his head that the key to winning was having a ballpark with the same dimensions as

Yankee Stadium. He built "Pennant Porch" in the right field corner, reducing the distance down the line to 296 feet. Baseball responded by passing a rule that no new fences could be built within 325 feet from the plate. The porch lasted for two exhibition games.

According to baseball analyst and Kansas City local Bill James, Finley had a line painted where the porch had been. Anytime a ball landed or was caught on the other side of the line, the P.A. announcer told everyone it would have been a homer in Yankee Stadium.

Writes James: "It is said that the practice of making this announcement came to an end in the eleventh inning on May 2, when the Minnesota Twins became the first team in baseball history to hit four consecutive home runs. It is said that following the home runs by Oliva, Allison, Hall and Killebrew, Earl Battey drove the ball to the wall.... The announcer dutifully intoned 'That ball would have been a home run ... in Yankee Stadium.' The announcement was discontinued the next day."

In 1964 it is reported that Finley paid the Beatles more money for a single performance at Municipal Stadium than he was paying his entire ball club for the season. Kansas City is not the hippest place, however, and ticket sales for the Fab Four were slow.

In 1965, Satchel Paige came back and pitched three scoreless innings for the A's at the age of 59. He registered one K versus the Boston Red Sox.

Royals Stadium
American League 1973–present (Royals). Site of the 1973 All-Star Game: July 24, National League 7, American League 1, attendance 40,849. Owned by Jackson County, Missouri. *Location:* Blue Ridge Cutoff (first base side), Arrowhead Stadium (home plate), Interstate 435 (third base), Interstate 70 (center field). *Architect:* Joe Spear. *Cost of construction:* $70 million. *Dimensions:* Left field, 330 feet;

left center, 385 feet; center field, 410 feet; right center, 385 feet; right field, 330 feet. 60 feet from home plate to the backstop. *Fences:* 12 feet all the way around. *Turf:* Artificial (Astro Turf-8 Drainthru manufactured by Monsanto). *Cost of turf:* $1.7 million. *Seating capacity:* 40,762. Club boxes, 2616; lower boxes, 7605; lower reserved, 7633; upper boxes, 4543; upper reserved, 13,279; general admission, 5070; wheelchair reserved, 16. *First game:* April 10, 1973 (night, Kansas City 12, Texas 1, attendance, 39,464, temperature, 39 degrees F).

Has a 12-story scoreboard, and a 322-foot-wide water spectacular. The scoreboard contains 16,320 light bulbs, most of them on a 40-foot wide and 60-foot long grid.

The water display extends from center field to the right field corner. It is the largest privately funded fountain in the world.

Fans reach their seats via four circular ramps and four escalators. More than half of the seats are on the lower level. There is a two-level air-conditioned press box. The upper level houses seven broadcast units, while the lower level is reserved for print media. There are field and press box level photographer and television camera positions as well.

All of the seats point toward second base. The stadium houses the Royals' administrative offices.

Kennewick, Washington

Sanders-Jacobs Field
Northwest League circa 1955. *Dimensions:* Left field, 330 feet; center field, 400 feet; right field, 330 feet. *Seating capacity:* 2500.

Bomber Bowl
Northwest League circa 1985 (Tri-Cities). *Dimensions:* Left field, 350 feet; center field, 375 feet; right field, 350 feet. *Seating capacity:* 3000.

Royals Stadium, Kansas City, Mo. (Compliments of the Kansas City Royals.)

Kenosha, Wisconsin

Simmons Park

Home of Kenosha baseball since 1923; Midwest League 1984–present (Twins). *Location:* Sheridan Road. *Dimensions:* Left field, 335 feet; center field, 400 feet; right field, 335 feet. *Seating capacity:* 3500. *Record season attendance:* 87,672 (1984). *1986 season attendance:* 57,495. *1987 season attendance:* 58,197.

Says Jay Weiner in the *Minneapolis Star and Tribune,* "Simmons Field is a lovely, state fair kind of ballpark with a red and blue grandstand and bleachers down each foul line. It's the kind of place where baseball was born, and where men in straw hats once performed music by John Philip Sousa before industrial league games."

Just after pitcher-turned-plumbing-contractor Bob Lee won his quest to bring the Midwest League to Kenosha (pop. 77,000) in January 1984, work started readying Simmons Park for the spring. Until then Simmons Park had been the home of Kenosha's 50 Little League teams, and—back in the early

1920s—to semi-pro clubs like Simmons Bed Company and Nash Motors. By the 1980s the lights were rickety, the infield was skin, and there wasn't much need for outfield fences. The place was in terrible shape.

A ditch was dug near the railroad tracks and temporary tile was laid out just to drain the field so the work could begin. The entire field, infield and outfield, was resodded. Fences were erected and dugouts constructed. Billboard ads on the outfield fence were sold to 54 different businesses for $800 apiece, plus the cost of paint.

That's as far as the workers got when the season started. The clubhouses weren't finished until several weeks into the season, so ballplayers had to duck into trailers to dodge the public eye. Players went to and from the park wearing their uniforms.

Because of sogginess, the land behind the center field fence—which would later become the parking lot—could not support heavy machinery. The $60,000 scoreboard could not be erected until the end of June. That meant the public address announcer

Top: *The two-man grounds crew at Simmons Field, Kenosha, Wis., truly outstanding in their field.* Bottom: *The bleachers and concession stand at Simmons Field. (Both photos compliments of the Kenosha Twins.)*

David McGrath had to recite the count after every pitch. A portable ticket booth had to be wheeled to and from the park, and Greg Lee, the owner's 16-year-old son, was in charge of driving the Twins' starting pitchers home if they got knocked from the box early. During each seventh inning stretch President Lee led the fans in the singing of "Take Me Out to the Ballgame."

The team set their attendance record that year, offering imaginative promo-tions such as Banana Split Night, when Little Leaguers were invited to dig into a 200-foot banana split behind second base.

By the end of the 1984 season the ballpark looked great. The scoreboard was up, the beer garden was in use, the clubhouses were finished, and the Midwest League selected Simmons Park as their Most Improved Facility of the Year—the first time the award had ever been given to a franchise after its rookie year in the league.

By major league standards the 335-400-335 dimensions of the outfield seem normal enough, but they represent the largest playing field in the Midwest League, whose ballparks are known for their tininess. In Waterloo, for example, it's only 360 feet to the center field fence.

In 1987, Kenosha was ranked the fourth nicest facility in the league — the biggest complaint being the lights.

Beginning with the 1987 season, organ music added a major league flavor to games at Simmons Field. Kenoshans Robert and Virginia Dix donated a Lowry organ to the city of Kenosha for use during Twins games. Lucas Dix, age 2, sat at the organ for the picture in the *Kenosha News*.

Even by minor league standards the prices here are cheap — perhaps because Kenosha is within an hour's driving distance of three major league ballparks, one in Milwaukee and two in Chicago. For the '87 season, box seats at Simmons were $3, general admission $2. Parking was free — and for the first time there were places to park. Through '86, only 55 parking spaces were available in a lot next to Sheridan Road. The new lot offered 225 spots and was located beyond the outfield fence, with street access from 79th Street. Because of an easement granted by the Kenosha Achievement Center, fans could enter the Achievement Center lot and drive through the easternmost boundary of the Center's property near the railroad tracks to reach the new lot. For fans using the new lot a new ticket office was constructed by the right field fence near the beer garden.

In '86, many of Kenosha's streets were resurfaced. The old asphalt was recycled. Originally targeted for an industrial site near Highway 31, the asphalt was instead taken to Simmons and turned into the new parking lot.

Keokuk, Iowa

Perry Park

Home of the Westerns 1874 (independent), National Association 1875 (Westerns). *Location:* Block 34 of the Reeves, Perry and Williams addition to the original city of Keokuk. Currently, this would be known as North Nineteenth and Twentieth and Fulton and Franklin streets, between (Location has also been described as on the Walte Pasture just north of the present-day Rand Park.) *First National Association game:* May 4, 1875 (Chicago 12, Keokuk 1).

Named after Colonel C.H. Perry, who gave the right to use the property for baseball. The Perry family owned a number of tracts in the area.

Organized baseball in Keokuk got its start in 1874, when the Westerns played as an independent team. The big home game of the year was against the New York (Brooklyn) Mutuals. The Westerns got trounced 12–1, but nonetheless sought entrance and were accepted into the National Association for the following year.

The home opener was May 4, 1875. Fred Boardman, an umpire from Chicago, yelled "Play Ball" at 3 p.m., as 1500 watched from Perry Park's bleachers. They lost again 12–1, committing 12 errors in the field. Truth was, the Westerns only won one game in their entire stint in the National Association. They were ahead in the fourth inning of another game that was rained out.

After the record got to 1–12, Western's president John N. Irwin announced the club was disbanding, forfeiting the rest of its schedule.

High Banks Park

Western League 1885–87 (Kernals). *Location:* Crystal Glen. *First Western League game:* June 6, 1885 (Keokuk 10, Milwaukee 9).

The Kernals won the Western League pennant every year they were in it, thanks in a large part to second base-man Ed Fowler. Team manager Nick Curtis signed Fowler sight-unseen. When Curtis went to the station to meet Fowler's train, he almost swallowed his chaw. His new second base-man was a black man. But Curtis did not let prejudice stand in the way of signing a great ballplayer. Fowler became the first black man in organized baseball, and one of the best second basemen in the league.

Five of Keokuk's players went on to play in the big leagues. The catcher, Dan Dugdale, became the owner of the Chicago Cubs. He took his former teammate Fowler along and made him his head groundskeeper.

Hubinger Park

Iowa State League 1904–15 (Indians). *Location:* Behind the J.C. Hubinger mansion.

The highest position Keokuk ever finished during its stay in the Iowa State League was second in 1915. Probably the most celebrated player on Keokuk's team during this period was Alva "Buff" Williams of Carthage. He played for them from 1907 to 1908 before becoming the catcher of the Washington Senators, where he caught Walter Johnson. Williams ended up dying in Keokuk in 1933.

After the 1915 season, and the loss of lots of money, the franchise was sold to Ft. Dodge. It would be 15 years before the city again fielded a professional team.

Joyce Park

Mississippi Valley League 1930–34 (Indians), Western League 1935, Central Association 1947–49, Three-I League 1952–57, Midwest League 1958–62. *Seating capacity:* 2500.

In 1930, the Indians took over the financially distraught Marshalltown franchise. After finishing sixth during their initial campaign, Keokuk persuaded the St. Louis Cardinals to sponsor their team.

The Cardinals helped finance the placing of lights in Joyce Park, and assigned a top-notch manager in their organization, Bob Rice. Rice steered Keokuk to the 1931 pennant. They drew over 50,000 in attendance for the year.

In 1933, the Mississippi Valley League threatened to go under when four of its members folded. The new president of the league, Dr. C.R. Logan from Keokuk, quickly added three teams from Illinois, and the competition rating was raised from D to B.

The Cardinals switched their loyalties to the new Springfield team. Losing their manager and their financial support, Keokuk dropped out of the league following the 1934 season.

Joyce Park was sold by the Keokuk Baseball Association to Thomas H. Joyce in 1934. Joyce, in turn, gave it to the city. Besides the lighting installed by the Cardinals, Keokuk also had the outfield leveled and reseeded and equipped the infield with a drainage system. In 1935, Topeka moved their Class A Western League team to Keokuk. This team did not make any money either, and moved on after one season.

In 1947, Keokuk got backing from the Pirates and played for three years in the Central Association. In 1952, Keokuk joined the Three-I League as an independent. After two years, this team became a farm of the Cleveland Indians.

Big stars who played for Keokuk in Joyce Park include Gus Bell and Roger Maris.

Key West, Florida

Wickers Stadium

Florida State League 1971–circa 1975. *Constructed:* 1950. *Dimensions:* Left field, 330 feet; center field, 425 feet; right field, 315 feet. *Seating capacity:* 2500.

Kingsport, Tennessee

J. Fred Johnson Park

Appalachian League 1969–present (Mets). *Location:* Fort Henry Drive at Dobyns Bennett High School. *Built:* 1939. *Dimensions:* Left field, 335 feet; center field, 380 feet; right field, 310 feet. *Seating capacity:* 8000. *1987 season attendance:* 28,453.

In 1930, the city of Kingsport purchased 63 acres of land to be used as a citywide recreation area. In 1939, the ballpark and the Civic Auditorium were built on the site. The auditorium housed Kingsport's Parks and Recreation and Central Dispatch departments.

Since then, a swimming pool, tennis courts, a fire station, and the Tennessee Highway Patrol Building have been built in the park, along with Dobyns Bennett High School, whose teams play their home games in Johnson Park.

Kingston, New York

Dietz Memorial Stadium

North Atlantic League 1947, Colonial League 1950, Canadian-American League 1951 (Colonials). *Location:* Downtown. *Dimensions:* Football configuration. *Seating capacity:* 3000.

Built as a WPA project in the 1930s. Renamed after Staff Sergeant Robert Dietz, who was posthumously awarded the Congressional Medal of Honor during World War II. Since Dietz Stadium was designed for football, seating consisted of a lone linear set of bleachers down the first base line.

The park is still there and still used for local baseball. There are no outfield fences, but rather sharp grassy inclines indicating the edge of the playing field. In the days when it was used for pro baseball, snow fences determined home run distance.

Next to the playing field is a Friendly's

Restaurant. Across the street is the Pine Hill Trailways Station and the Dietz Stadium Diner and Restaurant.

Kinston, North Carolina

Parrott Field

Home of Kinston baseball before 1900. *Location:* Caswell Street, on the Happersville side of the former Parrott's Bridge.

The earliest memories of baseball in Kinston recall this open lot.

Name of park unknown

Location: East Street, north of Washington Avenue.

Home of Kinston's first professional baseball team. Games played here "years after" those at Parrott Field.

The Tater. On the Fourth of July, 1904, there was a good old-fashioned country brouhaha on East Street, at the game between the Kinston nine and New Bern. In the top of the ninth, Kinston ahead 1–0, New Bern had runners on first and third with two out. William F. Lewis and Elisha B. Lewis constituted the Kinston battery. With the runner on first going with the pitch, Elisha B. lazily pegged what appeared to be a baseball to second. The runner at third couldn't help trying to score, at which time Elisha B. tagged him out with the baseball. Huh? Wha'? Turned out the Kinston second baseman had a remarkably round potato in his glove.

The ensuing riot lasted all the way to the train station. A couple of Kinston rowdies stowed away on the New Bern train looking for trouble. They got the boot in Cove City, and had to walk all the way back.

Ten County Fairgrounds

Diamond here became home of pro ball in Kinston after team moved out of its East Street Park.

Westend Park

Virginia League (until 1932). *Loca-*

Signboard at Dietz Memorial Stadium, Kingston, N.Y. (Photo by David Pietrusza.)

tion: Across from the Kinston Power Plants. *Seating capacity:* 3000.

Grainger Stadium (I)

Coastal Plain League 1933–37 (Eagles, semi-pro). *Location:* Summit Avenue, behind Grainger High School.

The erection of this stadium was a community effort. After the 1937 season the whole structure was taken apart and moved to the present site, where it remained until 1951.

Grainger Stadium (II)

Virginia League circa 1938 (Eagles), Carolina League 1962–present. *Location:* Off Highway 11 and Route 70. *Dimensions:* Left field, 335 feet; center field, 390 feet; right field, 335 feet. *Seating capacity:* (1975) 3847; (1985) 4478. *1987 season attendance:* 68,199. *Rebuilt:* 1952.

The stands on Summit were moved to this site in 1938 after Mayor W.A. Graham supported a drive to get the WPA to help. The structure was wooden, making it one of the last wooden ballparks around, lasting until 1951.

The property was deeded by the Kinston City School Board to the city

of Kinston for 99 years—as long as it was used for baseball (as well as other sports). In 1951, a $150,000 bond issue was approved by the people of Kinston, and the current ballpark was constructed. It is also used for football.

Even today Kinston is a small tobacco, timber, and cotton city. This is not a favorite stop for ballplayers. Everything closes at nine o'clock. There are only two fast food restaurants open at night, a Pizza Hut and a Hardee's. The Kinston ballplayers usually live in one of the trailer parks.

Kissimmee, Florida

Osceola County Stadium

Florida State League 1985–present (Osceola Astros), spring home of the Houston Astros 1985–present. *Location:* Osceola Boulevard, Neptune Road, between Kissimmee and St. Cloud, one mile west of Florida Turnpike exit 65, 13 miles east of I-4, off U.S. 192. *Cost of construction:* $5.5 million. *Dimensions:* Left field, 330 feet; center field, 410 feet; right field, 330 feet. *Seating capacity:* 5800. *1987 Florida State League season atten-*

Osceola County Stadium (right) and the rest of the complex, Kissimmee, Fla. (Compliments of the Osceola County Stadium and Sports Complex.)

dance: 38,068. *Size of complex:* 80 acres. *Size of clubhouse:* 30,000 square feet.

The complex can also be used for business meetings, banquets, and theater. Spring facilities include four slices-of-a-pie practice fields with a control tower in the center.

Writes Boston Red Sox announcer Ken Coleman, "The Astros complex is almost beyond modern . . . it's where the Jetsons will be playing baseball in a few hundred years."

Knoxville, Tennessee

City Ballpark

Municipally owned. *Location:* Asylum Street, now Western Street, current location of Roddy Manufacturing (Coca-Cola). *Construction cost:* $3000.

Stands were built in three sections: one for blacks, one for white men and women nonsmokers, and a third for white men who smoked.

Bill Meyer Stadium (Caswell Park circa 1905-30, Smithson Stadium 1931-52, Knoxville Municipal Stadium 1953-56)

South Atlantic League 1957-63, Southern League 1964-67, 1972-present (White Sox, Blue Jays, K'Jays). *Location:* 633 Jessamine Street, off Magnolia Avenue. *Dimensions:* Left field, 330 feet; center field, 410 feet; right field, 330 feet. *Seating capacity:* (1960) 6700; (1975) 6900; (1985) 7000. *1987 season attendance:* 124,231. *Fire:* 1953. *Rebuilt:* 1931, 1953.

Named between 1931 and 1952 after City Councilman W.N. Smithson, who in '31 convinced the Knoxville council to tear down Caswell Park and build a modern stadium. Despite the name change and the new structure, Knoxvillians continued, for the most part, to call the place Caswell Park.

The new stadium was destroyed by fire in 1953 and again rebuilt. In 1957, the park was renamed after native son and former National League Manager of the Year Bill Meyer.

Meyer won the award in 1948, the year he skippered the Pittsburgh Pirates to an 83-71 record for part-owner

Two views of Bill Meyer Stadium, Knoxville, Tenn. (Compliments of the Knoxville Blue Jays.)

Bing Crosby. As a player, Meyer played most of his 113 major league games catching for the A's. He managed for many years in the Yankee organization, most notably for the AAA Newark Bears from 1943 to 1945. In retirement, Meyer returned to Knoxville and died at the age of 65 in his city of birth in 1957, the same year the ballpark's name was changed.

Hudson Field

Home of the University of Tennessee Volunteers (Southeastern Conference), present. *Location:* University of Tennessee, south campus. *Dimensions:* Left field, 350 feet; left center, 380 feet; center field, 400 feet; right center, 360 feet; right field, 330 feet. *Seating capacity:* 3000.

In 1987, the field added Triple-A quality lights and a permanent outfield fence designed to hold billboard advertising. The batting cage currently living in the left field corner will be moved behind the fence to make room for

*Highland Park Baseball Stadium, Kokomo, Ind. Picture taken opening day of the
1985 American Legion World Series. (Compliments of the Kokomo Parks and
Recreation Department.)*

additional bleachers in the near future.
The scoreboard peeks up over the right
field fence.

Photos of the ballpark show extremely tiny seating sections to the left
and right of home, so the 3000 seating
capacity figure given by the university
probably includes the room along the
foul lines for fans to sit or sprawl on a
grassy slope.

Kokomo, Indiana

Highland Park Baseball Stadium

Midwest League 1956–61. *Seating
capacity:* (1980) 700 (wooden bleachers); (1985) 4000 (aluminum bleachers).
Renovation: 1985 (New grandstand
cost $103,750 built by Grandstand Un-
limited). *Lights:* Hubbell Lighting
System. Seventy lights apiece on 65-
foot towers.

In 1985, this ballpark hosted the
American Legion Baseball World
Series. Kokomo became only the sec-
ond Indiana city to play host in the

60-year history of the Series.

From the time officers of Legion
Post 6 proposed the city as a site in
1983, until the Legion World Series
began play in Highland Park, $308,000
in improvements were made on the
facility, not including hundreds of
local volunteer hours. The playing field
was restored with 1600 square yards of
sod, an expensive but beautiful brick
dust infield, and Agralime warning
tracks. The ballpark drains very well.
New clubhouse facilities were built for
two ball clubs and the umpires in concrete block buildings. There was a new
two-story structure that held the press
box on top and a concession stand
below. New dugouts and restrooms
were constructed. Local firms donated
a modern scoreboard, air conditioning
for the concrete buildings, and a new
public address system. Kokomo Park
and Street Department employees did
much of the construction work.

Lafayette, Louisiana

Clark Field (Bull Stadium)
Evangeline League 1954 (Bulls),
Texas League circa 1975. *Constructed:*
1954. *Dimensions:* Left field, 325 feet;
center field, 370 feet; right field, 282
feet. *Seating capacity:* 6500. *First
game:* April 13, 1954.

Steel framework, a concrete base,
and wooden seats. Corrugated tin
fences boomed when a line-drive dented
them.

Clark Field was built in 1954 on land
that had once been a garbage dump and
a small lake. The trash was removed
and the lake was filled, both by the city.
The park was named after Dr. L.O.
Clark. It became an athletic complex,
the city sharing in its revenues. Football and softball were played here as
well as baseball. The grandstand was
made of steel, and had box seats and
concession stands. Dressing room facilities were added. The complex continued to be used by local teams even
when Lafayette fielded no professional
team.

Lakeland, Florida

Henley Field
Florida State League 1960, 1962–64,
spring home of the Detroit Tigers
1934–66. *Location:* Lakeland Hills
Boulevard, in back of Parker Lake.
Seating capacity: 3500.

Joker Marchant Stadium
Owned by the city of Lakeland.
Florida State League 1967–present
(Tigers), spring home of Detroit Tigers
1967–present. *Location:* Al Kaline
Drive off Lakeland Hills Boulevard
(one mile north of Henley Field). *Constructed:* 1966. *Cost of construction:*
$500,000. *Dimensions:* Left field, 340
feet; center field, 420 feet; right field,
340 feet. *Seating capacity:* (1975) 5000;
(1985) 6500. *1987 season attendance:*
61,255.

According to Boston Red Sox announcer Ken Coleman, "Without fail,
the P.A. announcer will implore everyone to 'kindly squeeze a little closer.'
This—along with such things as the
country music played between innings,
the grass fields, and swaying palms surrounding the park, and well-manicured
diamond itself—gives a game in Lakeland a special quality."

Named after the man instrumental in
getting it built.

Lancaster, Pennsylvania

**Franklin & Marshall College Foot-
ball Grounds**
Pennsylvania State League 1894–97
(Red Roses).

Used for Lancaster's first professional baseball team, the Red Roses.
This was Asa Bentley's club displaced
from Altoona.

Rossmere Park
Tri-State League 1900–14 (Roses).

Tri-State League also included Allentown, Wilmington, Trenton, Reading and Harrisburg.

Stumpf Field
Interstate League 1947 (Red Roses),
Eastern League 1958–61. *Seating capa-
city:* 4000.

The Interstate League franchise was
a farm of the A's, and the park was
described even then as old and beat up.

Las Vegas, Nevada

Roger Joe Barnson Field (Hustlin'
Rebel Field 1973–83)
Home of the University of Nevada at
Las Vegas Rebels 1973–present. *Location:* Northwest corner of the UNLV
campus. *Dimensions:* Left field, 335
feet; left center, 375 feet; center field,
400 feet; right center, 375 feet; right
field, 335 feet. *Seating capacity:* 5000.
First game: April 1973 (USC 9, Rebels

2, attendance: 1500). *Lights installed:* June 1982 by Stratton Electric of Las Vegas (eight standards, total of 144 fixtures with 1500 watt halide). *Cost of lights:* $180,000.

Park was renamed in 1983 to honor the UNLV assistant athletic director who had recently died in an automobile accident (March 14, 1980). Roger Barnson—a former star pitcher for Arizona State University—worked for 12 years in the UNLV athletic department.

The park, originally named Hustlin' Rebel Field (a pretty slick name), is located on the UNLV campus (33.5 acres in the metropolitan area south of the city of Las Vegas) and opened in April 1973. The attendance record at the park was set in May 1977, when a full house of 5000 watched the Kenny Rogers Celebrity–News Media softball game benefitting the Nevada Special Olympics.

In May 1977, three games between the Rebels and the University of Hawaii from Rebel Field were televised live in Hawaii.

Since July 1984, the infield grass has been Santa Ana Hybrid, and the infield dirt has been, according to the UNLV athletic department, "crushed brick added with a power stabilizer from Phoenix, Arizona."

In September 1984, a $155,000 scoreboard was installed by Young Electric Sign Company just out past the left field fence. The scoreboard is 36 feet high and is perhaps the most elaborate for amateur baseball in the country, with "message grams" running ticker-tape-style across the bottom. The sign on the bottom of the scoreboard reads, "UNLV, Roger Barnson Field."

The outfield fence at Barnson Field is a screen fence covered with vines.

Cashman Field
Pacific Coast League 1983–present. *Location:* Las Vegas Boulevard North, north of U.S. 95. *Dimensions:* Left field, 330 feet; center field, 422 feet; right field, 330 feet. *Seating capacity:*

10,000. *1987 season attendance:* 299,198. *Parking lot:* 2600 cars.

The ballpark is part of the Cashman Field Complex, which includes facilities for conventions and trade shows, a level of rooms of various sizes for business meetings, and a 2000-seat auditorium with a stage. The exhibit halls are adjacent to the ballpark grandstand, flush against the third base side. The auditorium is connected to the exhibit hall behind home plate.

Lawrenceville, Virginia

City Stadium
Virginia League circa 1950 (Cardinals). *Seating capacity:* 2100.

Leesburg, Florida

Venetian Gardens
Florida State League 1960–61. *Seating capacity:* 1500.

Leon, Mexico

Estadio Domingo Santana
Mexican League, Zona Sur, present (Bravos). *Dimensions:* Left field, 330 feet; center field, 400 feet; right field, 330 feet. *Seating capacity:* 7000.

Lethbridge, Alberta

Henderson Stadium
Pioneer League circa 1985 (franchise no longer exists). *Seating capacity:* 1500.

Lewiston, Idaho

Back in the old days, there was a ballpark built on an island in the middle of the Clearwater River. To get to the ball game, you had to take a boat. That was before the dam was built in

Cashman Field, Las Vegas, Nev. (Compliments of the Las Vegas News Bureau.)

the river. The site of that early diamond has been under water for years.

Bengal Field

Western International League 1937, 1952–54, Pioneer League 1939, Northwest League 1955–circa 1975. *Location:* Twelfth Avenue, 15th Street. *Constructed:* 1938. *Dimensions:* Left field, 335 feet; center field, 411 feet; right field, 308 feet. *Seating capacity:* 3500. Still in existence, used for football only.

In 1926, the plot of land that was to become Bengal Field was purchased by the Lewiston School District from the city, says Virgel Larson, that district's current assistant superintendent. The official owner of the land was the Lewiston High School Athletic Association. Twelfth Avenue originally ran through the plot, but was moved around the south end of the parcel of land to create space for an athletic facility.

In 1938, the WPA kicked in with funds for a new playing surface. Local citizens and businesses pooled their volunteer efforts and used government assistance to build a grandstand and install lights. In 1948, a section of 15th Street was abandoned by the city so the ballpark could be enlarged to its current size. Bengal Field was used for football, baseball and track until 1985. It is now football only.

During the time that Bengal Field hosted professional baseball, it provided the first minor league experience for future stars like Reggie Jackson and Rick Monday.

Little Falls, New York

Veterans Memorial Stadium

New York–Pennsylvania League 1977–present (Mets). *Location:* Exit 29A on the New York State Thruway. *Dimensions:* Left field, 378 feet; center field, 380 feet; right field, 373 feet. *Seating capacity:* 4000. *1987 season attendance:* 32,536.

From the stands, fans can see the mountains across the Mohawk River and the city dump. A splendid park. Tennis and basketball courts on the first base side, Little League fields behind

Top: *Bengal Field, Lewiston, Ida., in the snow, configured for football, as it looks today. (Compliments of the Lewiston Chamber of Commerce.)* Bottom: *Veterans Memorial Stadium, Little Falls, N.Y. Little Falls pitching coach advises a prospect in the V.M.S. bullpen. (Photo by David Pietrusza.)*

the left field fence. Rose bushes planted around the grounds give it a picnic-basket-and-handlebar-mustache feel. The field looks like a pool table—a phenomenal groundskeeping job for baseball at this level. Little Falls is a very small town (population 6156), and this is small-town baseball at its best. Let's hope there's always baseball here.

Little Rock, Arkansas

Lamar Porter Field
Location: Central Little Rock.

According to the Arkansas Department of Parks and Tourism, this is one of Little Rock's oldest ballparks. It has been the location for several movies made in Arkansas, most notably *A Soldier's Story* (1983), for which it was chosen because of its resemblance to parks of the '40s. The field is still used for Boys' Club programs.

Ray Winder Field (Travelers Field, Kavanaugh Field, Southern Association Park)

Southern Association 1960–61 (Arkansas Travelers), International League 1963, Pacific Coast League 1964–68, Texas League 1969–present (Arkansas Travelers). *Location:* Jonesboro Drive, War Memorial Park, Monroe Street, Eighth Street (later Interstate 630). *Constructed:* 1925. *Dimensions:* Left field, 325 feet; center field, 405 feet; right field, 300 feet. *Seating capacity:* (1960) 7500; (1975) 10,500; (1985) 6100. *1987 season attendance:* 256,365.

As of 1980, this field was home of a St. Louis Cardinals farm club.

Lodi, California

Lawrence Park
California League, late 1950s–circa 1985. *Seating capacity:* 2000.

Thanks to Mamie Van Doren (a sentiment long overdue), the Lodi team received more newspaper coverage in their first year than they did combined after that. The blonde movie star with the physically impossible shape—star of *High School Confidential* and *Sex Kittens Go to College*—was the recent bride of 19-year-old Lodi pitcher Lee Meyers. She declared Lodi her new base of operations, and the press followed her wherever she went. Van Doren later admitted feigning pregnancy to induce marriage.

Lodi, once known only for its Tokay grapes and its proximity to the Southern Pacific Railroad, with its population of 28,000, was one of the smallest communities in America to be supporting professional baseball. Crowds were comfortably large for a time, but this did not last. Word was the Cubs, with whom the community of Lodi had a working agreement, were interested exclusively in the development of talent and not in giving the community a winning ball club.

The team was sold to a Japanese group, became a farm club of the Oakland A's, and things only got worse. In 1970, the San Diego Padres bought the club and installed new management, but things continued to deteriorate. A large announcement of a guaranteed-win policy for ticket sales (fans saw a win or they got to come back for free) was greeted, by the team, with a 43–97 record. By 1971, a reporter from the *Los Angeles Times* was assigned to cover a game and almost missed the first inning because he couldn't find anyone who knew where the park was. Attendance that night was 158, and word was they had counted the bats and balls. The Lodi newspaper, which had only a one-man sports staff, had long since stopped covering the team.

In the late '60s and early '70s out on the right field fence, at the very top of the scoreboard, was a sign that read, "Hit This Sign, Win a Complete Shoe Wardrobe." In the five years the sign was up, there were two winners, the second being first baseman Jeff Pentland, who did it in 1971.

Lamar Porter Field, Little Rock, Ark. — a throwback to another time. (Compliments of the Arkansas Industrial Development Commission.)

In 1970, the commissioner of baseball, Bowie Kuhn, inspected the Lodi baseball facilities at Lawrence Park and said to the director of operations, "My God, can't you do something?" Kuhn was apparently particularly appalled at the clubhouses.

At that time, the lights were very poor, especially out in the left and right field corners, where outfielders seemed to disappear while chasing down doubles. The light poles were condemned, so it became illegal to put any more lights on them, and no one had the money for new towers. The legal condemnation of the poles also prohibited their being climbed, so the local firemen with their cherry picker had to be called in each time a bulb needed replacing.

Long Beach, California

49er Field
Home of the Long Beach State University 49ers (Pacific Coast Athletic Association, some games), present. *Seating capacity:* 1000.

Blair Field
Home of the Long Beach State University 49ers (Pacific Coast Athletic Association, some games), present. *Seating capacity:* 3000.

Los Angeles, California

Chutes Park
Pacific Coast League 1895-1911, California League 1903.
Located next to an amusement park.

Washington Park
Pacific Coast League 1912-25 (Angels). *Location:* Washington and Hill streets.
The Angels of the Pacific Coast League moved out of Washington Park after owner William Wrigley, Jr., failed to get permission from the city to build an underground parking lot beneath the playing field.

Wrigley Field
Pacific Coast League 1925-58 (Angels), American League 1961 (Angels). Originally owned by the Chicago Cubs, later by the Los Angeles Dodgers.

Location: East 42nd Place (home plate side), Avalon Boulevard (left field), East 41st Street (right field), San Pedro Street (first base). *Architect:* Zachary Taylor Davis (also designer of Wrigley Field and Comiskey Park in Chicago). *Construction cost:* $1.1 million. *Opened:* 1925. *Dedication:* September 27, 1925 (as a memorial to fallen soldiers of World War I). *Dimensions:* Left field, 340 feet; left center, 345 feet; center field, 412 feet; right center, 345 feet; right field, 339 feet. 56 feet from home plate to the backstop. *Seating capacity:* 20,457. Boxes, 8196; grandstand reserved, 10,261; bleacher, 2000. *Day game attendance record:* 19,722 (May 7, 1961, versus New York). *Doubleheader attendance record:* 16,297 (April 30, 1961, versus Kansas City). *Night game attendance record:* 19,930 (August 22, 1961, versus New York). *Twi-night doubleheader attendance record:* 9574 (May 19, 1961, versus Chicago). *Opening game attendance record:* 11,931 (April 27, 1961, versus Minnesota). *Season high (and low) attendance record:* 603,510 (1961). *First American League game:* April 27, 1961 (Minnesota 4, Los Angeles 2). *Last American League game:* October 1, 1961 (Cleveland 8, Los Angeles 5). *First night game:* July 22, 1932 (Angels 5, Seattle 4, 11 innings). *Torn down:* 1966.

As one might suspect, Wrigley Field once belonged to the Cubs. It was dedicated September 27, 1925, and was home until the 1950s to the Los Angeles Angels of the Pacific Coast League, then the Cubs' number one farm club. Fans took the old "S" cars to get there. In the 1920s, Wrigley Field was home of play in the "California Winter League." Black all-stars, big league all-stars, the best of the minor leagues and a few Mexican stars all formed teams and played each other. It was the highest quality baseball available on the coast.

In 1949, the ballpark was used as background for the filming of *It Happens Every Spring,* starring Ray Mil-

land as the college professor who cheats at baseball, wins 38 games on the mound using a foreign substance, gets away with it, and becomes a hero in his home town.

The Dodgers traded their Fort Worth minor league team to the Cubs for the Pacific Coast League Angels and Wrigley Field. In 1961, the Dodgers allowed the expansion Angels of the American League to use Wrigley Field, just as they would allow them to use Dodger Stadium from 1962 to 1965. The PCL team moved to Spokane.

In the expansion draft, the American League Angels kept in mind that they were to be playing their premiere season in a ballpark with 345-foot power alleys. They beefed up their lineup with hearty appetites like Steve Bilko, Ted Kluszewski, and Leon Wagner. A lot of home runs were hit all right, mostly by the opponents. The Angels finished eighth. Troubled relief pitcher Ryne Duren—known for thirst, thick spectacles, and warm-up pitches on the screen—lost 12 games for the Angels and only saved two. It was a strange lot to be wearing halos on their caps.

At the beginning of the season there were those who worried Wrigley Field's capacity of just over 20,000 would hurt the team's money-making capabilities—but the point turned out to be moot as they failed to draw 20,000 for a game all year.

The left field light tower came right up out of the outfield and was in play. This was more of a factor here than it was in some ballparks, because of the shallow fences.

Wrigley Field was torn down in 1966. The site was transformed into a playground named Gilbert Lindsay Park.

Los Angeles Memorial Coliseum

National League 1958–61 (Dodgers). Owned by the County of Los Angeles. *Location:* Santa Barbara Avenue (first base side), Hoover Avenue (third base),

Los Angeles, Calif.: The Los Angeles Memorial Coliseum. After playing in Ebbets Field, it must have been enough to make a grown man cry. The bottom photo shows the Coliseum in its natural state. (Top photo compliments of the Los Angeles Dodgers, Inc. Bottom photo supplied by the Los Angeles Coliseum Commission.)

Exposition Boulevard (left field), Figueroa Street (right field). *Groundbreaking:* December 21, 1921. *Architect:* John and Donald Parkinson. *Contractor:* Edwards, Wildey and Dixon Company (now known as the L.E. Dixon Company). *Construction completed:* May 1, 1923. *Construction cost:* $954,872.98. *Enlarged:* February 1930–May 1931 (for the Olympics). *Enlargement cost:* $950,293.88. *Dimensions:* Left field, 251 feet; left center, 320 feet; center field, 410 feet; right center, 385 feet; right field, 300 feet. 66 feet from home plate to the backstop. *Field dimensions (entire playing surface):* East to west (wall to wall) 680 feet, 2 inches; north to south (wall to wall), 324 feet, 2 inches; width of field (including track), 304 feet, 8 inches. Total of 4.5 acres. *Fences:* 42-foot screen in left, held in place by two 60-foot support towers. Left center, 8 feet; center field, 6 feet; right field, 6 feet. *Seating capacity:* 1921 (Olympics), 74,000; 1932 (Olympics), 105,000; for baseball, 93,600. *Exhibition game attendance record:* 93,103 (May 7, 1959, versus New York Yankees, Roy Campanella Night). *World Series attendance record:* 92,706 (alltime record), Game 5, October 6, 1959, Chicago 1, Los Angeles 0, Koufax loses heartbreaker to Bob Shaw. *Day game (Regular season) attendance record:* 78,672 (April 18, 1958, versus San Francisco). *Doubleheader attendance record:* 39,432 (September 6, 1959, versus Chicago). *Night game attendance record:* 67,550 (April 12, 1960, versus Chicago). *Twi-night doubleheader attendance record:* 72,140 (August 16, 1961, versus Cincinnati). *Opening game attendance record:* 78,672 (April 18, 1958, versus San Francisco). *Season high attendance record:* 2,253,887 (1960). *Season low attendance record:* 1,804,250 (1961). *First game:* April 18, 1958 (Los Angeles 6, San Francisco 5). *Last game:* September 20, 1961 (night, Los Angeles 3, Chicago 3, 13 innings, suspended). *First football game:* October 6, 1923, University of Southern

California versus Pomona College (attendance, 12,836).

This site was used for a public entertainment facility since the 1890s, when it was known as Agricultural Park, home of horse racing, fairs, saloons and other amusements. In the early part of the twentieth century, the area was known as Exposition Park, with a museum and gardens (and an armory during the war). At least part of the site was composed of gravel pit.

Dodger pitcher Clem Labine said, "I used to make good pitches in the Los Angeles Coliseum and someone would hit it off that screen in left. It was hard to adjust to. For some hitters, the games were like batting practice."

After the intimacy of Ebbets Field, the Coliseum came as a shock to Dodger players. The Olympic playing surface at the base of the bowl was the same size as the whole plot of land that held Ebbets Field, stands and all. "It was a very difficult move, very upsetting," said Labine. "Nobody understood those freeways, and nobody could deal with that ballpark.

"I knew it was a different game when I couldn't throw the ball in the stands because I couldn't reach it."

There was a huge tunnel behind home plate, which must have looked great when marathon runners entered through it. During a baseball game it looked more like a huge mouth eager to eat left-handers alive.

The 79 rows of seats in the bowl rise 110 feet above the ground — 143 feet above the playing field, which is sunken. Everyone knew that the dimensions were going to hurt Duke Snider's home run productivity. The move and a bad knee reduced the Duke's numbers from 40 homers to 15. But the same folks thought the Coliseum would make Gil Hodges break Ruth's record. Wrong. Hodges hit line drives, which were turned into singles by the Chinese screen. What the Dodgers needed was a guy who could hit cans of corn to left every time.

The home run breakdown was as follows:

	left	ctr.	right
1958	182	3	8
1959	132	1	39
1960	155	3	28
1961	147	7	38

But the fans came out. Despite the heat. In the summer the Coliseum really baked players and fans. During the first year of baseball, 1958, 1,845,000 came to see the Dodgers play, almost twice the attendance at Ebbets Field the previous season, and the attendance figure broke the 2 million mark for the first time in the franchise's history the following year.

Of course, it isn't the structure's — or its designers' — fault that the Coliseum was silly when used for baseball. It is a grand structure, and one of our greatest sports arenas.

The largest attendance at the Coliseum for a single event was 134,254 for a Billy Graham religious rally on September 8, 1963. The attendance record for a sporting event here is 105,236 for the USC versus Notre Dame football game November 10, 1957.

The record attendance for the Olympics was 104,022, on August 9, 1984, and the largest pro football attendance was 102,368 for the L.A. Rams versus the San Francisco 49ers on December 6, 1947.

Dodger Stadium (Chavez Ravine)

National League 1962–present (Dodgers), American League 1962–65 (Angels). Owned by the Los Angeles Dodgers. *Location:* Park encircled by Stadium Way. Pasadena Freeway (first base side), Elysian Park Avenue (home plate), Scott Road (third base), Solano Canyon Road (right field). *Architect:* Captain Emil Praeger. *Construction cost:* $23 million. *Dimensions:* Left field, 330 feet; left center, 370 feet; center field, 400 feet; right center, 370 feet; right field, 330 feet. 75 feet from home plate to the backstop. *Fences:* Under four feet down the lines, eight feet in center. *Seating capacity:* 56,000. Dugout boxes, 264; boxes, 24,476; club boxes, 1468; reserved, 19,322; general admission, 10,470. *Dodgers season high attendance record:* 3,608,881 (1982, all-time record). *Angels day game attendance record:* 44,912 (June 3, 1962, versus New York). *Angels day doubleheader attendance record:* 12,873 (June 10, 1962, versus Kansas City). *Angels night game attendance record:* 53,591 (July 13, 1962, versus New York). *Angels twi-night doubleheader attendance record:* 18,902 (May 19, 1965, versus Minnesota). *Angels opening game attendance record:* 21,864 (April 11, 1963, versus Chicago). *Angels season high attendance record:* 1,144,063 (1962). *Angels season low attendance record:* 566,727 (1965). *First National League game:* April 10, 1962 (Cincinnati 6, Los Angeles 3, attendance 52,564). *First American League game:* April 17, 1962 (Kansas City 5, Los Angeles 3). *Last American League game:* September 22, 1965 (Los Angeles 2, Boston 0).

Maybe it's easier to forgive the Dodgers for ripping the heart out of Brooklyn, when you consider the Los Angeles Dodgers have, by far, the most successful franchise of all time. Or maybe not.

The Dodgers draw over three million per year all the time now. They were the first franchise to draw that figure, and they set the all-time baseball attendance record in 1982, when they drew 3,608,881.

Chavez Ravine was hills, gullies, washes and twisting roads when it was chosen as the site of the new Dodger ballpark. Before construction could begin, it was necessary to move over 8 million cubic yards of earth and a few feisty people. On August 22, 1957, two sheriffs suffered bites and bruises trying to evict the family of Manuel Arechiga from the ravine.

The stadium was constructed with

Dodger Stadium, Los Angeles, Calif. (Photo © 1985 Los Angeles Dodgers, Inc. Used with permission.)

building blocks, 21,000 pre-cast concrete units. Single units weighed up to 32 tons. The Dodger Stadium scoreboard is in right field. DiamondVision (added later) is in left. The ballpark was and is the only privately financed major league baseball stadium since Yankee Stadium opened in 1923.

The Dodgers brought the World Championship to Chavez Ravine in 1963, as they completed a four-game sweep of the New York Yankees on October 6, 1963. The Dodgers only got two hits in Game Four, but luckily one of them was an awesome Frank Howard home run into the second deck, the longest home run hit in Dodger Stadium up till that time.

The parking lot holds 16,000 cars on 21 terraced lots at five different levels. Fans can park their cars and enter the ballpark at the same level as their seats. Seating levels and parking levels are color coordinated. The four decks of seats (plus a "below ground level") have no obstructions. None of the decks is deeper than 20 rows.

Homers. The first home run here was

hit during the very first game on April 10, 1962, by Cincinnati outfielder Wally Post, providing the G.W.R.B.I.

Only two batted balls have been hit out of Dodger Stadium. Both of them were struck by Willie Stargell, off Alan Foster in 1969 and Andy Messersmith in 1973. The '69 blast was measured at 506 feet.

Only three players have hit home runs into the loge (second) level of seats at Dodger Stadium — because it is quite a poke from the plate, and because so little of it is in fair territory. On October 6, 1963, Frank Howard hit a World Series home run eight rows deep into the section, a blast estimated at 420 feet down the left field line. Dave Kingman did it June 4, 1976. (Kong hit three home runs in the game, drove in eight, and still failed to help his ball club.) Dave Parker is the only man to hit a loge-level homer down the right field line, June 6, 1984.

On May 25, 1979, eight home runs were hit in a game at Dodger Stadium, setting the ballpark record. Seven were hit by Dodgers: Dusty Baker, Rick

Sutcliffe, Steve Garvey, Gary Thomasson, Joe Ferguson, Derrel Thomas and Davey Lopes. **Koufax.** Sandy Koufax was an extraordinary pitcher by any criterion, but his record in Dodger Stadium is truly out of this world. Check out these win-loss records at home:

1962 13-3
1963 11-1
1964 12-2
1965 14-3
1966 13-5

Dodger Stadium's mound was known for its height, and it always was one of the best pitchers' parks in baseball, but these numbers are remarkable. It was also in his home park that Koufax pitched his perfect game, beating the Cubs on September 9, 1965. That year Koufax whiffed 382 opponents.

For their tenth anniversary in Dodger Stadium, the Dodgers honored two men for the construction of the ballpark: Captain Emil Praeger, who designed Dodger Stadium, and Jack Young, vice president and general manager of Vinnell, the company that constructed the structure.

Up until 1985, there had been only eleven rainouts in Dodger Stadium history—and only one prior to 1976.

In 1984, Dodger Stadium was home of the Olympic Games baseball competition. Japan won the gold medal, the United States won the silver and Chinese Taipai the bronze.

Dedeaux Field

Home of the University of Southern California Trojans 1974–present (Pac-10 Conference). *Location:* Northwest corner of the USC campus, near the intersection of Jefferson and Vermont streets. *Dimensions:* Left field, 335 feet; left center, 375 feet; center field, 395 feet; right center, 365 feet; right field, 335 feet. *Turf:* grass. *Seating capacity:* 1800.

The first game played at Dedeaux

Field took place March 30, 1974. Right-hander Russ McQueen threw a no-hitter for the Trojans and USC went on to sweep a doubleheader from the University of California.

Jackie Robinson Stadium

Home of the University of California at Los Angeles Bruins (Pac-10 Conference), present. *Seating capacity:* 1250.

Louisville, Kentucky

Name of park unknown

Location: Where Nineteenth and Duncan streets now intersect. *Dimensions:* Open field. Site of Louisville's first inter-town game, between the Louisvilles and the Nashville Cumberlands, July 19, 1865.

Several hundred attended this game, the men bewhiskered and the women in hoop skirts. The official scorer was Mrs. John Dickens, wife of the captain and shortstop of the Nashville Cumberlands.

Since no one in the crowd fully understood the game, they didn't know when it was over, and when it was over they didn't know who won until Mrs. Dickens climbed atop the scorer's table and announced Louisville the victor.

Eclipse Park (I)

Home of the Louisville Eclipse (semi-pro) circa 1874, American Association 1882–91 (Eclipse, Cyclones), National League 1892–93 (Colonels, Night Riders, Wanderers). *Location:* Magazine, 28th, 29th and Elliott streets. *First American Association game:* May 5, 1882. *Last American Association game:* September 27, 1891. *First National League game:* April 12, 1892. *Last National League game:* May 4, 1893. *Fire:* September 27, 1892 (use not interrupted).

As early as 1874, the Eclipse played local semi-pro competition such as the Olympics and the Eagles. The Olympics' home park was very close to Eclipse Park—though it is no longer known precisely where—and these two teams had a fierce rivalry, worthy even of national attention. If you were a man in Louisville at that time you probably rooted for either the Olympics or the Eclipse, with fights between the factions so common that some bars banned discussion of baseball, just as they might ban religion or politics.

In the 1880s, when the big league American Association played here, one of the star pitchers for the Eclipse was Tom Ramsey, a spitball pitcher who liked both his baseball and his diet nice and wet. Ramsey's liquid diet might easily have been described as habitual. Manager "Honest" John Kelly tried sobering Ramsey up—but the pitcher maintained only two states, drunk and hung over. He pitched lousy when hung over. Finally, Kelly wisened up and escorted Ramsey to the bar under the Eclipse Park grandstand before each of his starts, poured liquor into him until his eyes cleared, then sent him out to work his moist wizardry.

For a time, in the early 1890s, the Louisville National League team was known as the Night Riders, because of Kentucky's tobacco raids of that era. A tornado swept through town on March 27, 1890, killing 75, and the team became known temporarily as the Cyclones.

National League Park

National League 1876–77 (Eclipse). *Location:* Fourth, Sixth, Hill and Magnolia streets, current site of St. James Court. *First game:* April 25, 1876 (Chicago 4, Louisville 0, winning pitcher: Al Spalding). *Last game:* September 29, 1877. *Damaged by tornado:* 1876.

The grandstand ran east-west on the field's south side, and the bleachers (or "boards," as they were referred to at the time) were on the east side (Fourth Street). Behind the outfield fence was a small hill, where fans could sit and watch the game. The crowd was of the la-di-da variety, and expensive carriages parked along Fourth Street during games, their Who's-Who owners inside the ballpark.

The 1877 Louisville season was marred by a gambling scandal. It was learned from the wife of one of the guilty players that four of the Eclipse accepted $100 apiece to throw ball games. As a result, Louisville was dropped from the National League.

Eclipse Park (II)

National League 1893–99 (Colonels), Western Association 1901. *Location:* 28th Street and Broadway (across the street from previous site). *First game:* May 22, 1893. *Last National League game:* September 2, 1899 (Louisville 25, Washington 4). *First Western Association game:* April 25, 1901. *Last game:* June 30, 1901. *Fire:* 1899.

In 1893, property owners tried to stop the Louisville ball club from building the new park in their neighborhood, on the site of the old Kentucky and Indiana Company railroad switching yard and stockyard. They said it would be a nuisance, but the court ruled against them.

Having already put up with the ruffians for a few years across the street, at the original Eclipse Park, the locals knew what they were talking about. The Colonels could be a rowdy lot. Among their ranks was William B. (Farmer) Weaver, originally of Parkersburg, West Virginia. Legend has it that on July 4, 1893, Weaver decided to celebrate Independence Day in the middle of the ball game. He whipped out a revolver and placed five shots into a fly ball before catching it. Weaver hit .309 that year, best of his career.

Louisville joined the National League in 1892 when it expanded to twelve teams. After the 1899 season, when the league reverted to eight franchises, Louisville, along with Washington, Cleveland, and Baltimore, was dropped.

On July 19, 1897, Eclipse Park was the site of Honus Wagner's big league debut. He played center, handled his only chance, and went one for two. Louisville fans' only reaction was to laugh at Wagner because his knees were so far apart. The Flying Dutchman played three all-star quality seasons in Louisville and never once played shortstop. You could look it up.

Fire. The Louisville Colonels had been a solid franchise in the National League until their ballpark was completely destroyed by fire in 1899. The park was inactive at the time, so no one was injured.

Temporary but insufficient stands were erected. In August there was a near-riot as the ballpark proved grossly inadequate for the drawing power of a doubleheader against the Orioles.

A piece of history occurred at the final game at Eclipse Park, September 2, 1899, before makeshift fan accommodations. Washington outfielder Buck Freeman smacked his twenty-fifth home run of the year, second best ever in the NL, second to Ned Williamson's 27 (with the help of Lakefront Park in Chicago) in 1884. (The rest of the day was all Louisville, as they defeated Washington in their final major league home game 25-4.)

Owner Barney Dreyfuss became frustrated with turning away paying customers and ordered all games from the beginning of September to the end of the season played on the road.

The fire directly caused the dropping of the franchise from the League. Dreyfuss went to Pittsburgh, where he became the Pirates' president. Wagner went with him, and spent another year playing outfield, first and third before trying his hand at short.

Eclipse Park (III)

American Association (AAA) 1902–22 (Colonels). *Location:* Seventh and Kentucky streets.

The first owner of the American Association Colonels, George "White Wings" Tebeau, had some trouble finding a site for a ballpark. The old site at 28th and Broadway was no longer available. Tebeau got so far as to close a deal near the current intersection of Seventh and Algonquin, then far out in the country. After his purchase, and just as he was ready to start grading the field and building the grandstand, he discovered the streetcar company was unwilling to lengthen its tracks to the site.

Tebeau quickly found another spot, at Seventh and Kentucky streets. With three weeks to go before Opening Day, Tebeau built himself a ballpark. At the first game the fences and bleachers were up and the grandstand was four-fifths done. That ballpark, built so hastily, and as a last minute replacement, served Louisville for 21 years, until it was replaced in 1923 by Parkway Field.

Once Tebeau, infuriated by an umpire's call, went into the umpires' locker room, took the arbiter's civvies, and set them outside the grandstand on the streetcar tracks. A ballplayer who'd drawn turnstile duty that day retrieved the clothes once the owner of the club was gone.

Parkway Field (Colonels Field)

American Association 1923–at least 1940 (Colonels), Negro National League 1931 (White Sox), Negro Southern League 1932 (Black Caps), Negro American League 1949 (Buckeyes). *Location:* Eastern Parkway (left field), Brook Street (right field). *Dimensions:* Left field, 331 feet; center field, 512 feet; right field, 350 feet. *First game:* May 1, 1923.

Built in 1923 by William F. Knebelkamp, despite much criticism from his peers and the community. Baseball fever wasn't raging in 1923 Louisville. But all of that changed by the time the ballpark was finished, a thing of beauty, much larger than anything Louisville had seen before. Its deep concrete and steel single-decked grandstand had a large, heavy roof, and almost com-

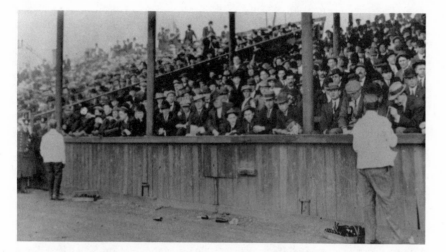

Eclipse Park (III), Louisville, Ky. Note the vendors, police and empties on the field. (From the R.G. Potter Collection, University of Louisville Photographic Archives. Used with permission.)

pletely encompassed foul territory.

According to A.H. Tarvin in *Seventy-Five Years on Louisville Diamonds,* "Parkway Field was opened on May 1, 1923, with much eclat. Villagers to a number that far overflowed the seating capacity tithered thither by automobile, streetcar, Shanks' mare and one venerable gentleman, so tradition says, was so inflicted with sciatica that he could not be placed in a machine or streetcar, so they toted him to the scene in a wheelbarrow, the early spring breezes toying playfully with his whiskers en route, and his hat blowing off, ever and anon, to add to the troubles of the young man who acted as propelling power."

The ballpark was built at the end of the streetcar line. There was a loop of tracks where the streetcars turned around just beyond the left field wall. Behind home plate were factories whose tall chimney stacks belched black smoke—smoke that sometimes

clung low over the field while a game was played. The parking lot was on the third base side. There were lights by 1937. Over the right field fence fans saw a billboard advertisement for Gold Medal Flour. The hand-operated scoreboard in left field was tall, as tall as the triple deck of signs that flanked it, three times as high as the fence anywhere else.

Parkway Field's grandstand was torn down in 1961, but the playing field remains, now used by the University of Louisville. The brick outfield wall is still intact. Center field is now 504 feet from home.

Cardinal Stadium (Fairgrounds Stadium 1957–82)

American Association 1957–62 (Colonels), 1982–present (Redbirds), International League 1968–72 (Colonels). *Location:* Off Interstate 65, on the site of the Kentucky State Fairgrounds. *Dimensions:* Left field, 340

Opposite: *Action at the plate in Eclipse Park (II), Louisville, Ky., sometime in the 1890s. (From the R.G. Potter Collection, University of Louisville Photographic Archives. Used with permission.)*

feet; center field, 410 feet; right field, 300 feet. *Turf:* (1957–81) grass; (1982–present) artificial. *Seating capacity:* (1957) 20,628; (1982) 32,500. *All-time minor league season attendance record:* 1,052,438. *1987 season attendance:* 516,329.

Between 1972 and 1981, the park was used by the University of Louisville and the Commonwealth of Kentucky, primarily for football. In the fall of 1981, over $4 million was raised by businesses and fans of baseball in Louisville for renovations. The first minor league ball in Louisville in a decade began play in spring 1982. New press boxes dangled from underneath the grandstand roof. The Redbirds, a farm team of the St. Louis Cardinals, drew 868,418 in 1982, breaking the old minor league attendance record of 675,063, held by the 1946 San Francisco Seals. The Redbirds broke their own record in 1983, drawing 1,052,438. From 1982–87, Louisville holds down the top five places for all-time minor league season attendance.

Lynchburg, Virginia

Hill City Park
Location: Park Avenue, between Orchard and Forest streets, a short distance from the fairgrounds.

By 1886, over 100 amateur baseball teams were operating in Lynchburg — the Hill City, as it is called — said *The Lynchburg Virginian* that year, quoting "a base ballist." It was the city's centennial year, and local business leaders decided it was time they had their own professional baseball team. The Lynchburg Base Ball Association was formed, officers were elected, and shares of stock were sold at $10 apiece. Construction began on a ballfield on a plot of land leased to the association by a man named A. Tunstall. The city's first enclosed baseball pavilion was built conveniently on the end of a car line.

All but one of the professionals had previous pro ball experience. The team wore silver-gray uniforms with maroon trim. They played the first game at Hill City Park on May 6, 1886. Seven hundred paid to get in, with another 700 watching for free over the low outfield fence. The opponents were the Pastimes, Lynchburg's strongest amateur club. It was a mismatch. The pros won 36–3. The game was mercifully stopped after five innings. By June, the team had a franchise in the short-lived State League.

City Stadium
Virginia League circa 1950 (Cardinals, Shoemakers, Senators), Carolina League 1966–present (Red Sox). *Location:* Just off U.S. Route 29. *Dimensions:* Left field, 325 feet; center field, 390 feet; right field, 325 feet. *Seating capacity:* 4164. *1987 season attendance:* 88,370.

In 1983, 18-year-old Dwight Gooden went 19–4 and struck out 300 for Lynchburg.

McCook, Nebraska

Cibola Stadium
Nebraska State League (Class D) circa 1957 (Braves). *Seating capacity:* 1000.

Built as part of the McCook County Fairgrounds (total size, one-quarter of a mile square), at the northern edge of town where the plains began. Baseball dressing rooms were in the armory, one-half mile south of the ballpark. The ballpark was in the southernmost portion of the grounds, closest to McCook. Home plate faced north so fans saw the plains over the outfield fences. In his autobiography, *A False Spring,* Pat Jordan describes the field as "rock-hard dirt and scattered clumps of tall dried grasses." An unpainted wooden fence separated this playing surface from the fairgrounds proper. Lights were mounted on "about a dozen or so" surrounding telephone poles. Jordan goes on: "A 10-foot-high fence of chicken wire separated the field of play from the temporary stands along the first-base line, behind home plate and along the thirdbase line ... consisting of metal supports and 10 inclining rows of long wooden planks. The planks clattered and groaned when stepped or sat on.... There was a much smaller section of stands along the left field foul line directly behind a single picnic bench that served as the home team bullpen. Unlike seats in the other stands, which cost 75 cents (in 1957), the left field seats cost only a quarter. They were reserved for the Mexican and Indian migrant workers.... Behind the left field stands was a small wooden building.... At night, with a game in progress, it became a refreshment stand on one side and rest rooms on the other. The rest rooms were directly below the highest part of the left field stands and so were always in shadows. The refreshment side was well-lighted and faced an open gravel space that was the stadium's parking lot."

McKeesport, Pennsylvania

Cycler Park

Negro East-West League 1932 (Homestead Grays, some games). *Dimensions:* Left field, 393 feet; center field, 440 feet; right field, 325 feet.

Macon, Georgia

Luther Williams Field

Southern Association 1961, South Atlantic League 1962–63, 1980s, Southern League 1964, 1966–67 (Pirates). *Dimensions:* Left field, 330 feet; center field, 405 feet; right field, 330 feet. *Seating capacity:* (1960) 5000; (1985) 3000.

In 1976, Luther Williams Field was

used in the making of the film *Bingo Long's Traveling All-Star and Motor Kings.* The film was not appreciated by the former Negro League stars who saw it, as it portrayed the antics of a clown team. Such acts did exist, but they were relatively few and seldom played in a league. A film of the Harlem Globetrotters would inadequately represent NBA basketball.

The Sally League franchise that played here until 1987 moved to Augusta, Georgia.

Claude Smith Field

Home of the Mercer University Bears (Trans-America Conference), present. *Dimensions:* Left field, 330 feet; right field, 315 feet. *Seating capacity:* 2000.

Madison, Wisconsin

Breese Stevens Field

Home of the Blues circa 1930, Three-I League 1940–42 (Blues), used for Industrial League play during World War II. *Location:* East Washington Avenue, Brearly Street, Mifflin Street.

Said Tom Butler, sports columnist for the *Wisconsin State Journal:* "A particularly pleasant memory I have of Breese Stevens was the tantalizing aroma that wafted over East Washington Avenue from Gardner's Bakery across the street. Ever since those days I always associate the smell of baking bread and rolls with baseball."

The land for Breese Stevens Field was purchased by the city of Madison in 1923. In 1925, the brick grandstand was constructed. A chain link fence covered with canvas encircled the block.

In 1934, home plate was turned from facing Brearly Street to facing East Washington Avenue, and a stone wall was built around the grounds with stone quarried out of Hoyt Park. A football press box was added along the third base line in 1939, and this was the way the park remained for over 40 years.

Configured for football and track and field, Breese Stevens Field had the short dimension in right when set up for baseball. A single-deck, roofed grandstand wrapped from home plate around the oval to almost straightaway center, with open bleachers extending all the way down the extremely long left field foul line.

In the 1930s the park was used by the Madison Blues, who played teams like the Sheboygan Chairmakers. In those days the Blues were a semi-pro team, and the biggest crowds showed up for exhibition games against such big league competition as the three Chicago clubs (Cubs, American Giants, and White Sox), the Detroit Tigers, the St. Louis Cardinals, and the Kansas City Monarchs.

In the late 1930s the Blues joined the Three-I League, but World War II, and then the movement of the Braves to Milwaukee, ended minor league ball in Madison until the 1980s. During the war the park was used by the Industrial League. According to Tom Butler, one of the longest home runs ever hit at Breese Stevens Field was by Jug Girard in an Industrial League game.

Until the 1960s, Breese Stevens Field was the only outdoor arena in Madison with lights. It housed University of Wisconsin football, city track meets, midget car racing, boxing and wrestling.

In 1981, with the major league baseball strike in progress, Breese Stevens Field was dying a slow death. That summer the National Baseball Congress state tournament was held there. Madison's superintendent of parks, Dan Stapay, issued a directive that spectator seating beneath the covered portion of the grandstand wouldn't be allowed for reasons of safety and liability. Fans were only allowed to sit in the long open section of seats that ran along the third base line.

Preservation planner Katherine H. Rankin inspected the site in 1981 and wrote to Daniel Stapay begging that the park be saved. "I realize," she wrote, "that the costs of repair would be high, because the building has suffered from many years of neglect. But even though the design of the building is more functional than it is artistic, the grandstand has architectural elements and details that would be impossible to duplicate in this day and age, such as the terra trim around the windows and doors. It is unlikely the replacement structure would match the existing in architectural quality or in design compatibility with the stone walls. And it would be impossible to replace the historical associations that the existing grandstand has for the people of Madison."

Warner Park

Midwest League 1982–present (Muskies). *Location:* Sherman Avenue. *Dimensions:* Left field, 320 feet; center field, 390 feet; right field, 320 feet. *Seating capacity:* 3400. *Record season attendance:* 131,646 (1983). *1987 season attendance:* 84,381.

The ballpark was constructed by the Park Division of the city of Madison's Department of Public Works in 1956–57. It was used for high school and local sports before becoming a minor league ballpark.

The Muskies (named after a kind of fish) are a farm club of the Oakland Athletics.

Marblehead, Massachusetts

Seaside Park

Used for local baseball, present. *Location:* Atlantic Avenue, near the ocean.

Marshallton, Delaware

Eden Park

Location: Second and Adams.

Seaside Park, Marblehead, Mass. (Photo by David Pietrusza.)

Marshallton is a town near Wilmington. In the 1920s, Eden Park was the home of the black ball club the Rosedales. The star of the team was Judy Johnson.

Martinsville, Virginia

English Field
Appalachian League 1988 (Phillies). *Location:* Commonwealth Boulevard. *Dimensions:* Left field, 320 feet; center field, 370 feet; right field, 320 feet. *Seating capacity:* 3200.

Massena, New York

Alco Field
Canadian-American League 1936 (Ramblers, partial season).
Shared a disastrous franchise with Watertown.

Medford, Oregon

Miles Field
Northwest League 1979–present (A's). *Location:* State Highway 99, ½

mile south of town. *Dimensions:* Left field, 332 feet; center field, 384 feet; right field, 344 feet. *Seating capacity:* 3300. *1987 season attendance:* 72,729.

Medicine Hat, Alberta

Athletic Park
Pioneer League 1978–present (Blue Jays). *Location:* 100 Second Street. *Dimensions:* Left field, 350 feet; center field, 380 feet; right field, 350 feet. *Seating capacity:* 3400. *1987 season attendance:* 25,948.

Melbourne, Florida

Melbourne Regional Airport Complex
Spring home of the Minnesota Twins' farm system, present. *Location:* South side of NASA Boulevard.

Memphis, Tennessee

Central Park
League Alliance 1877 (Red Stockings).

Memphis's first exposure to organized ball. The Red Stockings went 25–6 before going broke and disbanding in mid–July. The team blamed poor press coverage.

First baseman Oscar Walker led the '77 Red Stockings in hitting at .350. Their top pitcher was William Buckalow (16–4).

The city did not field another pro team until 1884. In the interim, Memphis's top inter- and intra-city semi-pro teams were the Blues (sponsored by the Louisville and Nashville Railroad), the Riverdales and the Reds.

Olympic Park (later renamed Citizens Park)

Southern League 1884–89, 1892–95 (Leaguers 1884–87, Grays 1888–89, Giants 1892–95). *Location:* Current site of the Memphis Area Transit Authority Bus Terminal. *First Southern League game:* May 4, 1884 (Memphis defeated Birmingham).

In 1886, Memphis pitcher Eddie Knouff was a lone bright spot in a dismal season. He struck out a city record 390 and won 24 of the Leaguers' 44 victories.

In 1888, the team's name was changed to the Grays, because of the color of their uniforms. That year, future Hall of Famers Kid Nichols and Buck Ewing played for the club.

In 1894, the team won the city's only nineteenth century pennant. The team folded in mid–June of the following year, for lack of funds. For the next five years there would be nothing but amateur ball in Memphis.

Russwood Park (Red Elm Park)

Southern Association 1901–59 (Leaguers 1901–07, Turtles 1907–14, Chicks 1915–59). *Location:* Jefferson and Madison avenues, at Edgeway and Dunlaps streets. Currently the site of a medical center. *Built:* 1896. *Refurbished:* 1921. *Dimensions:* (Before inner fence) left field, 424 feet; center field, 366 feet; right field, 301 feet.

Seating capacity: (1896) 3000; (1915) 6500; (1921) 11,000. *Record season attendance:* 361,174 (1948). *First night game:* May 13, 1943 (Knoxville 4, Memphis 3, attendance 4167). *Last game:* April 17, 1960 (exhibition game, Cleveland Indians 2, Chicago White Sox 1, attendance 7279). *Fire:* April 17, 1960 (Easter Sunday).

Professional baseball returned to Memphis in 1901, as the city earned a franchise in the Southern Association. In their first year of competition the Leaguers played a benefit game against the amateur Memphis Chicks, and defeated them 4–2 before 5000 fans at Red Elm Park. Receipts from the game went to the family of Captain Fred Brennan, a fireman who had died in the line of duty.

Behind the pitching of Harry McIntyre, the Memphis team took home the Southern Association pennant in 1903 and 1904.

Before the start of the 1906 season, an unusual game took place in Red Elm Park. The Leaguers played an exhibition game against the Philadelphia Athletics, the eccentric Rube Waddell on the mound. Ahead 5–2 in the ninth, men on second and third, one out, Waddell ordered his fielders to the dugout, except for his catcher and an infielder. Connie Mack tried to talk sense to the boy, but Rube was insistent. So, since the game didn't count, Mack let the strange one have his way. Waddell, of course, struck out the remaining two batters to end the game.

In 1907, the club became known as the Turtles, because of the turtle-back shape of the new diamond at Red Elm Park. For six years the team was awful. In 1915, the name was changed to the Chicks, partially in an attempt to change the club's luck.

The new name didn't have anything to do with hatching eggs. Memphis was the home of the Chickasaw Indian nation, as well as the Chickasaw Guard, a military drill team that won various marching championships in the 1870s

Top: *Russwood Park, Memphis, Tenn., in the 1960s from the air: lopsided, out of whack, and lovable. Note the outer fence in left with its hand-operated scoreboard.* Bottom: *The queue for admittance to Russwood, some time in the late 1940s. A grandstand ticket cost a dollar. (Both photos compliments of the Memphis Chicks.)*

and 1880s. There had also been an amateur club known as the Chicks from Memphis for many years. That same year, 1915, Red Elm Park became Russwood Park. The change was the idea of team owner Russell E. Gardner. He probably named the park after himself, but he claimed it was because of the rusty color of the grandstand.

The 1921 season brought another pennant to Memphis as well as a major refurbishment to Russwood Stadium. Seating capacity was raised from 6500 to 11,000. That year, Memphis led the league in attendance with 254,725.

In 1944, the Memphis Chicks featured the league-MVP play of one-armed Pete Gray. He hit .333 and stole 68 bases.

In 1947, it was Ted Kluszewski who hit .377. On July 28, a crowd of 6736 saw Kluszewski go eight for ten in a doubleheader sweep of the New Orleans Pelicans.

Fire. On April 17, 1960, only three days before the Blues were scheduled to play their home opener against Chattanooga, the last baseball game was played in Russwood Stadium. It was an exhibition game between the Chicago White Sox and the Cleveland Indians. Rocky Colavito homered to win the game for the Indians, 2-1. After the game, when almost everyone had gone home, the ballpark caught fire—and soon the city had a dangerous, raging inferno on its hands. Four former Chicks played for the White Sox that day. They were Ted Kluszewski, Luis Aparicio, Sammy Esposito and Dixie Upright. Upright was one of the first to spot the fire that Easter Sunday evening.

The Memphis Fire Department eventually issued a five-alarm, which at that time was the highest used. It meant every available firefighter was called into service and all off-duty men were ordered back to their posts.

Over 30 fire engines responded. Flames shot hundreds of feet into the air. Egg-sized embers were propelled throughout the midtown area. The wind hampered firefighting efforts, gusting over 20 miles per hour.

Two hospitals, the Baptist and the John Gaston, were forced to evacuate some floors because smoke from the blaze entered those buildings. At Baptist Hospital, one male patient was moved to the maternity ward, and was teased about the incident for days.

Sixteen businesses were destroyed by the fire, and both hospitals were severely damaged.

Fire Captain Gail Goforth was one of six firefighters who went inside Russwood Stadium to fight the fire and almost didn't get out. For the first time in his eighteen years as a fireman, he was scared. He and the five others had gotten under the grandstand on the third base side, trying to head the fire off. Above them, heavy steel girders

bent with the heat, and the grandstand began to collapse. They backed out just before the whole thing fell.

Martin Park (Lewis Park)
Negro National League 1924-25, 1927, 1929-30 (Red Sox), Negro Southern League 1932 (Red Sox), Negro American League 1937-41, 1943-50 (Red Sox). *Location:* Crump Boulevard and Danny Thomas Avenue, current site of a truck terminal.

Hodges Field
Southern Association 1960 (Chicks). *Dimensions:* Left field, 335 feet; left center, 356 feet; right center, 279 feet; right field, 204 feet.

A high school football facility used in the emergency following the Russwood fire. Memphis lost their home opener here 11-8 to Birmingham. Eleven home runs were hit during the game, a Southern Association record. There was a reason for that.

The right field line measured only 204 feet to the fence. The wall out there was 40 feet high, but that didn't do anything to keep fly balls in. It was the shortest distance to a home run fence in organized baseball since the White Stockings moved out of Chicago's Lakefront Park 75 years before.

Home runs at Hodges Field were so easy to hit that Association and Chicks officials revised the ground rules, making hits over that wall ground rule doubles.

Tobey Park
Southern Association 1960 (Chicks). The Chicks eventually gave up on Hodges Field and moved to Tobey Park, where there was room for three outfielders. Tobey Park was another Park Commission facility.

The team also played five of their 1960 "home" games in Columbus, Georgia.

As had happened in Louisville many years before (*see* Eclipse Park II), the Memphis franchise was destroyed by

Chicks Stadium, Memphis, Tenn. (Compliments of the Memphis Chicks.)

the chaos following the fire at their home park (*see* Russwood Park). The Chicks disbanded after the 1960 season. Organized ball didn't return to the Bluff City until 1968.

Chicks Stadium (Blues Stadium, Tim McCarver Stadium)

Texas League 1968–73 (Blues), International League 1974–76 (Blues), Southern League 1978–present (Chicks). *Location:* 800 Home Run Lane, at State Fairgrounds, near Liberty Bowl. *Constructed:* 1967. *Dimensions:* Left field, 322.7 feet; left center, 348 feet; center field, 399.45 feet; right center, 335.5 feet; right field, 324.3 feet. *Seating capacity:* (1975) 6900; (1985) 10,000. *1968 season attendance:* 141,418. *1987 season attendance:* 215,749.

For a time this ballpark was known as Tim McCarver Stadium after the native son who became Lefty Carlton's personal catcher. McCarver now works out of the broadcast booth at Shea Stadium.

Over 9000 showed up Opening Night in 1978 to see former Memphis great Pete Gray throw out the first pitch and the Chicks beat Nashville 4–2. Blues

Stadium was originally a Park Commission field designed for high school play.

Nat Buring Field

Home of the Memphis State University Tigers (Metro Conference), present. *Dimensions:* Left field, 335 feet; left center, 365 feet; center field, 395 feet; right center, 365 feet; right field, 335 feet. *Seating capacity:* 2000.

Mérida, Mexico

Estadio de Beisbol Kukulcan

Mexican League, Zona Sur, present (Leones de Yucatan). *Dimensions:* Left field, 340 feet; center field, 400 feet; right field, 335 feet. *Seating capacity:* 15,000.

Mesa, Arizona

Hohokam Park

Chicago Cubs spring training home since at least 1980. *Seating capacity:* (Original) 4000; (current) 8000.

Park is named after an extinct Indian tribe. Called by Ron Fimrite in *Sports*

Illustrated "a funky architectural jumble that keeps growing like Topsy." No beer sold in the stands.

Mesa Baseball Complex

Current spring home of the California Angels. *Location:* 4125 East McKellips Road, Brown Road, Val Vista Drive, Greenfield Road, ten miles from downtown Mesa. *Construction cost:* $1.2 million. *Size of complex:* 28 acres. This facility was financed by the city of Mesa and the Golden West Baseball Company. The city contributed the land and the lights. There are 3½ practice fields. In addition to spring training, the complex hosts camp and summer recreation programs.

Mexico City, Mexico

Social Security Stadium (Parque Deportivo del Seguro Social)
Mexican League, Zona Sur, present (Tigres, Diablos Rojos, two franchises). *Location:* Avenue Cuauhtemoc 462. *Dimensions:* Left field, 330 feet; center field, 400 feet; right field, 340 feet. *Seating capacity:* 25,000.

Miami, Florida

Orange Bowl

Location: 17th Avenue, near Route 836. Former home of the National Football League's Miami Dolphins. This facility set the all-time International League game attendance record August 7, 1950, as 57,313 watched Satchel Paige take the mound.

Miami Stadium

International League 1956–60, Florida State League 1962–present (Marlins), spring home of the Baltimore Orioles 1959–present. *Location:* 2301 NW Tenth Avenue, NW Twelfth Avenue, Route 836. *Constructed:* 1949. *Dimensions:* Left field, 330 feet; center field, 400 feet; right field, 330 feet.

Seating capacity: (1960) 13,500; (1975) 9548; (1985) 9532. *1987 Florida State League attendance:* 35,934.

Many teams never play night games in the spring. Not Baltimore. Half their games at Miami Stadium are under the lights. Palm trees grow out of the paved walkway circling the outer stadium. The grandstand is distinctive because of its high, rounded roof. In the 1950s it was not uncommon for temporary bleachers to be set up in the outfield for spring training games, especially when the Yankees were in.

Sunblazer Field

Home of the Florida International University Golden Panthers (independent schedule), present. *Dimensions:* Left field, 325 feet; center field, 400 feet; right field, 327 feet. *Seating capacity:* 1500.

Middletown, Connecticut

Fort Hill Grounds

National Association 1872 (Mansfields).

The Mansfields of Middletown joined the National Association in the second year of its existence.

Lisa L. Broberg, director of the Middlesex County Historical Society, recently discovered a reminiscence by one George Arbuckle Craig (1858–1934). Mr. Craig gave a talk entitled "My First Conscious Recollection" to the Conversational Club. An excerpt of Craig's talk was graciously provided by the Historical Society, typed by Ms. Broberg on a "cantankerous manual typewriter."

"The base ball fields of those days were indifferent affairs. The first upon which I can remember playing was on the Pike property since spoiled by the running through it of Lawn Avenue and the lateral avenues, while the first big-fellows field was on the crown of Washington Street hill now occupied by the residences of the late William H. Burrows, the late Miss Townsend, Miss

Binney, and others. Park Place and Lincoln Street have since cut up this good field. I remember its western boundary was thorn hedge which offered only discouragement to small boys who wished by their presence to testify their approval of so fine a recreation as that furnished by the game of base ball.

"The Mansfields had a most creditable career, doing battle with the best nines in the land and always giving a good account of themselves. (*The team was 5-19*—M.B.) When the team disbanded, primarily for financial reasons, some of the players went to other cities where they made fame for themselves, and one, when no longer a player, became a noted newspaper writer on sports. The club's best playing field was a fenced enclosure on Fort Hill, east of the factory now owned by the Omo Manufacturing Company. The founder, manager and supporter of the Mansfields was Ben Douglas who afterward filled about the same relationships to clubs in Springfield, Hartford and Providence, his nine in the last named city narrowly failing of winning the national championship.

"The clubs which engaged my most mature attention were the Unity and the Excelsior, the latter name being conferred upon us by the above named Ben Douglas. The game developed rapidly, finding great favor with the public, and notable changes were constantly making more playable and attractive. At first pitchers were required to deliver the ball to the batter with arm perfectly straight. Of course, under this law, no great speed was attainable although it was astonishing just what could be done in this respect. The best straight arm pitcher it was my lot to know was Clarence Bacon, Wesleyan '78 and father of the two noted Wesleyan athletes, Roger and Everett Bacon.

"Not every ball was called a ball or a strike, but the umpire took his time and called such as he chose leaving ball after ball unnamed until the indignant pitcher goaded him into some pronouncement. And the batter might not take his base until seven balls were called. The pitcher's box was only 45 ft. from the plate, until the introduction of the swifter pitching made it just to put the hurler 50 feet away from his prey. Gloves, masks and chest protectors were unknown, and when first introduced were regarded with considerable disfavor and derision — effeminate appliances calculated to make the game appear much too ladylike.

"A later change in the rules permitted the pitcher to deliver the ball from any point below his waist and this change brought in the underhand throw and pitching which was really swift, for the practiced arm could throw a very swift ball while keeping well within the restriction. Sometime in here a rule was made which called a ball fair, wherever it went, which struck in front of the base line. Some remarkably skillful batters were developed who could adroitly bat so that the ball after striking in front of the line would bound sharply back of it beyond the reach of all players except the harried catcher and generally impossible for him to field. This style of batting would be impossible with present day pitching.

"Balls of two kinds were used — dead and lively, the choice for a game being subject for agreement between contestants. Scores were much larger than now because pitching had not been so developed, but for all the free batting home runs bore only a small ratio to totals. The batter was allowed to call for his favorite ball and as he stepped to the plate announced "high ball," "low ball," or "knee ball," as he preferred and the umpire was governed by his expressed wish.

"The greatest change in the game came about with the introduction of curved pitching. The throwing of a curved ball is a wonderful performance and it is difficult to say which is the greater achievement, to throw such a ball or to hit one after it is thrown to you. . . . Now every boy on the sand lot can throw a curved ball and most of them can also hit curved balls. I shall always marvel at either feat."

The Mansfields were named after General Joseph King Fenno Mansfield, hero of the Mexican-American War and a leading Union general who was killed at the battle of the Antietam in Sharpsburg, Maryland. General Mansfield was pretty important to Middletown. The Historical Society Headquarters are in his home.

Middletown, Ohio

Rathman Park (People's Base Ball Park)
Primary home of community baseball in Middletown circa 1911–present. *Location:* Beside the Middletown Hydraulic Canal, adjacent to the City Water Works and Hook Field Municipal Airport (currently known as north of Tytus Avenue between Main Street and the Verity Parkway, adjacent to Smith Park). *Size of site:* 3.87 acres.

In 1911 the Middletown Baseball and Athletic Association acquired this land from the old Wolverton estate. On March 16, 1921, the association donated the land—with its diamond and diminutive wooden grandstand behind home—to the city for public use. At that time it was named Rathman Park after Emil Rathman, a recently deceased community leader (and funeral parlor operator) who had been instrumental in getting the park constructed. Lights were later added, and the site remains a modern ball field.

Armco Field
Used by the Armco Steel Corporation semi-pro Industrial League teams (KIO League) circa 1900–circa 1950. *Location:* Parkview Avenue (right field), Grove Street (left field). Current site of the Armco General Offices Complex. *Lights:* Late 1930s.

Armco Field had an eight-row wooden grandstand behind home and along the baselines past the bases, a bandstand in the left field corner, and elm trees in the outfield, in play, growing in front of the outfield lights. Beyond the left field fence and across Grove Street was the three-story Grove Street School.

In the 1920s the Cincinnati Reds came to town every year and played the Armco nine. In 1926 Armco won, and the Reds got vengeance repeatedly, punishing the Armco squad during their yearly meeting.

The great football matches of Middletown were played here for many years as well, with the field set up so that one end zone covered the third base line while the other was out in right field.

Midland, Texas

Angels Stadium (Municipal Stadium)
Texas League 1972–present (Angels). *Location:* Hogan Park, Lamesa Road and Loop 250. *Last renovation:* 1972. *Dimensions:* Left field, 310 feet; center field, 405 feet; right field, 300 feet. *Seating capacity:* (1975) 3500; (1985) 3000. *1987 season attendance:* 137,910. Located in Lakeland's largest park (620 acres). Along with Angels Stadium, Hogan Park holds a 27-hole golf course, 13 softball fields, and 11 soccer fields.

Milwaukee, Wisconsin

It has been reported that a baseball-like game was played as early as 1836 at what became North Milwaukee Street and East Wisconsin Avenue, using a ball made of deerhide, yarn, and rubber.

State Fair Grounds (Camp Scott 1861–66)

Site of Milwaukee baseball 1859–66. Home of the Cream Citys 1865–66. *Location:* On Spring Street (now Wisconsin Avenue) hill, today a part of the Marquette University campus.

Site of the first organized baseball game in Milwaukee history between teams of amateurs—not youngsters, either, but a "surprising cross-section of (Milwaukee's) business and professional community," writes Harry H. Anderson in *Milwaukee History*. Players included 48-year-old Rufus King, a newspaperman and civic leader, and—heading the opposing team—banker John L. Hathaway.

They played November 30, 1859, then again December 10. The second game, ending the season, was played under conditions more suitable for sledding.

In 1858, Abraham Lincoln gave a memorable address from this very spot. By 1861, with war in the wind, the field was called Camp Scott, and was used for both military drilling and baseball. It was here that, after the Civil War, the Cream Citys played their first two seasons. The team was named after the color of bricks made in Milwaukee.

Camp Reno

Home of the Cream Citys 1867–75. *Location:* Prospect Avenue, near the lakefront.

The ballpark at Camp Reno was built by John Plankinton, whose streetcar line ran out to the site. An enclosed ballpark was constructed in Milwaukee for the first time, an investment that paid for itself through baseball gate receipts alone, not even counting extra transit income. Once the ballpark was paid for, Plankinton built the Cream Citys a clubhouse and took responsibility for field maintenance. In return he received exclusive concessionaire's rights. Attendance was good. The Cream Citys of the 1860s were a "northwestern" powerhouse.

West End Grounds

Home of the West End Club 1876–77, independent schedule 1876, League Alliance 1877. *Location:* Wells Avenue, near the outer limits.

Milwaukee Base-Ball Grounds

National League 1878 (Grays). *Location:* West Clybourn, West Michigan, North Tenth, and Eleventh streets (today, underneath the Marquette Interchange of the freeway system). *First game:* May 14, 1878. *Last game:* September 14, 1878.

This park housed a bad team. The Grays went 15–45, led the league in errors, with a fielding average in last place by 30 points. The star of the team was pitcher Sam Weaver, who pitched a no-hitter that year on the road. The catcher was Charley Bennett, who later lost his legs and had a ballpark in Detroit named after him. After the season, the National League took Milwaukee's franchise away and gave it to Troy. The town took the lousiness, and then the loss, of the Grays bitterly—so bitterly there was no professional ball in Milwaukee for six years, until 1884.

Wright Street Grounds

Northwest League 1884, Union Association 1884 (Unions, partial season), Western League 1885–86, Northwestern Association 1887–88. *Location:* West Clarke, North Eleventh, North Twelfth, and West Wright streets. *First Union Association game:* September 27, 1884. *Last Union Association game:* October 12, 1884 (Milwaukee 5, Cincinnati 2, attendance: 4000+).

In addition to its short stint as the home of the Milwaukee Unions, the Wright Street Grounds became a showcase for big league baseball twice in 1885, as the neutral site of two National League games: Chicago-Buffalo on September 4, and Chicago-Providence on September 25.

The Milwaukee team played 12 games of Union Association competition. They went 8–4.

Borchert Field in Milwaukee, Wis., looking at peace with its community. (Photo by A.F. Toepfer, furnished by the Milwaukee County Historical Society.)

Borchert Field (Athletic Park 1887–1894, Brewer Field 1902–1918)

Western Association 1887–94 (Creams, Brewers), American Association 1891 (Brewers, major league), 1902–52 (Brewers, minor league), Negro National League 1923 (Bears, partial season). *Location:* North Seventh Avenue (first base), West Chambers Street (home), North Eighth Avenue (third base), West Burleigh Street (center field). *Dimensions:* Left field, 266 feet; center field, 395 feet; right field, 266 feet. *Fences:* Right field, 60 feet (1941–52). *Seating capacity:* 10,000.

In the late 1880s the Irish sat on the first base side, the Germans over by third. Unwritten law demanded the Creams' third baseman be German, and the first baseman Irish.

Back in those days, the site was turned into an ice skating rink in the winter. A dressing room for skaters was built near the left field foul pole.

The grandstand was turned in a tight horseshoe behind home so that seats all faced home plate, those sitting out past first and third base sitting with their backs to the outfield. Unless you sat behind home, you could only see half of the vast rectangular outfield. It was a flimsy pop down the lines for a homer and forget-about-it to center.

The stands were so close to the action that screen fences from first to third had to be put up to protect box seat spectators, instead of just behind home, as would have been customary. The grandstand was deeply roofed, which further restricted the vision of those sitting up near the top. There were frequent obstructing poles supporting the roof. To make matters even worse, in later years, the lights were put on the field—the roof wouldn't support their weight—in front of the grandstand, held aloft by telephone poles.

White Rocks and Goat Doo. In 1919 the park was named Borchert Field. Otto Borchert, the man all of Milwaukee loved to hate, had just bought the team. After taking some sun in his ballpark's center field pasture before games when the stands were crowded, he would, using his walking stick, stroll

slowly to his seat, making sure everyone noticed him. Borchert transformed
the skaters' dressing room in left into a
chicken coop. He bred White Rocks.

Before Prohibition, Borchert had
the good sense to put in a bar directly
behind home plate so that the thirstiest
of the thirsty wouldn't miss anything.

A goat was kept at the ballpark for
many years, the pet of pitcher Ralph
Cutting. During road trips he grazed in
the infield and saved mowing costs. At
night the goat stayed on the ballpark
roof. In the press box, reporters complained of the reek. Soon after Cutting
retired, the goat was asked to take up
residence elsewhere.

Borchert died giving a speech to the
Elks Club in 1927, and no one ever
changed the name of his ballpark.

**The Movable Fence and Removable
Roof.** In 1941, owner Bill Veeck got
sick of having a team that couldn't exploit his ballpark's 266-foot right field
foul line the way the visitors could. He
had a 60-foot chicken wire screen fence
built out there.

The following year, Veeck tried to
pull a fast one. He had the fence in
right mounted on a motor-driven hydraulic unit. When the home team was
up the fence was moved into foul territory.

Veeck got away with it for a whole
game. Reaction was swift, and a rule
was passed against the moving fence
before the next game began.

On June 15, 1944, during the seventh
inning of a game against Columbus, a
windstorm ripped the roof off the first
base side, blacking out the lights. A
panic sent fans streaming onto the
playing field. All in all, 35 persons were
injured. Due to structural weakness,
the roof was never replaced. The first
base side became the sun seats.

Despite the park's decaying condition, Veeck did not break ground for a
new park until 1950 — and by that time
he was lobbying for a major league
franchise. The Borchert Field lot is still
used as a community playground.

Milwaukee Park (Lloyd Street Ball
Park)

Western Association 1895-99
(Brewers), American League 1900-01
(Brewers), Western League 1902-03
(Creams). *Owned by:* Fred C. Gross.
Location: West Lloyd Street, between
North 16th and North 17th streets. *First
game:* May 2, 1895 (Minneapolis 4,
Milwaukee 3, attendance: 5000). *First
Major League game:* May 4, 1901
(Chicago 11, Milwaukee 3, attendance:
3000). *Last American League game:*
September 12, 1901 (split doubleheader
with Chicago, attendance: 1200). *Rec-
ord single game attendance:* 10,000
(estimated, versus Philadelphia, May
26, 1901).

A single-deck park, with a press box
atop a tower behind home. Viewing the
action from the top of the billboarded
wooden center field fence, the steeple
of the Cross Lutheran Church rose
above the wooden grandstand. The
grandstand was less than ten rows
deep, and was shorter than the open
bleachers on either side. Instead of a
warning track there were dangerous
wooden supports holding the fence up.
There was a short incline to the very
short fence in right. The manager of
the Brewers from 1897 to 1900 was
Connie Mack, and the star pitcher was
Rube Waddell.

At the turn of the century Milwaukee
had a population of about 300,000, and
was drawing just under 100,000 per
season to ball games. For their only big
league season (1901) attendance was
139,034. But that wasn't enough. On
December 3, 1901, the American League
franchise was taken away from Milwaukee and given to St. Louis, where it
remained for 52 years.

County Stadium

National League 1953-65 (Braves),
American League 1968-69 (White Sox,
nine games each season), 1970-present
(Brewers). Owned by the County of
Milwaukee. *Location:* Blue Mountain
Road (home plate side), Harnischfeger

Road (third base), Interstate 94 (left field). *Groundbreaking:* October 19, 1950. *Dimensions:* Left field, 315 (previously 320) feet; left center, 362 feet; center field, 402 feet; right center, 362 feet; right field, 315 feet. 60 feet from home plate to the backstop. *Fences:* (1953) Four feet all the way around. (1957) Ten feet. *Seating capacity:* (1953) 36,011 (28,111 permanent, 7900 portable). (1954) 43,394. (1974) 46,625, broken down as follows: field boxes, 5336; lower reserved, 18,583; deluxe mezzanine, 76; mezzanine and loge boxes, 738; upper boxes, 3853; upper reserved, 11,039; bleachers, 7000. (1975) 53,192. *Parking lot:* 11,000 cars and buses. *Stadium area:* 84 acres. *Braves day game attendance record:* 48,642 (September 27, 1959, versus Philadelphia). *Braves doubleheader attendance record:* 47,604 (September 3, 1956, versus Cincinnati). *Braves night game attendance record:* 46,944 (August 27, 1954, versus New York). *Braves twinight doubleheader attendance record:* 36,241 (August 12, 1953, versus St. Louis). *Braves opening game attendance record:* 43,640 (April 12, 1955, versus Cincinnati). *Braves season high attendance record:* 2,215,404 (1957). *Braves season low attendance record:* 555,584 (1965). *Brewers Opening Day attendance record:* 55,887 (April 15, 1988, Yankees 7, Brewers 1, winning pitcher: Tommy John). *First game:* April 6, 1953 (Milwaukee versus Boston Red Sox, exhibition). *First National League game:* April 14, 1953 (Milwaukee 3, St. Louis 2, 10 innings, attendance 34,357). *Last National League game:* September 22, 1965 (Los Angeles 7, Milwaukee 6, 11 innings). *First American League game (White Sox):* May 15, 1968 (California 5, Chicago 4, 5 innings, rain). *First American League game (Brewers):* April 7, 1970 (California 12, Milwaukee 0).

Before 1954, patients and staff of a hospital on a nearby hill could watch games for free over the right field fence. After the 1953 season, four sets of bleachers were built in the outfield, blocking the view. Today, the grandstand is completely double-decked. The park is known for its bratwurst and its healthy co-educational sunbathing scene.

The outfield wall was constructed in 1961, the same year that permanent bleachers were put in center field. Slow increments over the years have brought County Stadium's seating capacity from 36,011 when it opened to its current 53,192.

This is the house where Henry Aaron started and finished his quietly awesome onslaught. Millions of martial arts students should study the movements of Aaron. He could kill you with his wrists alone.

Speaking of strong wrists, Willie Mays once used County Stadium as the venue for one of his most tremendous feats: hitting four home runs in a single game. He did it on April 30, 1961. Each blast traveled over 400 feet.

While playing here Warren Spahn won 20 games nine times.

It was here on May 26, 1959, that Pittsburgh Pirates left-hander Harvey Haddix pitched 12-plus innings of perfect ball before losing the ball game in the thirteenth on an unearned run.

This was the site of the 1955 All-Star Game (July 12), won by the National League 6–5 in the twelfth inning on a Stan Musial home run.

The All-Star Game was played at County Stadium again on July 15, 1975, and again the National League won (6–3)—though this time they were the visitors.

Minneapolis, Minnesota

Hiawatha Park
Western League 1882–83, 1895, Northwestern League 1884, 1886–87, Western Association 1888–91. *Location:* Hennepin Avenue, Fifth Street, in back of the West Hotel.

On these grounds, Elmer Foster and Walter Wilmot gained fame as hitters, outfielders, and base runners—before playing in the National League.

In those days the Mill City (pop. 68,000) was filled with stories of Foster, playing center field, making pirouetting backhand grabs against the wooden fence. A St. Paul tall tale tells of Foster's most famous catch, the time during an extra-inning game in the dusk, when he dashed toward right field in pursuit of a sinking line drive, only to haul in a sparrow instead of the ball.

By the mid-1890s, the expansion of loop buildings forced team owners to look elsewhere for a site.

Minnehaha Driving Park

Western League 1895 (St. Paul, two Sunday games), 1896–99, 1901, American Association 1902–10 (Sundays only). *Location:* Minnehaha Avenue, between 34th and 38th streets.

When a petition by residents of the area near the new Nicollet Park demanded a stop to Sunday baseball, Minneapolis moved its Sunday games to the one-mile race track in Minnehaha Driving Park, which they converted into a ballpark.

The problem with the rural site was that the car line didn't run out that far. Not everyone with a yearning for baseball had the scratch to rattle out in a gig. The baseball promoters went to work and came up with almost 150 reasons why the extension of the Minnehaha line to 34th Street was essential to the well-being of South Minneapolis. The streetcar company officials were impressed, the thing was done, and the ballpark was used regularly on Sundays until 1910.

When a court injunction barred St. Paul from playing Sunday games on their home grounds, they played two games in Minneapolis' Minnehaha Park back in 1895. The Minneapolis Brewers of the American Association played their Sunday games here until

the ban on Sunday ball was lifted in 1910.

Nicollet Park

Western League 1896–99, 1901 (Millers), American League 1900, American Association 1902–1955 (Millers). *Location:* West 30th Street, later Lake Street (left field), Blaisdell Avenue (third base), West 31st Avenue (first base), Nicollet Avenue (right field). *Dimensions:* Left field, 334 feet; center field, 432 feet; right center, 328 feet; right field, 279 feet. 88 feet from home plate to the backstop. *Fences:* Left field, 12 feet; center field (scoreboard), 40 feet; right field (before 1935), 25 feet, (after 1935) 30 feet. *Last game:* September 28, 1955 (Millers 9, Rochester Red Wings 4, Minneapolis wins the Junior World Series, attendance 9927). *Torn down:* 1956.

It was here that Wheaties first used their slogan "Breakfast of Champions." The words were part of a 1933 billboard ad on the outfield fence following a year in which the Millers won the pennant. This was a "Final Jeopardy" answer once, so it must be true.

The Minneapolis Millers (Minneapolis is the Mill City) moved into brand new Nicollet Park in 1896, and won the pennant in the Western League their first year there.

The highlight of that season was the power hitting of slugger Perry Werden, who hit 49 home runs. This was the organized baseball record until Babe Ruth hit 59 in 1921. The current professional baseball record for most home runs in a season still belongs to someone who played at Nicollet Park, Joe Hauser, who hit 69 home runs for the Millers of the American Association in 1933. The right field corner was less than 280 feet from home, and it was only 328 feet to the alley.

The Riot. In 1906, the Millers were in a vicious pennant race with Columbus, and the end of the season was approaching. The two teams were a game apart, Minneapolis ahead, when they began a series at Nicollet Park. American Association president Joseph D. O'Brien made the mistake of assigning a rookie umpire to officiate the crucial series. He was Brick Owens, who later went on to have a distinguished career as a big league umpire. Owens worked the game alone, as was the custom of the day. But this day he was green and astigmatic, blowing a couple of key calls that gave the game to the Ohio team.

There were 9000 very angry fans at the scene, and several hundred rushed the field to kill the umpire. Owens had to be removed from the premises by the police.

The next day the Minnesota fans came armed. The instant that Owens appeared on the field, he had to start ducking. Eggs, tomatoes, sunglasses, and a couple of canes came flying out of the grandstand in the general direction of Owens' skull. The umpire declared a forfeit in favor of Columbus. And that's when the *real* riot started.

Owens might have actually been torn apart by the angry crowd if not for Minnesota favorite and former Yale football great Pudge Heffelfinger, who wrapped his arms around the umpire and screamed out that anyone touching the umpire was going to have to deal with him. The cops had been expecting trouble, so Heffelfinger led Owens into a nearby paddywagon and off they went, leaving the angry milling crowd nothing to do but kick the dirt.

The league president suspended the Millers' manager, Mike Kelley — who was in Minneapolis between longer stints as the St. Paul skipper — for inciting to riot. Kelley compensated during home games by having a hole cut in the back of the dugout so he could manage from beneath the grandstand. Fans boycotted Nicollet Park for the rest of the season. The Millers never recovered and ended up finishing third.

Nicollet Park's grandstand was distinctive because of the chimney on the roof. Fans entered the ballpark through a house that held the Millers' offices.

The original wooden grandstand was very small, with only the seats directly behind home being roofed over. There were bleacher seats along the first and third base lines. When the stands were filled fans sat on the field, in the foul territory between the seats and the playing field, or along the outfield fences. Fans sat so close to home plate that it's a wonder no one was killed by a line drive. The dugout on the first base side was built into the base of the wooden grandstand, and said HOME TEAM across the top of it, just to avoid any confusion.

After 1935, a 16-foot screen was placed on top of the 30-foot fence in right field. As is the case in Fenway Park, balls striking this screen were home runs.

The block is the current site of the Norwood Bank Building. There is a plaque just outside the entrance commemorating the location of Nicollet Park.

Metropolitan Stadium

American Association 1956–60 (Millers), American League 1961–81 (Minnesota Twins). Site of the 1965 All-Star Game (National League 6, American League 5, attendance: 46,706). Also former home of the National Football League's Vikings. *Location:* Bloomington. Cedar Avenue (first base side), 24th Avenue (third base), Killebrew Drive (center field). *Groundbreaking:* June 1955. *Opened:* April 22, 1956. *Construction cost (including 1960 enlargement):* $8.5 million. *Dimensions:* Left field, 346 feet; left center, 365 feet; center field, 430 feet; right center, 365 feet; right field, 330 feet. 60 feet from home plate to the backstop. *Fences:* (1961) Eight feet all the way around. (1977) Twelve feet in left field, eight feet elsewhere. *Surface:* grass. *Scoreboard:* 135 feet long, 50 feet high (clock on top: 16 feet wide, 18 feet high, for a total height at the top of

Metropolitan Stadium, Minneapolis, Minn. (Compliments of the Minnesota Twins.)

the clock of 68 feet). *Lights:* (Infield) 200 footcandles; (outfield) 100 footcandles. *Seating capacity:* (1956) 21,698; (1961) 45,919, broken down as follows: plush boxes, 116; football press box, 88; field boxes, 6797; lower boxes, 2744; lower reserved, 7641; upper boxes, 3062; upper reserved, 3409; third tier boxes, 1359; third tier reserved, 1729; general admission, 18,974. *Record single game attendance:* 50,596 (Game 7, 1965 World Series, October 14, Los Angeles 2, Minnesota 0, winning pitcher: Sandy Koufax). *Size of site:* 152 acres. *Parking lot capacity:* 14,500 cars. *First American Association League game:* April 22, 1956 (Wichita 5, Minneapolis 3, attendance 18,366). *First American League game:* April 21, 1961 (Washington 5, Minnesota 3). *Last American League game:* September 30, 1981. *Torn down:* 1984–85.

In 1954, when the St. Louis Browns became the Baltimore Orioles—marking the first major league franchise change in many years—Minneapolis officials were told expansion was coming, but that they couldn't get a big league team unless they had an appropriate ballpark. The city had the

Met built, using the money of local investors, by the beginning of the 1956 season. It would be five years before Minnesota got the Twins. Until then the Met was used by the Millers, who'd finally quit Nicollet Park.

Metropolitan Stadium, built on the rolling land above the Minnesota River Valley, was dedicated in September 1955. A fire in February 1956 destroyed part of the stands. The damage was rebuilt in time for the '56 season.

When the ballpark first opened it held a little over 20,000, just fine for AAA ball, but insufficient for the majors. In 1960, when American League expansion to Minnesota became definite, the double deck of seats in left was built (costing $1.2 million), raising seating capacity to over 40,000.

At the first major league game here, April 21, 1961, Minnesota Governor Elmer Anderson threw out the first ball. During the first few years the Twins averaged a respectable 1.4 million fans per season.

Ballpark Customization by Erickson. During the entire 25 years that the Met was used in the land of 10,000 lakes, it had the same head groundskeeper. His name was Dick Erickson, and he wasn't afraid to customize his ballpark to the needs of the Twins.

When notoriously slow-of-foot Harmon Killebrew played third, the infield was tilted so that slow rollers down the third base line rolled foul. When sinkerball pitchers Dave Goltz and Geoff Zahn were on the Twins' staff, the ground in front of home was left soft, to take the steam out of many ground balls and avoid the high hop.

Before the 1965 World Series with the roadrunner Dodgers coming to town, Erickson mixed lots of sand with the dirt between first and second. When Walter Alston complained, the umpires made Erickson's crew remove a whole wheelbarrow full of dirt from the field. (That infield sat upon rich black soil where wheat once grew.)

Other attempts were made to customize the Met to the Twins. For one year there was a short inside fence built in left that was supposed to help Killebrew hit more home runs, but Harmon was traded to Kansas City that year, opponents seemed to use the short fence a lot more than the Twins did, and the fence came down.

Killebrew hit the longest home run ever at the Met in 1961 off a misguided attempt at a knuckleball by Lou Burdette of the Angels. The ball traveled an estimated 520 feet and landed nine rows deep in the upper deck of the left field grandstand.

On June 9, 1966, the whole Twin ball club was home-run happy, at least for one inning. During that inning, against the Athletics, the Twins smacked five home runs.

In addition to Killebrew's home runs, the Met is best remembered by the fans of the Twin Cities area for its "brats" (bratwurst) and its lousy recording of "The Star-Spangled Banner."

On August 26, 1962, Jack Kralick of the Twins no-hit Kansas City 1–0. The no-hitter was saved by a great defensive play made by Bob Allison.

The 1965 pennant was the only one ever to fly over the Met. The Dodgers ended up beating the Twins in the World Series in seven games, the 2–0 final game victory in Minnesota going to Sandy Koufax.

This was the first of the second wave ('50s and '60s) of big ballparks to be torn down. It was in dismal repair near the end. In 1981, broken railings on the third deck overlooking the left field bleachers created a distinct safety hazard. When the stadium was torn down the street behind the old right field fence had its named changed to Killebrew Drive.

Hubert H. Humphrey Metrodome

American League 1982–present (Minnesota Twins). Also the home of the Minnesota Vikings, and the University of Minnesota football team. *Location:* Eleventh Avenue South (right field), 900 Fifth Street South (first base), Chicago Avenue South (third base), Fourth Street South (left field). *Nickname:* The Homerdome. *Groundbreaking:* December 20, 1979. *Construction cost:* $62 million. *Dimensions:* Left field, 343 feet; left center, 385 feet; center field, 408 feet; right center, 367 feet; left field, 327 feet. *Fences:* Left field, 13 feet; center field, 7 feet; right field, 23 feet. *Turf:* Artificial (SporTurf and pad glued to asphalt base. Thickest pad in the major leagues.). *Scoreboard:* 66 feet wide, 18 feet high (illuminated with 18,000 light bulbs). *Roof:* Ten acres of Teflon Coated Fibreglass, 1/32 of an inch thick. Maximum height: 195 feet (16 stories). Supported by air pressure supplied by 20 electric fans, each operated by a 90 horsepower engine. *Concession stands:* 39. *Seating capacity:* (Baseball) 55,122; (football) 62,000. *Luxury boxes:* 115. *Single game attendance record:* 55,257 (Game Two, 1987 World Series, Minnesota 8, St. Louis 4). *Size of site:* 20 acres. *Press levels:* Two.

That 23-foot "fence" in right is actually folded up football seats covered

The Hubert H. Humphrey Metrodome, Minneapolis, Minn. (Compliments of the Minnesota Twins.)

with a plastic sheet. The wall is known as the "trash bag."

The wall was not always there. It replaced a seven-foot wall — the same as the one out in left — because too many home runs were being hit.

The power alley in right, 367 feet, still makes the ballpark a great place for left-handed power-hitters (thus the nickname "Homerdome").

Another reason for the early success of power-hitters here was that the air conditioning did not work until halfway through its second season of use. The place was called "the sweat box." Balls flew out in bunches.

The pitcher's mound can be raised and lowered (for football games and other events) with the press of a button. **The World's Loudest Ballpark.** The roof of the dome is white and bathed in an orange light. Fly balls frequently disappear into the quilting, making the outfield hazardous, usually for the visitors. The Metrodome was thought of as a bad ballpark until it proved in 1987 to cause an unprecedented home team advantage. The Minnesota fans made the ballpark seem like an intimidating thing with their racket and

their Homer Hankies in the '87 World Series. A Minnesota Pollution Control Agency sound meter was placed in the Metrodome for Game 1 of the Series. According to *The Sporting News,* the meter read 118 decibels for Dan Gladden's grand slam in the fourth inning, about the noise made by a jet taking off. The average background noise for the game was 80 decibels, about the sound of a garbage disposal. No wonder the Twins won the series by winning all four games at home.

The story goes that it was so loud in the Metrodome during the second game of the 1987 American League Championship Series that Tiger manager Sparky Anderson threw up.

In a recent *New Yorker* article covering the 1987 World Series, Roger Angell wrote that the sound effects were something like being in "an I.R.T. express car with the Purdue Marching Band during a rush-hour rehearsal of 'The Stars and Stripes Forever.'" Among the park's other "eccentricities," Angell mentioned "an outfield so poorly illuminated that distant players look like lurking strangers at the foot of an alley."

Dick Siebert Field, Minneapolis, Minn. (Compliments of the University of Minnesota.)

Once the Roof Came Down; Once the Ball Didn't. There is now a plexiglass barrier above the left field wall, such as one might expect to see above hockey boards—so folks in the front row can see without outfielders falling into their laps.

Among the unusual occurrences in the Metrodome are the collapse of the roof in 1982, and the fly ball by the Twins' Randy Bush in 1983 that struck the roof and then was caught by Toronto Blue Jays catcher Buck Martinez. Bush was called out.

Dave Kingman hit a ball in 1984 that went through a hole in the roof. Finally one had been hit that never came down—and Kingman was given a ground rule double.

Dick Siebert Field

Home of the University of Minnesota Golden Gophers (Big Ten Conference, present). *Location:* 1606 Eighth Street SE, on the University of Minnesota campus. *Turf:* grass. *Seating capacity:* 2500.

This is the Gophers' on-campus facility, which has an electronic scoreboard, a roofed grandstand and bleachers. There's plenty of foul territory and no lights. Former home of Dave Winfield, who led his senior team—with both his hitting and his pitching (.385, 9–1, 2.74)—into the College World Series in 1973. The Gophers now play their night games at the Metrodome.

Missoula, Montana

City Park

Home of Missoula baseball 1913–33. *Location:* Higgins, Railroad, and Pattee streets, near the Northern Pacific Depot. Since 1936, the site of the Missoulian newspaper plant.

Telephone poles and barbed wire. Antiquated by the time the WPA provided funds to replace it.

Campbell Field

Home of University of Montana baseball 1947–69, Pioneer League 1956–60 (Timberjacks, Mavericks). Owned by the University of Montana (1947–69). *Built:* 1934 (WPA funded). *Dimensions:* Left field, 325 feet; center field, 385 feet; right field, 315 feet.

Seating capacity: (1934) 550; (1956) 1200. *Lights:* 1947. *Burned:* August 1969.

Named after Senator John L. Campbell, an avid sportsman and state legislator, who pushed to have a WPA-funded park built in the Garden City. During the 1930s, the park was used by the semi-pro Montana State League. Until 1942, Campbell Field was the home of the American Legion Junior baseball.

In the late '50s, the Timberjacks of the Pioneer League played here. Jack McKeon, a member of that team, is now the vice-president of the San Diego Padres.

Lindborg-Cregg Field

Used for American Legion baseball. *Built:* 1985.

A modern, lighted park. Legion officials have started a campaign to build a 3000-seat grandstand in anticipation of a return of pro ball to Missoula.

Mobile, Alabama

Hartwell Field (Monroe Park, League Park)

Southern League circa 1960. *Location:* Ann and Tennessee streets. *Dimensions:* Left field, 335 feet; center field, 406 feet; right field, 335 feet. *Seating capacity:* 11,000.

There was once a huge scoreboard out in left field, but it was destroyed during a hurricane when it was hit by lightning and caught fire.

Eddie Stanky Field

Home of the University of South Alabama Jaguars (Sun Belt Conference) 1980–present. *Dimensions:* Left field, 330 feet; left center, 375 feet; center field, 400 feet; right center, 375 feet; right field, 330 feet. *Seating capacity:* 5000. Record single game attendance: 4231 (May 8, 1923, versus the University of Miami). *First game:*

March 8, 1980 (doubleheader versus the University of Alabama).

A 21-row roofless grandstand stretches from first to third, with a small air conditioned press box mounted on top. This was the site of the World's Largest Pie Fight (3000 participants), certified by Guinness.

Modesto, California

Del Webb Field

California League 1946–64. *Seating capacity:* 3500.

John Thurman Field

California League 1966–present (A's). *Location:* Tuolomne Boulevard and Neece Drive. *Dimensions:* Left field, 325 feet; center field, 370 feet; right field, 300 feet. *Seating capacity:* 2500. *1987 season attendance:* 78,357.

Monclova, Mexico

Estadio Monclova

Mexican League, Zona Norte (Acereros). *Dimensions:* Left field, 330 feet; center field, 390 feet; right field, 330 feet. *Seating capacity:* 8000.

Monessen, Pennsylvania

Page Park

Negro National League (Homestead Grays, some games).

The great Josh Gibson, one of the greatest catchers of all time, once hit a home run in Page Park that was supposedly measured at 513 feet.

Monroe, Louisiana

Name of park unknown

Gulf Coast League 1907. *Location:* Site of the Swartz swimming pool.

Casino Park (Stovall Park, Ramona Park)

Negro Southern League 1932 (Monarchs). *Location:* Renwick, South 29th and DeSiard streets, Missouri Pacific Railroad tracks. *Dimensions:* Left field, 360 feet; center field, 450 feet; right field, 350 feet.

Monterrey, Mexico

Cuauhtemoc y Famosa

Mexican League, Zona Norte, present (Sultanes). *Dimensions:* Left field, 330 feet; center field, 400 feet; right field, 330 feet. *Seating capacity:* 6000.

Montgomery, Alabama

College Hill Park

Negro Southern League 1932 (Grey Sox). *Location:* Alabama State University.

Cramton Bowl

Negro Southern League 1932 (Grey Sox, some games). *Location:* Madison Avenue, Hillard Street.

Football stadium that hosted the seventh game of the touring 1943 Negro League World Series.

Paterson Field

Southern League 1972–circa 1980 (Rebels). *Location:* Madison Avenue. *Built:* 1949. *Dimensions:* Left field, 330 feet; center field, 380 feet; right field, 330 feet. *Seating capacity:* 6000.

Current home of the NCAA Division II College World Series. Rebels were a farm team of the Detroit Tigers.

Montreal, Quebec

Atwater Park

International League 1890 (two franchises), 1897–1917, Eastern Canada League (Class B) 1922–23, Quebec-Ontario-Vermont League 1924–27.

Two different teams tried to make it financially playing at Atwater Park in 1890, but neither succeeded. The first team managed only three home games, and the league collapsed before the second could get rolling. Atwater Park was used for minor league baseball again in 1897 when Rochester, New York's, Culver Field burned. The Rochester team moved to Montreal, where they stayed — with the exception of part of the 1902 season, when they moved temporarily to Worcester, Massachusetts — until 1917 when World War I interrupted minor league play.

Hector Racine Stadium (Delorimier Downs, Royals Stadium)

International League 1928–60 (Royals). *Location:* 2101 Ontario Street East; Parthenais, Lariviere, Delorimier streets. *Dimensions:* Left field, 340 feet; center field, 440 feet; right field, 293 feet. *Seating capacity:* 20,142. *Single game attendance record:* 24,458 (1941 playoff game). *Season attendance record:* 600,000+ (1948). *First game:* May 5, 1928 (Royals 7, Reading 4, paid attendance 17,757). *Torn down:* 1971.

In 1946, the Royals' star was Jackie Robinson, who lit up the Delorimier Downs. A crowd of 15,745 saw Robinson make his home debut in the white man's game, and everyone could tell right away that, all things being equal, he wasn't going to be in the minor leagues for very long. Other Dodger stars like Don Newcombe and Duke Snider also finished up their minor league days here, and the Royals were always the team to beat in the International League during the late 1940s and the 1950s. They won the pennant in 1945, 1946, 1948, 1951, 1952, 1955, and 1958.

Pal Razor Blades cut a hole in their outfield fence advertisement, right through the wall. Anyone hitting a ball through the hole won a two-year supply of blades.

Parc Jarry

National League 1969–76 (Expos). Owned by the City of Montreal. *Loca-*

tion: Rue Faillon (first base side), Rue St. Laurent (right field), Rue Jarry (left field), Canadian Pacific Railroad (third base). *Dimensions:* Left field, 340 feet; left center, 368 feet; center field, 417 feet; right center, 368 feet; right field, 340 feet. 62 feet from home plate to the backstop. *Fences:* Eight feet all the way around. *Seating capacity:* 28,000. Field boxes, 6584; field reserved, 2140; lower reserved, 8320; grandstand reserved, 3706; bleacher, 7250. *Parking lot:* 5000 cars. *Day game attendance record:* 34,331 (September 15, 1973, versus Philadelphia). *Doubleheader attendance record:* 30,416 (July 7, 1974, versus Los Angeles). *Night game attendance record:* 28,702 (May 23, 1970, versus Pittsburgh). *Twi-night doubleheader attendance record:* 28,818 (June 25, 1969, versus St. Louis). *Opening game attendance record:* 29,184 (April 14, 1969, versus St. Louis). *Season high attendance record:* 1,424,683 (1970). *Season low attendance record:* 1,019,134 (1974). *First game:* April 14, 1969 (Montreal 8, St. Louis 7, attendance 29,184). *Last game:* September 26, 1976.

Jarry Park is still there, used as a police rifle range and as a picnic site for large companies — though never both at the same time. The location of the park was described by Stanley G. Triggs of the McCord Museum in Montreal as "roughly north of the Mountain, beside the railway tracks leading to the Laurentians."

The park had been used as a recreation field with 3000 seats before the single deck of roofless stands was built in 1968. There was also a dull-looking set of bleachers in left field.

Stade Olympique

National League 1977–present (Expos). *Location:* Rue Sherbrooke (left field), Rue Pius IX (third base), Avenue Pierre-de-Coubertin (first base), Rue Viau (right field). *Construction cost:* $770 million(!). *Dimensions:* Left field, 325 feet; center field, 404 feet; right field, 325 feet. *Turf:* Artificial. *Seating capacity:* 59,149. *First game:* April 15, 1977 (Philadelphia Phillies 7, Montreal Expos 2, attendance 57,592).

Fans in Olympic Stadium are farther back from the action than they had been in Jarry Park. The roof is a soft rose color (with white splotches).

Team emblems are painted on the outfield walls. The scoreboard is computerized. The lights are good. On the scoreboard, the Expos' positions are listed in French, the visitors' positions in English.

Food and refreshments are overpriced by United States standards.

On the east side of the park are the Olympic pool and velodrome, gift shop, and tour headquarters. Expos officials are on the south side of the stadium at street level. There's a plaque for Jackie Robinson, a Montreal minor leaguer in 1946. The main walk around the park is above street level.

The longest home run in the history of Olympic Stadium was struck April 4, 1988, the first Opening Day ever in Montreal, by Darryl Strawberry. The ball struck the rim of the original roof, where the old roof meets the new, where the lights are attached. The ball struck 340 feet out and 160 feet up, and would have traveled an estimated 525 feet in the air if unobstructed. It was Strawberry's second home run of the day, and the Mets went on to win the ball game 10–8.

By far more money has been spent on the construction of the Olympic Stadium than on any other venue for major league baseball. Every step of the way, the construction of this arena was plagued by labor strikes, foul weather, lousy planning, and other problems. The roof was not installed until years after it was originally planned to make its debut. The tower next to the park was partially built, then sat that way for years waiting to be finished, during which time it occasionally caught fire, offering a diversion to the (usually chilly) Expos fans.

Muncie, Indiana

Ball State Diamond

Home of the Ball State University Cardinals (Mid-American Conference), present. Summer home of the Muncie Chiefs of the Great Lakes Summer Collegiate League. *Dimensions:* Left field, 330 feet; left center, 365 feet; center field, 400 feet; right center, 365 feet; right field, 330 feet. *Seating capacity:* 1200 (bleacher seats).

The outfield fence here is screen, and the hitting background is provided by thick, dark shrubbery planted on the other side of that fence from left to right center.

Beyond that fence is the Cardinals' practice field. The brick dust infield soaks up the rain. The dugouts have individual storage areas and their own restrooms.

On the frequent occasion when the weather isn't nice enough for practice, the team uses a nearby hangar-type structure called the Field Sports Building.

The most famous ballplayer to come out of the Ball State baseball program is Merv Rettenmund.

Myrtle Beach, South Carolina

Coastal Carolina College Field

South Atlantic League 1987–present (Blue Jays). *Location:* Campus of the University of South Carolina—Coastal Carolina College Branch, between the towns of Myrtle Beach and Conway. *Dimensions:* Left field, 315 feet; center field, 400 feet; right field, 315 feet. *Seating capacity:* 3200. *1987 season attendance:* 74,179.

Nashua, New Hampshire

Before 1937, baseball in Nashua was played most frequently on the upper part of the Common. This area became a parking lot and access roads for Holman Stadium.

Holman Stadium (Holman Memorial Field)

New England League 1946–49, Eastern League circa 1985 (Pirates), used for local baseball and football 1937–present. *Location:* Amherst and Merrimack streets, Sargent Avenue. *Architect:* Phillip Avery of Boston. *Dedicated:* September 23, 1937. *Dimensions:* Left field, 345 feet; center field, 400 feet; right field, 330 feet. *Seating capacity:* 5500.

Holman Stadium and Fieldhouse was built in 1937 with several hundred thousands of dollars in WPA funds and $60,000 under bequest of Charles Frank Holman, who dedicated the sports facilities—via a trust in his will—to the youth and people of Nashua in memory of his parents. So it says on the two plaques on either side of the front gate.

Holman's father had been a penniless traveling salesman when he came to Nashua, but went on to build a large confectionery business. He was elected mayor in 1878.

The ballpark was built on the site of a grant made in 1673 to the Ancient and Honorable Artillery Company of Boston. For 250 years the land had been known as Artillery Pond. Work began on the ballpark on April 28, 1936, when 30 men began to clean, grade and compact the land. The park opened September 23, 1937.

The dedication ceremony for the playing field and the impressive brick and concrete grandstand took place at 4:30 p.m., and preceded a 5:00 city championship baseball game between the "Card Shop" and "St. Louis" nines. Holman's pastor, Rev. William T. Knapp of the Pilgrim Congregational Church, opened the ceremonies by reading the invocation. The J.F. McElwain Band then played "America." George M. French, Esq., administrator of the Holman estate, spoke briefly. Mayor Alvin A. Lucier followed. The final speaker was Thomas J. Leonard, Esq., representing the Nashua Knights

of Columbus, who had donated funds
for permanent bleachers to go with the
grandstand. The new park had lights,
locker rooms for players, and restrooms for fans. An electric public address system was set up so that everyone could hear the speeches. School
children were admitted to the bleachers
for free that day. The Salvation Army
Band donated their services, playing
selections from the grandstand in between innings.

Since it opened in September, most
of the first events here were high school
football games. A beautiful gate
marked the front entrance. The playing
field was completely enclosed by a wire
fence. Ball games could be watched
from outside the premises until the ivy
that had been planted grew into a living
obstruction.

At the time the playing field was the
largest in New England. It was later
diminished by an inner fence. The
original boundaries are marked now by
tall trees.

Park was used recently by the Eastern League. Nashua is currently without pro baseball.

Nashville, Tennessee

The story has it that baseball was introduced to Nashville in 1862 by the occupying Union army, but there is no
record of specific games being played.

Sulphur Dell

First used for baseball 1876, Southern
League 1885–1963 (Fishermen, Volunteers). *Location:* Jackson Street (left
field), 900 Fifth Avenue North, formerly Summer Street (third base), Tennessee Central Railroad tracks (first
base), Fourth Avenue North, formerly
Cherry Street (right field). *Dimensions:*
Left field, 334 feet; center field, 421
feet; right field, 262 feet. *Fences:* (1927)
16 feet all around. (1931) 16 feet in left
and center, 46 feet in right (30-foot
screen on top of 16-foot wooden fence).

Seating capacity: 7000. *Rebuilt:* 1926,
diamond repositioned.

The first reported baseball game ever
played in Nashville took place in 1876,
the nation's centennial year. According
to Joe Hatcher in the *Tennessean,* "One
team represented North Nashville, the
other carried the colors of the Linck's
Hotel, an establishment that stood near
the railroad station near the Cumberland River. Scene of the game was the
old Sulphur Spring Bottom, later
named Sulphur Dell by Grantland
Rice, famed *Tennessean* sports editor."
This was the site of the historic sulphur
spring and salt lick that attracted
buffalo, Indians, hunters, and eventually the pioneers who settled on the
bluff above the "Big Salt Lick" or
"French Lick," as traders called it.

The playing surface was far below
street level, down inside a hole. Baseball was played on that site more or less
continuously until 1963, at which time
it was the oldest ballpark in use.
Nashville took a liking to the place,
maybe because it was so strange. It
wasn't flat and it wasn't big enough.

No matter how you configured it,
there was going to be an easy home run
someplace. Until 1926, the short right
field was on Fifth Avenue. After 1925,
when the diamond was moved, the
short right field was on Fourth Avenue—a short iron for Nashville sluggers like Jim Poole, Babe Barna, and
Wes Fleming. Poole was an aging first
baseman when he played for Nashville,
but he had the perfect swing to lift fly
balls over the short right field fence,
while Fleming and Barna struck blows
that not only cleared the fence but the
street on the other side of the fence,
striking the ice house or plopping into
the coal yard.

The best Nashville teams played in
the 1940s under manager Larry Gilbert,
who also owned stock in the team.
Gilbert's teams won four Southern
League pennants and three Dixie Series
against the Texas League pennant winners.

A Relief Map. According to Philip Lowry in *Green Cathedrals,* "Sulphur Dell had the craziest right field in history. Right fielders were called mountain goats because they had to go up and down the irregular hills in right center and right. The incline in right rose 25 feet, beginning gradually behind first, then rising sharply at a 45 degree angle, then leveling off at a 10 foot wide shelf one-third of the way up the incline, and then continuing at a 45 degree angle to the fence.

"Fielders used to play on the shelf, 235 feet from the plate. When overflow crowds were attracted to a game, a rope was extended in front of the shelf, and fans sat on the upper ⅔ of the incline, reducing right field to 235 rather than 262.... Embankments began in left at 301 and in right at 224."

The ballpark was only 440 yards from the Cumberland River. Sulphur Dell flooded in the spring. The city dump was so near that its odor was clear for most games. Fans sometimes called the park "the dump." Outfielders called it "Suffer Hell."

Some outfielders handled the Dump better than others. Multi-levels in the outfield gave fielding a new dimension some players never got the hang of at all, like jugglers who can't juggle objects of different weights. Some mastered the hills and made them their own. First and foremost among the latter group is Doc Wiseman, known as the Goat, who could snare drives running uphill, downhill and sidehill.

The original Sulphur Dell was a wooden structure, with an open press box on top of the roof. It looked more like a concession stand or a booth of chance in a carnival, and it was inevitably filled at game time with straw-hatted men looking bored and hot, their ties all snug and in place.

In addition to baseball, the stadium held rock concerts, auto racing, barbecue fund-raisers, and circuses. The hole has now been filled up and paved over, and functions as a state government parking lot.

Wilson Park

Negro National League 1930, 1933–34 (Elite Giants), Negro Southern League 1932 (Elite Giants). *Location:* South Nashville, Trimble Bottom section.

Named after the president of the Negro National League, Thomas T. Wilson. A picture of Wilson Park appears on the cover of *I Remember Tom,* a booklet written by James Hendrix about his memories of Wilson and published by the Black Music Foundation. The park grandstand is a big single deck with a large roof, easily big enough to accommodate AAA ball.

According to Hendrix:

"Wilson Park, at that time (1930s), was ideally located. To the north of the park was Old Meharry Medical College, and a couple of blocks to the east was Waldon College, and further south was the Fairgrounds. When ever there would be a game, the word of mouth promotion would guarantee a good attendance. The nearby residents would may as well be in attendance, because the loud speakers would broadcast all the details and the enthusiasm of the crowd for miles around. The activities at Wilson Park soon became so widespread that the white spectators outnumbered the black spectators. Sulphur Dell, the whiteowned park, near downtown Nashville, would hold some of their spring training sessions at Wilson Park. It was larger and the April showers would not flood Wilson Park, as it did Sulphur Dell. During some of these sessions, I met Babe Ruth, Lou Gehrig, and some of the other members of the New York Yankee Ball Team."

The Wilson family lived in a little house on the southeastern side of the field. Wilson had a happy-go-lucky attitude when it came to the competitive side of baseball. After a defeat, he'd get on the loudspeaker himself and say, "We can't win 'em all." It was here that

Roy Campanella made his last stop before becoming a Dodger.

According to Hendrix, Wilson dropped out of baseball in 1946 because of ill health. Integration had arrived anyway, the beginning of the end for black baseball. For a while, there was dog racing in Wilson Park, then the Paradise Ballroom was built on the lot and performers like Cab Calloway, Lionel Hampton, Sarah Vaughn, and Dinah Washington came to perform. Wilson died in 1947.

Hershel Greer Stadium

American Association 1978–present (Sounds). *Location:* On the slopes of Fort Negley, once St. Cloud Hill. Wedgewood exit on Interstate 65. *Dimensions:* Left field, 330 feet; center field, 405 feet; right field, 330 feet. *Seating capacity:* 16,000. *1987 season attendance:* 378,715.

New Britain, Connecticut

Beehive Field

Eastern League 1983–present (Red Sox). Owned by the City of New Britain. *Location:* Willow Brook Park, on Route 72. *Built:* 1982. *Construction cost:* $4.5 million. *Officially dedicated:* July 25, 1983. *Dimensions:* Left field, 330 feet; center field, 420 feet; right field, 330 feet. *Fences:* (1982) Eight feet all the way around. (1988) Left field, 16 feet; center field, eight feet; right field, 16 feet. *Seating capacity:* 3500. *1987 season attendance:* 83,338. *First Eastern League game:* April 22, 1983.

The complex includes football, soccer, and track and field facilities, a softball field, and Beehive Field, a baseball diamond. The fields were put on the site of the old New Britain High School athletic facilities. The New Britain High School campus is very close to Willow Brook Park. The football field holds over 10,000, the baseball field about a third of that in two open bleachers set up along both foul lines.

There was a single set of small open bleachers along the foul line of the softball field as well, sandwiched between the other two fields.

The name Beehive Field was chosen as the winner of a contest, from 79 entries. A symbol of a beehive, along with the motto, "Industry fills the hive and enjoys the honey," was adapted as the town emblem in March of 1873 by the Town Council. The name-the-ballpark contest was co-sponsored by the city Parks and Recreation Department and the *New Britain Herald.*

Present at the July 1983 dedication ceremony, in his Cleveland Indians uniform, was Hall of Famer Bob Feller. Also present were Mayor William J. McNamara, former featherweight boxing champ Willie Pep, and other city officials.

The site continued to serve New Britain High School athletics, just as it had before.

An Old-Fashioned Ballpark. The ballpark, considering it was built in 1982, is remarkably quaint. Its grandstand has seven rows and the roof behind home is supported by thick obstructing beams.

The press box sits on top of the open bleachers beside third base. Apparently the roof isn't strong enough to support it. Beehive Field looks for all the world like a ballpark built four decades earlier. The outfield fences have advertisement billboards. The signs are double-decked in right and left near the foul poles.

New Haven, Connecticut

Brewster Park (formerly Brewster Race Track)

National Association 1875. *Location:* Howard, West Park and Whalley avenues, Elm and Pendleton streets.

The New Havens of 1875, managed by Charlie Gould, went 7–40 in league play, with a team batting average of .203.

In addition to its use by the National Association, Brewster Park was used twice in 1877 by Hartford of the National League. This was not just a ballpark, but a public park on land donated by the Brewster family, and former site of the Brewster estate.

Weiss Park

Home of New Haven baseball, Depression era.

New Orleans, Louisiana

The Delachaise Estate

Location: Near today's Louisiana Avenue.

This was a cleared field where the first baseball game important enough for press coverage was played in New Orleans. The game was played in July 1859 by teams who were members of the high society Louisiana Baseball Club.

Name of park unknown

Location: Midway between the main part of the city and the suburb of Carrollton on St. Charles Avenue. This is now part of New Orleans proper. *Seating capacity:* 4000.

Used 1870–73 by the amateur and loosely organized Louisiana State Base Ball Association. A *Chicago Tribune* reporter in New Orleans reported on May 7, 1870, that the St. Charles Avenue facility was "the finest arranged ball park in America." Of course, he hadn't been to New York, and Al Spalding was yet to get into the act.

Baseball fever lasted only two years. By 1873 the Louisiana State Base Ball Association dissolved. In October of that year the *New Orleans Daily Picayune* officially pronounced baseball dead.

Athletic Park (Crescent City Base Ball Park, Sportsman's Park)

Southern League 1887–1900 (Pelicans), Southern Association 1901–15 (Pelicans). *Location:* Banks and Carrollton streets, opposite what is now Jesuit High School. *Built:* 1880. *Renovated:* 1887. *Seating capacity:* (1887) 5000.

In January of 1880, interest in baseball in New Orleans was rekindled by a visit to town from the Hop Bitters team of Rochester, New York, and their leader, Asa T. Soule — creator and sole proponent of his cure-all potion, "Hop Bitters, the Invalid's Friend and Hope."

The ball club gave New Orleans their first taste of pro baseball. Local promoters quickly formed a Park Association to finance construction of the Crescent City Base Ball Park so that thousands, paying 25 cents a head, could come out and watch the Rochesterians play local competition. By the time the Hop Bitters left town — after a busy two-month stay — a local Sunday league had been formed, and crowds continued to pack the new ballpark.

But New Orleans' second bout with baseball fever was also short-lived. By 1884, the park was empty. A game between the Brennans and the Lone Stars of the Crescent City League yielded $2.70 after the rent was paid.

In 1887, Toby Hart got New Orleans its first minor league franchise, in the Southern League. The new Pelicans played in Crescent City Park, which had been enlarged to seat 5000. The playing field had been leveled, and the lines had reportedly been drawn correct to "the hundredth of an inch." Five thousand showed up Opening Day.

The "Father" of the Pelicans was Abner Powell. Powell first came to New Orleans to pitch for and manage the 1887 team. He stayed in town until he died in 1953. In 1901, Powell became so infuriated by the performance of his team that he went to North Carolina, bought a new team for $12,000, brought it back to New Orleans, and fired the old team.

In 1887, crowds remained large and enthusiastic. The Pelicans were the lowest-paid team in the league—with a team payroll under $2000 a year—as well as the rowdiest lowlifes. (In July of 1887 a *New Orleans Times-Democrat* headline read "More Lushing by the Home Team," and the report read that the Pelicans had been observed "pretty well tanked up.") However, they were also the best ballplayers. While the Pelicans flourished, the rest of the Southern League struggled. Seven times before the turn of the century the circuit failed to complete its season. During four years there was no play at all. The Pelicans always made the most money—and they spent most of it keeping the rest of the league afloat. Powell, who owned the Pelicans by the 1890s, was forced to buy three other Southern League teams during that decade to keep the league from falling apart.

Because of the New Orleans' frequent summer thundershowers, Powell invented the infield cover. Because of the many rainouts, he invented the raincheck. He was one of the first to use Ladies' Day as a promotion.

On June 15, 1907, Pelican pitcher Moxie Manuel pitched both ends of a doubleheader at Athletic Park. He won both nine-inning games by the same 1–0 score, allowing a total of eight hits on the day.

By 1914, the Pelicans' general manager was Julius Heinemann, who got his start with the club vending soft drinks in the grandstand. It was he who decided the ballpark should be moved down the street to a preferable site.

When it was decided that this site would no longer be used for baseball, the grandstand was dismantled and carried piecemeal down Carrollton to Tulane Avenue, where it was turned into Pelican Stadium and renamed for Heinemann. Heinemann ended up losing his fortune in the 1929 Stock Market crash and committed suicide in 1930.

New Orleans Base Ball Park
Built: 1884.

In the autumn of 1884, the New Orleans Base Ball Park was built expressly for the professional games being promoted by the managers of the World's Cotton Centennial and Industrial Exposition. Major league teams came down for post-season barnstorming in 1884 and 1885. In November of 1885, 8000 showed up to see the Sunday afternoon game between the New York Giants and the then–American Association champion St. Louis Browns. The *New Orleans Daily Picayune* of November 20, 1885, reported, "In the crowd were many prominent citizens, judges, lawyers, doctors, merchants, laborers, politicians and representatives of every other class that goes to make up the population of a large city."

Pelican Stadium (Julius Heinemann
Stadium, Municipal Park, Larry Gilbert Stadium)

Southern Association 1915–57 (Pelicans), Negro American League 1941 (Stars). *Location:* Tulane Avenue (left field), South Carrollton Street (third base), Gravier Street (first base), Pierce Street (right field). Currently the site of the Fountain Bay Motor Hotel. *Dimensions:* Left field, 427 feet; center field, 405 feet; right field, 418 feet. *First game:* April 13, 1915. *Last game:* September 1, 1957 (Sunday afternoon, Memphis 7, New Orleans 3, attendance: 941). *Torn down:* October 1957.

The manager of the Pelicans from 1922 to 1938 was Larry Gilbert. He had been the first New Orleans native to play in the major leagues, as well as the first to play in a World Series.

In 1923, the Pelicans won the Southern Association pennant. The second baseman for that club was Cotton Knaupp, who on August 8, 1916, became the only player in the Southern Association to make an unassisted triple play.

On August 12, 1935, Eddie Rose

gained national fame by killing a pigeon with a fly ball.

Pelican left-fielder Cob Jarvis hit the final home run in Pelican Stadium. Memphis right-hander Bill Darden threw the last pitch. Peanuts Lowry was the last Pelican skipper to manage in Pelican Stadium. In that last game he inserted himself in the lineup in the eighth inning as a pinch hitter and kayed. In 1957, the Pelicans finished last. Their season attendance was a dismal 66,151.

Lousy baseball wasn't the only reason people stopped going to Pelican Stadium. There was also a local ban on black ballplayers and a resulting boycott by black fans.

Between the 1964 and 1965 baseball seasons the park was completely renovated. The oldest ballpark in New Orleans was made to look the newest. The ballpark was renamed for Larry Gilbert, the long-time Pelicans manager who had died earlier in 1965.

The dedication ceremonies were held at 3:30 p.m. on May 23, 1965, between games of a NORD-Maison Blanche Babe Ruth League doubleheader. The new ballpark had an open steel grandstand. The field was enclosed by chain link fencing nine feet high, running 960 feet around the park, replacing the old weatherbeaten wooden fence.

The previous lighting system was replaced by a mercury vapor system that doubled the previous lighting power. The new grandstand was entirely screened in, eliminating the possibility of any fan getting struck by a foul ball.

City Park Stadium

Southern Association 1958–59 (Pelicans). *Location:* City Park. *Final game:* September 7, 1959 (attendance: 229).

The Pelicans of the Southern Association were a dying tradition. This was so when the team finished their days in Pelican Stadium, and the situation only got worse after they moved to City

Park Stadium. The stadium was built for football, shaped like a horseshoe, and had the infield tucked straightaway in an end zone, so that both lines were short and center field went on forever. They removed the goal post for baseball, but the 440-yard track was left in place. The track was mostly in fair territory and came into play most frequently down the lines, where it crossed just behind first and third base. The stadium was surrounded by trees on all sides. A screen was built at the end of the left field line to keep line drives on the playing field, but none was built down the right field line, where balls were allowed to fly into the stands unencumbered. The seats were wooden bleacher benches, 37 rows of them to the upper lip of the bowl.

The last Pelican game in New Orleans was played on Labor Day, 1959, and nobody noticed.

Berhman Park

Location: West Bank, one block from Shirley Drive.

New Westminster, British Columbia

Queens Park Stadium

Northwest League circa 1974. *Dimensions:* Left field, 346 feet; center field, 433 feet; right field, 297 feet. *Seating capacity:* 5804.

New York, New York

Around 1842 Alexander Cartwright and a group of young gentlemen who were to become the Knickerbockers devised the rules to baseball while playing games in a lot at 27th Street and Madison Avenue — near the current site of Madison Square Park. This lot was used by the Knickerbockers until the city's residential and commercial community forced them to secure a permanent site in Hoboken, New Jersey.

The scoreboard at Berhman Park, New Orleans, La., worse for wear and tear.
(Photo by Wanda Boudreaux.)

St. George Cricket Club

Home of the Washington Club (later the Gotham Club) 1853.

The first mention of a baseball game in the New York press comes in 1853. Stories in *Spirit* and the *New York Mercury* reported a game at the St. George Cricket Club between the Washington Club and the visiting Knickerbockers.

Fashion Race Course (National Course)

Used for New York-Brooklyn series in 1858. *Location:* Willets Point, County of Queens (in what is now Flushing Meadow Park a few hundred yards from the site of Shea Stadium). *Seating capacity:* 12,000.

There had never been an admission charge for a baseball game until 1858, when a series of All-Star games was played between teams from Brooklyn and New York. For the events, the Fashion Race Course on Willets Point was remodeled and fifty cents charged at the gate to pay for the refurbishment. The park was chosen because of its seating capacity and its geographic neutrality.

The opening game, July 20, 1858, drew between 1500 and 2000. The game had been originally scheduled for a week earlier but had been postponed by rain. The New Yorkers beat Brooklyn 22–18, 8–29, 29–18, with each crowd being a little bit smaller than the one before.

This was four summers before William Cammeyer built the Union Grounds, the first enclosed ballpark, in Brooklyn.

Fashion Beats Boston. The racetrack, formerly the National Course, had been renamed in 1856 after the great northern mare. In December 1841, Fashion and a horse named Boston had run a four-mile race in New York City that drew a crowd of 70,000. It was the race of the decade, and Fashion won by a little more than a length.

In early 1854, S.J. Carter of New Orleans, William W. Boyden of Tennessee, and native New Yorker Lovell Purdy spent $85,000 and purchased the 141-acre Willets farm, now Flushing Meadow Park, then considered the Newtown section of Queens County, Long Island. Over $165,000 was spent on the building of the track. A grandstand was built to seat 12,000, and there was standing room for 38,000 more. For one year the National Course was a big success, but the novelty wore off and the popularity quickly dissipated toward failure.

Name of park unknown

Home of the Morrisania Unions 1866. *Location:* Near the old Melrose Station of the Harlem Railroad, close to the current location of Yankee Stadium.

The Unions were one team of many who claimed to be the 1866 World Champions. Baseball, in its infancy, was still disorganized.

Polo Grounds (I)

First used for baseball 1880, National League 1883–88 (Gothams, 1883–85, Giants), American Association 1883–85 (Metropolitans). *Location:* 110th Street, 112th Street, Fifth and Sixth avenues. *First game:* September 29, 1880 (Metropolitans versus Washington Nationals). *First National League game:* May 1, 1883 (New York 7, Boston 5). *Last National League game:* October 13, 1888 (Indianapolis 6, New York 4). *First American Association game:* May 12, 1883 (Philadelphia 11, New York 4). *Last American Association game:* October 1, 1885 (New York 5, Cincinnati 1). *Last game (World Series):* October 20, 1888 (New York NL 6, St. Louis AA 4).

The original Polo Grounds on 110th Street was a wooden enclosure ornately festooned with strung pennants. The grandstand and playing field were on the land of newspaper tycoon James Gordon Bennett, who had formerly reserved the use of the land for his polo-playing buddies.

The wooden grandstand was double-decked and went from first to third, making it one of the largest of its day, comparable in every way with Lakefront Park in Chicago and the Grand Pavilion in Boston. Bleachers extended down the foul lines to the outfield fences — fences too tall to be easily scaled.

Crowds for baseball and polo differed. Polo attracted the upper crust. For baseball, in the 1880s, the bleachers were known as Burkeville, and were filled with the sons of Irish immigrants.

Four American flags waved from evenly spaced poles atop the upper deck. The largest flagpole of all stuck right up out of the field in straightaway center, not deep enough to avoid causing the center fielder worry. From the top of this pole flew, not an American flag, but a white pennant with a simple NEW YORK written across it.

The foul lines did not make it all the way to the fences, but stopped about 180 feet out. The "foul poles" came right up out of the field at the end of the lime line, standing slightly taller than a man. They had colorful flags attached to their top, and did not look unlike "pins" on a golf course.

There were no dugouts. Players sat on benches in front of the grandstand just on the home plate side of first and third.

On days when the park was crowded, fans sat or stood on the field, between the grandstand and the foul lines, and in front of the outfield fences. The fence in right field was a distance from home that would strike a modern eye as familiar, but out in left the pasture went on and on, so deep that left field eventually held a second baseball diamond. Before that, however, deep left field was where the carriages were parked. The finest ladies sat on top of their barouches in left, where the fence was an avenue block (maybe 800 feet)

from home, while beneath them bookies turned the enclosed cabin into a rolling office.

From a distance, one could tell the widely spaced positions of the women by their colorful parasols.

When crowds on the field threatened to overwhelm games, policemen were assigned to keep fans back as far as possible. With no law authority present, fields of play tended to shrink as the game went on. Fans, giving themselves breathing room and a better view, inched closer to the outfielders' backs.

Baseball was played on the Polo Grounds even when it was still used for polo. The first baseball game was played September 29, 1880, between the non-affiliated New York Metropolitans and the Washington Nationals. The Polo Grounds was not converted to baseball until three years later, by John B. Day.

Day owned the Mets, a team he had entered in the 1883 American Association. He also owned the National League team in Troy, which he moved to New York. Day's new baseball grounds were to be the home of both teams, but he didn't own the grounds. He leased them from owner James Gordon Bennett through his business, the Metropolitan Exhibition Company. Baseball no longer allows one man to own two major league baseball teams, although there are those who own several non-competitive minor league teams.

The first National League game there, May 1, 1883, saw the newborn Giants defeat Boston 7-5. It was Roger Connor's triple off the right field wall that knocked in the winning run. (By 1886, that fence was covered with billboard advertisements, the largest of which promoted A.G. Spalding and Bros. Athletic Goods, and there were bleacher seats sitting in front of it.) The game was attended by former president U.S. Grant, who, along with the estimated 15,000 others attending the game, was entertained by Grafulia's (later Cappa's) Seventh Regiment Band. It was the largest crowd in New York baseball history up to that time.

In the first American Association game, eleven days later, Athletics pitcher Bobby Mathews beat Tim Keefe of the Mets 11-4. Mathews had also been the winning pitcher of the first National Association game in Fort Wayne, Indiana, in 1871.

On May 28, 1883, bareknuckle heavyweight champion John L. Sullivan was paid $1200 to pitch an exhibition (2:19 of work) for the Metropolitans against a picked nine before a "comfortably filled" house of 4000, all of whom paid double the normal admission price.

According to the New York Times the following day, "Such decorum was observed by (the Polo Grounds') male occupants that the sprinkling of ladies seemed not out of place.... (Sullivan's) breadth of shoulder, thick legs, and expansive rump distinguished him from every other player on the field. Whenever he took his place at the pitchers' plate or at the bat the spectators craned their necks and watched every movement he made. As a balltosser, Mr. Sullivan's ability was gauged exactly by the boy who remarked, disgustedly, 'No good.'"

A fixture on the right wing of the ladies' pavilion was Helen Dauvray (Mrs. John Montgomery) Ward, who "could score (a game) as well as any man," and was accompanied by her friend Mrs. Helm. Mrs. Ward was the wife of the Giants' shortstop.

When there were conflicts in scheduling, as there seemed to be during most of the 1884 season, the Metropolitans played their games in a lot they called Metropolitan Park between 107th and 109th Street along the East River.

In 1884, the old Polo Grounds was the site of the first fully sanctioned World Series, between the National League champions, the Providence Grays, and the American Association champions, the Mets. Grays ace Charles

"Ol' Hoss" Radbourne, who had won 60 games during that regular season, swept the Mets in the best-of-five, 6-0, 3-1, 12-2.

Punishing the Mets. Owner Day became so infuriated by his team's humiliation that he set out to destroy the team. He "traded" all of the Mets' best players to the Giants, and scheduled Mets games for early in the morning when no one would want to show up. In the meantime, he wholeheartedly promoted the Giants.

But the worst degradation the Mets had to endure was the division of the Polo Grounds into two playing fields, separated only by a canvas fence. The Mets had to play their games in what had once been deep left field, while the Giants got to play in the usual field. Evidence of shoddy construction was everywhere in the new park, but nowhere quite so much as in the infield, where decaying garbage had been used as fill. The playing field literally stank.

By the end of the 1885 season, during which the Mets went 44-64, the American Association insisted Day sell the Mets to someone who would treat them nicer. He did—to Erastus Wiman, who moved the team to Staten Island.

Characters. In the meantime, Giants fans (or "cranks," as they were then called) were already getting a reputation as a bunch of characters. One such gentleman, Frank H. Wood, was known as "Well! Well! Well!" because that was his favorite cry. He used his exclamation to convey both celebration and woe. Once, it was said, Mr. Wood made the mistake of singing his trademark, only to be deluged by the miscellaneous projectiles of nearby music lovers.

Zane Grey, the famous writer of Westerns, was so impressed by Mr. Wood during a visit to see the Giants that he named a character after him in his baseball story The Redheaded Outfield.

Other well-known Giants fans of the time were De Wolf Hopper, the actor

The original Polo Grounds, New York, N.Y., Opening Day, 1888. New York Giants versus the Philadelphia Phillies. (Photo furnished by the National Baseball Library in Cooperstown, New York.)

who made a career out of reciting "Casey at the Bat," and Miss Maggie Cline, the Giants' favorite buxom young lady.

Wrong Side of the Political Fence. The Giants played their last game at the Old Polo Grounds on October 20, 1888, defeating St. Louis of the American Association 6–4 in the fifth game of that year's World Series. There was no ceremony. No one knew it would be the last game.

Day did not learn until February 1889 that the Polo Grounds was to be torn down. His lease never had been too secure. Certain aldermen were disappointed with the number of free passes they were given, and retaliated by trying to get a street cut through the site. This had been prevented for a few years by the generous bribing of Tammany officials.

When the end came, it came swiftly and unexpectedly. A court order was obtained to bring down the Polo Grounds, and it was done. Day's last-minute plea—in the form of a $10,000 "donation" to city charities—was ig-

nored. While the Giants played on borrowed ground in Jersey City and then at St. George Grounds on Staten Island for 25 games, waiting for their new park further uptown to be completed, the old Polo Grounds was leveled for the completion of the 111th Street extension.

Home plate was at the current site of Frawley Circle, at the northeast corner of Central Park. Currently occupying that land are the Lincoln Correctional Facility, Colony Fried Chicken, apartment houses and a public school.

Metropolitan Park

American Association 1884 (Metropolitans, some games). *Location:* 107th and 109th streets, First Avenue, East River.

St. George Grounds

American Association 1886–87 (Metropolitans), National League 1889 (Giants, some games). *Location:* Staten Island, St. George section, on the harbor.

In the summer of 1886, there was a big construction project underway on the little island out in New York Harbor, easily visible from the St. George Grounds grandstand. The Statue of Liberty was being assembled out there. The double-decked grandstand behind home was linear, like those at racetracks. Ladies dressed to the tee clustered as deep as they could get on the grandstand's first base side.

The Giants were forced to use this former home of the Mets for the first 25 home games of the 1889 season. They'd been booted from the Polo Grounds, and Manhattan Field wasn't ready.

The Giants' stay on Staten Island was a soggy one. The same rains that caused the Johnstown floods of 1889 made the outfield here so wet that boards were placed out there to provide some kind of footing. The Giants, especially pitcher Ned Crane, did well in Staten Island, and one of the big reasons was that the Giants' outfielders ran well on wood.

The field was owned by millionaire promotor Erastmus Wiman, who also, conveniently enough, owned a ferry from Manhattan to Staten Island. Here is one of Wiman's advertisements for the St. George Grounds during the time the Mets were playing there:

St. George Beautiful Grounds,
Staten Island
20 Minutes from The Battery
Seventh Regiment Band
Fairyland ,Concerts Every Evening
Water Fireworks, Illuminated Geysers
Easy of Access
Baseball and Lacrosse Every Afternoon
Restaurant by Purssell
A Breath of Fresh Air for 10 Cents
A Delightful Sail Down the Bay
Day and Evening Attractions

"Illuminated Geysers" have appeared since in major league baseball parks, most recently the display in Kansas City's Royals Stadium.

Wild West Grounds

American Association 1887 (some games). *Location:* Staten Island, in the Tomkinsville section.

Used by the Mets when the perpetually soggy St. George Grounds was flooded or being used by another event.

Manhattan Field

National League 1889-90 (Giants), American Association 1890 (Brooklyn Gladiators, seven games). *Location:* 155th Street (first base), Coogan's Bluff (third base), Eighth Avenue (right field), Brotherhood Park, later Polo Grounds II (center field). *Depth of lower tier:* 50 feet. *Depth of upper tier:* 31 feet. *Seating capacity:* 15,000 (Grandstand, 5500; bleacher, 9500). *First game:* July 8, 1889 (New York 7, Pittsburgh 5). *Last game:* September 10, 1890 (Boston 8, New York 5).

The Giants had just finished a 25-home-game stint on Staten Island, waiting for their new park to be completed. The flooding problems that had plagued the Giants on Staten Island returned in September 1889 when the Hudson and East rivers overflowed their banks and with them Manhattan Field. The Giants were oblivious to the hardship and won the pennant, drawing 201,662 for the year. In 1890, with the formation of the Players League, a second park was built beside the first, so close that Mike Tiernan of the Giants hit the ball from Manhattan Park into Brotherhood Park next door — a field that would eventually be known as the new Polo Grounds. In those days ball games were scheduled head to head, instead of alternating home stands as in today's scheduling for two-franchise cities. When Tiernan hit his famous home run, he received a hand from the crowds in both parks.

The Gemini Factor. New York always had a thing about putting their ballparks next to one another. There were two parks side by side in the Old Polo Grounds for a time. Even later, when Yankee Stadium was built, it was felt important that crowds going to the Polo Grounds be able to *see* the new structure, and only a river separated the ballparks.

The Players League had the better of the two ballparks (Manhattan Field had sharp inclines in center and right field, making the grounds hazardous to an outfielder's health), so, when the Brotherhood folded after a year, the National League team moved next door, changed the name of Brotherhood Park to the Polo Grounds, and Manhattan Field was forgotten.

Maspeth Ball Grounds (Long Island Recreation Grounds)

American Association 1890 (Brooklyn Trolley Dodgers, Sundays only). *Location:* In the Maspeth section of Queens.

Polo Grounds (II) (Brotherhood Park 1890, Brush Stadium 1911–19)

Players League 1890, National League 1891–1957 (Giants), American League 1913–22 (Yankees), home of the Cuban Giants 1940s, National League 1962–63 (Mets). Site of Game 1 of the 1946 Negro League World Series. Owned by the New York Giants. *Location:* Eighth Avenue (center field side), East 155th Street (first base), Harlem River Speedway (home plate), East 157th Street (third base). *Grandstand destroyed by fire:* 1911. *Re-opened in steel and concrete:* June 28, 1911. *Formal dedication of new park:* April 19, 1912. *Dimensions:* Left field, 280 feet; left center, 450 feet; center field, 475 feet (once 483); right center, 450 feet; right field, 258 feet. 74 feet from home plate to the backstop. *Fences:* (1911) Left field, 10 feet; center field, 20 feet; right center, 10 feet; right field, 12 feet. (1923) Left field, 17 feet; left center, 18 feet; center field (clubhouse), 60 feet; right center, 12 feet; right field, 10½ feet. *Seating capacity:* (1923) 55,987. Field boxes, 2730; lower reserved, 12,617; upper boxes, 1084; upper reserved, 5138; lower general admission,

27,500; upper general admission, 2318; bleacher, 4600. *Giants day game attendance record:* 54,992 (April 30, 1941, versus St. Louis). *Giants doubleheader attendance record:* 60,747 (May 3, 1937, versus Brooklyn). *Giants night game attendance record:* 51,790 (May 27, 1957, versus Brooklyn). *Giants opening game attendance record:* 54,393 (April 14, 1936, versus Brooklyn). *Giants season high attendance record:* 1,600,793 (1947). *Giants season low attendance record:* 258,618 (1918). *Mets day game attendance record:* 35,264 (July 14, 1962, versus Los Angeles). *Mets doubleheader attendance record:* 54,360 (May 30, 1962, versus Los Angeles). *Mets night game attendance record:* 49,431 (May 3, 1963, versus San Francisco). *Mets twinight doubleheader attendance record:* 16,540 (August 19, 1962, versus Pittsburgh). *Mets opening game attendance record:* 25,251 (April 9, 1963, versus St. Louis). *Mets season high attendance record:* 1,080,108 (1963). *Mets season low attendance record:* 922,530 (1962). *First Players League game:* April 19, 1890 (Philadelphia 12, New York 11). *Last Players League game:* September 18, 1890 (Brooklyn 8, New York 7). *First National League game (Giants):* April 22, 1891 (Boston 4, New York 3). *Last Giants game:* September 29, 1957 (Pittsburgh 9, New York 1). *First Mets game:* April 13, 1962 (Pittsburgh 4, New York 3). *Last National League game (Mets):* September 18, 1963 (Philadelphia 5, New York 1). *First American League game:* April 17, 1913 (Washington 9, New York 3). *Last American League game:* September 10, 1922 (doubleheader, New York 10, Philadelphia 3; New York 2, Philadelphia 1).

This plot of land, once a seventeenth century farm given to John Lion Gardiner by the king of England, passed from generation to generation to James J. Coogan, the 1890 Manhattan borough president. Eighteen-ninety was the first year that the land under Coogan's Bluff held a ballpark. It was called Brotherhood Park, used by the Players League, and sat next to Manhattan Field where the Giants played. When the Players League dissolved, the Giants moved next door to this park and stayed for 67 years. Because the Giants played there, the park became known as the new Polo Grounds. From the start the playing field was rectangular, to fit between Coogan's Bluff and Manhattan Field. There were high fences all the way around, and the grandstand was single-decked, though there were open roof seats. By the time the National League used the park it had a full-fledged upper deck.

The Seeley and Rappleyea Cafe. In 1890, the bar under the grandstand was known as the Seeley and Rappleyea Cafe, offering "fine wines, liquors and cigars, whiskey, and James Everhard's Celebrated Lager Bier." The bar was positioned to give a view of the field's right side. A former Giant and Met, Dasher Troy, tended bar. In 1893, there were complaints that the bar was unsightly and a nuisance, particularly to the women who passed, so the bar was closed for the end of that season. The no-alcohol rule lasted a year, failing to survive an 1894 heat wave. In the scorecards of the day, published by Harry M. Stevens, there were advertisements for $15 suits. In those days the Giants were owned by Andrew Freedman, who thought nothing of putting his non–starting roster players on duty elsewhere in the park. In 1896, as a rookie, Giants pitcher James Bentley "Cy" Seymour was assigned by Freedman to gate duty. After a few innings, Seymour snuck away from his post to watch the game. Freedman caught him and fined him $10.

Bleachers were installed in deep center field around that time. The seats were known as "the cigar boxes" because of their size and shape. Since the grandstand curved into fair territory a few feet and the bullpens behind were in play, it was possible for a home run ball to go too far, clear the stands,

and be caught on the other side by an outfielder chasing into the bullpen.

In 1907, Opening Day at the Polo Grounds turned into a near-riot as fans took advantage of a lack of police presence. The New York City Police Commissioner said that the grounds constituted a private amusement park and refused to allow his men to patrol there. With the Giants losing badly in the ninth inning, fans began to run onto the field. Bottles, snowballs, and seat cushions were hurled. Hall of Fame umpire Bill Klem declared a forfeit.

1908. The following year, in 1908, the Polo Grounds were the site of the Merkle Boner, and the greatest pennant race ever. The 1908 pennant race was such a doozy that Giants owner John T. Brush began to expand seating capacity, changing aspects of the grounds that had been unchanged for as long as anyone could remember. According to the September 8 edition of the *New York Evening Telegram:*

"So much had the surroundings of the Polo Grounds been changed this afternoon six score 'old fans' who had occupied seats since the days of the Brotherhood in 1890 were ousted from their positions and wandered aimlessly around the grandstand and bleachers looking for available sites to preempt for another 20 years. This field was opened to the public in 1890 and has not changed since then.

"In the 'Roost,' as it was called, in the right corner of the field bleachers, something like 50 patrons have sat year after year, and they were turned out today simply because baseball has become so popular that the Polo Grounds could not accommodate the spectators.

"To take the place of 1000 bleacher seats which have been withdrawn, there is a new stand that will accommodate 3000 fans."

By the end of the season Brush had added 7000 new seats, creating a seating capacity of close to 30,000. According to the *New York Evening Mail,* this made the Polo Grounds the third

Polo Grounds, New York, N.Y., 1896. Fans in the outfield. (Photo by Byron, the Byron Collection, Museum of the City of New York.)

largest sporting arena in the nation, behind the bowls of Harvard and Yale.

The Merkle Boner (best described in G.H. Fleming's *The Unforgettable Season*) resulted initially in a riot and mass confusion, then later, at the end of the season, in a one-game playoff against the hated Cubs for the National League pennant. These were the days before advance sales, and a quarter of a million people showed up at the park, creating a dangerous human gridlock. One man died when he fell from the el, above and behind the left field stands. There was a scramble to take the place the man had involuntarily vacated. One fan put a board between the el platform and the Polo Grounds fence so the brave could walk the plank and drop into the ballpark. According to the *New York Evening Telegram,* "From the pressbox, the skyline everywhere was human heads. They were located on grandstand, roofs, fences, 'L' structures, electric light poles and in the distance on smokestacks, chimneys, advertising signs and coping of apartment houses."

After the game, which the Cubs won, a Giant fan expressed his displeasure by striking Cub manager Frank Chance, injuring the Peerless Leader's neck.

John T. Brush. During the first decade of the twentieth century, the Giants were owned by John T. Brush, an orphan who fought with the First New York Artillery in the Civil War and went on to own successful clothing stores in Boston, Troy, and Indianapolis. It was he who provided the big bucks behind John McGraw's Giant Dynasty. He was drawn to New York by the stage. He married an actress, joined the Lambs Club, and was quick to give a free pass to the wooden Polo Grounds to any actor who didn't have a matinee that day. He was a man with style, and kept it even in his old age. By 1911, he was confined to a wheelchair by locomotor ataxia.

That April his ballpark burned. Only the cigar boxes were left standing.

The fire took place early in the morning, so there were no injuries, but the place was in total ruin. Brush went there by train with his wife, Elsie, to survey the still-smoldering wreckage. He took one look and became determined to build a bigger and better park, in steel and concrete—the biggest in the country. Elsie said she was with him 100 percent, so the thing was done. While the Giants temporarily used Hilltop Park, Brush negotiated a long-term lease with the owner of the land, Mrs. Harriet Coogan.

He built the new park on a cost-plus basis. Brush said that quality fans of New York city deserved "this mammoth structure ... a model for all subsequent Base Ball structures." Brush hated anything dull and gave his ornamental new grandstand some grand touches. The coat of arms for each National League city was emblazoned upon the grandstand's summit. The Giants were back by June, using the grounds beneath Coogan's Bluff even as construction continued.

Undaunted by the confusion and changes of scenery, the Giants kept winning. The new park literally rose around them as they played. By October 14, 1911, for the first game of the World Series against the Athletics—a rematch of the 1905 all-shutout classic—the new stadium held 38,281. The new park was the now-familiar horseshoe-shaped classic, with its soft home run touches down the lines, enhanced by an upper deck overhang like the one in Tiger Stadium, and an infinite pasture in center, where outfielders were allowed to chase unhindered, like pedigreed pooches after a frisbee. In 1923, the bleachers in center were built and the seating capacity reached over 55,000.

The Polo Grounds Through the Years. In 1915, the Giants' announced Women Suffrage Day. They sold a suffrage organization many tickets at a reduced price. The ladies resold the tickets at regular prices and made a profit of $3000. According to the Giants' president, Harry Hempstead, his club made an extra $2500 out of the deal and split the cash with the visiting

Chicago club. Hempstead knew that it paid doubly to have the suffragettes on his side, as they could be militant agitators.

For a time there were flower beds in right and center field, but Giants manager John McGraw had them ripped out. Players—no doubt hearing voices of conscience dating back to their youth—refused to charge into the flower beds after balls, and instead tippy-toed through the flowers, not wanting to uproot anything, while an inside-the-park home run was being coursed.

On Memorial Day, 1921, the five-foot-high Eddie Grant Memorial was dedicated in center field at the base of the clubhouse wall. Eddie Grant was a former Giant killed in action in the Argonne Forest October 5, 1918.

When the Giants first moved to the Polo Grounds, upper Harlem and Washington Heights had been considered suburban communities, but by 1920 this was no longer so. With the growth of the city and the expansion of mass transit, the Polo Grounds was very much in the city of New York. To some degree, natural boundaries kept the Polo Grounds from affecting its community say, in the way Yankee Stadium did. The river was on one side, Coogan's Bluff on another, and there was nothing but railroad repair sheds to the north and a major highway to the east. No string of bars popped up across the street when the ballparks were built. There really wasn't an "across the street." The residential section nearest to the Polo Grounds was separated from the ballpark by the bluff. The only businesses that benefitted from the Giants playing where they did were the Uptown dance halls and casinos of New York's pre–Prohibition era, south of 155th Street.

In those days, there was an attempt by the Stoneham family, owners of the club and the park—though the Coogans still owned the land upon which the park was built—to keep the Polo

Grounds as busy as possible. In the 1920s, the park hosted college and pro football games, international soccer matches (which drew over 50,000), tennis, midget auto racing, outdoor opera—and there was once a skating rink in the outfield.

According to Horace Stoneham in Roger Angell's *Five Seasons,* "I think we had every sport at the Polo Grounds except polo. I did my best to arrange that, but we never could work it out."

In 1929, the Polo Grounds became the first park to have a public address system. A microphone was attached to the mask of the home-plate umpire.

The outfield walls were covered with advertisements (such as Botany clothes, Stahl-Meyer hot dogs, GEM razor blades, Old Gold cigarettes, and Lifebuoy soap) until 1948, when the fences were painted the same green as the rest of the park. There were plenty of signs out there on August 1, 1945, when Mel Ott hit his 500th home run.

According to Fred Stein in his book *Under Coogan's Bluff:*

"The outfield walls were probably the most difficult to play of any major league ball park and not only because of their sharp angles. The right field wall presented a solid stretch of concrete where most drives struck. Accordingly, a hard drive off the wall was likely to rebound back towards the infield. Balls hit not quite so hard often caromed off towards center field, and softer drives, particularly those that just reached the wall, usually bounced off towards right center field or continued bouncing along the wall.

"The left field wall was even more difficult to play. Compounding the problems encountered in playing the carom, the left field wall had a corrugated iron door on its gate which caused particularly unpredictable rebounds. Judgement on fly balls was complicated further because this was the sun field. In addition, the upper deck facing extended well out past the lower deck. This meant that in cases where fly balls just missed the upper deck there was a split second during which the fielder frequently lost sight of the ball.

"Normally, distances from home plate are indicated by painted numerals on the wall which have no effect on outfield play. But not in the Polo Grounds. Because of the slanted view of the outfield walls from behind the plate, signs on the walls could not be read. Instead, markers were placed along the bottom of the walls to indicate distances from home plate. Made of tin or sheet steel and about 15 inches off the ground, they were set about two or three inches from the wall. When a drive struck a marker the rebound would behave unpredictably—either stopping dead or rolling along the base of the wall."

On July 6, 1942, the Polo Grounds was the site of the first night All-Star Game. The game wasn't scheduled that way, but a lengthy rain delay made it a necessity. The game finally got started at 7:22 p.m. The American League was winning 3–1 when the game was called for a wartime blackout test at 9:30.

In the 1940s, the Cuban Stars moved to the Polo Grounds, and changed their name to the Cuban Giants. The black team was owned by bigwig Alex Pompez (*see* Dyckman Oval). When integration came, Pompez signed a working relationship with Horace Stoneham, the first time a Negro League team formally became a major league farm club.

It was in a Negro League game in 1948 that Luke Easter became the first man ever to hit a home run into the Polo Grounds' center field bleachers. Joe Adcock repeated the accomplishment April 29, 1953, off Jim Hearn. It was done twice after that, coincidentally on consecutive days, June 17 and 18, 1962, by Lou Brock and Henry Aaron.

The Greatest Offensive Moment in Baseball History. *"The Giants Win the Pennant! The Giants Win the Pennant!*

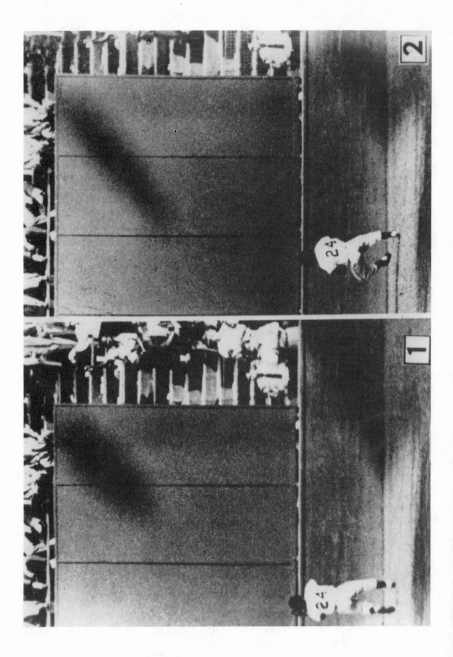

The Giants Win the Pennant! The Giants Win the Pennant! The Giants Win the Pennant!" **The Greatest Defensive Moment in Baseball History.** The clubhouses and the ball club's front office were in center field. Twin staircases led the ballplayers from deepest center up to the clubhouse entrances. The clubhouse wall was 60 feet high. No one ever hit a ball over it. In fact, no ball ever struck the clubhouse wall on the fly. It was just to the right field side of the alley leading back to the clubhouse steps that Willie Mays made the greatest catch in the history of baseball.

There are those that say Mays made greater catches—and this alone is hard to believe—but we know he never made one more important. The Catch (a proper noun) in all likelihood won the Giants a World Series game. The score was tied 2–2 in the eighth inning, men on first and second, when the Catch was made. The Indians failed to score in the inning. Eyewitnesses (3,786,987 report being there) claim Wertz's shot was low, not a towering drive. Mays must have started heading for the place where the ball was going to come down while pitcher Don Liddle was winding up—and he probably would have made the Catch even if he weren't wearing a glove.

Track and field records are broken every day. All athletics have improved greatly in the last 35 years. Could today's slick young outfielder make the Catch routinely? We'll never know. There is no 460 right center anymore. The devaluation of the homer has limited our ability to measure an outfielder's skills.

Mays spun and threw a strike to second after the Catch. The Throw kept Indian base runner Larry Doby from scoring from second after tagging up. **Some Called It Home.** The Polo Grounds always was a place where people lived. For years a caretaker named Matty Schwab lived with his family in an apartment built for him by owner Horace Stoneham under Section 31 in left field. In 1962 and 1963, the Mets' groundskeepers painted the Schwab apartment pink, installed a shower, and used it as their personal clubhouse.

Even Stoneham was known to spend great chunks of time at the park without going home. Many was the time he and a friend or a sports writer or two would retire to his office-apartment above the clubhouse in straightaway center for a drink or ten, fall asleep whenever, and wake the next day to the thunderously painful sounds of batting practice.

Fans in the Polo Grounds often saw the little faces peering out of the windows in that green wall, 500 feet from home plate, and had no idea who was out there. Those faces could have belonged to the phantoms of the ballpark.

Having clubhouses in center offered moments of poignancy unavailable in most parks: a humiliated pitcher walking to the showers after an early hook, or the unforgettable sight of the Giants running for their lives after their final home game in New York, chased by those infuriated by their abandonment.

In the late '40s and early '50s, when Leo Durocher was Giant manager, his wife was actress Laraine Day, who brought Hollywood celebrities to the ballpark with her. Her box seat became known as "Celebrity Corner."

The land, once known as Harlem Meadow, is the current site of the Polo Grounds Housing Project, whose four towers stand over 30 stories.

Hilltop Park
American League 1903–1912 (Highlanders, Yankees), National League 1911 (Giants, some games). *Location:* 165th Street (first base side), 168th

The Catch, 1954, at the Polo Grounds, New York, N.Y. Willie Mays, in the deepest of all centers, has corralled Vic Wertz's line drive and is whirling for the Throw.

The "New" Polo Grounds, New York, N.Y. (Photo furnished by the National Baseball Library in Cooperstown, New York.)

Street (left field), Fort Washington Avenue (third base), Broadway (right field). *Seating capacity:* 15,000. *First American League game:* April 30, 1903 (New York 6, Washington 2). *Last American League game:* October 5, 1912 (New York 8, Washington 6). *First National League game:* April 15, 1911 (New York 6, Brooklyn 3). *Last National League game:* May 30, 1911 (morning/afternoon doubleheader, New York 4, Brooklyn 1; New York 3, Brooklyn 0).

It was a struggle to establish an American League franchise in the country's largest city. In New York, without the proper political connections, it could be next to impossible to secure a suitable site for a ballpark. Andrew Freedman owned the Giants, as well as the lease to every plot upon which a competitor could build a park, so odds were against anyone who chose to compete. Even after Freedman sold his controlling interest in the club, he promised to use his prominent real estate role to protect the Giants.

Despite Freedman's promise, Ban

Johnson and his American League presumed a ballpark would be built if the need were there and established a franchise in New York, signing up ballplayers even before choosing appropriate owners. In December 1902, the American League found a lot on 142nd Street and Lenox Avenue that Freedman didn't own. The land was better for the fact that the new subway was putting in a station within walking distance. But the lot was expensive, beyond the means of the Junior Circuit, so aid from other interested parties was sought. League representatives urged I.R.T. Construction Company contractor John B. McDonald to buy the site and lease it to the ball club, convincing him the field could promote subway traffic. McDonald took the proposal to August Belmont II, the principal financier of the subway construction. Belmont was persuaded to support the plan. Then the idea was vetoed by the I.R.T. director, and plans for the East Side site were abandoned. The I.R.T. director was Andrew Freedman.

Ban Johnson, after running into similar difficulties with several more proposed ballpark sites, realized he needed a political bigwig (i.e. gangster) on his side to do battle with Freedman. It was March 1903, less than two months before the season would start. Johnson's problems were solved when Tammany Hall front man Joseph Gordon, representing William Devery and Frank Farrell, approached him with a deal. Lots had been lined up at 165th Street and Broadway where the American League team could build their ballpark, if Gordon were granted the franchise. Johnson sold the New York franchise to the Gordon syndicate for $18,000, and he had his site.

Farrell was an ex-saloonkeeper who owned 250 pool halls across the city. He was known as a syndicate bookie, and as bag man for Boss Sullivan, syndicate chieftain.

The lots Gordon rented (for $10,000 a year) were in an underdeveloped section of town and belonged to the New York Institute for the Blind. The land was a mess. It wasn't level—it really was on top of a hill—and it consisted of a lot of weeds growing atop a rockpile. Even after an enormous amount of excavation, after the ballpark was built there, the land never lost its slumlike appearance. Local district leader Thomas McAvoy nabbed the $200,000 excavating and $75,000 building contracts.

Problems down the line included accessibility to the site. Only one train line went past, a solid 50-minute ride from Wall Street and City Hall. Owners hoped completion of a new West Side Subway in 1904 would help the problem. As it turned out, the second subway line to the park wasn't completed until the 1906 season, when the average travel time was cut in half.

Naturally, Andrew Freedman did his best to sabotage the efforts of the new league. He circulated petitions to stir up community opposition to the park. Petitions said the ballpark's presence would encourage the existence of saloons, disorderly conduct, and the community's demoralization.

The Washington Heights Board of Improvements denied the petition by a three-to-two vote. Freedman requested that the city run streets through the site. Opposition continued even after the park was built, but the new team had friends in City Hall to protect their investment.

In the November elections, friends of the Highlanders were defeated by Washington Heights residents, angry about the new park.

A Flimsy Edifice. Hilltop park cost only $75,000 to build. It was the last ballpark to cost anywhere near that figure. The ballpark building craze of 1909 would change America's image of what a ballpark was supposed to be, and it would pass the New York American League team by. The Highlanders—who got their name because Joseph Gordon was their president and the Gordon Highlanders were the best known regiment in the British army—would be the last team to rebuild in concrete and steel. By the time they did they were known as the Yankees, and they built the grandest of concert halls for the music of ash and sphere: Yankee Stadium.

Hilltop consisted of a flimsy edifice, free of ornamentation, made entirely of wood except for a masonry foundation. It had a seating capacity of 16,000, including 1500 25-cent seats. The field was dirt thrown on top of rock, and no money was ever put into upkeep. The place was about to collapse when the club was sold for $460,000 to Colonel Jacob Ruppert, a brewer, and Colonel Tillinghast Huston, an engineer-contractor.

A useful feature was parking lots for carriages and cars inside the grounds behind the grandstand. The owners originally pledged to keep the outfield fences clear of unsightly advertisements. There were ads all over the outfield walls by 1907.

Hilltop Park, New York, N.Y. (Compliments of the New York Yankees.)

When the Highlanders made their debut at Hilltop Park on April 30, 1903, 16,000 showed up—a capacity crowd. Ban Johnson arranged for each fan to receive an American flag while going through the turnstiles. At three o'clock, the ballplayers queued up on the field and marched from the outfield toward home, where they stood at attention while the 69th Regiment Band played "Washington Post March," followed by "The Star-Spangled Banner."

On the first club to play in Hilltop Park, Wee Willie Keeler hit .315, and Jack Chesbro won 21 games, as the Highlanders finished just within the first division.

The site of the ballpark is currently occupied, as it has been since 1925, by the Presbyterian Hospital, with the maternity ward along the former first base line.

Dyckman Oval (Inwood Hill Park Playground)
Negro National League 1922, 1923–30 (Cuban Stars, Cuban Stars West), Eastern Colored League 1923–28 (Cuban Stars East, Bacharach Giants), Negro American League 1929 (Cuban

Stars East), Negro East-West League 1932 (Cuban Stars). *Location:* In Inwood Hill Park. 214th Street (left field), Seaman Street (first base).

Owner of the Cuban Stars Alessandro Pompez (pom-PAY) installed lights in Dyckman Oval in 1930, making it the first ballpark in New York equipped for night games.

Cuban Stars games were frequented by Harlem nightclub entertainers like Louis Armstrong, Eubie Blake, Count Basie, Lionel Hampton, Cab Calloway, and the Mills Brothers.

The ballpark functioned as Harlem's amusement park to the north, at the very tip of Manhattan. Pompez was one of the richest men in New York, having made his fortune running numbers for the Dutch Schultz mob.

By the 1940s, Pompez had moved his team to the Polo Grounds, where the money was better. The team name was changed to the Cuban Giants.

Dyckman Oval is still a ball field. The round ticket booth is freshly and colorfully painted at the entrance, and a foundation for five rows of concrete seats stands around the infield, now shrunken to Little League size. The lights are gone and the oval-shaped plot has been divided into three playing fields.

One of the most beautiful locations in Manhattan, the oval is on a low plain, the only flatland for miles, surrounded by rocky and woody hills, with the blue span of the Henry Hudson Bridge crossing the gorge of the Spuyten Duyvil Creek to the Bronx beyond left field.

Catholic Protectory Oval

Eastern Colored League 1923–26 (Lincoln Giants), Negro National League 1935–36 (Cubans). *Location:* The Bronx. East Tremont Avenue, Unionport Road.

Sometimes referred to by old-time ballplayers as the "Catholic Protection" or "Capital Texture," the park was so small that no one could hit a triple there except Cool Papa Bell—and even then there were always complaints he'd missed second.

Dexter Park (Bushwick Park, Sterling Oval) *see* Brooklyn, New York

Jasper Oval (Hebrew Orphan Asylum Oval)

Eastern Colored League 1920s (Bacharach Giants, some games). *Location:* West 138th and West 136th streets, Convent Avenue, St. Nicholas Terrace, on the campus of the City College of New York.

This was an all-dirt CCNY athletic field and probably didn't have much or any seating. It had been an athletic field a long time, since the nineteenth century, when the closest building was the Hebrew Orphan Asylum, on the other side of Amsterdam Avenue to the west. The asylum was big enough to hold 1200 orphans.

In the late teens, CCNY built their athletic stadium in between this field and the asylum. The asylum became an army hall. Lewisohn Stadium across Convent Avenue dwarfed Jasper Field. The land is now the site of CCNY's indoor athletic complex, which includes

the college Hall of Fame.

At the site of the Hebrew Asylum now is the Schiff School (formerly PS 192) and a paved playground with a big backstop and a concrete grandstand big enough to hold 750 people. The little kids that play there swatting a rubber ball with a broomstick (even though there's a drizzle) say the park doesn't have a name.

Lewisohn Stadium

Home of City College of New York baseball circa 1910s and 1920s. *Location:* Amsterdam and Convent avenues, West 136th and 138th streets, on the campus of the City College of New York.

A tri-oval with a pillared amphitheater around the Amsterdam Avenue side, the side that faced the imposing Hebrew Orphan Asylum. Used by the college for baseball, football and track and field. At the corner of Convent Avenue and 138th Street, the northeast corner of the grounds, was the entrance to the campus, celebrated by an ornamented gate over Convent Avenue. Across 138th Street was the main campus. Across Convent Avenue was Jasper Oval (see above). Kitty-corner to the south was the Sacred Heart Convent. The Stadium was on the current site of the CCNY library. Like Jasper Oval, Lewisohn Stadium's playing field was completely dirt.

Yankee Stadium

American League 1923–73, 1975–present (Yankees), Negro National League 1936–48 (Black Yankees). Also used, until 1973, for Giants football. Owned by the New York Yankees. *Location:* East 157th Street (first base side), River Avenue (right field), East 161st Street (left field), Ruppert Place (third base). *Land purchased (20 acres):* February 5, 1921. *Construction costs:* (1927) $2.5 million. *Dimensions:* (1973) Left field, 301 feet; left center, 457 feet; center field, 461 feet; right center, 367 feet; right field, 296 feet. 82 feet

Lewisohn Stadium, 1942. Copy of CCNY yearbook photo by Maria Grasso.

between home plate and the backstop. (1988) Left field, 318 feet; left center, 399 feet; center field, 417 feet; right field, 310 feet. *Seating capacity:* (1973) 67,224, broken down as follows: loge, 135; lower boxes, 10,459; lower grandstand, 14,543; mezzanine boxes, 3995; mezzanine reserved, 8785; upper boxes, 4857; upper grandstand, 10,712; bleacher, 13,738. (1975) 57,545. *"New" Yankee Stadium regular season single game attendance record:* 55,802 (April 5, 1988, New York 8, Minnesota 0, Opening Day). *First game:* April 18, 1923 (New York 4, Boston 1). *Last game in "Old" Yankee Stadium:* September 30, 1973 (Detroit 8, New York 4). *Lights installed:* 1946.

It's unclear why the Yankees left the Polo Grounds. Maybe they were asked to leave because the Giants were jealous of their popularity. Maybe they wanted to leave to avoid the possibility of future rent hikes by the landlord Giants. Maybe Ban Johnson, president of the American League, was trying to drive the Yankee owners, Colonels Ruppert and Huston, out of baseball. We know it was February 6, 1921, that the Yankees publicly announced the purchase of 10 West Bronx acres, right across the river from the Polo Grounds. The $675,000 chunk of land, resting 16 minutes by subway from Times Square, had belonged to the estate of William Waldorf Astor. The site was particularly pleasing to Colonel Ruppert, who picked it out, because it was right across the Harlem River from the Polo Grounds, in full view of fans watching Giant games. It was the same site that had been considered and rejected in 1890 by the Players League, who chose the eventual location of the Polo Grounds instead, and by the American League in 1903, before the construction of Hilltop Park. Back then the land was considered too far from the beaten path, but the growing roots of New York's public transportation system (specifically, the recently completed Jerome Avenue, Bronx extension of the Lexington Avenue subway), had brought the beaten path to the Bronx.

The Yankees announced the proposed stadium would be shaped like the Yale Bowl, and enclosed with towering embattlements. Unless you bought a ticket, the release said, you'd have to be in an airplane to see the action. Silently, the Yankees designed a ballpark that favored left-handed power.

Yankee Stadium, New York, N.Y., Opening Day, 1923. (Photo furnished by the National Baseball Library in Cooperstown, N.Y.)

An early proposed model showed a stadium triple-decked and roofed all the way around. This illustration has appeared in several books as an accurate model of the early stadium – yet the creature never existed.

When first constructed, the triple-decked grandstand made it to neither foul pole, and you could see the game fine, though from quite a distance, from both the roofs of the buildings across River Avenue and the trains passing behind right field. Always the right field seats were reachable by batted balls (that being the direction Ruth hit them), while Death Valley bulged outward in left. (Only recently, accommodating Dave Winfield and then Jack Clark, has the left center fence been brought in nearer to home than 400 feet.)

The construction materials were as follows: earth (for grading), 45,000 cubic yards; Pacific Coast fir lumber, 1 million feet (shipped through the Panama Canal); concrete, 20,000 cubic yards; reinforcing steel, 800 tons; structural steel, 2200 tons; steel casings, 135,000; maple lumber, 400,000 pieces; and brass screws, 1 million.

The Yankees' new home was the first baseball park to be called a stadium. According to Steven A. Riess in *Touching Base,* the change in terminology indicated a new willingness to acknowledge baseball's urban setting. "The rustic titles and the layouts of earlier parks were rural metaphors, which had reinforced the agrarian ideology of baseball." The site's name no longer reflected the plot of land upon which it was built, the field of play, as would be the case if it were known as "grounds," or "field," but rather the structure around the playing field. Yankee Stadium's name not only tells us that the structure is the thing, but brags about its size. More so then – but even now, for certain – Yankee Stadium boggles through size alone. Like New York. It is a beautiful place, but impresses one first by its awesome size. Compared to Yankee Stadium, most other ballparks look small and kind of cruddy.

The stadium's presence had an immediate favorable effect on property values in the neighborhood, especially to the blocks immediately east of the structure. Small restaurants, parking lots, bars and a theater opened. Drug-

Yankee Stadium, New York, N.Y., as it looked in 1926—the original design, with a dirt track running through the outfield. Note that the upper decks of the grandstand do not make it as far as the foul poles. (Photo furnished by the National Baseball Library in Cooperstown, N.Y.)

stores installed lunch counters. In 1923, the Concourse Plaza Hotel opened nearby, and catered to visiting ball clubs.

The home opener was perfect. As 60,000 watched, Babe Ruth baptized the citadel with a game-winning homer.

During its first season, there were 20 inside-the-park home runs hit in Yankee Stadium. The outfielders just hadn't figured it out yet.

Appropriately, the Giants and the Yankees met in that year's World Series. For the games at the new stadium, Giants manager John McGraw refused to allow his players to dress in the Yankees' visiting clubhouse. Instead, the National League pennant-winners used their own clubhouse and took cabs across the Central Bridge to the game.

Murderer's Row and the House Ruth Begrudgingly Moved Into. On April 13, 1927, Opening Day for the greatest baseball team of all time, the jam around Yankee Stadium began before

noon. The unreserved seats were filled by three. Along River Avenue, in the back of the park, New York's Finest formed lines, allowing only ticket-holders to pass.

According to the *New York World,* "By game time the vast structure was packed solid. Rows of men were standing in back of the seats and along the runways. Such a crowd had never seen a baseball game or any other kind of game in New York."

Yankee general manager Ed Barrow said the club wanted to sell even more tickets, but couldn't without breaking fire and police rules against clogging the runways.

Seventy-two thousand attended the game. These consisted of 62,000 paid admissions, 9000 invited guests, and 1000 who had passes. It is still the New York City Opening Day attendance record—one not apt to be broken soon due to diminishing ballpark capacities.

The Seventh Regiment Band played loudly. Ushers wore red coats and tried to maintain order, the older ones closer to the field. (Career-wise, ushers work their way down the ladder. In a ballpark, the higher the seats, the smaller the tip.)

At 3:25, Yankee skipper Miller Huggins went to the A's dugout, Pied Piper to the photo corps. He was greeted on the top step by Connie Mack, a man imitating a stick figure. As the tiny Huggins posed, arm around the stringbean Mack, they looked like Mutt and Jeff.

The band began to oompah, and the teams marched onto the field in columns of four. According to the *New York World,* the Athletics wore "blue silk blouses, quite snappy...." The band and the ballplayers marched into Yankee Stadium's cow pasture of an outfield and were joined there by a southpaw in civvies pushing a four-foot-high baseball. After the playing of the National Anthem, mayor Jimmy Walker—sitting in Colonel Ruppert's box—threw out the first ball to "little Eddie Bennett, the Yankee mascot." His Honor, knowing a photo opportunity when he saw it, threw out the first ball twice, just to make sure everybody got a good shot. Mayor Walker liked it at Yankee Stadium. The composer of "The Sidewalks of New York" was later married in center field. A man announced the starting batteries through a megaphone, and the game began. There was no electronic public address system until the mid-1930s.

In 1927, Ruppert reduced the price of his 22,000 bleacher tickets from 75 cents to 50 cents. It was a popular move. Ruppert had, by far, the most 50-cent seats in the majors, but he made the move work by keeping the seats filled. As late as 1985, bleacher seats at Yankee Stadium cost only $1.50, less than a Big Beer—still the largest number of cheap seats in the majors.

Until 1928, the triple-decked grandstand reached neither foul pole. The bleachers surrounded the outfield, which was graded so the playing sur-face sloped upward approaching the outfield wall. A dirt track cut through the outfield. By the beginning of the 1928 season, the grandstand was extended beyond the left field foul pole. In 1937 and 1938, the triple decking would be extended past the foul pole in right as well, presenting the possibility of "upper-deck homers" in both directions. At that time the old wooden bleachers were torn down and were replaced by the enlarged grandstand. Babe Ruth hit most of his home runs into that wooden bleacher, which had been known as Ruthville. Separating the wooden bleachers from the playing field had been a ten-foot chicken wire fence. Outfielders poked their throwing-hand fingers through the holes as they watched a Ruthian blast fall into Ruthville. (To see Yankee Stadium the way it looked when Ruth played there, watch the movie *The Winning Team,* with Ronald Reagan as Grover Cleveland Alexander. The producers used shots of the old, old Yankee Stadium in their rear projections.)

Later, they would call Yankee Stadium "The House That Ruth Built," but as of May 14, 1927, Ruth himself claimed he preferred hitting in the Polo Grounds, where he had swatted 54 and 59 home runs in 1920 and 1921.

"Yes, (the Polo Grounds) is a good ball park to hit in. All the parks are good except the Stadium. There is no background there at all. But the best of them is the Polo Grounds. Boy, how I used to sock 'em in there. I cried when they took me out of the Polo Grounds," Ruth said to a *New York Sun* reporter. Of course, the Babe changed his tune by the end of the 1927 season when his home run total registered 60.

In the 1930s and 1940s the Yankees made extra money by renting out their ballpark to the Black Yankees during road trips. The Black Yankees, owned by Bill Robinson, were year after year the worst ball club in town, perennially finishing last in the Negro National League.

On October 6, 1943, Game 2 of the World Series was temporarily halted by a low-swooping army plane that came dangerously close to clipping the upper deck. In 1945, on Opening Day, members of the Communist party picketed Yankee Stadium carrying signs that called for the integration of the major leagues.

The first night game was not played in Yankee Stadium until 1946. In 1953, the ballpark was sold to Earl and Arnold Johnson of Kansas City. In 1955, John Williams Cox bought the ballpark, sold the land to the Knights of Columbus, and left the structure to Rice University in 1962. Yankee Stadium got its first message scoreboard in 1959. It was painted a fresh blue and white in 1966, and those are the colors it has remained. In 1972, the Yankees signed a 30-year lease to play in the new Yankee Stadium starting in 1976.

The old Yankee Stadium had a 15-foot brick-lined vault beneath second base which contained the electronic equipment necessary to run a boxing ring-press area on the infield.

The Monuments. Since 1932, the greatest Yankees have been honored with monuments in Yankee Stadium's outfield. The first to receive such an honor was Miller Huggins, the little man who managed the Yankees to three World Championships and six American League flags. Huggins died suddenly in 1931. His monument, which looked to many, especially young children, like a gravestone, was dedicated on Memorial Day, 1932. In 1941, Lou Gehrig was posthumously honored in a center field ceremony, and Babe Ruth received his, also posthumously, in 1949. The initial three monuments sat on the playing field ten feet in front of the wall in straightaway center, part of the hitter's background, in front of the flagpole, also in play. Long drives rolled behind the monuments and had to be retrieved, offering delightful moments of comedy or tragedy. No outfielder looked good

when a ball got rattling around the "gravestones." Fans were allowed to exit the stadium through a gate in center on the warning track, thus allowing the plaques to be read.

•

MILLER JAMES HUGGINS. *Manager of the New York Yankees, 1918–1929. Pennant winners 1921-22-23-26-27-28. World Champions 1923, 1927 and 1928. As a tribute to a splendid character who made priceless contributions to baseball and on this field brought glory to the New York club of the American League, this memorial erected by Col. Jacob Ruppert and baseball writers of New York, May 30, 1932.*

•

HENRY LOUIS GEHRIG. *June 19, 1902–June 2, 1941. A man, a gentleman, and a great ballplayer whose amazing record of 2,130 consecutive games should stand for all time. This memorial is a tribute from the Yankee players to their beloved captain and team mate.*

•

GEORGE HERMAN "BABE" RUTH. *1895–1948. A great ball player, a great man, a great American. Erected by the Yankees and the New York Baseball Writers, April 19, 1949.*

•

In 1969, plaques were put out there in honor of Joe DiMaggio and Mickey Mantle. When Yankee Stadium was torn down and rebuilt, 1974–75, the monuments and plaques were moved into Memorial Park. Plaques were added commemorating Jacob Ruppert, Edward Grant Barrow, Joe McCarthy, Casey Stengel, Thurman Munson *(Our captain and leader has not left us today, tomorrow, this year, next ... our endeavors will reflect our love and admiration for him),* Elston Howard and Roger Maris.

Two other plaques, placed by the Knights of Columbus, commemorate the masses said by Pope Paul VI in 1965 and Pope John Paul II in 1979.

Lou Gehrig, top, *then Babe Ruth say goodbye in Yankee Stadium, New York, N.Y.*

The Bronx County Building. Since 1933, the Bronx skyline beyond the Yankee Stadium bleachers and the el has been dominated by the Bronx County Building, where the borough's courthouse is located.

The structure, two blocks from the ballpark at 861 Grand Concourse, was dedicated June 15, 1934, by Bronx president James J. Lyons.

The 161st Street Station on the D and 4 lines is populated by locals, lawyers, and, on game day, Yankee fans.

Rain Delay. During a rain delay in August 1987, 200 general admissions (mostly day care groups and their harried adult supervisors) sat crowded up under the small roof over the third deck. A Yankee blue tarp, matching the outfield walls and the mostly unfilled seats, covered the infield. Above the right field bleachers, Diamond-Vision showed Ruth and Gehrig and the Murderer's Row. The whole Yankee history was shown. Gehrig's farewell. Ruth's farewell. Larsen's perfect game. Mantle and Maris. Reggie. Thurman Munson trying to get up and

Top: *Old Yankee Stadium, New York, N.Y., as it looked in the 1960s. (Compliments of the New York Yankees.)* Bottom: *New Yankee Stadium, retaining the magic of the original. That thing sticking up out of the ground near the main entrance is a huge baseball bat, business end down. (Compliments of the New York Convention and Visitors Bureau.)*

falling and trying to get up. Righetti on the Fourth of July. If, by some chance, you didn't already know the glory of Yankee tradition, the Yankees reminded you every five minutes. If there's a Yankee team in heaven, you know they gotta helluva nine.

The roof is smaller than it used to be, and its hanging facade has been removed—though a replica of that facade sits atop the billboards and scoreboards over the bleachers. The kids under the roof could see right down into Monument Park, between the bullpens in left, out of whose center grew the Yankee Stadium flagpole. Out in the right field bleachers (the left field version isn't used until the other is full), a few diehards were standing all the way in the back, with their backs pressed against the wall beneath the BUD and CITIBANK signs. They were the only ones who couldn't see the TV. Outside there's a walkway where there used to be a street, and the wall behind the bleachers blocks the view of the playing field from the elevated train, preventing the casual viewing that used to go on out there. Some things are the same, like the view of the game from the back of the lower or middle deck. In *Five Seasons,* Roger Angell called this view "a narrow, skyless slot of intense green, framed between the black of the overhang mezzanine and the black of the seated crowd below: a game vista that an auto-mechanic might have from under a stalled DeSoto." The refurbishment cost over $100 million, three times the construction cost of Royals Stadium in Kansas City—but the refurbishment was necessary. If the new Yankee Stadium had not been built, the Yanks would be playing in the Meadowlands by now.

The children up here in general admission, who—like New York—came in all different sizes and colors and shapes, reflected no disappointment or frustration about the dingy weather or the lack of a ball game. The ballpark was infinitely preferable to wherever they would have been otherwise. For them it was a social scene. They had box lunches or hot dogs to eat, Cokes to be drunk. It was Yankee Clipboard Day, the last weekday day game of the season, so everyone fourteen and under got a back-to-school clipboard. Then the Yankee History video ended and John Fogerty's "Centerfield" segued into Yankee organist Eddie Layton's version of "New York, New York." How different this crowd was from the Friday night version (against the Red Sox maybe) when the average fan seemed an adolescent 25 and looking for trouble. As this rain delay grew longer, one mostly heard the sound of children laughing.

At 1:35, a half-hour after the game was to begin, it was still so dark that the lights were having a noticeable effect, and the clouds were ready to touch the top of the Bronx County Building in right. It was still raining. Nonetheless, the grounds crew came out to remove the tarp. There was a small cry of approval. Most had found other ways to occupy themselves, and didn't notice. Without a game to distract the fans, the ballpark had become the thing. Sand was poured on the infield, while water on the outfield was raked toward the drainage holes. Ron Guidry started to warm up in the Yankee bullpen.

After 2½ innings, the rains came again. The grounds crew quickly rolled the tarp back into place and then surrounded it and grabbed it at the edges to straighten it. Some wind got up under the tarp and for a moment it looked as if they were trying to corral an ocean wave.

There'll be no baseball today. Hold on to your raincheck.

Olympic Field

Eastern Colored League 1928 (Lincoln Giants), Negro American League 1929 (Lincoln Giants). *Location:* East 138th and East 135th streets, Madison and Fifth avenues, current site of the Riverton Apartments.

John J. Downing Stadium (Randalls Island Stadium, Triborough Stadium)

Negro National League 1938 (Black Yankees). *Location:* Eastern Parkway, Vesta Avenue, Sutter Avenue, Powell Street, on Randalls Island. Also home of the North American Soccer League's Cosmos in 1975, and the World Football League's Stars in 1974.

Park still exists. When Ebbets Field was torn down, the light towers were moved here.

59th Street Sandlot

Negro National League 1939 (Cubans). *Location:* East 59th and East 60th streets, First Avenue and Sutton Place.

The Cubans played beneath the approach ramps to the 59th Street Bridge. Ballpark expert Philip Lowry delights in saying the Astrodome was the second ballpark with a roof.

Infield was made of dark gray cinder and ash, which, if you've ever played in the stuff, is great for bunting, but terrible for running—and no doubt cool from being in the shade.

William A. Shea Municipal Stadium

National League 1964–present (Mets), American Legue 1974–75 (Yankees). Owned by the city of New York. Designed by Praeger-Kavanaugh-Waterbury. *Location:* Willets Point, Flushing Meadow Park. Grand Central Parkway (first base side), Van Wyck Expressway (third base), 126th Street (left field), Roosevelt Avenue (right field). *Dimensions:* Left field, 341 feet; left center, 371 feet; center field, 410 feet; right center, 371 feet; right field, 341 feet. 70 feet from home plate to the backstop. *Seating capacity:* 55,101. Field boxes, 10,583; loge boxes, 2272; loge reserved, 6582; press level boxes, 1086; mezzanine boxes, 3660; mezzanine reserved, 10,542; upper boxes, 4020; upper reserved and general admission, 16,356. *Mets single game attendance record:* 57,175 (June 13, 1965, versus Los Angeles). *Mets season attendance record:* 3,027,121 (1987). *Yankees day game attendance record:* 50,828 (August 3, 1974, versus Boston). *Yankees doubleheader attendance record:* 42,915 (July 14, 1974, versus Oakland). *Yankees night game attendance record:* 33,784 (September 17, 1974, versus Baltimore). *Yankees twi-night doubleheader attendance record:* 46,448 (September 24, 1974, versus Boston). *Yankees opening game attendance record:* 26,212 (Detroit, April 11, 1975). *First National League game:* April 17, 1964 (Pittsburgh 4, New York 3). *First American League game:* April 6, 1974 (New York 6, Cleveland 1).

Shea was never that great to look at, with its cookie-cutter shape, view of Flushing, and the seats (except for the corporate field boxes) set back too far from the field—but that doesn't mean it can't be a great place to be. Shea is far more innocently joyous than Yankee Stadium. Watch. It's April 1985 . . . *Gooden into the seventh with a no-hitter going against the Phils on a Friday night in front of a packed house . . . the crowd singing "Take Me Out to the Ball Game" at the top of its lungs, louder than it has ever been sung before, during the seventh inning stretch . . . then, on the Number 7 train after the victory—a three-hit shutout by the Doc—everyone on the packed car sings "God Bless America" feeling like they're in a Frank Capra movie . . .* You see? Innocent joy.

William Shea and the Return of the National League. Ground was broken on October 28, 1961, for Shea Stadium, a ballpark that would replace the decrepit Polo Grounds as the home of the Mets. It opened 29 months later with 24 ramps and 21 escalators. The park's opening coincided with the 1964 New York World's Fair next door, and Shea Stadium was the unisphere of stadia. It was built on the site of both the 1939–40 and 1964–65 World's Fairs. The escalators went all the way to the top, the highest and most sophisticated escalator system ever built up till that time.

The Mets had been brought to town by William Shea, when the National League expanded to ten teams in 1962. Shea is the thriving attorney (his firm employs over 400 lawyers) who was appointed chairman of Mayor Robert Wagner's Baseball Commission and brought National League baseball back to New York, following the abandonment of the city by the Giants and Dodgers.

The Mets, originally, were owned by Mrs. Joan Payson, who was about as much like a mother hen (behind those wacky sunglasses) as an owner could be.

Out in right field, behind the home run fence, was a huge scoreboard, which, despite being mostly advertisement, was radically new in its information-giving capabilities in 1964. It was 86 feet (seven stories) tall and 175 feet long. It took 80 miles of wiring to make it operate. At the time the Mets hawked like a carnival barker, "An attraction in itself is the Stadiarama Scoreboard which keeps fans advised of games elsewhere, helps fans on the scene keep score, shows pictures, responds in brilliant colors to music played on the stadium organ, and actually has a memory."

Everything at the new ballpark was not perfect. As of June during the opening season, there was still no telephone service to the structure.

Six weeks after Shea opened in 1964 the San Francisco Giants were in town for a doubleheader, an event that took nine hours and 52 minutes to accomplish. The first game lasted 23 innings. There were 47 strikeouts in the game by 12 pitchers, a triple play, and 15 consecutive scoreless innings. For awhile Willie Mays played shortstop. The twin bill was not finished until 11:25 at night. Since there were no phones, the press had to messenger their reports to the World's Fair, where they could be called in.

On June 21 of that year Jim Bunning pitched a perfect game against the Mets, a "that figures" kind of way to make it into the record books. Right from the start, the Mets had developed a tradition of losing. They lost a lot and they lost big. Sometimes they lost in bizarre ways. Casey Stengel was their manager and public relations man extraordinaire. He called the Mets the Amazin's, a name that's stuck, at least among New York's considerable press. They won only 53 games in their third year, their first at Shea, but only the Dodgers outdrew them in the National League, and they outdrew the Yankees by 400,000 fans. Because of Casey, and the joy of having a team to root for that

wasn't steeped in tradition, there was something going on at Shea. It wasn't completely serious, but it sure was a lot of fun. At Yankee Stadium there was a rule: no banners. Shea had a Banner Day. Here came the Ebbets Field people, their broken hearts just mending, who thought of their ball club as family. Sure they yelled and went berserk when their boys messed up, but they always forgave and they always came back.

In the summer of 1965, just before celebrating his seventy-fifth birthday, Casey slipped and fell at Toots Shor's and fractured his hip. At Shea the next day, over 50,000 sang "Happy Birthday" to Casey as the ol' perfessor watched from a hospital bed.

The losing tradition has not lasted. It left for awhile in the early Tom Seaver years, came back, then left again with the arrival of Gooden and Strawberry— hopefully to stay. The Mets have brought New York two World Championships (in 1969 and 1986) and a National League pennant (in 1973). These are numbers a Chicago Cubs fan would die for, but merely enough to whet the appetite of a town that's used to dynasties.

Home Opener '88. Brand new in 1988, across the blue stadium's outer facade is a piece of minimal(ist) art, a squiggly line here, a dot there. At first it looks like chaos, then arranges in the brain into a pitcher winding up. (The first night game of the year reveals the squiggly lines to be made of neon lights, green and red, making one fan comment from the number 7 train, "Shea looks like a brand new Mexican restaurant.") On the other side is a similar neon design, this one of a batter. Gone are the big white letter slogans that crossed the outer stadium in years past, like, "Watch the Stars Come Out," "Catch the Rising Stars," "Ya Gotta Believe," etc. With the Mets established as yearly contenders, such slogans are no longer necessary.

From the top of the stadium there's a

Shea Stadium, New York, N.Y., as it looked when used for American League play. (Compliments of the New York Yankees.)

view of the Throgs Neck and White-stone bridges, Flushing Bay, LaGuardia Airport—whose traffic will inevitably make Keith Hernandez step out of the batter's box at least once per game—and the skyline of New York, predominantly the World Trade Center and the Empire State Building. Surrounding the park are the multitude of expressways that seem to converge here.

It is 47 degrees at game time, which is seasonable anyplace else, but bitter at Shea, with its unmistakable April wind off the bay. Day games are tolerable if you bundle, but early-season night games can be cruel. But, unlike Candlestick, Shea enjoys improving weather by May.

On the field the Rocky Point High School Golden Eagles Marching Band and the Joint Services Color Guard stand in formation. In straightaway center is a bag of balloons, in Mets blue and orange, ready to go.

Just to the right of the balloons is the big red apple sticking out of its upturned black top hat. It will recede

before the game starts, only to emerge again in case of a Met home run. DiamondVision is behind the picnic area, and the bullpens behind the left field fence. Out in right is the huge scoreboard, still mostly advertising.

Vice-president George Bush throws out the first ball to Gary Carter, accompanied on the mound by Bill Shea. Shea Stadium is celebrating its twenty-fifth anniversary.

Between innings the P.A. system plays instrumental oldies: "Rebel Rouser" by Duane Eddy, "Tequila" by The Champs, and "Wipe Out" by the Surfaris. Listen for "The Peter Gunn Theme" upon future visits.

The red apple gets to rise from its top hat sheath in the second inning as an uncannily smooth Darryl Strawberry deposits a Pascual Perez fastball in front of the scoreboard. That proves to be all the Mets need, though they get more, as Ron Darling completes his shutout just as the chill gets through the last layer of clothing.

Lads from Liverpool. Here's where, in the summer of 1965, the Beatles helicoptered in, played, and left, all in plenty of time to fit in an hour TV special. The stage was set up between second base and the mound. No one heard the Beatles. Not a note. There were 53,275 people there, and all of them were screaming thirteen-year-old girls wearing harlequin-framed glasses. Five rows of wooden horses surrounded the field between the grandstand and the Fab Four. Five hundred of New York's Finest were there. Plans were for the Beatles not to announce their final tune so that an armored car could grab them and whisk them away at the end of the show, before the fans had an opportunity to charge. But Paul forgot and said, "And now, for our lust num-buh..." and a wild scene ensued, cops grabbing four and five girls apiece, hauling them back into the seats.

A year later, on August 23, 1966, the Beatles played a return engagement. But it was the summer after John's unfortunate Beatles-are-more-popular-than-Jesus remarks. Only 46,000 were there and the energy level was noticeably down. Some people even heard the music. Six days later the Beatles gave their last concert at Candlestick Park in San Francisco.

Shea's been used for other rock concerts, too, concerts that used the new technology so everyone could hear. Everyone in Queens, that is. Grand Funk *(We proceeded to tear the hotel down!)* Railroad on July 9, 1971, drew 47,200. The Who drew 70,346 and 69,976 for two shows on October 12 and 13, 1982, and the Police drew 66,404 on August 18, 1983.

Shea has also been the home of international soccer matches, boxing (Nino Benvenuti versus Emile Griffith, middleweight championship fight, September 29, 1967; Sugar Ray Leonard versus Roberto Duran, WBC welterweight title bout, June 20, 1980), professional wrestling, a cricket match (drawing 4197 in 1978, better than some Mets dates that year), Pope John Paul II on tour October 3, 1979, college football,

roller derby, and, of course, Joe Namath and Jets football. The New York Football Giants (1975) and the New York Yankees (1974–75) played here while Yankee Stadium was being rebuilt.

Newark, Delaware

Delaware Field
   Home of the University of Delaware Fightin' Blue Hens (Yankee Conference) 1965–present. *Seating capacity:* 500.

Newark, New Jersey

Wiedenmeyer Park (Davids' Stadium 1926–31, Bear Stadium 1932–33, Ruppert Stadium 1934–67)
   International League 1912–25, 1931–49 (Bears), Negro National League 1936–48 (Eagles). Site of Games 2, 6 and 7 of the 1946 Negro League World Series. *Location:* Hamburg Place (now 262 Wilson Avenue), Avenue K. Current site of an industrial park. *Dimensions:* (1936) Left field, 305 feet; center field, 410 feet; right field, 305 feet. *Fire:* 1926. *Torn down:* 1967.
   In 1915, the Newark Feds went head-to-head with the city's International League franchise and won. The IL team relocated in mid-season in Harrisburg, Pennsylvania. Wiedenmeyer Park burned in 1926 and became Ruppert Stadium. For one game in 1904, this ballpark was home field for the New York Highlanders of the American League. They played Detroit here on July 17.

Effa and the Eagles. The steadiest occupants of the site were the Newark Eagles of the Negro National League. They were owned by Abe and Effa Manley — but it was Effa who was really in charge. Too much in charge sometimes. It was agreed by all, however, that Effa Manley was quite a dish, and a very difficult woman to say no to. She once experimented with giving signals to Eagles batters from her box seat. Crossed legs meant bunt; uncrossed, swing away. That lasted until there was a serious beaning.

Effa drove the real manager, Biz Mackey, crazy—once ordering him to change his starting rotation so she could show her girlfriends what a hunk one of her pitchers was.

She wanted Satchel Paige to pitch for her and paid $5000 for his contract, but Satch split for Latin America instead. Later Effa admitted that Paige wouldn't report to Newark unless she agreed to be his "sideline girlfriend."

At Ruppert Stadium, right field was the largest of the outfields. The outfield bellied out from the foul pole in right. Distances were kept short in left by bleachers that went from the left field corner to center.

The death of Negro League baseball following Jackie Robinson's debut in the National League can be accurately plotted by the attendance figures for the Newark Eagles: (1946) 120,000; (1947) 57,000; (1948) 35,000, at which point the Manleys got out of the baseball business.

Harrison Field

Federal League 1915 (Peppers), American League 1918 (New York Yankees, Sundays only), National League 1918 (Brooklyn Dodgers, New York Giants, Sundays only). *Location:* Harrison, New Jersey. Middlesex, Second, Third, and Burlington streets. *Fire:* August 23, 1924.

In 1915 in Newark the Federal League was competing for attendance with a Triple-A franchise. The Peppers attempted to stimulate attendance by combining bike races with baseball games. It didn't work.

Railroad tracks (the Hudson & Manhattan, and the Pennsylvania) ran along both sides of the park, which was only a block from the Passaic River.

Newark Schools Stadium

Eastern Colored League 1926 (Stars). *Location:* North Tenth Street, Bloomfield, Roseville, and First avenues.

A football stadium. When set up for baseball, distances down the lines were so short that balls hit over the fence there were ground rule doubles.

Meadowbrook Oval

Negro National League 1934–35 (Dodgers). *Location:* South Orange Avenue, 12th Street. *Dimensions:* Left field, 300 feet; center field, 380 feet; right field, 300 feet. *Fences:* Twelve feet all the way around.

Newark, New York

Colbern Park

New York–Pennsylvania League 1968–87 (Orioles). *Dimensions:* Left field, 330 feet; center field, 390 feet; right field, 330 feet. *Seating capacity:* 2000.

Karl Zimmermann in *Upstate* magazine describes Colbern Park as "dowdy" and "little," with "its box seats (relics of some grander, long-gone stadium), its dugouts painted Orioles orange, (and) its left field stanchion out in the middle of 'live' foul territory well-padded against careening outfielders."

This franchise was moved to Erie, Pennsylvania, for the 1988 season.

Newport, Kentucky

Wiedemann Park

Ohio State League 1914 (Brewers), also home of the semi-pro Wiedemann team. *Location:* 11th and Lowell streets. Currently the foot of the Shortway Bridge. *Seating capacity:* 4000. *Cost of construction:* $14,000.

A year after nearby Covington, Kentucky, failed in its attempt to bring organized baseball to Cincinnati's Kentucky suburbs via the outlaw Federal League, Newport gave it a shot. The

Colbern Park, Newark, N.Y. Note the single row of box seats behind the backstop. (Photo by David Pietrusza.)

town, behind magnate Charles W. Sturr, acquired a franchise in the Ohio State League, and fielded a team transferred intact from a defunct Marion, Ohio, franchise.

The Brewers started the season on the road, winning one and losing one against Chillicothe. With the team on the road, Newport officials made plans for the Home Opener. County employees were to be given a half-day off. A parade committee was formed. Local businessmen offered a $25 prize to the company that could fit the most employees on their float. Here's the way *The Kentucky Post* described the Home Opener:

"Undaunted by the chilly breezes from the Licking River, several thousand fans of Newport stuck through the game ... and saw the home boys defeat Chillicothe in a well-played game by a score of 5 to 4. The baseball parade that preceded the game was a fine one and the teams were cheered repeatedly as they paraded the streets before the contest. The streets were gaily decorated with flags, and the auto parade made a fine showing. The entire force of the city and county officials took part in the parade. Commissioner

of Public Property Herman Riesenberg made a hit by having his men wear red, white and blue hats."

The team got off to a good start but soon floundered, and the fans stopped coming. On June 11, it was announced that the directors of the Newport Exhibition Company had decided to give up on their attempt to supply minor league baseball to the people of Newport at popular prices. The franchise was moved to Paris, was rechristened the Paris Orphans, and continued to do poorly, both on the field and at the gate. As had been the case in other communities (*see* Fort Wayne, Indiana, and Covington, Kentucky), there was an inverse relationship between pre-season hoopla and long-term team success.

Wiedemann Park later became well known for softball. It was the first ballpark in the Cincinnati area to have lights, and was the home of Newport High School football until 1936.

Newport News, Virginia

League Park
Virginia League circa 1910 (Pilots). *Seating capacity:* 3000.

City Park
Virginia League circa 1916 (Ship-
builders). Seating capacity: 3250.

Horowitz Field
Virginia League circa 1928 (Ship-
builders). Seating capacity: 3000.

War Memorial Stadium
Piedmont League 1948-55 (Baby
Dodgers), Carolina League 1963-71,
1974, 1976-present (Peninsula Senators
1963, Peninsula Grays 1964-68, Peninsula Astros 1969-70, Peninsula Phillies
1971, Peninsula Pennants 1974, Peninsula Pilots 1976-85, Peninsula White
Sox 1986-87, Virginia Generals 1988-
present). Built: 1947. Location: Pem-
broke Avenue. Dimensions: Left field,
335 feet; center field, 400 feet; right
field, 335 feet. Seating capacity: 4600.
Record Carolina League attendance:
102,424 (1965, first place). Record
Carolina League low attendance: 27,406
(1984, third place). 1987 season attendance: 88,620.

Wayne Johnson of the Newport
News Baby Dodgers faced the Norfolk
Tars' Whitey Ford in the very first game
played in War Memorial Stadium in
1948. Tim Thompson, who still comes
out to the ballpark on a regular basis,
was the catcher that year for the
Dodgers. Don Otten arrived a year
later, maybe the tallest pro ball player
ever at seven feet even. Otten switched
to a larger ball and made some money
in the National Basketball Association.

Niagara Falls, New York

24th Street Stadium
Home of baseball in Niagara Falls
before 1936.

Sal Maglie Stadium (Hyde Park
Stadium 1936-83)
P.O.N.Y. League 1939-40, Middle
Atlantic League 1946-47, 1950-51, In-
ternational League 1967-68 (Buffalo
Bisons), New York-Pennsylvania

League 1969-78 (Pirates), 1983-present
(White Sox). Architect: Ben Long
(originally designed for track and
field). Dimensions: Left field, 327 feet;
center field, 410 feet; right field, 327
feet. Seating capacity: 4000.

On Saturday, October 17, 1936,
President Roosevelt dedicated Niagara
Falls' new ballpark with a speech from
the playing field, before over 7000 spectators: "This particular stadium may be
called boondoggling, but it's pretty
good boondoggling in creating such
projects as these. The government
policy is to think not only of the practical necessities of public works, including water systems, sewage disposal
plants, and similar projects, but to
develop that kind of thing which is
useful to us and our children in recreational life."

Used for track and field and football,
Hyde Park Stadium did not host minor
league baseball until 1967, after city
riots drove the Bisons out of Buffalo.
For minor league baseball, the park was
extensively refurbished. Sod, fences,
lights, and paint were all new, through
the efforts of mayor E. Dent Lackey
and city manager David O'Hara.

The highlight of the Bisons' two-year
stay was the exhibition game played
against the Washington Senators in
1968, which drew over 7000, the biggest
crowd since the F.D.R. dedication.

By the winter of 1982, Hyde Park
Stadium was showing its age. The
Niagara Gazette called for its refurbishment. Only seven of the original
eight light towers were standing. The
eighth had been knocked down in a
wind storm a few years before. Baseball was returning to Hyde Park Stadium after a five-year absence. There
were worries that the park might not be
safe, and mayor Michael C. O'Laugh-
lin was wondering where the money
would come from. The field needed
work, and though the green-on-green
paint job was wearing well, the signs of
the walls still advertised the defunct
Pirates.

So the park was fixed up. On June 21, 1983, the park was officially renamed Sal Maglie Stadium, and the "Barber" was there, along with a little over 500 fans. The crowd wasn't so big, but they went home happy. Chuck Tanner's son Bruce made his pro debut for the Niagara Falls White Sox, blanking the Newark Orioles over the final three innings, as the home team rallied from behind to win 6–4.

The refurbishment didn't make everyone happy. Karl Zimmermann, writing in *Upstate* magazine, called it "a ballpark not worthy of the famous native son to whom the blue-green concrete mass of crumbling Art Deco detailing had recently been dedicated."

There was a municipal swimming pool as part of the complex, and, according to Zimmermann, foul balls often "ended their trajectories with a splash."

Norfolk, Virginia

For the first half of the twentieth century, Norfolk minor league teams (always known as the Tars, usually playing in the Virginia League) played in ballparks known as *Lafayette Park, League Park, Bain Field, High Rock Park,* and *Myers Field,* each with a seating capacity of around 7000.

Metropolitan Park
International League 1971–present (Tidewater Tides). *Location:* Interstate 64, Military Highway. *Dimensions:* Left field, 341 feet; center field, 410 feet; right field, 341 feet. *Seating capacity:* 6216. *Built:* 1970. *Single game attendance record:* 6466 (May 5, 1970, versus Syracuse Chiefs). *1987 season attendance:* 175,104.

Bud Metheny Baseball Complex
Home of the Old Dominion Monarchs (Sun Belt Conference), present. *Dimensions:* Left field, 320 feet; left center, 375 feet; center field, 395 feet; right center, 375 feet; right field, 320 feet. *Seating capacity:* 3000.

Equipped with lights, the Old Dominion ballpark, named after the longtime coach, is called "Bud's Place" by the students there. It has locker rooms, concession stands, offices, and a fully enclosed press box.

Arthur "Bud" Metheny was Old Dominion's baseball coach 1948–80. He had a 441–369 record. In 1983, he was voted into the College Baseball Coaches Hall of Fame in Dallas. Metheny started for the New York Yankees in the second and last games of the 1943 World Series. He was a Yankee from 1938 to 1946.

Norman, Oklahoma

Dale Mitchell Park
Home of the University of Oklahoma Sooners (Big Eight Conference), present. *Seating capacity:* 2500.

Nuevo Laredo, Mexico

La Junta
Mexican League, Zona Norte, present (Tecolotes de los dos Laredos). *Dimensions:* Left field, 330 feet; center field, 400 feet; right field, 330 feet. *Seating capacity:* 7000.

West Martin Field
Mexican League, Zona Norte, present (Tecolotes de los dos Laredos). *Dimensions:* Left field, 330 feet; center field, 400 feet; right field, 330 feet. *Seating capacity:* 6000.

Nuevo Laredo, Mexico, and Laredo, Texas, are directly across the Rio Grande from one another.

Oakland, California

Oaks Park (Emeryville Park)
Pacific Coast League 1913–57 (Oaks). *Location:* Emeryville, California, be-

tween Oakland and Berkeley. 1120 Park Avenue (left field), San Pablo Avenue (third base), 45th Street (first base), Watts Street (right field), current site of a soft drink bottler. *Built:* 1913. *Dimensions:* Left field, 335 feet; center field, 407 feet; right field, 329 feet. *Size of plot:* Seven acres. *Record season attendance:* 550,000 (1948). *Torn down:* 1957.

A long, low grandstand surrounded the field, except in left field, where there were billboard signs for Mortensen's Rug Cleaning and Calo Cat and Dog Food. The roof was small, covering only the seats directly behind home, but it was large enough to have a press box sitting on top. Near the end of this ballpark's life, when it was pretty run down, the left field fence deteriorated each time a ball struck it—splintering a lot for line drives, less for fly balls.

Oakland-Alameda County Coliseum

American League 1968–present (Athletics). Owned by Alameda County. *Location:* Hegenberger Road (first base side), Nimitz Freeway (home plate), 66th Avenue (third base), San Leandro Boulevard (center field). *Dimensions:* Left field, 330 feet; left center, 375 feet; center field, 400 feet; right center, 375 feet; right field, 330 feet. (1968) 90 feet between home plate and the backstop; (1969) 60 feet. *Fences:* (1968) Eight feet all the way around; (1981) Ten feet. *Seating capacity:* 48,621. Lower reserved, 15,377; loge boxes, 1488; second deck reserved, 11,219; third deck reserved, 13,537; bleacher, 7000. *First game:* April 17, 1968 (night, Baltimore 4, Oakland 1). *Surface:* Grass.

Built inside a hole in the ground so it can barely be seen from the outside. Has a tremendous amount of foul territory, so batters rarely get a second chance after hitting a foul pop. Home of the A's dynasty of the early '70s, and currently the stage for the Canseco-

McGwire Show. Architecturally drab, but a good deal warmer than Candlestick on the other side of the bay.

Ogden, Utah

John Affleck Park

Home of Ogden baseball circa 1975. *Nickname:* John Affliction Park.

This was another one of those parks set up so that the sun set in batters' faces, a factor known to warp players for life. For a while the minor leagues were sprinkled with athletes who would answer gripes by saying, "You think this is bad, you shoulda played in Ogden."

Ogdensburg, New York

Winter Park (currently Father Martin Park)

Canadian-American League 1936–1940 (Colts), Border League 1946–51. *Dimensions:* short left field fence. *Seating capacity:* 1800. *Lights:* 1946 (constructed by Bradley & Williams of Syracuse). *Cost of lights:* $17,500.

The president of the Canadian-American League was Father Harold J. Martin, from South Boston. Before becoming a priest, he was a pitcher on the Fordham University baseball team that featured the Fordham Flash, Frankie Frisch. He went on to play pro ball and got as high as the Eastern League before he found something else to do with his life. He joined the priesthood.

Martin couldn't get baseball out of his blood and continued to play semi-pro ball in Ogdensburg under the name O'Reilly. Martin's bishop happened to watch "O'Reilly" pitch one day, and after the game questioned him about his activities. Martin explained that he was making $75 a game, all of it going toward the new recreation center. The elder man looked Martin in the eye and asked if the team needed a $50 first baseman.

Oakland-Alameda Coliseum, Oakland, Calif. (Compliments of the Oakland A's.)

The priest's pitching days were through after his eyesight was damaged by ammonia fumes while he pulled an unconscious man from a burning building.

There are stories told that Martin would give away everything that was given him. He worked in a mission church so cold he left it at night to sleep in the hospital. He owned no coat, so one day a rich man gave him one. The minister promptly gave the coat to a derelict who lived in the church, a man Martin said needed it more.

"Spencer Tracy should play the role," says baseball historian David Pietrusza. "Father Martin got Ogdensburg's recreation center built. It was Winter Park."

When pro baseball came to town in the form of a Canadian-American League franchise in 1936, this is where they played — and Martin was given ⅓ ownership of the ballclub.

Because of the way the streets were, the fence in left field was very short, and it was not uncommon for home runs to smack off the houses on the other side of that fence. Local Barney Hearn says, "You could urinate over that left field fence."

Lights were not installed at Winter Park until 1946, when a Border League franchise played here. When that league folded, after the single campaign, the Winter Park lights were removed and sold to Valley Field in Quebec City, Quebec.

The site still holds an athletic field, called Father Martin Park, but there are no lights or stands.

Oklahoma City, Oklahoma

Stiles Park

Home of Oklahoma City baseball circa 1890–1900. *Location:* Northeast Eighth and Harrison streets.

The first settlers in Oklahoma came to Indian Territory in the famous rush of 1889. The run began April 22 at noon, and almost instantly there was baseball. That first summer there were two ballparks with temporary seating used, one west and one east of Oklahoma City. The first permanent grandstand in town was built the following year at Stiles Park, and this facility served as the community's premiere baseball diamond until the turn of the century.

Colcord Park

Independent 1902–03, Southwestern League 1904 (Metropolitans), Western Association (Class C) 1905–08 (Metropolitans), Texas League (Class C) 1909–11, Oklahoma State League (Class D) 1912 (partial season). *Location:* West of Delmar Garden, along the bank of the North Canadian River, near Western and Exchange avenues, at the current site of the Public Market.

According to a memo in the Oklahoma Historical Society's files, "The establishment of a modern park at Delmar Garden and the probability of a line of the street car system being laid to that place revived interest in the year 1902, and a baseball club was formed that proposed promotion of a permanent league. Seymour C. Heyman was elected president." Heyman was a clothing merchant and a civic leader who had been president of the Oklahoma Chamber of Commerce in 1903. Delmar Garden was "a popular amusement center." Baseball left Oklahoma City in the middle of the 1912 season and did not return until six years later, this time a mile down the river.

Western League Park (I)

Western League 1918–23 (Indians). *Location:* On the bank of the North Canadian River, about a mile south of where Colcord Park was located.

It was Seymour Heyman again who saw to it that there was baseball in Oklahoma City. He found a Western League team in Hutchinson, Kansas, that was looking to move.

The ball club was run by John Holland, Sr., who had been manager and part-owner since 1910, when the club played its games in St. Joseph, Missouri. A fiercely competitive man, Holland seldom smiled and was known to linger at the ballpark long after a game was over, brooding about a defeat. His other character references? Well, he'd been fired from the Santa Fe Railroad and traded by at least three minor league baseball teams when he decided to get into management. Holland led the Indians to a Western League pennant in '23. When the team moved the following season, the new park was named after Holland.

State Fairgrounds

Western League 1923 (Indians, some games). *Location:* Northeast Eighth and Eastern streets.

The Indians won the Western League pennant by half a game in 1923. The pennant-winner was determined the last day of the season on a muddy field set up before the grandstand at the State Fairgrounds—the use of which was necessitated by a flood. (At Western League Park the water was up to the fourth row of the grandstand.) About ten games were played at the Fairgrounds site, but for the championship game that field was too wet also, so a new diamond was marked off out in the outfield.

This fairgrounds site now holds a football stadium used by Douglass High School.

Holland Park (Western League Park [II], Tribe Park, Texas League Park)

Western League 1924–32, Texas League 1933–42, 1946–57. *Location:* NW Fourth Street, Pennsylvania Street, current site of a waterworks. *Dimensions:* Left field, 335 feet; center field, 385 feet; right field, 337 feet. *Seating capacity:* 8500.

Evidence indicates John Holland chose this site for his new ballpark because of its access to the Linwood streetcar line, showing foreknowledge of Oklahoma City's 1930s growth pattern. In 1933, Holland, who was originally from El Paso, realized a dream by moving his team into the Texas League. When Shreveport's ballpark burned down, Holland took their spot. He died in 1936 following a stroke, after watching his ball club barely survive the Depression. In 1934, for example, attendance dropped to 52,610. By 1935, it was back up to 121,289. In 1942, the ball club was run by John Holland, Jr., and this time it was the war that was destroying minor league baseball. In 1942, the Indians drew under 37,000 for the year. The whole Texas League disbanded from 1943 to 1945.

Ma. Beginning in 1940, the manager of the Indians was Rogers Hornsby, the most famous baseball personality to wear an Oklahoma City uniform. He quit in the middle of the 1941 season (June 23) because the Indians were having trouble meeting payroll. On a team filled with gruff men who cursed and scratched and spit brown liquid, Rajah was on the coarse side.

But there was one Oklahoma Indian fan who called Hornsby "Honey" and got away with it. That was Mrs. Ella Barham, who was then in her early sixties. Mrs. Barham never missed a game at Holland Field. She'd been thoroughly addicted to watching baseball games since she was ten and the neighborhood boys wouldn't let her play. They said it was okay if she watched while she did her sewing — and that is what the woman had done since. A lot of the players probably didn't know her name. They just called her "Ma" and she beamed with maternal joy when she looked at all of her boys, no matter how they acted, and that included the chaw-chewing skipper. It also included pitcher Hub Kittle, who wore his hat on the back of his head, chewed a cigar, and had this expression on his face like he knew something you didn't, probably about women.

Mrs. Barham had a house at 209 Northwest Second Street, but eventually she moved in with Mrs. M.J. Weinand, 1501 Northwest Fourth Street, because it was a shorter walk to the ballpark. Having no radio, Ma listened to road games in the lobby of the Noll Hotel. In 1939, she baked Indian Manager Wilcy Moore a birthday cake, delivering it with a timid knock at the clubhouse door. Moore invited her in to meet the boys, and she was a part of the family from that day forward.

She remained a fixture around Holland Field until the late '40s.

In 1941, 6000 people attending Holland Field on Aluminum Night brought along six truckloads of the important "defense metal." A contest was held to see who could bring in the most aluminum. Trembly Bakery won with 19 pounds (three gunny sacks full) of milk bottle tops. C.J. French and C.J. French, Jr., won a $25 savings bond for bringing in 16 pounds of aluminum window molding. A schoolteacher named C.A. Morris brought in 15½ pounds of pots and pans, thus leading to the next day's headline in the paper, "It All Pans Out Fine at Holland Field."

Baseball Returns After the War. Attendance was up when baseball came back to Holland Field in 1946. For the resumption of play in the Texas League, 120,334 showed up — more than triple the 1942 attendance.

A fan could choose from six different kinds of beer at Holland Field: Griesedieck Brothers, Silver Fox, Progress, Gold Seal Premium, Muehlebach Pilsner, and Falstaff. Many ordered a Griesedieck because they just liked to say it.

In 1949, the ballpark became Texas League Park. The team became part of Bill Veeck's Cleveland Indian farm system. Veeck put some money into the Oklahoma City ballpark. Everything got a fresh coat of paint, and 700 new box seats were installed.

The stadium was roofed and single-decked, with many obstructions supporting the roof. Until the '40s, at least, fans were allowed to sit on folding chairs on the field in front of the stands, on either side of the dugout — as well as stand up on the roof, where the press box was built behind home. These practices were stopped for safety reasons.

All-Sports Stadium

American Association 1962–present (89ers). *Location:* May Avenue, 10th Street (State Fairgrounds). *Built:* 1958,

1962. *Dimensions:* Left field, 343 feet; center field, 420 feet; right field, 343 feet. *Cost of scoreboard:* (1962) $48,000; (1983) $200,000, computerized, with updated statistic capabilities, a dot race, animation, and graphics. *Lights:* Eight towers, between 120–135 feet high. Each tower has 500 bulbs, each of 500-watt strength. *Seating capacity:* (1958) 3000; (1975) 11,000; (1985) 12,000. *Record season attendance:* 370,087 (1985). *1987 season attendance:* 277,722. *First American Association game:* April 19, 1962 (Omaha 6, Oklahoma 5).

In July 1958, Roy (father of Cot) Deal, head of the Oklahoma City Amateur Baseball Association, went to the city council proposing the construction of a new ballpark on the State Fairgrounds. Deal and his group had purchased the lights and part of the bleachers to Texas League Park. Deal asked the city for $5000 to move the structures he already had, grade a ballfield, and build a concrete grandstand and backstop. The park would seat 3000. The city sold some property in the northwest corner of Oklahoma City and used those funds to finance the ballpark.

Community cooperation got All-Sports Stadium built in 1958. The Oklahoma Gas and Electric power crews erected the light towers. Companies sold materials at cost, and craftsmen donated time.

In 1961, the city council obtained an American Association franchise. The new ballpark was improved to AAA standards. A contest was held — a 100-word-or-less essay contest — to name the new team. Grade school teacher Mrs. Velma Petree submitted the winning essay, in which she noted that "the name 89ers ... stands for pioneers starting from nothing to build a future."

Many thought All-Sports Stadium resembled Holland Park. Both ballparks pointed in the same direction and gave views of the city skyline from the stands. Both parks had the clubhouses down the right field line. But this playing field was bigger, the scoreboard was in left instead of right, and the outfield fence had only one deck of signs instead of two.

Opening Night. The park was finished and ready for baseball in the nick of time. The doors opened at 5 p.m., Thursday, April 19. Trucks were still sprinkling the parking lot and the approach roads. The scoreboard was filled with electricians who were completing the wiring. That afternoon the new 89ers had been given a parade through downtown. Over 10,000 learned a valuable lesson in the heartbreak of baseball as the new ball club blew a three-run lead in the ninth and lost to Omaha.

In 1984, All-Sports Stadium became one of the first minor league ballparks to have luxury boxes. They are leased both to companies for the season (at $6000 per annum) and to private groups on a nightly basis ($250 per game).

In 1985, the ballpark received a new sound system. Speakers were placed on top of the left field fence for equal distribution of sound throughout the park.

In 1986, All-Sports Stadium received some sprucing up. Thirty new light fixtures ($30,000 worth) were installed. The clubhouse facilities were renovated, as was the picnic area on the hill along the left field line. The "hilltop terrace" was constructed prior to 1986 to add a festive atmosphere. Concessions are sold out there. Bring your own blanket.

Once a year there's a Beach Boys concert after an 89ers game.

Old Orchard Beach, Maine

The Ballpark

International League 1984–88 (Maine Guides, Maine Phillies). *Location:* One Park Way. *Dimensions:* Left field, 327 feet; center field, 402 feet; right field,

327 feet. *Fences:* Eight feet all the way around. *Turf:* Grass. *Seating capacity:* (1985) 5000; (present) 5500. *Single game attendance record:* 6215 (July 23, 1984, versus Pawtucket). *Season attendance record:* 183,289 (1984). *1987 season attendance:* 104,219.

Omaha, Nebraska

Johnnie Rosenblatt Stadium (Omaha Baseball Park)
American Association 1969–present (Royals). *Location:* Deer Park Boulevard, later Grover Street (left field), South 13th Street (third base), B Street, later Bert Murphy Drive (first base), Tenth Street (right field), Henry Dorley Zoo (center field). *Built:* 1950. *Dimensions:* Left field, 343 feet; center field, 420 feet; right field, 343 feet. *Fences:* Nine feet all the way around. *Seating capacity:* (1975) 14,000; (1985) 15,000. *1987 season attendance:* 251,995.

Oneonta, New York

Damaschke Field (Elm Park, Neahwa Park)
Eastern League 1924 (Giants, partial season), Canadian-American League 1939–51 (Indians, Red Sox), New York–Pennsylvania League 1966–present (Yankees). *Location:* Main Street and Neahwa Place. *Dimensions:* Left field, 337 feet; center field, 403 feet; right field, 341 feet. *Seating capacity:* 4000. *1987 season attendance:* 48,903.

Damaschke (pronounced like what you would use to open your Damasch) Field is a ballpark for teetotallers. You can't buy alcoholic beverages inside, and you're not allowed to carry them in.

Baseball has been played on this site since 1903. That year Louis R. Morris donated the land, then known as Elm Park, to the City of Oneonta. The community first got to see minor league baseball here when the Eastern League

Utica franchise moved here August 1, 1924, to finish the season before moving again. In the 1940s, Neahwa Park, as it was then known, housed the Red Soxes' Class C team. During that time the name was changed to honor E.C. "Dutch" Damaschke, vice president of the Oneonta Red Sox of the Canadian-American League and chairman of the city of Oneonta's Recreation Committee.

Today, Damaschke Field is a bit on the beat-up side, but it's a great place to eat. The sausage and peppers at the concession stand are particularly good.

Orlando, Florida

Tinker Field
Florida State League 1946–61, 1963–72, Southern League 1973–present. Spring home of the Minnesota Twins 1963–present. *Location:* 287 S. Tampa Avenue, Colyer Street, Orange Blossom. *Renovation:* 1963. *Dimensions:* (1963) Left field, 332 feet; center field, 412 feet; right field, 332 feet. *Seating capacity:* (1960) 3500; (1985) 6000. *1987 season attendance:* 69,656.

Before crowded games, the public address announcer at Tinker Field says, "Please move closer together in your seats so we can get more people in." And everyone moves closer.

The Twins have trained in Orlando since 1961, their first year. As the Senators they trained here for 25 years before that, starting in 1936.

Tinker Field sits beside the huge Citrus Bowl football stadium and has a three-ton memorial to Clark Griffith. Five hundred wooden seats from Griffith Park are in Tinker Field, at the top of the covered grandstand.

University of Central Florida Baseball Complex
Home of the University of Central Florida Knights (independent schedule), present. *Seating capacity:* 2800.

Top: *Damaschke Field, Oneonta, N.Y., as it looked back in the days when it was known as Neahwa Park. (Photo from the personal collection of David Pietrusza.)* Bottom: *Boardwalk and Baseball at Baseball City, Orlando, Fla. Here's the main playing field's press box (top level) and the Stadium Club Restaurant (lower level), along with the seats behind home. (Photo by David Pietrusza.)*

Baseball City

Florida State League 1988–present (Baseball City Royals). Spring home of the Kansas City Royals 1988–present. *Location:* Routes 4 and 27. *Seating capacity:* 6500.

It's a baseball park. No, it's an amusement park.

It's a baseball park *and* an amusement park! Two parks in one!

Competing for tourist dollars with EPCOT and Sea World, Baseball City offers you a heck of a lot more than just baseball. There's "A Taste of Cooperstown," a 1000-square-foot showcase of memorabilia; 30 rides, including the awesome Monster and Florida Hurricane; a Boardwalk with theaters and eateries; and Professor Bubbles' Magical Factory.

The main stadium is the most sophisticated in baseball. It has a press box that seats more than some spring training facilities put together.

There is even a practice field with bleachers and a grandstand with a canvas roof behind home, so that a thousand or so people can sit comfortably and watch the B squad play its game.

Orono, Maine

Mahaney Diamond

Home of the University of Maine Black Bears (East Coast Athletic Conference), present. *Dimensions:* Left field, 330 feet; left center, 375 feet; center field, 400 feet; right center, 375 feet; right field, 330 feet. *Seating capacity:* 4000.

In 1987, a new entrance was built onto Mahaney Diamond, brick piers with connecting gates, beneath an arching sign spelling out MAHANEY DIAMOND, and a shrub-lined plaza between the gate and the grandstand. New lights were installed at about the same time so the diamond would conform to NCAA Regional Playoff standards. Two new metal stands, holding 670 apiece, were installed in 1986, raising the total seating capacity to 4000. The field was last re-sodded in 1984. At that time drainage was improved. A new warning track was built, and both dugouts got new water coolers. There are plans to install, by the 1989 season, a new building that would serve as (downstairs) new clubhouses and (upstairs) new athletic department offices. The building would be on the third base side. There are also plans for new restrooms. All of this is to be paid for by Larry K. Mahaney, class of 1951, former assistant baseball coach, now president of Webber Oil.

Osceola County, Florida *see* Kissimmee, Florida

Oswego, New York

Richardson Park

Empire State League 1905-07.

Torn down before the construction of Otis Field, and replaced by the county's public works garage.

Otis Field

Canadian-American League 1936-38 (Netherlands). *Built:* 1931. *Dimensions:* Left field, 550 feet; center field, 585 feet; right field, 428 feet. *Seating capacity:* 2000. *Lights:* 1936-39.

This site was used for semi-pro and youth baseball as early as 1931, but according to David Pietrusza, it didn't have outfield fences and seats until 1936, when the Netherlands of the Can-Am League began to play here.

It had a skin infield, despite suggestions from infielders that grass infields reduced bad hops. Because of the huge dimensions, only two balls were ever hit out of Otis Field.

The park was originally built as a semi-pro field over a garbage dump. It was named after Oswego mayor John Otis. The Can-Am team was owned by the Netherland Ice Cream and Milk Company, and therefore, in a fit of shameless commercialism, was named the Netherlands.

The lights were installed when the Netherlands moved in, making this the first field in the Can-Am League to have lights. However, the lights were so poor that they were removed two years later.

In the 1940s the ballpark was not used and the people of Oswego began to slowly but steadily dismantle it, taking the boards for firewood. (This isn't the only time the poor have taken apart their ballpark for firewood. *See* Boaco, Nicaragua.)

The grandstand was torn down in the 1950s so the site could be used for the Creighton Elementary School. The construction of the school turned out to be a big mistake. Someone forgot that the site had once been a dump, and

the new construction had serious settling problems.

Ottawa, Ontario

Lansdowne Stadium

Canadian-American League 1936-40
(Senators, Braves), Border League
1947-50, International League 1951-54.
Current home of the Canadian Football League's Roughriders. *Built:* 1909
(for football). *Construction cost:*
$100,000. *Seating capacity:* (1909-60)
10,000, (1961) 17,301.

A football stadium. When it was
used for baseball the short field was in
right. For a while no baseball fence was
built in left field, so balls hit past the
left-fielder rolled all the way to the back
of the far end zone. There were many
inside-the-park home runs. The fence
was not constructed until the middle of
the 1936 Canadian-American League
season.

During World War II, games were
played here while troops were stationed
at the ballpark, with barracks under the
stands and training on the field.

In 1966 the original grandstand —
which had been expanded in 1961 — was
demolished for the construction of the
Civic Centre (the city of Ottawa's
Centennial Project), which includes a
large exhibition hall and the new
Astroturf football stadium, seating
14,842.

Paintsville, Kentucky

Central Park

Site of a Negro Baseball Hall of
History game between former mem-
bers of the Paintsville Yankees and the
Pikeville Brewers on June 21, 1982.

Palatka, Florida

Azalea Bowl

Florida State League 1956-62 (Aza-
leas). *Seating capacity:* 2700.

Named after the town flower. Referred to by the players of the time
simply as "the Bowl." Built at the edge
of a swamp. Stands were ten rows high.
Crowds were predominantly black,
and sat in the segregated bleachers
along the left field line. Occasionally a
snake would slither out of the swamp
and under the outfield fence. Time was
called until the thing could be blud-
geoned to death with a Louisville
Slugger.

In *A False Spring,* Pat Jordan described another enemy that sometimes
crawled under the fence: tendrils and
vines from the foliage that hung over it.
"Often," he noted, "when an outfielder
chased a ball to the wall, those perverse
vines would tangle in his spikes and trip
him up."

The Azalea Bowl site is still designated as a baseball park on Palatka
maps, but the facility has not been used
for years. The grandstand is no longer
there.

Palm Springs, California

Angels Stadium

California League 1986-present (Angels). *Location:* Sunrise Way and
Baristo Road. *Dimensions:* Left field,
360 feet; center field, 408 feet; right
field, 360 feet. *Seating capacity:* 5185.
1987 season attendance: 52,313.

Paterson, New Jersey

Hinchliffe Stadium

Negro National League 1936-37,
1939-45 (Black Yankees). *Location:*
Walnut, Spruce and Liberty streets.

Still standing. Used for community
baseball.

Pawtucket, Rhode Island

McCoy Stadium

International League 1973-present
(Red Sox). *Constructed:* 1941 (WPA).

Location: School Street exit on Route 95 North. *Dimensions:* Left field, 325 feet; center field, 380 feet; right field, 325 feet. *Fences:* 16 feet all the way around. *Turf:* Grass. *Seating capacity:* (1975) 6500; (1985) 5810; (present) 6010. *Season attendance record:* 220,838 (1987). *Single game attendance record:* 9389 (July 1, 1982, versus Columbus).

Pennington Gap, Virginia

Leeman Field
Appalachian League 1937–40 (Lee Bears).

Last of the minor league ballparks with no outfield fence, where all homers were inside-the-parkers – and anything over an outfielder's head was at least a triple.

An August 1, 1938, issue of *Minor League Digest* said it was 1200 feet to the center field fence (900 feet to left and 600 to right), winning the 1938 Moot Stat Award.

Peoria, Illinois

Sylvan Park
Independent 1878 (Reds), Northwestern League 1879–82 (Reds), Interstate League 1883. *Location:* Approximately the current location of St. Augustine Manor, formerly the Proctor Home.

In 1878, when the Peoria Reds played an independent schedule against big league competition from Boston, Detroit, Cincinnati, St. Louis and Louisville, the ace of their pitching staff was 24-year-old Hoss Radbourne. The exact 1878 record of the future Hall of Famer is unknown, but he was undefeated.

Lake View Park
Northwestern League 1883–84, 1891, Central Inter-State League 1888–89, Western Inter-State League 1890, Illinois-Iowa League 1892, Western League 1898–1904, Three-I League

1905–17, 1919–22 (Distillers). *Location:* Across the street from the eventual site of Woodruff Field. *Seating capacity:* 2000.

Fancy grandstand.

In 1898, the ace of the Peoria pitching staff was Iron Man McGinnity. It was his last stop before arriving in the bigs at Baltimore the following year. He was 27 when he played for the Distillers.

In 1922, the last year Lake View was used for professional baseball, McGinnity returned to town, pitching for Danville of the Three-I League. The park was packed to see the Iron Man shut out Peoria 2–0 in the second game of a doubleheader. He was 51.

McGinnity ended his career with Dubuque of the Mississippi Valley League in 1925 and died four years later.

Woodruff Field
Three-I League 1923–35, 1937 (Tractors), 1953–57. *Location:* North Adams Street. *Seating capacity:* 8100. Grandstand, 2600; bleachers, 5500. *First game:* May 7, 1923. *Construction cost:* $50,000. *Lights:* 1930 (replaced 1953, fourteen 90-foot light towers). *Cost of lights:* (1930) $8000.

Park was built by the city across the street from 50-year-old Lake View Park, and named after a longtime Peoria mayor E.N. Woodruff. On Opening Day there was a parade (featuring several American Flags and a bunch of ballplayers who couldn't keep in step if their lives depended on it) that ended with a dedication at home plate.

The original ballpark had no press box. It would be added later on top of the roof behind home. The original fences were made of cinder block but were too deep for the modern game. An inner fence made of wood was later added. Railroad tracks ran past the first base side of the grandstand.

The Fall and Rise of Woodruff Field. The Depression ended baseball in Peoria in 1937. For 16 years, Woodruff

Field was a deteriorating arena, infrequently used. Paul King, sports editor of the *Peoria Journal Star,* notes that "the state semi-pro tournament was held there once. The Pittsburgh Pirates played there in an exhibition game, in 1938, against their Bloomington club in the Three-I League." The field was also used for the annual Knights of Columbus barbecue.

King goes on: "The park slowly acquired warts. The lighting system grew moldy. The grandstand roof fell apart. The seating disintegrated. The place, which owned such a proud heritage, became almost an eyesore.

"Then, after 15 years out of professional baseball, Peoria suddenly was back. A local group, headed by Bert Sanders, a Hiram Walker Distillery executive, plucked off a Three-I franchise, thus restoring the venerable league to eight-team status."

By March 1, 1953, the new Peoria team, with headquarters in the old Jefferson Hotel, had already received $30,000 in pledges from local citizens to pay for the remodeling of Woodruff Field. The team sent a scouting mission to visit Lanphier Park in Springfield to inspect the lights. The team's first manager was longtime Cardinal third baseman Whitey Kurowski, who gave frequent speeches around town to drum up support. A week later the winner of the "Name the Team" contest was announced. "Chiefs" was the victor. More press attention, however, was focused on Woodruff's new lights, which team general manager Carl Roth promised were going to be the best in the Three-I League. Also in the first week of March, preliminary work started on Woodruff Field. Old boards were removed. Local unions pledged free support in the rebuilding of the grandstand roof, the replacement of the lights, and the grandstand's new plumbing system. That spring the ballpark was completely transformed, largely through volunteer efforts. The Lambda Chi Alpha fraternity of Brad-

ley University voluntarily raked the entire field in preparation for fresh sodding. Those bills that did crop up were paid for out of donated and invested funds. Four hundred shares of Peoria Chiefs stock were sold to the community at $10 a share. Forty-five electricians joined to erect the light towers and get them functioning. Two thousand six hundred theater-type seats were put in the brick grandstand, while bleacher seats increased the total capacity to 10,100 — but 2000 of this consisted of bleachers borrowed from Bradley University, and those had to be returned two weeks into the season.

Opening night at the new Woodruff Field drew 7518. They watched Peoria strand 19 base runners, give up five home runs, and bow to Evansville 13–7. That year, Roger Maris played in the Three-I League for Keokuk. He hit 32 home runs, including a few over Woodruff Field's notably short right field fence.

During the five years that baseball returned to Peoria and Woodruff Field in the '50s, attendance steadily declined. In '53, 124,866 attended games, most in the league. In '54 that figure dropped to 78,497. In '57 it further plummeted to 54,737.

On August 12, 1957, 795 fans at Woodruff Field watched the first-place Peoria Chiefs' pitcher Don Nichols become a 20-game winner in a 10–7 Three-I League victory over the Cedar Rapids Raiders. All of his victories were in relief.

Baseball left Peoria at the end of that season and didn't return until April 15, 1983. The ballpark was sold to the Hyster Company in the late '50s. The state high school baseball tournament was held there briefly, but by 1970 the park had again "developed warts," and this time the case was terminal. The grandstand was torn down completely in the late '70s, but the site is still used for youth baseball.

Meinen Field, Peoria, Ill., at night. (Compliments of the Peoria Chiefs.)

Meinen Field
Midwest League 1983–present (Chiefs). *Location:* 1524 West Nebraska Street. *Dimensions:* Left field, 335 feet; center field, 385 feet; right field, 335 feet. *Seating capacity:* 5000. *Record season attendance:* 195,832 (1987).

When the park was built, the light tower next to the third base dugout was placed so that it inhibited the view of just about everybody sitting on that side of the grandstand. There is currently talk of moving the tower back and adding lights to compensate for the additional distance. Also on the drawing board is a 40-foot fence in left, a new press box, a new infield tarp, and additional restrooms and concession stands. The restroom situation has been critical when crowds are big. There's more than one way to keep a crowd on the edge of their seats.

Perth, Ontario

Perth Collegiate Institute Park
(P.C.I. Park)
St. Lawrence (Outlaw) League, be-

fore 1936, Canadian-American League (Class C) 1936 (Blue Cats, Royals). Owned by the Perth School Board. *Construction cost:* $3000. *Dimensions:* Left field, no fence (row of maple trees, 335 feet); center field, 420 feet; right field, 320 feet. *Fences:* Right field, four feet (snow fence). *Seating capacity:* 1500.

This was a high school field with bleachers constructed beside it for minor league play. The site had been used as an athletic field by P.C.I. since before the turn of the century. In 1936, this was considered the worst park in the Canadian-American League. At that time the infield was skin, a hard clay surface that was lightning quick. The outfield, likewise, was known for its hardness and speed.

There was no fence in left, just a row of maples. Batters couldn't hit the ball over, but they could hit the ball through.

Park is still used by the school district.

Petersburg, Virginia

Day Field
Virginia League circa 1911 (Broncos). *Seating capacity:* 3000.

Parkinson Park
Virginia League circa 1913 (Goobers). *Seating capacity:* 2800.

McKenzie Street Park
Virginia League circa 1919 (Trunkmakers). *Seating capacity:* 4000.

Shepherd Stadium
Virginia League circa 1941 (Generals). *Seating capacity:* 3500.

Philadelphia, Pennsylvania

Name of park unknown
Location: 15th Street and Columbia Avenue.

On October 1, 1866, this was the site of "The Great Game for the Championship of the United States." *Attendance:* 30,000. *Score:* Philadelphia Athletics 18, Brooklyn Atlantics 9. Scorecards, some of the first ever, were printed for this game.

Athletics Park
National Association 1871–75 (Athletics, White Stockings, two franchises), National League 1876 (Athletics), American Association 1883–91 (Athletics). *Location:* 25th, 29th and Master streets, Jefferson Avenue. *First National Association game (Athletics):* May 15, 1871. *First National Association game (White Stockings):* May 1, 1873. *Last National Association game (White Stockings):* October 25, 1875. *Last National Association game (Athletics):* October 28, 1875. *First National League game:* April 22, 1876 (Boston 6, Philadelphia 5. First National League game ever played, as all others scheduled for this day were rained out.). *Last National League game:* September 16, 1876. *Last American Association game:* October 5, 1891.

In 1871, a Philadelphia writer praised the Athletics' press facilities. "The reporters' stand will be placed directly back of the catcher," he wrote, "and will be sufficiently elevated to be out of the reach of strong foul balls that may chance their way."

An illustration of this park appears in the April 30, 1873, *New York Daily Graphic.* It was 500 feet to the center field fence, but the enclosure was narrow at the sides. The wooden stands were roofed on the right side as far as first base, and open the rest of the way down the line to the outfield fence. The American flag flew behind the far end of the grandstand while the 1871 National Association pennant flew from atop a pole behind the grandstand near first base, closer to the action than the Stars and Stripes. The pennant-bearing flagpole was beside a large tree, which grew right outside the park.

On Saturday afternoon, April 22, 1876, this was the site of the first-ever National League game. A large turnout saw Boston beat the Athletics 6–5, in a game that featured 26 errors and took 2:05 to play.

The Athletics' franchise was unsuccessful and did not last until the end of the year. Neither did George Armstrong Custer.

In 1883, the Athletics, now in the American Association, returned to the Jefferson Street ballpark, which was fixed up for the occasion. It was reported that "landscape gardeners" made the playing field as "level as a billiard table." A printed invitation was sent to Henry Chadwick, the sports writer and inventor of the box score, announcing that the Athletics had, "at cost of many thousand dollars, fitted the . . . park in first class order to cater to respectable audiences."

That year, every Thursday was Ladies' Day.

Oakdale Park
American Association 1882 (Athletics). *Location:* Eleventh and Hunt-

ingdon streets. *First game:* May 2, 1882. A's moved from here to the park abandoned six years before on Jefferson Avenue.

Recreation Park

National League 1883-86 (Phillies). *Location:* 23rd and 25th streets, Ridge Pike, Columbia Avenue. *First game:* May 1, 1883 (Providence 4, Philadelphia 3, winning pitcher Ol' Hoss Radbourne, attendance 1000). *Last game:* October 9, 1886 (doubleheader, Philadelphia 5, Detroit 1; Philadelphia 6, Detroit 1, 6 innings, darkness).

The franchise moved from Worcester to Philadelphia at the beginning of the 1883 season. Alfred J. Reach bought and transferred the franchise. Instead of keeping the former name, the Brown Stockings, Reach gave the new Philadelphia Nationals the moniker "Phillies." For the 1884 season, $2000 was spent on improvements. New players' benches were installed and bat racks for both teams were put in. In the reserved seat section the seats had numbers and the aisles were carpeted. Everything was painted, and flags flew everywhere.

The most common complaint about this ballpark was the financial distress caused by the loss of batted balls into the "Corinthean reservoir."

Keystone Park

Union Association 1884 (Keystones). *Location:* Wharton, Broad, Moore and Eleventh streets. *First game:* April 17, 1884. *Last game:* August 7, 1884.

Baker Bowl (Huntingdon Grounds, Philadelphia Park, National League Park)

National League 1887-1938 (Phillies). Also home of the National Football League (Eagles) 1933-35. Owned by the Philadelphia Phillies. *Construction cost:* (1887) $80,000. *Location:* Broad Street (right field), Huntingdon Avenue (first base), 15th Street (third base), Lehigh Avenue (left field). *Di-*mensions: Left field, 341 feet; center field, 408 feet; right field, 272-280 feet. *Fences:* (1887) 15 feet all the way around. (1895-1929) Left field, 40 feet. (1929-38) 60 feet. *Seating capacity:* (1895) 18,800. Field boxes, 2000; field stand reserved, 2500; grandstand, 11,300; bleacher, 3000. *First game:* April 30, 1887 (Philadelphia 15, New York 9). *Last game:* June 30, 1938 (New York 14, Philadelphia 1). *Burned:* August 6, 1894. *Torn down:* 1950.

This park was the successor to Lakefront Park in Chicago as the best big league baseball facility when it was built. It was the worst—by far—when it was finally abandoned. Considered proud and huge when dedicated, it was a bitter town joke by the time it rusted away. At its largest it held 20,000, half the size of other parks of the 1930s.

Built on a Dump. Alfred J. Reach, owner of the Phillies, and his partner, Colonel John I. Rogers, opened up their grand new ballpark on April 30, 1887. The site had formerly been a dump with a creek running through. Team manager Harry Wright raised the American flag on the center field flagpole while a military band played. Twenty thousand saw the Phillies trounce Tim Keefe and the New York Giants 15-9, in a slugfest that would prove representative of the offensive ball often played on this site in the years to come.

On August 6, 1894, a spark from a plumber's torch started a fire that destroyed the Huntingdon Grounds grandstand. The place went up completely. Even neighboring property was singed. $80,000 in damage resulted—and all of it was repaired, plus $40,000 in improvements.

The grandstand was replaced in concrete and steel, the first ever of this type. In 1896, when it reopened, the park was again being called "the best athletic ground in the world." At that time seating capacity was 16,000, with room for 4000 standees.

The steel grandstand, built in 1894 and 1895 to replace the wooden one that burned, was the first cantilevered construction in ballpark history. There were no obstructing beams. (Philadelphia would be prouder of this point if the ballpark hadn't repeatedly fallen apart while in use.) At this time, only 5500 seats were atop steel and concrete construction. The rest of the park was wood. (Also installed were several scheming poltergeists.) Stands went from foul pole to foul pole. There were simple bleachers in left, and a 40-foot sign in right advertising A.J. Reach Sporting Goods. This was understandable, as Reach owned both the Phillies and Philadelphia Park.

In the 1890s the Phillies franchise was the cheapest of the cheap. Players' passes were not honored. It was in the players' contract that they could be used to work at the gate. Players not starting that day were frequently employed in taking tickets.

A Few, Ahem, Eccentricities. Because of the shape and relief of the land upon which it was built, as well as some poor baseball sensibilities, the park had some odd dimensions and features.

There was a hump in deep center field, a sort of speed bump, caused by the underground Philadelphia and Reading Railroad tunnel beneath. It was the only major league outfield ever to rumble.

An unusual alley was formed in center field by the end of the left field bleachers, the front of the clubhouse, and the right field fence.

At the foul pole, the right field fence was only 272 feet away (it later got to be as far as 280 feet and 6 inches away when home plate was moved closer to the grandstand), and did not get much deeper in the right-center power alley. Left-handed hitters loved it, but the park was good for hitters in general. The outfield had fences that changed angles frequently, turning the arena into a goofy pinball machine.

Less skilled outfielders had nightmares about those walls, as they would later about the walls of Forbes Field

in Pittsburgh and Fenway Park in Boston. For example, Hack Wilson, playing for the Cubs in right field, liked to drink in Philadelphia. In 1930, when Hack hit 56 homers and knocked in an all-time record 190 runs, he could come into Baker Bowl with a hangover, go the other way for a couple of easy homers, and still have a bad day, chasing those "vulgarity balls off that vulgarity wall."

The center field "wall" was the stone and mortar foundation for the building that held the clubhouses. That's the sort of surface that efficiently removes the outfielders' skin upon contact.

For a while there was a small deck of seats on top of the clubhouse (probably for the 1915 World Series) and the seats in left extended in front of the clubhouse completely. But the rooftop and straightaway center seats were removed. There was a swimming pool in the basement of the clubhouse until World War I. It was quite a poke out there. No one ever hit a ball over the clubhouse roof, but Rogers Hornsby came the closest. He hit a home run through a clubhouse window in 1929. (That's the same clubhouse window Phillies manager Art Fletcher used to hang out the "Catfish Klem" sign after Umpire Bill Klem gave him the boot. It got a laugh from the sparse and bored crowd and cost Fletcher a hefty fine.) Part of the time there was an embanked 15-foot-wide bicycle track rimming the outfield.

The right field wall was made of rusting iron and bore the dents of the many balls that struck it. Atop the wall was a screen. Everything was in play. Pop-ups were out of there, line drives bounced back in bizarre ways. With the coming of the rabbit-ball era of the 1920s and 1930s, Baker Bowl's dimensions became ridiculous. As Roger Angell put it in his book *Five Seasons,* "The field was better suited for a smaller, narrower game — croquet, perhaps."

During the early part of the twentieth century, the Phillies were bad.

Philadelphia, Pa.: Baker Bowl's famous wall and its many dents as it appeared in 1938. For awhile a huge advertisement reading "Lifebuoy Health Soap Stops B.O." covered that wall. (Temple University Libraries Photojournalism Collection.)

According to a Philadelphia sports writer of the time, the most memorable event at Philadelphia Park between 1903 and 1911 was the birth of a baby boy in the ladies' room.

In 1910, Horace Fogel, the Phillies' owner, started a campaign to change the name of the club. He thought Phillies was too trite. The Quakers — as they were sometimes called — stood for peaceful people who refused to fight. Fogel pleaded with the press, "Why don't you fellows call the club the Live Wires!" In 1914, Fogel was ousted as a troublemaker.

The club passed into the hands of William Baker, who earned a reputation for cheapness, for which his deteriorating namesake became a symbol. It's not clear if the name of the park was ever officially changed to Baker Bowl. Nobody ever bothered to repaint the signs outside the park, which read, from construction to demolition, "National League Park."

Tragedy. On August 6, 1903, the ballpark became the site of one of baseball's greatest tragedies. During the game that day, a fight broke out on 15th Street behind the left field stands. Fans rushed to the top of the stands to get a bird's eye view of the action many feet below. Rotten joists gave way and hundreds of fans crashed down onto the street. Twelve were killed, 232 injured. Many lawsuits ensued. Shortly before the accident the former owners had assured the recent purchasers — a syndicate that included Barney Dreyfuss — that the ballpark was safe.

The ballpark was closed while repairs were being made. The Phillies played their interim home games in Columbia Park, the home of Ben Shibe's Philadelphia Athletics.

This was not the last time poor conditions at the ballpark resulted in death. Twenty-four years later, during a game between the Phillies and the Cardinals on May 14, 1927, an entire section of the right field stands collapsed with the weight of the crowd. Thousands of fans fell on top of those below. It was miraculous that the carnage wasn't worse. Many were injured, but there was only one death, a casualty not of the grandstand's collapse but of the following stampede onto the playing field. (Baker Bowl was not the only grandstand to collapse during a game, causing mayhem and death. *See* Cincinnati, 1884.)

Amazingly, the ballpark was not condemned right then and there, but was repaired. The Phillies got another ten years of use out of it.

Like the accommodations for the fans, those for the players became increasingly seedy as the years went by. As a cynical sports writer of the 1920s put it, "National League players will be pleased to learn that the visiting dressing room at Baker Bowl is being completely refurbished for next season — brand new nails are being installed on which to hang their clothes."

World Series Play. The ballpark was the site of three World Series games, games 1, 2, and 5 of the 1915 Series, which the Phillies lost to Boston in five games.

Game 1, on October 8, was played before 19,343, packing them in. The crowd saw Grover Cleveland Alexander scatter eight singles with that bread-and-butter sinker for a 3–1 victory, the Phillies' last World Series victory for many years. Crowds were 20,306 for each of the other two games.

On October 3, 1924, Baker Bowl was the site of Game 1 of the first "Colored World Series" between the Kansas City Monarchs of the Negro National League and the nearby (Yeadon/Darby) Hilldale team of the Eastern Colored League. Attendance for the game was a sellout 18,500.

The Natural Impulse of All Boys. In 1923, in a case that was in the papers, an 11-year-old boy named Reuben Berman was held in a house of detention overnight for keeping a baseball hit into Baker Bowl's bleachers. According to baseball historian Harold Seymour, the judge ruled that "a boy who gets a baseball in the bleachers to take home as a souvenir is acting on the natural impulse of all boys and is not guilty of larceny." Baseball would never be the same. Teams had no way of making fans, especially the young ones, give foul balls back. From that point on, every time one was hit out of play, the scramble was on.

Slugfest City. In 1934, Baker Bowl became the site of the first game to be played in Philadelphia on a Sunday. By that time the bowl was inflating batting averages and earned run averages alike. Baseball was a hitters' sport in 1930 — as never before or since — all over the major leagues, but nowhere like in Baker Bowl.

The highest team earned run average of all time was recorded by the 1930 Phillies, who allowed 6.7 *earned* runs per game. To put that figure in perspective, the Phillies hit .315 as a team that year, yet finished in last place, 52–102. Phillie right-fielder Chuck Klein drove in 170 runs, made 250 hits, scored 158 runs, hit .383, and had 40 home runs. Sometimes one of his line drives would strike one of Baker Bowl's steel girders, causing a rain of rust to fall on spectators below. Klein once hit a line drive through the right field wall — knocking a hole through a rust spot — for a ground rule double. For many years, Klein was not inducted into the Hall of Fame because his statistics were thought to reflect his ballpark more than his abilities. His mastery of the Baker Bowl wall is reflected in the 44 assists he had in 1930, a major league record.

When you looked out over the right field wall in the 1930s, the sky was dominated by the Coke sign and the huge chimney stack at the edge of the rail yards.

It was here that the Phillies fans first earned a reputation for crankiness, the sort of folks who would boo their grandmother if she took the collar. In the 1920s and 1930s most ballparks were new and had a buffer zone built between the stands and the action. In Baker Bowl the fans were within spitting

Baker Bowl, Philadelphia, Pa. The p.a. announcer uses good old fashioned lung power to give the starting lineups during infield practice. Note the seats on top of and in front of the clubhouse in center field. (Temple University Libraries Photojournalism Collection.)

distance. This intimacy contributed toward Phillies fans' reputation as the nastiest in baseball. These were the grandparents of present-day Phillies fans who waited until Mike Schmidt hit his 500th home run before they gave him a hand.

At late as 1925 no mower was used to groom Baker Bowl's surface. That job was done by sheep who, along with a ram, had their own living quarters under the stands, maintained by longtime greenskeeper Sam Payne. The ram got the axe when he tried to butt Phillies secretary Bill Shetsline. The sheep were gone soon thereafter, and a mower was purchased. Payne remained the Bowl groundskeeper until he was 80, supervising his crew from a sitting position near the end.

During the 1929 season, Baker Bowl almost came to an end. That year the local real estate tycoon Reymold H. Greenberg wanted to buy Baker Bowl, tear it down, and put up buildings. Greenberg planned to buy the Phillies,

with co-owner and new manager Ty Cobb, move the team into Shibe Park, and use the Baker Bowl site for more lucrative things. William F. Baker, who had only a year to live, leased Baker Bowl from the estate of Charles W. Murphy—but with Baker's approval, Greenberg and Cobb could have purchased the site cheaply. Then a funny thing happened. The Phillies began to win—and win and win and win. They returned from a long road trip out of the cellar for the first time in ages. By the time the team came home, Baker raised the price of the team and the park $100,000. Cobb walked out of the deal and went home, and Greenberg sought real estate elsewhere.

The Boys from the Press. In 1936, Red Smith covered the Phillies, the year after lightning hit the Baker Bowl flagpole and split it like a hair. In most ballparks back then the press box was tucked under the roof, but in Baker Bowl the press sat in a section only ten yards deep into the second deck.

Years later, Smith wrote, "Baker Bowl had the charm of a city dump, but not the size. If the right-fielder had beer on his breath, as he frequently did, the first baseman could smell it. For that matter, the whole team smelled most of the time, even though a sign covering the wall in right boasted, 'The Phillies Use Lifebuoy.'" About one day in particular, Smith wrote, "(In the press area) the flower of Philadelphia letters drowsed over scorebooks and whiled away the afternoon throwing peanuts at the head of Sam Baumgartner of the *Philadelphia Inquirer,* who sat in the front row. Running out of peanuts that day when the Cubs were in town, somebody started throwing paper cups of water. The water dripped into the box area below." When Phillies president Gerry Nugent came up to the press area to complain, saying, "You must remember, we have patrons downstairs," Chicago scribe Warren Brown threw a sheet of paper into his typer and said, "My God, what a story!"

These same reporters had a reputation for flicking cigarette butts out of their section onto helpless millinery.

From 1933 to 1935, Baker Bowl was home of the National Football League's brand new Philadelphia Eagles. During their stay there, the team went 3-11-1. They drew as many as 18,000 for a loss to the Giants, but only 1750 for a loss to the Portsmouth Spartans in 1933.

When the Baker Bowl was abandoned in 1938, the Phillies again shared accommodations with the A's in Shibe Park, a situation that would continue until the 1954 season, when the A's moved to Kansas City. The site became a "sink for forlorn entertainment projects." For a while, Baker Bowl was used for midget auto races, an ice skating rink was put in, and then the site served as a used car lot.

The poltergeists did not leave just because the Phillies had. On November 26, 1950, 200 feet of the brick wall surrounding the old Phillies ballpark collapsed with a roar and completely blocked 15th Street, very near the site of the 1903 disaster. Police said that the 20-foot-high wall had been weakened by the wind and rain.

By 1958, all that was left of the ballpark, according to the *Sunday Bulletin,* was "a knee high hedge of bricks along LeHigh Avenue that once were part of the left field wall. The once hallowed playing surface is now a parking lot." Hallowed seems like a strong word. It only goes to show how time heals.

Brotherhood Park

Players League 1890, American Association 1891 (Athletics). *Location:* 35th Street and Dauphin.

University of Pennsylvania

National League 1894 (Phillies). *Location:* 37th, 39th and Spruce streets.

Temporary home of the Phillies after the fire at the Huntingdon Grounds.

Columbia Park

American League 1901–08 (Athletics), National League 1903 (Phillies). *Location:* 29th, 30th and Oxford streets, Columbia Avenue. *Seating capacity:* 15,000. *First game:* April 26, 1901 (Washington 5, Philadelphia 1). *First National League game:* August 20, 1903. *Last game:* October 3, 1908 (doubleheader, Philadelphia 8, Boston 7; Boston 5, Philadelphia 0).

Ban Johnson, while forming the American League, sent Connie Mack, recently fired as the manager of the Pirates, to Philadelphia to look for someone interested in buying a ball club and building a park for it to play in. Mack found Ben Shibe, a baseball manufacturer.

The proposition was iffy, which probably explains why the park Shibe built was so small: no great loss if things didn't work out.

The park had a wooden grandstand from first to third, with open bleachers extending down the foul lines. It was

It's 1939 and there's no more baseball at Baker Bowl, Philadelphia, Pa., now missing its upper deck and set up for the auto races. (Photo used with permission from the Historical Society of Pennsylvania.)

used by the Phillies only in August and September of 1903, after the first Baker Bowl tragedy.

The park was built in a section of Philadelphia called Brewerytown. Columbia Park air always carried the aroma of yeast and hops.

On October 9, 1905, this was the site of the first game of the first World Series played in the current format (best of seven, between the American and National League pennant winners). The game, between the Giants and the Athletics, was a classic in its own right. The Giants were dressed in black, the A's in white. The crowd spilled out of the stand and into the outfield. Fans numbered 17,995 for the classic.

On the mound, two former college rivals faced each other. Eddie Plank (Gettysburg) pitched for the A's, while Christy Mathewson (Bucknell) chucked for the Giants. Mathewson won the duel 3-0. Allowing four hits and walking none, this was the first of his three shutout victories in the five-game series. For the three games combined, Mathewson allowed no runs, gave up 14 hits, struck out 18, and walked one.

All five games were shutouts.

Athletics attendance nearly tripled during their eight-year stay here, necessitating the early move to larger quarters, and the construction of a baseball landmark.

Shibe Park (Connie Mack Stadium 1953-70)

American League 1909-54 (Athletics), National League 1927, 1938-70 (Phillies). Also home of the National Football League 1920s (Frankford Yellow Jackets, some games), 1940-42, 1944-57 (Eagles, total record 58-35-6). Owned by the Athletics, then the Phillies. *Location:* Lehigh Avenue (first base side), 21st Street (third base), Somerset Street (left field), 20th Street (right field). Six blocks from Baker Bowl, in the Swampoodle section. *Dimensions:* (1909) Left field, 360 feet; left center, 393 feet; center field, 515 feet; right center, 393 feet; right field, 360 feet. (1930) Left field, 334 feet; left center, 387 feet; center field, 447 feet; right center, 390 feet; right field, 329 feet. (1909) 90 feet from home plate to the backstop; (1956) 78 feet; (1960) 60 feet. *Seating capacity:* (1909) 20,000; (1925) 33,608, broken down as follows: boxes, 8147, reserved grandstand, 3233; general admission, 18,928; bleacher, 3300. *Phillies day game attendance record:* 36,765 (October 2, 1949, versus Brooklyn). *Phillies doubleheader attendance record:* 40,720 (May 11, 1947, versus Brooklyn). *Phillies night game attendance record:* 40,007. *Phillies twi-night doubleheader attendance record:* 39,705 (August 11, 1952, versus Brooklyn). *Phillies opening game attendance record:* 37,667 (April 16, 1957, versus Brooklyn). *Phillies season high attendance record:* 1,425,891 (1964). *Phillies season low attendance record:* 207,177 (1940). *Athletics day game attendance record:* 37,534 (May 16, 1937, versus New York). *Athletics doubleheader attendance record:* 38,800 (July 13, 1931, versus Washington). *Athletics night game attendance record:* 37,383 (June 27, 1947, versus New York). *Athletics twi-night doubleheader attendance record:* 37,684 (July 15, 1948, versus Cleveland). *Athletics opening game attendance record:* 32,825 (April 20, 1927, versus New York. Over 10,000 were turned away. This represented the highest attendance ever to see a game in Philadelphia up until that time. The A's won the game 8–5. Babe Ruth came to the plate four times and failed to hit the ball out of the infield.). *Athletics season high attendance record:* 945,076 (1948). *Athletics season low attendance record:* 146,223 (1915). *First American League game:* April 12, 1909 (Philadelphia 8, Boston 1). *First night game:* May 16, 1939. *Last American League game:* September 19, 1954 (New York 4, Philadelphia 2). *First National League game (with Phillies as a regular tenant):* July 4, 1938 (doubleheader, Boston 10, Philadelphia 5; Phildelphia 10, Boston 2). *Last National League game:* October 1, 1970 (Philadelphia 2, Montreal 1, 10 innings).

In 1909, many thought Connie Mack (team manager and already part club owner) and majority stockholder Ben

Shibe were being over-optimistic when they opened their first-of-its-kind concrete and steel structure. But Shibe had underestimated the Athletics' drawing power when he built Columbia Park, and he wasn't going to let it happen again.

Shibe Park was so big and beautiful that every big league owner wanted one just like it. In the next five years, Comiskey Park, Ebbets Field, Forbes Field, Fenway Park, Braves Field, and Wrigley Field were built on new sites while other owners replaced their old parks with new concrete and steel fan accommodations (Polo Grounds, Crosley Field, League Park in Cleveland, Navin Field). The era of the wooden ballpark was over.

The place held 20,000 when it opened, with room for expansion. Over 30,000 showed up Opening Day, and the standing room crowd was allowed to spill onto the field. Nobody questioned the size of Shibe's ballpark any longer. On the day of a big game Lehigh Avenue became gridlocked.

There had also been criticism that the park had been built too far from downtown Philadelphia. Little did those critics know that one day the city would overrun Shibe Park, squeeze it to death and force the Phillies to build Veterans Stadium even further from the city's center.

The new concrete and steel construction was not the only fire prevention aspect of Shibe Park. There were water plugs throughout the stands, enabling maintenance people to conveniently hose everything down to clean it, or to extinguish any fire that might start. No fires ever broke out, however, and hosing down the whole park turned out to be a messy proposition—all of that water had to run off somewhere—so over the years the water plugs rusted over with disuse, and the ballpark's only firefighting water came from the same hoses that were used to sprinkle the infield.

When built in 1909, the fence in right

field was only 12 feet high, so folks could crowd upon the rooftops across 20th Street to see the game for free. During the Depression, the height of the field wall was increased with corrugated iron to prevent freeloading. From 1934 to 1956, the right field wall measured 50 feet tall, 13 feet higher than the Green Monster in Fenway.

We Want Beer! During the first decade of Shibe Park's existence, signs such as "White Rock" and "Regal Shoes" were painted on the outfield fence, in two six-foot-tall rows.

The park was originally single-decked. The upper deck was added in 1925 along with seats out in left field. The grandstand had a tower with a dome. Inside the dome was Connie Mack's office.

Between 1927 and 1950, the prices at Shibe Park stayed the same. Mack was manager and owner by this time so box seats stayed $2.20, while bleachers cost half of that.

At the 1929 World Series, the Prohibition crowd chanted "We want beer!"

On June 3, 1932, Lou Gehrig hit four home runs in a single game here.

Mack in Civvies with Scorecard. On May 16, 1939, Connie Mack, age 76, president and manager of the Athletics, hosted the first American League night game. A crowd of 15,109 watched the Indians beat the A's 8-3 in 10 innings. The Phillies also played seven night games that year.

Mack was the last manager to work in his street clothes. He could easily be spotted in the A's dugout—since he appeared to be six foot nine, weighing 75 pounds—and he always carried a scorecard, which he waved from the top step to position his outfielders.

From 1925 to 1933, this was the home field of Lefty Grove, perhaps the greatest left-handed pitcher in the history of the game. Between 1927 and 1933, Grove went 20-12, 24-8, 20-6, 28-5, 31-4, 25-10, and 24-8. Not bad.

In 1951, Shibe Park hosted the American League's first Opening Night. The A's lost their opener under the lights to the Senators 5-1 on April 17.

In 1956, when Yankee Stadium got a new scoreboard, the old one was moved to Shibe and placed in front of the wall in right. It was 50 feet high. On top of the scoreboard was a Ballantine Beer ad, the top of which was 60 feet off the ground. On top of the ad was a Longines clock, reaching 75 feet high. Balls striking the clock were home runs, whereas balls striking the beer ad were still in play. The only ball to clear the scoreboard in right center was hit by Richie "Dick" Allen.

While Richie Ashburn played here (1948-59) the groundskeepers used to build up the third base line to help keep his bunts fair, and the chalk line became known as "Ashburn's Ridge."

The Phillies first played here in 1927, temporary tenant after the second Baker Bowl collapse. They became permanent tenants when Baker Bowl was abandoned in 1938.

When the Athletics moved to Kansas City, the Phillies purchased this park for $2 million.

From the mid-fifties to 1970, Connie Mack Stadium's surrounding neighborhood changed, for the worse, hurting attendance. Near the end of the park's life, a successful attempt was made to get more parking space to attract fans. But the creation of the new parking lots caused further deterioration of the neighborhood, and even fewer fans showed up at the ballpark. The park had a fire due to arson the year after its abandonment and was torn down in 1976. Though many plans have been made to use the site, the seven-acre lot is still vacant.

Chessline Park

Eastern Colored League 1928 (Tigers). *Location:* South Philadelphia.

Passon Field

Negro National League 1934-35 (Stars, Bacharach Giants). *Location:* Spruce, Locust, 48th, and 49th streets.

Shibe Park/Connie Mack Stadium, Philadelphia, Pa. (Compliments of the Philadelphia Phillies.)

Penmar Park

Home of the All-Phillies semi-pro team 1933, Negro National League 1936–48 (Stars), Negro American League 1949–50 (Stars). *Location:* 44th Street, Parkside Avenue. *Dimensions:* Left field, 330 feet; center field, 410 feet; right field, 310 feet. *Lights installed:* 1933.

Out in center field, past the fence, was the main roadhouse to the Pennsylvania Railroad. This was no coincidence. The railroad built the park in the 1920s to be used by their YMCA. The tracks were so close that smoke from locomotives occasionally hid fly balls from their prospective captors.

Veterans Stadium

National League 1971–present (Phillies). Also home of the National Football League 1971–86 (Eagles). Owned by the city of Philadelphia. *Location:* Pattison Avenue (first base side), Broad Street (third base), Packer Street (left field), Seventh Street (right field). *Nickname:* The Vet. *Groundbreaking:* November 2, 1967. *Cost of construc-*

tion: $50 million. *Dedicated:* April 4, 1971. *Dimensions:* Left field, 330 feet; left center, 371 feet; center field, 408 feeet; right center, 371 feet; right field, 330 feet. 60 feet from home plate to the backstop. *Fences:* Twelve feet all the way around. *Turf:* Artificial. *Ramps:* Two miles' worth. *Seating capacity:* 56,581. Super boxes, 254; deluxe boxes, 1004; field boxes, 8957; terrace boxes, 8800; loge boxes, 5711; upper reserved, 17,979; general admission, 13,876. For football, 66,592. *First game:* April 10, 1971 (Philadelphia 4, Montreal 1, attendance 55,352, winning pitcher Jim Bunning, first ball dropped to catcher Mike Ryan from a helicopter).

Built on a 74-acre site in South Philadelphia, the Vet is part of a sports complex that includes R.F.K. Stadium and the Spectrum indoor arena, home of the Flyers and 76ers. The Phillies, Eagles and 76ers have offices inside the Vet. It's been the home field of Mike Schmidt, the greatest third baseman ever, and, from 1972 to 1986, 300-game-winner Steve Carlton. Your basic cookie-cutter, with blue-green artificial

Two views of Veterans Stadium, Philadelphia, Pa. (Top photo compliments of the Philadelphia Eagles. Bottom photo by David Pietrusza.)

turf, and yellow and orange seats—like playing baseball in a big McDonalds.

In 1985, 27 luxurious penthouse suites were built atop the south side of the stadium. In 1986, 24 more were built on the north side. Thirty-eight boxes opened on the west side for 1987. Fans in the superboxes are served a buffet-style dinner before the game. Above the first base line is the ritzy Stadium Restaurant.

There's one step between the parking lots and the entrance gates. Otherwise the ballpark is completely wheelchair accessible. The best seats for the handicapped are those reached from Gate D.

To get from the airport to the Vet, take I-95 north about six miles to the Broad Street exit, go straight on Broad two lights to Pattison.

There has never been a no-hitter pitched in the Vet.

David Pietrusza reports: "The Vet has some interesting statuary out front—a statue of Connie Mack, and a huge piece showing a runner sliding into home. At the 200 level, just under an overhang, dozens of TV sets are mounted for the fans. I'm not sure why since there is a big DiamondVision Screen anyway. A 'Food Court' runs the gamut of cuisines—Chinese, Mexican, Italian, Hoagies, Cheesesteaks, to the smallest hot dogs in baseball. Beverage prices are out of sight, and vendors make a point of asking for the IDs of even clearly middle-aged fans."

Between the 1987 and 1988 seasons the Vet received a new Astroturf-8 self-draining carpet, a hydraulic pitching mound (for which a ten-foot hole was dug to hold the underground equipment necessary to make the mound lower three feet), and a new lighting system (which cut the number of light bulbs illuminating the field from 1600 to 800) that uses computer technology to make sure each and every fixture is pointing in the right direction.

Outside the stadium many trees and shrubs were planted, and a serpentine-shaped wall was built at the street entrance between Gates A and B. The wall is decorated with a "Welcome to the Vet" graphic, and three flagpoles flying the city of Philadelphia, the Eagles, and the Phillies flags.

Phoenix, Arizona

Phoenix Municipal Stadium
Pacific Coast League 1966–present (Roadrunners, Firebirds), spring home of the Oakland Athletics, present. *Location:* 5999 East Van Buren Street, Mill Avenue, Galvin Parkway. *Dimensions:* Left field, 345 feet; center field, 410 feet; right field, 345 feet. *Seating capacity:* 10,000. *1987 season attendance:* 183,798.

On April 16, 1986, the Calgary Cannons beat the Firebirds 21–3. Everyone in the Calgary lineup had at least two hits. The most amazing thing about the game was that it took only 2:42 to play. It was Calgary's only win in Phoenix during 1986.

Fans have a view of Camelback Mountain over the left field fence.

According to Ron Fimrite in *Sports Illustrated,* Phoenix fans strip down when the weather's hot. The park "can look like a sanctuary for recumbent nudists. Arizona has its share of geezers, that's certain, but there's also enough college youths on the premises to give the place that beach blanket look."

Pittsburgh, Pennsylvania

Recreation Park (Union Park 1884)
International Association 1876 (Alleghenys), Union Association 1884, American Association 1885–86, National League 1887–90 (Alleghenys 1887–89, Innocents). *Location:* 1200 Allegheny Avenue; Pennsylvania and Grant avenues, North Avenue West, Boquet (now Behan) Street, and the Fort Wayne Railroad tracks (outfield). *Seating capacity:* (1876) 2500. *First Union Association game:* August 25, 1884. *Last Union Association game:* August 30, 1884. *First American Association game:* April 28, 1885. *Last American Association game:* October 12, 1886 (Pittsburgh 7, New York 2, 7 innings, darkness). *First National League game:* April 30, 1887 (Pittsburgh 6, Chicago 2). *Last National League game:* September 30, 1890 (Pittsburgh 10, Philadelphia 1).

In 1884 the Brotherhood team played here in the city of Allegheny just down the river a bit from Exposition Park where the Pirates played. Allegheny had two teams, and they both claimed to be from Pittsburgh—just like New Jersey's present professional football teams who feign New York residency. Allegheny City officially became part of Pittsburgh on December 9, 1907.

In 1889, Ned Hanlon managed the Pittsburgh team, and one of his players was Billy Sunday, later to become a famous evangelist. The Pittsburgh Innocents of 1890 averaged 411 spectators per game.

Recreation Park was also the home of Western University of Pennsylvania (now the University of Pittsburgh) football and was used for bicycle racing. By the end of the 1890s, this arena was known as the Coliseum, and its baseball days were through.

Exposition Park

American Association 1882–84 (Alleghenys), Players League 1890 (Burghers), National League 1891–1909 (Pirates), Federal League 1914 (Rebels). *Location:* Allegheny City. River Avenue, Cremo Street, South Avenue (first base), School Street (third base), Grant Street. *First American Association game:* May 10, 1882. *Last American Association game:* October 15, 1884. *First Players League game:* April 19, 1890 (Chicago 10, Pittsburgh 2). *Last Players League game:* October 4, 1890 (doubleheader, Pittsburgh 10, Boston 6; Boston 7, Pittsburgh 3). *First National League game:* April 22, 1891 (Chicago 7, Pittsburgh 6, 10 innings). *Last National League game:* June 29, 1909 (Pittsburgh 8, Chicago 1). *First Federal League game:* April 14, 1914. *Last Federal League game:* October 2, 1915. *Refurbished:* 1890.

Located right on the Allegheny, near the covered bridge between Pittsburgh's Exposition Buildings and the lower part of Allegheny City, near "the Point" (where the Allegheny and Monongahela rivers converge to form the Ohio), Exposition Park doubled as a bike track when the home team was on the road. The site for the ballpark was made available when the Allegheny Tradesmen's Industrial Institute burned and the ruins were razed. In addition to baseball and bike racing, the park housed circuses and other large tent shows.

When the Pirates began to play at Exposition Park in 1891, they had a new catcher on the team, tall and thin Connie Mack from Brookfield, Massachusetts. To enhance a Pirate spot-

starter's chances of victory, the ever-alert Mack used to put the next day's baseballs in the icebox overnight to freeze the hits out of them.

Visiting ballplayers stayed at the Monongahela Hotel in Pittsburgh, then rode in open carriages across the river to Allegheny City. To reach the bridge they had to pass the public market place, which could be a very dangerous thing for a ball club to do, especially if they happened to be McGraw's Giants. Pittsburgh rowdies gave visiting teams the razz all along that route, but passing through the market was the worst, because there were so many throwable vegetables handy.

One year, the Giants displayed a huge banner from their horse-drawn bus, proclaiming themselves World Champions. It didn't survive the trip to the ballpark. Throwing things at the visitors was absolutely acceptable behavior during these barbaric parades. Patrolman Dutch Schultz was known to congratulate youngsters who displayed promising aim by nailing a visiting star.

On July 22, 1899, Clarence "Ginger" Beaumont went six for six and scored six runs in a game against the Phillies.

Honus and the Kids. While playing shortstop at Exposition Park—and some outfield early on—Honus Wagner led the National League in hitting six times. He was to do it twice more after the Pirates moved to Forbes Field.

Honus was loved by the kids, and vice versa. He was known as the only Pirate who would help kids sneak into the ballpark free, opening a gate accidentally on purpose, giving a wink, then folding his arms with his back turned. He'd wait until a self-chosen number of kids had scampered in, then shut the gate quietly and go on with his warm-ups.

Famous for a similar reason was Patrolman George Gates, whose beat was to guard the "Carriage Gate" to

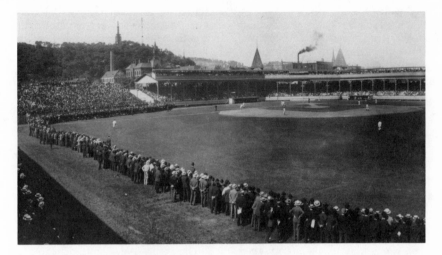

Exposition Park, Pittsburgh, Pa. August 23, 1904: Pittsburgh versus New York. Attendance 15,935. (Photo by George R. Lawrence. Used with permission from the Carnegie Library of Pittsburgh [Pennsylvania Dept.].)

Exposition Park on South Avenue. According to William M. Rimmel of the *Pittsburgh Post-Gazette,* one or two kids snuck in with each carriage that entered, and nobody got snagged unless they were brutally obvious about it. Gates did not like to be shown up.

Sometimes the cop lost interest in this game of pretend deception, opened the gate, and said, "Take it easy . . . don't go in all at once . . . there are a lot of seats."

The kids that didn't make it inside, or weren't up to trying, sat on the side of Monument Hill, behind the grandstand. Not everybody went up there. The climb was steep enough so that you had to get on all fours at times. You could see only part of the playing field from a lot of the lower perches, but they were free, and popular.

Speaking of games of deception, the rocky side of Monument Hill provided some of the classic truant *vs.* truant officer match-ups of all time. Some days, kids were getting dragged off the hill left and right. Some days the truant officers watched the game and everyone ate cookies (ten cents a bag) or soda

crackers (five cents) from the bakery at the foot of the hill. Kids playing hooky and the officials out to nab them ignored their differences in the light of a greater spectacle. (Maybe a bowlegged shortshop who did it all, or something.)

On Saturdays and Sundays, the side of the hill was covered with grown-ups too, folks showing up early for key spots upon the rocky perches offering the best view. (You could never see the entire infield because of the grandstand and the grandstand roof. Luckily, there was a gap between the two, so choice spots on the hill showed the battery or maybe the first base line.)

As one sat in the stands at "Expo" Park, or on Monument Hill, the river was over the left field fence, just on the other side of the railroad tracks. The fences were high all the way around in the outfield and carried painted advertisements. They were so far out that no ball was ever batted over the fence in left or center.

Wet Grounds. When the Allegheny River overflowed its banks, Exposition Park went under. (This had been a particular problem in 1882, when home games were washed out until well into May.) The strange thing is, once they played a doubleheader there anyway. It happened on the Fourth of July in 1902. Ten thousand fans showed up for the morning half of a doubleheader and found a foot of water in the outfield. There had been a heavy rain and the sewers had backed up. Not wanting to turn away all of those paying customers, the morning game was played, anything hit into the water being a ground rule single. Matters got worse for the second game that afternoon. The water continued to rise and eventually came up to within 20 feet of second base. A boy was busy with towels, drying the balls when they came out of the lagoon. The umpire gave the pitcher a dry ball for every other delivery. (The next day the press referred to the body of outfield water as Lake Dreyfuss, after the Pirate owner.) Despite conditions, there was only one wild throw, which slipped out of Claude Ritchey's hand as he was releasing it, and there was a sensational one-hand grab of player-manager Fred Clarke's menacing drive by Superba centerfielder Cozy Dolan, who was knee-deep and on the move at the time. Being the better swimmers, the Pirates swept the Superbas of Brooklyn. Eventually, floodgates were put on the sewers, but they didn't always work, and the outfield was almost always marshy. In both 1900 and 1901, the wind took the ballpark's roof off.

In the spring of Expo's final season, 1908, *Sporting Life* reported on President Dreyfuss' continuing efforts to maintain a dry field:

"A contract was signed yesterday by Dreyfuss with the Pittsburgh Waterproof Company for a tarpaulin to cover the entire playing field. The tarpaulin will contain 1800 yards of brown parafinned duck and will cost $2000. The center of the tarpaulin will be attached to a truck 10 × 15 feet and 3 feet high. Before and after a game in threatening weather, the truck will be run out and the playing ground covered with the tarpaulin. The tarpaulin will protect the field, and there should be no more deferred games on account of wet grounds, unless rain should fall during the progress of a game."

There's never been a World Series for triples like the one in 1903—the first Fall Classic pitting American and National League pennant-winners. Four games were played in Exposition Park, and in them there were 17 triples, 12 by Boston.

On Saturday, August 5, 1905, a crowd of 18,383 (a local record to that date) watched the Pirates play a crucial game against the Giants. In the ninth inning, score tied 5–5, the Giants lost an argument at third base and forfeited the game. But the New Yorkers ended up winning the pennant that year nonetheless, beating the Pirates by one game.

According to Regis M. Welsh in the *Pittsburgh Press,* "...Pittsburgh had a trainer who also acted as a 'bouncer'—James M. 'Red' Mason—who became manager of such boxers as Harry Greb, Buck Crouse, Cuddy Demarco, Red Robinson, Al Grayber, Kid Tyler, Bricky Ryan and Val Gruenenwald.

"(Later) 'Red' was, for years, one of the loudest of Forbes Field's rooters...."

On April 29, 1908, President William Howard Taft threw out the first ball Opening Day. Wagner doubled that day, but the Bucs lost to the Cubs, 8–3.

After Forbes Field was built, the Exposition Field grandstand was torn down. The site now holds what has been described as "truck warehouses and terminals" and "a carloading and distributing plant." Part of the grounds are still used for carnivals and smaller tent shows.

Washington Park

The city of Pittsburgh was induced to turn Washington Park in the lower Hill District over to the Pittsburgh

Playground Association in 1903, and the PPA erected a woodframe recreation center on a former dumping ground.

According to Rob Ruck in his book *Sandlot Seasons*, "An athletic field and bleachers were built, and in 1908 a more modern center was constructed. The first fully equipped playground and athletic field in the city, Washington Park became a center for baseball, boxing, basketball, and football for the next forty-odd years. Its name still evokes fond memories in many parts of the city."

This was a racially mixed playground, about one-third black in the 1930s.

Forbes Field

National League 1909–70 (Pirates), Negro National League 1939–48 (Grays). Site of four Negro League World Series games, Game 2 in 1942, Games 4 and 5 in 1944, and Game 2 in 1945. Site of the 1944 and 1959 All-Star Games. Owned by the Pittsburgh Pirates. *Location:* Boquet Street (first base side), Sennott Street (third base), Schenley Park (outfield). *Groundbreaking:* March 1, 1909. *Construction cost:* $2 million. *Dimensions:* Left field, 365 feet; left center, 457 feet; center field, 435 feet; right center, 416 feet; right field, 300 feet (originally 376 feet). (1909) 110 feet from home plate to the backstop; (1938) 84 feet; (1959) 75 feet. *Fences:* Left and center field, 12 feet; right field, 9½ feet. *Seating capacity:* (1909) 25,000; (1925) 35,000, broken down as follows: boxes, 6120; grandstand reserved, 10,350; general admission, 15,030; bleacher, 3500. *Day game attendance record:* 44,932 (September 23, 1956, versus Brooklyn). *Doubleheader attendance record:* 43,586 (August 31, 1938, versus New York). *Night game attendance record:* 42,254 (August 12, 1940, versus Cincinnati). *Twinight doubleheader attendance record:* 34,673 (August 16, 1960, versus Philadelphia). *Opening game attendance record:* 38,546 (April 20, 1948, versus

Chicago). *Season high attendance record:* 1,705,828 (1960). *Season low attendance record:* 139,620 (1914). *First game:* June 30, 1909 (Chicago 3, Pittsburgh 2, attendance: 30,338). *First night game:* June 4, 1940. *Last game:* June 28, 1970 (doubleheader, Pittsburgh 3, Chicago 2; Pittsburgh 4, Chicago 1, attendance: 40,918).

Natt Moll was the state inspector assigned in 1971 to see that the dismantling of Forbes Field was done according to contract. It was a sad job for him, because this was the same Natt Moll who had, for years, been the ballpark's public address announcer. The P.A. system during the '20s—when he had the job and the lungs—was his megaphone. His biggest thrill was announcing the lineups for the 1925 World Series.

In 1971 he had to sit in a temporary office in the left field corner and watch the crashing of the headache ball, listen to the hiss of acetylene torches, and watch Forbes Field come down, girder by girder. The pigeons that had long used those girders for nests (and fans for target practice) were going to have to find a new home.

The Beginning: 1909. To build his new ballpark, Pirate owner Barney Dreyfuss bought a section of Schenley Farms—later to become Schenley Park—guided in his purchase by friend Andrew Carnegie. There was nothing there but cows, a livery stable and a hothouse. Nearby was Pittsburgh's best residential section. The ballpark would be a thing of luxury. Since a ravine ran through the area, the first thing that had to be done to make the land suitable for baseball was level it off.

The first use of the site as an athletic field came before the rocks were taken out, on October 31, 1908, when the gridiron eleven of Penn defeated Carnegie Tech. Forbes Field was named after a British general who fought in the French and Indian War.

The 1910 *Reach Guide* said, "The

Forbes Field, Pittsburgh, Pa., Monday, July 5, 1909. Independence Day was being celebrated with the traditional fireworks, balloon ascensions from Schenley Park, and a doubleheader at Forbes Field. The Pirates beat Cincinnati twice that day, 2–0 behind Nick Maddox, and 6–1 with Vic Willis pitching. There were 17,805 fans at the first game, 23,502 at the second. The bridge at the entrance to Forbes Field was known as the Bellefield Bridge, or sometimes the Carnegie Library Bridge. It crossed St. Pierre's Ravine. The ravine was filled in 1912, forming Schenley Park Plaza, but the bridge remained—and remains—beneath the Schenley Memorial Fountain, dedicated September 2, 1918. Notice that the flag is at half-mast. Two days earlier Judge Christopher Magee had dropped dead while attending a ball game. (Photo used with permission from the Carnegie Library of Pittsburgh [Pennsylvania Dept.].)

formal opening of Forbes Field was an historic event, the full significance of which could be better felt than described. Words must also fail to picture to the mind's eye adequately the splendors of the magnificent pile President Dreyfuss erected as a tribute to the national game, a beneficence to Pittsburgh and an enduring monument to himself. For architectural beauty, imposing size, solid construction and for public comfort and convenience, it has not its superior in the world." Nor would it for over a decade.

Following that opener *Baseball Magazine* wrote:

"The second grand division (of the grandstand) is the balcony, supported and suspended on steel trusses, the front row being over the fifth row of the lower deck. Here there are twelve tiers or steps, rising more rapidly than those below, so as to provide a perfect view of the diamond. The seats in this balcony, numbering 5500, are also approached by level ways or passages from the rear and to the center of the deck in a manner similar to those below. This deck is also provided with toilets. The new park is the greatest achievement in civil engineering—and as beautiful as well as secure a construction as has been undertaken in this country since baseball first began to be the national pastime."

Forbes Field had been made an

ornate thing, with elevators, electric lights, telephones, ramps instead of steps, and maids in the ladies' john. These were innovations in fan comfort. Season box seats cost $100.00, *plus* general admission prices per attended game—and for this you got an easily removable brass sign to put on your box.

Forbes Field, in keeping with its neighborhood, had a diminutive bleacher section and a large grandstand. Very upper-crust. After all, overlooking the left field stands was the University of Pittsburgh's Cathedral of Learning.

There was a crowd of 30,338 for that first game. Mayor William A. Magee, sitting in Box 137, threw out the first ball. The Chicago Cubs sent the fans home blue by beating the Pirates 3-2—but the Bucs won the pennant and the World Series that year.

Hot Dog Panic. In 1927 Bozeman Bulger of the *New York Evening World* reported:

"The man at Forbes Field in charge of the refreshment stand says that the favorite foods of Pittsburgh fans are small hamburger steaks stuck in a round roll and the regulation hot dog. The Pitt fan goes in rather strong for soda pop, buttermilk and sweet milk. The temper of the crowd, they tell me, reflects the way the fans have been fed. When they have had time to eat well they are easy on the umpires and much more tolerant to visiting players. Dreyfuss has arranged his refreshment layout so it is the first thing seen by incoming fans. His is the only stand where customers have to buy hot dog and hamburger tickets in advance. This arrangement works nicely ordinarily, but one day last summer (1926) it resulted in the first hot dog panic in history. A heavy rain caused suspension of play, and there was a great rush for hamburgers and hot dogs. The ticket-sellers sold their little checks by the yard—they look like subway tickets—and then the hot dogs ran out!

The only thing that stopped the clamoring was the resumption of play. Barney Dreyfuss declares very gravely that he has taken such precautions that there can never be another hot dog scandal in his park."

Lotsa Triples. The first home run in Forbes Field was not struck until July 5, 1909, by Mike Mitchell of Cincinnati. The final homer was hit in the last game played at Forbes Field in 1970 by Al Oliver.

This was never a park known for its home runs, but rather for its triples. In 1983, L. Robert Davids in *Insider's Baseball* noted that "since 1900 the Pirates have led the league in triples 40 times and have finished second 23 times. Most of the domination was caused by Forbes Field.... The size and configuration of this park was conducive to batted balls rolling a long way and to outfielders running to no end while chasing the ball and then throwing to very deep cut-off men. The fences, near the right field foul pole, were at such great distances that many potential home runs became very long outs; or if they were line drives they went for three bases or sometimes for four. Ten Pirates hit Inside the Park Home Runs in 1925."

In those early days, Dreyfuss was out to make money in addition to his baseball income, and frequently rented out the arena to other events. These included horse shows, which were never good for the infield.

In 1951, Forbes Field was used in the making of *Angels in the Outfield,* a motion picture starring Paul Douglas, along with real Pirates like Ralph Kiner. (Kiner was the biggest draw in Pirates history. On July 5, 1948, he hit three home runs in Forbes Field for the third time in two years.)

Not counting the complete shrinkage of Braves Field's once massive lawn in 1928, the first inner fence, a fence built specifically to make home runs easier to hit, was built in left field at Forbes Field in 1947. The fence reduced the home run

Forbes Field, Pittsburgh, Pa. (Photo used with permission from the Carnegie Library of Pittsburgh [Pennsylvania Dept.].)

distance by 30 feet. The unkempt area between the old and new fence was known as Greenberg Gardens in honor of Hank Greenberg, for whom it was designed. The area was later known as Kiner's Korner, after Ralph. (Today Kiner is the New York Mets' TV announcer. His interview show after Mets broadcasts is known as *Kiner's Korner.*)

The World Series. The World Series, and the World Championship (following Game 7), came to Pittsburgh the first year baseball was played in Forbes Field. It was in that series that Cobb, a base runner at first, taunted Wagner: "Look out, Banjo, watch out, you Krauthead, here I come, I'm coming down!"

When Cobb ran, Wagner took the throw, and put the tag on the Georgia Peach's teeth, loosening a few that Cobb needed. There was no more name calling. Of course, the tag being that high, Cobb was safe at second base.

In 1925, the Pirates again won the World Series, defeating the Washington Senators and Walter Johnson in Game 7 in the rain. Johnson was knocked out of the box in the first, and Pittsburgh won 9–7 in a slugfest, before 42,856 at Forbes Field.

Two years later the Pirates won the National League pennant but were swept in four games straight in the World Series by the greatest team ever, the '27 Yankees.

Then, of course, there was 1960. That year Bill Mazeroski hit the only home run to win a World Series in the history of baseball, off Ralph Terry. Maz led off the ninth with the score tied and smacked Terry's second pitch.

Paige: The Legend. Every legend unaffiliated with a public relations firm had to—at least once—do something legendary. The Babe really hit one out for the crippled kid. Willie Mays really did make that catch at the end of the airplane runway. It only took Reggie three swings. There's some discrepancy about what Satchel Paige did and didn't do during his 42-year (1924–65) career in professional baseball. But he did, at least once, do something legendary in front of plenty of witnesses, some of whom took the time to write down their observations on the day.

It was July 21, 1942, and the scene was Forbes Field, where Paige's Kansas City Monarchs were playing the local Homestead Grays and the great Josh Gibson. Years earlier Paige and Gibson had been teammates (Paige and every black ballplayer had been teammates at one time or another), and Satchel told Josh that one day he would strike him out with the bases loaded in front of a big crowd. With one man on, two out and Gibson third down in the batting order, Paige saw his opportunity to set up the scenario of his dreams. The pitcher walked the next two batters intentionally so that he could pitch to Gibson with the bases loaded. With the scene set, Satchel made sure Josh remembered what he had said years before, and Josh did. Then Satchel made sure that everyone in the ballpark knew what was going to happen. "Three fast balls, Josh," Satchel said — and that was all it took. The third strike was called.

Wall Still Stands. Though Forbes Field is gone, and the land upon which it stood now belongs to the University of Pittsburgh, a portion of the ballpark's center field fence — the part with 457 painted on it — still stands where it always stood.

According to a university publicist, "We kept the wall because Forbes Field was an integral part of Oakland (section of Pittsburgh) for so long. When Forbes Quadrangle and the Graduate School of Business were put on (the site of the ballpark) we tried to maintain some historical and architectural integrity."

The Forbes Quadrangle is a huge classroom and administrative offices building. On the ground floor, preserved under lucite, is the home plate from Forbes Field's last game.

On May 25, 1935, Babe Ruth of the Braves, 41 years old, hit three home runs in a game, numbers 712, 713, and 714. The last home run cleared Forbes Field's right field roof, which had never been done before. With that wallop under his tortured belt, the Babe circled the bases, went into the dugout, through the tunnel, to the clubhouse, and called it a career. After that, there was a plaque on the right-field wall commemorating the feat. After Barney Dreyfuss died a memorial to him was put up in center. Kids were allowed to walk around on the field mornings before night games, so any kid worth his salt knew what it said on those plaques. A lot of kids sat in the bleachers, of course, where the hot dogs were grilled black, unlike the boiled wieners available in the grandstand.

According to Pittsburgh sports writer Pete Bishop, Forbes Field, "like Howdy Doody, Frankie Avalon and being one of Dr. Salk's polio vaccine 'guinea pigs,' is part of the days when fun was where you found it and, it seems, there were more spots in which to find it."

There was never a no-hitter in Forbes Field.

Ammon Field

City Recreational League 1920s (Crawfords), Negro National League 1922 (Keystones). *Location:* Bedford Avenue, on the north side of Pittsburgh.

In the 1920s, this was the home of the Crawfords, still a sandlot team playing in the City Recreational League. During that time, Charlie Hughes was the second baseman, and a gutter ran across second base that filled up whenever it rained. Charlie was his own ground crew, out there raking and digging to no avail. The gutter always came back. He finally gave up raking and became the greatest bad-hop fielder his teammates had ever seen. He was like a magician who could frequently pluck baseballs from his ear. Gus Greenlee was about to "adopt" this ball club, and things for the Crawfords would never be the same.

McKinley Park

Home of 18th Ward, black sandlot club, 1920s–50s.

The 18th Ward team represented the Beltzhoover community south of the Monongahela River, which extended from the top of Mount Washington down to the 72-acre McKinley Park, where they played. Black Beltzhooverites were few and far between — only about 200 of them altogether — before the First World War, but that figure more than tripled during the 1920s. By 1930 the black population in the neighborhood was 1500, and remained less than 2000 during the entire time the 18th Ward ball club existed. The 18th Ward played a 48-game schedule against white competition in the South Hills League, one of the big sandlot leagues in the city (the other was the Greater Pittsburgh League). Every once in a while the Homestead Grays or the Newark Eagles appeared at the McKinley Park ballpark, and the crowd was in the thousands.

The people of Beltzhoover were racially mixed and so were the crowds at McKinley Park. According to Rob Ruck in *Sandlot Seasons,* crowds "reflected the racial proportions of the community fairly closely, with as many whites as blacks in attendance. At the games (whites and blacks) stood or sat next to each other and cheered for the same team. On July 4th, they attended doubleheaders at McKinley Park and also competed in 50- and 100-yard dashes, egg races, ball throwing contests, and needle threading and fat people races for prizes provided by the Montooth Hotel, the McKinley Drugstore, and Goldsmith's Store."

Grays Field

Negro American League 1929 (Grays). *Location:* Homewood and Long avenues, at the Pennsylvania Railroad tracks, in the Homewood section.

Gus Greenlee Field (Crawford Recreation Center)

Negro East-West League 1932 (Grays), Negro National League (Grays 1935–38, Crawfords 1933–38, two franchises 1935–38). *Location:* The Hill District. 2500 Bedford Avenue. Wylie and Crawford avenues, Fitzpatrick Street, current site of the Pittsburgh Housing Authority projects. West of Municipal Hospital and east of the Lincoln Cemetery. *First game:* April 29, 1932. *Lights:* 1933. *Torn down:* December 10, 1938.

William A. (Gus) Greenlee, Black Pittsburgh's "Mr. Big," relocated a number of buried bodies, obtained zoning modifications on a plot of land formerly owned by the Empress Brick Company on Bedford Avenue where the "little Crawfords" (a.k.a. "the bath house gang") played their games, and here he built his ballpark. He was at last free of white stadium owners whose facilities he rented during the white clubs' road trips. Greenlee knew his Crawfords were clearly inferior to the Grays and sought to make them competitive. He obtained Satchel Paige in 1931 and Josh Gibson in 1932, then bought two seven-passenger Lincolns for travel. Greenlee, who made his fortune running numbers, smoked a big cigar and could often be seen tending bar at his own establishment, Greenlee's Crawford Bar and Grille.

Fourteen railcars of cement, 75 tons of steel and $100,000 went into Greenlee Field, a red brick beauty. Six months after the Bedford Land and Improvement Company broke ground, the park was finished. The Crawfords played one exhibition game against a white semi-pro club called the Vandergrifts earlier, but the park did not officially open until April 30, 1932. Bands played. The mayor was there. So were the county commissioners and the city council. The dedication was read and the first ball was thrown out by *Pittsburgh Courier* editor Robert Vann. The crowd of 5000 gave Greenlee a standing ovation, then settled back to watch the Black Yankees beat the Crawfords and Satchel Paige 1-0, the only run scoring in the ninth inning. Five future Hall of Famers played on that ball club: Paige, Bell, Gibson, Judy Johnson and Oscar Charleston.

On Thanksgiving Day, 1932, a very important football game was played between the 1931 Black Football Champions, Wilberforce College, and West Virginia State. Buses were chartered. Motorcades were arranged, convoys of alumni came from all directions. Greenlee Field became a focal point that day for the black middle class of the Northeast.

The total park attendance for its first year (1932) was 119,000, over 65,000 of which came from baseball.

The ballpark was kept busy. For six years (1933-38) Greenlee Field was home to two teams in the Negro National League. There was a ball game there every summer day.

In the 1930s, the Crawfords were drawing over 200,000 per year. Promotions were run to stimulate attendance. A Ford sedan was given away. Season passes were awarded. Jesse Owens once raced a thoroughbred race horse at Greenlee. The race was rigged with a horse that reared at the sound of the starting gun, and Owens was gone.

The Crawfords never made much money. The story goes that Josh saw Joe Garagiola in a major league uniform and realized the meaning of prejudice.

Kennard Field

Home of the Oakland Barons and the Terrace Village (housing complex) sandlot team during the late 1940s and early 1950s.

The Terrace Village team was a black sandlot team who drew 3000 to 4000 fans for games against the 18th Ward. The concession stand for these games consisted of 12 cases of pop on ice, and bagged peanuts behind the backstop.

Three Rivers Stadium

National League 1970-present (Pirates). Owned by the city of Pittsburgh. *Location:* Park encircled by Stadium Circle. General Robinson Street (left field). Address: 400 Stadium Circle. *Groundbreaking:* April 25, 1968. *Construction cost:* $55 million. *Cost of scoreboard:* $1.5 million. *Dimensions:* Left field, 340 feet; left center, 385 feet; center field, 410 feet; right center, 385 feet; right field, 340 feet. 60 feet from home plate to the backstop. *Surface:* Astroturf. *Seating capacity:* 50,235. Special boxes, 954; lower boxes, 8058; loge boxes, 7288; upper boxes, 2848; upper reserved, 13,800; general admission, 17,287. *Record attendance for a three-game series:* 127,717 (June 27, 28, 29, 1988, versus New York). *First game:* July 16, 1970 (night, Cincinnati 3, Pittsburgh 2).

The first game here on July 16, 1970, represented the first time a major league baseball game had been played on artificial turf outside. Boo, hiss.

On October 13, 1971, Three Rivers hosted the first World Series night game. A crowd of 51,378 watched the Pirates beat the Orioles 4-3 in Game 4.

This was the site of the 1974 All-Star Game, in which the National clobbered the American League 7-2.

The ballpark is the site of the "Stadium Hall-of-Fame" commemorating the national history of baseball and football, as well as Pittsburgh's overall sports heritage. At the Hall-of-Fame there are conducted tours and multimedia exhibits.

The playing field (fair territory, in other words) measures 120,000 square feet. The entire area of the field is 140,000 square feet.

The Stadium Club has a restaurant that will hold 700 patrons and a cocktail lounge that holds another 100.

The stadium was discussed, planned, scrapped, planned again and built over a ten-year period. Federal funds and money earned from smart investments by the Stadium Authority got Three

Three Rivers Stadium, Pittsburgh, Pa. (Compliments of Three Rivers Stadium.)

Rivers built.

Three Rivers Stadium was the site of the 1971 World Series between the Pirates and the Baltimore Orioles. Behind the remarkable hitting, fielding and throwing of Roberto Clemente, the Pirates won all three home games and then Game 7 on the road. Another cookie-cutter.

Pittsfield, Massachusetts

Wahconah Park

New York State League 1894 (one month), Eastern League 1919–30 (Hillies), 1965–present (Cubs), Canadian-American League 1940 (Electrics, Phillies, partial season). *Location:* North and Wahconah streets, near Berkshire Hospital, north of downtown. *Dimensions:* (1940s) Left field, 352 feet; center field, 362 feet; right field, 333 feet. (Present) Left field, 339 feet; center field, 411 feet; right field, 339 feet. *Seating capacity:* 4000. *1987 season attendance:* 51,551. *Lights:* 1946. *Major renovation:* 1949, 1976. *Cost of renovation:* (1949) $114,000, (1976) $700,000.

Baseball was played on this site as early as 1892. Though it's been refurbished about once a decade for who knows how long, no one has ever changed the configuration of the diamond. After 97 years of squinting, the sun still sets over the left field fence. Night games here start late to avoid the dangerous situation.

In 1919, the 50-acre plot was sold to the city of Pittsfield. The Hillies of the Eastern League took up residency here and stayed until 1930.

In 1927 a dyke was built in the outfield to prevent flooding from the Housatonic River. That same year, repairs were made on the crumbling grandstand. (The waters have never been successfully held back. Much of an extensive 1976 refurbishment, financed by federal funds, went to holding back the Housatonic.)

As a Depression-buster in 1931, 1300 men regraded the field. The field was made smooth, and $25,000 in wages were pumped into the community.

The park was falling apart—a condition it found itself in regularly—in 1940 when the Canadian-American League

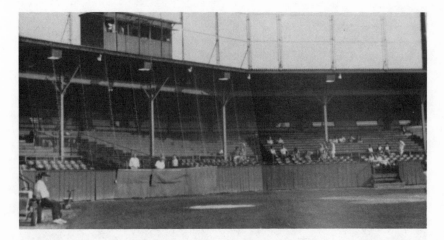

Wahconah Park, Pittsfield, Mass., as it appeared in 1987. (Photo by David Pietrusza.)

franchise finished out their season here, and (not counting the 1976 spruce-up) was most recently rebuilt in 1950.

Today the park is charmingly old with lots of green-painted wood, the grandstand slightly raised for better viewing. Not too many people go there, so it's easy to get a seat in the front row.

In other parks that point the wrong way, late starts for night games have hurt sales because fans eat at home before coming to the park—but this is not true at Wahconah Park. According to the foremost aficionado of New York state ballpark cuisine, David Pietrusza, the food at present day Wahconah park is very good. "It's the only park I've been to that serves white wine," he says. Bring a date.

Dorothy Demming Field

Canadian-American League (Class C) 1940 (Electrics, partial season).

Known for tremendous dust swirls that made baseball hard to play and watch, this field was little more than a playground.

The Canadian-American League team that played here was owned by William Connelly from Albany. The owner planned a new stadium for his club but went broke—the whole franchise folding after a year—before ground was broken. At the end of the season, the Electrics were playing their games at Wahconah Park, which had already been there as long as anyone could remember.

Just a field, some bleachers, and a wire fence.

Plant City, Florida

Plant City Stadium

Spring training home of the Cincinnati Reds 1988–present. *Location:* Parks Road. *Seating capacity:* 3500.

The Reds played fourteen games in Plant City in 1988. Season tickets were $84. The grandstand was constructed in 4 months, 28 days. The park opened for '88 spring training without a fully functioning scoreboard.

Pocatello, Idaho

Legion Park

Home of Pocatello American Legion ball circa 1926. *Location:* Current site of Idaho State University.

This field was carved out of the sagebrush by neighborhood boys, led by R.B. "Dube" Bistline, who later went on to coach the Pocatello American Legion team.

Overland Park

Twilight League (semi-pro) 1930s. *Location:* Oak Street, current site of the oil tanks. Railroad-owned.

Halliwell Park (I)

Pioneer League 1939–63. *Location:* North Sixth Street, current site of the Osco Buttrey Shopping Center.

Named after longtime president of the Pioneer League, John Phillip (Jack) Halliwell. After the league folded, the ballpark was used by amateur local baseball and football teams until the late 1960s, when a new Halliwell Park was constructed at a different location.

Halliwell Park (II)

Pioneer League 1987–present (Gems). *Location:* 1100 West Alameda Road, Hawthorne School area. *Dimensions:* Left field, 340 feet; center field, 410 feet; right field, 340 feet. *Seating capacity:* 2000. *1987 season attendance:* 18,790.

Port Charlotte, Florida

Charlotte County Stadium

Part of $5.6 million, 82-acre training complex owned by Charlotte County. Spring home of the Texas Rangers, 1987–present, Florida State League 1987–present (Rangers), Gulf Coast League 1987–present (Rangers). *Location:* 2300 El Jobean Road, Biscayne Drive. *Groundbreaking:* April 9, 1986. *Opened:* March 1987. *Seating capacity:* 5000.

Five full fields in addition to the stadium.

Port St. Lucie, Florida

Port St. Lucie County Complex
(Club Met)

Spring training home of the New York Mets (National League) 1988–present, Florida State League 1988–present (Mets). *Location:* Prima Vista Boulevard, off I-95 — complex has its own exit. *Dimensions:* Left field, 341 feet; left center, 371 feet; center field, 410 feet; right center, 371 feet; right field, 341 feet (same as Shea Stadium). *Seating capacity:* 8000 (6000 reserved, 2000 bleacher). *First game:* March 5, 1988 (Los Angeles Dodgers 5, Mets 2, exhibition, attendance 6649).

The Mets' new spring training complex consists of 6½ fields on 100 acres of land, including a modern 8000-seat stadium — so modern that it looks like it's about to take off. The single-decked grandstand has something perched on top of it that is probably the roof, but looks more like a UFO, or an inverted satellite dish. The press box is attached to the roof's lower lip. The outfield fences are screen-covered with a dark blue mesh, as is the tall hitters' background in center. Look hard at the hitters' background and you can see trees on the other side of it. The fences are the same distance as those at Shea, and this is true of the home run distances in all six full fields. (The half field consists of an infield and short outfield for infield and baserunning drills.) Four of the full fields form the quarters of a pie with an observation tower in the center, a configuration that has become popular among the new Florida spring training super-duper complexes. This one, too, has the ultimate facilities for the players off the field too, with saunas and whirlpools and a training room better equipped than many city hospitals.

Early Problems. At the first spring training game in the new ballpark (March 1988) there were some problems, as might be expected. The glass designed to protect the television camera directly behind home turned out to be vulnerable to baseballs, which repeatedly cracked it. Three or four attempts were made to keep the plate held together with electrical tape until the sheet looked like an aerial photograph of Kennedy International Airport. Finally the behind-home camera was abandoned until the protective sheet could be replaced with a sturdier material.

Also in that first game, the sprinkler system, set on a timer, went off in the middle of the eighth inning and had to be turned off by hand, while the Mets outfielders got soaked.

Portland, Oregon

Lucky Beavers Stadium (Vaughn Street Ballpark)

Northwest League 1901–02, Pacific Coast League 1903–55 (Beavers). *Built:* Spring 1901. *Location:* 2409 NW Vaughn Street (first base), NW 25th Avenue (third base), NW 24th Street (right field). *Dimensions:* Left field, 331 feet; center field, 368 feet; right field, 315 feet. *Fences:* Left field, 20 feet; center field, 20 feet; right field, 30 feet. *Seating capacity:* (1912–55) 12,000. *Torn down:* 1956.

Park was built on a four-block site owned by F.I. Fuller's Portland Railway Company, and developed in conjunction with a rival trolley company, C.F. Swigeat's City & Surburban Lines. The competitors joined forces on this project, correctly assuming the ballpark would help both of their businesses.

When the park was first used the only grandstand was very small and directly behind home. This structure lasted only four years and was demolished during the construction of the 440 track used in the National Track and Field Games of the 1905 Lewis and Clark Exposition.

In 1912, the Vaughn Street park took on the look for which it is best remembered: still a wooden structure, but fully enclosed with a seating capacity of 12,000. In addition to the grandstand there was a set of bleachers in straightaway center field.

According to baseball historian Mike Maras in *The Ballpark Bulletin,* "Outfield bleachers were added, right field seats were extended from home plate to the first base area, and the covered grandstand seating extended along the third base line all the way to the left field bleachers. Except for minor changes and additions, the park remained intact until its final season in 1955." By that time it was the oldest active park in the Pacific Coast League, and it was torn down the year after it was abandoned. Out past the right field fence was the Electric Steel Foundry, whose black smoke hung thick over the field like so much gloom.

L.H. Gregory covered the Beavers when they played at Lucky Beavers Stadium. Here's what Gregory had to say in *The Portland Oregonian* about the Vaughn Street facility on the eve of its abandonment:

"Stands and field were so closely adjacent that customers had a feeling of intimacy with the players. Only in the closing years was the main grandstand badly run down. One spring, near the end, the fire marshall even gestured toward closing it as a fire hazard unless a costly sprinkler system was installed. It never was and he didn't carry out his threat.... With the Portland baseball club's departure from Vaughn Street, more than just an era comes to a close—a way of life is ending. Vaughn Street grew in the simple days when wood stands were good enough; it gives way to a complex era of steel and concrete, of formality in design and in living."

Since the park was made of wood, it was always catching fire. In 1947, the left field bleachers burned. Luckily everyone caught baseball fever that year, and the Beavers drew 421,000 paying customers even without their left field seats. During most of the time

Pilot Stadium, Portland Oregon, as it looks today. (Compliments of the University of Portland.)

it was used, there was talk of replacing it. After the '47 fire, talk of a new steel and concrete park sprouted up, as city officials threatened to fine or condemn Lucky Beavers Stadium, but the Beavers stayed for eight more years.

Civic Stadium (Multnomah Stadium)
Pacific Coast League circa 1956–60, 1977–present (Beavers), Northwest League circa 1975 (Beavers), home of the Portland State University Vikings (Pac-10 Conference, Northern Division), present. *Location:* 1844 SW Morrison Street, SW 18th and SW 20th avenues, at Salmon Street. *Opened:* October 9, 1926 (used exclusively for football until 1956). *Dimensions:* Left field, 302 feet; center field, 393 feet; right field, 336 feet. *Seating capacity:* (1975) 30,000; (1985) 26,912. *1987 season attendance:* 154,989.
A football stadium with the short field in left. Large J-shaped grandstand goes from foul pole to foul pole.

Pilot Stadium
Home of the University of Portland Pilots (Pac-10 Conference, Northern Division), present. *Seating capacity:* 1200.
Refurbished between the 1987 and

1988 seasons. Three small sets of all-wood bleachers were replaced by wood-on-concrete bleachers. New dugouts and a new press box also were added.
The stadium sits adjacent to a domed arena. The University of Portland has had a baseball program since 1923.

Portsmouth, Virginia

Washington Street Park
Virginia League 1910s (Merrimacs). *Seating capacity:* 3500.

Bland Park
Virginia League 1910s (Cubs). *Seating capacity:* 4000.

Sewanee Stadium
Virginia League 1920s (Truckers). *Seating capacity:* 5000.
In 1923, Hack Wilson won the Virginia League Triple Crown while playing for Portsmouth.

Portsmouth Stadium
Virginia League circa 1927 (Truckers). *Seating capacity:* 10,000.

Name of park unknown.
Home of the Portsmouth Fire Fighters circa 1933.

In April of 1933, the Portsmouth Fire Fighters played an exhibition game against the great Detroit Stars. The crowd was in the hundreds. There was a barbeque. Soft drinks were sold. The captain of the local nine was 19-year-old Ray Dandridge. That day, in a losing cause, Dandridge hit an awesome home run and made a spectacular catch in the outfield. He played so well that afterwards the Stars asked Ray's dad if they could take his son Ray along with them. The elder Dandridge saw an opportunity to keep Ray out of the textile mills that had left him an invalid. So Ray packed his bags and, by way of Mexico, ended up in the Hall of Fame — the most popular American player ever to play south of the border.

Frank Lawrence Stadium

Owned and operated by the Portsmouth Parks and Recreation Department. Piedmont League 1945–55 (Cubs). Also, Carolina League ball and high school football. *Location:* Queens Street at Williamsburg Avenue. *Opened:* Easter Sunday, 1941. *Seating capacity:* For baseball, 7500 (6000 grandstand, 1500 removable bleachers). For football, 5500.

Portsmouth native and original owner of the Portsmouth professional baseball team, Frank Lawrence, was the president of the American National Bank and the Minor League Association. He was involved in the construction and design of the ballpark that bore his name. When set up for baseball, the park had a huge set of football bleachers in left center. There was a small baseball scoreboard in right center.

This area is currently represented by the Tidewater Tides.

Princeton, West Virginia

Princeton Recreation Complex

Appalachian League 1988 (Pirates). *Location:* Near the downtown exit to U.S. 460. *Dimensions:* Left field, 340 feet; center field, 400 feet; right field, 340 feet. *Seating capacity:* 1500.

Providence, Rhode Island

Adelaide Park

Location: Broad, Hamilton, and Sackett streets; Adelaide and Elwood avenues. *Built:* 1875.

Used twice in 1875 for National Association games involving New Haven, Boston, Hartford, and Brooklyn.

Messer Park

National League 1878–85 (Grays). *Location:* East of Olneyville, near the present site of Bridgham Middle School. Hudson, Ropes, Wood and Messer streets. *First National League game:* May 1, 1878. *Last National League game:* September 9, 1885.

In 1879, except for games with Boston and Chicago, the Grays drew miserably, with a total home attendance for the year of 43,000, and total receipts of $12,516. That did not cover expenses.

Attendance wasn't even helped by the park's convenience to public transportation. The park was adjacent to three horsecar lines, one of which built a spur right up to the gate. In return for the anticipated business — which turned out to be next to nil — the local trolley line paid for grading the field.

The magnificence of Ol' Hoss Radbourne was surely wasted on this town. By 1884, when Hoss went 60–12, the Grays were drawing less than a thousand fans even to crucial games.

An earlier star of the Grays was pitcher John Montgomery Ward, a native of Bellefonte, Pennsylvania. In 1879, at the age of 19, Ward won 47, lost 17.

The Grays' hitting stars during their 1878 pennant-winning season were Paul Hines (.357) and James Henry "Orator Jim" O'Rourke (.348).

The grandstand was rectangular and elevated, like those at racetracks.

Bleachers stood next to the grandstand on the first base side. Foul territory went on forever. The seats were divided into eight sections of ten rows apiece beneath a supported roof.

Kinsley Park
International League 1925 (Grays), Eastern League 1926–27 (Grays). *Location:* Acorn Street opposite the Nicholson File Company.

The star of the 1925 Grays was Jimmie Foxx, while Rube Marquard won headlines for the 1926 Grays, who played in a lower minor league.

In 1927, Tim O'Neil, Providence's renowned organizer, organized an exhibition baseball game at Kinsley Field featuring Babe Ruth and Lou Gehrig: the Larrupin' Lous versus the Bustin' Babes. The game was ended before nine innings were up after fans collected all the foul balls for autographs. Neither Babe nor Lou got to hit a home run in Kinsley.

Pulaski, Virginia

Calfee Park
Virginia League circa 1950 (Counts), Appalachian League 1969–present (Braves). *Location:* Fifth and Pierce streets. *Dimensions:* Left field, 335 feet; center field, 390 feet; right field, 291 feet. *Seating capacity:* (1950) 2500; (1969) 2000. *1987 season attendance:* 15,248.

Pullman, Washington

Arthur "Buck" Bailey Field I
Home of the Washington State University Cougars (Pac-10 Conference, Northern Division) before 1980. *Location:* At the current site of Mooberry Track, located next to Hollingbery Fieldhouse, on the campus of Washington State University.

Named after the WSU coach (1927–42, 1946–61), who compiled a record during his 32 years at the helm of

603–325–5 (.649). In 1980, the track team and baseball team switched facilities. Baseball moved to the site of the old Martin Field, while this site was converted into a track and field facility.

Arthur "Buck" Bailey Field II
Home of the Washington State University Cougars (Pac-10 Conference, Northern Division) 1980–present. *Location:* Southeast of the Beasley Performing Arts Coliseum, on the campus of Washington State University. *Dimensions:* Left field, 335 feet; center field, 400 feet; right field, 330 feet. *Seating capacity:* 3500. *First night game:* May 11, 1984 (Washington State 3, Washington 2). *Cost of lights:* $250,000.

Washington State University got its first electronic baseball scoreboard in 1981. The addition of lights in 1984 was the long-standing dream of current WSU baseball coach Chuck "Bobo" Brayton. The lights were taken from Sick's Stadium in Seattle when that park was razed. Also taken from Sick's were some bleacher seats. Seating consists of aluminum chairback seats, aluminum bleachers, and box seats.

This site had formerly been Martin Field, home of WSU's track and field meets. During the transition from track to baseball, 16 feet of dirt were excavated from the site. That dirt went toward the landscaping of the WSU golf course.

Quebec City, Quebec

Municipal Stadium
Provincial League, Canadian-American League (Class C) late 1930s–circa 1942 (Athletics, Royals, Braves, Alouettes), Eastern League 1971. *Dimensions:* Left field, 317 feet; center field, 372 feet; right field, 317 feet. *Seating capacity:* 7500.

See Three Rivers, Quebec.

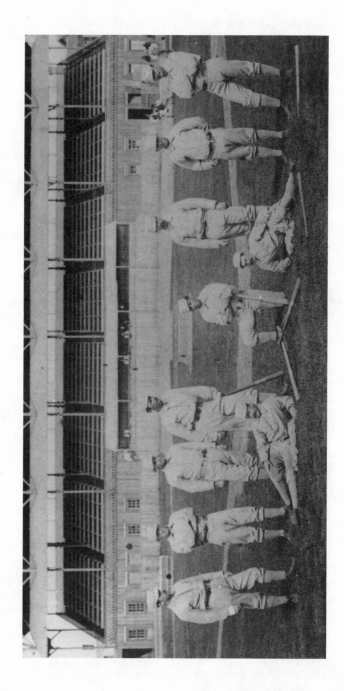

Top: *The scene at Bailey Field, Pullman, Wash.* Bottom: *The first night game at Bailey Field, May 11, 1984. (Both photos compliments of the Washington State University Intercollegiate Athletic Office.)*

Opposite: *The pennant-winning 1879 Providence Grays in front of the grandstand at Messer Park, Providence, R.I. Left to right: T. York, left field; John Montgomery Ward, pitcher (47–17 that year); J. Start, first base; E. Gross, catcher; Jack Farrell (lying down), second base (came to the club mid-season and only played 12 games); George Wright (kneeling), shortstop; Bobby Mathews (lying down), pitcher (the winning pitcher of the very first National Association game played in 1871 in Fort Wayne, Indiana); James Henry O'Rourke, right field (hit .348); M. McGreary, second base; Paul Hines, center field (hit .357). (Photo from the Rhode Island collection of the Providence Public Library; used with permission.)*

Municipal Stadium, or Stade Municipal, *Quebec City, Quebec, Canada. An exact duplicate of the ballpark in Three Rivers, Quebec, built during the Depression through Canada's version of the* WPA *to look like the front of a high school. (Photo from the private collection of David Pietrusza.)*

Quincy, Illinois

Q Stadium
Midwest League 1960–circa 1972.
Seating capacity: 3500.

Raleigh, North Carolina

Devereaux Meadow
Carolina League 1958–71. *Location:* West and Peace streets, Downtown Boulevard. *Dimensions:* Left field, 310 feet; center field, 400 feet; right field, 370 feet. *Fences:* 40 feet all the way around. *Seating capacity:* 4000. *Constructed:* 1939 (WPA project). *Torn down:* 1979.

In November 1987, Raleigh voters narrowly approved a $3.5 million bond issue for a new baseball stadium, according to *Baseball America*. Recruitment began for a franchise. A site was chosen for the park. Then there was a problem. The National Association, the governing body of the minor leagues, stipulates that franchises must be 35 miles apart, home plate to home plate — and Raleigh's proposed site is just 15 miles from Durham Athletic

Park, home of Miles Wolff's Bulls. Back to the drawing board.

Rapid City, South Dakota

Floyd Fitzgerald Stadium (Sioux Park Stadium)
Constructed: Spring 1957. *First game:* mid–June, 1957. *1957 season attendance:* 38,000 (21-game schedule, 1800 per game).

Back when it was known as Sioux Park Stadium, this field was home of the Basin League, a summer program for college players and managers. Now the ballpark is used exclusively for American Legion ball.

In 1957, Rapid City's first year in the Basin League, there was a wet spring, slowing up the construction of the new ballpark. Still, Sioux City Stadium was ready for the Basin League's mid–June start. There were three rows of box seats ($1.50) and eight rows of bench general admission seats (90 cents) from first to third. No roof. An early sign on the right center field fence advertised the Rushmore Motel. The park had no

permanent box office, refreshment
stands or clubhouses, and instead
operated out of sheds.

Star of the Rapid City Chiefs in 1957
was Frank Howard, then an All-Amer-
ican basketball player at Ohio State.

Reading, Pennsylvania

*Reading Municipal Memorial Sta-
dium*
Eastern League 1950–present (Phillies). *Location:* Centre Avenue (Route
61), just off the bypass. *Dimensions:*
Left field, 339 feet; center field, 411
feet; right field, 339 feet. *Seating capacity:* (1960) 8000, (1985) 8200. *1987
season attendance:* 100,895. *Refurbished:* 1987.

Craig Stein, who purchased the
Reading Phillies from Joe Buzas in December 1986, operated the club under a
lease arrangement in 1987, and refurbished the stadium for the 1988 season.
According to the *Albany Times Union,*
"Replacing the wood bleachers in the
large grandstand are nearly 5000 seats
of major league quality, dressed up in
attractive blue and red. The box seats
have a perk to beat even the big leagues.
Cup holders between every seat."

The Reading ballpark received a partial grandstand roof, new reserved and
box seats, more concession areas, and
a new electronic scoreboard. The improvements were paid for by both the
city of Reading and the Reading Phillies.

There is talk that the outfield fences
will be brought in to match those in
Veteran's Stadium in Philadelphia. The
power alleys now are very deep, and
Reading Phillies management feels that
some of the Reading ballplayers' power
stats inadequately reflect their power.

Screen fences with wooden billboards
leaning against them determine home
runs, while the entire complex is surrounded by a sturdy and attractive
brick wall. Out past the wooden fence,
inside the brick wall in left field is a hill,

where more advertising, such as the
Marlboro man, can be found.

Before the refurbishment, the grandstand had no roof, and the box seats
were folding chairs unattached to the
concrete floor. There were two press
boxes, one atop the grandstand behind
home (for baseball) and another atop
the bleachers along the third base line
(for football). The scoreboard was still
hand-operated and there were no warning tracks. Instead of a dirt track to
warn outfielders there were embankments. The flagpole was in front of the
fence in center and had to be covered at
the bottom with padding material.

Redwood, California

Rohnert Park Stadium
California League circa 1985. *Dimensions:* Left field, 330 feet; center
field, 400 feet; right field, 330 feet.
Seating capacity: 3500.

Reno, Nevada

Moana Municipal Stadium (formerly Moana Park)
California League 1955–64, 1966–
present (Silver Sox). *Location:* Moana
Lane, five blocks from U.S. 395's Exit
64. *Dimensions:* Left field, 339 feet;
center field, 420 feet; right field, 339
feet. *Seating capacity:* (1960) 3000;
(1985) 4500. *1987 season attendance:*
109,002.

An oddity in ballpark design. The
stands along the first base line are
roofed, while those directly behind
home are open bleachers with two rows
of box seats at the bottom.

Light towers stick up out of the
ground on either side of the behind-
home bleachers. Suspended between
the light towers above the backstop is a
net to further prevent foul balls from
leaving the premises. From the looks of
it, it may also catch a few low-flying
birds. Moana looks like it's set up for a
player-fan volleyball game.

Piccole Field
Home of the University of Nevada at Reno Wolfpack (West Coast Athletic Conference), present. *Seating capacity:* 1000.

Richmond, Virginia

Richmond Fairgrounds
Location: Franklin, Belvidere, Main and Laurel streets—current site of Monroe Park.

Used twice in 1875 for National Association games between Boston and Washington. On April 30, after one of these games played before a crowd of 1500, the *Richmond Dispatch* reported that "the ground had been laid off directly in front of the grandstand and to the left of the judges' stand." The grounds' roadways were lined with parked hacks and other vehicles. Poor police representation resulted in problems keeping fans off of the playing field.

Boschen Field
Home of baseball 1870s. *Location:* Currently Clay and Lombardy streets.

The first professional baseball team in Richmond was operated in the 1870s by a shoemaker named Henry Boschen, who had been advised by a doctor to seek out outdoor recreation. Everyone in town knew "Daddy" Boschen's shoe factory on Broad Street, between Second and Third streets. The team played their games at Boschen Field, opposite the Richmond, Fredericksburg & Potomac Railroad yards—not far from Mrs. Kidd's "Pin Money Pickle" factory.

Boschen not only owned the field and managed the team, but was also its star pitcher. Along with others nationwide, Boschen took credit for the invention of the spitter.

The beloved Pop Tate was backstop for Boschen's upshoot, on a team that included Jim Powell (nephew of the Powell who ran the old Richmond Theater), Barefoot R.F. Butler, Billy Nash, and Puss Luck.

Virginia Park
Eastern League, American Association 1884 (Virginias). *Location:* In a vacant lot outside the city limits, currently Lombardy and Franklin streets, Allen and Park avenues. *First American Association game:* August 5, 1884. *Last American Association game:* October 15, 1884.

The June 20, 1883, edition of the *Richmond Dispatch* reported that the previous day the Virginia Baseball Club had been founded, with William C. Seddon as its president, and was seeking a charter in an organized league. According to that paper, "A committee of three were appointed to secure suitable grounds."

The site chosen by the committee was to become the original Virginia Park. The park was located where Otway Allen's Farm had once been, at the current site of the General Fitzhugh Lee Monument at the west end of Franklin Street, extending all the way to Cary Street. It was a large field.

It was here that John L. Sullivan, the bare-knuckles champ of the time, crashed the gate even though local ruffian Lonnie Graves was "collecting pasteboards." Men came to the ballpark in carriage, hack, or "shank's mare," to root for the Dugan "brothers" battery. William, the pitcher, and Edward, the catcher, were actually unrelated. Between innings and after the game there was a mad rush for a spot at the brass bar beneath the grandstand for bock, lager, and 100 proof. From that old ballpark went Billy Nash to the Boston Red Stockings and Pop Tate to the Baltimore Orioles. Nash, who came out of Boschen's shoe factory (see Boschen Field), played 15 major league seasons (.275, 1072 runs, 1606 hits, 977 RBI's, 249 stolen bases), yet upon his death in 1929 the Richmond paper gave him a tiny obit that failed to mention he was a native.

A game famous in Richmond for many years was played at Virginia Park between Boschen's Richmonders and the Virginia Club of Sodden, a team composed of men Boschen trained from his factory. During that game Billy Barfoot got the good wood on a Charlie Ferguson inshoot and drove it against the outfield fence so hard that it snapped off the top of a wooden plank.

The Virginias entered the Eastern League at the beginning of the 1884 season. The Richmond *Dispatch* of May 14, 1884, described a typical game at Virginia Park:

"The first of three games between the Harrisburgs and the Virginias was played at Virginia Park yesterday afternoon. The game was called at 4:45, the Harrisburgs at bat. Weidel and Munyon formed the battery for the Harrisburgs while the Dugan brothers filled a similar position for the Virginias. There were about a thousand persons out to witness the game, and the weather and all circumstances were propitious for good sport. The game commenced in favor of the Virginias, they being able to score one run in the first inning, while the Harrisburgs in this, and in all succeeding innings, were blanked.... The Virginias, on the whole, played a good game, with but a few errors, while the Harrisburgs had a much larger number of errors and muffed a number of balls. This, in a measure, was owing to the fact that they were unacquainted with this ground. The game resulted in a 11-0 victory for the Virginias.

"The full [box] score could not be obtained for the reason that the official scorer was in such a hurry to leave the ground that he would not take time to let the *Dispatch* reporter get a copy of it. He promised to come to the office last night and bring it, but he did not put in an appearance...."

In the Eastern League, the Virginias played competition from Pennsylvania, Delaware and New Jersey. On August 5, when Washington dropped out of the American Association, a big league, the Virginias received an invitation to join. It was an opportunity too good to pass up.

The rest of the season proved difficult for the Virginias, as they were outclassed by their upgraded competition. They won only 12 of 42, and finished tenth on a field of 13. They led the league in only one category: errors per game. The following year the team played in another "Eastern League" and dominated. After the 1885 season Pop Tate and Bill Nash were sold to the Boston Nationals and the Richmond team broke up. There wouldn't be baseball in town again until 1890.

Mayo Island Park

Home of the Giants 1890, 1892, Virginia League 1921–30, Eastern League 1931–32 (Byrds), Piedmont League (Class B) 1933–41. *Location:* Mayo Island. On the east side of the 14th Street (Mayo) Bridge, hard against the Southern Railroad tracks and the Virginia Boat Club facility. *Dimensions:* (1921) Left field, 294 feet; center field, 400 feet; right field, 356 feet. *Seating capacity:* 4200. *First game:* March 25, 1890. *Lights:* 1933. *Fire:* 1924; May 25, 1941.

Here's how the *Dispatch* described Richmond's new ballpark, Opening Day, 1890: "Newly made and graded, the grounds were quite firm, and there was very little either of slipping or miring.... The space back of home plate was well covered with sawdust, and the heavy city street-roller, with six mules hitched to it, was on duty the whole day and did effective service."

The team that played here was owned by Main Street restaurateur Charles "Squire" Donati. The team competed locally for the most part, played an exhibition against big league competition now and again, and was rarely successful. The Giants, as they were called, only managed to complete one season, 1890, their first.

Baseball would return to Mayo Island

in 1921, and this time it would stay for twenty years.

The Illuminations of Mooers. Baseball in Richmond would not have survived the Depression had it not been for Eddie Mooers, who had played for Richmond in 1917, and who, along with his brother Willard, had run an auto dealership in town since 1924. Mooers paid the ball club's debts, moved the team into the Piedmont League and installed lights in Island Park, later renamed Tate Field after Pop Tate.

New lights in 1933 saved the Depression franchise. By 1934, according to baseball writer Oscar Eddleton, 15 of 19 minor leagues had lights in one or more of their parks. Baseball purists in the majors were very slow to realize the financial necessity of lights—and the big leagues played exclusively during the day until 1935. (*See* Cincinnati, Ohio.)

The field was used until 1941, when a fire forced the Colts to play most of the season on the road while Mooers built a new ballpark (Mooers Field) for the opening of the 1942 season. The land fell into disuse until bought by a trucking concern in 1957, and is today used by a trucking company and a trailer-repair business.

West End Park

Virginia League 1894–96 (Bluebirds). *Location:* Near the end of the Main Street car line, near Laurel Street.

In 1894, W.B. Bradley, a South Richmond construction magnate, bought a franchise for Richmond in the new Virginia League. He called his team the Crows and outfitted them in black uniforms. Bradley built a ballpark convenient to public transportation. The Crows won the pennant and regularly packed West End Park during their second season. But in 1896 the team was not as successful and interest lagged.

Broad Street Park (I)

Atlantic League 1897–99 (Johnnie Rebs, Bluebirds), Virginia League 1900, Virginia-Carolina League 1901, Virginia League (Class C) 1906–12 (Lawmakers, Colts). *Location:* Broad Street between Lombardy and Allen avenues. *Seating capacity:* 4800. *Attendance record:* 19,000 (doubleheader versus Danville, 1908).

Park was built by W.B. Bradley on land leased from the Richmond, Fredericksburg and Potomac Railroad. Boys used to gather in a triangular lot where Allen Avenue dead-ends at Broad, because that's where home runs went, and "chislers" got in free for retrieving a ball.

In 1906, baseball got a brand new start in Richmond in a brand new Virginia League. The season opened on April 26th, preceded by the city's first motorcade—all eight cars of it.

The outfield fence in right was built flush to the corners of a house so that the side wall of the house became part of the fence. The game could be watched from either the ground- or top-floor window.

Lee Park (Boulevard Field)

United States League (outlaw) 1912 (Rebels), Virginia League 1917–21 (Climbers). *Location:* North Boulevard, Moore Street. *Seating capacity:* 4400.

The outlaw United States League (which was pretending to be a "third major league") franchise in Richmond was owned by E.C. Landgraf, who built a park for his Rebels in 28 days. The Rebels didn't play much longer than that. The problem was they didn't play anything like big leaguers, and neither did the rest of the league of has-beens and never-wases. The United States League was out of business by June 24, 1912, but the Rebels didn't make it that far. A headline in the June 4 issue of the *Richmond Times-Dispatch* read, "Players Determined Not to Play Again Until They Are Paid."

Virginia League baseball moved to this park in 1917, at which time it was enlarged. It was used until early in the

1921 season, when a shake-up in management left a landlord and a tenant who weren't speaking. The ball club moved back to Mayo Island, where ball had been played back in the 1890s.

Broad Street Park (II)

Virginia League 1913-14 (Colts), International League 1915-16 (Virginians, Climbers). *Location:* Addison and Broad streets, current site of the Science Museum. *Renovated:* 1914.

Another W.B. Bradley creation, also built on Richmond, Fredericksburg and Potomac Railroad land. In 1914, the Virginia League franchise was moved to Rocky Mount, North Carolina, so that Jack Dunn could bring his (International League) Baltimore Orioles to Richmond, chased out of Baltimore by the Federal League. Dunn refurbished the Broad Street Park abandoned by the Colts.

For the first time, Richmond fans went through turnstiles to see a game. Before that, attendance had to be counted by hand. The Broad Street Park was used only through the 1916 season, when the railroad company decided they needed it to build a new terminal.

City Stadium

Eastern League 1931-32 (Byrds, some games). *Constructed:* circa 1930.

Used for big games when a parking lot was needed. Parking on Mayo Island had proven to be a problem.

Mooers Field

Piedmont League 1942-53 (Colts). *Location:* Roseneath, Norfolk, Belleville, and Carlton streets. *Dimensions:* Left field, 335 feet; center field, 380 feet; right field, 330 feet. *Seating capacity:* 4300.

The Diamond (Parker Field 1953-84)

International League 1953-64, 1966-present (Virginians, Braves). *Location:* 3001 North Boulevard. *Built:* 1934, 1985. *Construction cost:* (1985) $8

million. Rebuilt from September 1984 to April 1985, re-opened April 17, 1985. *Dimensions:* (1966) Left field, 325 feet; center field, 400 feet; right field, 325 feet. (1988) Left field, 330 feet; center field, 402 feet; right field, 330 feet. *Fences:* (1985) Ten feet all the way around. *Surface:* Grass. *Seating capacity:* (1960) 9500, (1975) 9588, (1985) 12,148. Field level box seats, 3205; superboxes, 130; reserved seats (first ten rows in upper deck), 2218; general admission seats (rows 11-30 in upper deck), 6595. *Single game attendance record:* 15,864 (April 28, 1983, exhibition game versus the Atlanta Braves). *Season attendance record:* 403,252 (1986). *1987 season attendance:* 332,440.

$200,000 was raised in a couple of hours on January 5, 1954, so that Parker Field could be readied for AAA-level baseball. In 1985, when the park was completely rebuilt, the scoreboard was moved to Pitt Field so it could be used by the University of Richmond baseball team.

Of the $8 million required to transform Parker Field into the Diamond, $4 million came from the city of Richmond and the counties of Henrico and Chesterfield. The other $4 million came from private and corporate donations. The Braves drew 1.1 million fans during the first three years of the Diamond's existence.

Pitt Field

Home of the University of Richmond Spiders (Colonial Athletic Association), present. *Dimensions:* Left field, 328 feet; right field, 328 feet. *Fences:* Left field, 8 feet; center field, 10 feet; right field, 8 feet. *Seating capacity:* 600. *Renovated:* 1985.

The Spiders play on a field made of Bermuda grass, featuring red clay and sand baselines. There is a new (1985) drainage system, so that standing water is no longer a problem in the outfield. Outside the playing field, the facility boasts astroturfed bullpens, a batting cage along the third base line, and

Top: *Parker Field, Richmond, Va.* Bottom: *The Diamond, or Parker Field reincarnated. (Both photos compliments of the Richmond Braves.)*

new dugouts with plenty of storage space.

The electronic scoreboard that stands behind the left center fence once stood in Parker Field. It was donated in 1985 by the Richmond Braves. Behind home plate, between the two sets of bleachers, is a two-story press and scout viewing area. The improvements have enhanced the University of Richmond's recruiting ability for their baseball program.

Riverhead, New York

Riverhead Stadium (Wivchar Stadium)
Home of Negro National League games. *Location:* Long Island. Harrison and Roanoke avenues, School Street, Old Country Road. *Dimensions:* Left field, 325 feet; left center, 410 feet; center field, 500 feet; right center, 410 feet; right field, 325 feet. *Fences:* Ten feet all the way around.

Riverside, California

Riverside Sports Complex
California League 1988–present (Red Wave). *Location:* 1000 Blaine Avenue. *Dimensions:* Left field, 330 feet; center field, 400 feet; right field, 330 feet. *Seating capacity:* 3500.
Franchise moved here from Salinas, California.

Roanoke, Virginia

Maher Field
Virginia League circa 1940 (Tigers), Piedmont League (Class B) 1943–52 (Red Sox, Rosox). *Location:* Adjacent to Victory Stadium. *Seating capacity:* 3000-3500. *Record season high attendance:* 139,000 (rounded figure, 1949). *Record season low attendance:* 43,000 (rounded figure, 1952).
In a recent interview by John Pugh in *The Roanoker,* former Red Sox pitcher

Bill Slack remembered what it used to be like in Class B ball in the 1940s:

"My first game in pro ball we were losing 1–0 with two out in the [bottom of the] ninth. Sheriff Robinson [later a coach for the New York Mets], a .180 hitter, was up for us. Everybody figured we were as good as beaten. Robinson promptly hit a three-run homer. The fans went wild, and when Robinson rounded third, they started pouring onto the field to congratulate him. When he reached home plate, fans were waiting with money in their hands. They started shoving five and 10 dollar bills into his pockets as he made his way from home plate to the dugout. I had never seen anything like it. I just stood there in awe of that kind of fan reaction. When Robinson got to the clubhouse, he counted his money — and found they had given him $160. I sat there looking at all of that money on the table, still hearing all that tumult, the players all whooping it up. I thought, 'This has got to be one of the best baseball towns in America.'

"There was a little restaurant near the park where a lot of ballplayers would go after the game. The fans sometimes came over and they were always nice. There was a big boarding house where 10 of us players lived; so it was a close team, and close to the fans. Maher Field was a very good playing field. The only drawback was that the clubhouse was about 100 yards behind the center field gate, over near Victory Stadium."

The greatest game ever at Maher Field was played May 25, 1949. By the seventh inning stretch, the Newport News Dodgers had taken a 13–4 lead over the Rosox. Roanoke rallied for four runs in the bottom of the seventh, and the Dodgers scored once in the eighth. The Rosox now trailed 14–8, and scored five times in the eighth to pull within one. After holding the Dodgers scoreless in the ninth, the Rosox had two on with two out, Charley Maxwell coming up. Maxwell was easily the most popular Rosox player ever. He was outgoing, married a local girl, and on this day smashed a towering three-run homer to win the game 16–14. The Rosox had needed 12 runs in the final three innings to secure the victory. Maxwell went 4-for-6 on the day with 6 RBIs. For the year, he hit .345 and knocked in 112. Experts say he could have hit .400 if he hadn't been a sucker for high heat. (Maxwell was called up to the majors late in the 1950 season and stayed for 14 years.)

The team folded operations after the 1952 season. Owner LeRoy Schneider was tired of pouring money into the club to keep it functioning. Maher Field was deserted, and was left for years to deteriorate until there were those so young they thought of it only as an eyesore with a peeling pale-green cinderblock wall in left and a handful of worn seats around home, unaware that it had ever been an attractive place to play ball.

The year after the Roanoke Red Sox folded, nearby Salem, Virginia, received a franchise in the Appalachian League, and the Rosox were hardly missed.

Rochester, Minnesota

Mayo Field

Rochester's premiere baseball field 1904–1920s, 1946–present. *Location:* At the confluence of the Zumbro River and Bear Creek. *Lights:* 1949. *Current grandstand built:* 1951. *Cost of current grandstand:* $80,000.

In 1904 the Doctors Mayo—whose clinic is Rochester's best-known feature—donated to the city the land where Mayo Field was built. The donation came with the following condition:

"Said premises shall always be used for the playing of baseball, football, and any and all athletic work, games, sports, and exhibitions, permitting under the Laws of the State of Minnesota, whether admission fee or price

is charged or not, for the holding of legal gatherings and assemblages, for school, college, agricultural fairs and exhibits, fairs and exhibits of animals and fowls, school athletic work, games and exhibits, for any and all educational, charitable, instructive, or entertaining purpose or purposes and for purpose beneficial to the City of Rochester, Minnesota and the residents thereof."

In Mayo Field's early years, it was already used for all of the area's major athletic contests. The grandstand was on the south end of the field near the Van Dusen garage, configured so that too many foul balls went into the river.

The site fell into relative disuse (no baseball) from the 1920s until the end of World War II. Rochester's baseball was played elsewhere.

In 1945, the Utility Department traded the Mayo Field site to the Parks Department in exchange for the land (formerly Mill Pond) where the current light plant stands. The diamond was moved to the other end of the field, a $9600 rest room-concession stand-office building behind it. There were open bleachers on either side of the building. In 1946, the adjacent area—which has been, since 1962, the Park and Recreation Department headquarters and parking lot—was used as a skating rink.

In 1951, a grandstand (the current one) was built above the office building and between the open bleachers behind home plate. The new grandstand forced two light towers to be moved further from the field, and that necessitated the addition of new light fixtures.

The stadium was last refurbished in 1973. $10,000 was put into sandblasting and painting the grandstand, resodding the infield, and repairing the outfield fences.

Mayo Field continues to be used for semi-pro, American Legion, and V.F.W. ball. It is the site of league play between Rochester's three high schools.

Baseball in Rochester, N.Y., was so popular as early as 1860 that songs were written about clubs like the Live Oaks. (Sheet music cover from the Lester S. Levy Collection of Sheet Music, Special Collections, Milton S. Eisenhower Library, The Johns Hopkins University. Used by permission.)

Rochester, New York

Rochester's lively interest in baseball dates back as far as 1858, when the big rivalry in town was between the two best amateur teams, the Flour City Nine and the Live Oaks. The Oaks even had their own song, the "Live Oak Polka."

Hop Bitters Grounds

International Association 1880 (Hop Bitters), New York State League 1885 (Hop Bitters). *Location:* North Union Street at Weld Street, on the west side of Union, north of Main Street.

The Hop Bitters Grounds and ball club were owned and operated by Asa T. Soule, creator and head promoter of a nostrum called "Hop Bitters, the Invalid's Friend and Hope." Soule never let on that he lacked faith in his tonic; in fact, he made his ballplayers take a teaspoonful apiece before games, and doubled the dosage after losses. His motto was "We shall march from victory to victory." During the winter, Soule took his team south for barn-

storming tours. In New Orleans they caused quite a sensation, and a ballpark was built just for their two-month stay.

On June 10, 1885, there was Ladies Day at the Hop Bitters Grounds.

Stars of the team while in Rochester were Big Dan Brouthers and Buck Ewing — both later Hall of Famers — who were the first baseman and the catcher respectively.

Culver Field

Eastern League 1886–89 (Broncos), American Association 1890, Eastern League 1891–92, 1898–1907 (Beau Brummels). *Location:* University Avenue (current site of the Gleason Works), Russell Street, Culver Road. Northwest corner of University and Culver. *Fire:* 1892.

According to Jack Burgess in the *Rochester Times Union,* the site of Culver Field "had been a woods and was owned, I believe, by the Culver family after whom Culver Road is named. A couple of young enthusiasts, headed by Charley Vick, whose folks founded the Vick Seed Company, mapped out the grounds...."

The ballpark was built in 1886 and destroyed by fire in 1892. It was rebuilt in 1898 and remained in use until 1907 when Gleason Works took over the site.

Rochester fielded its only big league team in 1890, when they had a franchise in the American Association. The AA was one of three big leagues operating that year, the year of the Players League. It was the Brotherhood rebellion that forced the American Association to relocate many of its teams — bringing major league baseball to upstate New York and Ohio. Along with Rochester, Syracuse and Toledo received franchises for the 1890 season. All were gone by the following year. This was the last year the American Association functioned as a major circuit, though a league by that name has existed for many years at the AAA level.

All but four American Association teams went out of business in 1890, and the remaining quartet joined the National League. The Players League folded, and the eldest league functioned alone with 12 teams until 1899.

The Players League had stolen some of the biggest stars of the game, including Buck Ewing and Hoss Radbourne. The American Association's strategy, along with relocating to cities that hadn't previously had major league ball, was to give the ballplayers more money while charging fans less for admission. This kind of thinking never makes good business.

The 1890 team — which had no recorded nickname — was owned by General Henry Brinker and managed by Patrick Powers. They went 63-63 on the season and finished just out of the first division, fifth in an eight-team loop.

The star pitcher for Rochester was Bob Barr, a 34-year-old journeyman right-hander, who went 28-24. Barr pitched for five years in the majors —

no two in a row with the same club. This was Barr's only winning season.

The hitting star was centerfielder Sandy Griffin, who led the team in home runs with five, and in hitting (.307).

Baseball was not enjoying peak popularity in the 1890s. Cap Anson was *still* playing first base for Chicago in the National League, knocking in 100 runs a year, and Jack Glasscock and Mike Tiernan were smacking the horsehide for the New York Giants.

Still, the biggest stars of the deadball era had yet to start playing. Cy Young was in his rookie season in 1890. Honus Wagner didn't make it to the major league level until 1897. Christy Mathewson premiered at the turn of the century, Ty Cobb in 1905.

In 1890, Benjamin Harrison was president of the United States, his administration sandwiched by the two Grover Cleveland efforts. This was the year the last major battle between native Americans and United States troops was fought at Wounded Knee. The troops won. This was the year the first execution by electrocution was performed (in Auburn, New York).

The Rochester teams' uniforms were heavy, baggy and made of wool, worn with quilted knickers — with hip-length wool sweaters for warm-ups. It was believed that sweating cleansed the impurities from the body, so these heavy uniforms — warm-ups and all — were worn even during the dog days.

Catchers wore no protection. No mask. No cup. Nothing. These were *men*. The number of balls required for a walk had just been lowered from five to four. Pitchers got a running start, like a bowler in cricket, from a box — the box pitchers are still getting knocked out of — only 50 feet from the plate.

The rule allowing pitchers to deliver the ball overhand had been instituted only six years before. There were other differences in the rules, but the biggest difference was the level of violence.

Spikes were sharpened for high

slides. With only one umpire to watch the games, runners were routinely tripped as they tried to advance. Brawls were commonplace. The quantity of tobacco chewed was about the same.

After 1890, Culver Field returned to being the home of minor league ball. The huge fire that destroyed Culver Field left Rochester without baseball for much of that decade. When the grandstand was rebuilt in 1898, the job was flimsy. In 1906, during an Eastern League contest, the right field stands collapsed. The owner of the Rochester ball club, Charles T. Chapin's Rochester Baseball and Amusement Company, suffered many lawsuits.

Riverside Park
Eastern League 1895–97 (Brownies). *Location:* On the east bank of the Genesee River, north of Norton Street, opposite the present site of Seneca Park.

The team that played here was named the Brownies in honor of hometown boy George Eastman's new camera.

Jones Square
American Association 1890 (some games). *Location:* Plymouth Avenue at Lorimer Street.

Windsor Beach
American Association 1890 (some games). *Location:* Irondequoit, across city line. Current site of Norcrest Drive. At the mouth of the Genesee River at Lake Ontario.

Ontario Beach Grounds
Circa 1898. *Location:* Charlotte (cha-LOT) section. Beach Avenue.

Used once for a National League game between Brooklyn and Cleveland. There is still a large athletic field (two diamonds) across Beach Avenue from the Ontario Beach bath-house.

Bay Street Park
Eastern League 1908–1911, International League 1912–28 (Beau Brummels, Hustlers, Red Wings). *Location:* South side of Bay Street, east of Webster Avenue.

The outfield was big enough for cars and carriages to park out there, in front of a billboard sign that read: "Fone 519 For Carriage Service." The first home run (an inside-the-parker) was struck in 1908 by the Beau Brummels' Ross "Tex" Erwin. The 1916 Rochester Hustlers featured Carmen Hill, the first professional pitcher to wear spectacles.

At the 1913 home opener, six men desperate to see the action from the outfield actually constructed a wooden perch on the outfield fence so they could see over the carriages parked in the outfield.

Only one ball was ever struck over the scoreboard at the Bay Street Park. Appropriately enough, it was hit by Babe Ruth, when he was a pitcher for the International League Baltimore Orioles.

Silver Stadium (Red Wing Stadium 1929–67)
International League 1929–present. *Location:* 500 Norton Street (first base), Clinton Avenue (third base), Joseph Avenue (right field), Bastian Street (left field). *Built:* 1928. *Refurbished:* 1986. *Refurbishing cost:* $4.5 million. *Dimensions:* (1988) Left field, 320 feet; center field, 415 feet; right field, 315 feet. *Surface:* Grass. *Seating capacity:* (1960) 14,475; (1975) 12,500; (1985) 13,080. *Single game attendance record:* 19,006 (May 5, 1931, Newark Bears 4, Rochester 1). Second place, 18,681 (May 4, 1949, versus Jersey City). *Season attendance record:* 443,533 (1949). *1987 season attendance:* 315,807. *First game:* May 2, 1929 (Reading Keys 2, Rochester 0, attendance: 15,127). *First night game:* August 18, 1933, Baltimore 12, Rochester 3, attendance, 15,000.

The first home run at Red Wing Stadium was struck only two days after it opened, by the Red Wings' Rip Collins, while playing the Jersey City Cats.

A Sunday doubleheader at Red Wing Stadium, Rochester, N.Y., on August 30, 1931, attendance 18,000. (Photo from the private collection of Kevin Johnston at The Clubhouse.)

When originally built, the bleachers beyond the grandstand in left field wrapped around the foul pole so home runs could be caught. The bleachers' size was greatly diminished by the reconfiguration in that corner, which enabled a triple deck of advertisement signs to go all the way from the foul pole to the side of the scoreboard in left center.

The elongated bleachers did not last long and were soon altered to their current size, fitting nicely between the end of the grandstand and the left field corner.

Grandma's Button Read, "Luke's Our Boy!" In 1959 Luke Easter, the former Cleveland Indian first baseman—who was close to fifty at the time—led the Red Wings in homers. (According to the *Baseball Encyclopedia,* Easter was born in 1915, but Easter admitted to being 52 years old in 1963, by then almost exclusively a pinch hitter specializing in instant victory.) He also hit Red Wing Stadium's most awesome home run, striking the top of the right field light tower.

He couldn't run, but AAA pitching looked fat. Another shot of Easter's went just foul and rolled forever down Norton Street that same year. He was a huge man whose friendliness, community spirit, and timely exhibitions of power made him, by far, the most popular Red Wing of all time.

As a player in the Negro Leagues, Easter had been the first to hit a home run into the center field bleachers at the Polo Grounds. Years later, with the Cleveland Indians, his shot into the top of the upper deck at Municipal Stadium was said to be the longest home run ever struck in that park.

Faces in the Crowd. During the 1960s, Red Wing Stadium's resident character was Victor "Red" Smith, an elderly bespectacled man who came to every game, and walked back and forth along the grandstand aisle, waving his cap in the air, shouting "YA! YA! YA! YA!" It was a rally cry that lit up the faces of Red Wing fans no matter what the score.

Among the others during those days who never missed a game was Mrs. Walter Fox, who always brought her scorebook and sat in her season box,

Top: *Red Wing Stadium, Rochester, N.Y., 1934. The first inner fence has been built in right, to keep the new light tower off of the playing field. Later this fence would be drawn in even further. (Photo from the private collection of Kevin Johnston at The Clubhouse, Rochester, N.Y.)* Bottom: *Silver Stadium, 1987. (Photo by Bernie Liberatore, compliments of the Rochester Baseball Club.)*

usually with her daughter Dorothy. Her records were so complete and so accurate that, on occasion, she was consulted by the International League for statistical information.

For as long as anyone could remember, spry Corky Yannock (known to the fans who loved him as Augie) had been sprinkling the infield. Dick Sierens had been cutting the grass.

As the last stop before the majors in the Baltimore Orioles' farm system, Silver Stadium was home to many future stars—like Bobby Grich, Don Baylor, Boog Powell, Cal Ripken, and Davey Johnson.

On August 18, 1968, the name of the ballpark was changed to Silver Stadium, in honor of Morrie Silver, a man who had twice almost single-handedly saved the Red Wings from bankruptcy. The Wings lost that night, after the dedication ceremony, 2-1, to the Jacksonville Suns.

Following the 1986 season, the grandstand at Silver Stadium received a much-needed refurbishment. Seats were replaced and everything was painted. Just to the left of straightaway center, at the deepest part of the ballpark, the old hand-operated scoreboard was finally replaced by a fully electric version. There remained a triple deck of signs in left, in front of the bullpens. The foundation of the stadium was rebuilt, and a new wine and beer garden was installed in the open area between the front gate and the grandstand.

In the summer of 1987, the refurbished Silver Stadium was used for a Grateful Dead concert. For weeks afterward, fielders complained about damage done to the field by Deadheads pretending they were falling leaves.

Rockford, Illinois

The Commons

Home of the Forest Citys, 1865. *Location:* North side of Whitman and Church streets.

The Forest Citys organized August 10, 1865, representing 150 Rockford businessmen who liked to play ball. All of the expenses to carry on the pastime were met by merchants and manufacturers.

Fairgrounds Park

Home of the Forest Citys 1866-70, National Association 1871, Western Association circa 1890s. *Location:* Acorn Street, Kilburn Avenue, the St. Paul Railroad, Mulberry Street. *Dimensions:* No outfield fence. *Seating capacity:* 300-500. *First National Association game:* May 5, 1871. *Last National Association game:* September 26, 1871.

The games in the summer of 1865 were played on the commons just north of the Whitman and Church streets intersection. In 1866, a retired dentist named Dr. Norman introduced his community to the concept of seating for the viewing of baseball when he had benches for the ladies hauled to Fairgrounds Park from Brown's Hall before a game against nearby Freeport. The ladies said at the time that the seats were built like church pews and were the last word in discomfort.

The Forest Citys took the field back then in white, stiff-bosom shirts with paper collars, long white canton flannel trousers, woolly side out, tied with strings at the ankles. There was a blue star on the crown of their white caps. These were the days when a man claimed to feel renewed health after a therapeutic sweat.

In 1866, Dr. Norman promoted a tournament at Fairgrounds Park. He charged 25 cents, the first admission charge in Rockford history for baseball. Doubleheaders were held daily. Businesses closed at noon so that workers could play or watch. Many of the teams that would five years later be in the National Association attended Norman's tournament. Teams from Philadelphia, New York, Brooklyn (Atlantics), Milwaukee (Cream Citys), Chicago (White Stockings), Pecatonica, Boston, and Cincinnati (Red Stockings). The winners, predictably enough, were the Red Stockings. The trophy was a mahogany baseball bat whose business end was engraved silver. The consolation prize, a tin horn, went to Pecatonica. The true trophy was the keg, and everyone was a winner. In fact, there was so much beer that the police department and volunteer firemen had to be called to help finish the celebration, which they did without complaint.

Some of the celebrities who played for Rockford were Cap Anson, Al Spalding and Bob Addy. Bob married his wife, Ida, while a second baseman for the Forest Citys. Between seasons he ran a tin shop on West State Street. Will B. Bourbon was the treasurer of the club. The first nine had day jobs and practiced only at night. Their "clubhouse" was over the Haskell Seed Store, just north of Ashton and North Main streets.

By 1869, the Rockford nine were considered one of the best teams in the "northwest." Overall, they were 26–10. These weren't gamblers or ringers, but local amateurs, and Rockford was proud of them. That year, the Forest City club tied the unbeaten Cincinnati Red Stockings in a 12-inning game called by Harry Wright on account of darkness. Because of the Red Stockings' presumed superiority, Rockford considered the tie a victory of sorts.

First and foremost among the stars of the early Rockford nine was Al G. Spalding of Byron, Illinois. His hurling accounted for the club's winning record. Spalding got so good that he skipped town in 1871 for the big money in Boston, where he went 21–10 as an opponent during Rockford's sole big league campaign. That year, Rockford went 6–20, last in the National Association. It wasn't Adrian (later Cap) Anson's fault. He made 43 hits and 30 runs in 25 games (.352). The manager was Hiram Waldo, Rockford bookstore owner and major team investor.

Let's let John Clifford tell about it. He was there:

"The team got good and it was but natural that Uncle Hi put money into the Forest Citys—especially after his clerk Al (Spalding) beat the Nationals of Washington, who had a reputation like that of today's [1934's] Yankees.

"The games were played at Fairgrounds Park, and a poorer field, to my mind, has never been known. There was a cluster of five trees around third base. The catcher was hemmed in by trees with the exception of a space about 30 by 50 feet. The umpire could not see a foul unless it was hit back of the plate or a few feet on either side of the base lines.

"Between the plate and second base the terrain was fairly level, but approaching third base there was a notable rise. From third to the plate there was a depression. The baserunner had to dig in for life.

"At the edge of the outfield was a deep gutter that drained a nearby quarter-mile track. Only Providence's protection kept more players from breaking legs in that trap. Bad as the playing field was, all of the stars of the day came there to do their stuff."

Mr. Clifford was asked to describe Fairgrounds Park's accommodations for fans:

"The bleachers were situated along first base and the plate. They held 300 to 500 persons, and were made of bridge planking. In the later years of the club's existence, there was built a grandstand, primarily to protect the scorers, who were Horace Buker, the jeweler, and Henry W. Price. The grandstand held 30 to 40 persons.

"The refreshment privilege was presided over by the Kellogg Brothers, John and Prentice. Lemonade and peanuts were all they had to offer. The price was five cents a glass. Gum was not available, except spruce and white wax, a derivative of kerosene oil."

The Grays versus the Locals. Mr. Clifford, a former Rockford resident who moved to Savanna, Illinois, in the 1930s, also recalled a game held in September of 1884 at Fairgrounds Park between the Providence Grays, managed by Harry Wright, and a selected local nine. A fellow commanding great respect, Frank Lander, footed the entire $400 bill for the game to be played. All of the Grays came to the exhibition except the one everyone wanted to see, Ol' Hoss Radbourne. Radbourne had been given a much-deserved rest after pitching 23 games in a row. Clifford noted that it was Grays manager Harry Wright's first appearance in Rockford in 15 years:

"When Harry Wright had last appeared on the old fair grounds, 1869, his full beard was auburn. At this game

I am describing his facial adornment was gray Dundrearies.

"The game finally got under way and at the end of the third inning the score stood 20 to 0 for Providence. At this time the Providence team began to kill time, waiting for darkness, but Harry Wright was a stickler for the ethics of the pastime and called his captain toward the bench and stated: 'I expect every man to do his best as though this were a regularly scheduled game and the player who does not will be short in his next paycheck.' The final score was 73 to 3 in favor of Providence."

Gentleman Jim Plays First. Former heavyweight champion Jim Corbett, the man who took John L. Sullivan's belt, came to Rockford in the summer of 1897 to play some ball for the Rockfords of the Western Association at Fairgrounds Park. Corbett played first base for one game on September 13, 1897, against Cedar Rapids. The total receipts for the game were $475. Corbett's share of the take was $213.52. It was the largest crowd of the year. The boxer had a respectable day. He went one for four at the plate, scored a run, and made one error in thirteen chances in the field. Rockford won the game 2 to 1. Time: 1:20. Fastest that season. Maybe somebody had to catch a train.

Legion Park
Home of the Industrial Leagues during the World War II years.

Marinelli Field
Midwest League 1988 (Expos). *Location:* Blackhawk Park. *Dimensions:* Left field, 330 feet; center field, 400 feet; right field, 330 feet. *Seating capacity:* 4200.
Home of a 1988 Midwest League expansion franchise.

Rocky Mount, North Carolina

Railroaders Park
Circa 1909 (Railroaders).
It was here that Jim Thorpe played

those professional baseball games that cost him his pair of Olympic gold medals. He played for the Rocky Mount Railroaders 1909–10, while attending Carlisle Institute. He won the golds in 1912, in the Olympic pentathlon and decathlon, but was later disqualified because of his professional status with the Railroaders. The Associated Press named Thorpe the greatest athlete of the first half of the century. Thorpe went on to play for the New York Giants. His gold medals were posthumously restored to him in 1982.

Tar Heel Park
Virginia League circa 1900 (Tar Heels). *Seating capacity:* 4500.

Briles Field
Virginia League circa 1915 (Downhomers, Rocks). *Seating capacity:* 3200.

Municipal Stadium
Piedmont League 1936–40 (Rocks), Coastal Plain League 1941, 1946–52, Bi-State League 1942, Carolina League 1962–(at least) 1972. *Constructed:* 1936. *Dimensions:* Left field, 350 feet; center field, 350 feet; right field, 346 feet. *Seating capacity:* 4500. *Cost of construction:* $30,000. *Torn down:* December 1987.
One of the most popular ballplayers to appear in a Rocky Mount uniform was Johnny Pesky, who broke into pro ball in 1940. In 1946 a tall, slow lefty named Bill Kennedy struck out 456 in 280 innings — and pitched the Rocks to a pennant.
Most people think of Municipal Stadium as a football stadium. For many years it was the home field of the Rocky Mount Senior High School Gryphons.

Rome, New York

League Park (formerly Murray's Park)
Canadian-American League 1936

(Watertown Grays, one game), 1937 (Colonels). *Location:* West Rome.

A sign out front said, "Welcome to League Park, Fort of the Rome Colonels." This was an old semi-pro park fixed up by the Colonels' owner, a former umpire named Knight. He spent so much money fixing up League Park (new fence, new bleachers, new grandstand roof, new concession stand) that he went broke and had to sell the club. His refurbished grounds were not used for minor league ball for even a full season.

Colonels Park

Canadian-American League 1938–1942, 1946–51 (Colonels). *Location:* Black River Boulevard, Pine Street. Downtown, current site of a senior citizen housing project. *Dedicated:* May 18, 1938 (Rome versus Gloversville, attendance 2661, Can-Am League record). *Construction cost:* $15,000. *Dimensions:* Left field, 360 feet; center field, 380 feet; right field, 320 feet. *Seating capacity:* 3500 (box seats, 80). *First night game:* June 11, 1942 (Rome 6, Quebec 5, attendance: 1023, season high, winning pitcher: Dale Matthewson). *Torn down:* 1952.

On March 31, 1938, Dr. Dan Mellen, new president of the Rome Colonels, announced the purchase of land for a new ballpark in the rear of Franklyn's Field, off Black River Boulevard. By the beginning of that year's Canadian-American League season, the place was built, an eight-row grandstand behind home, and four-row bleachers on either side. The skin diamond was noted for its hardness.

When the land was sold to a developer to turn into a housing project, he built a house for himself in what used to be left field.

After World War II a plaque was put upon Colonels Park's facade honoring the three Colonels that had been killed in action. That plaque now resides in Rome's VFW hall.

Sacramento, California

Edmonds Field (Moreing Field 1931–35, Cardinal Field 1936–circa 1945)

Pacific Coast League 1931–60. *Location:* Y Street (now Broadway), Riverside Street, and First Avenue, now the site of a supermarket. *Dimensions:* Left field, 326 feet; center field, 463 feet; right field, 326 feet. *Seating capacity:* 10,000. *Fire:* 1948. *Last used for baseball:* 1960.

St. Catherines, Ontario

Community Park

New York–Pennsylvania League 1986–present (Blue Jays). *Location:* Merritt Road at Seymour, next to Merritton High School. *Construction cost:* $750,000. *Dimensions:* Left field, 310 feet; center field, 400 feet; right field, 310 feet. *Seating capacity:* (1986) 530; (1987) 2000. *1987 season attendance:* 48,015.

During their first season in the NYP League, the St. Catherines Blue Jays played before a small grandstand along the first base line holding 530 people. The ballpark was enlarged in 1987 with bleacher seats on the other side of the field.

The town is particularly popular among black and Hispanic ballplayers, who find the Canadian community devoid of the all-too-familiar prejudices of other places.

St. Louis, Missouri

Sportsman's Park (Busch Stadium, 1953–66)

First used for baseball as an open lot in the 1860s. Enclosed stands built 1871. National Association 1875 (Brown Stockings), National League 1876–77, 1920–66 (Cardinals), American Association 1882–91, American League 1902–53 (Browns). *Location:* Dodier Street (first base side), Spring Street (third base), Sullivan Avenue (left field), Grand Avenue (right field). *Refurbished:* 1925. *Cost of refurbishment:* $500,000. *Dimensions:* (1961) Left field, 351 feet; center field, 426 feet; right field, 310 feet. 75 feet from home plate to the backstop. *Seating capacity:* (1909) 18,000. (1925) 30,500, broken down as follows: deluxe boxes, 128; boxes, 3617; grandstand reserved, 19,552; general admission, 2203; bleacher (left field), 2600; pavilion (right field), 2400. *Browns day game attendance record:* 34,625 (October 1, 1944, versus New York). *Browns doubleheader attendance record:* 31,932 (June 17, 1928, versus New York). *Browns night game attendance record:* 22,847 (May 24, 1940, versus Cleveland). *Browns opening game attendance record:* 19,561 (April 18, 1923, versus Detroit). *Browns season high attendance record:* 712,918 (1922). *Browns season low attendance record:* 80,922 (1935). *Cardinals day game attendance record:* 41,284 (September 15, 1935, versus New York). *Cardinals doubleheader attendance record:* 45,770 (July 12, 1931, versus Chicago). *Cardinals night game attendance record:* 33,323 (August 25, 1942, versus Brooklyn). *Cardinals opening game attendance record:* 26,246 (April 15, 1962, versus Chicago). *Cardinals season high attendance record:* 1,430,676 (1949). *Cardinals season low attendance record:* 256,171 (1933). *First National Association game:* May 6, 1875. *Last National Association game:* October 8, 1875. *First National League game:* May 5, 1876 (St. Louis 1, Chicago 0). *First National League night game:* June 4, 1940 (Brooklyn 10, Cards 1). *Last National League game:* May 8, 1966 (San Francisco 10, St. Louis 5). *First American Association game:* May 2, 1882 (St. Louis 9, Louisville 7). *Last American Association game:* October 4, 1891 (doubleheader, St. Louis 8, Louisville 0; Louisville 4, St. Louis 3, 8 innings). *First American League game:* April 23, 1902 (St. Louis 5, Cleveland 2). *First*

American League night game: May 24, 1940 (Cleveland 3, Browns 2, attendance: 25,562, winning pitcher: Bob Feller). *Last American League game:* September 27, 1953 (Chicago 2, St. Louis 1, 11 innings.

This plot of land housed major league baseball longer than any other spot, off and on for over 90 years. Counting games played here in the 1860s, when this was just an empty lot, the site was a ballpark for over a century. **The Beauty of the Stockholders' Pavilion.** On June 3, 1875, the *St. Louis Republican,* following a game between the St. Louis Brown Stockings and the Boston Red Stockings, wrote this about the ballpark:

"As early as two o'clock people began to file into the spacious stands and pavilions within the enclosure on Grand Avenue, and until half-past four o'clock the living stream poured through the gates and occupied every available seat and space of turf set apart for spectators. The attendance was not less than six thousand, and the stockholders' pavilion presented a most beautiful appearance, being nearly filled with the elite and St. Louis' fair sex."

When the ballpark on Grand Avenue fell into disuse after the failure of St. Louis' first attempt at maintaining a National League franchise, Alfred H. Spink helped organize the Sportsman's Park and Club Association, and it was this group that not only fixed the ballpark up for major league ball, but lent its name to the facility.

Von der Ahe. The field and the team (an American Association franchise, and then a National League franchise) soon became the property of Chris Von der Ahe. It was he who installed the first ladies' room in Sportsman's Park, in 1885.

Von der Ahe made a career for himself in beer and whiskey, and much of his profits went into his ball club. According to Douglas Wallop in his book, *Baseball: An Informal History:* "In no particular order, (Von der Ahe's) consuming interests were baseball, money, whiskey and women. Baseball at first was incidental. Among other enterprises, he owned a saloon and boarding house adjacent to the St. Louis ball park and he could not help noticing the baseball fans, both before and after the game, drank a lot of beer at his bar. Putting two and two together, Chris decided that baseball and beer might make splendid running mates. At first his interest was largely economic, but he soon found himself caught up with the team and added pageantry to the splendor of it all. Over the Golden Lion Saloon in St. Louis he ran up a golden ball inscribed 'Game Today,' or, if there was no game, a flag so informing the patrons."

Von der Ahe took out full-page advertisements in the St. Louis newspapers that read: "The Browns Are Here! The Hardest Hitters, the Finest Fielders, the Best Base Runners, the Coming Champions!"

Welch's Secret. In 1886, one of the highlights of the season for fans was watching outfielder Curt Welch making circus catches, robbing opponents of extra base hits. Later, his secret was revealed: he kept a stock of beer hidden behind the outfield billboards.

Baseball writer Robert Smith said of Sportsman's Park in the mid-1880s, "One could see a grandstand full of men in high-crowned derbies, plug hats, and odd little round cloth hats like the Rollo hats which in later years used to make small boys wretched on Sunday. There were ladies in the audience and a heavy sprinkling of kids, both in the grandstand and on the bleaching boards...."

The original park burned in 1891, signaling an end to St. Louis' participation in the American Association. The park was not completely rebuilt until 1893, but this time majestically, with seating for 10,000. Iron columns supported the grandstand roof, columns set back as far as possible for minimal obstruction. Von der Ahe gave the Lindell Railway Company 200 feet of land outside the grandstand for a loop.

The Spanish-American War came and went, taking wind out of baseball's sails. Many teams lost money, the Browns included. The 1890s were bad years for the remaining St. Louis baseball fans. The teams were horrible and there wasn't a lot to cheer about.

The Coney Island of the West. Von der Ahe sought to enhance his income by using his ballpark year-round. He put in a honky-tonk, amusement park rides, and a "wine room." He called his park "the Coney Island of the West." Von der Ahe put in a racetrack and rented it to local promoter Fred Foster for $10,000 for two years. These moves offended baseball purists — as did the Browns, a team about as vulgar and rowdy as they came.

Sometimes Browns games were combined with other events. Once the Browns hosted a Buffalo Bill Show, complete with Sitting Bull, in addition to the regular baseball game, all for a single 50-cent admission. Kids got in for two bits. *The Sporting News* was forced to write a piece called "The Prostitution of a Ball Park." The National League did nothing. It was Von der Ahe's ballpark. He could do as he pleased with it. The league had just about given up on the Browns' players too. Every time the league fined one of the St. Louis players for verbal or physical abuse upon their opponents, Von der Ahe quietly paid the fines for his boys and winked a keep-up-the-good-work wink.

Around this time, Von der Ahe announced a Ladies Day at the ballpark. Ladies were to be admitted free. Upon arriving, the ladies were shocked to find that they were expected to sit out in the broiling sun on plank bleacher seats. If they wanted to sit in the shade of the grandstand as they were accustomed to doing, they were going to have to pay a quarter.

Sportsman's Park, St. Louis, Mo. (Photo supplied by the National Baseball Library, Cooperstown, N.Y.)

St. Louis fans were known for their drinking abilities. On Sundays in particular, vendors were kept busy with the imbibing fans, who were probably trying to fortify themselves for the lousy baseball they were seeing.

Frequent Fires. All in all, there were five major fires at Sportsman's Park in the 1890s, compounding Von der Ahe's problems. The park had to be completely rebuilt once, and partially rebuilt three times before the fire in 1898 proved to be the last straw. The final fire had broken out during a game. Hundreds had been burned or trampled in the panic. The owner was up to his ears in lawsuits. Destroyed, along with the grandstand and half of the bleachers, were Von der Ahe's saloon, the club office, Von der Ahe's correspondence files and his extensive wardrobe.

In 1898, Von der Ahe lost the franchise. The Browns of the National League became the Cardinals and moved to Robison Field. Sportsman's Park was not used again until the formation of the American League, when it became home of the new Browns in 1902. In 1920, the Cardinals left Robison Field and became tenants of the Browns. St. Louis was a two-franchise town with one ballpark for the next 22 years.

"A Garish County-Fair Sort of Layout." During the first part of the twentieth century, Sportsman's Park grew slowly into the park now remembered as the old Busch Stadium. The grandstand was reinforced with steel and concrete in 1908, and it was this structure that served St. Louis baseball until 1966. A second deck was built behind the infield in 1909, and this upper deck was extended to the foul poles in 1925. The following year, bleachers were put in the outfield.

Red Smith wrote that Sportsman's Park had "a garish, county-fair sort of layout." In 1929 — when Smith covered the Browns from the park's press box, dangling from the roof over the second deck — a fat baritone named Jim Kelly announced the starting lineups to the crowds near the infield through a raised megaphone. Kelly then moved with the gait of a rotund man out to right field and then to left, where he announced just the starting batteries, because — as Smith biographer Ira Berkow put it — the long walk to the outfield sapped his enthusiasm for reading the complete lineups.

In the 1930s, a goat assisted the grounds crew in cutting the sizeable Sportsman's Park lawn.

The low pavilion, where homers to right were hit, was where the wagering took place. The outfield walls were covered with large ads for Philip Morris and Ivory Soap. During each game, a recording attached to Johnny the Bellhop's billboard on the lower right hand corner of the scoreboard sang out, "Call for Phil-ip Mor-ris." The Busch eagle flapped its wings after Cardinal homers.

Before and during the Depression, Sportsman's Park was poorly cared for. Many of the wooden seats, and the wooden ladder up to the press box, were ready to fall apart.

In the 1940s, Sportsman's Park remained the only big league arena with a Jim Crow section. The black-only right field pavilion, covered in front by a screen, was the only extended outfield seating in big league baseball where it was impossible to catch a home run.

That pavilion was not screened over when Babe Ruth played here against the Browns, and right field was an easy touch for him — as it was in Cleveland. In 1927, Ruth hit four homers into the pavilion.

The seats out in left field were bleachers, used by white people. The big hand-operated scoreboard sat atop the bleachers with big advertisements painted on it, and a clock perched on top.

On April 18, 1950, Sportsman's Park hosted the first major league home opener ever played at night. The Cards beat the Pirates 4-2. During the 1950s the Veeck family lived in Sportsman's Park, in an apartment fashioned for them. It was here, on August 19, 1951,

that ol' number 1/8 came to the plate for the first and only time: Eddie Gaedel, 3'7", 65 lbs.

From 1941 to 1963 this was the home field of one of baseball's greatest hitters, Stan Musial. Musial batted over .300 seventeen times. Speaking of great hitters, the last home run hit here was by Willie Mays, golfed over the pavilion on Mothers' Day Eve, 1966, the ballpark's final day. There were 17,803 there to say goodbye to the ballpark. After the game, a helicopter carried home plate to the new Busch Stadium. A bulldozer then crashed through the center field wall before the crowd had left. It seemed cruel — like lowering the casket into the grave while the widow looks on.

Red Stocking Park (Compton Park 1885–98)

National Association 1875 (Red Stockings). *Location:* Scott Street (right field), South Compton Avenue (first base), Gratiot Street (home plate), Atlantic Street (third base), Theresa Avenue (left field). *First National Association game:* May 4, 1875. *Last National Association game:* July 4, 1875. *Torn down:* 1898.

Athletic Park

National Association 1875 (Red Stockings, some games), National League 1876-77 (Brown Stockings, some games). *Location:* North Market, Bacon, and Coleman streets, St. Louis Avenue.

Lucas Park

National League 1879 (some games), Union Association 1884 (Maroons, some games). *Location:* 13th, 14th, Lucas, and Locust streets.

According to Bill James in *The Historical Abstract,* Henry Lucas was an enthusiastic millionaire who backed the Union Association and allowed the Maroons to play in a "small but pretentious ballpark on his private estate."

The Union Association's biggest

weakness was imbalance. Lucas' park, called "the Palace Park of America," was given extra features like reception and lecture facilities. The seating capacity was 10,000. But fans didn't come. The Maroons always won, so it wasn't interesting.

Union Association Park

Union Association 1884 (Maroons, some games), National League 1885 (Maroons, some games). *Location:* Cass and Jefferson avenues, West 25th and Madison streets. *First National League game:* April 30, 1885 (St. Louis 3, Chicago 2). *Last National League game:* June 5, 1885.

Lafayette Park

American Association 1880s (Browns, some games). *Location:* Missouri, Park, Mississippi, and Lafayette streets.

Robison Field (League Park, Cardinal Field, Vandeventer Lot)

National League 1885–86 (Maroons), 1899–1920 (Cardinals). *Location:* Vandeventer Avenue (first base), Natural Bridge Avenue (third base), Prairie Avenue (left field), Lexington Avenue (right field). *Dimensions:* (1890) Left field, 470 feet; center field, 500 feet; right field, 290 feet. (1909) Left field, 380 feet; center field, 435 feet; right field, 290 feet. 120 feet from home plate to the backstop. *First National League game:* June 6, 1885. *Last National League game:* June 6, 1920 (St. Louis 5, Chicago 2).

Named after Cardinal owners Stanley and Frank Robison.

In 1913, when Schuyler "Skip" Britton became president of the Cardinals, he gave flowers away to ladies at the ballpark, and made scorecards (temporarily) complimentary.

Britton was one of the first to introduce a "lucky number" in the scorecards. Fans holding winning numbers got to see a game for free.

Britton's wife was actively involved,

publicly crying for more women to come out and see the Cardinals play. At her urging, Skip got a male singer to croon through a megaphone between innings, and the women came out like nowhere before. Some men didn't care for the way that crooner strutted, and criticized this "baseball cabaret."

Overhead had to be low because there wasn't any money. The Cardinals watched as every other team in the major leagues (except the Yankees, who shared) rebuilt their ballparks in concrete. The only public relations expenses the Cards incurred was that of taking reporters on the road.

First Knothole Gang. In 1917, in an attempt to reduce juvenile delinquency and sell stock, the Cardinals created the first knothole gang. Purchase of a $25 pair of shares of ball club stock entitled one St. Louis kid to a free season ticket. Later, the club became more generous, offering knothole club membership to kids through the YMCA, Protestant Sunday Schools, Catholic churches, Jewish welfare, and a black boys' club. In 1920, 64,000 free admissions were given to St. Louis kids. Surprise: there was a discipline problem in the stands. The Cardinals had opened an unprepared daycare center. A few toughs had to have their "passes" taken, and later problems subsided when groups of knothole members were required to bring adult supervision.

The Park was very rundown by the time the Cardinals finished using it in 1920. When the Browns of the American League agreed to let the Cards use their ballpark (Sportsman's Park) that year, Cardinal owner Sam Breadon sold this property and used the money to improve his ball club.

The last major league ball game played here—on June 6, 1920—represented the final big league contest in an old-fashioned wooden ballpark.

Handlan's Park (Laclede Park, Grand and Market Park)

Federal League 1914–15 (Terriers),

Negro National League 1920–21 (Giants, some games), 1920s (Stars, some games). *Location:* Laclede, Grand and Theresa avenues, Market Street. When used by the Terriers, the ballpark was named after Terrier owner Eugene Handlan. When used by the Negro National League, the park was known by its location.

Giants Park (Kuebler's Park)

Negro National League 1920–21 (Giants). *Location:* North Broadway, Clarence, East Taylor and Hall streets.

Stars Park (Dick Kent's Ballyard, Athletic Park [II])

Negro National League 1922–31 (Stars), Negro American League 1937, 1939, 1941 (Stars). *Location:* Compton, Laclede and Market streets, just down the street from Handlan's Park.

The clubs of the Negro Leagues drew from their communities in ways white baseball hadn't known in big cities for years. Across the street from Stars Park was Vashon High School, who annually played Sumner for the St. Louis High School football championship.

According to Donn Rogosin's *Invisible Men,* "a truly outstanding (baseball) player from Vashon, such as Quincy Trouppe, was automatically on the periphery of professional Negro baseball. Trouppe volunteered to be the Stars' third-string catcher and began to work out with the team regularly—a training which proved priceless."

Vandeventer Lot [II]

Negro National League 1920s (Stars, some games). *Location:* Grand, Vandeventer, Franklin, Spring, and Belle streets (different from site of Robison Field, also known as Vandeventer Lot).

Easton Street Park

Negro National League 1920s (Stars, some games). *Location:* Easton and Vandeventer streets, next to the stockyards.

Market Street Park

Negro National League 1920s (Stars, some games). *Location:* North Market and Elephant streets, at Broadway.

Busch Stadium (Busch Memorial Stadium)

National League 1966–present (Cardinals). Site of the 1966 All-Star Game (National League 2, American League 1, attendance: 49,936, July 12, 1966). Also the home of the St. Louis Cardinals of the National Football League until 1987–88. *Owned by:* Civic Center Corporation (subsidiary of the Anheuser-Busch Companies, Inc.). *Location:* Spruce Street (first base side), Stadium Plaza (third base), Walnut Street (left field), Broadway (right field). *Groundbreaking:* May 24, 1964. *Dimensions:* Left field, 330 feet; left center, 386 feet; center field, 414 feet; right center, 386 feet; right field, 330 feet. 64 feet between home plate and the backstop. *Fences:* 10½ feet all the way around. *Surface:* (1966) Grass. (1970) Artificial. (The dirt infield was maintained, 1970–73, then covered with artificial turf except for "sliding pits." Resurfaced with AstroTurf-8 in 1984.) *Lights:* 10 towers, 690 metal halide lights, 1500 watts each. *Seating capacity:* (1966) 50,126, broken down as follows: deluxe rooms, 312; lower boxes, 11,985; lower reserved, 10,046; upper boxes, 2646; upper reserved, 12,973; general admission, 8082; bleacher, 4082. (1987) 53,029 for baseball, 54,146 for football. *Parking lot:* 17,100 cars. *First game:* May 12, 1966 (night, St. Louis 4, Atlanta 3, 12 innings, attendance: 46,048, winning pitcher: Don Dennis).

Because of the new Busch Stadium's deep power alleys, this is a pitchers' park. The Cardinals can't play for the three-run homer like other clubs—the three-run homer never comes—so they rely on speed and sequential hitting, a batting order filled to the gills with lead-off hitters. It follows that the two Hall of Famers to play here (Gibson

Busch Stadium, St. Louis, Mo. (Compliments of Busch Stadium.)

and Brock) were a pitcher and a speedster.

Massive Redevelopment Project. The stadium opened in 1966, beginning an extensive downtown St. Louis redevelopment effort. The results have been many new office buildings, shopping malls, hotels, parking garages and other facilities. St. Louis is particularly proud of the National Bowling Hall of Fame.

Busch Stadium is owned and operated by Civic Center Corporation, one of the Anheuser-Busch Companies, Inc. The brewery was the largest single investor in the corporation that built the ballpark, and purchased the remaining shares of stock in 1981.

It's easy to pick Busch out of a group of aerial photographs of 1960s–'70s perfectly round cookie-cutter stadia. It's the one with the little "archways to the west" around its top. It's the one, not surprisingly, that you always see on the Budweiser commercials.

It's a tradition for the Clydesdales to make an appearance at each home opener, pulling around the field a beer wagon with a dalmatian perched on top.

There are two-foot chicken wire baskets on top of the outfield fences in left and right to keep fans from interfering with catchable home runs.

The playing field is 10 to 30 feet below street level. Open arches surround the stadium just below the roof. Within the structure is the St. Louis Sports Hall of Fame. Just outside the stadium stands a statue of Stan Musial, erected in 1968.

A massive seating replacement and installation project began in August 1986, and was completed before the home opener in 1987. Every seat was replaced. Every new seat was red.

Perfect Circle. The structure of the stadium itself covers 12 acres of land. It is almost perfectly circular, as close to perfect as the engineers could make it. It is a two-deck stadium, the seats about equally divided between the two. Before the St. Louis Football Cardinals of the NFL moved to Phoenix there were two sections of seats along the baselines (7200 seats altogether) that were moveable so they could be parallel to the football field.

Modern scoreboard: The color video

board is 22 feet by 30 feet, while the black-and-white matrix is 22 feet by 44 feet. The video shows photos, slow-motion replays, and live television. The matrix offers stats, graphics, and animated fun.

Even Busch Stadium's new playing surface, installed in 1984, is state-of-the-art, just like its shortstop. The surface is permeable, allowing rainwater to flow through into a sophisticated drainage system. Anyone want a used Zamboni?

St. Paul, Minnesota

Name of park unknown
Northwestern League 1884. *Location:* St. Clair, Oneida, and Duke streets, and the Short Line Railroad tracks.

St. Paul made its debut in organized ball in 1884, fielding a team in the disorganized Northwestern League. Starting the season with twelve teams, the league was down to six by August 11, three by August 18. The Minneapolis team disbanded September 5, so the league's last game was played between its two surviving members, St. Paul and Milwaukee, on September 7.

That was the year of the Union Association, the third major league, and the year the American Association expanded to twelve teams. There was too much baseball.

The Union Association—or the "Onion League," as the people of St. Paul called it—struggled as much as the Northwestern League, with franchises shifting and abandoned.

When the St. Paul team finished Northwestern League play, they went to Cincinnati to play a few exhibition games. While there, they were admitted to the Union Association to finish the season. St. Paul played eight games of major league ball in its history (1-6-1), all of them on the road.

Name of park unknown
Northwestern League 1886. *Location:*

Toronto, Jefferson, and Osceola streets, and the Short Line Railroad tracks.

St. Paul played an 80-game schedule, and finished fourth in a six-team league.

Name of park unknown
Northwestern League 1887. *Location:* Eaton Street, between Chicago and Plato streets, on the West Side.

Name of park unknown
Western Association 1888-91, Western League 1895-96 (Sunday only). *Location:* State and Eaton streets.

Leip's Park
Western Association 1888 (First two games only). *Location:* White Bear Lake, ten miles north of the city.

For the opening of the 1888 season both Eaton Street ballparks, the one on State and the one between Chicago and Plato, were underwater—so the first two games against the Chicago Maroons were played at Leip's Park. St. Paul won them both.

Dale and Aurora Grounds
Western League 1895-96.

In their first of five years under Charlie Comiskey, St. Paul finished second in an eight-team league. They finished third in 1896.

In May 1895, an injunction barred Sunday games here, forcing the team to use grounds on State and Eaton. During the first month of the injunction, St. Paul twice played Sunday games in Minneapolis' Minnehaha Driving Park.

Lexington Park
Western League 1897-1902, 1910-56 (Saints). *Location:* Lexington Avenue, now Lexington Parkway (left field), University Avenue (third base), Dunlap Street (first base), Fuller Avenue (right field), current site of a shopping center. *Dimensions:* Left field, 315 feet; center field, 470 feet; right field, 365 feet (fence atop embankment). *Last game:* September 5, 1956 (St. Paul 4, Minneapolis 0, attendance: 2227. *Fire:* 1906, 1914.

Top: *Lexington Park, St. Paul, Minn., 1925.* Bottom: *Lexington Park's score-board, 1935. (Photos supplied by the Minnesota Historical Society.)*

Miller Huggins, manager of Murderer's Row, played second base here, 1901–02. In 1951, a mean wind came along and blew down the right field fence. Behind the left field fence was the Coliseum Ballroom.

Downtown Stadium

Western League 1903–09 (Saints). *Location:* Robert, Minnesota, Twelfth and Thirteenth streets.

Midway Stadium

American Association 1957–60. *Location:* 1000 North Snelling Avenue. *Dimensions:* Left field, 321 feet; center field, 410 feet; right field, 321 feet. *Fences:* Center field, 16 feet. *Seating capacity:* 13,050. *First game:* April 25, 1957 (St. Paul loses both games of a doubleheader to Wichita).

St. Petersburg, Florida

The first organized baseball team in St. Petersburg played in an intertown amateur league just after the turn of the century. According to Karl Grismer's *The Story of St. Petersburg,* home games were played "on vacant lots south of the railroad tracks."

Name of park unknown

Home of the St. Petersburg Saints 1908-11. *Location:* Northeast side of Mirror Lake. *Built:* Autumn 1908. *First game:* October 29, 1908 (Cincinnati Reds 7, St. Petersburg Saints 0).

The first appearance of a big league baseball team in St. Petersburg occurred in 1908, when the Reds were on a barnstorming tour. Baseball was played on this site until 1911, when the field was flooded out by an expanding Mirror Lake.

Symonette Field

Home of the St. Petersburg Saints 1912-14. *Location:* Tangerine Avenue, just west of 40th Street.

Money to build this field was raised by public subscription.

Coffee Pot Park

Spring training home of the St. Louis Browns 1914, Philadelphia Phillies (all National League) 1915-18, Boston Braves 1921-37. *Location:* The head of Coffee Pot Bayou. *First game:* February 27, 1914 (Chicago Cubs 3, St. Louis Browns 2, exhibition, attendance: 4000).

The scoreboard was three feet high and sat atop the old plank fence in the outfield. Angled planks supported a platform in front of the scoreboard, where the operator sat—and walked back and forth to put the numbers up. Upon this ledge, Phillies sometimes posed for their publicity shots.

The ballpark got its name because it was built on the Coffee Pot Bayou. Free java was served to the fans.

Lang's Concept. In 1911, Albert Fielding Lang was the owner of a successful laundry business in Pittsburgh when he became ill. He was 41 years old; doctors told him he had only six months to live. Lang moved to St. Petersburg, a town of 3000, and his health promptly returned.

After hearing of big league spring camps being rained out in Arkansas, day after day, he invited clubs to train in St. Pete. In 1913, an arrangement was made with the St. Louis Browns to train in town for the spring of 1914. The city of St. Petersburg agreed to provide the diamond and pay transportation for 40 Browns. The Coffee Pot Bayou site was leased from Snell & Hamlett for three years, and the land was cleared of trees and palmettoes.

Lang lived to the age of 89, when he died of pneumonia. By that time he'd had a ballpark (on his own land) named after him for 14 years.

Moore Field

Florida State League 1920 (Saints), spring home of Indianapolis (American Association) 1921. *Location:* Fourth Street, Seventh Avenue South.

The Saints played here for one year before moving to the new park on the waterfront, on the site of the eventual Al Lang Stadium.

Al Lang Stadium (Al Lang Field, 1947-77)

Spring home of the Boston Braves 1921-37, St. Louis Cardinals 1938-present, also Florida State League 1921-46 (Saints), 1955-present (Cardinals), spring home of Mets 1960s and 1970s. *Location:* 180 Second Avenue S.E., First Street, First Avenue S.E., Bayshore Drive, Tampa Bay. *Built:* 1946, 1977. *Construction cost:* (1946) $300,000. *Dimensions:* Left field, 309 feet; center field, 400 feet; right field, 305 feet. *Seating capacity:* (1960) 6000; (1975) 7000; (1985) 8200. *First game in Al Lang Field:* March 12, 1947 (St. Louis Cardinals 10, New York Yankees 5, exhibition, attendance 7706).

In 1921, the city secured a plot of land on a 99-year lease from the Park Board for a ballpark. Located at the foot of First Avenue facing the waterfront, it was used as a spring training practice field. The movement to build a new ballpark on the site with a real grandstand—and to name that park after Al Lang—started in the late '30s but was postponed by the war.

Some argued baseball would detract from the overall beauty of the waterfront, as well as lowering the value of adjoining real estate. But they were wrong. By 1955, St. Petersburg's population would be 125,000 three seasons of the year and 325,000 in the spring. Real estate values soared.

Frying Bacon on the Bleachers. The 1947 dedication ceremony speakers were Sam Breadon, who first brought the Cardinals to St. Pete; president of the Yankees, Larry MacPhail; American League president Will Harridge; and Mayor George L. Patterson. Formal dedication was performed by the commissioner of baseball, Happy Chandler.

According to Red Sox announcer Ken Coleman, "The stadium . . . is all concrete, with stands sloping up in a steep, precarious angle. Also beware of the metal seats, which, under a hot Florida sun, can sizzle up and create a stifling, saunalike effect. . . . You can watch the game and at the same time catch glimpses of boats in the bay beyond the fence. The sloped stands offer an excellent view no matter where you sit."

Before the 1977 refurbishment that conventionalized the shape, the playing field was shaped like the Polo Grounds, hemmed in at the sides by Tampa Bay on the first base side and a major four-lane thoroughfare on the other. There was plenty of room in center and the corners, so much so that stands were put right on the field in deep right. Palm trees grew on the other side of the fence. There was also plenty of room on the lot behind the grandstand,

which was used as a dirt parking lot. The dimensions were so short down the lines that tall fences were built behind the stands to keep balls off roads and parked cars. Later on, a second practice diamond without an infield (called a half-field in today's high-tech spring training terminology) was put beyond the center field fence.

The park is the current home of the Singing Vendor. Check out his crooning act as he serves up the hot dogs.

Dome Built. The St. Petersburg–Tampa area has constructed a 45,000-seat Florida Suncoast Dome, in hopes of getting a major league expansion team sometime in the near future.

Stengel-Huggins Field (Miller Huggins Field, Crescent Lake Park)

Spring home of the New York Yankees 1925–61. *Location:* 13th Avenue, Fifth Street North.

According to Barbara Walder in the *New York Times,* Huggins-Stengel Field in the 1950s had a "single diamond, two tatty batting cages and basic bleachers. There players lazed through simple stretches on a dew-dropped field, the early morning mist covering their shoetops while the smell of fresh coffee wafted out of the tiny pine-paneled clubhouse, borne on billowing breezes through doors thrown open at each end, to writers and coaches sitting companionably in the spring sun."

Described as "little more than a high-school field," Stengel-Huggins Field had no outfield fences, and long balls struck through the gap in left center often rolled into the woods.

Busch Field

Spring home of St. Louis Cardinals mid-1960s.

Piper Fuller Park

Spring home of the Mets late 1960s.

Salem, Oregon

Chemeketa College Field

Northwest League 1979–present

Al Lang Stadium, St. Petersburg, Fla. (Compliments of the St. Petersburg Area Chamber of Commerce.)

(Dodgers). *Location:* Lancaster Drive, on the campus of Chemeketa Community College. *Dimensions:* Left field, 330 feet; center field, 413 feet; right field, 350 feet. *Seating capacity:* 3500. *1987 season attendance:* 34,181.

Salem, Virginia

Municipal Field
Virginia League circa 1950 (Tigers), Carolina League 1968–present (Buccaneers). *Location:* Two miles off Interstate 81 near downtown Salem. *Dimensions:* Left field, 320 feet; center field, 430 feet; right field, 320 feet. *Seating capacity:* 4000. *1987 season attendance:* 111,661.

Salinas, California

Municipal Stadium
California League circa 1987. *Dimensions:* Left field, 365 feet; center field, 401 feet; right field, 335 feet. *Seating capacity:* 3600.

Salt Lake City, Utah

Bonneville Park
Home of Salt Lake City's first pro baseball team 1915–1924.
This franchise moved to California, and the land on which Bonneville Park stood was sold.

Community Park (circa 1925–1945), Derks Field (1946–present).
Utah-Idaho League 1926–28, Pioneer League 1939–42, 1946–57, 1967–69, 1985–present (Trappers), Pacific Coast League 1958–65. *Location:* 13th South, West Temple and Harrison avenues, and Main Street. *Dimensions:* Left field, 350 feet; center field, 405 feet; right field, 365 feet. *Seating capacity:* (1947) 5000; (1958) 10,200. *Lights installed:* 1939. *Fire:* 1946.
A group of Salt Lake baseball fans purchased the materials and reconstructed the Bonneville Park facility on the eventual site of Derks Field.
Before the 1946 season the ballpark was renamed Derks Field, after John C. Derks, a long-time *Salt Lake Tribune* sports editor who brought pro-

fessional baseball back to town after a ten-year absence.

Later that season, the park was completely destroyed by fire. Because of enthusiastic community fund-raising, the city was able to reconstruct immediately. They built the Derks Field that still exists.

During the next 40 years Derks Field underwent some changes. In 1947, it had box seating from dugout to dugout and gold-painted grandstand seats for a combined capacity of 5000.

In 1958, the city approved a major expansion for the park. The seating capacity was more than doubled by adding box and grandstand seats all the way down each line. The dugouts and clubhouses were also completely renovated.

Part of that funding was earmarked for a roof. Derks Field had never had one, and the sun on summer afternoons could be intense. But there was debate among city officials and Derks Field was to remain roofless, the subject "on hold" to the present day.

After the refurbishment in '58, Derks Field was used for baseball only. Before that, football was played here — one set of goal posts on the third base line and another near the right field fence.

The original lights, installed in 1939, lasted until 1971, when a modernized lighting system was put in. In 1982, Derks Field sprouted a $150,000 scoreboard and message center in right field.

According to the publicity department of the current Salt Lake Trappers, "Even now, the city gives the ballpark a sprucing up on a regular basis and more improvements are forthcoming in the future."

Ute Field

Home of the University of Utah Utes (Western Athletic Conference), present. *Seating capacity:* 1000.

Saltillo, Mexico

Francisco I. Madero Parque

Mexican League, Zona Norte, present (Saraperos). *Dimensions:* Left field, 330 feet; center field, 400 feet; right field, 330 feet. *Seating capacity:* 8500.

San Antonio, Texas

League Park

Texas League circa 1930s. *Fire:* June 18, 1932. (Park burned, team moved.)

Mission Stadium

Texas League 1947–64. *Location:* 514 Mission Street (left field), Mitchell Street (first base), Steves Avenue (right field). *Opened:* 1947. *Dimensions:* Left field, 325 feet; center field, 400 feet; right field, 325 feet. *Fences:* 20 feet all the way around. *Seating capacity:* 7500. *Torn down:* 1974.

Like the street it was on, Mission Stadium was named after Mission Concepción. Topped by twin spires, the entrance building contained the club offices and ticket windows.

V.J. Keefe Memorial Stadium

Texas League 1968–present (Spurs, Missions). *Location:* St. Mary's University campus. *Built:* 1960. *Dimensions:* Left field, 300 feet; center field, 401 feet; right field, 305 feet. *Seating capacity:* (1975) 10,250; (1985) 3500.

On July 15 and 16, 1988, this was the site of the longest scoreless tie in pro ball history. The game started Friday night, was suspended after 25 scoreless innings at 2:30 a.m. on Saturday, and was completed later that day, the Missions beating the Jackson Mets 1–0 on Manny François's bases-loaded single in the 26th inning, thirteen minutes into the continuation. Total time for the game: 7:23.

According to Bill O'Neal in his book *The Texas League,* V.J. Keefe Memorial Stadium was the first college campus ballpark ever used as home for a pro baseball team. The park has been expanded and improved since pro ball moved in.

San Bernardino, California

Fiscalini Field
California League 1986–present (Spirit). *Location:* Highland Avenue. *Dimensions:* Left field, 330 feet; center field, 400 feet; right field, 330 feet. *Seating capacity:* 3000. *1987 season attendance:* 158,896.

A formerly independent operation — and the biggest draw in the league — the Spirit became affiliated with Seattle for the 1988 season.

San Cristobal de las Casas, Mexico

It was late September in the bleachers at Yankee Stadium. The pennant race was over. Only the loyal had turned out. Stretched across three rows of seats was statistical wizard, musician, and all-around swell fellow Rick Erickson, shooting the breeze with the regulars:

"The best bunt I've seen came in the late innings of a game in San Cristobal de las Casas, Chiapas, Mexico. It was a Sunday in early March, 1987, five long months since Jesse Orosco struck out Marty Barrett to end the 1986 World Series, and I was starving for baseball. The Mexican League season wouldn't open for another two weeks and by that time I'd be back in the States watching spring training games on the tube. In the meantime I wanted live baseball. Back in November, in Guaymas, I'd managed to pick up radio broadcasts of winter league games on my Walkman. I caught Willie Aikens name a few times, but never found out where the games were played. So in the end my only glimpse of Mexican *beisbol* was this local game in San Cris-

tobal, which, according to *Let's Go Mexico,* 'outdoes almost every other town in the republic for color, activity and sheer beauty.' I concur. In San Cristobal women breast-feed their babies with one hand, thrust merchandise into your face with the other; drunken men insist on addressing you as Mr. Anthropologist and demand to know why the United States is about to bomb Mexico; and at the ballpark, under the shaded concrete grandstand only eight or ten rows deep, a brass band toots and farts, vendors hawk dripping tacos in lieu of hot dogs, and everybody gets drunk. Sadly, a notorious tourist ailment kept me away from the *Tres Equis* beer and the goat tacos. The game was a pitchers' duel, decided by one run. I dimly recall a close play at the plate.

"And that bunt.

"It rolled fifteen feet down the third base line and died, and all hands were safe. Granted, the field wasn't exactly manicured — maybe the ball rolled into a crater. Still, it beat anything I'd seen in the major leagues in the last ten years.

"After the game, a few guys in their early twenties, each toting a flask, realized they had a gringo in their midst and sat down to talk baseball. For the next half-hour we re-lived the 1986 World Series, which they'd seen on TV via satellite dish: *"El Doctor no servía para nada,"* they observed. (Translation: Gooden was useless.) I agreed. They were anxious to ascertain that I had heard of and appreciated the performance of Mexican lefties Fernando Valenzuela and Teddy Higuera, and in fact I'd seen both of them pitch in New York. Meanwhile, the sun was sinking — it sets early in the mountains — and it was getting cold and I had to go, so to speak. Nevertheless, I left reluctantly. The ballpark, more than any other place in Mexico, felt like home."

San Diego, California

Lockling Square

Site of first organized baseball game in San Diego 1871. *Location:* C, D (now Broadway), Sixth, and Seventh streets.

This downtown vacant lot was used for baseball when San Diego's population was 2300. There were three organized baseball clubs in town: the Lone Stars, the Old San Diegos, and the Young Americans. At least six games were played during the summer of 1871, all of them on Saturday, the first on May 2.

An 1883 photograph of Lockling Square, from the San Diego Historical Society's Title Insurance and Trust Collection, shows a gathering of men in a flat spot, hilly desolation behind them, the soft hills spotted with plain square houses. Some of the men lean on bats. There are half as many boys in the picture, standing between the ballplayers or sitting behind them to peak between their legs. There are no women or girls to be seen—which is not to say that they weren't there. The men are divided up by teams, and have made a sloppy attempt to dress like teammates, creating "looks" more than uniforms. The team at the far right wears freshly boiled white shirts and dark pants; the group next to them, gray suits; and the men on the left side are vested. One man, at the precise center of the picture, is wearing a tall top hat—the only top hat among a variety of hat styles—and exceptionally wide baggy trousers. The umpire, no doubt.

There was a building boom in San Diego in the 1880s, and Lockling Square was turned into a social club and a house.

Driving Park

Location: Pacific Beach. Primary home of San Diego baseball late 1880s.

During this period, intratown baseball was also played at diamonds located at Third and A Street, Eleventh and J Street, Fourteenth and G Street, Fourteenth and N (Commercial) Street, near the current San Diego Police Department Headquarters, in Roseville on Point Loma, and on the beach in Coronado.

Recreation Park (I)

Primary home of San Diego baseball 1887-90. *Location:* Evans (now South 25th) and Newton streets.

Recreation Park (II)

Primary home of San Diego baseball 1891-92. *Location:* Present-day University and Normal streets.

Bay View Park

Primary home of San Diego baseball 1893-1901. *Location:* Logan Avenue and Beardsley (now South 22nd) Street.

Home of a series of semi-pro winter leagues with names like the Southern California League, the California Winter League, and the Southern League.

According to San Diego historian Frank Norris in *The Journal of San Diego History:*

"These leagues were much like today's Mexican and Caribbean Leagues; they provided a way for professional players to hone their skills, and also served as a training ground for developing local talent.... The popularity of the intercity leagues appears to have been strongest between 1898 and 1901. The high turnover of teams and players made the leagues appear unstable at times, but the lure of intercity baseball played by professionals drew large crowds to league games from November to March.... Perhaps the biggest highlight of the brief winter era came on March 3, 1901, when San Diego, with ace pitcher 'Dummy' Taylor on the mound, beat San Bernardino 1 to 0 in a fifteen-inning duel at Bay View Park. The game, doubly amazing because no errors were committed by either side, was hailed as 'the greatest game on record' at the time, and was recalled fondly by veteran fans decades afterwards."

Athletic Park

Primary home of San Diego baseball beginning 1902. *Location:* On the East End, as Bay View Park was, but further down the trolley car line.

When the Pacific Coast League formed in 1903, San Diego was hoping to be a charter member – but the new league passed. The city lacked a ballpark worthy of league play. After that, local interest in baseball dwindled.

Balboa Stadium

Primary home of San Diego baseball circa 1924.

A proposal was made about halfway through the 1924 Pacific Coast League season that the Salt Lake City franchise be moved to San Diego. League rules specified league play had to take place on a grass field with seating accommodation of 2500 or better. Balboa Stadium fulfilled neither requirement, and San Diego refused to build a new ballpark. The Salt Lake team stayed put.

Lane Field

Pacific Coast League 1936-58 (Padres). *Location:* 906 West Broadway (first base), Harbor Drive (third base), Pacific Coast Highway (right field), current site of a parking lot. *Built:* 1938 (WPA). *Dimensions:* Left field, 390 feet; center field, 500 feet; right field, 350 feet. 12 (!) feet from home plate to the backstop. *Fences:* 7 feet all the way around. *First game:* March 31, 1936 (San Diego 6, Seattle 2, attendance: 8178, winning pitcher: Herman Pillette). *Record season attendance:* 493,780 (1949). *Torn down:* 1958.

Built right on the Pacific, on tidelands property at the foot of Broadway. The ocean hit the beach on the other side of Harbor Drive, on the other side of the third base stands. Sitting up there, and looking out over the left field fence, one saw the Santa Fe

Railroad depot. The longest home run hit at Lane Field was smote in 1949 by Luke Easter – 500 feet on the fly, clearing the scoreboard in center field. **Many Infield Hits, No Passed Balls.** The park, named after former San Diego baseball magnate H. William "Hardrock Bill" Lane, had the shortest distance from home to the backstop in the history of organized ball. Wild pitches routinely bounced back to the catcher, and runners couldn't advance. Sitting behind home, twelve feet from the bat, could be hazardous in the early days of Lane Field, before they put up the screen. The distance from home to first – it was discovered at an absurdly late date – was only 87 feet.

The site currently holds a bar and its parking lot. The Santa Fe Railroad depot and the Pacific Ocean are still there.

Baseball moved directly from Lane Field into Westgate Park. By the time Lane Field was torn down in the late 1950s it was all but eaten away by termites.

Westgate Park

Pacific Coast League 1958-67 (Padres). *Owned by:* C. Arnholt Smith (also owner of Padres). *Location:* Mission Valley. Current site of Fashion Valley Shopping Center. *Seating capacity:* 8200 (5732 box, 2516 grandstand). *Parking lot:* 3000 cars. *First game:* April 29, 1958 (versus Phoenix, attendance: 4619). *Torn down:* 1968.

The grandstand was completely roofed over, and the grounds were beautified with trees, shrubs, flowers, and tropical plants. Named after owner C. Arnholt Smith's Westgate, California, Packing Corporation.

San Diego–Jack Murphy Stadium

Pacific Coast League 1968 (Padres), National League 1969-present (Padres). *Owned by:* The city of San Diego. *Location:* Interstate Route 8 (first base side), Stadium Way (third base), Friars Road (left field), Murphy

Canyon Road (right field). *Built:* 1967. *Construction cost:* $27 million. *Dimensions:* Left field, 330 feet; left center, 370 feet; center field, 410 feet; right center, 370 feet; right field, 330 feet. 60 feet from home plate to the backstop. *Fences:* (1967) 17 feet all the way around. (Present) 8½ feet. *Seating capacity:* (1967) 47,634, broken down as follows: lower boxes, 6394; lower reserved, 8183; press level, 1918; upper boxes, 11,224; general admission, 19,915. (1983) For baseball: 59,192, broken down as follows: upper deck, 12,901; press level, 2603; loge level, 12,587; plaza level, 24,708; field level, 6394. For football: 60,751. *Record Pacific Coast League season attendance:* 203,000 (1968). *Single game attendance record:* 58,359 (October 7, 1984, NLCS, versus Cubs). *First National League game:* April 8, 1969 (night, San Diego 2, Houston 1, attendance 23,270, winning pitcher: Dick Selma).

The stadium parking lot is one of the biggest in the world, and houses events of its own. Each year drag racing and skateboarding events are held here. Approaching the stadium are tree-lined walkways. The stadium includes a modern restaurant. Prior to the 1974 season, the Padres were bought by Ray Kroc of McDonalds hamburger fame. On September 22, 1969, Willie Mays hit his 600th home run here. This was the site of the 1978 All-Star Game, in which the Nationals beat the Americans 7–3. The stadium is the home of the San Diego Chargers of the National Football League, and the San Diego State University Aztecs football team. Site of the 1988 Super Bowl—and, of course, the original home of Ted Giannoulas, who dons his feathers professionally to become the Chicken. Here, on June 12, 1970, the Pirates' Dock Ellis pitched the first no-hitter ever at Jack Murphy Stadium, beating the Padres 2–0. Ellis later admitted he was under the influence of LSD that day. The catcher's glove looked so big he couldn't miss it.

Major Excavation. During construction 2.5 million cubic yards of earth had to be moved. (The earth was taken from the other side of Friars Road, from the high banks that formed the north rim of Mission Valley, and banked up to create the bowl in which the stadium sits. The grading alone cost $1.5 million and took from December 1965 to July 1966.) Fifteen hundred piles were driven. There are 2000 signs.

The ballpark was enlarged in 1983. Seats were added above the original bleachers in right and left center. Of the 59,192 the ballpark currently seats for baseball, 15,476 are between first and third, and 37,212 are in between the foul poles. The entire site takes up 166 acres of San Diego real estate, and 122 of that is parking lot. The stadium sits on a 15-acre plot, with the remainder taken up by drainage areas, other landscaped areas, and a practice field. The parking lot seats 17,800 automobiles, 120 buses. The field is illuminated by 1165 light fixtures: 365 incandescent 5000-watt fixtures, and 800 metallic arc fixtures of 1000 watts apiece. From the ground to the top level of seats is 109 feet. From the ground to the highest light bank is 146 feet. The park was constructed with 58,000 cubic yards of concrete that were poured in place, and 10,000 cubic yards of pre-cast and pre-stressed concrete. Also used were 108,000 tons of asphalt and 5000 tons of reinforcement steel.

San Francisco, California

Recreation Grounds
Used circa 1868.
San Francisco's first enclosed ballpark.

Name of park unknown
Pacific Coast League 1903–06. *Location:* Eighth and Harrison streets. *Destroyed:* 1906 (earthquake).

San Diego (Calif.)–Jack Murphy Stadium. (Compliments of the San Diego Padres.)

Recreation Park
Pacific Coast League 1907–13, 1915–30 (Seals). *Location:* 15th and Valencia streets. *Seating capacity:* 15,000.

Ewing Field
Pacific Coast League 1914 (Seals). Prohibitively prone to fog.

Seals Stadium
Pacific Coast League 1931–57 (Seals), National League 1958–59 (Giants). Owned by the San Francisco Giants. *Location:* Bryant Street (third base side), 16th Street (first base), Potrero Avenue (right field). *Construction cost:* $600,000. *Dimensions:* Left field, 360 feet; center field, 400 feet; right field, 365 feet. 56 feet from home plate to the backstop. *Fences:* Left field, 15 feet; center field (scoreboard), 31 feet; right field, 16 feet. *Light towers:* 122 feet. *Seating capacity:* 22,900. *Giants day game attendance record:* 23,192 (April 15, 1958, versus Los Angeles). *Giants doubleheader attendance record:* 22,721 (May 4, 1958, versus Pittsburgh). *Giants night game attendance record:* 23,115 (April 22, 1958, versus St. Louis). *Giants opening game attendance record:* 23,192 (April 15, 1958, versus Los Angeles). *Giants season high attendance record:* 1,422,130 (1959). *Giants season low attendance record:* 1,272,625 (1958). *First Pacific Coast League game:* April 7, 1931 (Seals 8, Portland 0). *Last Pacific Coast League game:* September 13, 1957 (Sacramento 14, Seals 7; attendance: 15,484). *First National League game:* April 15, 1958 (San Francisco 8, Los Angeles 0, winning pitcher: Ruben Gomez). *Last National League game:* September 20, 1959 (Los Angeles 8, San Francisco 2).

During Seals Stadium's Pacific Coast League era, there were white stars painted at the top of the right center field fence, bearing names like Al Lyons and Joe Brovia, indicating where these players hit home runs completely out of the park. There was no warning track at the base of the fence. The grandstand had no roof, and there were advertising billboards on top of the hitters' background in center. Bleachers sat in right field.

Here, Joe DiMaggio played his minor league ball during the '30s. DiMaggio hit in 61 straight games in 1933. The streak ended at Seals Stadium on July 26 when Oakland pitcher Ed Walsh,

Jr., put an 0–5 collar on him.
Peanut Protest. According to Art
Rust, Jr., in the *New York Daily News,*
it was in September 1950 that Seals
president Paul I. Fagan announced
there would be no more peanut sales at
Seals Stadium because of the cost of
cleaning up the shells — reportedly
$20,000 a year. More, Fagan claimed,
than the income from peanut sales.

As one might expect, all hell broke
loose. Within days fans were smuggling
their own peanuts into the ballpark and
throwing shells all over the place in
protest.

Fagan eventually gave in. The story
was earning him a national reputation
as a cheapskate. To make amends, he
gave away 18,000 free bags of peanuts.
In response, the Seals' janitorial crew
demanded a raise.

Candlestick Park
National League 1960–present. Site
of 1961 All-Star Game (National League
5, American League 4, 10 innings).
Owned by: The city of San Francisco.
Location: Giants Way (home plate
side), Gilman Street (left field), Jamestown Avenue (right field). *Dimensions:*
(1960) Left field, 330 feet; left center,
397 feet; center field, 420 feet; right
center, 397 feet; right field, 335 feet.
(Present) Left field, 335 feet; left
center, 365 feet; center field, 400 feet;
right center, 365 feet; right field, 335
feet. 65 feet from home plate to the
backstop. *Surface:* (1960) grass; (1971)
artificial turf; (1979) grass. *Seating
capacity:* (1960) 42,553; (1961) 43,765;
(1971) 59,083. Lower boxes, 8965;
lower reserved, 13,314; mezzanine
boxes, 504; upper boxes, 6681; upper
reserved, 22,708; general admission,
6911. *First game:* April 12, 1960 (San
Francisco 3, St. Louis 1, attendance:
42,269). *Refurbishment:* 1971.

Ever since it opened, Candlestick
Park has been recognized as the worst
ballpark in the National League. It's
cold. Bitter cold. All the time. Sometimes it's both foggy and cold. Giants

relief pitcher Stu Miller was blown
right off the mound during the 1961 All-
Star Game. By the seventh inning of
that game the fans were bundled in
blankets drinking hot cocoa — which
was particularly odd, considering that
22 had been treated earlier for heat exhaustion. At game time the temperature had been 81 degrees, and then it
had plummeted back to its chilly norm.

This kind of weather nightmare is
partly due to location — this home of
Mays, McCovey and Marichal is right
on the bay — but part of the problem is
the wacky thing they call San Francisco
summer. The temperature rarely gets
above 70 (which is why people had heat
exhaustion at 81) and there's a dense
fog until noon each day, which burns
off and is replaced by a warm but gentle
sunshine. At night it's like the winter-
time.

Candlestick originally was open in
center like Shea, but two decks of seats
enclosed the outfield starting in the
1972 season. The idea was to provide
extra seating for 49er games. Now
more people could suffer at once.

Viewing night baseball in Candlestick became such an unpopular thing
to do that management put heaters
beneath 20,000 seats.

Pop-ups offer thrills, adventure and
lost face to infielders. Mets third
baseman Rod Kanehl — an adventurous
lad to begin with — once raced back into
left after a pop-up that came down near
first. Ground balls are no fun either, as
the field is built on a landfill, settling
and growing new bad hops every day.

One of the *nice* things about Candlestick was the grassy lawn between
the outfield stands and the plexiglass
home run fences. Kids were allowed to
leave the seats and romp around in this
area chasing home runs. But, because
of drunken and violent behavior (most
memorably during a game against the
Dodgers in 1988), this area is now
blocked off to fans.

**Fab Four's Last Show, Liverpool
Lads Studio Bound.** It was here that

Candlestick Park, San Francisco, Calif. (Compliments of the San Francisco Giants.)

the Beatles played their last concert, on August 29, 1966—that is, if you don't count the rooftop gig. It was less than three years after they first played the Ed Sullivan Show.

San Jose, California

Luna Park
Home of San Jose baseball 1909–20. *Constructed by:* Ingersoll Amusement Company. *Construction cost:* $50,000. *First game:* November 14, 1909.

This park was the brainchild of San Jose real estate and transit tycoon Lewis E. Hanchett, who built it far enough from the center of town so that patrons would have to ride his street-cars. Fans rode the Fourteenth (now Seventeenth) Street line.

In addition to baseball, Luna Park was frequently the site of rodeos and balloon ascensions. There was also an amusement park with a roller coaster. The first ball game at Luna Park, on November 14, 1909, was part of a twin bill with a balloon ascension.

With the coming of World War I,

San Jose lost interest in baseball and balloons. In 1920, the site was bought by the National Axle Corporation, who built a $178,000 car axle plant.

Sodality Park
Home of San Jose baseball 1920–35. *Location:* On the bank of the Guadalupe River at San Carlos Street.

During the time Sodality Park was used for baseball, Babe Ruth, Lou Gehrig and Ty Cobb made appearances in exhibition games.

In 1926, San Jose fans paid $1.50 to see the Babe—and they did not go home disappointed. Ruth hit a home run that, according to the *San Jose News,* "sailed over the creek and over the CPC cannery buildings, and they never did find that ball."

Cobb's appearance in 1920 had not been as popular. He faced local pitcher Frank Juney. Juney was known for his (illegal) emery ball, which he used to deceive Cobb. After Cobb fanned, he took exception to Juney's junk. He and Juney began to jaw at one another. The crowd sided with the local boy, then later cheered when Cobb let a ball go between his legs in the outfield. According to the *San Jose News,* Cobb turned to chase the ball, then "kept on running out through the park gate and on to his hotel."

In 1935, Sodality Park was torn down to make way for the relocation of the Southern Pacific Railroad.

Municipal Stadium

California League 1962–present (Missions, Bees), home of San Jose State University Spartans (Pacific Coast Athletic Association), present. *Owned by:* The city of San Jose. *Location:* Tenth Street, Story Road. *Construction cost:* $80,000. *Dimensions:* Left field, 340 feet; center field, 390 feet; right field, 340 feet. *Seating capacity:* 5000. *Surface:* (1962) grass – bermuda grass in the outfield, a mixture in the infield; (1976) artificial. *1987 season attendance:* 69,120.

Before 1967, the winds whipped through Municipal Stadium on cold nights, making conditions uncomfortable. Then a $125,000, 27-foot steel cantilever roof was built by architect William Hedley, alleviating the problem.

San Juan, Puerto Rico

Estadio Sixto Escobar

Location: Avenida Munoz Rivera. *Dimensions:* Left field, 347 feet; center field, 385 feet; right field, 347 feet.

San Luis Potosi, Mexico

Estadio 20 De Noviembre

Mexican League, Zona Norte, present (Tuneros). *Dimensions:* Left field, 325 feet; center field, 405 feet; right field, 320 feet. *Seating capacity:* 6500.

Sanford, Florida

Memorial Stadium

Florida State League 1959–60. *Seating capacity:* 3200.

Santa Barbara, California

Campus Diamond

Home of the University of California at Santa Barbara Gauchos (Pacific Coast Athletic Association), present. *Seating capacity:* 1500.

Sarasota, Florida

Royals Complex

Gulf Coast League (Rookie), present (Astros, Reds, Royals, three franchises). *Location:* U.S. 301 and Adams Lane. *Dimensions:* Left field, 330 feet; center field, 410 feet; right field, 330 feet.

Ed Smith Complex

Gulf Coast League, present (Rangers, Yankees). *Dimensions:* Left field, 355 feet; center field, 400 feet; right field, 355 feet.

Payne Park

Spring training home of the New York Giants 1926, Boston Red Sox circa 1935–58 (except during World War II), Los Angeles Dodgers 1958 (some games), Chicago White Sox 1960–present, Gulf Coast League, present (White Sox). *Location:* U.S. 301, Adams Lane. *Built:* 1925. *Dimensions:* Left field, 355 feet; center field, 400 feet; right field, 355 feet. *Seating capacity:* 4950.

Payne Park is part of a spring training complex used since 1960 by the Chicago White Sox. The stands were originally built for John McGraw's Giants in the spring of 1926, and have gradually grown over the years to hold almost 5000. In 1988, Payne Park was scheduled to host its final baseball game.

In a 1986 city of Sarasota general obligation bond referendum, voters approved $8.5 million for a new 7500-seat ballpark to be built next to Payne Park, where the softball fields are. Plans are to move the softball fields into Payne Park.

One of the major complaints about Payne Park is the lack of legal parking, except on Sunday when the meters aren't read in the nearby municipal lot.

Savannah, Georgia

Grayson Stadium

Southeastern League 1926–28, South Atlantic League 1936–42, 1946–60, 1962, Southern League 1968–70, 1972–circa 1975, Dixie Association 1971. *Location:* Daffin Park, 1500 E. Victory Drive. *Built:* 1925. *Dimensions:* Left field, 290 feet; center field, 420 feet; right field, 310 feet. *Seating capacity:* (1960) 8995; (1975) 8109; (1985) 7500.

The 90-foot light tower in left field was in play all the way to the top. Once this was the second highest structure in play in baseball, surpassed only by the 125-foot flagpole in Tiger Stadium, Detroit. Now it is a ground rule home run if a ball strikes the Tiger Stadium flagpole above a certain point, and all of the highest objects in play are dangling from domes.

In 1976, Grayson Stadium was used in the making of the film *Bingo Long Travelling All-Star and Motor Kings.*

Daffin Park, in which Grayson Stadium is built, also has facilities for soccer, basketball, tennis (nine courts, three lighted), playgrounds, swimming pool, picnic area, lake pavilion, and a children's fishing hole. The park is also the home of the administrative offices of the Leisure Services Bureau.

Schenectady, New York

County Fairgrounds (Racing Park)

New York State League 1895 (partial season, team folded), 1899–1901. *Location:* Hamilton Hill.

Schenectady's ball club built their own grandstand and bleachers on the old fairgrounds, and used this field until they moved to Van Slyke Island (Island Park).

Island Park (later known as Columbus Park)

New York State League 1899–1904, Mohawk Giants (black team) circa 1913–16. *Location:* Van Slyke Island. *Built:* 1901.

The park was on an island in the Mohawk River and was reached by pontoon bridge. Van Slyke Island has since been joined to the mainland by tons of man-moved earth. The site is currently the Schenectady County Community College parking lot, in back of the Hotel Curler, partially beneath the eastern end of the Western Gateway Bridge.

It was here that, in 1913, black pitching ace Frank Wickware outdueled the white man with the incredibly long arms, Walter Johnson, 1–0. Wickware, who remained in Schenectady many years after his playing days were through, used to belittle opposing hitters by calling in the outfield. According to the *Schenectady Gazette,* "...there is no record that this bit of show-boating ever backfired."

After the First World War, the park was bought by the Knights of Columbus and renamed Columbus Park. In 1921, the Brooklyn Dodgers came to play the Knights of Columbus team in an exhibition game.

The park had two covered grandstands, one on either side of the infield. For big games fans circled the grounds on foot. In the early days there was no outfield fence to impede the view.

General Electric Athletic Association Field (G.E.A.A. Field)

Home of the General Electric Refrigerators.

Site, in 1927, of an exhibition game between the Cincinnati Reds and a team representing the Schenectady Police Department.

Alexander Field

Location: Union College.

On June 28, 1928, this was the site of an exhibition game between the

Schenectady Police Department and the Boston Braves. The game had to be called in the seventh inning because fans refused to give back foul balls and all three dozen balls were gone.

Central Park (Buck Ewing Park)
Canadian-American League (Class C) 1946.

While waiting for the construction of McNearney Stadium to be completed, the ball club played their home games on the "A" diamond in Central Park. No lights.

The park is still used for baseball. It is now known as Buck Ewing Park, not after the Hall of Famer but rather the Negro League star.

Schenectady Stadium (originally McNearney Stadium)
Canadian-American League 1946–50, Eastern League 1951–57 (Blue Jays). *Built:* 1946. *Roof added:* 1948. *Dimensions:* Left field, 320 feet; center field, 390 feet; right field, 320 feet. *Seating capacity:* 5000.

When minor league baseball started up again after World War II, the Utica team transferred to the Eastern League, and Schenectady replaced them in the Canadian-American League.

Schenectady Stadium was built in concrete and steel by the owners of the club, beer distributors Pete and Jim McNearney. Pete stayed with the club for the duration. Jim had to get out after he slugged Joe Riordan, the head of the Phillies farm system.

"The ballpark looks a lot like the beer distributorship," says ballpark expert David Pietrusza. "You can tell the structures had the same architect."

There was a full-service restaurant on top of the stands on the third base side. The turnstiles were coin operated, like subway turnstiles in New York. The ones in Schenectady Stadium took silver dollars.

Schenectady is the home of General Electric, so it should be no surprise that Schenectady Stadium has some of the best lights in the minor league. Here G.E. tested out the type of system that they eventually installed in Yankee Stadium.

In 1947, the ballpark was used almost as frequently for professional boxing as it was for baseball, as a series of bouts were promoted by MMP Enterprises.

Now Schenectady Stadium has been transformed into a pitch-and-putt golf course. It's been that way since 1958, but the shell of the structure is still there. It still looks like a ballpark from the outside, and the sign on the outside of the building still says, "Schenectady Stadium."

Scotia, New York

Glenotia Park
Location: Eastern tip of island in the Mohawk River, south of the foot of Sanders Avenue, just west of the Western Gateway Bridge, just south of Scotia village line. *Built:* 1907. Owned by the Scotia Athletic Association.

Glenotia Park, so named because it represented the town of Glenville and the village of Scotia, was built on an island in the Mohawk across from Schenectady by the Scotia Athletic Association, and opened July 1907. The SAA operated the park for about twelve years.

Here the Scotia locals played among each other or picked a nine to take on the (then formidable) Mohawk Giants or the Schenectady Knights of Columbus.

After World War I, the Knights of Columbus played their games on their own island, just down the river.

The bridge to Glenotia Park was dismantled each fall, so it wouldn't be swept away by the Mohawk's heavy ice flow.

Collins Park
Used for baseball in Scotia since 1920. Still there.

In the 1920s, the Philadelphia Phillies played an exhibition game against the General Electric Refrigerators at this park, just across the river from Schenectady. The St. Louis Browns played a Scotia Police team once, and in September of 1928, the Brooklyn Dodgers came to Collins Park to play a local nine.

Scottsdale, Arizona

Scottsdale Stadium

Spring home of the San Francisco Giants, present. *Location:* 7402 East Osborn Road, Scottsdale Road. *Seating capacity:* 4721.

According to Ron Fimrite in *Sports Illustrated,* "Scottsdale Stadium is no more a 'stadium,' in the current sense of the term, than the Old North Church is a cathedral.... Its green wooden stands are so close to the field you can hear the players chew their sunflower seeds."

The outfield fence is two levels of green plank with see-through slats between the boards.

Seattle, Washington

YMCA Park

Home of Seattle baseball before 1903. *Location:* 12th and Jefferson streets.

Madison Park Picnic Grounds

Site of Sunday baseball in Seattle before 1903. *Location:* Madison Park.

Name of park unknown

Home of Seattle baseball 1903–07. *Location:* Fifth Avenue and Republican Street.

Dugdale Park I (Band Box Park)

Northwestern League 1907–12 (Indians). *Location:* 13th and Yesler streets.

Dugdale Park II

Northwestern League 1913–18, International Northwest League 1919, Pacific International League 1920, Pacific Coast League 1921–32 (all teams called Indians). *Location:* Rainier and McClellan streets, same as Sick's Stadium. *Seating capacity:* 15,000. *Fire:* July 4, 1932.

Named after Seattle baseball magnate D.E. Dugdale, this wooden park is one of a surprisingly large number that burned after an Independence Day fireworks display.

Civic Field (Seattle Center's Municipal Stadium)

Pacific Coast League 1932–37 (Rainiers). *Location:* Republican and Harrison streets, Third and Fifth avenues North. *Seating capacity:* 15,000.

Built near Puget Sound, and darn windy because of it, Civic Field had no grass, not even in the outfield. Dusty during a drought, and muddy in the springtime.

The place is still used for high school football games.

Sick's Stadium

Pacific Coast League 1938–67 (Angels), American League 1969 (Pilots), Northwest League 1972–76. *Location:* 2700 Rainier Avenue South (first base side), Bayview Street (third base), South McClellan Street (right field), Empire Way (left field). *Dimensions:* Left field, 305 feet; left center, 345 feet; center field, 405 feet; right center, 345 feet; right field, 320 feet. *Seating capacity:* (1965) 15,000; (1969) 25,420, broken down as follows: field boxes, 1848; loge boxes, 5960; grandstand reserved, 7612; general admission, 10,000. *Pilots day game attendance record:* 21,900 (August 3, 1969, versus New York). *Pilots night game attendance record:* 20,490 (May 28, 1969, versus Baltimore). *Pilots twi-night doubleheader attendance record:* 18,147 (June 20, 1969, versus Kansas City). *Pilots opening game attendance:* 14,993

(April 11, 1969, versus Chicago). *Pilots 1969 season attendance:* 677,944. *First game:* June 15, 1938 (attendance: 12,000). *First night game:* June 16, 1938. *First Pilots game:* April 11, 1969 (Seattle 7, Chicago 0). *Last Pilots game:* October 2, 1969 (Oakland 3, Seattle 1).

The name Pilots was chosen by contest-winner Donald Nelson, who felt the name denoted leadership and combined the area's heritage on sea and in the air.

When the ballpark was razed, its lights were moved to Buck Bailey Field in Pullman, Washington, the home of the Washington State University Cougars.

Kingdome

American League 1977–present (Mariners). Current home of the National Football League's Seattle Seahawks, and the National Basketball Association's Seattle Supersonics. Former home of the North American Soccer League's Seattle Sounders. Site of the 1979 All-Star Game (National League 7, American League 6). *Location:* Fourth Avenue South (right field), South Royal Brougham Way (first base), Occidental Avenue South (third base), South King Street (left field), close to the Seattle waterfront. *Architect:* Naramore, Skilling and Praeger. *Construction cost:* $67 million. *Dimensions:* Left field, 316 feet; center field, 410 feet; right field, 316 feet. *Surface:* Artificial. *Seating capacity:* For baseball, 59,438; for football, 65,000. *Single game attendance record:* 58,905 (July 17, 1979, All-Star Game). *Season attendance record:* 1,338,000 (1977). *First game:* April 6, 1977 (Angels 7, Seattle 0, attendance 57,762, winning pitcher: Frank Tanana).

The Kingdome is built on 35.9 acres near ground where early settlers founded Seattle in 1853. It was conceived by mandate of the people of Seattle in March 1976. At the time of its opening, it featured the world's largest

self-supporting concrete roof.

In 1977, the power alleys at the Kingdome measured 375 feet. They were brought in ten feet in 1978 and then another eight in 1981, to 357 feet. Here's an arena that seems determined to be an easy home run touch. The fences may continue to creep inward until Seattle is playing in a Japanese-style ballpark.

The highest point of the dome rises 250 feet above the playing field. Construction required 443 tons of structural steel and 52,800 cubic yards of concrete. It is anchored by 1822 concrete-filled steel pipes and 42 wooden piles that extend 60 feet into hardpan.

It is considered to be a better place to watch baseball than the other domes, as the lighting is better and the seats are closer to the field.

On May 6, 1982, this was the site of Gaylord Perry's 300th victory as the "Ancient Mariner" beat the New York Yankees 7–3.

In addition to major sports, other events to have taken place in the Kingdome include auto racing, circuses, motorcycle racing, rodeos, and track and field meets.

Tubby Graves Field

Home of the University of Washington Huskies (Pac-10 Conference, Northern Division), present. *Seating capacity:* 1000.

Sedona, Arizona

Posse Grounds Community Park

Current home of local baseball. *Location:* Two miles west of town on Posse Grounds Road.

Sedona (population 8730) is in the heart of Central Arizona, 127 miles north of Phoenix and 27 miles south of Flagstaff. This is the only ballpark in town, also used for community picnics.

Sherbrooke, Quebec

Amadee Roy Stadium
Provincial League 1950–51, 1953–55 (Athletics). *Built:* 1953.

This park replaced the Provincial League stadium that burned on the morning of September 19, 1951. Amadee Roy was the second baseman, secretary and treasurer of the 1934 Sherbrooke Provincial League team. Torn down before 1982.

Shreveport, Louisiana

Shreveport's Texas League ballpark burned down on May 4, 1932, after a game against Galveston, and the town lost the franchise to Oklahoma City.

Spar Stadium (Gassers Park, Texas League Park)
Southern League 1959–61, Texas League 1972–85. *Location:* Harp (now Gary) Street, Sycamore, Walnut and Dove streets at Park Avenue. *Built:* 1935. *Dimensions:* Left field, 320 feet; center field, 410 feet; right field, 310 feet. *Seating capacity:* (1960) 9500; (1975) 8000; (1985) 3000.

Fairgrounds Field
Texas League 1986–present (Captains). *Location:* Off Interstate 20.

Recently replaced decaying Spar Stadium. State-of-the-art concrete and fibreglass ballpark. According to *The Bill James Baseball Abstract 1988,* this is one of baseball's worst parks for hitting.

Sioux Falls, South Dakota

The Flats
Site of the first reported ball game in Sioux Falls 1878. *Location:* Below Brewery Hill, south of the present site of the Crescent Creamery.

Game was played on the Fourth of July, between two local teams, probably picked especially for the occasion.

The Prairie
Home of Sioux Falls baseball circa 1884. *Location:* Current 10th Street and Prairie Avenue.

Howard Wood Field
Northern League 1946–53 (Canaries). *Location:* Washington High School.

Part of a cinder 440-oval ran through left field. This was the Washington High School football field, and was named after Coach Howard Wood, who coached WHS football from 1911 to 1943. The park was torn down in the 1950s and a new Howard Wood Field was constructed at a different site. In 1961, this new field was the site of a National Football League pre-season game between the brand-new Minnesota Vikings and Dallas Cowboys, the first professional football game in South Dakota history.

Packer Stadium (Sioux Falls Baseball Stadium)
Basin League 1960s (Packers).

Once home of a Cincinnati Reds farm team, now used exclusively for American Legion and Sioux Falls Amateur Baseball.

Smiths Falls, Ontario

Canadian Pacific Recreation Field
Canadian-American League (Class C) 1937 (Beavers), 1938 (Ottawa Braves, three games). *Dimensions:* Left field, 270 feet; center field, 410 feet; right field, 400 feet. *Seating capacity:* 2200.

The park was operated by the Canadian Pacific Railroad Employees Association, and it got good reviews during its sole year of pro ball, hosting a New York Class C farm team. Perth and Smiths Falls were too close for both to support baseball.

According to David Pietrusza, the infield was grass (uncommonly luxurious in this league), and flags bearing the names of the teams in the league flew from the grandstand roof. The

scoreboard was in center, and an auxiliary information board in left field
gave the names and numbers of that
day's opponents.

This field was last used for organized
baseball in July 1938, when an exhibition came to Ottawa's Lansdowne
Stadium, and the Braves had to play
three Can-Am League games in Smiths
Falls.

This plot of land, however, is still
used for baseball.

South Bend, Indiana

Goose pasture

Home of South Bend baseball 1860–
63 (Hoosiers). *Location:* Michigan
Street, LaSalle Avenue.

Henry Benjamin organized the Hoosiers, South Bend's first baseball team,
in the spring of 1860. They played on a
goose pasture, where German immigrants grazed their geese.

The Fairgrounds

Home of South Bend baseball 1864–
70. *Location:* On the western edge of
town.

One of the areas used most for
baseball during this time period.

Taylor's Field

Home of South Bend baseball 1871–
77 (Excelsiors, Rough and Readys,
Clippers). *Location:* Division Street
(currently Western Avenue), Carroll
and Bronson streets.

This field was developed to accommodate the large crowds that had been
attending games out at the Fairgrounds.
During the time Taylor's Field was
used, John Deacon's Greenstockings
became the dominant team in town.

Greenstocking Park (I)

Home of South Bend baseball 1878–
81 (Greenstockings). *Location:* Just
west of the old Laurel School. *Construction foreman:* Alex Staples. *Seating capacity:* 1500 (with room along
both of the foul lines for people in car-

riages to view the action).

The concept of John Deacon, this
was the first enclosed baseball facility
in Northern Indiana. On May 31, 1878,
the *South Bend Tribune* described
Greenstocking Park's grounds as "com-
modious, level as a floor with a clear
diamond and surrounded by a high
board fence."

On July 20, 1878, the *New York
Clipper* reported, "The Liberty Baseball Club of Chicago visited South
Bend July 5th and played a match game
in the afternoon with the Greenstocks
on the latter's grounds, which are said
to be the finest in the west, excelling the
grounds of the Chicago White Sox."

By that time, South Bend had already seen major league competition.
The Boston Red Stockings had come to
town to play the Greenstockings on
June 26.

The ballpark closed after three years
because incoming attractions demanded
a bigger cut of the take than Deacon
could afford.

Greenstocking Park (II)

Home of South Bend baseball 1886–
96 (Greenstockings). *Location:* Between Lafayette Boulevard and William Street near the south edge of town.
Construction foreman: Theodore
Knoblock. *Seating capacity:* 2000.

The roofed amphitheater was built
on land leased by John Deacon. As was
the case with the first Greenstocking
Park, the playing area was enclosed by
a high-board fence.

Again, the Greenstockings took on
major league competition. Five hundred extra seats (boosting the seating
capacity to 2500) were added—and
filled—for a game against Detroit of
the National League on August 3, 1887.

In addition to baseball, the ballpark
housed "moonlight dancing festivals,"
shooting tournaments, and foot races.
In 1888, the field was used for a Notre
Dame football game. The arena stood
until 1896, when the property was sold
for city real estate.

Springbrook Park (Playland Park 1920s–1950s)

Central League 1903–12, 1916–17, 1932 (Blue Sox), Southern Michigan League 1914–15. Home of South Bend baseball 1896–circa 1955 (Senators, other semi-pro and professional baseball, such as the Studebaker Athletics, Greenstockings, and Indestructos.) *Location:* Ironwood and Twyckenham drives, Lincoln Way East, and the St. Joseph River. *First game:* June 14, 1896.

On August 28, 1904, a game was played here under portable lights.

The ballpark changed names during the 1920s because of a change in ownership.

Singer Park

Home of South Bend Factory League baseball and other games 1910s–1920s. *Location:* Just north of Western Avenue.

Factory teams like the Singer Sewing Machine team played here. There were also stops here on barnstorming tours by the Chicago White Sox and the House of David.

A small roofed grandstand sat behind home, with jury box–type bleachers just to its first base side. There were longer bleachers along the third base line. The rest of the first base line held the "parking lot." Fans who came in automobiles could pull right up to the right field foul line and watch the game from the car.

Lippincott Park

Local ball 1929–40 (Studebaker Athletics, Hoosier Beer), Negro American League 1940s (American Giants, some games). *Location:* Ewing Avenue and Franklin Street. *Built by:* Studebaker Athletic Association. *Groundbreaking:* Spring, 1929. *Dedicated:* September 7, 1929. *Construction cost:* $25,000. *Seating capacity:* 4000.

Reportedly the Chicago-based American Giants of the Negro American League's "home away from home."

Stanley Coveleski Regional Stadium

Used for local ball starting July 2, 1987, Midwest League 1988–present (White Sox). *Location:* Beside historic Union Station. *Architects:* Hellmuth-Obata-Kassabaum, Inc. *Seating capacity:* 5200.

A group of South Bend baseball enthusiasts got together after the 1984 baseball season and formed the Michiana Professional Baseball Association. This group approached the city of South Bend with the idea of bringing back professional baseball. The city saw this as an excellent opportunity to spruce up a faded section of South Bend's inner city. The city Parks Department owned some land in the western part of downtown, purchased the surrounding lots, and plans for the park began. The area, known as Studebaker Corridor, included Union Station and the Studebaker Museum, and would receive additional redevelopment projects, of which the ballpark would be a mere cornerstone. Local businesses pitched in a hand for the new park, offering their facilities for fund-raisers and organizational meetings.

Ah, there's always a spoilsport. In this case it was Fair Tax, Inc., a zealous group of anti-ballpark people who knew who was really paying for the ballpark and did not like it one iota. They took the Michiana group to court a few times, but managed only some costly delays. The ballpark was built — and it was named after a longtime local favorite, Hall of Famer Stanley Coveleski.

The Pied Piper of South Bend. Coveleski won 215 games in the major leagues, 13 in a row once in 1925. He was long known for his wet pitches and their ability to fan Babe Ruth. From the time they first met on the playing field, Coveleski had Ruth's number.

Coveleski retired after the '28 season, after 16 years of pro ball, and moved to South Bend to stay. In the

An artist gives a bird's eye view of the Stanley Coveleski Regional Stadium in downtown South Bend, Indiana. (Compliments of the South Bend White Sox.)

1920 World Series he pitched three complete games for the Cleveland Indians allowing two runs. His series E.R.A. was 0.67. In 1929, he and his wife, Frances, bought a home on Napier Street from a pioneer family of South Bend named Napieralski. Stan opened a gas station on the west side of town, which quickly turned into the hangout of every ballplaying youngster in South Bend. Coveleski (a.k.a. the Pied Piper of South Bend) gave out free lessons daily. A fellow has to do something when he isn't pumping gas. When it came time to name the new ballpark, the choice was easy. Stan more than anyone had kept baseball alive in South Bend.

And the ballpark is gorgeous. The grandstand roof is dark blue and the outfield fence is high and padded green. The land is sculpted so that there are grassy knolls above the outfield fences. Above the right field foul pole giant sycamores overlook the playing field. The roofed grandstand is about 17 rows high at its tallest and extends out beyond first and third. Theater seats behind the plate, and a bit to either side, are painted blue, while the bleacher benches that make up the remainder of the stands are gray.

Spartanburg, South Carolina

Duncan Park
South Atlantic League 1938–40, 1973–present (Suns), Tri-State League 1946–55, Western Carolinas League 1963–72. *Location:* Duncan Park Drive at South Converse Street. *Dimensions:* Left field, 320 feet; center field, 385 feet; right field, 320 feet. *Lights installed:* 1936. *Lights:* (Originals) 160 demountable reflectors supported by ten timber poles, providing 20 candlepower on the mound, ten in the outfield. (1985) 93 metal halide lamps on 85-foot galvanized steel poles, installed by MUSCO, providing 70 candlepower on the mound, 54 in the outfield. *Seating capacity:* 2945. *1987 season attendance:* 36,286. *Record season attendance:* 173,010 (1966).

Duncan Park didn't change much

between 1936 and 1985. There were new lights, and the wooden fence was gone, but some of the advertisers on the billboard signs remained the same— like Smith's Drug Store and R.C. Cola, whose logos were painted on the outfield fence all that time.

According to Bill Veeck, in a 1966 edition of his syndicated column, "The park is clean and colorful. It has the finest ladies' room I've seen in minor league baseball (Pat took me on an early tour), a well-kept diamond and good concessions." Pat is Pat Williams, then Spartanburg general manager.

Spokane, Washington

The Spokane Grounds

Northwest League 1890–1900. *Location:* Twyckenham, "on the cable road." *Seating capacity:* 1000.

The Spokane team had won the 1889 Northwest League pennant, and the players were building a new ballfield out on the cable road. Manager John S. Barnes was in charge of construction, showing up at the site at seven o'clock each morning.

According to the April 15, 1890, edition of *The Spokane Falls Review:*

"A large force of carpenters is at work on the grand stand, and 'bleachers,' as the seats unprotected from the rays of the sun are called, and the whole place will be ready for the public by Saturday night.

"A dozen teams are constantly at work, hauling dirt from down the river for the infield, and the rocks have all been removed from the outfield. The ground is being worked as carefully as a ladies' flower bed, and will be almost perfect when completed.

"The grand stand will be divided into a place for ladies with gentlemen and a place for gentlemen only, and the directors and the newspaper reporters will be comfortably provided for. . . . Cushions will be provided at a trifling cost,

so there will be lots of comfort, besides good ball playing at the new grounds."

The Spokane team repeated as pennant winners in their first year at the new park. And business was sufficient so that everyone got paid.

Natatorium Park

Home of Spokane baseball circa 1901.

A team representing the Spokane Athletic Club played games here against teams from Walla Walla, Portland, corporation teams from San Francisco, and the University of California.

Natatorium Park was a real park, not a ballpark, and was the site of Spokane's largest society picnics.

Northwest League Grounds

Northwest League 1901–03. *Location:* About 100 yards from the junction of the O.R.&N. railroad and the Hillyard car line on the open prairie. *Seating capacity:* 1500.

Baseball was gaining in popularity fast. Estimates were that the team was losing $50 to $100 every Sunday because there was no place to put the people. The local paper, the *Spokesman,* called for the stands to be enlarged. The club agreed to cover part of the bleachers with an awning to make the grandstand section larger. The newspaper reported on June 20, 1901, that other planned improvements in the field included "placing a scoreboard in a more conspicuous place, probably in deep center field, and improving the condition of the center garden, which is considered very rank by the fielders of this league."

Recreation Park

Northwest League 1904–at least 1909, Idaho-Washington League 1923–36. *Owned by:* The city of Spokane. *Location:* Mission Avenue (north), Sinto Avenue (south), Normandie Street (west), Atlantic Street (east). Grandstand at northeast corner of the plot, at the corner of Mission and Atlantic.

Dimensions: right field, 250 feet.

Fans attending the games had five lines of streetcars near the grounds, with the Spokane Traction Company Line traveling right beside the park. The Washington Water Power Line on Division Street traveled within a block of the grandstand. There was some mild objection to construction by a handful of neighbors, but nothing that interfered with progress.

In 1909, baseball was more popular than ever in Spokane. The Northwest League team drew 58,000 to Recreation Park in the season's first four weeks. The new riches were put into helping the playing surface.

According to the May 19, 1909, issue of *The Spokesman Review:*

"...several teams and a force of men were put to work spreading a carload of sand and loam shipped from a Traction company from Freeman, Wash. This will be carefully scattered over the infield and daily rollings and packings will make it (a) much faster and liver [sic] infield.

"The old bleacher row will be completely covered over with the grandstand roof, adding 500 to the grandstand seating capacity. Work has already commenced on a big new tier of bleachers in right field which will probably accommodate 700 to 1000 more. This will give the grounds a new seating capacity of 6000, and enable the Recreation company to handle 7000 or maybe 8000 people, which, it is expected, will want to see the games in June."

The outfield fence was curved and made of eight-foot wooden slats. Advertisements were painted directly onto the wood.

Ferris Field

Western International League (Class B) 1937-41, 1946-57 (Indians, Hawks). *Record season attendance:* 204,000 (1938, Class B record).

Named after a former Spokane ballplayer, and member of the City Corporation Council, the "granddaddy of baseball in Spokane."

In 1946, the Spokane Indians were wiped out in a bus crash. Nine died and five were injured. Among the dead was the manager, Mel Cole. The bus crashed and rolled 500 feet to the bottom of Snoqualmie pass, where it burned.

The Interstate Fairgrouds Stadium

(Spokane Fairgrounds Park, Indians Stadium)

Pacific Coast League 1958-71, 1973-82, Northwest League 1972, 1983-present (Indians). *Location:* Interstate Fairgrounds Park, Havana exit on Interstate 90. *Dimensions:* Left field, 335 feet; center field, 411 feet; right field, 335 feet. *Seating capacity:* 10,000. *Record Pacific Coast League season attendance:* 270,000 (1958). *1987 attendance:* 113,865.

The 23-foot walls — painted everywhere but in straightaway center with a double deck of signs — make this park a pitcher's delight. There are seven extension signs above the fence, making the wall 28 feet high in those spots.

The stadium was built in 90 days in 1958 to accommodate the Dodgers' AAA affiliate, forced out of Los Angeles by big league expansion. The 1960 Spokane team had Frank Howard, Tommy Davis, Willie Davis and Maury Wills. The 1970 edition featured Bill Buckner, Davey Lopes, Bill Russell, Steve Garvey, Doyle Alexander, Charlie Hough, and Bobby Valentine, all managed by Tommy Lasorda.

There's a single-decked grandstand behind home, and roofless stands extending down the foul lines to the corners. The press box sits on top of the roof directly behind home.

The Dodgers sold their interest in the Spokane club after the 1971 season to an Albuquerque group, where the franchise went to stay. A local group operated a Northwest League (Class A) team out of Spokane for a year, before the Pacific Coast League moved back in, this time with a cluster of affiliations and confusion. Between 1973 and 1982, Spokane's professional baseball team was a farm club of the Brewers, Angels, Mariners and Rangers. In 1983, the franchise moved to Las Vegas and Spokane was back in Class A ball, this time with a Northwest League franchise owned first by Sunshine Baseball, Inc., and then by Bobby and Ken Brett, brothers of injury-prone Royal George. The county of Spokane, who still owns the park, split costs of refurbishing the park with the Bretts. In 1986, $50,000 worth of brand-new contoured box seats were installed, and overall, more than $200,000 was spent on improvements. After years in five figures, Spokane is drawing over 100,000 annually once again.

Pecarovich Field

Home of the Gonzaga University Bulldogs (Pac-10 Conference, Northern Division), present. *Seating capacity:* 2000.

Springfield, Illinois

Ball Grounds

Home of the Liberties 1876–77 (for most games). *Location:* In the first ward, between Tenth and Eleventh streets, and Lincoln and Enos avenues.

A railroad track ran past the ballpark. The field existed until at least 1883. The site became the Springfield Furniture Factory in 1890, and their building still stands today, used by Goodwill Industries.

Name of park unknown

Home of the Liberties 1876–77 (some games). *Location:* A field south of "Uncle" Jesse Dubois' orchard, believed to have been in the area of Lanphier Park.

Springfield got its first professional ball club in 1876. They were known as the Liberties, and though they belonged to no league, they played many of the teams in the newly formed National League.

President of the Liberties was Frank Myers, owner of the Wonder store on the north side of the square, while George Hodge, the town blacksmith, served as treasurer. Hodge's brother Dick was umpire for most of the home games, played usually at Eleventh and Enos, but sometimes near Dubois' orchard.

The record, painted with local nostalgia no doubt, says the Liberties held their own against Boston, Providence, and Buffalo, but admits that Cap Anson's Chicago White Stockings dominated.

Springfield was a popular stop for traveling major league ball clubs because of the one-day layover between scheduled games in Chicago and St. Louis.

The Liberties lasted for only two years, when Frank Myers packed up his team and moved them to Peoria. The city would be in and out of professional baseball for the next forty years.

Lanphier Park (Robin Roberts Stadium)

Three-I League 1925–1932 (Senators), 1935–49 (Brownies), Mississippi Valley League 1933, Central League 1934, Midwest League 1978–present (Redbirds). *Location:* Converse and Grand avenues, at 15th Street. *Built:* 1925. *Construction cost:* $49,000. *Rebuilt:* 1978. *Dimensions:* Left field, 320 feet; center field, 410 feet; right field, 320 feet. *Seating capacity:* 5000. *Record season attendance:* 154,148 (1987).

Springfield's spotty record as a professional baseball franchise continued until 1914, when it fizzled out altogether. Baseball did not return until 1925, but this time it came to stay, beginning what has been called the "Golden Age of Springfield Baseball."

In 1924, those advocating the return of baseball to Springfield found there was no money readily available to support a team. A citywide fund-raising drive was launched.

By February 1925, there was enough

money in the bank to start construction on Lanphier Park, and the ballpark was finished in time for the home opener.

On Opening Day, 1925, 9063 paying spectators and several hundred guests watched manager Bill Jackson and his Senators lose to Terre Haute. That team finished seventh and drew 128,000 for the year. The next year, the Senators nabbed the Three-I pennant and drew 128,000—then a record for Class B ball.

One highlight of the 1926 season was a game between Springfield and Peoria on July 21. The Senators won 33–23. There were ten out-of-the-park home runs, four triples and seven doubles. Eighteen batters walked, and there were eight errors.

Springfield's third year in the Three-I League proved that the honeymoon was over. The team finished a respectable third, but the novelty of the new ballpark had worn off. Attendance dropped to 75,000. Then the Depression struck and by 1932, the Three-I League went belly-up, taking the Springfield Senators with it.

After stints in the Mississippi Valley League, and the Central League, Springfield returned to a reformed Three-I League in 1935 as a farm club of the St. Louis Browns, and remained until 1949.

In May 1943, Lanphier hosted a Negro American League game featuring the Cincinnati Clowns.

When the park was built, it was neighbored by the city reservoir (whose sloping sides made a good sled run in winter) as well as the plant and athletic field of the Sangamon Electric Company. Between the reservoir and the ballpark was a lagoon that traced a lazy course through that area, where there were no streets and houses. The rest of the area was residential.

By 1950, the area had changed, but the ballpark remained the same. The reservoir was gone, replaced by Lanphier High School. The lazy lagoon had been filled and turned into a football field. The Sangamon Electric Company remained, and had expanded—so that there was no longer room for an athletic field. That space by then was used for company warehouses and parking.

Excluding a Class D experiment in 1950 in another ballpark, Lanphier Park went without pro baseball until 1978, when the New Orleans Pelicans of the Midwest League moved their franchise into a rebuilt Lanphier Park, renamed for Hall of Fame pitcher and native son Robin Roberts.

Jim Fitzpatrick Memorial Stadium
Mississippi Valley League 1950 (Class D). *Location:* Fourth and Stanford.

When Springfield lost its Three-I League franchise in 1949, local J.R. "Bud" Fitzpatrick built his own ballpark and enticed the Class D Mississippi League to move into it. The arrangement failed to click, however, and the franchise was gone by the following year.

The ballpark was named after Bud's son, Jim, who had become ill and died in 1946 at the age of 20.

Springfield, Massachusetts

Lot at the corner of Main and Lyman streets
Home of the Springfield Pioneers 1854.

As late as 1850, folks were still playing rounders in Springfield—but the British game's days were numbered. It was around that year that two former members of the New York Knickerbockers, players with the 1845 team,

Two halves of a panoramic view of Lanphier Park, Springfield, Ill., as it appeared in 1926. (Photos supplied by Sangamon Valley Collection, Lincoln Library, Springfield, Illinois.)

came to town with Cartwright's rules committed to memory. Baseball became the sport of choice from that day on.

In 1852, Springfield received its charter. Two years later teams such as the Hampden Pioneers began to play other towns, using the lot on Main and Lyman as their home grounds. There were no bleachers, but townsfolk had been known to bring along their own chairs so they could take a load off beside the foul line of their choice.

Hampden Park

International Association 1877, National Association 1878, Massachusetts Association 1884, Eastern League 1887, 1895–1900, Connecticut League 1902–1912 (Ponies). First used for baseball in 1853. *New grandstand built:* 1908. *Dimensions* (1908): Center field, 500 feet. Possibly 450 feet down the lines. *Seating capacity* (1867): 3000 (also a racetrack).

By the middle of the 1850s, the Pioneers were an organized group of amateurs — undisputedly Springfield's best nine. In 1859, the Pioneers clubbed Pittsfield, 56–4.

That same summer, on July 11, the nation's first college baseball game was played at Pittsfield, Amherst defeating Williams 66–32.

By this time the Pioneers were playing their home games at Hampden Park, which had been, until recently, nothing but 63 acres of pasture, part of the farms of Festus Stebbins and Horatio Sergeant.

The land had been purchased in 1853 for $15,405 by the Hampden Agricultural Society, an organization of business and professional men who directed the annual local meetings of the National Trotting Organization. It was turned into a recreation center for the entire valley.

A horse-racing track was laid out in the park for $10,000, and in 1867 $12,000 was spent building seating accommodations for 3000. Noted trotters and pacers raced on the Hampden mile track from 1867 to 1893. During those years, the park was also the site of bicycle races, running events, circuses, and fireworks displays.

Baseball was played here for the next 70 years. During that time, Springfield fielded teams in five different minor leagues, including the Eastern League and the International Association.

Hampden Park first saw big league action between 1872 and 1875, when it was used on occasion by Boston or Middletown for National Association games.

In the nineteenth century, Hampden Park was the site of many Yale-Harvard football games, dating back as far as 1875. In 1889, 20,000 came to the park to see the annual rivalry.

The Stars. Phil Powers, Lipman Pike, Sam Crane, and Arlie Latham were among Springfield's early baseball heroes. Pike was the Babe Ruth of his day. According to legend, he hit six home runs in one game during the 1866 season.

It was in Hampden Park that Hugh Duffy played his first professional game. Duffy went on to set the all-time major league record for a season batting average with .438 for Boston (National League) in 1894. In 1887, Duffy played for Springfield as a shortstop, catcher, and outfielder.

It was in Hampden Park that Fred Tenney was first used as a first baseman. He went on to become the greatest first baseman the world had known — until Lou Gehrig. Tenney had been a catcher, but manager Tom Burns of Springfield saw the possibilities of the left-handed Tenney at first base.

It was here that outfielder Fielder Jones blossomed as a ballplayer, and here that Dan Brouthers hit .416, the highest mark ever attained by a Springfield player.

Temple Cup. Springfield was the home of major league baseball only as refuge for the Boston Beaneaters of 1897 during the Temple Cup series.

In 1894, William C. Temple, a Pittsburgh sportsman, donated an expensive cup as prize for a post-season series between the National League pennant-winner and runner-up. The series ran for four years and never managed to cause much excitement. Some teams wanted to defend the cup they had won the previous year, even if they finished lower than second in the National League standings. Lopsided victories became the Temple Cup norm. By the final year of its existence, the series already had a bad reputation.

In 1897, Boston managed a slim pennant victory over John McGraw's Orioles. But the Beaneaters completely folded during post-season play.

By the end of the series, Boston had to move their games to Hampden Park for safety, so angry were the Boston fans, who sensed a dive.

The Beaneaters, with three 20-game winners, including Kid Nichols, yielded 54 runs in the series' five games. Springfield's sole exposure to big league ball was of the fishiest variety.

A new grandstand was built in Hampden Park in 1908, and fences were built to enclose the playing ground. According to a 1911 edition of the *Springfield Homestead,* "(Hampden Park) is now one of the largest fields in baseball parks in the (Connecticut) league. The distance from home plate to the fence in the rear of center field is 500 feet and the distance between the fence at left and right fields, about 450 feet." These dimensions may be defining a quadrangle, rather than giving the then-meaningless home run distances.

At that time, Springfield played in the Connecticut League along with New Haven, Waterbury, New Britain, and Bridgeport.

Forest Park

Home of the local "shop league" circa 1911.

Today, with 800 acres, Forest Park is the largest in Springfield. It has a kid-dieland zoo and a winter ice skating pond.

Pynchon Park

International League 1950–53 (Cubs), Eastern League 1957–65. *Location:* West Street. *Seating capacity:* 7500. *Last International League game:* September 7, 1953 (Syracuse Chiefs 11, Springfield Cubs 10).

Stanford, California

Sunken Diamond

Home of the Stanford University Cardinals 1931–present. *Location:* Stanford University campus, near Stanford Stadium. *Built:* 1931. *Dimensions:* (1931) Left field, 360 feet; center field, 500 feet; right field, 335 feet. (1966) Left field, 335 feet; center field, 400 feet; right field, 335 feet. *Fences:* (1978) Seven feet all the way around.

A constantly improving facility. The dugouts and the warning track were installed in 1970. In the 1980s, wooden bleachers were replaced with aluminum benches, financed by a "Buy-a-Bench Program" initiated by former Cardinal coach Ray Young. A 36' × 12' scoreboard was installed, financed by the Diamond Club. Cement steps were built leading to and from the field and an ultra-modern press box was put in. Most recently, the new Bud Klein Varsity Clubhouse was built, a structure next to the Sunken Diamond holding locker rooms, offices, restrooms, the ticket office, and training and equipment rooms.

Stillwater, Oklahoma

Allie Reynolds Stadium

Home of the Oklahoma State University Cowboys (Big Eight Conference), present. *Seating capacity:* 2800.

Named after the Oklahoma right-hander who went 182–107 for the Indians and the Yankees between 1942 and 1954.

Stockton, California

Banner Island

Stockton's "big diamond" before 1890. *Location:* Fremont and Lincoln streets. *Seating capacity:* 2000.

Banner Island received its name from the fact that one Captain Weber, during the Civil War, placed a tall flagpole at this spot, from which he flew the Stars and Stripes. The flagpole was so tall that it could be seen for miles around. Captain Weber placed a cannon at its base and fired it every time there was a Union victory in battle.

The baseball field there was fenced in, with a grandstand and bleachers for paid admissions. Many came with horses and rigs and surrounded the field to watch games.

Banner Island served Stockton's baseball community for over 50 years. Even after major baseball activity moved to Oak Park around 1890, the Banner Island diamond was still used by the recreation department for city league contests.

Ultimately, being private property, the field gave way to industry. Where the backstop used to be now stands the Blue Ribbon Dairy.

Other Parks. Baseball flourished in Stockton in the nineteenth century. Among the more popular sandlot fields of the 1870s and 1880s were Gypsy Camp, in present Constitution Square; the Hamilton Lot, where Weber School is now located; the Western Pacific, located at Ophir and Church streets; the Santa Fe lot at Worth and Sutter streets; the Cool corner at Worth and Madison streets; and the East Street diamond, in the present Holt Park. The East Street diamond was used extensively before the Santa Fe Railroad came through in 1896. It was located diagonally across present-day Wilson Way from the San Joaquin County General Hospital. When the hospital was moved to French Camp, the Detention Home for Youth was located on that corner and remained there until 1949.

Oak Park Baseball Field (Goodwater Grove, 1880s–circa 1915, Billy Hebert Field, 1950–present)

Used for baseball since at least 1890, California State League 1913–15, Pacific Coast League circa 1918–29, California League 1941, 1946–present (Ports, Mariners), home of the University of the Pacific Tigers (Pacific Coast Athletic Association) 1947–present. *Location:* Sutter and Alpine streets. *Dimensions:* Left field, 325 feet; center field, 390 feet; right field, 325 feet. *Seating capacity:* (1946) 5000; (1960) 4500; (1985) 6000. *Lights erected:* 1941, 1946.

Major baseball activity in Stockton was moved from Banner Island to Oak Park around 1890, when the streetcar line was extended from North Street. After almost a century, baseball is still there.

In the early days, the names most synonymous with Oak Park baseball were those of the Moreing brothers: Cy, Bill, Charley and Lou. They were interested in sports in general, but baseball in particular. They backed their baseball interest with the same kind of personal and financial backing that they offered all their endeavors. They were ranchers, grain-farmers, contractors and subdividers. Charley and Lou raised a million bushels of wheat in the Sacramento Valley during World War I. Cy and Bill built many of Stockton's streets, and were responsible for the subdivision around Yosemite Lake. Cy created and managed the Outlaw League. Bill was a premiere local pitcher. Charley and Lou owned the Pacific Coast League's Sacramento Senators. They played their Sunday games at Oak Park, giving Stockton their first taste of minor league ball. They built the Oak Park stands, improved the playing field, and donated to the city much good equipment when they left town in 1929.

From 1900 to the start of World War II, Oak Park was the home of the city's finest semi-pro ball. After the Senators stopped coming to town, the number-one attractions on that diamond were the American Legion and the Amblers Club.

Minor league baseball returned to Stockton in 1941, with the formation of the California State League. At that point, Oak Park was lighted for night baseball. The Stockton team was a farm of the Los Angeles Pacific Coast League team, and managed by Earl Hamilton.

The California State League finished out the 1941 season intact. Then the war broke out. Blackouts were declared in California. A lighted baseball stadium invited air raids. The league discontinued. Oak Park's lights were removed and sold to the Pollock shipbuilding company for war equipment. The park kept the poles and wiring—just the lamps were sold.

When the war was over, the California League started up again. Oak Park was relighted and additional stands were built to accommodate 5000 spectators. The Ports were well-supported and drew good crowds, winning the California State League pennant in 1946 and 1947.

Billy Hebert. Resolution Number 17,277 of the Stockton City Council, September 18, 1950:

"WHEREAS, DAN W. MORRISON, Mayor of the City of Stockton, and METROPOLITAN RECREATION COMMISSION suggest and recommend that the area presently known as the Oak Park Baseball Field be re-named 'Billy Hebert Field,' so as to distinguish it from the rest of Oak Park and to give it a singularity it does not have at the present time, and

"WHEREAS, the most popular suggestion has been to honor a young man, Billy Hebert, who learned his baseball in the Recreation Department boys' league, developed it playing Junior Legion ball for Karl Ross Post,

and was starting on the way to a promising professional career in the California League when called to duty in World War II and who was the first player in all of organized baseball to give his life for his country when he was killed in action in the South Pacific Theatre of War, and

"WHEREAS, the City Council agrees with the Mayor and said Metropolitan Recreation Commission and considers the name 'Billy Hebert Field' to be appropriate and commemorative; now therefore,

"BE IT RESOLVED BY THE COUNCIL OF THE CITY OF STOCKTON, AS FOLLOWS:

"That that certain area presently known as Oak Park Baseball Field located at Oak Park in the City of Stockton, be renamed 'Billy Hebert Field.'"

The original wooden grandstand burned sometime in the 1950s and was replaced by a brick and concrete structure. The outfield fence is irregularly shaped, jutting outward sharply in left center. Reminding one of Baker Bowl, a fieldhouse is built right into the center field fence. Two of the five outfield light towers, the two in straightaway center, beside the fieldhouse, rise from the playing field and are in play.

Suffolk, Virginia

Athletic Park
Virginia League circa 1939 (Nuts).
Seating capacity: 2200.

Smith Street Park
Virginia League 1940s (Wildcats).
Seating capacity: 2200.

Peanut Park
Virginia League 1940s (Goobers).
Seating capacity: 2500.

Sumter, South Carolina

Riley Park

South Atlantic League 1983–present
(Braves). *Location:* 615 Church Street,
½ mile north of U.S. 521 (Broad
Street). *Dimensions:* Left field, 337
feet; center field, 372 feet; right field,
338 feet. *Seating capacity:* 4000. *1987
season attendance:* 26,081.

Sun City, Arizona

Sun City Stadium

Spring home of the Milwaukee
Brewers 1973–85. *Location:* Grand
Avenue, 111th Street.

Ballpark in a retirement community.
The screen protecting fans from foul
balls went from foul pole to foul pole.
Many fans watched games from their
golf carts, parked on a runway behind
the stands.

Sun City Stadium, no longer in use,
was built on land owned by Del E.
Webb Development Company (there's
a Del Webb Stadium in Modesto,
California). At one time it was also the
home of a ladies' softball team known
as the Sun City Saints.

Sunbury, Pennsylvania

Memorial Park

Interstate League 1947 (Yankees).
Seating capacity: 3800.

An excellent park with scenery worth
painting, surrounded by mountains.

Syracuse, New York

Name of park unknown

Home of Syracuse baseball 1858.
Location: Otisco and Catherine streets.

Armory Park

Home of Syracuse baseball 1868.
Location: West Onondaga.

Driving Park

Home of Syracuse baseball 1868.
Location: Eighth Ward.

Lakeside Park

Home of the Syracuse Club 1876–77,
first used for baseball 1869, National
League 1879 (Stars, Sundays only).
Location: The town of Geddes, bordered by the New York Central tracks,
Hiawatha Boulevard, State Fair Boulevard and Onondaga Lake.

A park where you didn't have to
worry about the ball rolling very far.
The outfield was a soggy marsh of
weeds. The soil in the all-skin infield
had a salty texture, and the damp grass
was allowed to grow so long in the
outfield that balls could get lost in it.

Fans rode horse cars or mule-drawn
canal boats to the ballpark. George
Brackett managed the Stars. The hitting star for the team was Austin
Knickerbocker, who once hit four
home runs during a doubleheader. It's
unknown if this Austin Knickerbocker
is any relation to the Austin Knickerbocker from Bangall, New York, who
played 21 games for the 1947 Philadelphia Athletics.

After playing an independent schedule 1876–77, the Syracuse club joined
the International Association and
moved to Newell Park, where outfielders had an easier time keeping their
feet dry.

Newell Park

International Association 1878, National League 1879 (Stars). First used
for baseball in 1869. *Location:* East
Raynor, Mulberry, Groton, and South
Salina streets. *First National League
game:* May 28, 1879. *Last National
League game:* September 10, 1879.

In 1878, the Stars won the International Association pennant. Buoyed by
their success, they joined the National
League, where they found themselves
outclassed by the competition. In 1879,
the Stars went 15–27 and did not finish
the season.

Star Park

New York State League 1885 (Stars), International Association 1888 (Stars), American Association 1890, Eastern League 1902. *Location:* South Salina, Temple, Oneida and West Taylor streets. *First American Association game:* April 28, 1890. *Last American Association game:* October 6, 1890.

In 1885, manager John Ormsbee led the Syracuse team to the New York State League pennant.

In 1888, manager Pep Hackett led the Stars to the International Association pennant.

In 1890, during Syracuse's only year in the (then) major league American Association, the team played a wacky three-game series against Louisville. Syracuse won the first game, on a Sunday, by forfeit: Sunday baseball was illegal in Syracuse and the Louisville players chose to obey the law, feeling the wrath of their club's management was less severe than a trip to the hoosegow. Perhaps some of the Louisville squad, not known as altar boys to begin with, weren't playing under their real names. On Sunday night there was a long, soaking rain and the Monday afternoon game was played in mud so deep that it sometimes covered the tops of players' shoes. The third game of the series, on Tuesday, was drier and legal — but the Star Park bleachers collapsed, injuring 20. All in all, the Louisville nine was glad to get the hell out of there.

Athletic Field

Empire State League 1906. *Location:* Old Lakeside Boulevard, Marsh Road, Hiawatha Boulevard.

When it first opened, it was called up-to-date. When it closed, it was called deadly. In the fall of 1906, after its last baseball season was finished, the grandstand at Athletic Park collapsed during a Colgate-Syracuse football game, costing the life of Father Donovan, a Catholic priest from Binghamton.

Hallock Park

Eastern League 1907-19. *Location:* North Salina Street, not far from Onondaga Lake.

Grover Cleveland Alexander pitched here in 1910. He won 29, lost 14, for the third-place club, on his way up to the majors. He finished the season — and his minor league career — with 50 consecutive scoreless innings.

Archbold Stadium

Eastern League 1920 (Stars, some games).

Archbold was the Syracuse Orange football stadium before the building of the Carrier Dome. Baseball was played here at the beginning of the season until construction of the new Star Park was completed.

Star Park (II)

Eastern League 1920-27 (Stars). *Location:* West Genesee Street.

MacArthur Stadium (Municipal Stadium 1934-41)

International League 1961-present (Chiefs). *Location:* East Hiawatha Boulevard, Second Street North, and LeMoyne Park. *Built:* 1934. *Dimensions:* (1934) Left field, 335 feet; center field, 464 feet; right field, 335 feet. (1946) Left field, 320 feet; center field, 434 feet; right field, 320 feet. *Surface:* Grass. *Seating capacity:* (1975) 8000; (1985) 10,500. *Single game attendance record:* 13,087 (July 17, 1967, versus Jacksonville). *Season attendance record:* 288,141 (1947). *Fire:* May 15, 1969.

Because of a fire early in the 1969 season, MacArthur Stadium functioned for years without any stands directly behind home. The grandstand has since been completely rebuilt. The park was most recently refurbished between the 1987 and 1988 seasons. It looked like a bomb hit it right after the 1987 season, but all the seats were in and ready for the start of International League play in 1988.

A very high scoreboard and bill-

The scoreboard at MacArthur Stadium, Syracuse, N.Y. (Photo by David Pietrusza.)

boards are now in left center. The fences were moved in after the old wooden fences were blown down by a wind storm in 1945. The new stud and metal outfield fence was erected closer to home all the way around.

In the 1980s the Chiefs averaged a little under 200,000 a year in attendance.

Tabasco, Mexico

Centenario 27 de Febrero
Mexican League, Zona Sur, present (Ganaderos). *Dimensions:* Left field, 335 feet; center field, 370 feet; right field, 335 feet. *Seating capacity:* 7500.

Tacoma, Washington

Cheney Stadium
Pacific Coast League 1960–present (Tugs). *Built:* 1960. *Construction cost:* $840,000. *Location:* 2525 Bantz Boulevard. Easily accessible from Interstate Freeway 5 (Exit 132). *Dimensions:* Left field, 325 feet; center field, 425 feet; right field, 325 feet. *Seating capacity:* 8002 (once as high as 8500). *First game:* April 14, 1960.

The outfield is mowed to form a checkerboard pattern—the same grass-cutting technique used in San Francisco's Candlestick Park. The single-decked grandstand is boomerang-shaped, with seats painted the same color as the infield grass. Bleachers on both sides extend seating to the foul poles. There's a soccer field surrounded by a track and field oval and a softball field out beyond the right field fence. Parking facilities surround the park behind home and on the first base side.

Among the stars who played in Cheney Stadium are Willie McCovey, Juan Marichal, Dusty Rhodes, Matty and Jesus Alou, and Gaylord Perry.

When the Pacific Coast League's Phoenix franchise moved here in 1960, it was the first time the league had played in Tacoma since 1905.

Tallahassee, Florida

Dick Howser Stadium (Seminole Field before 1983, Seminole Stadium 1983–87)

Home of the Florida State University Seminoles, present. *Location:* Florida State University campus, adjacent to the football stadium. *Dimensions:* Left field, 340 feet; center field, 400 feet; right field, 320 feet. *Fences:* Right center, 20 feet; right field, 30 feet (screen). *Seating capacity:* 5000 + (2000, grandstand, 3000 +, bleachers). *Single game attendance record:* 6145 (1986, versus the University of Miami). *Renovated:* 1983. *Cost of renovation:* $1 million +. *Grounds chief:* Robert Barrett.

Seminole Field was transformed into a AAA-quality ballpark in 1982 when Florida State University spent over a million dollars fixing it up. It was christened March 28, 1983, before a game against Louisiana State University in front of 1305 fans. Modern concession stands were installed and vendors circulated among the crowd for the first time. Besides the new high-tech grandstand replacing the old wooden stands, a new drainage system was installed on the playing field, and a low spot behind second base was filled in.

Much, however, remained the same.

The bermuda grass stayed in place, and the old lighting system stayed, metal 1500-watt lights mounted on concrete standards. The new press box — accommodating home and visiting radio, television, and boosters — sits at the top of the grandstand behind home, tucked under the small roof.

The field is always kept groomed to professional quality.

Dick Howser. The first bill signed into law during the 1987 legislative season by Governor Bob Martinez legally changed the name of Seminole Stadium to Dick Howser Stadium, in honor of the former Florida State star who went on to be a major league player and manager before his death in 1987. Howser maintained a residence in Tallahassee throughout his college and professional career. He is buried in Tallahassee's Memorial Gardens.

On March 3, 1988, the ballpark was rededicated before an exhibition game against Howser's old Kansas City Royals. On that day the Seminoles unveiled their new $150,000 matrix scoreboard. The visit to the ballpark by the Royals was the fifth by a major league club, as the Yankees and Braves played the Seminoles twice apiece, as recently as 1985.

Tampa, Florida

Al Lopez Field

Florida State League 1957–present (Tarpons), spring home of Cincinnati Reds until 1987. *Location:* Dale Mabry Highway, and Tampa Bay Boulevard, adjacent to Tampa Stadium (home of the NFL's Buccaneers). *Built:* 1954. *Dimensions:* Left field, 342 feet; center field, 410 feet; right field, 342 feet. *Seating capacity:* (1960) 9000; (1985) 8500. *Record attendance:* 8359 (March 17, 1963, spring training, Cincinnati versus New York Yankees). *1987 season attendance:* 62,394.

The yellow concrete structure is dwarfed by the sleek and modern

Tampa Stadium next door. *Tampa Tribune* reporter Kathy Feeny calls Al Lopez Field a "squatty dinosaur"—a description applicable to Al himself in his latter catching days.

In 1987, a billboard in front of the entrance said, "Site of Tampa Bay Baseball Coliseum." The Cincinnati Reds, who used the park as their spring training headquarters, abandoned Al Lopez Field after the 1987 season, for a new park in Plant City. The Coliseum is a proposed major league facility that would take this ballpark's place.

The Tampa Tarpons, playing here in the 1950s and 1960s, provided minor league experience for Pete Rose, Tony Perez and Johnny Bench. In 1961, as a Tarpon, Rose hit .331—the first time he hit .300 in pro ball. That same year Rose hit a Florida State League record 30 triples.

On Monday, November 18, 1963, four days before he was assassinated, John F. Kennedy spoke at Al Lopez Field.

On December 9, 1969, an old C-46, piloted by Andrew P. Voyna, suffered engine failure after takeoff from Tampa International Airport, and belly-flopped, landing gear up, in the ballpark's parking lot.

Mayor Curtis Hixon of Tampa suggested the park be christened for Tampa native Al Lopez, who caught 1918 games in the major leagues, for the Dodgers, Braves, Pirates, and Indians. Lopez held the record for most major league games caught until 1987, when it was broken by Bob Boone. He also managed for 16 years.

Lopez was inducted into the Hall of Fame in 1977. He last appeared in uniform at the park that bore his name when he was the visiting manager of the Chicago White Sox.

When he retired from baseball in 1970, the ceremony was held at Al Lopez Field. Casey Stengel presented Lopez with a rocking chair. The Cincinnati Reds have held spring training in Tampa since 1931.

Red McEwen Field (USF Baseball Field 1966-1975)

Home of the University of South Florida Bulls (Sun Belt Conference) 1966-present. *Dimensions:* Left field, 340 feet; center field, 400 feet; right field, 340 feet. *Surface:* Artificial. *Seating capacity:* 1200. *Lights:* 1976. *First night game:* February 16, 1977 (University of South Florida 8, University of Tampa 7).

Park named after a man who never sang a song to Jean and who—as far as anybody's telling—never once wrote a sappy poem.

No, the park is named after a Tampa lawyer, sportsman and civic leader who was active in establishing the University of South Florida.

The field's lights were donated in 1976 by George Steinbrenner, principal owner of the New York Yankees. The concession stand, restrooms and utility shed were completed in 1982, thanks to donations of money and materials by Dick Wittcoff, Joe Hudson, John Allen, and Hugo Schmidt.

Tempe, Arizona

Diablo Stadium

Spring home of the Seattle Mariners, present. *Location:* 2525 South 48th Street. *Dimensions:* Left center, 420 feet; right center, 420 feet.

Gunfight at El Diablo? According to Ron Fimrite in *Sports Illustrated,* "Tempe Diablo Stadium, with its Spanish arches, looks like someplace the Magnificent Seven might have been called on to defend."

Packard Stadium

Home of the Arizona State University Sun Devils (Pac-10 Conference) 1974-present. *Built:* 1974. *Construction cost:* $1 million. *Dimensions:* Left field, 325 feet; left center, 370 feet; center field, 400 feet; right center, 370 feet; right field, 325 feet. *Fences:* Center field, 60 feet. *Surface:* (Infield)

Santa Anna Bermuda, (outfield) Common Bermuda and Nuts Edge, (infield skin) crushed brick. *Scoreboard:* Digital electronic with message center capabilities. *Lights:* 160 halide lamps (AAA-quality). *Sound system:* Ten speakers, powered by two 250-watt amplifiers. *Seating capacity:* 8000.

Park built and donated by alumni Guthrie and Peter Packard in honor of their late father, William Guthrie Packard, a prominent member of the publishing industry. The elder Packard had been active in church and community affairs in Arizona and Colorado.

The stands have newly added box seats, and the players' clubhouse facilities are state-of-the-art, with a weight room, players' lounge, sports medicine facility and various offices. As of 1987, box seats cost $3.00 and general admission was $2.50 — with a 50-cent increase for Pac-10 Conference games.

Terre Haute, Indiana

Before Terre Haute received its first enclosed ballpark in 1895, games of varying sophistication took place among locals in three open fields: between Sycamore Street and the Vandalia Railroad on Sixth Street; east of Eighth Street between Chestnut and Sycamore streets; and on the north side of Wabash west of Seventh Street. The first recorded ball game in Terre Haute took place on August 31, 1867, between two volunteer fire companies, the Eurekas defeating the Mohawks 83–61.

Athletics Park (Triple-I League Park)
Home of Terre Haute baseball 1895–1924 (some Three-I League). *Location:* East Wabash Avenue (U.S. Highway 40), between 25th and 27th streets, on the south side of Wabash, just west of the Topps Building. *Dimensions:* Left field, 440 feet; center field, 592 feet; right field, 440 feet. *Torn down:* 1925.

According to Richard C. Tuttle in the *Terre Haute Star,* "The field was surrounded by a high board fence, the stands and even the small grandstand, were wood.... When leaving the game, with Dad, A.O. Gillis offered us a ride in his electric ... my first and only ride in one of those fascinating soundless cars ... operated entirely by levers, speed, turning and braking."

Athletics Park was the minor league home of baseball greats like Three-Finger Brown, Branch Rickey, Charlie Root, Jim Elliott and Art Nehf. Vendors sold popcorn and peanuts from wicker baskets. According to Terre Haute attorney Mike McCormick, this land was originally part of a nine-hole golf course and was later used for circuses and aviation shows.

Memorial Stadium
Three-I League 1925–1932, 1935, 1937 (Tots), 1946–1956 (Phillies, Huts). *Location:* Just across the street from where Home Avenue now intersects with Wabash Avenue. *Opened:* Thanksgiving Day, 1924 (Wiley-Garfield football game). *Construction cost:* (1922–25) $450,000. *Seating capacity:* 20,000. *Record season attendance:* 133,648 (1947). *First used for baseball:* May 1925. *First game:* May 5, 1925 (Terre Haute Tots 5, Peoria Tractors 4, 11 innings, attendance: 8000, winning pitcher: Big Jim Elliot). *First game radio broadcast:* April 28, 1928 (play-by-play by Carl C. Jones, KGFO). *First night game:* June 8, 1931. *Last game:* July 4, 1956. *Rebuilt for football, reopened:* 1970.

This ballpark was built on the site of the old fairgrounds, on land that had been Terre Haute's horse racing center. The Vigo County Fair was held here from the turn of the century until 1917, and during those years, one of the fair's top attractions was "four-cornered Grand Circuit harness racing." The land was used for both trotting and pacing from 1887 until 1916.

Memorial Stadium was built by the city of Terre Haute in the memory of local men killed in World War I, on land leased by Vigo County to the city of Terre Haute on December 18, 1920, for as long as the city continued to maintain it as a public park. Construction on Memorial Stadium began in 1922. The concrete and steel structure (except for the bleachers, which were wood) was almost round, and seats went from foul pole to foul pole. The scoreboard was in left center. The main entrance resembled a Parisian arch, while smaller arches decorated the concrete outer grandstand facade.

Dedication Day. Harry H. Hamby of the *Terre Haute Star* attended Memorial Stadium's dedication ceremonies May 5, 1925, and later filed this report:

"No artist could paint such a picture as was presented yesterday when the huge bowl seemed practically filled with swaying colors of various hues. The dark clothes of the men contrasting with the bright and colorful attire of the women, gaily decorated boxes, banners floating, Old Glory flapping in the breeze with now and then a burst of sunlight peeping from out of the huge white clouds which drifted slowly by in the sky overhead."

Judge Landis was there (he called the ballpark "the finest of its kind for a city of this size"), a band played throughout the game, first balls were tossed by Landis and Terre Haute mayor Ora Davis. The game was scheduled for 3:30, but crowds had begun to arrive two hours earlier. By the time of the ceremonies, the stands were filled. It was a big day in Terre Haute.

Hamby reported, "For the first time in many years, business was at a standstill throughout the city during the afternoon. All of the schools were dismissed and truly all roads led to the stadium."

Terre Haute manager Whitcraft and his team marched down the third base line. The Peoria squad marched toward the infield from right field. As they lined up between home and their (as Dizzy Dean would say) respectable bases, the largest crowd in the history of Terre Haute gave them, and the ballpark, a spontaneous standing ovation. Boy Scouts unfurled the flag. The Chamber of Commerce band played the National Anthem, and the game began.

One of the highlights of the 1927 season was a 17-inning game won by Terre Haute over Decatur by a score of 3–2. Wally Marks — later to be dean of the Indiana State University School of Health, Physical Education and Recreation — pitched the entire 17 innings for Terre Haute. The Decatur pitcher, who also worked without relief, was Carl Hubbell, a loser that day.

When the park first opened, attendance was good, but before the stadium was ten years old, Terre Haute had been dropped from the Three-I League for lack of interest, and money. In 1930, the worst year of the Depression in Terre Haute, the *season* attendance at Memorial Stadium numbered 16,813.

In the late 1930s, Vern McMillan of McMillan Sporting Goods formed the Midwest Semi-pro Baseball Tournament, between factory teams from Terre Haute and neighboring towns. The stadium was also used for wrestling and boxing.

Crowds of 10,000 showed up for games, and some of that money went to fixing Memorial Stadium's roof, which had been badly in need of repair.

After World War II, Terre Haute once again played in the Three-I League, as baseball flourished everywhere. The ballplayers were back, and that meant peace.

Again, the franchise lasted about a decade before terminal apathy returned, this time losing a 1950s summer entertainment battle with those new one-eyed monsters that were invading living rooms across America.

In November 1966, the aging stadium was leased to Indiana State University for football, and was rebuilt as a gridiron stadium holding 22,500. The only thing remaining from the original ballpark is the Memorial Arch at the entrance.

Elm Grove Ball Park

Home of the North Terre Haute Greys, 1930s–1940s. *Location:* North Terre Haute. *Seating capacity:* 0 (fans sat on slope around field, which was down in a hole).

The North Terre Haute Greys played an independent schedule against other local nines from towns like West Terre Haute, Brazil, New Goshen, St. Bernice, Blackhawk, Seelyville and Rosedale. They played their games at the Elm Grove Ball Park, part of the Elm Grove Amusement Park.

The games were competitive, and the community's identification with their team was strong. It was not uncommon for the Greys to outdraw the Tots at Memorial Stadium. Umpires were picked from the spectators. Games were played on Sunday at 1:00 p.m. One new ball was provided for every game.

According to Judy Stedman Calvert in the *Northside Journal,* "Before each game the field was raked to loosen the dirt and then a piece of railroad track was drug over the dirt to smooth it down. If the field was wet, gasoline was poured on the dirt and burned to dry out the ground. The infield was dirt — no grass."

At the Elm Grove complex were also a swimming pool and a dance hall/roller-skating rink. Once, it is said, Greys outfielder Bus King jumped into the pool after a fly ball and threw a runner out at home plate.

In the early 1950s, the grove's trees were cut down and the diamond was removed so an artificial lake could be built for fishing. No lake could be built that would hold water, so this idea was scrapped and the site was turned into a trailer park.

According to Terre Haute's Mike McCormick, the land currently holds an eight-room motel.

Art Nehf Field

Home of Rose-Holman Institute, present (Division III). *Location:* On Rose-Holman campus on Route 40, on the eastern outskirts of the city.

Three Rivers, Quebec

Municipal Stadium

Canadian-American League 1938 (Royals), Provincial League 1951–55, Eastern League 1971–77. *Built:* 1938. *Dimensions:* Left field, 317 feet; center field, 372 feet; right field, 317 feet. *Seating capacity:* 6000.

During 1937 and 1938, the province of Quebec built a series of ballparks in a program like the United States' WPA — a Depression-buster that used local supplies and labor with funding assistance from the government. The ballpark, built in concrete and steel, is identical in dimensions and design to its namesake in Quebec City.

Nuns watched ball games from the convent in the outfield.

Tidewater, Virginia *see* Norfolk, Virginia

Toledo, Ohio

Presque Isle Park

Northwestern League 1883 (Blue Stockings, Maumees). *Location:* Near the mouth of the Maumee River and the bay, on what became the C&O coal loading docks.

In the first pro ball game in Toledo history, the local Blue Stockings beat Bay City, Michigan, 5–4, in 10 innings. Toledo went on to win the Northwestern League pennant that year.

A member of the Blue Stockings, Moses Walker, was the second black man to play organized baseball.

League Park

American Association 1884 (Blue Stockings). *Location:* 13th, 15th, and Monroe streets; Jefferson Avenue. *First American Association game:* May 14, 1884. *Last American Association game:* September 23, 1884.

Tri-State Fairgrounds

American Association 1884 (Blue Stockings, Sundays and holidays). *Location:* Then known as Frazier and Dorr streets, Woodstock and Ravensburg avenues. Now known as Oakwood and Upton avenues, Addington and Dorr streets.

Speranza Park

American Association 1890 (Maumees). *Location:* Cherry and Frederick streets, Franklin Avenue. *First American Association game:* May 1, 1890. *Last American Association game:* October 2, 1890.

Bay View Park

Inter-State League 1896–1901 (Swamp Angels, Mud Hens). *Location:* 3900 North Summit Street, Manhattan Boulevard, current site of a senior citizen-maintained golf course.

The Aquatic Fowl of Glass City. The Toledo Club first became known as the Mud Hens in 1896 when they played games in the mud of Bay View Park, with the wild ducks flying around the marshland. During the first half of that season they were known as the Swamp Angels.

Today's Mud Hens public relations department reminds us that Mud Hens are birds with "aquatic and very athletic characteristics." Maybe so, but that is not why the name was picked. Mud hens also have short wings and long legs. They're variously known as marsh hens and rails. Truth is, these were days before ground crews — and in the late nineteenth century the Toledo Club had to play in the slop.

Armory Park

Early 1900s. *Location:* Speilbush Avenue; Jackson, Erie and Orange streets.

Used twice by Detroit of the American League as home field.

Noah H. Swayne Field (Mud Hen Park)

American Association 1909–13, 1916–55 (Iron Men 1916–18, Mud Hens), South Michigan League 1914 (Soumichers). No baseball in 1915. Negro National League 1923 (Tigers, some games), Negro American League 1939 (Crawfords, some games). *Location:* Monroe Street (first base), Detroit Avenue (right field), Council Street (left field), New York Central Railroad tracks (right field). *Dimensions:* Left field, 472 feet; center field, 482 feet; right field, 327 feet. 72 feet from home plate to the backstop. *Seating capacity:* (1948) 14,800. *First game:* July 3, 1909. *First night game:* June 23, 1933 (Toledo 2, Columbus 1).

The Glass City had never had a real ballpark. When Swayne Field was built in 1909, it represented the tenth home of organized baseball since 1883. This was a city known for its bad baseball grounds, and sick of its image.

Swayne Field was named after the donor of the land and was the best minor league park of its time. It seated as many as 14,800 by the late 1940s. When you sat in the stands and looked out over the left field fence, you saw the Red Man Tobacco factory and piles of coal. Negro League slugger Sam Jethroe was the only man to hit a ball into the coal piles, far behind the left field fence. Kids who chased down the homers and turned in the ball got to sit in the bleachers for free. It was a good deal, but the competition was stiff, and a kid could wait a long time out there listening to the crowd through the fence.

Maybe the best time to go see the Mud Hens play was from 1926 to 1931 when Casey Stengel was their manager.

As one might suspect, the old per-fesser—yeah, he was old even back then—was a popular figure in town. He brought out the crowds with his antics, breaking losing streaks with weird lineups, sometimes pinch-hitting or putting himself in the outfield.

His methods worked. In 1927, the Mud Hens hit .310 as a club, won the pennant and then the Junior World Series. Hitting stars were Roy Grimes, Bevo LeBourveau, Bobby Veach, and Freddie Maguire.

Other stars to play for the Mud Hens: Bill Terry, Hack Wilson, and native son Roger Bresnahan.

Toledo played their American Association ball on Swayne Field until 1955, at which time the grandstand was torn down and replaced by a shopping center.

Monte Pearson made the first night game at Swayne something to remember, and the quality of the lights something to question. While beating Columbus 2-1, he struck out 15, seven in a row, under the brand new lamps.

Ned Skeldon Stadium (Lucas County Stadium, Lucas County Recreation Center)

Owned by Lucas County. International League 1965–present (Mud Hens). *Location:* 2901 Key Street, Maumee. *Built:* 1965. *Dimensions:* Left field, 325 feet; center field, 410 feet; right field, 325 feet. *Fences:* Six feet all the way around. *Surface:* Grass. *Seating capacity:* (1965) 8000, (1984) 12,000. *Single game attendance record:* 13,695 (July 14, 1966, versus Jacksonville). *Season attendance record:* 210,685 (1980). *Major refurbishment:* 1984.

Baseball returned to Toledo in the mid-sixties, when the struggling International League franchise in Richmond was moved.

The team had trouble drawing 100,000 fans for a season until the 1980s, when figures closer to 200,000 have been the average.

Native son Jamie Farr, Corporal Klinger on TV's *M*A*S*H**, has added unmeasurable publicity to the franchise—not just through the TV show, but also by posing in a Mud Hen uniform for promotional materials.

Toronto, Ontario

Jarvis Street Lacrosse Grounds

Canadian League 1885. *Location:* Jarvis and Wellesley.

Sunlight Park

Canadian League 1886–91. *Location:* Next to Sunlight Soap Works, Scadding Street, Kingston Road, Eastern Avenue, Queen Street. *Construction cost:* $7000. *Dimensions:* Deep. *Seating capacity:* 2000 (550 reserved). *First game:* May 22, 1886 (Toronto 10, Rochester 3, attendance: 5000).

Hanlan's Point (Maple Leaf Park)

International League 1897–1901, 1909–25. *Location:* On an island in the Don River. *Fire:* 1909.

Fans had to take a ferry to the ballpark.

It was here that Babe Ruth hit one of his earliest professional home runs, playing as a pitcher for Providence on September 5, 1914. It was his first regular season homer.

Diamond Park

International League 1902–07, 1909. *Location:* Fraser Avenue.

Maple Leaf Stadium

International League 1926–67 (Maple Leafs). *Location:* 555 Lakeshore Boulevard West, Stadium Road, Western Channel, Bathurst Street. *Construction cost:* $750,000. *Dimensions:* Left field, 311 feet; center field, 425 feet; right field, 310 feet. *Seating capacity:* 19,224. *Opening Day attendance record:* 22,216 (1953). *First game:* April 29, 1926 (Toronto 6, Reading 5, 10 innings). *First night game:* June 28, 1934 (Rochester 8, Toronto 2).

Ned Skeldon Stadium, Toledo, Oh. (Compliments of the Toledo Mud Hens.)

Along the Fleet Street flats on the lakefront of Lake Ontario, this land is currently a public park and picnic grounds. When the Maple Leafs went out of business, everything worth anything was auctioned off, including two home plates. (Does every ballpark have a spare home plate? Has one ever broken?)

Maple Leafs attendance in 1952 was 440,000, and Maple Leaf Stadium was considered a jewel among minor league ballparks. In 1967, just 67,000—thus the auction.

Exhibition Stadium (C.N.E. Stadium)

American League 1977–present (Blue Jays). Home of the Canadian Football League Argos 1959–present. *Location:* New Brunswick Way (right field), Lakeshore Boulevard (first base), Prince's Boulevard (third base), Gardiner Expressway (left field), across the street from the CNE amusement park. *Originally constructed:* 1879. *Fire:* 1906, 1947. *Construction of North Grandstand:* 1948 (cost: $3 million). *Construction of South Grandstand:*

1959 (cost: $650,000). *Reconfigured for baseball:* 1976 (Cost: $17.8 million). *Designer* (1976): Bill Sanford. *Dimensions:* Left field, 330 feet; left center, 375 feet; center field, 400 feet; right center, 375 feet; right field, 330 feet. *Fences:* Twelve feet all the way around. *Surface:* (1879–1971) grass; (1972) 3-M Tartan Turf; (1974) Monsanto (artificial) Turf. *First American League game:* April 7, 1977. *First beer served:* July 30, 1982.

Though the distance to the right field foul pole is marked as 330 feet, there has been conjecture that it is actually as close as 315 feet from home plate.

This site was the Toronto Fairgrounds as early as 1879, and was used for baseball as early as 1885, when Detroit of the National League came to town for a post-season exhibition game against a local team. In those days, the park was used mostly for parades, concerts, and track and field meets.

In the 1920s this was the site of motorcycle racing and horse shows. It was even used as a horse racing track for the annual Two-Year-Old Futurity race. In 1947 the stands burned completely but were immediately rebuilt, just as they had been after the all-consuming 1906 fire.

In the 1950s and 1960s stock car racing became the premiere attraction at CNE Stadium. The races were promoted by Ernie Lieberman, and the number-one driver was Ted Hogan. Special attractions were booked to accompany the races, such as the Three Stooges, Bob Hope, Ed Sullivan, and Red Skelton.

In 1959 the Argos of the Canadian Football League moved here from their previous home in Varsity Stadium on Bloor Street.

To prepare the ballpark for baseball, the south (first base side) stands were torn down and a new elbow-shaped grandstand was built, wrapping around the diamond, facing the big grandstand in left. The whole job was done for under $18 million, which left no money for a roof, or for a baseball scoreboard. The scoreboard is at the far end zone, many feet behind the right field home run fence. This is the only major league stadium where the only seats under a roof are those in the outfield.

Gull Skulled. It was here that Dave Winfield of the New York Yankees caused a furor when he killed a seagull with a thrown ball and somebody thought he did it on purpose. Winfield was arrested. Manager Billy Martin scoffed at the issue. "If he hit the bird on purpose, it was the first time he hit the cutoff man all year." Experts say it was only a matter of time before a gull got nailed. When the birds swoop in it can look like an Alfred Hitchcock movie.

The area under the stands is cramped. Since there are so many general admission seats, advice is to get there early and avoid waiting in long lines for tickets.

Fan Skulled. The first in line most games for the general admission seats in left field—known erroneously as "bleachers"' in Toronto, despite their roof—is Peter Everton. He's a young

man now, but when he was a kid he got hit on the head by a home run. A CAT scan revealed no brain damage, but Everton has had an addiction to the ballpark ever since.

On April 30, 1984, a game was called on account of wind. Never happened before or since.

SkyDome. Exhibition Stadium was not designed to serve major league baseball for very long. The Blue Jays have already gotten more than their money's worth out of the impromptu baseball park. As this is written a domed stadium is being built in Toronto, a mega-modern monster, probably the most expensive athletic facility ever built. Date of completion unknown. The place is to be called the SkyDome, and is being built very close to the site of Maple Leaf Stadium. The park's concessions (four fast-food restaurants and 20 concession booths) are to be operated by McDonalds.

Trenton, New Jersey

Dunn Field

Interstate League 1939–50 (Giants). *Seating capacity:* 3500.

The lights here were notoriously poor.

On July 16, 1947, the Giants were 10½ back, but won 49 of their next 55 to win the pennant.

Television was one of the big reasons the team folded. Another was the Roman Catholic Diocese, who owned the land the ballpark was on. They did not allow the Giants to renew their lease, so that the site could be sold to a supermarket chain.

Twice afterward, the voters of Trenton approved construction of a new multi-purpose stadium, but the job was never done. The supermarket at the site of Dunn Field was built, and has now been closed and boarded up for many years.

Exhibition Stadium, Toronto, Ontario. (Compliments of the Toronto Blue Jays.)

Tri-Cities, Washington   *see* Kenniwick, Washington

Troy, New York

"What an exciting moment it is when you can send the ball back whizzing . . . whence it came." — An anonymous Lansingburgh Haymaker of the 1860s

Village Green

Home of the Unions 1866. *Location:* Lansingburgh.

On August 15, 1866, the Unions ball club held a reorganization meeting, baseball play having been suspended for the Civil War. A club constitution and bylaws were drawn up. One article established ten cents as the fine for "profane language on the field of exercise."

Vail's Lot

Home of the Unions (Haymakers) 1867. *Location:* Lansingburgh.

The Unions were, by far, the strongest club in the Troy area — frequently scoring over 100 runs during a game. After clobbering the local competition, they went to New York City to play with the big boys.

Their first road trip got off to a rocky start as they took a shellacking from the Brooklyn Atlantics, 46–11. The Unions couldn't figure out the swift pitching of George "Charmer" Zettlein.

Not about to surrender, the Unions went over to the Union Grounds in Brooklyn and there beat the Mutuals 15–13. It was on that day — when the country bumpkins went to the big city and whupped the city slickers — that the Unions became the Haymakers.

When the New York Mutuals came to Lansingburgh on August 28, 1866, to avenge their defeat, the Haymakers fell behind early 9-0, but then went on to beat them again 32–18, in a game played on Vail's Lot.

In 1867, the Haymakers continued their success, defeating the Morrisania Unions 51–23, before 5000 spectators standing around the edge of Vail's Lot. The following afternoon and evening a victory picnic was held at Lansing's Grove. Sullivan's Band played for those who liked to "trip the light fantastic toe," and cars were provided for the Haymakers' Troy friends to get back home.

Rensselaer Park

Home of the Haymakers 1868, National Association 1871–72 (Haymakers, some games). *Location:* Lansingburgh. Then called South, Hill and Middle streets. Now called 108th and 111th streets and Eighth Avenue.

In 1868, the Haymakers' season was successful overall, but they lost the big game of the year, against the Cincinnati Red Stockings, by 18 runs. Fans grumbled. It wasn't fair. The Red Stockings, after all, were recruited professionals, while the Haymakers were hometown boys.

Bull's Head Tavern Grounds

Home of the Haymakers 1869–70, National Association 1871–72 (Haymakers, some games). *Location:* Batestown. Second, Sixth, and Glenn avenues, adjacent to the Bull's Head Tavern.

The Haymakers again lost to the Red Stockings in the big game of the year in 1869, 32–31. The game wasn't as closely matched as it sounds. The Red Stockings played lackadaisically, teasing the Haymakers and their crowd by keeping the score close.

Later that year, in the rematch in Cincinnati, home cooking broiled the Haymakers as the umpire made call after call absurdly in favor of the Reds. Haymaker pitcher Cherokee Fisher, angered at the injustice, stormed off the field — and the umpire declared the Red Stockings the winners by forfeit.

When the National Association of Baseball Players learned that the umpire had gambling friends who had stacked their pile on the Red Stockings, the forfeit was lifted and the game was declared a tie.

After this year many of the Haymakers retired from baseball, while others (Cherokee Fisher, Clipper Flynn, Mart King et al.) went to form the nucleus of the Chicago White Stockings. In 1870, the Haymakers fielded a team with a lot of unfamiliar faces.

The glory days of the Lansingburgh Haymakers were gone — though the Troy version did have unsuccessful franchises in the National Association and National League.

Center Island Grounds

National Association 1871–72 (Haymakers), National League 1880–81 (Trojans). *Location:* Part of Green Island, Albany County. Ballpark was literally in the middle of the Hudson River, near its junction with the Mohawk. *First National Association game:* May 9, 1871. *Last National Association game:* June 6, 1872. *First National League game:* May 18, 1880. *Last National League game:* September 30, 1881 (game held in driving rainstorm, attendance 12).

Putnam Grounds

National League 1879 (Trojans). *Location:* Fifteenth Street and Peoples Avenue. *First game:* May 28, 1879. *Last game:* August 26, 1879.

Troy Ball Club Grounds

National League 1882 (Trojans). *Location:* Nineteenth Street in Watervliet, New York, just across the Hudson from Troy. *First game:* May 20, 1882. *Last game:* August 26, 1882.

Tucson, Arizona

Elysian Grove Field

Home of Tucson baseball 1907–13. *Location:* Southwest corner of Simpson and South Main streets.

The first Tucson intra-city league played its games here, on a diamond beside the Elysian Grove Entertainment Park of Emanuel Drachman. The league consisted of Drachman's own team, a team representing the Southern Pacific Railroad, and "the Armstrong team." A member of the rail team was Hi Corbett, son of the owner of the J. Knox Corbett Lumber Company. Hi went on to run the family business, and to be Mr. Baseball in Tucson. (*See* Hi Corbett Field.)

Bulls Head Tavern Grounds, Troy, N.Y., 1870. Game in progress. (Photo by James Irving, supplied by the Museum of the State of New York.)

Blenman Park Field
Rio Grande Valley Association 1915. *Location:* Simpson Street, Blenman Park.

When Emanuel Drachman subdivided the land where his entertainment park and ballpark were built, Tucson's intra-city league was forced to move across Simpson Street.

Name of park unknown
Home of Tucson baseball 1916-27. *Location:* North of the Congress Street Bridge, on the east bank of the Santa Cruz River.

The park suffered from inadequate seating, and needed to be replaced when Tucson received its first professional baseball team in 1928.

Hi Corbett Field (Randolph Park Field 1928-51)
Arizona State League 1928-31 (Cowboys), Arizona-Texas League 1937-41, 1947-50 (Cowboys), Southwest International League 1951, Arizona-Mexico League 1952-58, Pacific Coast League 1969-present (Toros, Rangers), spring home of the Cleveland Indians 1947-present. *Location:* Randolph Park,

Alvernon Way. *Dimensions:* Left field, 366 feet; left center, 410 feet; center field, 392 feet; right center, 405 feet; right field, 348 feet. *Seating capacity:* 8500. *Lights:* 1939.

In 1927, the city of Tucson voted a bond issue to provide funds for a ballfield. Hi Corbett and Emanuel Drachman, appointed by the mayor, chose Randolph Park, the site of a crude and at times relatively flat city-owned golf course.

J.F. "Pop" McKale, later University of Arizona director of athletics, laid out the diamond, while Herbert F. Brown, builder and designer of many Tucson landmarks—the Pima County Courthouse, the Valley Bank Building—built the grandstand.

The team, the Cowboys, played in the Arizona State League (along with Phoenix, Miami, and Bisbee). Charged 75 cents admission. A few years later, Hi Corbett became president of the club. He was to remain *the* major figure in Tucson baseball for years.

After an interruption for the Depression, the Old Pueblo area again played professional baseball in the Arizona-Texas League starting in 1937, along with Albuquerque, El Paso, and Bisbee—an arrangement that remained until the '50s, with time out for World War II.

Since 1947, Hi Corbett Field (a name it took in 1951) has been the spring training home of the Cleveland Indians, an arrangement originally made possible because of Corbett's friendship with then Cleveland Indian owner Bill Veeck.

By 1969, when Tucson baseball was first elevated to the AAA level, the City Council spent $50,000 to improve the lighting at Hi Corbett Field. But this was not nearly enough money to take care of the problem old age had caused the park.

The playing field and lights were fine, but the fan accommodations were sorely lacking. The parking lot was too small, the restrooms were obsolete, the seats weren't comfortable.

With all of this, the ballpark was far more active than the average. Between spring training with the Indians, the Toros of the Pacific Coast League, and the University of Arizona baseball, 245 games per year were being played.

In 1972, the Tucson Baseball Commission approved $500,000 to fix up the park, and Hi Corbett Field is still being used—although again the ravages of time are apparent.

In 1985, Tucson was last in attendance in a 10-team Pacific Coast League.

Tulsa, Oklahoma

Texas League Park (Oiler Park, McNulty Park)
Texas League 1934–42, 1946–65, 1977, Pacific Coast League 1966–68, American Association 1969–circa 1975. *Location:* 4400 East 15th Street, Sandusky and Urbana avenues, 17th Street. *Built:* 1934. *Dimensions:* Left field, 330 feet; center field, 390 feet; right field, 330 feet. *Seating capacity:* 5194.

On April 3, 1977, the wooden grandstand here collapsed during an exhibition game, causing 17 fans to fall 20 feet to the ground. There were several serious injuries but no fatalities.

Tulsa County Stadium (originally Sutton Stadium)
Texas League 1981–present (Drillers). *Location:* In the center of Tulsa on the State Fairgrounds. *Dimensions:* Left field, 335 feet; center field, 400 feet; right field, 340 feet. *Seating capacity:* 7500. *Surface:* Artificial.

Center field pushes against the corner of a major intersection, with four lanes of traffic going in either direction. Home runs to all fields—except for dead center, probably—go into one of the two roads.

The fences are covered with advertisement signs everywhere except for straightaway center, where a dark blue fence provides the hitter's background. The American flag flies behind the hitting background. Just to the right field side of the flag is a wooden mock oil rig, which rests behind the fence. Then, just to the right of that is the electric scoreboard, a small one, with a Lite Beer advertisement sitting on top of it.

The seating is divided into three distinct structures, one behind the plate and one on either baseline. The smaller grandstand, behind home, is painted red—the other two are white.

The center grandstand holds the front gate. On top of its roof is a small screened-off area, with no seats, where photographers get a bird's-eye view. The two grandstands along the baselines are larger, and all three have roofs. The artificial surface still shows the ghosts of football lines, with the field set up from the left field corner to the right field corner—as well as soccer lines, with the field set up from left field to the first base line.

The State Fairgrounds that house Tulsa County Stadium are also home of a livestock barn display, a show ring, and an exposition center.

The ballpark was named Sutter

Tulsa County Stadium, Tulsa Okla. (Compliments of the Tulsa Drillers.)

Stadium in 1981 when it opened, after a local oil man who helped pay for the construction, but the name soon changed.

Tulsa County Stadium has recently been the home field of Dave Righetti, Ron Darling, Pete O'Brien, and Ruben Sierra.

Tuscaloosa, Alabama

Sewell-Thomas Field

Home of the University of Alabama Crimson Tide (Southeastern Conference), present. *Location:* Bryant Drive, at the campus of the University of Alabama. *Seating capacity:* 5000.

The University of Alabama is scheduled to begin construction of a new grandstand for their ballpark in 1989. When it's finished, increasing the seating to 7500, the park will become known as Sewell-Thomas Stadium.

The new stadium will have a brick surface to go with those of the Paul W. Bryant Museum and the Music and Speech Building, campus structures to which it will be adjacent.

Sewell-Thomas Field is named after two former Crimson Tide baseball coaches: Hall-of-Famer Joe Sewell, and Frank Thomas.

Twin Falls, Idaho

JayCee Stadium

Pioneer League 1939–41, 1946–55. *Built:* 1938.

Park was constructed on city-owned land upon which only dirt could grow because of seepage from the nearby canal. Grass grew only after repeated experiments and a complete resodding with a mixture of chemicals and compost.

Utica, New York

Braves Field (Ambrose McConnell Field 1943–50)
Canadian-American League 1939–42 (Braves), Eastern League 1943–50 (Braves). *Location:* Mohawk River/Barge Canal, current site of the entrance ramp to the New York State Thruway east. *Dimensions:* Left field, 389 feet; center field, 503 feet; right field, 400 feet. *Seating capacity:* 5000. *Lights:* 1939. *Cost of lights:* $10,000.

In 1939, Braves Field's first year as a minor league park — and the first year it operated with lights — the Utica Braves drew over 100,000. That represented a solid third of the league attendance, and the Braves were in last place.

That's why there's night ball.

The park was already old by that time. The bleacher seats were called "Splinter Haven." The park was so close to the Mohawk, fog often rolled over the expansive outfield.

Ambrose McConnell Field, as the ballpark was known before and after World War II, was named after the owner of the Canadian-American League franchise. McConnell died in 1942. He'd once been a major league second baseman, hitting .264 in 409 games for the Red Sox and White Sox between 1908 and 1911.

The ballpark was razed in the mid-1950s for New York State Thruway construction.

Murnane Field
New York–Pennsylvania League 1970s–circa 1985 (Blue Sox). *Dimensions:* Left field, 330 feet; center field, 400 feet; right field, 330 feet. *Seating*

capacity: 2000.
If you ever find yourself watching a game here, remember to check out the pizza.

Valdosta, Georgia

Billy Grant Field
Home of the Valdosta State College Blazers (Gulf South Conference), present. *Dimensions:* Left field, 330 feet; center field, 400 feet; right field, 332 feet. *Seating capacity:* 1000.

Vancouver, British Columbia

Athletic Park
Location: Birch and Hemlock streets, West Sixth and West Fifth avenues, across False Creek from where British Columbia Place Stadium still stands, current site of the Pacific Press Building. *Dimensions:* Left field, 383 feet; center field, 318 feet; right field, 232 feet.
Take two and go to right.

Capilano Stadium
Pacific Coast League 1956–62, 1965–69. *Seating capacity:* 8700.

Nat Bailey Stadium
Pacific Coast League 1978–present (Canadians). *Owned by:* Molson Brewery. *Location:* 4601 Ontario Street. *Dimensions:* Left field, 335 feet; left center, 367 feet; center field, 395 feet; right center, 362 feet; right field, 335 feet. *Seating capacity:* 7000. *1987 season attendance:* 338,614.
Until recently, this park still had a hand-operated scoreboard.

Vernon, California

Maier Park
Pacific Coast League 1909–12 (Tigers).
Park named after team owner Fred Maier.

Vero Beach, Florida

Holman Stadium (Dodgertown)
Florida State League 1980–present (Dodgers), spring home of the Los Angeles Dodgers 1948–present. Also the summer training camp of the National Football League's New Orleans Saints. *Location:* 4001 26th Street, 43rd Avenue, Walker Avenue. *Stadium dedicated:* 1953 (site used for baseball since 1948). *Dimensions:* Left field, 360 feet; center field, 410 feet; right field, 360 feet. *Seating capacity:* (1980) 5000; (1988) 6000. *Single game attendance record:* 8200 (March 19, 1979, Los Angeles Dodgers versus New York Yankees).

Surrounded on the outside by palm trees, the stands are low and boomerang-shaped, going from foul pole to foul pole. The press box, at the top of the roofless grandstand behind home, has the architectural feel of a pagoda. If you climbed to the top of the grandstand and looked out behind it, you'd see a pond, a parking lot, and a par five, dog leg to the right.

Holman Stadium was recently landscaped and renovated to seat 6000. It is part of a 450-acre baseball spring training complex known since 1965 as Dodgertown. The ballpark has no center field fence—just a rope. The Dodgers average about 6000 fans per home spring date, so Holman Stadium is usually close to or a little better than filled.

The complex is built on a former Naval Air Station. The station had been given to the city of Vero Beach following World War II by the United States government.

Local businessman Bud Holman convinced the Dodgers to rent the station as their spring training home, and the Dodgers have been there ever since. It was to Holman that the stadium was dedicated in 1953.

Surrounding Holman Stadium are two-and-a-half practice fields, a long row of batting cages with pitching machines, two golf courses, clubhouses, a restaurant, a lounge open to the public, a pro shop, swimming pools, tennis courts, a recreation room, and a movie theater for Dodger personnel. There is also a 70-acre citrus grove. The half-field is for infield practice, bunting practice, etc.

Since 1980, Holman Stadium has been the home of the Vero Beach Dodgers, Los Angeles' Class A farm team. Over their first six years, the local Dodgers averaged 80,000 spectators per year, more than four times the population of the city. The Dodgers won the Florida State League pennant in 1983.

Victoria, Texas

Riverside Park
Texas League 1958–61. *Seating capacity:* 5000.

Visalia, California

Name of park unknown
Location: Just east of St. Mary's Church.

According to *The Spread Eagle,* a newspaper published briefly in Visalia in the 1870s by F.R. Bequette and F. Sutherland, an amateur baseball club in 1873 played their games on a diamond just east of St. Mary's Catholic Church. There is no written record of a specific game being played here, but it is known that the pitcher and manager of the team was John Fisher.

Recreation Grounds
Home of the Empires 1879–1886. *Location:* Willis and Acequia streets beside the Visalia Normal School, one block east of Visalia's current city hall, southwest side of the school building.

The Normal School was a teacher's college—an ironic location for the ballpark, as Visalia was not the world's most civilized place in 1879. It was an

Top: *Dodgertown in Vero Beach, Florida. That's Holman Stadium at the top.* Bottom: *Holman Stadium. (Both photos compliments of the Los Angeles Dodgers.)*

Old West rootin'-tootin' outlaw-ridden double-swinging-doors-on-the-saloon kind of a place. Any gathering of men meant many weapons.

The popularity of amateur baseball during the 1870s was a primary cause for the halt of hooliganism and lawlessness that had plagued the community. For the first time there was something to do in town other than get drunk and start a fight. At least it gave some of the men an excuse to sober up now and again.

Victorious Match Followed by Banquet. According to an April 1879 issue of *The Weekly Visalia Delta:*

"BASEBALL Match—Last Sunday the Two Orphans, of Bakersfield, and the Empire club of Visalia played a match game at the Recreation grounds near the Visalia Normal School. The Empire club was organized last week and were without practice, while the Two Orphans is an old club.

"A large number of people were out on the grounds to witness the match.

Seats had been provided for the spectators, and the boys' brass band dispensed sweet music for the occasion.... The Bakersfield boys, as might have been expected, won the victory, making a score of 31 to 6 on the part of the Empires. After the match the Visalia boys took their visitors around town and tried to make their stay as pleasant as possible, and in the evening gave them a banquet in the Palace Hotel."

Suspiciously euphemistic. Sounds like the Two Orphans introduced the Empires to the local talent. The *Delta* went on to say, "Afterward, they (the Empires) strolled around town to a late hour, when they were taken to Tulare to meet the train. They expressed themselves as well satisfied with the reception they received in Visalia."

The game had been played by men without uniforms. The Empires didn't get uniforms until July. No gloves were worn, and the catcher caught the ball on the first bounce.

The Empire team was sponsored by the Empire Store. The owner was cattle baron Thomas Fowler, who was in the process of pouring his fortune down the fruitless Empire Mine at Mineral King. By 1880 the Empires had a rivalry against the second Visalia team, the Uglies. Other towns in the area came to town with their best nine. The Hanford Blue Stars and the Grangeville Plow Boys visited the Normal School field. By 1884, crowds as large as 2000 were showing up to watch games.

There were two roofed grandstands on either side of home plate, about thirty feet long and ten rows deep apiece — on the outer sides of the grandstands were open bleachers, which were slightly shorter and extended down the foul lines just past first and third base.

Fairgrounds

Home of Visalia baseball as of 1887. Central City League 1890–98. *Location:* South side of Visalia.

In 1887, fruit grower I.H. Thomas managed the town team, which leased four acres of the old fairgrounds for its diamond. Up to 600 showed up for games. The largest crowds appeared when the Fresno nine were in town.

Here is the *Visalia Times*'s biased description of a Fresno-Visalia baseball game in 1890:

"The pleasure of the occasion was marred by Manager Young (of Fresno) and his second baseman, Vincent. The former was guilty of using profane language on the diamond in the hearing of ladies, showing he is devoid of the instincts of a gentleman. He made a vulgar allusion, proving he is a blackguard, and finally he called the umpire a horse thief and a robber, giving evidence of hoodlum proclivities. Fresno had not put up the $250 forfeit, so the umpire could not fine him as he should have done."

The star pitcher for Visalia was Charley Button, and his battery-mate was Soapy Simpson — the first in a long line of Soapy Simpsons who played ball in Visalia.

In 1894, Charley Button almost ended the career and the life of an 18-year-old Fresno first baseman named Frank Chance. At a game at the fairgrounds, Button let an "inshoot" get away from him and seriously beaned Chance. The future Peerless Leader remained unconscious for several hours.

The Old Shooting Grounds

Valley League circa 1899. *Location:* Lincoln Oval.

M.J. Rouse, a farmer, agreed to enclose his old shooting grounds so it could be used as a ballpark. The field was just to the north of the high school then located in Lincoln Oval.

The first game was a home victory over Fresno. The *Visalia Times* explained that the Fresno team had been hoodooed into defeat. The team had "met a cross-eyed boy dressed in white on the shady side of the street on Sunday morning."

The Armory

Location: Northeast corner of Court and Acequia streets. (Acequia parallels Main Street one block to the south.)

According to the *Visalia Times-Delta,* this was the site of the first indoor baseball game ever played in 1908. It was an experiment that didn't work out very well. The team was then managed by M.J. Rouse, the farmer who owned the Old Shooting Grounds, and was back to playing outdoors before long.

Recreation Park

California League 1946–62 (Cubs 1946–52), 1968–present (Oaks). *Location:* 440 North Giddings Avenue; West Center, North School, Murray and North Jacob streets, north of Main Street and several blocks west of downtown. *Dimensions:* Left field, 320 feet; center field, 405 feet; right field, 320 feet. *Seating capacity:* (1960) 3000; (1985) 1500. *Lights:* 1946. *1987 season attendance:* 60,818.

In the late fall of 1921, members of the Visalia Commercial Club raised $24,000 by selling 60 shares of stock at $400 per share to buy 11 acres of the Keener Estate and equip it for baseball. George Cobb headed the committee that arranged the purchase. The land was ultimately given to the city and is today Visalia Park.

The original wooden structure served both softball and baseball between the 1920s and the 1960s. Professional baseball was played in Visalia for the first time in 1946. To get a franchise in the California League, a $30,000 lighting system was donated to Recreation Park by local citizens. There were 8 light towers installed, 6 of which were 70 feet high. Two were 80 feet. The taller ones stood over first and third base.

For the opening game in 1946, Mayor W.R. Beckwith tossed out the ball to start the game, and the Visalia High School band played. It was originally planned to give away a Chevy, but the contest was delayed because the car had not arrived. The stands were not completely painted, as the paint supply had run out. For the opener, the visiting Bakersfield team had to dress in their hotel because the home team was living in the visiting clubhouse due to a severe housing shortage in Visalia. By the middle of that season, everything was running smoothly.

The park was not rebuilt in concrete until the mid-1960s. For many years, the baseball fans of Visalia watched the park slowly fall apart.

Mary Anne Terstegge of the Annie Mitchell History Room at the Tulare County Free Library System describes those years:

"The deterioration became obvious in 1952. Jim McDaniel, playing left field for the Class C Cub team, fell through the left field fence when making a catch. With the ball in his glove, he landed outside the park. The game had to be held up while he walked around to the players' entrance to re-enter the ballpark. The park kept deteriorating until baseball there was impossible."

During the late 1950s an inner fence was put in so the diamond could be used for Little League and Babe Ruth League contests.

Waco, Texas

Katy Park

Texas League 1925–30. *First night game:* June 20, 1930.

Site of one of the first official league night games in 1930. The idea caught on quickly. By the end of that season every team in the Texas League except two (Beaumont and Wichita Falls) was playing under the lights.

Walla Walla, Washington

Borleske Field

Northwest League circa 1969. *Dimensions:* Left field, 335 feet; center field, 400 feet; right field, 325 feet. *Seating capacity:* 3500.

Washington, D.C.

Olympic Grounds (National Grounds)

National Association 1871–75 (Olympics), 1872–73 (Nationals). Built in 1870 by Mike Scanlon. *Location:* 16th, 17th and South streets NW. *Seating capacity:* 500. *First Olympics game:* May 4, 1871. *First Nationals game:* April 20, 1872. *Last Nationals game:* October 23, 1873. *Last Olympics game:* June 8, 1875.

The teams that played here were bad, starting a tradition.

White Lot

National Association 1871–72 (Olympics, some games). *Location:* Just southwest of the White House.

President Andrew Johnson attended games here in the 1860s.

Maryland Avenue Park

National Association 1871–72 (Olympics, some games). *Location:* Sixth and Seventh streets NE at Maryland Avenue.

Athletic Park

American Association 1884 (Nationals). *Location:* S, T, and Ninth streets NW. *First game:* May 1, 1884. *Last game:* August 5, 1884.

A photo from the archives of the National Baseball Library in Cooperstown shows a double-decked wooden grandstand flanked by shallow bleachers that go into the corners. The playing field is in terrible condition, with only sparse grass growing in the outfield.

Union Association Park

Union Association 1884. *Location:* B, C, and First streets NE, Delaware Avenue.

Capitol Park

National League 1886–89 (Senators). *Location:* Capitol Avenue (left field side), F Street (third base), Delaware Avenue (first base), G Street (right field)—on the current side of Union Station National Visitors Center. *Seating capacity:* 6000. *First game:* April 29, 1886 (Washington 6, Philadelphia 3). *Last game:* September 21, 1889 (Washington 4, Boston 4, 12 innings, darkness).

The Senators of the 1880s and Capitol Park were owned by Robert and Walter Hewitt. The field, built in a residential neighborhood, was squared off so that fair territory was shaped like a modern home plate, narrow at the sides. A sign on the straightaway center field fence read, "Schlitz's Milwaukee Lager is the beer!" Another, in left field, read, "M.I.S.T. for MALARIA."

This park was the neutral site of the "world series" game between Detroit of the National League and St. Louis of the American Association, on October 21, 1887. The attendance was 1261. Final score: St. Louis 11, Detroit 4. There were three home runs hit in the game, batters taking advantage of those close fences down the lines.

Jersey Street Park

National League 1886–89 (Senators, some games). *Location:* Jersey Street, Indiana Avenue North.

Redford Grounds

National League 1890s (Senators, some games). *Location:* Second Street NW.

American League Park

American League 1901–02. *Location:* 14th Street NE, Florida Avenue NE, Trinidad Avenue NE and Bladensberg Avenue NE. *Seating capacity:* 10,000+. *First game:* April 29, 1901 (Washington 5, Baltimore 2). *Last game:* September 27, 1902 (Washington 9, Philadelphia 4).

Franchise moved here from Kansas

City, as the American League made a go of it as the second major league.

Griffith Stadium (Beyer's Seventh Street Park, National Park 1892–1910)
American Association 1891, National League 1892–99, American League 1903–61 (Senators), Negro East-West League 1932 (Pilots), Negro National League 1936–48 (Elite Giants 1936–37, Homestead Grays 1937–48, half of home games, Black Senators 1938). *Owned by:* The Washington Senators. *Location:* Georgia Avenue (first base side), W Street NW (third base), 5th Street (left field), U Street NW (right field), current site of Howard University Hospital. *Dimensions:* (1911) Left field, 407 feet; left center, 391 feet; center field, 421 feet; right field, 328 feet. (1961) Left field, 388 feet; left center, 372 feet; center field, 421 feet; right field, 320 feet. 61 feet from home plate to the backstop. *Fences:* Left field, 12 feet; center field, 30 feet; right center, 41 feet (scoreboard); right field, 30 feet. *Burned:* March 17, 1911. *Refurbished:* 1911. *Lights installed:* 1941. *Seating capacity:* (1892) 6500. (1911) 27,410. Lower boxes, 3786; grandstand reserved, 8453; upper boxes, 923; upper reserved, 7112; general admission, 5636; bleacher, 1500. *Day game attendance record:* 31,728 (April 19, 1948, versus New York). *Doubleheader attendance record:* 35,563 (July 4, 1936, versus New York). *Night game attendance record:* 30,701 (June 17, 1947, versus Cleveland). *Opening game attendance record:* 31,728 (April 19, 1948, versus New York). *Season high attendance record:* 1,027,216 (1946). *Season low attendance record:* 89,682 (1917). *First American Association game:* April 13, 1891. *Last American Association game:* October 5, 1891. *First National League game:* April 16, 1892 (New York 6, Washington 5). *Last National League game:* October 14, 1899 (Washington 12, New York 9). *First American League game:* April 22, 1903

(Washington 3, New York 1). *Last American League game:* September 21, 1961 (Minnesota 6, Washington 3). *Torn down:* 1965.

In the spring of 1891, when this site was chosen for the new American Association ballpark, management was not bothered by the oak forest there. The trees were felled and stumped, the holes were filled in, and the ballpark was built. Baseball would be played on the cleared lot for the next 70 years.

As early as 1891 the Olympics put in a restaurant on their grounds so fans could go straight to the park from work without stopping for lunch first.

In the 1890s, when the park was called National Park and used for National League play, there was barbed wire on top of the outfield fence—presumably to keep freeloaders from sitting up there. It is said that Wee Willie Keeler once saved a game for his Baltimore Orioles by racing after a long drive to the fence and plunging his arm through the wire to make the catch, ripping his arm from the wrist to the elbow in the process.

The National League Washington team of the 1890s was an expansion club, owned by George and Jacob Earle Wagner. The park was owned by the National League at that time—which is why the American League was not allowed to use this park until 1903. Just as had been the case in New York, the National League was not going to make it easy for the new kid on the block to get a foothold in a major United States city.

Ladies Day Riot. In 1897, the Senators decided to try a Ladies Day promotion. Ladies would be allowed in free. Women needed to learn more about the sport, the Senators said. The place was packed with ladies who knew all they needed to know: home team pitcher Winnie Mercer was cute and the umpire was built for abuse.

Aware of the charming peculiarities of this game's audience—and his own appeal to the feminine crowd—Mercer picked trouble whenever he could with the umpire, an undeserving victim named Bill Carpenter.

Carpenter, to his credit, took Mercer's tongue for five innings before sending him to the showers. There was a riot in the stands. After the game, a group of the rowdier females charged onto the field and tackled Carpenter. He was beaten and his clothes were torn. In the stands the ladies became wild vandals, ripped out seats and broke windows.

Here's a twist: with a common enemy to deal with, the players came to the aid of the umpire and got him safely into the clubhouse. Later, he was escorted from the park in disguise. Management decided Ladies Day hadn't worked out, and did not try the experiment again.

There was no baseball on this site between 1900 and 1902. In the spring of 1903, the stands from American League Park on 14th and Bladensberg were moved onto this site—and the lot became the home of the Senators of the American League for the first time.

It was here that the first megaphone man, E. Lawrence Phillips, announced the starting lineups before the game for the first fifth of the twentieth century.

The Senators used to give a gold season pass to the United States president Teddy Roosevelt, the first to receive this gift. Then, in a great public relations move, they got President William Howard Taft to throw out the first ball, stamping government approval on the national game.

The ballpark was in a neighborhood which is now black working-class. When the park burned in 1911, it was rebuilt enough to reopen in eleven days.

Griffith became president of the club in 1920, and it was then that the name of the park changed. The park was greatly enlarged, the grandstand largely doubled-decked.

A common saying in Washington was, "Meet me by the tree," and that meant the big tree just outside the center field wall.

On the other side of the center field wall, in play, was a small box used to hold the flag. It was called, because of a physical resemblance, the Dog House. Once a Senator scored an inside-the-parker when his drive rolled inside the Dog House. A groundskeeper had forgotten to close the little door. Philadelphia outfielder Socks Seybold crawled in after the ball and got stuck. (Another source tells a remarkably similar story taking place in Baker Bowl. The tale may be tall.)

Homers Hard to Come By. The back wall of the left bleachers was cleared only three times by the batted ball. Mickey Mantle did it, and Josh Gibson did it twice.

Mickey Mantle hit the longest home run of all time on April 17, 1953, off Chuck Stobbs. Nobody saw the measurement (by Yankee public relations man Red Patterson), but it is said the ball traveled 565 feet.

Before 1950, the home run distances were 405 feet down the left field line, 420 to center, and 328 to right. In 1950, the addition of 1000 outfield box seats lessened the measurements in left field to under 400 feet. Griffith Stadium was not the sort of place to play if you were looking to show off your power stats.

In all of 1945—a war year—the Senators hit only one home run at home, and it was Joe Kuhel's inside-the-parker. Sam Rice (5'9", 150 lbs.) played for Washington for 19 seasons and never hit a ground rule home run in Griffith Stadium. He hit nine at home and they all stayed inside the fences. Buddy Myer hit 14 home runs during his career in Griffith Stadium, and only one of them made it over a barrier.

The concrete wall in right field was 30 feet high. The scoreboard was the same height as the wall. On top of the scoreboard was an advertisement sign that read variously, "National Bohemian Beer," "Old Georgetown Beer," "Chesterfield" or "Coca-Cola." When the sign advertised National Bohemian Beer, there was a huge three-dimen-

Griffith Stadium, Washington, D.C. Mantle's home run landed in one of the back yards behind the left-field bleachers. (Photo supplied by the National Baseball Library in Cooperstown, New York.)

sional beer bottle sticking up from the top of the sign. The top of that beer bottle was 56 feet above the ground.

In the early 1940s, Clark Griffith said that Josh Gibson of the Homestead Grays hit more home runs in a year into Griffith Stadium's left-field seats than did the whole American League who came to play the Senators.

In 1942 the Homestead Grays (winners of the Negro National League pennant in 1941) played Sunday games only at Griffith Stadium—the team played Saturdays at Forbes Field in Pittsburgh—yet drew 170,000 to Griffith Stadium.

The final game played at Griffith Stadium came September 21, 1961, as the expansion Senators played the old Senators, now known as the Minnesota Twins.

Standpipe Park

Eastern Colored League 1924 (Potomacs). *Location:* 16th and Euclid streets NW.

Robert F. Kennedy Stadium (D.C. Stadium, 1962–68)

American League 1962–71 (Senators). Owned by the United States government. *Location:* 22nd Street (home plate side), Independence Avenue (first base), East Capitol Street Bridge (center field), C Street NE (third base). *Dimensions:* Left field, 335 feet; left center, 381 feet; center field, 410 feet; right center, 378 feet; right field, 335 feet. 60 feet between home plate and the backstop. *Fences:* Seven feet all the way around. *Seating capacity:* 45,016. Lower boxes, 3533; lower reserved, 6567; mezzanine boxes, 1371; upper boxes, 7933; upper reserved, 7840; lower general admission, 7672; upper general admission, 10,100. *Day game attendance record:* 45,125 (April 7, 1969, versus New York). *Doubleheader attendance record:* 40,359 (June 14, 1964, versus Minnesota). *Night game attendance record:* 30,421 (July 31, 1962, versus New York). *Twi-night doubleheader attendance record:* 48,147 (August 1, 1962, versus New

Robert F. Kennedy Stadium, Washington, D.C., in the foreground; the Capitol Building and the Washington Monument are in the upper-left-hand corner. (Photo supplied by the District of Columbia Armory Board.)

York). *Opening game attendance record:* 45,125 (April 7, 1969, versus New York). *Season high attendance record:* 918,106 (1969). *Season low attendance record:* 535,604 (1963). *First game:* April 9, 1962 (Washington 4, Detroit 1). *Last game:* September 30, 1971 (night, New York 9, Washington 0, forfeit).

The first of the cookie-cutters, and the only federally owned ballpark ever used in the majors. Architecturally, the stadium was interesting in that it had only an upper deck in the outfield, sitting on top of a tall facade that functioned as the hitters' background in center, the scoreboard in right, and the back wall for the bullpens in left. The first home run struck into the outfield seats was by Roger Maris. All the way around, a wire barrier in front of the tall wall provided the home run barrier.

The Senators' fans got testy when the team split for Texas at the end of the 1971 season. The final game against the New York Yankees on September 30, 1971, was forfeited when angry fans stormed the field in the ninth inning and tore everything up.

Current site of Crackerjack Old-Timers' games and New York Mets pre-season exhibitions. Park no longer configures for baseball so there's an extremely close fence in left. Washington hopes to stay in consideration for major league expansion.

Waterbury, Connecticut

Municipal Stadium
Eastern League 1966–circa 1985 (Giants, Indians, franchise no longer exists). *Dimensions:* Left field, 335 feet; center field, 385 feet; right field, 338 feet. *Seating capacity:* 5000.

Waterloo, Iowa

Municipal Stadium
Three-I League 1946–56, Midwest League 1958–present. *Built:* 1946. *Location:* Park Road exit on Highway 20. *Dimensions:* Left field, 335 feet; center field, 360 feet; right field, 335 feet. *Seating capacity:* (1960) 5000; (1985) 6000. *Record season attendance:* 91,625

(1975). *1987 prices:* Box, $3.00; general admission, $2.50; bleachers, $1.50; senior citizens and children, half price. Season tickets: box, $80; general admission, $65; bleachers, $50. *1987 season attendance:* 68,081.

Municipal Stadium's first box seats were 1910 originals, transplanted from Comiskey Park. The White Sox were Waterloo's parent club, and were finally getting around to changing Comiskey's seats. Waterloo got the old ones. Current Waterloo Indians executive secretary and writer Jerry Klinkowitz still has a few of those chairs.

Waterloo is currently affiliated with the Cleveland Indians. Between the Indians and the White Sox, Waterloo was in the farm system of the Royals and the Red Sox.

Watertown, New York

Fairgrounds Stadium (Alex Duffy Fairgrounds)

Havana Red Sox (black team) 1920s, Canadian-American League (Class C) 1936, Border League 1946–50, New York–Pennsylvania League 1983– present (Pirates). *Dimensions:* Left field, 320 feet; center field, 380 feet; right field, 320 feet. *Seating capacity:* 4500. *Built:* 1851, 1947. *First used for baseball:* 1873. *Burned:* September, 1947.

At the time of this writing, Alex T. Duffy was 89 years old. He's been involved with the fairgrounds since 1915.

Between home and the backstop is the quarter-mile track for stock cars. Gates at opposite sides of the ballpark are built for the cars to come in and go out.

The Canadian-American League franchise that played here was a one-year fiasco. Things even got off to a bad start. The Boston Braves decided to put a farm team here but couldn't locate a place to play. Bob Quinn, Braves president, had to come to town to handle the situation himself. The first place they

considered, the old Knickerbocker Grounds, turned out to be condemned. Even after the fairgrounds allowed baseball to be played there, Quinn had to beg to have a fence put up. A week after the infield was laid, the fairgrounds had the horseshow in and the field was ruined. Opening Day attendance was 41. The franchise moved to Massena, New York, mid-season, but didn't stay long. Before long the Watertown Bucks were back to finish the season before dissolving for good.

The original grandstand at the fairgrounds, which had been standing since 1851, was burned in 1947 by an arsonist, immediately after a Border League playoff game.

Wausau, Wisconsin

Athletic Park

Midwest League 1975–present (Timbers). *Location:* Third Street. *Dimensions:* Left field, 318 feet; center field, 365 feet; right field, 316 feet. *Seating capacity:* 2500. *Record season attendance:* 63,461 (1975). *1987 season attendance:* 61,342.

West Lynn, Massachusetts

General Electric Field

On June 24, 1927, this was the site of an early night game. More than 5000 people watched a team from Lynn beat a team from Salem 7–2 in seven innings. The game featured a double play by the Lynn squad, several outstanding catches, and only two errors.

Seventeen years after George F. Cahill's last attempts to make night baseball a reality, playing under the lights was finally being taken seriously.

In attendance for the game was New England League president Claude B. Johnson, who predicted all leagues would have night baseball within five years. He was off by three years.

Bucky Harris and Goose Goslin of the Washington Senators were at the game, as well as Bill Carrigan of the Red Sox. Harris and Carrigan foresaw night exhibition games in the near future in the big leagues. Goslin said he was looking forward to playing in a night game.

Pre-game antics were supplied by baseball comedian Al Schacht.

West Palm Beach, Florida

Municipal Stadium

Florida State League 1968–present, spring home of the Milwaukee/Atlanta Braves 1963–present, and the Montreal Expos, present. *Location:* 715 Hank Aaron Drive, Palm Beach Lake Boulevard, I-95. *Built:* 1965. *Dimensions:* Left field, 310 feet; center field, 380 feet; right field, 310 feet. *Seating capacity:* (1975) 4500; (1985) 5000. *1987 Florida State League season attendance:* 110,633.

Wichita, Kansas

Lawrence Stadium (Dumont Stadium)

American Association circa 1970 (Aeros), Texas League 1986–present (Pilots). *Location:* Douglas and Maple streets, McLean Boulevard. *Built:* 1934. *Dimensions:* Left field, 340 feet; left center, 370 feet; center field, 410 feet; right center, 348 feet; right field, 312 feet. *Fences:* Ten feet all the way around. *Seating capacity:* 7635. *1987 season attendance:* 150,952.

Eck Stadium (Shocker Field, before 1985)

Home of the Wichita State University Shockers (Missouri Valley Conference) 1970s–present. *Location:* 21st Street, east edge of the Wichita State University campus. *Designer:* Law-Kingdon, Inc. *Construction cost* (1985): $700,000. *Dimensions:* Left field, 330

feet; left center, 375 feet; center field, 390 feet; right center, 375 feet; right field, 330 feet. *Fence:* Eight feet all the way around (cedar). *Seating capacity* (1985): 3407. *Surface:* AstroTurf-8. Joske 210 Olympic Sport System rubberized warning track.

Before 1985, when the stands were built and the name was changed to Eck Stadium, fans sat around this field on flatcars.

Named after Wichita businessman/philanthropist Rusty Eck.

Wichita Falls, Texas

Athletic Park

Texas League 1920–32 (Spudders).

When the wooden grandstand caught fire in the middle of a ball game from a carelessly tossed cigarette butt, all 3000 in attendance got out of the ballpark unhurt, but the park was ruined. In addition to the grandstand, 50 parked cars were totally or partially destroyed by the blaze.

In two weeks the grandstand was rebuilt, only to burn again on June 3, 1924. Again it was rebuilt—this time during a road trip so the Spudders did not even have to miss a date. Today, only the reserved seat section's concrete base remains.

Williamsport, Pennsylvania

Bowman Field

Eastern League circa 1960–present (Bills). *Location:* West Fourth Street. *Dimensions:* Left field, 345 feet; center field, 405 feet; right field, 350 feet. *Seating capacity:* 5200. *1987 season attendance:* 77,140.

In August of 1987, Williamsport Bills catcher Dave Bresnahan had a trick in his glove—a potato, peeled round. Rick Lundblade, of the Phillies, was the runner at third, Bresnahan's victim. The catcher threw his potato over his third baseman's head and into left field. When Lundblade tried to score, Bresnahan tagged him out with the real ball. Bills manager Orlando Gomez immediately took Bresnahan out of the game and the next day he was released from his contract. Chances are he was going to get released anyway. (This was not the first time the tater trick had been pulled. *See* Kinston, North Carolina.) Bresnahan went home to sell real estate but was invited back to Williamsport on May 30, 1980, Dave Bresnahan Day, where his number (59) was retired. One buck and one potato (peeled or not) got a fan through the turnstiles.

Lamade Stadium
Location: U.S. Route 15, 18 miles north of Interstate 80. *Dimensions:* Left field, 204 feet; center field, 204 feet; right field, 204 feet. *Seating capacity:* 10,000.

Home of the Little League World Series, which has been played in Williamsport since 1939. The ballpark was originally purchased by Little League Baseball from Lycoming College through the Williamsport Foundation with money made available by *Grit,* the national weekly newspaper.

Howard J. Lamade, for whom the park is named, was vice president and secretary for *Grit* at the time, and a member of the Little League Board of Directors until his death in 1958. The current grandstand, which replaced wooden bleachers, was built in 1968. Three years later additional seats were added down the baselines.

There is no admission charge to any Little League game. Tickets for World Series games are complimentary. No tickets are required for Section 7 in the stadium or the terraced hills surrounding the outfield fence, which provide an excellent vantage point for watching the games. More than 80,000 fans per year come to see the World Series. Since 1963 the finals have been broadcast from Lamade Stadium on ABC-TV.

Surrounding the stadium is a 44-acre complex that comprises the Little League Camp, where a kid can spend two weeks for $325.

Wilmington, Delaware

Union Association Park
Union Association 1884 (Quicksteps, July and August only). *Location:* Front Street (currently Lancaster Avenue) and Union Street, just outside the city limits.

Name of park unknown
Location: Second and DuPont streets.

Home of the (black) Rosedale club in the 1920s. The team featured future Hall-of-Famer Judy Johnson. Fans brought along crates to sit on and watch the game.

Harlan's Field
Location: Near Market Street Bridge.

The place was packed in the 1920s for black-versus-white barnstorming games.

Wilmington Park
Interstate League 1947 (Blue Rocks). *Seating capacity:* 7700.

How could you not root for a team named the Blue Rocks?

According to Randolph Linthurst in his book *The 1947 Trenton Giants,* "An impressive and first rate facility was in Wilmington. The team was owned by the Carpenter family, who owned the (Philadelphia) Phillies. Everything in Wilmington had to be first class."

Wilson, North Carolina

Name of park unknown
Home of Wilson baseball circa 1890–1900. *Location:* "...in a park ... in the area back of Bud Warren's house on Kenan Street..." *(The Wilson Daily Times).*

A team including Dick Cozart, Cal-

Lamade Stadium, Williamsport, Pa., in 1962 (top) and after the 1968 construction (bottom). (Photos compliments of Little League Baseball.)

vin Woodard and W.S. Harris played teams from neighboring towns. Ball was played at this site until about the turn of the century, when the growth of the town forced a move.

Name of park unknown

Home of Wilson baseball circa 1900–04. *Location:* Between Goldsboro and Lodge streets at the end of Spring Street (now Douglas Street). Current location of the Export Tobacco Company.

Wilson had an independent team that played other towns (Rocky Mount, Tarboro) without need of a formal league. Star pitchers for the Wilson nine of 1900 were Ashe Hines and Dolph Mangum.

Captain Whitehead's Farm

Home of Wilson baseball 1905 (some games). *Location:* Current site of the S.W. Anderson home.

Name of park unknown

Home of Wilson baseball 1905–09.

Location: The Rountree property. By this time the same crew—Will Moore in center, Steve Anderson at second, Bob Wilkins at third, Jim Wilkins over at first, Dolph Mangum and Ashe Hines on the mound—had been playing together for a long time.

Name of park unknown

Carolina League (semi-pro) 1909–17. *Location:* Current site of Dick Cozart's home.

One can't help noticing that there was a Dick Cozart on that 1890 team. It was at this field that Jim Thorpe was knocked cold by a catcher's peg. He was playing as a member of the visiting Rocky Mount team and had laid down a bunt fielded by the catcher, who put the peg on his nut. Boom, out went the lights.

League Park

Virginia League (Class B) 1920–25, 1927 (Tobacconists). *Location:* "In the area behind Dick's Hot Dog stand." *Seating capacity:* 5000.

Site of Wilson's first professional baseball. At the time Wilson was the smallest town to have Class B baseball. The Tobacconists won the Virginia League pennant in 1922, then lost a one-game baby World Series against the Sally League champion club from Charleston. Charleston's Pie Traynor hit a home run off George Quinn for the only run of the game.

Fleming Stadium (previously Municipal Stadium)

Coastal Plain League (Class D) 1939–41, 1946–52, Bi-State League (Class D) 1942 (partial season), Carolina League 1956–68 (always the Tobacconists). *Built:* 1939. *Seating capacity:* 3000. *Season attendance record:* 140,000+ (1947, Class D record).

In the early 1950s, Municipal Stadium was renamed Fleming Stadium following the passing of Allie Fleming, one of the Tobacconists' chief benefactors.

Winston-Salem, North Carolina

Ernie Shore Stadium

Carolina League circa 1960–present (Red Sox, Spirits). *Location:* 30th Street. *Dimensions:* Left field, 335 feet; center field, 400 feet; right field, 335 feet. *Seating capacity:* 4200. *1987 season attendance:* 133,263.

Named after the Red Sox and Yankee pitcher from East Bend, North Carolina.

Winter Haven, Florida

Chain O'Lakes Park

Florida State League 1971–present (Red Sox), spring training home of the Boston Red Sox 1966–present. *Location:* Cypress Gardens Boulevard, ½ block east of Interstate 95. *Built:* 1966. *Dimensions:* Left field, 360 feet; center field, 425 feet; right field, 360 feet. *Seating capacity:* 5000. *Single game attendance record:* 6196 (March 22, 1979, Boston Red Sox versus New York Yankees). *1987 Florida State League season attendance:* 30,711.

The ballpark is thus named because it is beside a series of lakes connected by canals. The two lakes closest to the park are Lake Shipp and Lake Lulu. The air smells of oranges because of the many nearby groves.

In 1987, 3000 grandstand seats were installed along with a $100,000 electronic scoreboard and a 750-foot clubhouse expansion.

Woodbridge, Virginia

Prince William County Stadium (Davis Ford Park)

Carolina League 1983–present (Prince William Pirates, Prince William Yankees). *Location:* Davis Ford Road. *Dimensions:* Left field, 315 feet; center field, 400 feet; right field, 315 feet. *Seating capacity:* 6000. Also used by the Continental-Interstate Football

Fleming Stadium, Wilson, N.C. A freshly painted throwback. (Compliments of the city of Wilson.)

League's Prince William Storm. *1984 season attendance:* 108,818. *1987 season attendance:* 105,749.

Before 1983, this franchise was known as the Alexandria Dukes. Prince William County Stadium is on the road between Woodbridge and Manassas. The park is part of a recreational complex that includes four lighted softball fields.

This is the closest professional baseball to Washington, D.C. (beating Baltimore 35 miles to 37).

As of 1984, the Pirates paid $5000 a year plus a percentage of the gate to the county, who built the stadium just for the franchise.

Worcester, Massachusetts

Home of Ernest Thayer, author of the most famous baseball poem of them all, "Casey at the Bat."

The old common

Primary home of Worcester round ball 1865. Home of local teams such as the Mechanics, the Uptons, and the Medways.

A variation of baseball called round ball was played before the Civil War in the old Worcester common. On holidays, three or four games went on at the same time.

Even after the Cartwright rules were

Getting up close at Chain o'Lakes Park, Winter Haven, Fla. (Compliments of the Winter Haven Red Sox.)

introduced to the community in the late 1850s, round ball remained the game of the day for many years. Conversion was slow.

The big difference between round ball and baseball was in the manner that outs were created. In round ball, a runner was out if "soaked," that is, struck by a thrown ball while off base. Soaking could be a painful business, making this the real man's game in Worcester, preferable to a game that featured sissified "tagging."

Agricultural Grounds

Home of the Irvings 1877–78, International Association 1879 (Worcesters), National League 1880–82 (Brown

Stockings). *Location:* Cedar, Russell, Highland, and Sever streets. *First National League game:* May 1, 1880 (Worcester 13, Troy 1, winning pitcher: Frederick Corey). *Last National League game:* September 29, 1882 (Troy 10, Worcester 7).

Worcester's first professional baseball team, the Irvings, flourished in 1877 and 1878. In 1879 the "Worcesters" played the town's first organized ball, in the International Association. It was the success of this team that led the community to seek a major league franchise.

Back in 1869, all you needed to get into the National League was $500 and residency in a city of more than 75,000.

Worcester had only one of the two. That fall, when the Brown Stockings of Worcester applied for admission to the National League, their population was only 58,291.

Not everyone wanted the Brown Stockings in the league. The Troy Haymakers preferred the admission of nearby Albany, but these two cities were too close together for the taste of National League president William C. Hulbert. Hulbert, seeking to keep Albany out as much as to get Worcester in, allowed the Massachusetts city to count its suburban population, pushing Greater Worcester over the minimum.

On May 1, 1880, the Worcesters started play in the majors, drawing 1000 people to the old Fair Grounds in Agricultural Park, across Agricultural Street from Elm Park. The area is now filled with houses, but from 1853 to 1899 it was the site of the fairgrounds of the Worcester Agricultural Society.

Russell Street, which now passes by Elm Park and the Saint Spyridon Greek Orthodox Church, was once the best dirt racetrack in New England.

Mayor Frank Kelly was at the Opening Day ceremonies on the Agricultural Grounds. He was an outspoken supporter of General Winfield Scott Hancock for the Democratic presidential nomination. That day he watched Brown Stocking right-hander Frederick Corey beat the Haymakers in a yawner, 13–1.

The First Perfect Game. The first perfect game in organized baseball history was pitched at the Agricultural Grounds on June 12, 1880. It was only the third no-hitter in history—but the first of four to be pitched that year in the National League.

This was the last season that pitchers were allowed to deliver the ball from 45 feet. It would be another four years before the pitchers would be allowed to throw overhand.

The gem was turned in by John Lee Richmond, who beat Cleveland that day, 1–0. That spring, Richmond had been the starting pitcher at Brown University, and was signed by Brown Stocking manager Frank Bancroft after school was over.

Richmond was a lefty with a nasty curveball. He was known as an agonizingly slow worker. He looked at each of his drowsing infielders individually between pitches, and sometimes gazed upward at the clouds or at the rooftops as if he were seeing them for the first time. Then, according to an article in *The Providence Journal* of the day, Richmond would commence "a painful working of the shoulders, as though something were biting him between the blades."

Richmond's accomplishment lost some of its shine when, five days later, John Montgomery Ward of Providence pitched another perfect game. Folks began to figure the 27 up, 27 down scenario would be a frequent one, not knowing that 24 years would pass before the next perfect game was pitched by Cy Young for Boston.

Opening Day pitcher and regular centerfielder Fred Corey led the 1880 National League in home runs with 6—and that about covers the Brown Stockings' highlights. They never played better than .500 ball. Their last game was played on September 29, 1882, when they lost to the Haymakers in the Agricultural Grounds, 10–7, before a crowd of 18. The spectators could have played a B-game.

In 1884, a professional team was organized in Worcester, but interest was slow. The team folded after a year and a half.

There is no photo or drawing of the playing field on the Agricultural Grounds, but we can surmise that Highland Street ran past left field and Cedar Street ran along the first base line, since this configuration would best take advantage of the racetrack's grandstand on the Elm Park side of the oval.

The only photo of the grounds shows the entrance gate, which is large

enough to allow the entrance of carriages.

Grove Street Grounds
New England Baseball Association
1888.
Worcester went without organized
baseball in 1886 and 1887. Then, in 1888
a team representing the city in the New
England Base Ball Association played
at the new enclosed grounds on Grove
Street. The grounds had been leased for
the purpose of baseball by the street
railroad company from Stephen Salis-
bury, Esq.
By the 1890s, Worcester had become—as far as baseball was concerned—suburban Boston.

Wytheville, Virginia

Withers Field (Wytheville Athletic
Field, before 1948)
Home of the Statesmen (Independent pro schedule 1948-50), Appalachian League 1954-55, 1957-65, 1967,
1969, circa 1971 (Statesmen, Twins),
1985-present (Cubs). *Location:* Monroe and Fourth streets. *Dimensions:*
Left field, 317 feet; center field, 380
feet; right field, 345 feet. *Seating
capacity:* 1700. *1987 season attendance:*
18,122.
The 1950 baseball season was cut
short and the '51 season was not played
at Withers Field because of the Wythe
County polio epidemic.
Tony Oliva batted .410 for Wytheville in 1961.

Yeadon, Pennsylvania

Hilldale Park (Darby Catholic School
Stadium)
Eastern Colored League 1923-27
(Hilldales), Negro American League
1929 (Hilldales), Negro East-West
League 1932 (Hilldales). *Location:*
Chester Avenue. *Dimensions:* Left
field, 315 feet; right field, 370 feet.

Built in a suburb of Philadelphia,
this park had a big tree beyond the
fence in right center. The tree was so
close to the fence that its branches
dangled well over onto the playing
field, and, according to the ground
rules, were in play. The Hilldales began
playing here in 1921, and played two
years of an independent schedule before latching on with the Eastern Colored League in 1923.
The Hilldales won the pennant in
1923 and 1924. The team had Judy
Johnson. Biz Mackey caught. John
Henry Lloyd played shortstop and
managed. The park eventually had to
be enlarged to accommodate racially
mixed crowds who were bored by the
A's and Phillies, and took the Chester
Avenue trolley to Yeadon.
Other landmarks near the school
were the Fels-Naphtha Soap Factory,
the Bell Avenue School, and the Holy
Cross Cemetery, according to former
local resident Jean Booth Chiemingo.

York, Pennsylvania

Memorial Park
Interstate League 1947 (White Roses).
Seating capacity: 3500.
The park was old and beat up.
The league had teams named White
Roses, Red Roses (Lancaster), and
Blue Rocks (Wilmington).

Yuma, Arizona

Baseball was played in Yuma as far
back as 1890—when the community
was little more than a cluster of shacks
in the desert—on flat pieces of land, on
infields made of sandy soil, because
that's all there was. Maybe there was
some hard-leafed scrub here and there,
but not much else.
By 1920, there was a ballpark in
Yuma with a small set of wooden
bleachers behind home. From atop the
seats flew the Stars and Stripes. Crowds

Top: *Baseball in Yuma, Ariz., circa 1920. (Compliments of the Yuma County Historical Society.)* Bottom: *Desert Hills Sports Center, Yuma, Ariz. (Compliments of the City of Yuma Department of Parks and Recreation.)*

easily filled the stands and spread out on foot along the foul lines. A sprinkling of men dressed like Butch Cassidy and the Sundance Kid would sit in the sand around the outfield.

In 1913, a game at the Yuma ball field was interrupted by the landing of an airplane. It was the first time an airplane had flown into the state of Arizona. The pilot was Robert Fowler, a competitor in the first trans-continental air race.

Kennedy Park

Spring home of the San Diego Padres 1969. *Location:* 16th Street and 3rd Avenue.

Temporary training site used by Padres while their permanent facility was under construction.

Desert Hills Sports Center (Ray Kroc Baseball Complex)

Spring home of the San Diego Padres 1970–present, Yakult Swallows (Japanese), present. *Location:* Avenue A at 35th Street. *Seating capacity:* 6800. *Construction cost:* $400,000. *First game:* March 7, 1970.

This spring training complex is located two miles from downtown Yuma and was built in 1969 and 1970 by the city. The entire complex (not counting the parking lot) comprises 40 acres.

There are four-and-a-half practice fields. In the decade following the opening of the complex, there was a 443 percent increase in Yuma's tourism industry. The park was also used by various school teams.

In March of 1971, 2232 fans came out to see the Padres play the Tokyo Orions. The game represented the first time a Japanese team had opened its spring training in the United States. The Yakult Swallows now use the complex every spring.

Zanesville, Ohio

Mark Grey Athletic Park (Farm Diamond)

Negro National League 1938 (Homestead Grays, one game). *Location:* Putnam Avenue. *Built:* 1918. *Dimensions:* Left field, 304 feet; center field, 386 feet; right field, 265 feet.

Bibliography

"Aberdeen and Baseball: A Long Love Affair." *Aberdeen* [S.D.] *American News,* June 23, 1976, p. 27.

Adelman, Melvin L. *A Sporting Time.* Chicago: University of Illinois Press, 1986, 389 pp., indexed. History of sports in New York City, 1820–1870.

Alexander, Charles C. *Ty Cobb.* New York: Oxford University Press, 1984, 272 pp., indexed. Contains descriptions of Bennett Park's transformation into Navin Field.

Allen, Barry. "Crimson Tide to Get Stadium It Really Deserves." *Baseball Times,* University, Ala. (Alabama Athletic Department), February 26, 27, 1988, p. 3.

Allen, Maury. "Labine's Heart Still in Brooklyn." *New York Post,* April 28, 1983, p. 63.

The American Institute of Architects' Guide to New York City.

Anderson, Harry H. "The Ancient Origins of Baseball in Milwaukee." *Milwaukee History,* Summer 1983, Vol. 6, Number 2, pp. 42–57.

Angell, Roger. *Five Seasons, A Baseball Companion.* New York: Popular Library, 1978, 412 pp. Read this twice, the second time very slowly.

————. "Get Out Your Handkerchiefs." *The New Yorker,* December 7, 1987, p. 51. Story of the Homer Hanky, the Homerdome, and the 1987 World Series.

————. "Tiger, Tiger." *The New Yorker,* December 3, 1984, pp. 54–99. Discussion of Tiger Stadium and its Detroit neighborhood by baseball's poet.

"The Annals of Big League Ball in Indy." *Indianapolis Monthly,* April 1983, pp. 38–9.

Arbuckle, Clyde. *Clyde Arbuckle's History of San Jose.* San Jose, Calif. Smith McKay, 1986.

Askew, Hiram T. "Billy Nash: First Richmond Baseball Great." *Richmond Quarterly,* Spring 1981, p. 34.

Atlas of the City of Worcester Massachusetts. Philadelphia: G.M. Hopkins, 1886.

"Attendance Record." *Spokesman Review,* Spokane, Wash., May 19, 1909, p. 17, col. 1. Story of new riches and planned improvements at Recreation Park.

Baier, Paul. "Bretts, County Spruce Up Teams' Image." *Spokane Business Examiner,* April 23, 1986, p. 1.

"Ball Park Lease Fixed." *Spokesman Review,* Spokane, Wash., March 16, 1904, p. 7, col. 4. Story of Recreation Park.

"Ball Park on North Side." *Spokesman Review,* Spokane, Wash., March 9, 1904, p. 7, col. 2. Site of Recreation Park is announced.

"The Ball Tossers." *Spokane Falls Review,* April 15, 1890. Construction of the Spokane Grounds on Cable Road.

Banton, O.T., ed. *History of Macon County, 1976.* Pp. 479–80. Short history of baseball in Decatur, Illinois.

"Barnes' Sluggers." *Spokane Falls Review,* October 15, 1890, p. 3, col. 1. Wrap-up of the Northwest League season.

Bartlett, Arthur. *Baseball and Mr. Spalding.* New York: Farrar, Straus and Young, 1951, 295 pp.

Barton, George A. *My Lifetime in Sports.* Minneapolis: Olympic, 1957. Contains stories of Nicollet Park.

"Baseball Enjoyed Illustrious Career in Memorial Stadium." *Terre Haute Star,* September 18, 1970, p. 27.

"Baseball Practice Begins at City Park at 11 A.M." *ADTT,* Alexandria, Louisiana, March 22, 1934, p. 7.

"Base Ball, the New Club and New Ball Grounds." *The Standard,* Brooklyn, N.Y., Saturday, April 19, 1869. Discussion of the enlargement of the Union Grounds in Brooklyn.

Beard, Randy. "Spartanburg Was a Long Time Ago." *Spartanburg* [S.C.] *Herald-Journal,* May 4, 1986, p. El. Hard times have fallen on Duncan Park.

Beasley, Kay. "Out to the Baseball Game at Old Sulphur Dell." *Nashville Banner,* April 23, 1986, p. A20.

Beedle, Steve. "Baseball—More Than a Hobby; a Way of Life." *Jackson Hole* [Wyo.] *Guide,* August 8, 1976, p. 17. An interview with Ben Mateosky.

Behrens, David. "The Artful Dodgers." *Newsday,* September 19, 1984, Part Two, p. 4.

Belval, Adolph. "North Side Had Two Ball Parks, Reservoir and Lazy Lagoon." *Illinois State Register,* May 17, 1951. The neighborhood around Lanphier Park in Springfield, Illinois, had changed a lot since the 1930s.

Bishop, Pete. "Old Forbes Field Wistfully Recalled." *Pittsburgh Post-Gazette,* June 13, 1975, p. 15.

Bittner, John. "Kokomo Renovates Baseball Field and Stadium." *Park Maintenance and Grounds Management.* April 1986, p. 10.

Blake, Ben W. "Parks, Leagues, Names Are All That Change." *Richmond Times-Dispatch,* April 16, 1985.

Blake, John, with Small, Jim, and Hawkins, Burt. *Texas Rangers 1985 Media Guide.* Arlington, Tex.: Texas Rangers, 1985. Data on Arlington Stadium.

Bluthardt, Bob. "Ballparks: A Quiz." *The National Pastime: A Review of Baseball History.* Cooperstown, N.Y.: Society for American Baseball Research, Vol. 1, Number 1, p. 77.

Bolton, Reginald Pelham. *Inwood Hill Park.* New York: Dyckman Institute, 1932. Contains map showing location of the Dyckman Oval.

Boswell, Thomas. *How Life Imitates the World Series.* New York: Penguin, 1983, 296 pp.

————. *Why Time Begins on Opening Day.* New York: Penguin, 1985, 300 pp.

Brady, Erik. "Buffalo Rates No. 1 in Field of Expansion." *USA Today.* April 14, 1988. Story about Pilot Field in Buffalo, New York.

Breen, William D. "A Fan's Memory Goes All the Way Back to Brooklyn-Baltimore Merger." *Brooklyn Eagle,* May 28, 1944.

Brosnan, Jim. *The Long Season.* New York: Penguin, 1983 (originally published Harper and Row, 1960), 278 pp. Daddy of *Ball Four* and all the other kiss-and-tell clubhouse books.

Brown, Jim. "Chattanooga's Engel Stadium." *Ballparks Bulletin,* Number 12, January 1988, p. 6. A history professor at Tougaloo College (Tougaloo, Mississippi) visits one of the oldest ballparks still in use.

————. "The Old and the New: Two Southern League Ballparks in Alabama." *Ballparks Bulletin,* Number 10, September 1987, pp. 6–7. Professor Brown goes to Rickwood Field and Joe W. Davis Stadium.

Bruce, Janet. *The Kansas City Monarchs: Champions of Black Baseball.* Kansas City: University Press of Kansas, 1985, 176 pp., indexed. Talks about those many years when Kansas City was a two-franchise town.

Buck, Durward. "Remember the Day Ruth Led Braves in Game Here?" *The Fayetteville Observer,* April 3, 1960, p. 10A. Story of 1935 exhibition game in Fayetteville, North Carolina, featuring an aged Babe Ruth.

Bulger, Bozeman. *New York Evening World,* June 7, 1927. Article describing the concessions at Forbes Field.

Burgess, Jack. "Stout Hearted Pioneers Gambled Against Big Odds to Give City Baseball Teams, Frank Rutz Points Out." *Rochester* [N.Y.] *Times Union,* December 7, 1937. Information on the building of Culver Field.

Burns, Edward. "New Wrigley Field Blooms in Scenic Beauty—and Scoffers Rush to Apologize." *Chicago Sunday Tribune,* September 12, 1937.

Butler, Tom. "A Part of History Will Die When Breese Stevens Falls." *Wisconsin State Journal,* June 9, 1981. Dread of the inevitable destruction of Breese Stevens Field in Madison.

Calvert, Judy Stedman. "North Terre Haute Greys." *Northside Journal,* May 11, 1982. Description of Elm Grove Ball Park, where the swimming pool was in play.

Campbell, Bill. "Ainsworth Field ... Crumbling Monument to Baseball." *Erie Press,* May 20, 1972, p. 16.

Cannon, Jack. "Black Hills Bitten by Baseball Bug." *The Rapid City* [S.D.] *Daily Journal,* August 18, 1957, p. 19. Description of Sioux Park Stadium and Basin League play.

Caraher, Pat. "Bailey Field Lights." *Washington State University Hilltopics,* Pullman, Wash., June 1984, p. 24.

Casper, Jim. "New Simmons Parking Benefits Twins Fans." *Kenosha* [Wis.] *News,* April 9, 1987, p. 20.

Cervenka, Mike. "Tidbits from Clark and Addison." *Ballparks Bulletin,* Number 10, September 1987, p. 8. Celebration of the 50th anniversary of the ivy on the walls of Wrigley Field.

Cheek, George. "Crack of Bats in Spokane Recalls Bygone Days." *The Spokesman Review,* Spokane, Wash., April 13, 1952, p. 5.

"The Chicago Base-ball Grounds." *Harper's Weekly,* May 12, 1883, p. 299. Discussion of Lakefront Park.

Christ, Bob. "Hi Corbett Field Lacking for Charm and Memories." *Arizona Daily Star,* July 21, 1985, p. 1D.

Christine, Bill. "Forbes Field Fades into Memory." *Pittsburgh Press,* June 28, 1970, Section 4, p. 3.

"Civic Stadium Over the Years." *Eugene* [Ore.] *Emeralds Souvenir Program,* 1983.

Clifton, Merritt. *Disorganized Baseball: The Provincial League from LaRogue to Les Expos.* Richford, Vt.: SAMISDAT, 1982, 36 pp. Story of an integrated Canadian minor league in the 1930s and 1940s by a baseball historian from Quebec.

Club, Bench, Bar and Professional Life, a Journal for Club Men and Women. Providence, R.I.: 1896. "Compiled by Prominent Rhode Islanders and Men of Note."

Coffin, Tristram Potter. *The Old Ball Game.* New York: Herder and Herder, 1971, 206 pp., indexed. Still wondering if this is the same Tristram Coffin who starred in serial films in the forties. Maybe there's a bunch of Tristram Coffins.

Cohen, Stan. *Kanawha County Images.* Kanawha County Bicentennial, Inc., 1987. Contains early ballpark history of Charleston, West Virginia.

Coleman, Ken, with Valenti, Dan. *Grapefruit League Road Trip.* Lexington, Mass. Stephen Greene, 1988, 161 pp. A tourist's guide to spring training, by the long-time Boston Red Sox announcer.

"'Comiskey Field,' Name Selected for Playground." *Dubuque Telegraph-Herald,* May 15, 1929, p. 1.

Conley, Patrick T., and Campbell, Paul. *Providence, a Pictorial History.* Norfolk, Va.: Donning, 1982.

Connolly, Francis J. "Baseball's Golden Age." *Worcester* [Mass.] *Magazine,* April 2, 1980.

Connor, Anthony J. *Voices from Cooperstown.* New York: Collier, 1982, 333 pp., indexed. Anecdotes of Hall of Famers in their own words.

Connors, Joseph. "Baseball Game of 62 Years Ago Recalled in Full." *Brooklyn Eagle,* March 4, 1945.

Cook, Ron. "Revitalized Buffalo Has Major Goals." *Pittsburgh Press,* April 13, 1988. Story about Pilot Field in Buffalo, New York.

Couch, Dick. "New Home for Rainbows." *Honolulu Star-Bulletin,* September 12, 1975. Story about members of the University of Hawaii football team trying to get a sneak peak at the inside of Aloha Stadium before it officially opened.

Crane, Jeffrey. "Play Ball!" *Chandler Arizonian,* Chandler, Ariz., March 7, 1986, p. A1. Story of the first spring game played at Compadre Stadium.

Cuneo, Pat. "Homers Not Cheap — Just a Tad Short." *Times-News,* Erie, Pa., July 4, 1981. A surveyor discovers the distance markers on Ainsworth Field's outfield fences overstate the matter.

Dalrymple, Bob. "Riverview Was Home to the Industrial League." *Clinton Giants 1987 Souvenir Program.* A discussion of Riverview Stadium in Clinton, Iowa, during World War II.

Davids, L. Robert, ed. *Insider's Baseball.* New York: Charles Scribner's, 274 pp.

"Dayton Baseball Club to Play on West Side Field." *Dayton* [Oh.] *Journal,* January 11, 1934, p. 1.

Decker, Bob. "Baseball Under the Big Sky." *Montana Magazine,* May-June 1987, pp. 6–13. Baseball in Montana, especially from the bleachers in Helena, where sometimes the scenery is so beautiful you can't watch the game.

Dickey, Glenn. *The History of American League Baseball.* New York: Stein and Day, 319 pp., indexed.

Donaghey, Don. "Cobb Named Manager, But Deal Fizzled." *The Sunday Bulletin,* Philadelphia, Pa., August 6, 1950, Sports Section, p. 3.

_____. "20th Anniversary of Phillies Departure Brings Fond, Sad Recollections of Old Baker Bowl." *Sunday Bulletin,* Philadelphia, Pa., July 6, 1958, Sports Section, p. 3.

Doty, Kay. "Maury Doerr Recalls the Golden Days of Minor League Baseball in the Valley." *Valley News,* September 18, 1986, p. 8. History of baseball in Twin Falls, Idaho.

Durant, John. *The Story of Baseball.* New York: Hastings, 1973, 312 pp., indexed.

Durkin, Jack. "Dinneen, Doyle, Wiltse and Walsh Among City's Best on Diamond." *Syracuse Herald-American,* August 15, 1948.

Durso, Joseph. *Baseball and the American Dream.* St. Louis: Sporting News, 1986, 263 pp. Wonderful book. Not a history of baseball, but the story of the corner of America where baseball has lived since the Civil War.

"Earlier Ball Park." *Indianapolis Times,* April 26, 1937, p. 9, col. 7. Discussion of where professional baseball was played in Indianapolis before 1880.

"1886 — The Golden Era of Springfield — 1911." *Springfield* [Mass.] *Homestead,* May 22, 24, 27, 1911, p. 74. Description of Hampden Park, the nineteenth century home of baseball in Springfield.

Einstein, Charles, ed. *The Baseball Reader.* New York: Lippincott and Crowell, 1980, 361 pp.

Endicott, William. "Take Me Out to the Ballgame — But You'll Have to Find It." *Los Angeles Times,* May 30, 1971. Story of Lawrence Park in Lodi, Calif., and the sad truth that many local residents don't know where it is. Makes you understand why John Fogerty wrote that Creedence song—maybe he got stuck in Lodi looking for the ballpark.

"Enlarge the Stand." *Spokesman Review,* Spokane, Wash., June 20, 1901, p. 5, col. 3. Concerns the proposed expansion of the seating at the Northwest League ballpark.

"Fan Recalls Babe's 'First'." *Fayetteville News and Observer,* August 20, 1973, p. 23. Story of Babe Ruth's first home run as a professional in Fayetteville, North Carolina. So what if it was in an inter-squad game?

Feeny, Kathy. "Al Lopez Field Shines in Springtime." *Tampa* [Fla.] *Tribune,* March 26, 1987. Pete Rose and his Reds chat it up with fans and a reporter before a spring training game at Al Lopez Field, where Tony Perez and Rose played minor league ball.

Fimrite, Ron. "It's Easy to Get Stuck on the Cactus League." *Sports Illustrated,* February 15, 1988, pp. 30–34. Spring training in Arizona.

Finch, Robert L., ed. *The Story of Minor League Baseball.* Columbus, Oh.: Stoneham, 744 pp., indexed.

"First Playground: Oval Site Acquired by City Twenty-five Years Ago." *East Orange Record,* July 8, 1932. History of the Grove Street Oval in East Orange, New Jersey.

Fleming, G.H. *Murderer's Row.* New York: William Morrow, 1985, 399 pp., indexed. Assembled here are the day-by-day contemporary accounts of the 1927 New York Yankees and Ruth's 60 by the New York press. The Babe was everything you've heard and more. What a guy!

Forbell, George U. "Time Rolls Back Curtains of 60 Years When Mr. Forbell Thinks of Baseball." *Brooklyn Eagle,* December 26, 1943. It had not been a happy Christmas. An old man remembers Eastern Park in 1883. The title of the piece may be the first line of the great American novel.

Foust, Tom. "Renovation for Hi Corbett, Commission Seeks Facelift." *Arizona Daily Star,* March 10, 1972, p. 1C.

Gee, Bill. "Golden Moments at the Old Stadium...." *Honolulu Star-Bulletin,* September 12, 1975, page D-6. Memories of the Honolulu Stadium on the eve of the opening of Aloha Stadium.

Geise, George. "His Home Was Home Plate." *Great Falls Tribune,* October 25, 1987, p. 1E. Story of Logan Hurlburt and his love affair with Legion Park.

Gifford, Barry. *The Neighborhood of Baseball.* New York: E.P. Dutton, 205 pp., indexed. A personal history of the Cubs.

Gill, Hamilton A. "Recalls Old Capitoline and Baseball Stars." *Brooklyn Eagle,* April 8, 1934.

Gleason, James P. "Official Scorer Gladly Tells All About Original Pioneers." *Brooklyn Eagle,* November 19, 1944. Description of play in Red Hook's Ryan's Oval.

Godown, Marian, and Rawchuck, Alberta. *Yesterday's Fort Myers.* Miami, Fla: E.A. Seemann, 1975. History of Fort Myers, Florida. Could the ladies be using *noms de plume?*

"Goff and Burns Again." *Spokesman Review,* Spokane, Wash., April 3, 1901. Construction of a Northwest League ballpark is discussed.

Grabowski, Gary. "Clubhouse Construction Remains Ahead of Schedule." *Herald,* New Britain, Conn., February 22, 1983. Story of the construction of Beehive Field.

Graham, Frank. *The Brooklyn Dodgers—An Informal History.* New York: G.P. Putnam's, 1945, 278 pp., illustrated.

Greenberg, Eric Rolfe. *The Celebrant.* New York: Everest, 1983, 272 pp. Well-researched and -written historical novel about the Giants of McGraw and Mathewson.

Grismer, Karl H. *The Story of Fort Myers.* St. Petersburg, Fla.: St. Petersburg Printing, 1949 edition.

_____. *The Story of St. Petersburg.* St. Petersburg, Fla.: St. Petersburg Printing, 1924.

Guthrie, Wayne. "Playoff Is Old Time Plague." *Indianapolis News,* September 12, 1954, p. 9. Description of an 1897 game to decide the Western League pennant.

Hagood, J. Hurley, and Hagood, Roberta. *Hannibal, Too.* Walsworth, 1986.

Halstead, Joseph S. "Baseball-Mail Delivery Are Both Within His Ken." *Brooklyn Eagle,* December 12, 1943. Description of beer games between drivers and conductors.

Hamby, Harry H. "Baseball Was Game That Day." *Terre Haute Star,* September 18, 1970, p. 12. Reprinted from *Star* article May 5, 1925, regarding the dedication ceremonies at Memorial Stadium.

Hanna, Charles. "Metropolitan Stadium." *Greater Minneapolis,* April 1966, Vol. 18, Number 4, no pagination.

Hart, Arthur. "And Now—Prune Pickers vs. Melon Eaters." *Idaho Statesman,* June 15, 1981. History of baseball in Boise, Idaho.

_____. "Boiseans' Interest in Baseball Was Spirited." *Idaho Statesman,* October 4, 1982.

Harvey, Paul III. "Baseball Not New for Civic." *Eugene* [Ore.] *Register-Guard,* December 10, 1968, p. 3B.

Hatcher, Joe. "Remembering Old Times: The Vols & Sulphur Dell." *The Tennessean,* Nashville, Tennessee, January 22, 1978.

Hayes, Ron. "Idaho Played in First Legion Series." *Lewiston* [Ida.] *Tribune,* August 29, 1973. Story of early Legion ball in Pocatello, Idaho.

"He Cheated Death, Put Florida on Baseball Map." *New York Times,* March 2, 1955. Story of Al Lang, who turned St. Petersburg into a spring training capital.

Heldreth, Joe. "Wytheville Is Baseball Town." *Southwest Virginia Enterprise,* July 20, 1967. Story of baseball at Withers Field in Wytheville, Va.

Hendrix, James. *I Remember Tom.* Nashville, Tenn.: Black Music Foundation, 1983, 17 pp. Booklet containing one man's remembrances of Thomas T. Wilson, president of the Negro National League.

Herold, Larry. "Take Me Out to the Ballpark." *Dallas,* October 1983, pp. 49–54. Difficulties in operating and maintaining the sports arenas (including Texas Stadium) in the Dallas–Ft. Worth area.

Herschell, William. "Evolution of Baseball in Indianapolis." *Indianapolis News,* April 9, 1932.

Hilton, Bob. "Rockford Pioneering in Organizing Industrial Sports." *Rockford* [Ill.] *Register-Republic,* December 24, 1955.

Hilton, George W. "Milwaukee's Charter Membership in the American League." *Historical Messenger of the Milwaukee Historical Society,* Spring 1974, pp. 2–117.

Holmes, John. "Florida Lures the Majors with New Springtime Homes." *Insight,* September 21, 1987, p. 15. Major League teams are trading in their old spring training homes for new ultramodern complexes tailor-made to the ball clubs' needs.

_____. "The New Arenas of Debate." *Insight,* September 21, 1987, p. 8. Description of a rash of new stadia being built to draw—or keep—major league franchises.

Holmes, Tommy. *The Dodgers.* New York: Macmillan, 1975, 192 pp.

Honig, Donald. *Baseball America.* New York: Macmillan, 1985, 342 pp., indexed. Based on hundreds of hours of interviews with ballplayers from all eras, this book takes an analytical yet nostalgic look at America and its pastime.

Hosmer, Howard. *Monroe County, 1821–1921.* Rochester, N.Y.: Rochester and Museum and Science Center, 1971. History of Rochester, N.Y.

"H.S. 'Hi' Corbett, Granddaddy of Baseball in Tucson." *Magazine Tucson,* Tucson, Ariz., Volume 5, May 1952, pp. 26, 40.

Hunt, Marshall. *Daily News,* August 17, 1927. Description of a Babe Ruth home run over the roof of Comiskey Park.

Husted, Bob. "Dayton Ducks to Buy Site of Ball Park." *The Dayton* [Oh.] *Journal,* March 28, 1937, Sports Section, p. 1.

"It's Always Been a Baseball Town." *Lancaster* [Pa.] *Sunday News,* September 2, 1979.

Izenberg, Jerry. "Ol' Faithful." *New York Post,* October 6, 1986. Article about Fenway Park.

James, Bill. *The Baseball Abstract 1982.* New York: Ballantine, 1982, 213 pp.

————. *The Bill James Baseball Abstract 1986.* New York: Ballantine, 340 pp.

————. *The Bill James Historical Abstract,* New York: Villard, 721 pp., indexed. Baseball's premiere number-cruncher takes a look at the big picture. Enlightening—and often funny as hell.

James, G. Watson, Jr. "It's Batter Up Time!" *Richmond Times-Dispatch,* March 31, 1935, p. 6, col. 1. Discussion of nineteenth century baseball in Richmond.

Jedick, Peter. *League Park.* Cleveland, Oh.: Western Reserve Historical Society, 1978, 27 pp.

Jensen, Paul, ed. *1985 Chicago White Sox Media Guide.* Chicago: Chicago White Sox Public Relations Department, 1985.

Jones, Kenneth. "In the Good Old Days, Peoria Had One of the Top Baseball Teams Anyplace." *Peoria Journal Star,* April 12, 1984, pp. D10–11.

Jordan, Jimmy. "Forbes Field Is Coming Down." *Pittsburgh Post-Gazette,* October 12, 1971.

Jordan, Pat. *A False Spring.* New York: Dodd, Mead, 1975, 277 pp. Autobiographical novel about a boy who grows up, sort of, while bombing out in the minor leagues.

Kahn, Roger. "Bums' Rush Turns into a Big Bonanza." *The Sporting News 1983 Baseball Yearbook,* p. 26.

Karr, Gary. "Ex-Groundskeeper Remembers City's 'Boys of Summer.'" *Charleston* [W. Va.] *Daily Mail,* March 6, 1987, p. 1A.

Kerrane, Kevin, and Grossinger, Richard, eds. *Baseball Diamonds.* Garden City, N.Y.: Anchor, 1980, 419 pp.

Kimball, George. "Opening Day at Fenway." In *Baseball Diamonds,* ed. by Kevin Kerrane and Richard Grossinger. Garden City, N.Y.: Anchor, 1980, p. 314.

King, Paul. "'53–57: Rebuilding a Ballpark." *Peoria Journal Star,* April 12, 1984, p. D17. The *Journal Star*'s Sports Editor discusses the refurbishment of Peoria's Woodruff Field, in preparation for a five-year stint in the Three-I League.

Kissane, Leedice. "Baseball in Its Hey-day in Pocatello Tended to Tie Community Together." *Idaho State Journal,* July 22, 1979, p. C12.

Klinger, Henry L. "Remembers When Our Dodgers Were the Bridegrooms." *Brooklyn Eagle,* May 7, 1944.

————. "Reminds Us of Atlantic League Team." *Brooklyn Eagle,* January 8, 1953.

Kourtakis, Bob. "Kobs Field." *Lansing State Journal,* April 17, 1988. Story of the diamond at Michigan State University.

Kovach, John M. "Ballparks: Past and Present." *Stanley Coveleski Regional Stadium 1987 Souvenir Program,* South Bend, Ind., pp. 26–7.

Kramp, Gordon. "Good News from Cleveland." *Ballparks Bulletin,* Number 12, January 1988, p. 13. A celebration of the historical value of The Mistake by the Lake.

Kuehn, Bill. "50 Golden Years." *Clinton Giants 1987 Souvenir Program.* Clinton, Iowa. Article about the 50th anniversary of Riverview Stadium.

Kuklick, Bruce. "Progress Report — *Shibe Park: A History, 1908-1976* — Tentative Chapter Outline for the Book." *Ballparks Bulletin,* Number 10, September 1987, pp. 9–11.

League Park Pointers. Cleveland, Oh.: The Cleveland Ball Club Company, 1914. Subtitled: "For the Guidance of the Sixth City American League Base Ball Devotees."

Leitner, Irving A. *Baseball: Diamond in the Rough.* New York: Criterion, 226 pp.

Levine, Peter. *A.G. Spalding and the Rise of Baseball.* New York: Oxford University Press, 1985, 184 pp., indexed. A major new biography of one of baseball's founding fathers by a professor of history at Michigan State University.

Levy, Lester S. *Picture the Song.* Baltimore: Johns Hopkins University Press, 1976.

Lindstrom, Don. "Ray of Hope Grows Dim for Breese." *Wisconsin State Journal,* July 31, 1981. Gloominess reigns as Madison's funky ol' ballpark readies for abandonment and decay.

Linthurst, Randolph. *The 1947 Trenton Giants.* Self-published.

Littwin, Mike. "25 Years Ago . . . Baseball Headed West." *The Sporting News 1983 Baseball Yearbook,* p. 21.

Lowry, Philip J. *Green Cathedrals.* Society for American Baseball Research, 1986, 157 pp. A must for any baseball reference library. Especially helpful on obscure nineteenth century and Negro League ballparks.

————. "Mysteries Within Green Cathedrals." *The Ballparks Bulletin,* Number 10, September 1987, pp. 3–5. Discussion of the largest structures in baseball "in play" if struck by a batted ball.

McAuley, Regis. "Corbett Mound Rebuilt." *Tucson Daily Citizen,* January 21, 1969. And so was every other mound in the United States — with the possible exception of the one at Dodger Stadium.

McCarthy, William. *Rochester Diamond Echoes.* Rochester, New York: 1949.

McGoff, Parker (Paddy). "Bay Ridge Diamond Star Was Fat, Fast and Frisky." *Brooklyn Eagle,* August 20, 1944. Talk of play at Ambrose Park.

McGraw, Mrs. John J. *The Real McGraw,* ed. by Arthur Mann. New York: David McKay, 1953, 336 pp.

MacIntyre, John. "Lots of TLC Goes into Simmons Field." *Kenosha* [Wis.] *News,* April 10, 1986.

McKelvey, Blake. *The Flower City.* Cambridge: Harvard University Press, 1949. Book about Rochester, New York.

Mantle, Mickey. *The Education of a Baseball Player.* New York: Simon and Schuster, 219 pp., indexed.

Maras, Mike. "Old Vaughn Street." *Ballparks Bulletin,* Number 12, January 1988, p. 28. Discussion of Lucky Beavers Stadium in Portland, Oregon.

Markle, A.R. "Early Days of Baseball in Terre Haute." *Terre Haute Star,* April 24, 1955.

Mathewson, Christy. *Baseball in a Pinch or Baseball from the Inside.* New York: G.P. Putnam's, 1912. Reprint: Briarcliff Manor, N.Y.: Stein and Day/Scarborough, 306 pp., illus. Edited by Vic Ziegel and Neil Offen, with a foreword by John N. Wheeler. This edition has an introduction by Red Smith.

Mayhill, Tom. "The Boys of Summer." *Indianapolis Monthly,* April 1985, pp. 46–50. Discussion of Indianapolis's Federal League franchise in 1914.

Mittman, Dick. "City Had Its Own Major Leaguers 72 Years Ago." *Indianapolis Times,* April 19, 1959, p. 24, col. 1. Story of how Indianapolis joined the National League in 1887.

_____. "Openers Here a Century Old." *Indianapolis News,* April 18, 1978, p. 27, col. 3. Article on the beginning of the 1878 baseball season in Indianapolis.

Mona, Dave. "Memories of the Met." *Minneapolis/St. Paul,* April 1981, pp. 77–83, 142–144. A fan recalls the good old days when the Twins played outdoors.

"Municipal Athletic Park Opened." *Dubuque Telegraph-Herald,* April 30, 1914, p. 1.

Nash, Bruce, and Zullo, Allan. *The Baseball Hall of Shame.* New York: Pocket, 1985, 189 pp. Contains discussions on bad ballparks, the L.A. Coliseum, Colt Stadium, Baker Bowl, etc.

Nealon, Clark, et al. "The Campaign for Major League Baseball in Houston." *The Houston Review: History and Culture of the Gulf Coast,* Vol. 8, Number 1, 1985, pp. 3–47.

Neft, David S., and Cohen, Richard M. *The Sports Encyclopedia—Baseball.* New York: St. Martin's, 1985, 574 pp. Useful for its information concerning the rise and fall of the Player's League.

Nergal, Ory Mazar, ed. *The Encyclopedia of American Cities.* New York: E.P. Dutton, 1980, 416 pp., indexed. Information on every U.S. city that, in 1980, had a population of over 100,000.

"New Ball Park to Be Closer In." *Spokesman Review,* Spokane, Wash., February 9, 1904, p. 3, col. 1. Talk of construction of Recreation Park.

Nichols, Max. "It Happened at the Met." *Greater Minneapolis,* April 1966, Vol. 18, Number 4, no pagination.

Nightingale, Dave. "Comiskey: Still a Pitcher's Haven." *The Sporting News 1983 All-Star Special,* April 4, 1983, p. 21.

Nussbaum, Lowell. Column. *Indianapolis Star,* August 3, 1949, p. 19, col. 1. Item on South Street Park, home of the Indianapolis Browns of 1878.

Obojski, Robert. *Bush League.* New York: Macmillan, 1975, 418 pp., indexed. History of the minor leagues.

"Old 39th St. Assays the Diamond Dust From the 'Nineties." *Brooklyn Eagle,* August 12, 1945.

O'Neal, Bill. *The Texas League: A Century of Baseball.* Austin: Eakin, 1987.

"Once Home of Pioneer Ball." *Idaho State Journal,* October 28, 1979, p. C12. Story and photo of Halliwell Park in Pocatello, Idaho.

Osterland, Albert. "Baseball Loomed Large in Old East New York." *Brooklyn Eagle,* November 26, 1943.

Overfield, Joe. "Offermann Died Lonely Death." *Bisongram,* October 1987, Vol. 3, Number 6, p. 17. Obit of the ballpark that served Buffalo for 71 straight years. By the historian of the Buffalo Bisons.

Palmer, Edwin O. *History of Hollywood.* Arthur H. Cawston, 1937. Background on Arthur Gilmore, whose son built Gilmore Stadium in Hollywood.

Pardon, John F. *The Cities of Professional Baseball.* Handbound volume in the National Baseball Library in Cooperstown, N.Y.

Parker, Bob. "Fort Wayne Had Notable Baseball History; First Major League Game Played Here." *Old Fort News,* Allen County-Fort Wayne [Ind.] Historical Society Museum, Vol. 30, Number 3, Summer 1967.

Peterson, Robert W. *Only the Ball Was White.* Englewood Cliffs, N.J.: Prentice-Hall, 1970, 406 pp., indexed. History of the Negro Leagues.

Petree, Patrick K. *Old Times to the Goodtimes.* Oklahoma City: Sonic Industries, 1980, 130 pp. A history of professional baseball in Oklahoma City.

Pippen, Rodger H. "Fayetteville Was the Site of Babe's 1st Homer in O.B." *Fayetteville* [N.C.] *News-Post,* April 5, 1952, p. 6.

Pitoniak, Scott. "Bisons Will Unwrap 19,500-Seat Pilot Field, a Marriage of Old and New Stadiums." *Sunday Democrat and Chronicle,* Rochester, N.Y., April 3, 1988, p. 13E. Story of Buffalo's new park.

Poore, Jim. "History Hasn't Been Kind to Boise Baseball." *Idaho Statesman,* September 12, 1986, p. B1.

Porter, David L. *Biographical Dictionary of American Sports: Baseball.* Westport, Conn.: Greenwood, 1987, 713 pp., indexed. Author is history and political science professor at William Penn College in Oskaloosa, Iowa.

Potts, Mark. "Prince William Pirates on Upswing." *Washington Post,* June 17, 1985.

Pozar, Stephen M., and Purvis, Jean B. *Butler: A Pictorial History,* 1980. Includes history of the Butler [Pa.] Tigers and Pullman Park where they played.

Pugh, John. "Roanoke's Last Team." *The Roanoker,* April 1987, p. 30. Story of the Rosox of the 1940s, and Maher Field, their home grounds.

Ready, Milton. *Asheville, Land of the Sky.* Windsor Publications—History Books Division, John M. Phillips, Publisher.

Reichler, Joseph L. *The Baseball Encyclopedia.* Sixth edition. New York: Macmillan, 1985, 2733 pp. Every baseball stat known to man. A truly awesome—and heavy—book. Cannot be read in bed.

_____. *Baseball's Greatest Moments.* New York: Crown, 1979, 264 pp.

Reis, Jim. "Pieces of the Past." *Kentucky Post,* April 25, 1983, p. 18. Story of Wiedemann Park in Newport, Kentucky—home of the 1914 Newport Brewers of the Ohio State League.

_____. "Professional Baseball Didn't Last Long in Covington." *Kentucky Post,* October 4, 1982, p. 22. Story of Covington's short-lived stint in the 1913 outlaw Federal League.

Remington, John L. *The Red Wings—A Love Story.* Rochester, N.Y.: Hawk Dynasty, 37 pp. The history of Rochester baseball. Includes a photo of Culver Field, where the 1890 American Association team played.

Rice, Franklin P. *Dictionary of Worcester* [Mass.] *and its Vicinity.* Second issue. Reprinted from the *Worcester Commercial.* Worcester: F.S. Blanchard, 1893.

Richter, Francis C. *Richter's History and Records of Base Ball.* Philadelphia: Francis C. Richter, 1914, 306 pp.

Riess, Steven A. *Touching Base.* Westport, Conn.: Greenwood, 1980, 269 pp., indexed. The influence of baseball upon the communities in which it is played.

Rimmel, William M. "The Early Days of Pirate Baseball." *Pittsburgh Post-Gazette,* date unknown. Information from copy of partial page concerns Hans Wagner and the cop sneaking kids into Expo.

Ritter, Brad. "Old College Field Matures with Grace." *State News,* May 23, 1980, p. 1E. Story of Michigan State University's baseball field in East Lansing.

Ritter, Lawrence S. *The Glory of Their Times.* New enlarged edition. New York: William Morrow, 1984, 360 pp., indexed.

_____, and Honig, Donald. *The Image of Their Greatness.* New York: Crown,

1979, 374 pp., indexed. An illustrated history of baseball from 1900 to the present.

Rivers, Don, with Lewis, Miss Audrey, and Daline, Gordon. *Southtown Personalities.* Minneapolis: American, 1934. Memories of Minneapolis, including those of the baseball grounds "out in the country" at Minnehaha Driving Park.

Robinson, Don. "City Approves $50,000 for Hi Corbett Field." *Arizona Daily Star,* November 13, 1968.

Rochester History. Vol. 24, No. 3, 1962, p. 33.

Rodman, Bob. "29 Years of Minor League Baseball." *Eugene* [Ore.] *Register-Guard,* June 17, 1981, p. 1E.

Rogosin, Donn. *Invisible Men.* New York: Atheneum, 1985, 283 pp., indexed. Life in the Negro Leagues.

Rolfe, Shelley. "Virginians to Virginians." *Richmond Times-Dispatch,* April 4, 1954, section F, p. 1, col. 1. History of Richmond baseball.

Rose, William Ganson. *Cleveland, the Making of a City.* Cleveland: World.

Rozin, Skip. "At the Park." *Audubon,* September 1984, Vol. 86, Number 5, pp. 22-27. Essay on and beautiful photographs of Wrigley Field, Chicago.

Ruck, Rob. *Sandlot Seasons.* Chicago: University of Illinois Press, 1987, 239 pp., indexed. A history of sports in black Pittsburgh, where neighborhoods have names like Homestead and Garfield.

Ryan, James A. "Bloomer Boss Files Protest of 3-2 Victory." *Clinton Herald,* May 10, 1937. Description of the first game ever played at Riverview Stadium in Clinton, Iowa.

Ryder, Robert. "Ryder Thinks Up a Few for Hot Stove League." *Brooklyn Eagle,* January 27, 1944.

"S.J. Recalls 'Greats.'" *San Jose News,* July 20, 1973, p. 39. Story of visits by Ruth, Gehrig, and Cobb to Sodality Park.

Salant, Nathan, *This Date in New York Yankees History.* New York: Stein and Day, 1983, 401 pp.

Sandomir, Richard. "House of Dreams." *Sports, Inc.,* April 11, 1988. Story about Pilot Field in Buffalo, New York.

Santoro, Joe. "Taking You Out to the Ballgame One Last Time." *News-Press,* Fort Myers Fla., April 5, 1987, p. B1.

Sapakoff, Gene. "College Park: Improved with Age, but Is It Good Enough?" *Post-Courier,* Charleston, South Carolina, p. 13C. Charleston keeps putting money into their old ballpark, and it's still an old ballpark.

Scher, Jon. "After Bisons' Departure, Deserted Rockpile Faces Uncertain Future." *Baseball America,* July 10, 1988, p. 19. What to do about War Memorial Stadium in Buffalo, New York?

Scherrer, Anton. "Our Town." *Indianapolis Times,* January 16, 1940. Description of why Indianapolis lost their 1889 National League franchise.

Schlossberg, Dan. *The Baseball Catalog.* Middle Village, N.Y.: Jonathan David, 1980, 310 pp. A smorgasbord of baseball history, served up in tasty little chunks.

Schubel, George. *Illustrated History of Greater Ridgewood.* Brooklyn: Ridgewood Times, 1913, 276 pp., indexed. Contains a photo of Ridgewood Park in Brooklyn.

Schwartz, Paul. "Eastern League's Best Is Now Even Better." *Albany Times Union,* May 8, 1988. Article about Reading Municipal Stadium.

Scribner, Robert L. "Two Out, and—?" *Virginia Cavalcade,* Spring 1954, p. 18. The history of baseball in Richmond.

Seagram's Sports Almanac. New York: Masthead, 1962, 252 pp., indexed.

Seymour, Harold. *Baseball—The Early Years.* New York: Oxford University Press, 1960, 373 pp., indexed.

_____. *Baseball—The Golden Age.* New York: Oxford University Press, 1971, 492 pp., indexed. Together, the above two volumes represent the most comprehensive history of our national pastime by any single author.

Shannon, Bill, and Kaminsky, George. *The Ballparks.* New York: Hawthorne, 1975, 276 pp., indexed. Good book. Comes with a foreword by Monte Irvin.

Shewark, Maria, ed. *New York Mets 1988 Yearbook.* Article celebrating the 25th anniversary of Shea Stadium.

Simpson, Allan, ed. *Baseball America's 1988 Directory.* Durham, N.C.: 1988, 160 pp.

Smith, Red. *The Red Smith Reader.* New York: Random House, 1982. 308 pp. Here are assembled many of our greatest sportswriter's daily prose poems.

Smith, Robert. *Baseball.* New York: Simon and Schuster, 1947, 362 pp.

_____. *Illustrated History of Baseball.* New York: Madison Square/Grosset and Dunlap, 1973, 302 pp., indexed.

_____. *Pioneers of Baseball.* Boston: Little, Brown, 1978, 180 pp.

Solomon, Michael. "Hudson Field." *Annual Report of the City of Dayton, Ohio,* pp. 24–25.

Somers, Dale A. *The Rise of Sports in New Orleans 1850-1900.* Baton Rouge: Louisiana State University Press, 1972, 320 pp., indexed.

Spatter, Sam. "City's New Stadium Welcomes Sports Fans." *Pittsburgh Post-Gazette,* date unknown (approximately May or June, 1970).

Spink, J.G. Taylor. *Judge Landis and Twenty-five Years of Baseball.* New York: Thomas Y. Crowell, 1947, 306 pp., indexed.

Sprague, George M. "Mr. Sprague, 80, Knows Locations." *Brooklyn Eagle,* November 6, 1949. He draws maps, too. Here, it's of Capitoline Grounds and its surrounding streets.

"Stadium Architect Pleased Despite Loss." *Pacific Business News,* September 15, 1975. The story of the building of Aloha Stadium in Honolulu.

Stahlberg, Mike. "Ems Real Cl(AAA)ssy in Season's Opener." *Eugene* [Ore.] *Register-Guard,* April 27, 1969, p. 1. The Pacific Coast League comes to Eugene.

Stein, Fred. *Under Coogan's Bluff.* Glenshaw, Pa.: Chapter and Cask, 145 pp. A fan's recollections of the New York Giants under Terry and Ott.

Svendsen, Marlys A. *Davenport, a Pictorial History, 1836-1986.* St. Louis: G. Bradley, 1987 (second printing, revised). Includes photo and history of Municipal (later John O'Connell) Stadium in Davenport, Iowa.

Tarvin, A.H. *Seventy-five Years of Louisville Diamonds.* Louisville, Ky.: Schuhmann, 1940.

Terrell, Bob. "Asheville's McCormick Field Filled with History." *1985 Asheville Tourists Program.*

Thorn, John, ed. *The National Pastime.* Vol. 1, No. 1, Fall 1982, Cooperstown, N.Y.: Society for American Baseball Research, 87 pp. Contains a rare shot of Baker Bowl.

_____, and Palmer, Pete. *The Hidden Game of Baseball.* Garden City, N.Y.: Doubleday, 1984, 419 pp. Slide-rule baseball. Two guys in search of the ultimate stat.

Timmons, Grady. "Luckman: There's No One Like It." *Honolulu Star-Bulletin,* September 12, 1975. Story about the architect of Aloha Stadium in Honolulu.

Torrence, Bruce T. *Hollywood, the First 100 Years.* Hollywood Chamber of Commerce, 1979. Contains the history of the Gilmore family.

Tuckey, Ken. "Stein Regime Taking Shape with R-Phils." *Reading* [Pa.] *Eagle,* October 18, 1987. A story of how the new owner of the Reading Phillies plans to refurbish Reading Municipal Memorial Stadium.

Tune, Jerry. "Stadium's History an Old One." *Honolulu Star-Bulletin,* September 12, 1975, p. D4. Story about the building of Aloha Stadium.

Turkin, Hy, and Thompson, S.C. *The Official Encyclopedia of Baseball.* Seventh revised edition, with revisions by Pete Palmer. Cranbury, N.J.: A.S. Barnes, 737 pp. Buy two. The first one wears out.

Tuttle, Richard C. "Bleachers." *Terre Haute Star,* January 11, 1982. The *Star*'s assistant editor recalls a visit to the ballpark around 1930, and a ride in an electric car.

Updike, John. *Assorted Prose.* New York: Alfred A. Knopf, 1960.

Vanaman, Tina. "Inside the Vet." *Phillies Today,* 1988, p. 45. Discussion of improvements at the Vet.

Vidmer, Richards. *New York Times,* August 17, 1927. Description of a Babe Ruth home run over the roof of Comiskey Park.

"Visalia Has Been Fond of Baseball Since 1879 Team." *Visalia* [Calif.] *Times-Delta,* June 25, 1959, p. 2.

Voight, David Quentin. *American Baseball.* Vols. 1 and 2. Norman: University of Oklahoma Press, 1966 and 1983, 336 pp., and 350 pp. (respectively), indexed. Next to Seymour, this professor of sociology at Albright College in Reading, Pennsylvania, has written America's most thorough baseball history.

Walder, Barbara. "Spring Training the Way It Used to Be." *New York Times,* March 27, 1988, p. S10. Description of St. Petersburg days of yore, the smell of coffee in the air.

Wallop, Douglas. *Baseball—An Informal History.* New York: W.W. Norton, 1969, 263 pp., indexed.

Weber, Dan. "To a Kid It Was Heaven—the Covington Ball Park." *Kentucky Post,* September 21, 1981, p. 8.

Weber, Pete. "Shedding a Tear for War Memorial." *Bisongram,* October 1987, Vol. 3, Number 6, p. 14. Buffalo says goodbye to the Rockpile.

Welsh, Regis M. "How It All Began for Pirates." *Pittsburgh Press,* September 26, 1960, p. 25.

West, Bernard. "Baseball History in Wilson Begins Way Back in the 1890's." *Wilson Daily Times,* May 6, 1955, p. 5. History of baseball in Wilson, North Carolina.

West, Richard. "The History of Baseball in an In-and-Out Town." *Illinois Times,* April 14–20, 1978, The in-and-out town is Springfield, Ill.

Westlake, Charles W. *Columbus Baseball History 1876-1981.* Columbus, Oh.: 1981, 21 pp. Privately published booklet containing photos of Neil Park and Red Bird Stadium (later Jet Stadium, Franklin County Stadium and Cooper Stadium).

Whalen, Frank. "Tells of Pitcher Who Mistook Second Baseman for Batter." *Brooklyn Eagle,* August 13, 1944. As it turns out, he mistook the second baseman for a runner going from first to second.

"Where Old Time Nines Used to Play." *Brooklyn Eagle,* June 9, 1946.

Whiteford, Mike. "A Baseball Tradition That Began Here in 1910." *Charleston Wheelers Professional Baseball Souvenir Program 1987,* p. 22.

Wiegel, Art. *You're in Royal Country.* Fort Myers Chamber of Commerce, 1983, pp. 5–7. Story of the Kansas City Royals' love affair with Fort Myers, now estranged.

Williams, Robert L. *Gaston County: A Pictorial History.* Norfolk, Va.: Donning, 1981. Contains photo of Sims Park in Gastonia, North Carolina.

Willis, Art. "Duncan Park—Old and New Lighting." *The Paper,* Spartanburg, S.C., August 14, 1985, p. 26.

Wolcott, Bill. "FDR's 'Boondoggle' Needs Refurbishing for New White Sox." *Niagara Gazette,* January 30, 1982, p. 1A. Minor league baseball was returning to Niagara Falls, and Hyde Park Stadium needed fixing up.

_____. "Maglie's Night." *Niagara Gazette,* June 22, 1983, p. 10. Story of the dedication of Sal Maglie Stadium (née Hyde Park Stadium) in Niagara Falls.

Wolfe, Harry. "Brooklyn Active in Popularizing National Pastime." *Brooklyn Eagle,* January 2, 1944.

_____. "Brooklyn Started Off by Being Champs As This Epistolary History Demonstrates." *Brooklyn Eagle,* August 2, 1944.

Wulf, Steve. "Hearts on the Diamond." *Sports Illustrated,* August 11, 1986.

Yarrow, Andrew L. "Nostalgic Show Recalls the Brooklyn Dodgers." *New York Times,* October 12, 1986, p. 68. Article reviewing excellent Dodgers exhibition produced by the Brooklyn Historical Society.

Young, Dick. "Ebbets Field: Where Bums Became Kings." *New York Post,* May 24, 1983. A man who worked the Dodgers beat for many years remembers.

Zimmermann, Karl. "The Old Ball Game." *Upstate,* April 3, 1988, p. 4. A fan's tour of upstate New York ballparks.

Index

Numbers in bold refer to photographs.

INDEX

2